Rodale's Chemical-Free Yard & Garden

Rodale's Chemical-Free Yard & Garden

THE ULTIMATE AUTHORITY ON SUCCESSFUL ORGANIC GARDENING

WINGS BOOKS
New York • Avenel, New Jersey

This 1995 edition is published by Wings Books,
distributed by Random House Value Publishing, Inc.,
40 Engelhard Avenue, Avenel, New Jersey 07001,
by arrangement with Rodale Press, Inc.

Random House
New York • Toronto • London • Sydney • Auckland

Printed and bound in the United States of America

Library of Congress Cataloging-in-Publication Data

Rodale's chemical-free yard and garden : the ultimate authority on
    successful organic gardening / [Anna Carr . . . et al.; Fern Marshall
    Bradley, editor].
        p.   cm.
    Cover title: Rodale's chemical-free yard & garden.
    Originally published: Emmaus, PA : Rodale Press, c1991.
    Includes bibliographical references (p. 431) and index.
    ISBN 0-517-12243-X
    1. Organic gardening. I. Carr, Anna, 1955-   . II. Bradley,
Fern Marshall. III. Rodale Press. IV. Title: Chemical-free yard
and garden. V. Title: Rodale's chemical-free yard & garden.
SB453.5.R635   1994
635'.0484–dc20   94-31447
                                                                CIP

8 7 6 5 4 3 2 1

Contents

About the Authors

ANNA CARR is the author of *Good Neighbors: Companion Planting for Gardeners, Rodale's Color Handbook of Garden Insects,* and coauthor of *Rodale's Garden Insect, Disease, and Weed Identification Guide. Horticulture* magazine has called Anna Carr "a rare and valuable garden writer." She continues to experiment with new organic techniques in her home garden, one of the finest and most creative in eastern Pennsylvania.

MIRANDA SMITH is a multi-talented author who is currently studying creative writing at Burlington College in Vermont. She is the author of *Greenhouse Gardening* and coauthor of *Rodale's Garden Insect, Disease, and Weed Identification Guide.* Smith is currently editing a production manual for northeastern organic farmers for the federally sponsored Low Impact Sustainable Agriculture (LISA) program. Since 1971, she has gained broad experience and knowledge of organic practices by managing greenhouses and gardens on organic farms and by teaching organic farming and gardening techniques in both eastern and western United States and Canada.

LINDA A. GILKESON, Ph.D., is the director of research for Applied Bio-nomics Ltd., a biological control firm in British Columbia, Canada. Gilkeson has a doctorate in entomology from McGill University, Montreal. Her gardening background includes eight years managing a small organic produce and herb farm. In addition, she is an award-winning garden writer who has penned articles for *Harrowsmith* magazine as well as scientific papers on biological control.

JOSEPH SMILLIE is an ecological farming consultant who specializes in soil fertility, composting systems, and orchard management. He is the coauthor of *The Soul of Soil: A Guide to Ecological Soil Management* and *The Orchard Almanac.* He is a founding member of the Organic Foods Production Association of North America (OFPANA). As a consultant, Smillie has worked with farmers and extension agents in the United States, Canada, South and Central America, China, India, and Switzerland. When he's not traveling, he cares for his garden and orchard on a high plateau in Quebec, Canada.

BILL WOLF is the founder and president of the Necessary Trading Company in New Castle, Virginia, which specializes in agricultural consulting and distribution of biologically safe farm and garden supplies. Wolf serves on the board of directors of OFPANA and conducts workshops and seminars on biological soil management and natural pest control. He does consulting work on soils management and natural pest control and has farmed organically for more than a decade.

FERN MARSHALL BRADLEY is a garden editor for Rodale Books. She has a bachelor's degree in plant science from Cornell University and a master's degree in horticulture from Rutgers University. Bradley gained extensive practical experience with organic gardening while managing a large market garden on an organic farm in western New Jersey. She currently helps her 5-year-old son tend his organic garden at their home in Emmaus, Pennsylvania.

Acknowledgments

Michael LaChance and the staff of the Necessary Trading Company provided much assistance in the researching, writing, and manuscript preparation for chapter 4.

Dr. Peter R. Hemstad of the University of Minnesota, Paul M. Otten of North Star Gardens, and many others helped compile the listings of insect- and disease-resistant fruit cultivars.

Kevin Morris of the National Turfgrass Evaluation Program in Beltsville, Maryland, helped compile the listing of insect- and disease-resistant grass cultivars.

Introduction

Concern for the environment has finally come of age. Problems caused by pollution, hazardous waste, and resource depletion touch everyone's lives. The state of the environment is a top public concern. But we all feel helpless and frustrated in the face of problems as vast as acid rain, groundwater pollution, and global warming. How can one person help?

One place to start is in your own backyard. Gardening is a direct way to improve your health and make a small contribution to solving environmental problems. Raising your own fruits and vegetables saves energy and resources used to transport food from distant agricultural regions to your grocery store. Gardening is good exercise, and the fresh foods you grow are rich in vitamins and minerals. Planting trees, shrubs, and flowering plants helps counteract the release of carbon dioxide that many scientists believe is the major cause of global warming.

But if gardening is going to be part of the solution to the environmental crisis, you must make sure it's not also part of the problem. How? By gardening chemical-free.

What is chemical-free gardening? When we talk about using chemicals in the garden, we generally are referring to synthetic products like granulated fertilizers derived from petro-

leum and potent herbicides and insecticides created in laboratories.

It's not so easy to say whether other garden products should be labeled chemicals. For example, one of the substances widely used for insect control in organic gardens is rotenone. Rotenone is a poisonous substance that kills a broad range of insects and is also toxic to humans. It is extracted from a plant. So should we call it a chemical or not?

In this book, we have chosen to label *any* toxic substances used to kill insects, weeds, and plant disease organisms as chemicals, regardless of whether they were created by man or by nature. Some of these substances, such as a homemade garlic oil spray, are not toxic to humans (although a garlic spray certainly would irritate your eyes or upset your stomach if swallowed). We also discuss the use of natural mineral elements, such as sulfur and chelated zinc sprays, as organic fertilizers. These could also be called chemicals. Yet, all the substances and control methods described in this book are considered acceptable for use in organic gardens.

What, then, is organic gardening, and how is it different from chemical-free gardening? *Organic* means using our understanding of nature as a guide for gardening and living and caring for the plants in our yards and gardens without using synthetic chemical pesticides or synthetic fertilizers. *Chemical-free* means using no chemicals, and therefore sets an even stricter standard than organic.

The chemicals described in this book are acceptable to organic gardeners because they are derived from natural sources. Also, they are generally less toxic to humans than most synthetic pesticides and break down relatively quickly in the environment to harmless substances. However, they are described as the "last resort" in this book because they do have adverse effects on the environment: They may kill nonpest species or be toxic to animals.

MAKING THE SWITCH TO CHEMICAL-FREE

If you're a conventional gardener who's turned to this book for help in making a transition to organic gardening, you may feel uncertain about whether you can successfully change your approach to gardening. Trying to completely stop using chemicals in your garden may seem impossible. We've chosen to name this book *Rodale's Chemical-Free Yard and Garden* not because we expect you to drop the use of all chemicals immediately, but rather as a reminder of a goal worth striving for. Organic gardeners do sometimes use chemicals in their gardens. However, they try to use other, less invasive techniques first, and they reserve the use of toxins as the last resort. This book will help you decide what the best course of action is if flea beetles are swarming on your cabbage, or if your roses are suffering from powdery mildew. And as you gain experience, you'll find that the occasions when you need to use chemicals become fewer. If you're a seasoned organic gardener, you may already be close to, or have achieved, a truly chemical-free garden.

The standards used in writing this book are the standards that have always guided Rodale books. We advocate a sustainable approach to gardening based on enriching the soil with organic matter and using naturally occurring fertilizers that are mined from the earth or extracted from plants or animals. We recommend pest control methods that make the best use of plants' natural defenses, that encourage populations of naturally occurring pest enemies, and that use poisons derived from plant sources as a last resort.

We advocate organic methods for many reasons. The widespread use of synthetic fertilizers and pesticides in agriculture has increased productivity, but at great environmental cost. Groundwater supplies can be tainted by agricultural run-off containing soluble fertilizers and pesticides. Repeated pesticide applications can create a double problem: Pest insects may become resistant, while their natural enemies are killed by the pesticides. The long-term effects on human and animal health from pesticide residues on food crops, as well as their general accumulation in the environment, are still largely unknown, but evidence is accumulating that their use carries significant risk.

There are more personal reasons to strive for a chemical-free yard and garden. Using chemicals is in conflict with the very reasons you garden: enjoyment of nature's beauty and improving your health through exercise and raising fresh, nutritious food. It's hard to appreciate the beauty of your garden from behind a spray mask, whatever you're spraying. And apart from the risk that may be present in residues around your yard or on your food crops, there is risk in the simple act of applying pesticides. So take off the mask and learn about all the alternatives to managing your garden with chemicals. Enrich your soil naturally, grow plants that are well adapted to your local conditions, and encourage populations of pest predators and parasites. As you do, you'll discover the best reason not to use chemicals in your garden: You just don't need to.

How to Use This Book

Rodale's Chemical-Free Yard and Garden is designed to help both beginning and experienced gardeners learn to use organic techniques and methods as effectively as possible. It has much to offer to longtime organic gardeners as well as those who are trying to make the switch from using synthetic fertilizers and pesticides. The book opens with an easy-to-follow system that explains the fundamentals of organic gardening. From there, it continues with in-depth information on organic gardening methods and products, including the pros and cons of various methods, the proper way to apply products, and how to make many of them yourself. In addition, there is a troubleshooting encyclopedia for quick tips on fertilizing and pest and disease control for vegetables, flowers, fruit, trees and shrubs, and the lawn.

CHEMICAL-FREE GARDEN MANAGEMENT

Part 1 will be particularly helpful for gardeners making the transition to organic practices. Chapter 1 describes eight fundamentals of organic gardening. If you're new to organic gardening, or to gardening in general, be sure to read this chapter first to get an understanding of the basics. Chapter 2 tells you how to develop a plan for caring for your yard and garden organically and how to use garden records as a tool in managing your garden. This chapter is intended especially for new organic gardeners, but experienced gardeners will also find interesting and useful information that will help them better organize their gardening tasks. Chapter 3 provides month-by-month schedules of care to help you keep track of gardening tasks throughout the year.

CHEMICAL-FREE GARDEN TECHNIQUES

In part 2, you'll find systems for improving your soil organically, as well as for controlling weeds, diseases, and insects. Read these chapters straight through if you want a thorough overview of the topic, or use them for spot reference. The introduction of each of these chapters provides a summary of the system.

You'll find that the systems for controlling pests—weeds, diseases, and insects—all follow the same progression. They begin with the controls that are the least invasive, meaning those that have the fewest harmful effects on the natural balance in your yard and garden, and end with those that are most invasive. Organic gardeners use this as an order of priority, starting with the least invasive technique and moving to a more invasive one, if necessary, for acceptable control.

Cultural controls are discussed first. These involve only modifications to standard gardening practices such as seeding, mulching, and fertilizing. Try reading, or at least skimming, the sections on cultural controls in chapters 5, 6, and 7 *before* problems arise in your garden. Since these techniques are mainly preventive, they will help save you the time and expense later on of bringing a pest problem back into balance. Because they help prevent problems, they also help you avoid using more invasive methods that disturb the natural balance in your garden and that may require the use of toxins.

For insects, biological control methods come next. Biological controls use natural enemies of pest insects such as lady beetles or lacewings to keep pest populations in check. Physical controls are next in line for weed, disease, and insect controls. These stop or kill pests through physical means: hand pulling weeds and trapping insects, for example. Finally, chemical controls, which employ organically acceptable toxins to kill pests, are described last.

CHEMICAL-FREE GARDEN GUIDES

The guides in part 3 are designed for quick problem solving. Each area of your yard and garden is covered in a chapter, including vegetables, flowers, fruit, trees and shrubs, and the lawn. If you have a pest problem on a particular plant, look up that plant (they are listed alphabetically within chapters). Below the plant name, you'll find short descriptions of symptoms of several of the most common insect and disease problems that trouble that plant. Look for the symptoms that most closely match the condition of your plants. Following the symptoms, you'll find several control measures listed, with the least invasive controls listed first. All the controls suggested in the plant guides are described in detail in part 2 of the book. If you need more information about any of the controls given, look up that control in the index.

PART ONE

Chemical-Free Garden Management

CHAPTER ONE

The Eight-Point System for Successful Organic Gardening

By Miranda Smith

Organic gardening is a system inspired by processes that exist in nature. In the wild, a system of checks and balances keeps insects and diseases under control, and soil fertility is naturally replenished and renewed. Organic gardeners strive for a similar balance in their gardens by mimicking natural tactics. They understand that healthy, productive gardens depend on diverse populations of insects, microorganisms, animals, and plants—both harmful and helpful —just as any wild meadow or forest would. By carefully nurturing the soil, tending their crops, and practicing environmentally sound methods for controlling insects, diseases, and weeds, organic gardeners create attractive, bountiful gardens without using dangerous chemicals.

Perhaps the biggest difference between organic and conventional gardeners is their attitudes toward using chemicals in the garden. Conventional gardeners rely on synthetic chemicals as an important source of plant nutrition and for quick-fix remedies for pest problems.

For organic gardeners, strict standards limit the use of chemicals. The organic gardener will use natural mineral supplements to boost soil fertility and botanically derived poisons to fight pests—but only as a last resort. The organic gardener looks first to long-term biological processes to solve fertility and pest problems.

The eight-point system presented here will help you implement these natural processes in your yard and garden. It is not a set of step-by-step instructions. Every garden is different, and every gardener faces unique problems. You may be a gardener who wants to switch from using synthetic fertilizers and pesticides to using natural soil amendments and pest control methods. Perhaps you have an organic vegetable garden and now hope to find new ways to care for your lawn without chemicals. You may be a seasoned organic gardener or someone who has never gardened before.

Whatever your level of experience, however, the eight-point system will help you make decisions, avoid problems, keep up with your gardening tasks, improve your results, and move toward a chemical-free approach to gardening. Subsequent chapters explain the nuts and bolts of applying these common principles of organic gardening to your particular situation.

It's up to you to adapt the system to your yard and garden. Read through the system now, and use what you can. If it's November, you can do a thorough garden cleanup. If it's January, make a garden plan and put it in action when the growing season starts. But if it's May, don't despair. It's never too late—or too early—to start a compost pile and to begin applying the principles of pest prevention and organic control in your newly planted garden.

GARDEN WITH A PLAN

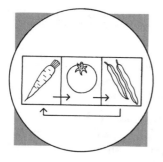

Gardening organically means more than not using synthetic fertilizers and pesticides. Planning in advance, reading about new techniques, and gathering the materials you'll need will make chemical-free gardening easier than you may have expected. Even if you're a mostly organic gardener who wants to make one small switch, like giving up herbicides for your lawn, planning is essential to success.

You may not think that planning has much to do with gardening. After all, the reasons you garden are probably to get outdoors, to get exercise, and to produce beautiful plants and good-tasting food—not to sit inside reading and writing. But organic gardeners must be knowledgeable about disease prevention, biological control of insects, organic soil management, resistant cultivars, and more. So, some advance thinking and research can be an important step in creating a healthy, productive garden.

Set your goals.   Start by sitting down with a map of your garden and listing everything you'd like to change, start new, or improve in your garden.

Learn the basics.   Read about what you plan to do before you do it. Find out what tools and equipment you'll need, what cultivars may work best for your purpose, and what growing methods you want to use.

Schedule your activities.   Write out a plan of what you'll do when in your garden. Decide what you'll do in the coming season, and also tentatively map out how you'll achieve your long-term goals—say, for the next three years.

Adjust the garden design.   Your garden may have plants that are hard to care for organically—disease-prone roses, for example. Or, you may be looking for a way to improve poor soil quickly. Changing your plant choices and growing methods may provide solutions.

Take inventory.   Make a list of supplies

and tools on hand and compare it to your notes about what you think you'll need. Make a shopping list, then buy what you need in advance. When a problem crops up in midseason, you may not have time to shop, and many of the products you need may only be available through mail-order catalogs.

MAKE COMPOST

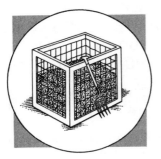

Healthy soil is the basis on which you'll build a flourishing, chemical-free garden, and compost is key to creating healthy soil. Compost is a mix of decomposed plant materials that improves soil structure, provides nutrients for plant growth, and encourages beneficial soil organisms. Best of all, it's free and easy to make. If you don't have a compost pile, building one should be a top priority. If you do have one, why not consider starting another?

Compost is the natural garden elixir that can help every plant in your yard—from the most delicate rose to the tallest oak tree—be healthier and more productive. It's hard to believe that something made of little more than decomposed plant debris can make such a dramatic difference in your garden.

Start a compost pile. There's nothing very complicated about making compost. Almost any backyard and kitchen will produce the basic raw materials needed for successful composting. Early spring is a good time to start a compost pile, but there's no reason not to start one, whatever the season. In colder climates, a pile started in fall or winter may be frozen until spring, but at least you'll be off to a good start. Just remember to turn the pile in March or April to get the composting process restarted, and you'll have compost ready for side-dressing your gardens during the summer.

Work with nature. Using a compost activator, a mix of trace elements and microorganisms, can give your pile a boost. Or, if you're ambitious about composting, think about buying earthworms—one of nature's best compost processors.

Tend your compost regularly. Turning your compost and checking temperature and moisture regularly will help the materials break down more rapidly. However, this isn't a necessity—if you don't have the time or ability to turn the pile, it will just take longer to get finished compost.

Look for outside sources. Don't just use the materials in your yard. There are plenty of inexpensive or free sources of compost materials in most neighborhoods. Ask nongardening neighbors if you can have their leaves or grass clippings, or see if restaurants or markets will let you pick up vegetable trimmings.

FEED THE SOIL

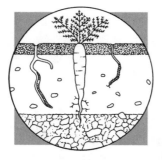

Adding "health food" to the soil is one of the first steps you'll take as an organic gardener, and one that you'll repeat through the years. Adding compost, aged manure, green manure crops, and other soil amendments will create a soil rich in humus and microorganisms, which will nurture healthy plants. You should also examine your soil and have it tested to determine what problems it has. There are many organic fertilizers you can use to supplement plant growth while you work to correct your soil's problems and improve its structure.

If you're a gardener who is making the switch to organic soil care, you'll be changing your approach and attitude toward using fertilizers. They will become the supplement to your main program of enriching the soil naturally. Organic gardeners feed the soil first and offer plants fertilizer as a nutrient "snack."

Learn about your soil. There are several simple tests you can do yourself to learn about the condition of your soil. In some cases, they may give you all the information you need to decide on a soil management strategy. However, if you suspect your soil has nutrient imbalances, it's best to have samples analyzed and follow recommendations from a soil testing laboratory.

Correct soil imbalances. Use natural soil amendments to feed and improve your soil. Many garden soils don't contain enough organic matter, especially if they've been treated with synthetic chemical fertilizers. A critical step in improving soil is adding compost and other organic materials.

Use a long-term approach. Restoring soil health may take several seasons. The time required will depend on the condition of the yard and garden when you begin. Even if you are starting with land that has never been chemically treated but has been neglected in one way or another, it will take some time for the soil to come into full health.

Maintain soil health. Once your soil is balanced, you can help keep it that way by using good gardening practices. Planting green manure crops, continuing to add organic matter, and mulching to help protect the soil will yield a rich soil that produces lush, healthy plants.

Give extra helpings as needed. Use organic fertilizers to help supply nutrients that may be in short supply during your soil-building process. Bonemeal, rock phosphate, fish emulsion, and other fertilizers will feed your plants directly, supplementing the nutrients gradually being released in the soil by the breakdown of organic matter. You can also use organic fertilizers to help your plants if they are under stress or just to make them look their finest.

KEEP THE GARDEN CLEAN

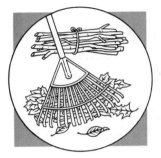

Garden sanitation protects plants against pests and diseases. Clearing crop waste out of the vegetable garden, pruning diseased branches from trees and shrubs, and composting diseased plant matter in a hot compost pile not only helps the appearance of your garden, it also makes for a healthy garden. Having a clean garden not only means clearing out dead and diseased plants, but also carefully inspecting any newly bought plants to ensure that they aren't carriers of disease or insects. Make garden cleanup part of your usual gardening routine, rather than a once-in-the-fall extravaganza.

Some people have difficulty believing that a garden can be "clean." After all, gardens are full of things like soil, old leaves, and rotting tomatoes. And that's not counting all the little squirmy things in the soil like worms, mites, and nematodes. Believe it or not, it's all these little squishy things that help to keep the garden clean. But the soil animals and microorganisms can't do it all. To practice organic gardening well, you are going to have to participate, too.

Don't import diseases. The gardener can be a disease carrier by inadvertently tracking in diseases from other areas! Change your shoes and clothes, sterilize your tools, and wash your hands before moving from a disease-ridden area to a healthy one.

Make sure newcomers are healthy. Buy only certified disease-free planting stock, and check all new plants carefully for both diseases and pests before putting them in the garden.

Nip diseases in the bud. Remove diseased annual plants and sickly branches from perennials, shrubs, and trees before the pathogens infect the rest of the garden.

Heat up the compost pile. High temperatures are essential to kill disease organisms. Make sure your compost pile is working fast and hot if you plan to add material from plants that have suffered from fungal or bacterial diseases.

Handle viruses with care. Put plants afflicted with viral diseases in sealed containers in your trash. Then work to control the conditions that made their attack possible in the garden.

Keep the neighborhood clean. Patrol the areas around your garden and clear away any plants hosting pests and diseases. Ask your neighbors to do the same if their yards contain plants that could spread pest problems to your property.

LEARN TO MANAGE PEST PROBLEMS

The nonchemical approach to pest control is management, not eradication. Managing pests means using a variety of preventive tactics to outwit insects and other pests before they damage your plants. If a pest problem still becomes severe, there are several botanical pesticides considered acceptable for organic gardeners—but these are toxic substances, only for use as a last resort. If chemical sprays (even if they're organic) have been your first defense against pests, experiment with other methods. You may be surprised by how effective they are.

The idea behind most organic techniques is to sidestep the insect problem one way or another or to let natural controls kill off the pests. Keeping plants healthy, timing plantings to avoid peak pest activity, eliminating pest hiding places, covering plants to keep pests away, encouraging or importing appropriate predators, and trapping pests are all parts of a good pest management system. Pests can never be entirely eliminated. Even in the best of gardens, some pests are present. But an effective pest management system can keep them within acceptable levels.

Healthy plants can fight back. Keep your plants well-fed and watered to help them resist or tolerate insect damage. Strong potato plants under attack by Colorado potato beetles can lose a great deal of leaf surface without suffering diminished yield. Choose resistant cultivars to give your plants a head start in the battle against insects. And when possible, time plantings to avoid exposing susceptible crops to a particular pest.

Encourage the good bugs. Encourage pest parasites and predators by planting mint, dill, daisies, and other nectar plants around your garden or just by leaving weedy patches where goldenrod, lamb's-quarters, and Queen-Anne's-lace are growing. These plants will provide a food supply for the good bugs and encourage them to stick around. You can also buy and release many of these good bugs in your garden if they don't seem to be present naturally.

Use germ warfare. Check gardening supply catalogs for disease organisms (*Bacillus thuringiensis* is one) that infect and kill cabbage caterpillars, grasshoppers, and Japanese beetles. If your supply of compost is low, you can buy the insect-parasitic nematodes it would contain to help control soil-borne larvae of many pests.

Barricade the garden. You can prevent many flying insects from landing for dinner or egg laying by covering plants with a light, translucent material. Barricade crops with cheesecloth or plastic tunnels or with floating row covers, such as Reemay.

Trap the bad bugs. Trap flying adult bugs with pheromone traps or yellow sticky traps. You can buy or make specialized traps that lure and trap apple maggot flies, Japanese beetles, and other pests.

Use natural insecticides as a last resort.

Natural pesticides, even those that degrade very quickly or do not injure mammals, are still toxic. Pyrethrin, rotenone, ryania, and sabadilla kill more than one insect species. In addition to the pests, victims can include pollinating insects such as bees, butterflies, and harmless flies, as well as the parasites and predators you are trying to encourage.

PRACTICE DISEASE PREVENTION

Prevention and protection are the keys to organic disease control. However, rather than using pesticides as both blanket preventives and cures, organic gardeners try to use good gardening practices to manage disease in the yard and garden. Natural poisons are used only when disease outbreaks occur that are serious enough to ruin the harvest or kill the affected plants.

The organic formula for preventing disease problems includes keeping plants healthy, keeping the garden clean, rotating crops, and planting resistant cultivars. If you keep the garden environment healthy and provide a balanced regimen of water and nutrients, your plants will be robust and vigorous enough to resist most bacterial, fungal, and viral infections, as well as other garden disorders.

If you're new to organic gardening, you may have to change your attitude toward plant disease problems. A few black spots on plant leaves won't ruin your garden's beauty, and blemished apples still taste delicious. Just remember the benefits of avoiding chemical sprays, and save them for the circumstances when using a fungicidal spray could literally be a life-or-death choice—for your plants.

Take advantage of built-in defense. Whenever possible, use disease-resistant or tolerant species and cultivars that are appropriate to your climate and season length. Many tomato cultivars are resistant to Fusarium and Verticillium wilts, and sour cherry trees are much less prone to disease problems than most sweet cherry cultivars.

Provide an optimum environment. You can't do much about the weather, but you can take steps to ensure that plants remain healthy and vigorous. Protect warm-loving crops with covers when the weather is cold. Water when the rains don't come. Give plants a well-balanced, general organic fertilizer if they show deficiency symptoms, and thin plants when they are too crowded.

Practice good sanitation. Scrutinize all new plants you bring into the garden to avoid importing diseases. Remember to wash and sterilize tools that you have used around diseased plants. Clean up the garden regularly, and put diseased plant materials in the trash or a hot compost pile.

Rotate crops. Changing the location of disease-prone crops every year helps prevent plant disease organisms from building up large populations. Remove and destroy any diseased weeds you spot in the area surrounding the garden, as disease could spread from them to your garden plants.

Use good cultural techniques. Don't handle plants when they're wet. Disease organisms spread readily from plant to plant in moist conditions. And be gentle when you pick and cultivate so you don't create wounds where disease organisms can gain entry.

Use natural poisons as a last resort. Copper- and sulfur-based sprays and dusts can help prevent disease problems, but they can also damage plant tissue. Reserve them for fighting disease organisms that could wipe out yields or kill your plants.

BANISH WEEDS

Organic gardeners don't have weed-choked gardens, and they don't spend endless hours hoeing or pulling weeds. The organic gardener's first line of attack against weeds is to prevent them from getting a foothold in the garden. For existing weed problems, organic gardeners begin by identifying the weed, and then use specific techniques that will be most effective for eradicating that plant. So, set aside some time for good old-fashioned weeding and learn about other techniques for controlling weeds that don't require a hoe and a strong back.

Chemical-free gardeners know that weeds aren't all bad. They may shelter pest predators or serve as a trap crop for pests. Rather than blasting weeds with synthetic herbicides, organic gardeners take a more benign, long-term approach that eventually results in fewer weeds, which means much less time spent weeding.

Identify the problem plants. Identifying dominant weed types in each area of the garden will help you select the most effective control strategy. Simply pulling or tilling under annual weeds may work fine, but the same techniques could actually worsen problems with perennial weeds.

Prevent weed problems from starting. To keep the seed reservoir in the soil from overwhelming you, pull out weeds before they set seed. Use mulches and cover crops to prevent weeds from flourishing in the bare spots in your garden.

Select appropriate controls.   Hand pulling weeds and cultivating the soil are still two of the best ways to beat weeds. But heavy mulching or use of some simple organic herbicidal methods may work better on certain tough perennials.

Keep up the attack.   Solving a tough weed problem may take more than one gardening season. Take heart in knowing that as weed populations decline, the yearly weed worry will become smaller and smaller.

KEEP RECORDS

Keeping records will help you plan crop rotations, evaluate the performance of new cultivars, and reap the rewards of your own experience. Taking notes and making quick diagrams is a habit that takes perseverance to start, but one that organic gardeners can't do without. So take along a pencil and paper whenever you visit the garden: You'll usually see something worth remembering.

It may be hard to remember to take notes regularly while you're gardening, but it's even harder to remember what you did last April when you're about to order seeds in January or plant your vegetable beds in May. Find a record-keeping style that suits you and stick with it. The value of records may not become apparent until you've kept them for a couple of years. Comparing soil progress or the severity of a certain pest from year to year can be invaluable in planning garden strategy for the upcoming season.

List crop rotations.   Rotation is critical in prevention and control of some diseases and insects. It's best not to count on your memory in planning your vegetable garden rotation.

Maintain soil records.   Your soil test re-cords, along with records of what type of fertilizers and soil amendments you applied when, are good reference materials to have as you pursue a multiyear project of improving your soil's health.

Have a weather diary.   Notes on weather conditions can help you diagnose environmental disorders and figure out when and how much supplementary watering your garden will need.

Use comparison records.   Comparison records will help you determine the best cultivars for your garden and also the best season for growing various crops. They may also help you to determine which pest control methods work best for you over time.

CHAPTER TWO

Garden Planning and Record Keeping

By Miranda Smith

On a cold January day, you gather seed catalogs and gardening books and settle in to make your garden plans. You calculate how much seed to order and how many transplants to raise and play with color schemes for a flower border. But do you try to anticipate what insects may devour your plants this year or consider what mineral supplements might boost yields in your vegetable garden? If you aspire to garden without using chemicals, anticipating problems and planning preventive measures is as important as the yearly catalog shopping ritual.

Planning is the keystone of a gardening system that helps you avoid pest damage and mineral deficiencies, eliminating the need for quick-fix chemicals. Staying ahead of the game can make a world of difference in organic gardening. Testing your soil and following through on recommendations for adding organic matter and amendments yield healthy, vigorous plants—without the use of quick-release chemical fertilizers. Planting resistant cultivars is a basic organic tactic for preventing disease, but finding those cultivars may require forethought. Altering your garden design and using mulches and cover crops are other techniques that may reduce problems too often solved by reaching for a container of hazardous chemicals. Many of the chemical-free techniques described in this book emphasize *prevention*, and that means thinking and acting in advance.

Sound complicated? It can be, but if you make a sound plan, the work will be both manageable and fun. And your investment of a day or two of planning in winter and early spring will be more than repaid by the hours saved and the cost—both monetary and environmental—of chemicals left unsprayed come summer.

MAKING A GARDEN PLAN

If you're a seasoned chemical-free gardener, making a plan that uses organic methods is

Getting Psyched to Make the Switch

What makes an organic gardener different from a conventional gardener? The obvious difference is that organic gardeners don't use synthetic pesticides and fertilizers, but perhaps the most important difference is attitude. Organic gardeners take the long view. Rather than buying bags of chemical fertilizer to apply on the spot, they save yard waste (like leaves and grass clippings) and kitchen scraps, and build a compost pile to create a first-rate soil amendment and slow-release fertilizer for later seasons. Instead of spraying cabbage loopers with a toxic insecticide, they spray the bacterium *Bacillus thuringiensis,* which is harmful only to caterpillars. They know they'll see some additional damage before the bacterial population builds up enough to overwhelm the pests, but they'll accept that as a small price to protect their health and the health of the environment.

If you've never gardened organically, you may be afraid your beautiful gardens will be overrun by pests and weeds while you're learning how to make the switch. Not so! For one thing, you don't have to give up all the familiar techniques overnight. You can scale back your use of fertilizers and pest control products gradually.

The first thing you may want to work on is the all-important attitude adjustment. You'll need to be enthusiastic about being in your garden, because switching to organic methods may mean extra work, at least at first. Invest some time in observing your garden. Start to learn how to identify pest insects, and also the beneficial insects that are your pest-control allies. If you don't already have a compost pile, find a good location and get one started. Get in the habit of taking regular garden-patrol walks to pull weeds and look for early signs of pest problems. Think of the extra physical effort your garden will require (hoeing, spreading mulch, turning compost) as a benefit to your health, as well as your garden's. As you slowly change your habits, you can phase out your old ways. Within a season or two, you'll see that what seemed to be a major switch is really many small changes in your gardening methods that will soon seem easy and familiar.

---

probably second nature. But if you're a gardener who's making the transition, the garden plan you create may include techniques you've never tried before. To come up with a good transition plan, you have to take your own situation into account. For example, a transition plan for a small flower garden where the only chemicals applied have been small amounts of artificial fertilizers will be simpler than one for a large backyard orchard where many different fungicides and insecticides have been routinely used year after year. To help you grasp the big picture and understand the basic areas where you'll need to make some changes, see "Getting Psyched to Make the Switch" above.

Set Your Goals

Your first step will be to decide what changes or additions you want to make in your garden. Getting more organic matter into your vegetable garden soil may be a top priority. Your list also may include weaning your flower bed soils from chemical fertilizer, growing spray-free fruit, or revitalizing a drab lawn.

You'll need a map of your garden to refer to when you sit down at your desk or kitchen table ready to plan. (See "How to Make a Garden Map" on page 20.) You'll also need pencil and paper. This book, gardening catalogs, and other books or magazine articles will be helpful.

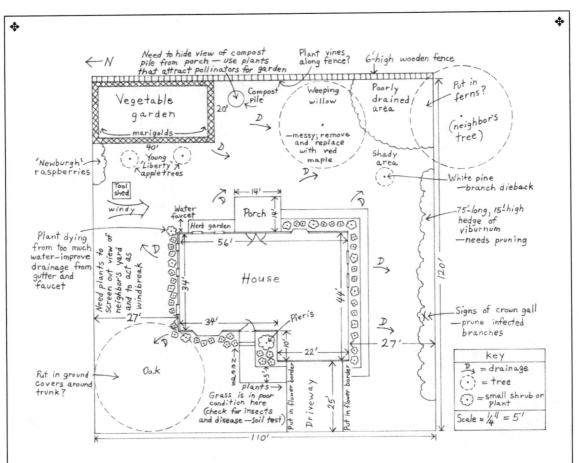

How to Make a Garden Map

Since most of us do our garden planning indoors during winter, it's helpful to have a garden map to refer to as we figure out our goals and plan of action. A garden map should include information about the dimensions and contents of existing plantings and notes on soil types around the yard.

You'll need to know the dimensions of your site before you draw. The easiest way to measure your yard is to use a flexible 25- or 50-foot measuring tape. Or, you can measure the average length of your stride and pace out your yard (this may be more convenient if you're trying to take measurements on a frosty winter day). Either way, take notes of the total dimensions of your property and of the square footage of your lawn, your vegetable garden, and flower beds. These measurements will be useful when you're calculating your needs for soil amendments or for some biological control agents.

It's easiest to draw your property accurately in miniature if you use graph paper. Let each square represent one square foot of your property (or more, if you have a large property). After you draw the map, fill in any information you have about soil characteristics or cultivar names of trees or perennial plantings. Your map will be a catalyst as you prepare a list of gardening goals. You can write up your goals on a separate sheet of paper, or make notes right on your map about problems that need attention and features you'd like to add or change.

Study your map and write down all the goals that pop into your head. This is your own private brainstorming session (or the whole family may contribute). Don't worry yet about how and when you'll accomplish all the changes. (See "Garden Brainstorming," below, for inspiration in setting your goals.) Once you have a complete list, you'll move on to doing a little research and scheduling a plan of action.

Learn the Basics

Depending on your past experience, getting the background you need to turn your list of goals into a schedule of activities may take ½ hour or a full day. It's important to understand the scope of a project before you embark on it. For example, growing spray-free fruit may mean planting new disease-resistant cultivars, making insect traps, and scheduling sprays of dormant oil or biological controls. Revitalizing your lawn may require aerating it, spreading organic matter, weeding diligently, and reseeding bare patches.

See part 2, "Chemical-Free Garden Techniques," for a wealth of information that will relate to your garden goals. Also, refer to "The Chemical-Free Gardener's Library," on page 431,

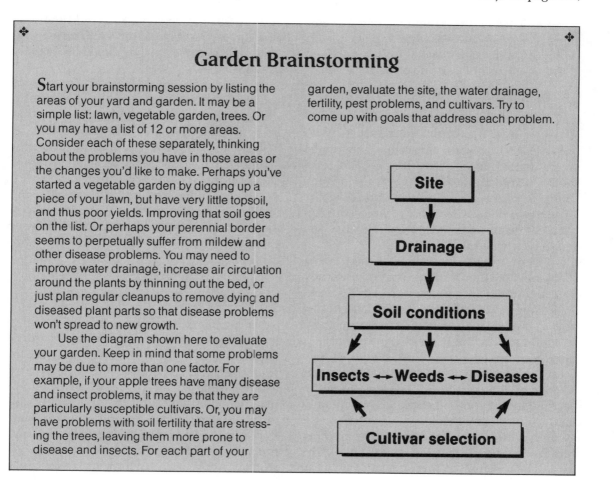

Garden Brainstorming

Start your brainstorming session by listing the areas of your yard and garden. It may be a simple list: lawn, vegetable garden, trees. Or you may have a list of 12 or more areas. Consider each of these separately, thinking about the problems you have in those areas or the changes you'd like to make. Perhaps you've started a vegetable garden by digging up a piece of your lawn, but have very little topsoil, and thus poor yields. Improving that soil goes on the list. Or perhaps your perennial border seems to perpetually suffer from mildew and other disease problems. You may need to improve water drainage, increase air circulation around the plants by thinning out the bed, or just plan regular cleanups to remove dying and diseased plant parts so that disease problems won't spread to new growth.

Use the diagram shown here to evaluate your garden. Keep in mind that some problems may be due to more than one factor. For example, if your apple trees have many disease and insect problems, it may be that they are particularly susceptible cultivars. Or, you may have problems with soil fertility that are stressing the trees, leaving them more prone to disease and insects. For each part of your garden, evaluate the site, the water drainage, fertility, pest problems, and cultivars. Try to come up with goals that address each problem.

Site → **Drainage** → **Soil conditions** → **Insects ↔ Weeds ↔ Diseases** ← **Cultivar selection**

for many other titles of helpful books and periodicals.

As you read, jot down how long it may take to complete a project and what special materials or tools you may need. These notes will help later as you draw up a schedule and shopping list. If your garden budget is a concern, check prices of plants, supplies, and tools now, so you can approximate the cost of a project and consider it as you make a schedule.

Schedule Your Activities

You're now ready to create a tentative schedule of activities. It may help you to refer to chapter 3, "Month-by-Month Garden Management," to get a picture of when to plant, prune, apply organic matter and fertilizer, and perform other garden tasks in your area.

Be Realistic

Only you know how much time, work, and money you can put into your garden. With experience, most gardeners come to expect the yearly paring down of lavish plans and learn not to be disappointed that they can't do everything in one season. But you can avoid the frustration of having to leave projects unfinished if you are as realistic as possible when you make your schedule.

Wise gardeners know that they can't overhaul their yards or gardens in a few weekends, and accordingly stagger the work. For example, in a large yard with widely separated growing areas, it might be smart to start an enclosed compost pile by the main garden in spring. A month or two later you can start an open pile near the berries that grow in an out-of-the-way corner of the yard. This two-step process of starting the compost piles spreads out the work and makes it manageable.

Apply this staggered approach to any other major changes you plan to make. It will be easier, for instance, to meet a goal of building sides for one raised bed each weekend rather than one of converting all 1,000 square feet of vegetable garden into raised beds by sundown on Sunday. Pace yourself to make gardening a pleasant—not strenuous—experience.

Include Long-Term Plans

Planning for the future by creating a tentative year-by-year schedule of activities can help with organization. For example, you could plan to apply rock phosphate, greensand, and manure to the garden this year and finished compost the next. You could begin double-digging and/or enclosing one or two growing beds in spring, another two in fall, two the following spring, and the final two that fall. You could gradually add disease-resistant apple cultivars to your backyard orchard—one or two each year for three years.

If you're experimenting with organic pest control, you may want to test the new techniques only in one area of your yard at first. Perhaps you'll feel more comfortable mastering new techniques for a season in the vegetable garden before you tackle the challenges of using chemical-free methods on your fruit trees.

Plan for your own particular situation and realize that you'll probably make adjustments as the years go by. You'll be well repaid for your efforts in more successful and enjoyable gardening.

Adjusting Garden Design

Gardening chemical-free may mean changing your garden design as well as your gardening practices. You may discover that some of your fruit trees are just too difficult to grow without using chemical sprays and decide to plant some resistant cultivars. Or, you may want to try tilling in a shaded portion of your lawn that seems more prone to disease problems and replacing it with a shade-tolerant, trouble-free ground cover. When you're making your schedule,

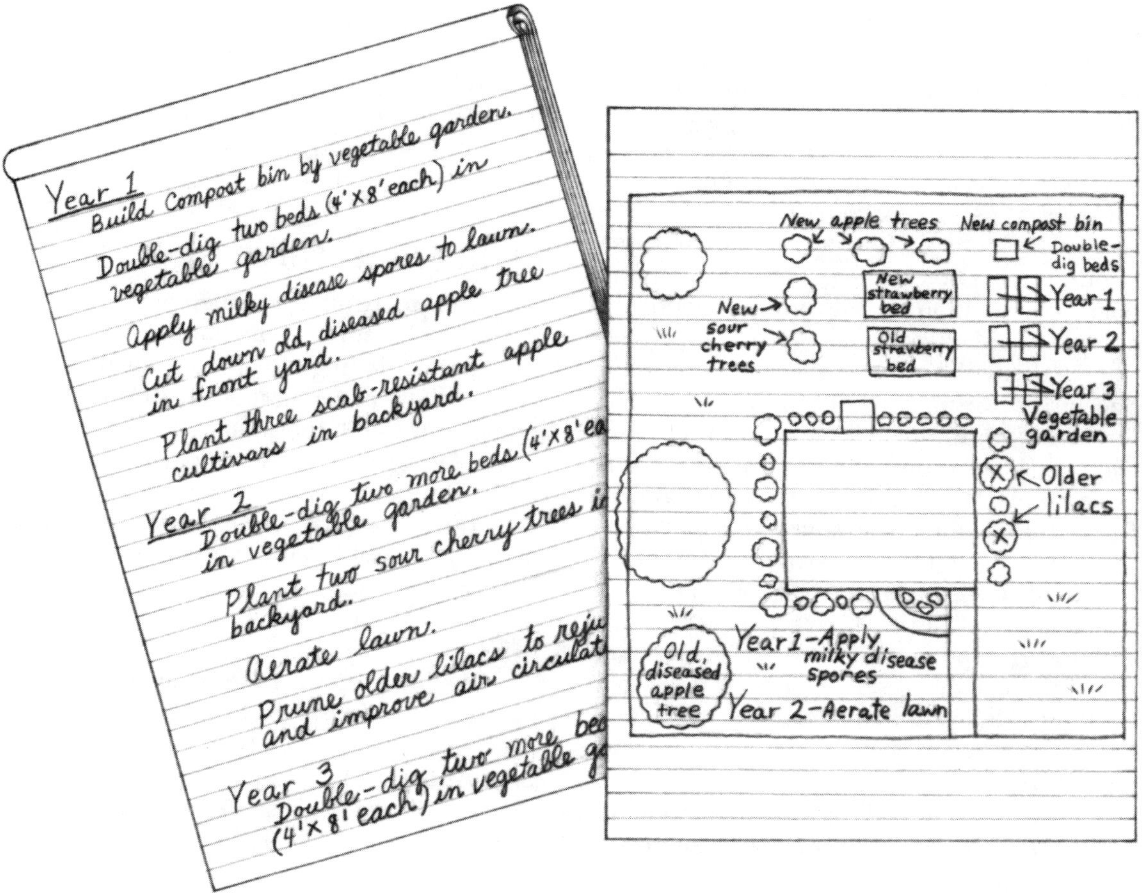

The handwritten notes read:

Year 1
Build compost bin by vegetable garden.
Double-dig two beds (4'×8' each) in vegetable garden.
Apply milky disease spores to lawn.
Cut down old, diseased apple tree in front yard.
Plant three scab-resistant apple cultivars in backyard.

Year 2
Double-dig two more beds (4'×8' ea) in vegetable garden.
Plant two sour cherry trees in backyard.
Aerate lawn.
Prune older lilacs to rejuv and improve air circulat

Year 3
Double-dig two more bed (4'×8' each) in vegetable ga

The sketch labels:
New apple trees   New compost bin
Double-dig beds
New sour cherry trees
New strawberry bed
Old strawberry bed
Year 1 / Year 2 / Year 3
Vegetable garden
Older lilacs
Old, diseased apple tree
Year 1—Apply milky disease spores
Year 2—Aerate lawn

Drawing a simple sketch of your property while working on your long-term plan of action may help you decide what changes to tackle right away and what to put off for future gardening seasons. Try to spread the work of major changes—like converting your vegetable garden to raised beds—over two or three years.

keep in mind that changes in design often require a considerable investment of time and/or money.

Beds Make Better Gardens

One change many gardeners make when converting to organic vegetable growing is to create raised beds in their vegetable gardens. While raised beds are not essential to successful organic gardening, they do have many advantages.

Closely planted beds are planned for weed, disease, and pest control. These intensive beds are actually easier to keep tidy than rows and are certainly more attractive. In a 3-foot-wide bed, everything is within arm's reach. The leaves of adjacent plants shade the soil, reducing weed growth. Obviously, a bed of mixed carrot, radish, and lettuce seedlings shouldn't be seeded so thickly that nothing else can get through; you *will* have to weed in the beginning of the season. But if you plant a little more thickly than usual, you can begin thinning (and eating) young plants within only a month or so. By the time the crops are almost mature, the soil is so shaded that few new weeds can survive.

The diversity of plants in a raised bed may also help provide some natural pest protection for your crops. Mixing your crops may make it harder for pests to find and eat their target plants. See the box "To Repel or to Attract?" on page 169, for more details on the benefits of companion planting.

Diversity also reduces the chance that pests and disease organisms will build to epidemic levels. If the troublemakers can't easily move from one host to another, more of them will die. For example, Mexican bean beetles may have difficulty finding their food source in a bed interplanted with snap beans, potatoes, and herbs.

Crop diversity can also be good for the soil. The traditional pairing of nitrogen-loving corn with nitrogen-providing beans is a good example of the way that diversity protects soils from becoming deficient in a particular nutrient.

Making Beds

You can make beds by simply marking off 3-by-5-foot sections of garden with space for pathways left between them. But by taking the extra step of raising the beds, either by double-digging or simply moving topsoil from the aisles to the growing area, you'll create a lighter, deeper, more nutrient-rich and water-absorbent soil environment. To maintain these benefits, regard beds as permanent. Don't walk on them or break them down at the end of the season. Double-digging is often preferable to simply heaping up topsoil to form beds. However, it requires so much effort and time that you shouldn't expect to convert a large garden to raised beds in a single season. A reasonable plan is to double-dig one or two beds in early spring and late fall, when the weather is cool. For step-by-step instructions on how to double-dig a garden bed, see "Starting with New Beds or Lawns" on page 67.

Building sides on beds is optional. Some gardeners prefer to leave the sides open and rake and reshape the beds every season. Others prefer the permanent shape and support provided by materials like landscaping ties, cement blocks, rocks, or bricks.

Taking Inventory

After you've made a garden plan, take stock of your garden supplies and tools. If you're new to organic gardening, chances are you'll need to buy some new materials that are effective, environmentally sound substitutes for chemical pesticides and fertilizers. Even if you're a longtime organic gardener, it's useful to take a yearly inventory to see what you've run out of or what new tools or supplies you'll need if you're starting a new project.

Garden Supplies

Organic gardeners use many of the same basic supplies as conventional gardeners, but they also use a range of alternatives to synthetically formulated fertilizers and pesticides. Consider the following categories as you inventory your garden supplies.

Organic soil amendments and fertilizers. No more bags of chemical fertilizer for the chemical-free gardener. You'll be using compost, mineral supplements, and possibly foliar feeds to nourish your soil and crops. You may be able to find free local sources of organic matter if you can't generate enough compost from the materials in your yard. Rock phosphate, greensand, bonemeal, and many other substances that boost the content of specific nutrients are commercially available.

Barriers and traps. These are essential items for preventing or combating insect and disease problems. Barriers keep insects from reaching plants. For example, you can spread floating row covers over many crops to barricade them from flying insects. Tree bands block or capture some fruit tree pests. Copper strips can be an effective barrier against slugs. Insect traps usually serve best as monitors of pest populations. You can make some of these barriers and traps yourself with simple materials; others are available commercially. Many are preventive controls, so you must have them on hand before a problem develops.

Sprays and dusts. Some insecticidal or insect-repelling sprays can be made at home from soap, garlic, and other substances. Diatomaceous earth is used as an insecticidal dust. There are several botanical poisons sold as sprays or dusts. Copper and sulfur compounds are used in natural sprays that help prevent and treat fungal and bacterial disease problems. If you plan to use sprays and dusts, also make sure you have the proper equipment to protect your health and safety (see "Spray Safely!" on page 220). Even though botanical poisons are natural substances that break down in the environment within several days, they are toxic—to insects and to people—at the time you apply them.

Biocontrols. Biocontrols include insects, bacteria, fungi, viruses, and nematodes that are predators or parasites of plant pests. The most widely used of these, *Bacillus thuringiensis,* or BT, is generally available at garden centers. However, many other biocontrol agents must be specially ordered from insectaries. Timing in releasing these agents is important. It may also be important to plan to make plantings of shelter or attracting crops to encourage native or released biocontrols.

Hand and Power Tools

New techniques may call for new tools. Turning a compost pile, double-digging a garden bed, and working with cover crops all are easier and a lot more fun if you have the right tools.

Digging tools. Spading forks are invaluable for aerating the soil. Just plunge the fork into a bed and wiggle it around, and you've added important air channels without dislodging any top soil. Spades with rectangular, fairly flat blades are more useful than shovels for most garden digging.

Shovels and manure forks are handy for the compost pile. Some gardeners buy compost-aerating tools, but others just stick the manure fork into different parts of the pile and lift slightly to let in new air.

Weeding tools. Weeding becomes much less of a chore with a sharp tool that is easy to manipulate. Different people like different tools, and you'll probably want to try several before investing in any. Two popular cultivating tools are an oscillating hoe, which has sharp edges on both sides of the swiveling blade, and a small, swan-neck, fixed-blade hoe. If you keep these tools sharp, you'll find it nearly effortless to sever crowns of weed seedlings from their roots. You'll also need a short-handled cultivating tool for spot weeding in closely planted beds.

Pruning tools. Pruning tools are essential for chemical-free gardeners. Keeping trees and shrubs well-pruned promotes vigorous growth and good health, and pruning out diseased wood frequently helps to control disease problems. However, make sure you have high-quality, sharp pruning tools, because a poor pruning job can leave slow-healing wounds that are ideal entry sites for disease organisms.

Tillers. Rotary tillers are a common sight in most gardener's sheds; chances are you may already own one. But, if you are in the market for one, try out various types before spending your money, as tillers differ a great deal. Those with the tines mounted under the motor are best for heavy work like breaking up ground for new beds. Small tillers are fairly lightweight and can be used in close quarters for jobs like cultivating around perennials.

Sprayers and dusters. Sprayers are important pieces of equipment in the chemical-free gardener's arsenal. Rather than filling them with pesticides, however, you'll use them more frequently for foliar nutrient sprays.

Sprayers for the home gardener include: small, handheld models for watering and feeding seedlings; stationary, manually pumped compressed-air sprayers for small greenhouses; and backpack sprayers for large greenhouses, the orchard, and gardens.

Dusters are handy for dry materials. Some of the new ones are designed to handle large particles such as rock powders. They are also convenient tools for applying powdery substances like diatomaceous earth to infested plants.

Seed-sowing aids. Several wheeled seeding tools are available. By changing interior disks, you can plant seeds of various sizes and at various spacings. If you routinely plant large areas, a seeder can be a great time-saver.

A canvas bag seed spreader is a handy aid for sowing grass and cover crop seed. With the bag hung over your shoulder, you turn a handle attached to a gear mechanism at the bottom of the bag, and quickly and evenly sow large areas as you walk.

Watering equipment. Lack of water is one of the most common causes of poor plant growth, and weakened plants are easy targets for pests. A good watering system is a wise investment for the chemical-free gardener. The least expensive way to start out is with a long wand and some fancy spray nozzles.

Drip irrigation systems and soaker hoses are invaluable for dry periods when you want to conserve water. Not only are they valuable water-saving devices, but once installed, they are a labor-saving way to water the garden.

Garden Shopping List

Once you know what you have and what you need, make your shopping list and order or buy your supplies and tools *now.* Shop with the assumption that the same pests and problems that bothered your plants last year will be back again. If you wait to shop until you see the damage, you may not get around to buying the nonchemical remedy. You'll probably discover that many of the supplies you need are not available at your local garden center. Many of these materials are produced by small companies that are not part of the distribution network that supplies most garden centers. These organic supply companies are listed in "Sources" on page 426.

KEEPING GARDEN RECORDS

Your transition to chemical-free gardening will be easier if you keep records. Before, you may have given the garden fairly uniform treatments; if you spread a chemical fertilizer, it was likely that you spread it everywhere. If you sprayed a pesticide, chances are it was a broad-spectrum chemical that killed many species of pests on several different crops. Some people who use chemical fertilizers plant the same crops in the same locations year after year because they aren't particularly concerned about changing and balancing nutrient demands on the soil or preventing pests and disease populations from building up. But with nonchemical growing, all of that changes. You're going to want to keep track of each area in order to plan well for the coming years.

Starting on page 434, you'll find blank forms that you can photocopy to create your own garden workbook. Or, you may want to devise your own chart and record book formats or use a garden diary book or planning calendar.

Rotation Records

You may find it relatively easy to remember where the plants in your vegetable garden were growing last year, but could you remember three years' worth of rotations? Controlling pests and diseases often hinges on rotations at least that long, and it's nearly impossible to remember details of rotations without records. Keep-

Location	Year 1	Year 2	Year 3	Year 4
Bed 1	Pumpkins (cover crop – hairy vetch)	Tomatoes (cover crop –) oats	Broccoli followed by Carrots (winter mulch)	Onions (spring) Lettuce (fall) (cover crop –) clover
Bed 2	Tomatoes (cover crop – hairy vetch)	Onions (spring) Broccoli (fall) (cover crop – oats –)	Beans followed by beets (cover crop –) clover	Butternut squash (cover crop –) clover
Bed 3	Sweet corn (cover crop – hairy vetch)	Dried beans (winter mulch)	Onions (spring) Spinach (fall) (winter mulch)	Tomatoes (cover crop –) clover

Rotating crops in your vegetable garden is an important way to prevent disease organisms from building up large populations that could infest your plants. Keeping clear and accurate records of your rotations is essential for success. This record was prepared using the worksheet on page 434.

ing track of rotations is doubly difficult if you're combating more than one problem. For example, you may need to control both club root, which affects cabbage family plants, and onion root maggot in a particular bed.

Recording areas where nutrients seem poor, where particular weeds are thriving, and where insect populations have built up all helps with rotational plans. For example, if flea beetles did damage in a particular bed last year, it would be foolhardy to direct seed cabbage there, even if the rotational plan calls for it. Early peas or members of a plant family that are not susceptible to flea beetles may be a better rotational choice.

Soil Records

Keep records from all the soil tests you do. And beyond that, note quantities, locations, and dates of fertilizers and amendments you've added to the garden. You are going to need to know whether manure or compost was used in a par-

ticular area, how much lime you spread, and where you sprayed with certain nutrients, particularly trace elements. Without records to refer to, you may inadvertently create mineral imbalances in your garden soils. After all, a tiny bit of boron can correct a deficiency, but just a little bit more can make the area toxic. (See "More Can Be Worse," on page 80, for other examples of how soil minerals can become overabundant or deficient as a result of poor fertilizing or liming practices).

Weather Diary

Records are useful even in the current season. If you keep track of sun, rain, cloud cover, humidity levels, and temperature, you'll be more likely to spot an environmentally caused disorder and refrain from blaming it completely on poor nutrition or a disease. Tipburn on lettuce and blossom-end rot on tomatoes are disorders that are environmentally caused, but commonly misdiagnosed as diseases.

Cultivar Comparison Records

Comparing the performance of one cultivar against another and noting the best season for each cultivar you grow will help you improve your garden's appearance and yield. For example, by making notes about different lettuce cultivars, you'll eventually know which ones are more resistant to hot weather, less attractive to pests, preferred at the dinner table, and relatively frost-tolerant. Records of bloom time of your perennials will enable you to figure out what new species to plant to fill in gaps in bloom in your beds. You may generally remember the really outstanding qualities of a particular cultivar, but may forget some of the small details that can help when placing seed orders and figuring out planting schedules.

Aside from their practical nature, record books can be highly amusing. Slightly frivolous jottings as well as the business-at-hand notes are fun to read throughout the years. Like an old diary, an old record book evokes pleasant memories while it helps increase your understanding of the chemical-free gardening system.

CHAPTER THREE

Month-by-Month Garden Management

By Anna Carr

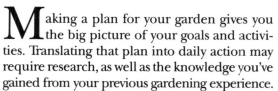

Making a plan for your garden gives you the big picture of your goals and activities. Translating that plan into daily action may require research, as well as the knowledge you've gained from your previous gardening experience.

Information on seed packets, in catalogs, and in brochures from your local Cooperative Extension Service office will help you decide when to plant various food crops and ornamentals. Your garden records will also be a valuable source of information about the best times to plant in your particular area.

You can use the calendar presented in this chapter to help you anticipate problems and spread the work of gardening more evenly through the seasons. We've taken a regional approach and combined the USDA Plant Hardiness Zones into three areas—short season, midlength season, and long season. Refer to the map on page 30 to determine in what region your garden lies.

Use the calendar for spot reference or for detailed planning. If you're trying to plan your weekends for the month of May, study the May list—as well as April and June—while you figure your strategy. In fact, you'll occasionally find a reminder in one month to complete a task—such as pruning fruit trees—if you didn't get around to it during the previous month. You may also notice suggestions for a garden technique or pest control measure (such as putting boards under melons to control rot) listed under another region that will also apply to your garden.

As you look through the calendar, you'll notice that while spring is undeniably the busiest time in the garden, there are plenty of garden chores that can be reserved for less hectic times in fall and winter. Plan ahead and do as much preventive maintenance as possible. Prepare new beds and holes for trees and shrubs in midsummer or late fall, and add lime and rock fertilizers, so you need only apply the quick release fertilizers at planting time next spring.

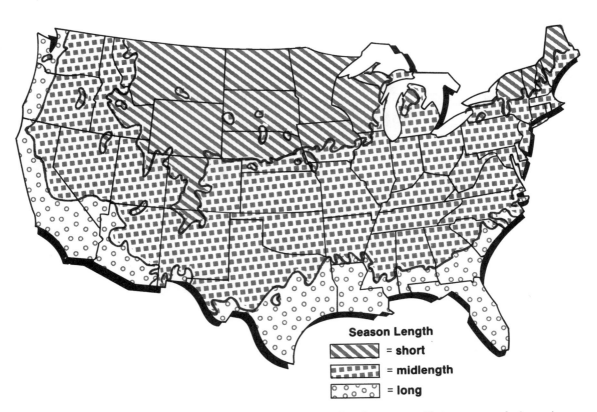

Season Length

- ▨ = **short**
- ▧ = **midlength**
- ○ = **long**

The map shown here illustrates the boundaries of the short-season, midlength-season, and long-season gardening regions. It is based on the USDA Plant Hardiness Zone Map. The short-season region corresponds to Zones 1–4; the midlength-season region to Zones 5–7; and the long-season region to Zones 8–11.

Practice pest control during all seasons—even in the dead of winter you can check trees and shrubs for scale and other overwintering pests and take steps to eliminate them. Dig or till the vegetable patch in the fall and clean up thoroughly to cut down on next year's pest problems. Make use of as many labor-saving practices as possible: Reduce weeding by using mulches. Protect crops with netting and floating row covers where appropriate. Set up automatic drip irrigation systems.

Also, remember that keeping records is easier if it's a year-round activity. Every month's list in this calendar could have a line that says "Write it down." To stay current with your gar-den and weather observations, get your hands on the largest calendar you can find and hang it—with a pencil permanently attached—in the garage or shed near your seeds and tools. Then, before you take off your boots after a morning in the garden, stop and jot down what you've done. Record the first sightings of pests and the occurrence of plant disease. Mark the days when you turn your compost pile. If you've just applied the first of several sprayings or feedings, pencil in the approximate times of the next applications. You can use these notes to periodically update your permanent workbook, which in time will become your personal week-by-week garden management guide.

JANUARY

SHORT SEASON

❧ Make plant and seed selections with an eye toward cold hardiness and short-season production. Plants not suited to your climate will be the first to succumb to pest and disease damage.

❧ Check stored dahlia tubers, gladiolus corms, and tuberous begonias; mist if they seem dry, and discard rotten ones.

❧ Hold off pruning roses, fruit trees, and bramble fruits this month, or you may induce winter injury.

❧ Check perennials for signs of frost heaving. Cover with more mulch if necessary.

❧ Shake snow from the lower branches of evergreen trees and from the tops of shrubs. Use a broom or rake to gently knock the snow from higher tree limbs.

❧ Use sand or birdseed to provide traction on icy walkways instead of de-icing salts: Salts can burn your lawn and other plantings.

MIDLENGTH SEASON

❧ If you have a thaw this month, turn the compost heap.

❧ Harvest the rest of your winter root crops, such as carrots and parsnips.

❧ Check stored dahlia tubers, gladiolus corms, and tuberous begonias; mist if they seem dry, and discard rotten ones.

❧ Hold off pruning roses, fruit trees, and bramble fruits this month, or you may induce winter injury.

❧ Check perennials for signs of frost heaving. Cover with more mulch if necessary.

❧ Use sand or birdseed to provide traction on icy walkways instead of de-icing salts: Salts can burn your lawn and other plantings.

LONG SEASON

❧ Dig or till in the green manure crop on your vegetable beds. Use a bioactivator to help speed breakdown. If you didn't sow a green manure crop, top-dress the beds with compost or well-rotted manure.

❧ Renew mulches on all your garden pathways now to help suppress newly germinating weeds.

❧ Apply insect-parasitic nematodes to wireworm-infested soil so it will be ready for spring planting.

❧ Cut back roses and strip off remaining leaves to prevent black spot and other diseases. Clean up debris.

❧ Now is a good time to prune grape vines, as they will bleed readily if pruned later than February or March.

❧ Prune fruit trees, including apples, cherries, peaches, and pears. Apply dormant oil after pruning to help control many insect pests.

❧ Spray ornamental trees and shrubs with dormant oil to control aphids and scale.

❧ Dig out weeds in the lawn.

FEBRUARY

SHORT SEASON

🐦 Run a germination check on your stored vegetable seeds before you sow them indoors. Don't use seeds with poor germination rates: Seedlings may be weak and more prone to insect and disease problems.

🐦 Prepare a soil mix for starting seeds and raising vegetable and annual flower transplants indoors.

🐦 Prune fruit and ornamental trees and scrape away egg masses from trunks and nearby rocks and debris.

🐦 Check rodent guards around fruit trees; replace if they are damaged.

MIDLENGTH SEASON

🐦 Run a germination check on your stored vegetable seeds before you sow them indoors. Don't use seeds with poor germination rates: Seedlings may be weak and more prone to insect and disease problems.

🐦 Prepare a soil mix for starting seeds and raising vegetable and annual flower transplants indoors.

🐦 If the weather warms near the end of the month, rake off mulch on one bed to get ready for planting spring greens and onions.

🐦 Prune fruit, nut, and shade trees before dormancy ends.

🐦 Use dormant oil spray to help control scale on trees and shrubs.

🐦 Rake the lawn near the end of the month.

LONG SEASON

🐦 Till or dig in green manure crops if you haven't already.

🐦 If you took a short winter break from your regular garden monitoring walks, now is the time to revive the habit. Check for insect damage and weed, disease, or fertility problems.

🐦 Turn the compost heap.

🐦 If necessary, take soil samples for soil tests.

🐦 Check stored begonia and caladium tubers for evidence of drying or decay. Cut out and discard any soft or rotten areas, then allow the healthy portion of the roots to dry before returning the tubers to storage.

🐦 Prune grape vines and fruit trees if you didn't do so last month.

🐦 Rake mulch away from bramble fruits such as blackberries and raspberries.

🐦 Begin spraying fruit trees with copper or sulfur fungicides if you had disease problems last season that can be prevented by this treatment.

🐦 Prune off damaged branches on ornamental trees and shrubs. Fertilize, as needed.

🐦 Cut roses back if you didn't do so last month. Fertilize.

🐦 Continue to weed the lawn and run a soil test if you're unsure about your soil's health. Rake in rock fertilizers and lime, as needed.

MARCH

SHORT SEASON

❧ If the ground is too wet for planting, start peas indoors in peat pots or soil blocks. They'll get off to a strong start and can be set out a week or two later.

❧ If you let your compost pile freeze up during the winter, turn it thoroughly now and add some fresh manure or soil to help restart the composting process.

❧ Mulch all garden pathways now to help suppress weeds.

❧ Prune fruit and ornamental trees if you haven't already done so. Remove diseased or infested branches. Also prune out glassy-looking masses of tent caterpillar eggs on your trees or on nearby wild fruit trees to reduce feeding damage in spring.

❧ Spray orchard and ornamental trees and shrubs with dormant oil to control scale and other overwintering pests.

❧ Prune blueberry bushes, bramble fruits, and grape vines late in the month, before new growth begins.

❧ Fertilize trees and shrubs when they leaf out.

❧ Prune hydrangeas and other shrubs that bloom on new wood.

❧ Rake the lawn to remove dead material.

MIDLENGTH SEASON

❧ Turn under green manure crops in vegetable and annual flower beds. If you didn't sow a green manure crop, top-dress the beds with compost or well-rotted manure.

❧ Mulch all garden pathways now to help suppress weeds.

❧ Add rock fertilizers and well-rotted manure to perennial beds.

❧ Gradually remove winter mulch from roses; fertilize near the end of the month.

❧ Prune any winter-damaged canes from rose bushes.

❧ Prune hibiscus, buddleia, and other shrubs that bloom on new growth.

❧ Scrape away loose bark on apple trees to expose codling moth cocoons.

❧ When the ground has thawed, feed fruit trees with compost, well-rotted manure, and rock fertilizers.

❧ Prune blueberry bushes, bramble fruits, and grape vines early in the month, before they break dormancy.

❧ If you spray dormant oil, be sure to do so before trees and shrubs break dormancy.

LONG SEASON

❧ Side-dress asparagus and rhubarb with a light application of compost or well-rotted manure.

❧ Scatter a mixture of granular BTK (*Bacillus thuringiensis* var. *kurstaki*), moist bran, and molasses over the soil one week before planting to control cutworms in vegetable and flower beds.

❧ Cover new vegetable seedlings and transplants with floating row covers to help prevent insect pest damage.

❧ Clean up litter around grape vines and bramble fruits and fertilize.

❧ Prune and feed summer-blooming shrubs such as crape myrtle and hibiscus to promote new growth.

❧ Feed azaleas, camellias, and clematis.

❧ Rake and reseed the lawn. Cut winter grass short.

APRIL

SHORT SEASON

🐛 If you planted a green manure crop on your beds last fall, till or dig it in early this month. Otherwise, spread compost or well-rotted manure on your vegetable garden and till or dig it in as soon as the soil is dry enough to work.

🐛 Lightly side-dress asparagus and rhubarb with compost or well-rotted manure.

🐛 Start taking regular garden monitoring walks to check for early signs of insect damage and weed, disease, and fertility problems.

🐛 Fertilize perennials before or during bloom, using a balanced organic fertilizer.

🐛 Uncover and fertilize established roses.

🐛 Prune winter-damaged canes from roses.

🐛 Near the end of the month, mulch berry canes with well-rotted manure and peat.

🐛 Prune bramble fruits and blueberries if you haven't already done so.

🐛 Check fruit and ornamental trees for borers; probe in borer holes with wire to kill them.

🐛 Weed and fill in bare patches of existing lawns.

🐛 Fertilize the lawn late in the month.

MIDLENGTH SEASON

🐛 Lightly side-dress asparagus and rhubarb with compost or well-rotted manure.

🐛 Scatter a mixture of granular BTK (*Bacillus thuringiensis* var. *kurstaki*), moist bran, and molasses over soil one week before planting to control cutworms in vegetable and flower beds.

🐛 Cover cool-season transplants with floating row covers to protect them from many flying insect pests. If you aren't using covers, apply insect-parasitic nematodes to the soil as you sow or set out broccoli, cabbage, and other plants that may be attacked by root maggots.

🐛 Start taking regular garden monitoring walks to check for early signs of insect damage and weed, disease, and fertility problems.

🐛 Feed perennials with bonemeal and manure.

🐛 Begin a spray program of copper or sulfur fungicides for your fruit crops if you've had previous problems with diseases.

🐛 Check your lawn for white grubs. Apply milky disease spores if you discover a white grub infestation.

🐛 Prepare new lawn areas now if planting warm-season grasses. Fertilize the lawn late in the month.

LONG SEASON

🐛 Spray with BTK (*Bacillus thuringiensis* var. *kurstaki*) if your plants are being damaged by chewing caterpillars.

🐛 Lay down organic mulch around young vegetable plants after the soil warms.

🐛 Remove spent blossoms on perennials to encourage further flowering.

🐛 Spread compost on perennial borders. Use care around plants such as delphiniums, whose crowns should not be smothered.

🐛 After fruit set, top-dress fruit trees with an organic fertilizer high in nitrogen and phosphorus.

🐛 Apply sticky bands around trees trunks to stop climbing pests.

🐛 Rake back mulch from azaleas and rhododendrons, and prune after flowering.

🐛 Check your lawn for white grubs. Apply milky disease spores if you discover a white grub infestation.

MAY

SHORT SEASON

ɞ Use floating row covers to protect young vegetable transplants from frost damage.

ɞ Scatter a mixture of granular BTK (*Bacillus thuringiensis* var. *kurstaki*), moist bran, and molasses over soil one week before planting to control cutworms in vegetable and flower beds.

ɞ Spray with BTK if your plants are being damaged by chewing caterpillars.

ɞ Fertilize bulbs with bonemeal after blooming.

ɞ Plant drought-tolerant annuals around bulbs, so that bulbs will be less likely to rot from overly moist soil conditions.

ɞ After petal fall, spray summer oil to control aphids, scale, and some caterpillar pests on fruit trees.

ɞ Mulch young evergreens with aged sawdust or composted bark chips to keep out weeds.

ɞ Fertilize spring-flowering shrubs.

ɞ Prune lilacs, forsythias, and other shrubs that bloom on old wood after they finish flowering.

ɞ Check your lawn for white grubs. Apply milky disease spores if you discover a white grub infestation.

MIDLENGTH SEASON

ɞ Spray with BTK (*Bacillus thuringiensis* var. *kurstaki*) if your plants are being damaged by chewing caterpillars.

ɞ Protect eggplant, melon, and cucumber seedlings with floating row covers as you plant.

ɞ Begin feeding roses every two weeks to encourage full growth and flowering.

ɞ After petal fall, spray fruit trees with summer oil to control aphids, scale, and some caterpillar pests.

ɞ Prune azaleas and other flowering shrubs after blossoming; fertilize, and replace mulch.

LONG SEASON

ɞ Keep checking for pests in the vegetable garden—destroy eggs of bean beetles, Colorado potato beetles, and squash bugs.

ɞ If grasshoppers have been a severe problem in the past, apply grasshopper bait now.

ɞ Set up bird netting on cherry trees, blueberries, and bramble fruits.

ɞ Thin fruits on orchard trees. Apply seaweed spray.

ɞ Mulch ornamental trees and shrubs to prevent water stress. Give vigorously growing trees a second feeding.

ɞ Keep newly seeded lawn areas well-watered to ensure good germination and establishment.

ɞ Give established lawns their main feeding.

JUNE

SHORT SEASON

❧ Cover beans, cucumbers, and melons with floating row covers as you plant.

❧ Weed the asparagus bed carefully after harvest is complete to avoid injuring roots.

❧ If you plan on lifting tulip or hyacinth bulbs, do so now, when foliage begins to turn brown.

❧ Begin feeding roses every two weeks to encourage full growth and flowering.

❧ Cover grape vines, cherry trees, and blueberry and bramble bushes with bird netting.

❧ Thin fruit on fruit trees and clean up fallen fruit after June drop.

❧ Apply sticky bands to fruit trees to catch insect pests that climb the trunks.

❧ Treat lawns infested with cutworms, armyworms, or sod webworms with parasitic nematodes.

MIDLENGTH SEASON

❧ Stake tomatoes and feed with manure tea or liquid seaweed to prevent blossom drop.

❧ Mulch peas and other cool-season vegetable crops. Keep them well-watered and fed as temperatures rise this month.

❧ Weed the asparagus bed carefully after harvest is complete to avoid injuring roots.

❧ Cover grape vines, cherry trees, and blueberry and bramble bushes with bird netting.

❧ Apply sticky bands to fruit trees to catch insect pests that climb the trunks.

❧ Thin fruit on trees and clean up fallen fruit after June drop.

❧ Hang sticky red traps to catch apple maggot flies.

❧ Feed and mulch summer-flowering shrubs after blossoms have faded.

LONG SEASON

❧ As early potatoes blossom and mature, reduce watering. Keep Colorado potato beetles in check by handpicking eggs and larvae or spraying with BTSD (*Bacillus thuringiensis* var. *san diego*).

❧ As mulches around your plants break down, add a fresh layer. Side-dress heavy-feeding crops with balanced organic fertilizer as you mulch.

❧ Carefully weed the asparagus bed after harvest is complete, and put down a deep mulch of chopped leaves or other organic material to help conserve moisture.

❧ Solarize the soil of vegetable beds if they've had problems with disease organisms or persistent weeds.

❧ Pinch back annual and perennial flowers to encourage continued blossoming.

❧ Keep fruit trees and ornamentals well-watered.

❧ There's still time to fertilize your lawn. Check for pests such as mole crickets and fire ants and take steps to control them while they are still young.

JULY

SHORT SEASON

🐛 Now that the soil has thoroughly warmed, mulch the vegetable garden.

🐛 Remove floating row covers from cucumbers and melons as soon as they start to bloom unless you plan to hand pollinate.

🐛 Stake tomatoes and tall flowers.

🐛 Solarize the soil of vegetable beds if they've had problems with disease organisms or persistent weeds.

🐛 Divide irises after flowering, and fertilize with bonemeal and compost as you replant.

🐛 Continue to spray BTK (*Bacillus thuringiensis* var. *kurstaki*) to control caterpillar pests.

🐛 Check fruit crops for pest damage or rot and destroy any infested fruit.

🐛 Check bramble fruits for disease and destroy sickly canes. Handpick Japanese beetles.

🐛 Check soil pH in your lawn and growing beds now. If you need to add balancing materials, do so in the fall.

🐛 Continue to apply parasitic nematodes every three weeks as needed on pest-ridden lawns.

MIDLENGTH SEASON

🐛 Put boards under growing melons to reduce the chances of rot and to deter slugs, sowbugs, and other pests.

🐛 Solarize the soil of vegetable beds if they've had problems with disease organisms or persistent weeds.

🐛 Remove floating row covers from cucumbers and melons as soon as they start to bloom unless you plan to hand pollinate.

🐛 Check soil pH in your lawn and growing beds now. If you need to add balancing materials, do so in the fall.

🐛 Withhold water from onions as soon as tops start to dry and fall over. Lift the bulbs when tops are entirely brown.

🐛 Remove spent blooms from perennials and annuals to encourage further flowering.

🐛 Check fruit crops for pest damage or rot, and destroy any infested fruit.

🐛 Check lawn for sod webworms and other pests and take proper steps to control them.

LONG SEASON

🐛 Set up screens to shade lettuce and other heat-sensitive vegetables from the sun.

🐛 Keep up weekly BTK (*Bacillus thuringiensis* var. *kurstaki*) sprays if caterpillar pests are seriously damaging cabbage family crops.

🐛 Remove diseased plants from the garden so healthy plants remain uninfected. Burn diseased plant parts, bury them in a hot compost pile, or put them in sealed containers for disposal with household trash.

🐛 Water all garden beds deeply.

🐛 Check for budworms on geraniums, nicotiana, and petunias; spray with BTK if severely infested.

🐛 Pinch back chrysanthemums to encourage bushy growth.

🐛 Spray fruit trees with liquid seaweed to help them withstand heat stress.

🐛 Keep warm-season grasses well-watered.

AUGUST

SHORT SEASON

To lessen the chance of pest infestations, don't follow spring and summer vegetables with a second planting of a crop from the same family. Plant fall broccoli and cabbage crops far away from your earlier crop.

Pull weeds before they set seed.

Remove spent blooms from perennials and annuals to encourage further flowering.

Renew mulches around fruit trees and provide support for sagging branches.

Monitor caterpillar pests and treat as needed.

Give roses their last feeding of the summer.

Stop fertilizing ornamentals, unless they show deficiency symptoms, so they will harden fully before winter.

Seed new lawns near the end of the month.

MIDLENGTH SEASON

Pinch off blossoms from winter squash and melons so energy won't be wasted on fruit formed too late to mature before cold weather.

As mulches around your plants break down, add a fresh layer. Side-dress heavy-feeding crops with balanced organic fertilizer as you mulch.

Mark healthiest vegetable and flower plants for saving seed.

Lift and divide daylilies and irises to share with friends. Be sure to check plants for signs of borers and destroy any infested plants.

Give roses their last feeding of the summer.

Replace sticky bands around fruit trees and check for pests.

LONG SEASON

Transplant and sow fall crops now so plants will be large enough to withstand snail damage during cool weather.

Renew mulches in vegetable and flower beds to help control weeds and conserve soil moisture.

Feed and lightly prune roses.

Check young fruit trees for scale and treat infestations with insecticidal soap or summer oil sprays.

Check soil pH in your lawn and growing beds now. If you need to add balancing materials, do so in the fall.

Continue to water the lawn deeply and thoroughly to encourage deep rooting and best growth.

SEPTEMBER

SHORT SEASON

🌱 After harvesting, take special care to pull and destroy squash, melon, cucumber, tomato, and bean plants that might harbor disease. Burn diseased plant parts, bury them in a hot compost pile, or put them in sealed containers for disposal with household trash.

🌱 Remove all black plastic mulch from vegetable beds as part of your fall garden cleanup.

🌱 Dig and fertilize vegetable beds as last crops are harvested, and plant a green manure crop.

🌱 Cut back perennials after frost.

🌱 Lift dahlia tubers, gladiolus corms, and tuberous begonias after frost. Let them dry thoroughly before you store them for next year.

🌱 Prune out spent bramble canes after fruiting.

🌱 Give the lawn its main feeding.

MIDLENGTH SEASON

🌱 Mulch heat-loving crops like eggplants, melons, and peppers and cover with floating row covers to help prolong their production.

🌱 Pinch back tomatoes early in the month, so no new fruit starts to form. Keep plants well-watered.

🌱 Cover fall cabbage family crops with floating row covers or spray regularly with BTK (*Bacillus thuringiensis* var. *kurstaki*) to prevent looper and cabbageworm damage.

🌱 Double-dig and enrich new garden beds for next year.

🌱 Fertilize fall vegetables, especially where previous crops may have depleted soil nutrients.

🌱 Marigolds, calendulas, and many other flowering annuals can be trimmed, lifted, and brought indoors to be enjoyed this fall.

🌱 Rake up and destroy fallen fruit.

🌱 Prune out spent bramble canes after fruiting.

🌱 Seed new lawns now if you're planting cool season grasses.

LONG SEASON

🌱 Cover fall cabbage family crops with floating row covers or spray regularly with BTK (*Bacillus thuringiensis* var. *kurstaki*) to prevent looper and cabbageworm damage.

🌱 Double-dig and enrich new garden beds for next year.

🌱 Lift and divide daylilies and irises to share with friends. Be sure to check plants for signs of borers and destroy any infested plants.

🌱 Gently bend raspberry canes to the ground and pin them in place to encourage layering.

🌱 Prune water sprouts from orchard trees and clean up fallen fruit.

🌱 Don't fertilize your lawn now. Growth is slowing, and warm-season grasses will soon be shutting down for the winter.

OCTOBER

SHORT SEASON

❧ Dig new beds, as needed, and protect them with a winter mulch or green manure crop.

❧ Pick up fallen fruit and debris to control codling moths and other pests.

❧ Wrap the trunks of fruit trees and young shade trees to protect them from sunscald and animal damage.

❧ Apply lime and rock fertilizers to the lawn and garden, as needed.

❧ Don't let fallen leaves remain on the grass. Rake, chop, and compost them.

❧ Sharpen lawn mower blades when you do your end-of-season mower maintenance.

MIDLENGTH SEASON

❧ Do your major fall cleanup this month. Remove dead and diseased plant parts from all parts of the garden and burn them, bury them in a hot compost pile, or put them in sealed containers for disposal with household trash.

❧ Remove all black plastic mulch from vegetable beds as part of your fall garden cleanup.

❧ Cultivate garden soil to expose pests to freezing temperatures.

❧ Enrich empty vegetable beds with rock fertilizers and lime, and plant a winter green manure crop.

❧ Cut back perennials after frost.

❧ Lift dahlias, gladiolus corms, and tuberous begonias after frost.

❧ Give the lawn its main feeding and reseed bare patches.

LONG SEASON

❧ Plant a green manure crop on empty beds.

❧ Fertilize vegetable and flower gardens with rock fertilizers and apply lime, as needed.

❧ Enrich perennial beds with compost and bonemeal.

❧ Rake up and destroy fallen fruit.

❧ Prune evergreens for shaping.

❧ Cut warm-season grass very short and over-seed with winter grass such as bluegrass or rye.

NOVEMBER

SHORT SEASON

🍂 Mulch the asparagus bed with chopped leaves or straw to protect crowns from frost.

🍂 Check stored vegetables for rot.

🍂 If you plan to test your soil, take samples early this month for nutrient analysis.

🍂 Mulch bramble fruits as they go dormant.

🍂 Continue watering young trees and shrubs until the ground freezes.

🍂 Apply an antidesiccant such as Wilt-Pruf to young trees and shrubs in windy spots.

🍂 Prepare a hole now for planting your live Christmas tree.

🍂 In preparation for winter snowfall, stake or prop up the heaviest branches of large evergreens. Yews and other foundation shrubs should be tied up or protected with snow boards to prevent damage.

🍂 It's not too late to fertilize the lawn if you didn't do so last month.

MIDLENGTH SEASON

🍂 Apply lime and rock fertilizers to the garden where necessary.

🍂 Mulch overwintering carrots and parsnips with clean straw.

🍂 If moles and mice are prevalent, place tulip bulbs in wire cages as you plant them.

🍂 Get a head start on spring weeding by clearing weeds from beds now.

🍂 Wrap the trunks of fruit trees and young shade trees to protect them from sunscald and animal damage.

🍂 Mulch bramble fruits as they go dormant.

🍂 Check lilacs for scale and cut away severely infested branches; wait until late winter to spray with lime sulfur or dormant oil.

🍂 Sharpen lawn mower blades when you do your end-of-season mower maintenance.

LONG SEASON

🍂 Continue spraying BTK (*Bacillus thuringiensis* var. *kurstaki*) on cabbage family plants if you have caterpillar problems.

🍂 Fertilize winter vegetables generously where the soil has already supported many earlier harvests.

🍂 Provide good wind protection for winter vegetable crops.

🍂 Plant a winter green manure crop on empty beds.

🍂 Mulch bramble fruits as they go dormant.

🍂 Work in bonemeal and rich compost as you plant spring bulbs.

🍂 Mark diseased tree limbs, but wait until they are dormant to begin pruning.

DECEMBER

SHORT SEASON

❧ Make compost in a covered garbage can during winter. Be sure to add soil or commercially available microorganisms to speed decomposition.

❧ Keep watering perennials and newly planted trees until the ground freezes.

❧ Mulch orchard trees, shrubs, roses, and other perennials once the ground has frozen.

MIDLENGTH SEASON

❧ Check stored potatoes, onions, and other vegetables for signs of spoilage and throw out any rotten ones.

❧ Take soil samples for testing before the garden beds freeze solid.

❧ Keep watering perennials and newly planted trees until the ground freezes.

❧ Mulch orchard trees, shrubs, roses, and other perennials once the ground has frozen.

❧ Spray orchard and ornamental trees with dormant oil if the weather allows.

LONG SEASON

❧ Destroy diseased plants by burning or burying deeply in a hot compost heap, or put them in sealed containers for disposal with household trash.

❧ Take up black plastic mulch from vegetable beds and store it for the winter.

❧ Enrich the soil with bonemeal and other rock fertilizers, and mulch any beds not planted in green manure crops.

❧ Fertilize perennials with compost and rock fertilizers as blooming ends; water plants well before dormancy sets in.

❧ Cut back chrysanthemums to 6 inches; cut straggly perennials to the ground.

❧ Get a head start on spring weeding by clearing weeds from beds now.

❧ Spray fruit and ornamental trees with dormant oil to control scale, spider mites, and overwintering insect eggs.

❧ Begin winter pruning once trees are thoroughly dormant.

❧ Keep leaves raked off the lawn so the grass doesn't yellow.

❧ Sharpen lawn mower blades when you do your end-of-season mower maintenance.

PART TWO

Chemical-Free Garden Techniques

CHAPTER FOUR

Soil Improvement and Fertilizing

By Bill Wolf

Healthy soil is the key to successful organic gardening, so it's not surprising that soil improvement and fertilizing programs are at the heart of a chemical-free gardening system. The basic principle that organic gardeners live by is to feed the soil and let the soil feed the plants.

Soil is the source of essential nutrients such as nitrogen, potassium, and phosphorus that plants need for growth and development. Plants also absorb water from the soil and draw physical support for their growth by spreading their roots through the soil. The challenge for the organic gardener is to balance the soil so that it provides all the conditions plants need to thrive.

Adding organic matter—various forms of living or dead plant and animal material—to the soil is the keystone of soil fertility. Organic matter supplies raw materials to earthworms and naturally occurring bacteria, fungi, and other microorganisms in the soil. These organ-isms digest organic matter in a process known as the decay cycle. The decay cycle breaks down the complex compounds in the plant material into forms that can be absorbed by plant roots, creating a natural recycling process. Enriching the soil with organic matter also improves soil structure, which in turn improves the soil's capacity to hold water and nutrients and to release them to plant roots as needed.

Gardeners can go a long way toward having properly nourished plants by simply adding appropriate amounts of organic matter to the soil each year. This practice alone will solve many problems commonly found in garden soils.

Keeping air in the soil is also essential to a healthy balance. Soil air can be thought of as an important fertilizer, because it feeds the soil organisms that make the nitrogen and decay cycles flow. Gently handling the soil to increase crumb structure and air and pore space is part of the balancing process.

When gardeners feed plants by adding synthetic fertilizers to the soil, they bypass these natural cycles and throw the soil out of balance. This has detrimental side effects. Synthetic fertilizers are highly soluble and may leach through the soil and end up polluting groundwater. Synthetic fertilizers do not encourage soil microorganisms, so their populations are altered. This interferes with the breakdown of organic matter, eventually causing soil structure and water-holding capacity to decline.

Organic gardeners opt to feed the soil before feeding the plants. They tend the soil in ways that invigorate soil organisms. This approach not only assists the plants' food production efforts, but helps them meet the stresses of insect damage, disease infection, and drought.

An organic soil improvement and fertilizing system has the following steps.

🐾 *Learn about your soil.* It's critical to examine and test your soil to determine whether it has good physical structure, sufficient biological activity to support plant growth with organic methods, and sufficient mineral reserves to produce healthy plants.

🐾 *Correct soil imbalances.* Adding proper amounts of balancing soil amendments will correct your soil's problems. This may be a two- to four-year process, depending on your soil's initial condition.

🐾 *Maintain soil balance.* Adding materials to maintain the level of soil organic matter is the key to keeping your soil in balance. A steady supply of organic matter feeds soil microorganisms and other life forms, which in turn help process the nutrients in organic matter into forms that your plants can use.

🐾 *Feed your plants.* Plants growing in a balanced, healthy soil may grow perfectly well without additional fertilizer in most situations. Thus, a plant-feeding program is an optional step used when you decide the extra effort is worthwhile.

Healthy soil won't happen overnight, or even in one growing season. If you're a gardener who has relied on chemical fertilizers, you may wonder if it's worth two or more years of effort to increase soil organic matter. But improving your soil organically will do more in the long term than reduce your fertilizer bill. A healthy, balanced soil will be easier to dig or till, will require less irrigation, and will support plants that are more tolerant of insect and disease problems.

LEARN ABOUT YOUR SOIL

To manage a healthy soil, you must understand the relationships between all its components—texture, mineral content, organic matter level, mix and population of organisms, air, and water. If you aren't familiar with these components, see "Soil Science Simplified," on the opposite page, for some quick explanations.

One question that most home gardeners ask themselves is, "Should I be adding anything to the soil this spring?" The best way to answer that question is to investigate your soil: to learn about its structure and content by observation and testing.

Having Your Soil Tested

The most precise way to evaluate your soil is to submit several soil samples from your yard for soil analysis. Privately run soil testing laboratories and the Cooperative Extension Service perform soil analyses for home gardeners and offer recommendations on soil improvement based on the results of their tests.

Preparing a Soil Sample

You may want to collect many samples from around your yard and combine them to submit

Soil Science Simplified

All soils are a mix of minerals, organic matter, living organisms, water, and air. They all play a part in creating an environment that allows plant roots to grow and take up water and nutrients to support growth.

Minerals. These very small fragments of rock are the most abundant component of the soil. The fragments are classified as sand, silt, or clay, depending on the size. The mix of sizes gives the soil a particular texture and influences how well the soil holds water and allows it to drain.

Organic matter. This is the fresh and decaying remains of plants and animals that become part of the soil. As plants grow and die, their tops and roots are digested by microorganisms living in the soil. This process of digestion eventually transforms the nutrients in the plant matter into forms that can be absorbed by plant roots, creating a recycling system in the soil. Decayed organic matter, called humus, also plays a role in the soil's water-holding capacity.

Living organisms. These include soil-dwelling mammals and reptiles, earthworms, insects, mites, nematodes, and soil microorganisms. Their activity creates channels in the soil for air and water. They also are the prime force in the decay cycle that replenishes soil's natural fertility. Some are also pests that damage the plants in our yards and gardens.

Water and air. Obviously, plants need to take up water to grow and survive. Water is also the carrier for dissolved nutrients that plants need for growth and development. Plant roots and soil organisms need air to function properly, and air is actually a food source for some soil microorganisms.

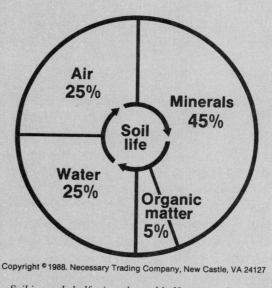

Copyright © 1988. Necessary Trading Company, New Castle, VA 24127

Soil is nearly half minerals, and half water and air. Organic matter makes up only a small percentage of the soil but has a large impact on soil fertility. Soil life, including mammals, reptiles, insects, and microorganisms, plays an important role in the decay cycle.

for a single test and report. Or, you may want to prepare separate samples from your vegetable garden soil, your lawn, and an area where you hope to create a flower border, for example. However, you'll have to pay three times as much to get the three separate sets of recommendations.

Follow these steps to prepare a sample that will accurately reflect the content of your soil.

1. Scrape away any surface litter or plant growth from a small area of soil. Use a soil probe to cut a core of soil or dig a hole with a stainless steel trowel or other tool (if you don't have stainless steel tools, you can use a large stainless steel spoon) and collect a slice of soil from the side of the hole. For cultivated areas, collect a core or slice to a depth of 6 inches. For lawns, collect your samples only from the top 4 inches of soil.

2. Repeat the sampling procedure at 10 to 15 different locations around your yard or the particular area you are sampling.

3. Mix the soil cores or slices in a clean plastic or stainless steel container.

4. Place the mixed sample in a plastic container or bag and put it in the bag supplied by your Cooperative Extension Service or the soil testing laboratory for shipment.

It is very important not to touch the sample with soft steel, galvanized, or brass tools, or with your bare skin. The content of some minerals in soil is so small that minerals picked up from these metals or your skin could throw off test results.

You'll send your sample, along with an information sheet concerning your soil's his-

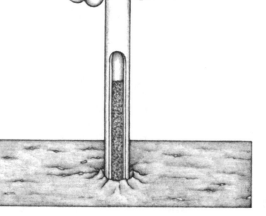

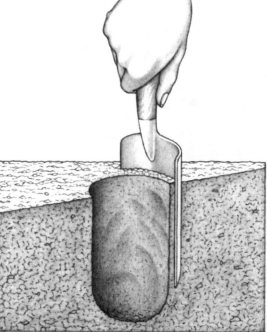

To collect a soil sample with a soil probe, first push the probe straight down into the soil to the proper depth. Then pull it completely out of the soil and remove the sample from the probe. If you're using a trowel, begin by digging a hole at least 6 inches deep. Then use the trowel to cut a slice of soil from the side of the hole: The slice is the soil sample.

tory and your future gardening plans, to the testing laboratory by mail. Be sure to write on the information form that you want recommendations for organic soil amendments.

Choosing a Testing Service

Soil testing labs, whether public or private, perform chemical analyses of the samples you submit to determine soil pH and levels of several mineral elements in the soil. The most common soil tests are pH, magnesium, phosphorus, potassium, and calcium levels, along with organic matter content. Some private testing laboratories also analyze micronutrient content, including zinc, manganese, iron, copper, and boron. These tests provide reasonable estimates of how much of these nutrients is likely to be available to plants, but not necessarily of the total quantity of nutrients in the soil. (See "The Mineral Side of Soil," on page 62, for an explanation of how minerals in the soil are taken up by plant roots.)

Cooperative Extension Soil Tests

The soil analysis offered by the Cooperative Extension Service is the least expensive available. For about $5 (or for free in some states), your state Extension Service will analyze your soil and make fertilizer recommendations. Cooperative Extension soil test kits are available from your local Cooperative Extension office or at many garden centers. Their analysis will probably not be as complete as that offered by private testing laboratories.

Private Laboratory Soil Tests

Private soil test labs charge $30 to $45 for their analyses. However, you will often find that the extra money you spend in using a reputable private soil testing laboratory will translate to a more complete soil test and final report. It may also be easier to find a soil lab that is familiar with making organic, rather than chemical, fertilizer recommendations. See "Soil Testing Services," on page 52, for the names and addresses of several private soil test laboratories.

Interpreting Recommendations

After analyzing your soil, the test lab will send you a report on the results of their analysis and recommendations for improving your soil.

Test results may include soil pH, organic matter content, and content of calcium, magnesium, phosphorus, potassium, sodium, sulfur, and trace minerals.

The recommendations the labs make are based on results of the research programs on plant responses to additions of these amendments. This research is complicated and hence expensive (it's a good part of why soil tests cost as much as they do). Making the recommendations is an imprecise science because the researchers must try to relate the data from the research soils they study to your individual soil. However, all soils are different: They are a complex mixture of minerals, organic matter, living organisms, water, and air. They do not all respond equally to applications of minerals or organic materials.

Typically, soil fertility studies are performed on soils that have not had much organic matter added to them. Soil analysis of such low organic

Soil Testing Services

A & L Agricultural Labs
7621 White Pine Road
Richmond, VA 23237

Biosystem Consultants
P.O. Box 43
Lorane, OR 97451

Cook's Consulting
RD 2, Box 13
Lowville, NY 13367

Erth-Rite
RD 1, Box 243
Gap, PA 17527

Peaceful Valley Farm Supply
P.O. Box 2209
Grass Valley, CA 95945

matter soils may be more accurate because organic matter makes the soil more biologically diverse and complex.

If you have built up your soil's organic matter content, the soil test results and recommendations you receive may be less than fully accurate. However, the advantages of gardening in high organic matter soils far outweigh this small disadvantage of less accurate soil test recommendations.

What practical measures can you take to correct for possible inaccuracies in the recommendations you receive? In general, if you have been adding organic matter regularly to your soil for years and had healthy crops and good yields, don't add as much nitrogen, phosphorus, and potassium as recommended. Because your soil will use the soil amendments you add more efficiently, and also because organic soil amendments are less likely to leach quickly out of the rooting zone, you can reduce the recommended amounts by as much as 75 percent. For example, if the recommendation you receive is for 2.5 pounds of nitrogen per 1,000 square feet of garden, you could add just 1 pound per 1,000 square feet.

If you are just beginning an organic soil management program, be prepared to add soil-building materials in the amounts recommended by the testing service. Once again, ask clearly for recommendations for organic amendments. That way, you won't have to guess whether to add smaller amounts than those on the lab report.

Testing the Soil Yourself

Another way you can learn about the condition of your soil is to try several simple tests that rely not on precise chemical analysis, but rather on your observations of the soil. With these tests, there is little or no cost and no waiting for results.

Testing Soil Condition

Simple observation skills go a long way in helping you learn about the general conditions of your soil. The color of your soil, the feel of it between your fingers, and the types of plants—especially weeds—that grow in it can tell you lots about your soil. Does your soil feel sticky or have bluish gray flecks in it? These are indicators of poor drainage. Are there lots of dandelions and plantain growing in your lawn? This could mean the soil has become compacted. These indicators are usually enough to tell you whether you have a problem serious enough to deserve a change in strategy or whether you should continue your present soil management program.

The squeeze test. This test will help you determine the texture of your soil, that is, the relative amounts of sand, silt, and clay. ("The Physical Side of Soil," on page 54, explains the importance of soil texture.) Do this test two or three days after a rainy spell. Take a loose ball of soil about the size of a Ping-Pong ball in the palm of your hand. Gently squeeze the mixture between the ball of your thumb and the lower outside edge of your index finger. Sand feels gritty, silt feels like moist talcum powder, and clay feels slippery.

Squeeze the ball in your hand, and release. If it crumbles, it has a reasonably balanced texture. If the soil ball can hold its shape, it has a substantial percentage of clay. If you can roll it into a sausage shape, it has even more clay.

Run your other hand firmly over the handful of soil. If you see scratch marks on the surface of the soil, there is a sizable proportion of sand present. If the soil feels greasy, this indicates silt.

The shake-up test. Another way to check your soil type is to measure the relative proportions of sand, silt, and clay in a sample of your soil. Gather a representative sample of your soil by collecting soil samples from several sites in your yard. Put about 1 cup of the combined sample in a quart jar, fill it with water, add a dash of nonsudsing dishwasher soap, and shake it until the soil is well mixed, about 10 seconds. Then let the jar stand for at least 24 hours. The soil will settle in layers with the sand on the bottom, the silt layer next, and the clay layer on the top. Compare the percentages you estimate with the soil texture triangle on page 55.

The root test. Plant roots are another indicator of your soil's general condition. Use a trowel to dig up a few plants, such as some

(continued on page 56)

Do You Need a Professional Soil Test?

When is it worthwhile for home gardeners to pay for a private soil lab test? To answer that question for yourself, start by thinking about the general condition of your plants for the past several years. Are they all in fair health? If there have been some problems, are these found in just one area, among only a few types of plants? If yields have been disappointing, if the lawn is filled with weeds, if plants are suffering from repeated disease problems, or if they show deficiency symptoms, you should consider testing your soil. Some deficiency or combination of deficiencies may well be the problem.

Also, if your observations and home tests of your soil indicate a problem that could be corrected by adding lime, rock phosphate, greensand, gypsum, sulfur, borax, or Epsom salts, get a professional soil test before you act. If you add too much of any of these materials, you can create problems that won't be easy to correct. If you add too little, you won't fix the problem.

You can't go wrong if you stick to adding composted organic matter. If most of the plants in your landscape are healthy, and you maintain your soils by adding compost, soil tests are an option, not a necessity.

The Physical Side of Soil

Your soil's physical structure influences how well plants grow in many different ways. Soil structure determines how well water is retained in the soil and how well it drains, how much air is available in the soil, and how easily minerals are released for uptake by plant roots.

Many factors contribute to the creation of soil structure. Soil water freezes and thaws, plant roots grow and die, earthworms move through the soil. All these processes contribute to formation of soil pores and formation of soil clumps, or aggregates. Soil structure is also affected by soil pH, the amount of humus in the soil, and the combination of minerals in the soil.

Ideally, soil pore spaces should vary in size and be evenly distributed. The ideal soil is well-granulated—the soil particles clump together in clusters with air spaces between them. Soil with sufficient organic matter will have this quality. Walking on the soil or driving yard and garden equipment over it causes these important pore spaces to collapse.

Soil texture. Sand, silt, and clay are tiny fragments of rock that make up nearly half the material in the soil. They are not necessarily different in composition, but are different in size. Sand particles are just large enough to be seen with the naked eye. Silt particles are smaller than sand particles, and clay particles are the smallest mineral particles in soil. The relative proportions of these three types of particles determine soil texture, which is a key indicator of your soil's potential productivity. The soil texture triangle shown here diagrams the relationships between sand, silt, and clay content and the resulting texture.

Knowing the proportions of sand, silt, and clay is useful for understanding the management techniques you'll use to improve your soil. Because sand particles are so coarse, and because the spaces between them are com-

paratively large, they do not tend to granulate, or stick together. Thus, sandy soils often do not hold enough water to support the growth of many kinds of plants. Sandy soils may also tend to be less fertile because they have less surface area where nutrients can be held. At the other end of the texture scale, clay soils are rich in very tiny particles that adhere to each other when wet. This can cause the soil surface to crust over, or a clay hardpan to form deeper in the soil when the clay particles wet and stick together and then dry into a hard, dense layer.

Soil structure. The arrangement of soil particles in the soil is referred to as the soil structure. It's desirable to have lots of pore spaces in the soil so water can drain through it, and oxygen and carbon dioxide can easily move from the air above into the spaces below. Pore space can vary from 30 to 50 percent of the volume of a soil.

Soil air. Oxygen is critical in the soil because many beneficial soil organisms cannot live without it. Gaseous nitrogen, another component of soil air, is a raw material for nitrogen-fixing bacteria that manufacture protein materials. These are later broken down to yield nitrogen compounds that can be absorbed by plant roots. Plant roots also "breathe" and need good air exchange between soil air and the atmosphere for good development.

Soil water. Water also occupies soil pore space. Plant roots absorb this water and pass it on to leaves and stems, where it serves as a coolant and as an essential part of all plant cells. Water is also the carrier for mineral nutrients, allowing them to enter plant roots and be transported through the plants. If soil doesn't drain well, water occupies all the soil pore space. This suffocates the plants because their roots cannot get the air they need for normal functioning.

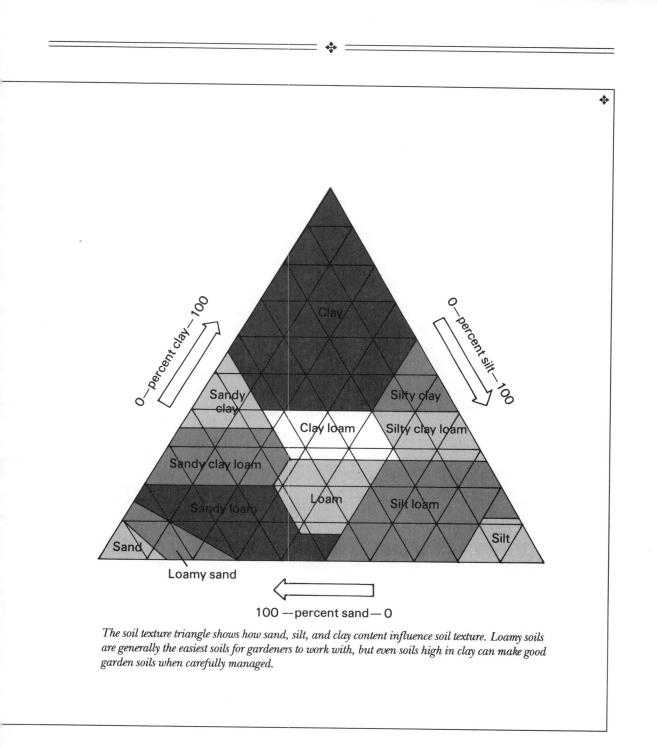

The soil texture triangle shows how sand, silt, and clay content influence soil texture. Loamy soils are generally the easiest soils for gardeners to work with, but even soils high in clay can make good garden soils when carefully managed.

annual flowers and vegetables. Even a small shrub can be lifted out and inspected in the early spring when its stored energy reserves are at a high level. Carefully lift the flower and vegetable plants and remove the soil from around the roots. Try to save as much of the root system as you can. If your soil is healthy, you should see strong, well-branched roots with plentiful root hairs. (Use a hand lens to look for root hairs.) Look for nodules (small swellings) on the roots of legumes like beans or peas. On other types of plants, if roots have a clubbed appearance, it may indicate problems caused by microbial pathogens and nematodes.

The root ball should be almost as big as the aboveground portion of the plant. Are the roots concentrated in the surface layer, making the root ball look flattened? This could mean your soil has a compaction or drainage problem. When you examine shrub roots, be content to check just the general depth and spread of the root systems. For all types of plants, you want to see strong, well-branched roots with plentiful root hairs.

Also check the roots of your lawn grass. Use a sharp knife to outline a square-foot section of turf, and cut down into the soil at least 6 inches. Carefully lift out and turn over the section. If the roots of your grass only extend into the first 2 inches of soil, you likely have problems with soil compaction. You may need to add organic material, and you definitely need to aerate the soil. If the lawn grass roots extend 4 to 6 inches deep, your soil is probably in good shape. You need only continue with your annual lawn management program. If the roots are sticking out of the bottom of the square, then your soil is physically in excellent condition. When you're done looking at the roots, carefully tuck the square of sod into place again, tamp it down, and water well to encourage rerooting.

The perc test. This test is an easy way to assess how quickly water drains through your soil.

Begin by digging a hole 6 inches across and 1 foot deep. Fill the hole with water and let it drain. As soon as the water has drained completely, fill it again. This time, keep track of how long it takes for the hole to drain. If it takes more than 4 hours, you have a drainage problem that needs attention.

The watering test. A variation on the perc test will tell you if your soil drains too rapidly. Start by watering a small area of your lawn or garden bed very thoroughly. Two days later, dig a small, 6-inch-deep hole where you watered. If the soil already is dry to the bottom of the hole, your soil likely doesn't retain enough water for good plant growth.

Another way to monitor soil moisture is to use a manual or automatic moisture sensor. These are small, electronic devices that measure available water in the soil, letting you know how long water levels are adequate for your plants' needs. If a meter indicates that the soil needs rewatering only a few days after you've watered thoroughly or after a soaking rain has fallen, then you need to improve your soil's water retention capacity.

The weed test. The types of weeds growing in your yard and garden can give you many clues about your soil's condition. For example, soils with a crust or a hardpan problem often have the following weeds growing in them: horse nettle, morning-glory, quackgrass, chamomile, field mustard, pineapple weed, and pennycress. See the table "Weeds as Soil Indicators," on page 60, for a complete listing of possible relationships between weeds and soil conditions.

The earthworm test. The earthworm population is a good general indicator of the biological activity in your soil. When you do this test, be sure the soil temperature is at least 55°F, has a moisture content of at least 25 percent, and hasn't been recently dug or tilled. Dig a hole 1 foot across and 1 foot deep, piling the soil on a ground cloth or layer of newspapers. Then filter through that soil with your hands, or put it through a coarse sieve as you refill the hole, and count the earthworms. If you find at least ten earthworms, your soil is in good shape. (Ten earthworms in a 1-by-1-foot hole is equivalent to 500,000 earthworms per acre.) If you find fewer than five earthworms, you probably have low biological activity in your soil. Possible reasons for low earthworm counts include a lack of organic matter for them to feed on, soil that is too acid or alkaline, or some kind of mineral imbalance.

The undercover test. The best way to learn about some aspects of your soil is to get right down into it. If you plan to plant a new fruit tree or shrub, kill two birds with one stone and check out your soil as you prepare the hole. Your new plant will benefit from the extra-large planting hole, and you'll get some valuable information about what's happening beneath the soil surface.

Dig a hole at least 2 feet down and 2 feet across so you can get a view down into it. If you pile the soil onto a tarp as you dig, the hole can be more neatly refilled when you are done. Look at the color of your soil as you dig. Generally, dark browns, reds, and tans indicate good

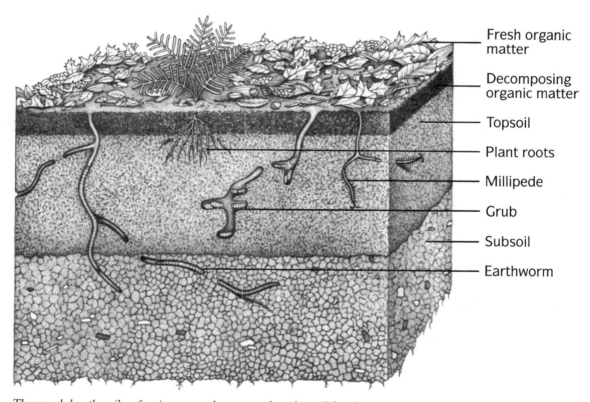

Fresh organic matter

Decomposing organic matter

Topsoil

Plant roots

Millipede

Grub

Subsoil

Earthworm

The scene below the soil surface in your garden may not be as beautiful as the view aboveground, but it's a fascinating and complex picture. In a healthy soil, the topsoil is filled with plant roots, organic matter in various stages of decomposition, and soil animals and insects. Subsoil is lighter in color than topsoil, because it contains less organic matter. Almost all biotic activity occurs in the top 1 foot of the soil. Earthworms and roots of some plant species will extend down into the subsoil.

soils. Soils that have a high humus content will usually be darker in color than soils low in humus. Soil color is also a clue to drainage. Tinges of blue and gray indicate poor aeration, often the result of poor water drainage. Generally, brown soils will drain much better than gray-colored soils. This is even true for a brown clay soil compared to a gray sandy soil, even though it is usually assumed that clay soils drain more poorly than sandy ones. Brown and red colors reflect the oxidized iron content of the soil.

You'll probably be breathing deeply as you dig, so notice how your soil smells. Soil with a high humus content usually has an appealing "earthy" smell, which is actually the odor produced by a type of soil microorganism called actinomycetes. Another cue to high humus content is living creatures. Earthworms and other soil organisms should abound in a healthy soil, especially in the late spring. If you have sufficient organic material in your soil, you will also see other small animals as you dig your hole. The presence of sow bugs, millipedes, and other soil organisms indicates there is sufficient organic material in your soil to keep them in attendance. Again, the absence of these creatures is an indicator that there is a problem—often simply a low level of organic material.

When you finish digging, step into the hole. Take a look at the layers of the soil. This exposed vertical surface of the soil is called a soil profile. From the top down, you will see first the organic matter of the rooting zone. This topsoil layer will be noticeably darker than the subsoil below. If that darker topsoil layer is more than 6 inches thick, you have a good base of topsoil for growing healthy plants.

Look down the successive layers of your soil. You may see a distinct boundary layer of clay materials at a certain level. These deposits will be slick when moist or very hard and dry. This is called a hardpan. It can restrict the downward progress of plant roots and reduce plant growth. Those layers can also indicate compaction caused by repeated plowing or tilling to a given depth over the years. A layer like this can be broken up by digging through it with a garden fork or chisel plow.

If you can see plant roots, observe their growth patterns. Roots of perennials should travel straight down and disappear into the lower levels of the soil. If you see a particular level where they stop growing downward or turn sideways, this is another indicator of a compaction problem.

Testing Soil pH

Soil pH is an index of the relative acidity of your soil. See "The Mineral Side of Soil," on page 62, for an explanation of the importance of soil pH. Checking soil pH yourself is a relatively easy task, and keeping pH in its proper range can be critical in solving other mineral-related problems in your soil. You can test pH at any time of year, using any of the following methods.

Portable pH meters. The best and most accurate meters for home use cost $45 or more. Many of the portable pH meters on the market do not stay accurate, so your initial investment in a quality meter pays off. Good-quality pH meters are available through garden supply catalogs. The procedure for getting a pH reading involves adding a soil sample to distilled water and inserting a sensing probe into the solution. (Distilled water is available at your local grocery store or drug store.) You'll get the best results if you follow the directions that come with the meter.

You'll find a portable pH meter a handy device, especially if you have a large yard or many different plantings that have varying pH requirements. You can spot changes in pH before they become serious, allowing you to figure out why a pH change is occurring in the first place. If you have many plants on your property and you are interested in keeping them as healthy as you can, a well-built pH meter is a good investment that will serve you for years.

Litmus paper. Litmus paper contains a pH-sensitive dye. It is commercially available from scientific and gardening supply catalogs. The strips are almost as accurate as pH meters and much less expensive.

Prepare a soil sample for litmus testing by making a slurry of your soil and some distilled water in a clean dish. The slurry should be a thick mud that will slide slowly off a spoon or spatula. Let it stand for an hour or so. If it thickens too much as it stands, add a little more distilled water to get to the right consistency again. Then place the strip of litmus paper directly into the slurry. Leave it there for at least a full minute. Remove the strip and rinse it with distilled water. You can then match its color to the chart that comes with the litmus papers. Each color represents a different pH level.

Home pH test kits. All commercial soil test kits sold for home use will include a pH test of some type. These tests give you a good pH reading if you follow the instructions exactly. See page 63, for details on using home soil testing kits.

Plant indicators. As you refine your observation skills, you may be able to tell the pH of your soil by taking an inventory of the wild plants growing in it. All plants grow best in soil conditions that suit them, so different weeds, shrubs, and trees will thrive in different types of soil. Thus, the presence of a particular plant can be an indicator of pH. If your soil is acid, you may expect to find acid soil–adapted weeds such as sorrel or horsetail. An abundance of stands of hemlock, red spruce, oak, and white pine suggest acid soil, as do ferns, blueberries, rhododendrons, and bayberries. Plants adapted to alkaline soil include true chamomile, field peppergrass, bladder campion, and goosefoot. Refer to the table "Weeds as Soil Indicators," on page 60, for more examples of weeds that give clues to pH conditions.

The most versatile and practical plant indicators of soil pH are white and red clover, which have long been acknowledged as signs of fertile and near neutral or moderately acid soil. Because these clovers need calcium, ground in which they thrive should be good for growing vegetables. A rich, well-balanced soil will also support burdock, lamb's-quarters, chicory, purslane, and dandelions—so if you have any of these other weeds, consider it a compliment and not just a nuisance.

Groundwater and pH. Another pH indicator is the groundwater under your soil. If the groundwater in your area is hard, there is likely plenty of lime (calcium) in your soil, tipping it toward the neutral or alkaline side of the scale. You can suspect that your pH may lean on the acid side of the scale if your area receives lots of rain and you know your local soils are naturally low in lime.

Testing Soil Minerals

A mineral disorder can be caused by either an excess or a lack of a certain nutrient. Plants can also show mineral deficiencies when the mineral is present in the soil but unavailable to the plants because of an improper pH level. An imbalance between various nutrients can also make certain minerals unavailable for absorption by plant roots.

Consequently, you must determine if your soil has any excesses or deficiencies of any of the major or minor nutrients needed by plants to produce food. If you do find a clear indicator of an excess or a deficiency, then take steps to correct it.

There are three ways to check whether your plants are getting an adequate supply of the individual minerals they need for proper growth: Observe your plants, do a chemical analysis of your soil, or have your plants' nutrient content analyzed. You may want to use some combination of these three methods as you learn about your soil.

Clues from Your Plants. Home garden-

Weeds as Soil Indicators

Weeds, like cultivated plants, differ in their requirements for light, water, and nutrients. But since we don't plant weeds or take special measures to meet their growing needs, they naturally end up growing in the niches in our yards and gardens where the existing light, drainage, and nutrient conditions suit them best. We can take advantage of this by using the weeds as indicators of the soil conditions in the areas where they are growing.

Common Name	Botanical Name	Indicates
Bracken	*Pteridium aquilinum*	Tilled or cultivated soil
Buttercups	*Ranunculus* spp.	Tilled or cultivated soil
Canada thistle	*Cirsium arvense*	Heavy clay soil
Chickweed, common	*Stellaria media*	Tilled or cultivated soil with high fertility or humus unless weeds are pale and stunted, then fertility is low
Coltsfoot	*Tussilago farfara*	Heavy clay soil; waterlogged or poorly drained; acid or low lime
Dandelion	*Taraxacum officinale*	Heavy clay soil; tilled or cultivated; acid or low lime, especially on lawns
Docks	*Rumex* spp.	Waterlogged or poorly drained soil; acid or low lime
Field bindweed	*Convolvulus arvensis*	Hardpan or crusty surface with light sand texture
Garden sorrel	*Rumex acetosa*	Waterlogged or poorly drained soil; acid or low lime
Hawkweeds	*Hieracium* spp.	Acid or low-lime soil
Horsetail	*Equisetum arvense*	Sandy light soil; acid or low lime
Knapweeds	*Centaurea* spp.	Acid or low-lime soil with high potassium
Knotweed	*Polygonum aviculare*	Tilled or cultivated soil; acid or low lime
Lamb's-quarters	*Chenopodium album*	Tilled or cultivated soil with high fertility or humus unless weeds are pale and stunted, then fertility is low
Meadowsweet	*Spiraea latifolia*	Wet or waterlogged soil
Mosses	Musci class	Waterlogged or poorly drained soil; acid or low lime
Mullein, common	*Verbascum thapsus*	Neglected, uncultivated soil; acid or low lime; low fertility

Common Name	Botanical Name	Indicates
Mustards	*Brassica* spp.	Hardpan or crusty surface; dry, often with thin topsoil
Nettles	*Urtica* spp.	Tilled or cultivated soil; acid or low lime
Oxeye daisy	*Chrysanthemum leucanthemum*	Waterlogged or poorly drained soil that has been neglected or uncultivated, acid or low lime with low fertility
Pennycress	*Thlaspi arvense*	Hardpan or crusty surface; high lime
Pigweeds	*Amaranthus* spp.	Tilled or cultivated soil with high fertility or humus unless weeds are pale and stunted, then low fertility is indicated
Pineapple weed	*Matricaria matricarioides*	Hardpan or crusty surface
Plantains	*Plantago* spp.	Heavy clay soil; waterlogged or poorly drained; tilled or cultivated; acid or low lime, especially on lawns
Prickly lettuce	*Lactuca serriola*	Tilled or cultivated soil
Quackgrass	*Agropyron repens*	Hardpan or crusty surface
Sheep sorrel	*Rumex acetosella*	Sandy light soil; acid or low lime
Shepherd's purse	*Capsella bursa-pastoris*	Saline soil
Silvery cinquefoil	*Potentilla argentea*	Dry soil often with thin topsoil; acid or low lime
Sowthistle, common	*Sonchus oleraceus*	Heavy clay soil
Yarrow	*Achillea millefolium*	Low potassium

SOURCE: From *The Soul of Soil: A Guide to Ecological Soil Management* by Grace Gershuny and Joseph Smillie, Gaia Services, 1986, adapted from "Weeds as Indicators of Soil Conditions" by Stuart B. Hill and Jennifer Ramsay, *The MacDonald Journal*, June 1977.

ers may find that the most common mineral-related problems in their gardens are due to an excess of either nitrogen, potassium, or magnesium. Excessive soil nitrogen may be the result of overfertilizing; excessive potassium, from too much fresh manure or wood ashes; excess magnesium, from too much dolomitic limestone.

The condition of your plants may reflect this. For example, tomatoes that are taking up excessive nitrogen may have lots of lush foliage and few flowers or fruits.

If your soil is mineral-deficient, your plants generally give some evidence of this also. For example, apple trees that aren't getting enough

The Mineral Side of Soil

Many common soil minerals are used by plants to make structural compounds or food reserves, or as part of enzymes or other substances that are necessary for proper growth and developments.

Nitrogen, phosphorus, potassium, calcium, magnesium, and sulfur are considered the major plant nutrients or minerals. Minerals such as boron, iron, cobalt, and sodium are called micronutrients, or trace elements, not because they are unimportant, but because they are needed in much smaller amounts.

Nutrient availability. Most nutrients exist in the soil in far greater quantities than crops require, but in forms that are unavailable to plants. Plants obtain nutrients through their roots, and roots can only absorb nutrients that are dissolved in water. Therefore, insoluble compounds are not available to plants. The amount of potassium and phosphorus in available forms in many soils is apt to be only 1 percent of the total weight of these elements in the soil.

Soil pH. Extremes of acidity and alkalinity affect the availability of soil nutrients. This is why soil pH is so frequently mentioned as a requirement for plant growth. Soil pH is simply a measurement of the acidity or alkalinity of the soil. It is not a rating of the amount of minerals in the soil. Soil pH is rated on a scale that spans from 0 (very acid) to 14.0 (very alkaline); 7.0 is the relative level that is considered neutral: not acid or alkaline. Most plants grow best when soil pH is between 6.0 and 7.0. Problems are likely to appear when pH drops below 5.0 or exceeds 8.0.

At low soil pH, essential minerals such as phosphorus and potassium are less available to plants. Phosphorus also tends to be unavailable at high pH because it is chemically bound to calcium. Acidic conditions are also unfavorable because many heavy metals, such as lead and cadmium, dissolve more readily and can enter plant tissue in harmful amounts. Acid soil is also inhospitable to many beneficial soil microorganisms.

Synthetic chemical fertilizers contain plant nutrients in forms that are readily absorbed by plants. However, these forms are easily absorbed because they are very soluble, so they are also easily lost from the soil by leaching. They also often cause the soil pH to surge to more acid levels in the immediate zone where they are applied. This is detrimental to soil organisms, which like all living things, are sensitive to the acidity or alkalinity of their environment.

magnesium often drop fruit before it ripens.

Unfortunately, the symptoms of each of the major and minor soil nutrient imbalances are not unique to each element. They can also be confused with cultural problems such as overwatering. For example, yellowing of the leaves may be the result of any one of several nutrient deficiencies. As a result, you need to be able to determine whether your plant is actually suffering from a soil excess or deficiency or is simply being overwatered. It may take several years of observation and practice before you'll know your soils and plants well enough to recognize mineral imbalances from plant symptoms alone. "Plant Symptoms of Mineral Imbalances," on page 64, is a guide to some of the more commonly observed symptoms of deficiencies or excesses. Keep in mind that some of these symptoms closely resemble those of disease problems. Be sure your plants are not suffering from attack by fungi, bacteria, or viruses. For clues on figuring out whether your plant is suffering from disease, see "Know Your Enemy" on page 129.

To generalize, nutrient-imbalanced crops will be more susceptible to insect and disease problems, grow slowly, and have below-average yields. As the imbalance worsens, these subtle signs are accompanied by symptoms that are diagnostic for each nutrient. Look for:

❧ Curling leaves, death of the growing tips, or other symptoms that are either apparent over the entire plant or located in just one area, such as the bottom leaves

❧ Leaves of the entire plant tending to be smaller than normal

❧ Abnormal leaf color for the plant species at that time of year

Remember, the symptoms of each of the major and minor soil nutrient imbalances are not unique. You can get yellowing of the leaves from a number of different individual excesses or deficiencies, from a combination of deficiencies, or simply from overwatering the plant. The visual analysis is the easiest first step, but often other issues need to be considered if a simple answer doesn't appear.

Commercial Home Test Kits. There are many soil test kits on the market for home use. I don't recommend using them to determine possible mineral problems in your soil. These kits will give you less accurate results than those from a professional soil lab, because soil labs factor in individual differences in soil samples, such as the moisture content and the soil density, when doing analyses.

The more sophisticated home test kits, such as the Lamotte garden kit (cost: approximately $40), will give fairly accurate results. This kit contains materials and directions for testing the content of nitrogen, phosphorus, potassium, calcium, magnesium, and for determining soil pH. If your home results indicate soil imbalances, you may want to confirm the results with a professional soil test.

When dealing with mineral deficiencies, you can generally solve small problems by adding organic matter and letting natural decay processes improve mineral availability. If you have a serious problem, then you need a professional assessment to be sure you know exactly what is wrong and how to correct it without creating some other imbalance.

Leaf Analysis. Plant analysis is not a do-it-yourself test. Many Cooperative Extension Service offices and some private labs will analyze samples of leaf tissue for nutrient content. This type of testing may give more accurate results for certain nutrients, including nitrogen, than soil analysis does. The labs analyze the nutrient content in the samples and compare the readings with compiled research data that show the normal range of nutrients required for optimal growth of that species. Based on that comparison, they make recommendations for treatment.

Most labs require from 30 to 40 leaves from a group of plants in one area of the garden. Choose leaves that are newly matured and have no signs of damage or stress. If possible, take them from the upper part of the plant. Put the leaves in a paper bag as you pick them. If you plan to send them through the mail for analysis, you'll have to dry them first. Do this by placing the open bag on a clean surface and let it sit for about 24 hours. Don't put the bag in a room that is very dusty, or one where chemicals are stored, as dust or chemicals could contaminate the samples.

Follow the instructions for mailing provided by the lab. Generally, you'll have to put the dried leaves in a box or mailing envelope, keeping samples from different plants separate.

The Cooperative Extension Service plant

(continued on page 66)

Plant Symptoms of Mineral Imbalances

If your plants are lacking essential minerals, they may not be able to grow or develop properly. When their natural internal processes are not functioning correctly, they may show outward signs that resemble disease problems. Use the following listings of symptoms and possible causes as one part of your assessment of your soil's nutrient condition. Remember that soil and foliar testing are more reliable ways to determine whether your soil is deficient in some minerals needed for plant growth.

Symptoms	Possible Causes
LEAVES	
Small terminal or tip growth ceases	Zinc deficiency
Thin and brittle	Magnesium deficiency
Mottling, blotches or necrotic areas	Zinc deficiency
Curled upward, elongation practically ceases	Iron or magnesium deficiency; insect damage
Curled downward	Boron deficiency; insect damage
Collapsed spots on young leaves	Zinc or manganese deficiency
Dead tips	Phosphorus deficiency; excess chlorine
Firing tips	Nitrogen deficiency
Color loss at tips, striping between veins	Magnesium deficiency
Dead tips and margins	Leaf burn caused by wind, frost, excess salts, or lack of water
Scorched margins	Potassium deficiency
Yellowed, streaked, or striped margins	Phosphorus deficiency; excess boron
Brown margins (lower leaves affected first)	Potassium deficiency
Scalloped appearance	Calcium deficiency
Yellow veins with pale green between	Nitrogen deficiency
Green veins with yellow between (young leaves first)	Iron deficiency
Green veins with color loss between	Iron, manganese, magnesium, molybdenum deficiencies; fungus; virus; insect or mite damage; low temperatures; toxic materials in air or soil; excessive water, copper, manganese, or zinc

Symptoms	Possible Causes
Grayish brown to bronze leaves; brown spotting	Magnesium deficiency
Green-and-white or yellow-and-white mottling, ring spots or mosaic pattern over entire leaf	Virus
Abnormal dark green color	Calcium deficiency
Purplish color	Phosphorus deficiency
Purplish red color	Magnesium deficiency
Blanched color	Copper deficiency
Yellow streaks on midribs and edges	Virus
Yellow-green overall, uniform chlorosis	Nitrogen deficiency

STEMS

Hard and brittle	Sulfur deficiency
Weak	Calcium or potassium deficiency

BUDS

Dried out and dying or absent	Calcium deficiency
Premature drop but stems are stiff and erect	Zinc or calcium deficiency
Reduced formation, necrotic at margins and tips	Zinc deficiency
Light green color	Boron deficiency

TWIGS

Dying back or development of brown spots	Zinc or copper deficiency
Weak, or petioles develop brown spots	Magnesium deficiency

FRUIT

Poor development or lack of development	Phosphorus or iron deficiency
Delayed maturity	Phosphorus deficiency
Shriveled	Potassium deficiency
Sour	Copper deficiency

analysis kit consists of a bag, mailing envelope, and instructions. Check in your telephone book under city or county government to find the phone number and address of your local Extension Service. The cost of the plant analysis kit is generally from $10 to $15.

A & L Agricultural Labs and Brookside Labs offer plant tissue testing for home gardeners. The cost is approximately $25. See "Soil Testing Services," on page 52, for addresses and phone numbers of these laboratories.

CORRECTING SOIL IMBALANCES

The second step in improving your soil is to correct soil imbalances. Gather all the data you've collected: soil test recommendations, notes from your observations of your soil and plants, and pH readings. Now you'll put your knowledge of the three components of soil—physical, biological, and mineral—together. This is because when you start adding materials to your soil, in most cases, all three components are affected by each action you take.

There are no overnight, or even single-season, organic solutions for an imbalanced soil. If you are a conventional gardener making the transition to organic gardening, this may be a hard lesson to accept. Organic gardeners don't look for a 50-pound bag solution. They look for a two, three, or four-year program that will result in a fertile, rich, soil. However, this doesn't mean your plants have to suffer during the soil building program. You can supplement your soil building program with organic fertilizers to meet your plants' needs for nutrients. For details on using organic fertilizers, see "Feeding Your Plants" on page 84.

Improving Soil Structure

If your soil assessment has turned up problems with the physical side of your soil—compaction, low humus, poor drainage, or poor water and air retention—the solution is to add organic matter. This will be a repeating theme in your soil management program. Organic materials are the proper prescription for many soil problems and imbalances. See "Understanding Organic Matter," on page 70, for a description of how organic matter affects your soils.

However, you'll need to decide what organic materials to use, how much to apply, and how to incorporate them into your soil. Spreading chopped leaves around shrubs is fine, but spreading them on your lawn is less than acceptable. See "Organic Soil Amendments and Mulches," on page 86, for more information about the materials you can use to improve your soil.

Increasing Organic Matter Content

As a rule of thumb, if you add about 1 inch of fine organic matter to a garden every year, you will gradually increase that soil's organic matter content. One inch of compost or other fine-textured organic material, such as mowed buckwheat, spread over the soil surface equals about 5 percent of the volume of the first foot of that soil. If you use a bulkier material like chopped leaves or straw, then you might need to apply 4 inches of material to get the same results. And this task is easier in the cooler North than it is in the hot South, where the organic material can break down twice as fast because average higher temperatures lead to faster rates of organic matter breakdown.

In general, the application rates for organic materials that I suggest are appropriate for most soils in the Midwest, Northeast, and parts of the Northwest. In the southern and far western United States, these soils require up to twice as much organic materials than listed here.

Organic matter spans the gamut from fresh plant material to fully decayed compost. And the degree of decay of the organic matter you use relates to how long it persists when added to the soil. On the average, fresh organic matter—

such as grass clippings, kitchen garbage, and green weeds—worked into the soil will be 50 percent decayed in just two months. See "The Biological Side of Soil," on page 78, for a full explanation of the decay cycle that drives this transformation. The material is 75 percent decayed after 4 months, and about 87 percent decayed after 6 months.

Dry materials decompose more slowly than moist. So, for example, if you dig chopped dried leaves into your garden, it may take 4 or 5 months for them to be halfway along the path of transformation to humus.

Keeping the Cycle Cooking

The decay process works best if there is a constant supply of food for the soil microorganisms that act as the decay "machine." So it's a good idea to mulch an area where you've incorporated partially decayed material with dry organic matter that will decompose slowly. The mulch serves two functions. First, it protects the decomposing organic matter beneath from excessive heat, which can actually cause some organic compounds to volatilize and be lost from the soil. Second, it provides a longer-term food source for the populations of soil microorganisms that are stimulated by the dug-in organic matter.

No matter where you live or what kind of soil you have, there is one cardinal rule in your efforts to increase the organic content of your soil. Once you've added whatever material your soil needs, there should be not one square inch of bare soil left anywhere on your property. It should be covered with grass, a ground cover, the plants themselves, or mulch. Bare soil loses humus much faster than covered soil because the nutrients created by the decomposition of the organic matter are leached away more readily. In addition, the impact of raindrops on bare soil can destroy the loose soil structure you have worked to obtain. For more detail on the types of materials to use for mulch, see "Organic Soil Amendments and Mulches" on page 86.

Getting Organic Matter into the Soil

In situations where the soil is in poor condition in the beginning, you'll need to make a liberal application of compost, manure, chopped leaves, peat moss, and/or any other organic material that will provide the necessary materials for humus formation. You can do this job any time of the year, but fall is generally the time most gardeners prefer. Your garden beds are then likely to have either few or no plants, and by applying the material to the soil in the fall, you give it a few months during the winter to begin the decay cycle. That means that in the spring, when plants are looking for nutrients, the organic material has already begun to break down, making nutrients available to your plants.

It is relatively easy to increase the humus content of vegetable gardens because they are usually cleared of plants every year. It's the rest of your landscape that poses problems. How do you increase the organic material under an existing lawn? Or around trees and shrubs? Wherever you have existing plants, including lawn grasses, shrubs, or perennials, you can lay compost or other decayed organic material on the surface. In a few months, the soil organisms will have begun to work that organic material down into the soil.

The other method for gardens and around trees and shrubs is to use some kind of organic mulch and let it break down naturally, giving the soil an organic material boost as it does. This can be done at any convenient time of year. Remember, a soil filled with plants also is gaining organic matter from the growth and decay of the plant root systems. However, that may not be adequate to give the soil the amount of organic material it needs.

Starting with New Beds or Lawns

If you are about to start a new flower garden or lawn, you can dig the organic material into the soil as you prepare those areas for

(continued on page 70)

Compost: Nature's Black Magic

It may seem like magic—a pile of leaves, grass clippings, pulled weeds, and kitchen scraps turns into a wonderful, dark, uniform organic soil amendment—compost. But making compost doesn't require a magician's tricks, just a little tinkering with the natural decay cycle.

In the soil, microorganisms, nematodes, and earthworms consume organic matter and break it down into simpler compounds. They require air, moisture, and heat to do so. The same process happens in a compost pile. It just happens faster (in an active pile) because the microorganisms have a diverse supply of raw materials to digest and optimal conditions for their work.

The Magic Formula

You can make compost one of two ways—by the active method or the passive method. The active method, of course, requires more work. With either method, the first step is to make a compost pile. You can build wooden or concrete block bins or buy a commercially made plastic bin to hold your pile in place. Or you can just layer the materials in a heap. An easy way to keep a passive pile contained is to set up a heavy chicken wire cylinder as a frame.

Follow these simple guidelines for successful composting:

Location. Select a shady, well-drained spot for your pile.

Season. It's best to compost when temperatures are above 50°F. At lower temperatures, your pile will not be active, or may freeze. Of course, you can restart the compost pile in spring by turning it and adjusting the moisture content.

Preparation. Clear away sod or other surface cover at the site, loosen the soil with a spading fork, and put down a base layer of brush or wood chips.

Materials. Materials you can use include garden wastes, grass clippings, kitchen scraps, manure, newspaper, and sawdust. Never include meat scraps or fats, which attract dogs and rodents. It's also best not to add kitchen scraps that are heavy with oil, as oils take longer to break down and can slow the composting process.

Layering. Alternate layers of plant material such as chopped leaves or straw with nitrogen-rich layers of kitchen scraps mixed with manure or blood meal. If you don't have nitrogen-rich materials, don't worry. Your compost will just take longer to finish.

Activating. Add an activator that contains microorganisms and growth stimulants to boost your pile's activity. You can use topsoil, fresh manure, or a commercial compost activator such as BioActivator.

Shredding. Shred materials to make better compost more quickly.

Moisture. Keep compost moist, but not wet; it should feel as damp as a squeezed-out sponge. Cover loose piles or open bins with plastic or heavy canvas so they won't become waterlogged by rain. If your compost is too dry, use water with kelp extract added to moisten it; this will help stimulate biotic activity.

Minerals. Add the fertilizers your garden needs directly to the compost as you add layers of plant material to the pile. It saves a step in your garden work and makes richer humus. Try adding colloidal or rock phosphate and kelp or fish meal.

Size. Size can vary. A pile 3 feet square heaped 5 feet high can yield almost a ton of compost. The ideal size for an active compost pile is 4 feet by 4 feet by 4 feet.

Aerating. The microorganisms that drive the composting process need air. Fluff or turn the pile regularly to keep microorganisms active, and to prevent the pile from overheating.

Active or Passive?

If you want your compost to stay active, you must turn it every week or so to add oxygen and keep the decomposition rate high. The inside temperature of an active pile can reach 170°F. If you are composting diseased plant material or weeds that have set seed, you must keep the pile at or above 160°F to kill disease organisms and weed seeds. Otherwise, a range of from 140° to 150°F is ideal. You can use a compost thermometer to monitor the temperature of the pile. Plan to turn the pile whenever the temperature of the center of the pile exceeds 140°F.

Of course, you can't just flip a compost pile like a pancake. Turning a pile means mixing

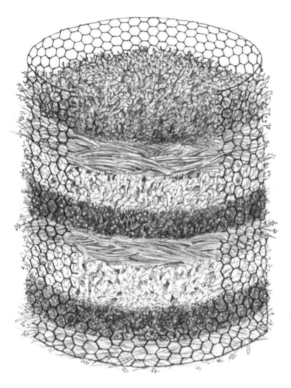

The principles of making compost are the same whether you build a permanent wooden compost bin or rig a temporary wire cage to contain your pile. Build your pile in layers, alternating dry materials like hay or chopped leaves with moist, high-nitrogen materials such as kitchen scraps, manure, or grass clippings. Turning the pile periodically will speed its transformation into finished compost.

and loosening the materials that make up the pile. If you have more than one compost bin, you can turn a pile by forking the material from one bin into another. Moving the pile in this way will let in air and remix the materials, which will stimulate a new flush of microbial activity. If you just have a single loose compost pile, you can turn it by using a spading or manure fork to lift material, shake it, and try to redistribute it in the pile.

If you don't want to worry about turning your compost, build a passive pile. A passive

compost pile is simply a pile of organic material that is left to sit until the material decomposes slowly over time—usually one to two years. Making leaf mold is an example of this. Most homeowners have passive piles tucked somewhere in the far reaches of their backyards. This approach may not produce as much compost for the garden, but it does work, and at least it's a good method for recycling yard wastes.

Many communities now collect yard waste from residents and compost it en masse. If municipal yard waste is available in your area, it can be an excellent source of organic matter. However, not all municipal programs actually compost the yard waste, some just stockpile it. Keep in mind that unless your municipal maintenance department is turning and monitoring the material to keep it active, it may not be truly composted. If you collect some for your home garden, put it in an active pile to kill off any disease organisms it may contain. Active composting will also help break down pesticide residues that could be in the material.

Computing Compost Coverage

Recommendations for spreading compost or other soil amendments are often given in terms of spreading a layer of a given thickness. But how do you know how much material to spread to end up with such a layer? The ratio to remember is 9 cubic feet of compost per 100 square feet of garden yields a 1-inch layer. Here's how to apply the ratio to your garden.

1. First, measure the area you want to cover with compost and determine the total square footage.

2. Divide by 100.

3. Multiply by the thickness of the layer you want to spread.

4. Multiply that number by 9. This will tell you how many cubic feet of compost you need.

A handy "measuring cup" for compost is a 30-gallon garbage can. It holds about 4 cubic feet (or about 50 pounds) of finished compost. You can also measure the volume of your garden cart and use it as your measuring device.

Understanding Organic Matter

Often gardeners and homeowners do not realize that adding organic material to lawns or gardens is really a major fertilizing step. Organic matter can supply nearly all the nitrogen and sulfur, and more than one-third the phosphorus needed by the plants in your landscape, as well as significant quantities of the other nutrients. Organic matter must first decompose to make specific plant nutrients available to plant roots. Therefore, as the rate of organic matter decomposition increases, quantities of nitrogen, phosphorus, potassium, calcium, magnesium, and other plant nutrients rise in the soil solution.

You can also lessen virtually all soil structure problems by adding organic matter to your soil. In a soil with a good organic matter content, most soil components are in proper supply and balance, because organic matter:

❧ Supplies more nutrients for plants by providing more surfaces where nutrients can be held in reserve in the soil

❧ Facilitates better drainage

❧ Stores more water

❧ Permits more air drainage

❧ Increases the activity and numbers of soil microorganisms

❧ Helps decrease problems caused by plant diseases and insects

❧ Encourages earthworms

There is a catch here, unfortunately. Organic material in the soil does not persist. Soil organisms consume organic compounds at varying rates, depending on the environmental conditions in and around the soil. For example, it is very difficult to maintain humus in clay soils in areas near the equator because of the large populations of microorganisms found in these clays (as opposed to the lower populations in sand) and the higher average temperatures, which cause the organic material to be consumed faster. On the other hand, how much humus is processed by the microbiotic population in your soil also depends a lot on your gardening practices.

The microorganisms in your soil will consume humus at a higher rate when it is tilled excessively (several times a year in seedbed preparation and for weed control) or when it is left exposed to the elements. These practices will exhaust soil fertility and destroy structure. To retard the loss of humus content, cultivate soil lightly, mulch during the growing season, and provide either a mulch or a cover crop during the winter. These practices will encourage a gradual increase in the soil's humus content over the years.

Can you have too much organic material in your soil? Too much fresh organic matter, such as plant residues and manure, uses up soil oxygen and can consume most of the nitrogen needed for plant growth. The overabundance of organic matter can stimulate excessive multiplication of microorganisms and bacteria, which then consume so much nitrogen and other plant nutrients that they lower soil fertility until an equilibrium is restored when this flux of microbial growth diminishes. Nitrogen loss can also come from too much water, which depletes nitrogen and other mineral nutrients by leaching them out of the upper soils where your plant roots are concentrated. Maintaining 5 to 6 percent organic matter in your soil is a good goal.

planting. You can also add organic matter to a vegetable garden each year by digging in material before planting. However, be sure to do this job only when the soil is in proper condition for digging or tilling, or you'll do more harm than good as you add the organic matter. See "Don't Dig In!" on page 73, for an explanation of how cultivation affects soil structure and soil organisms.

You can get organic material into your soil the easy way, by rotary tilling it in, or the more difficult and time-consuming way, by double-digging it in. As with lots of things in life, the more difficult technique is the best way to do the job. Double-digging is especially important if you have a hardpan below your topsoil. There is no getting around the fact that double-digging is hard work. But if you are willing to spend the time and energy, your plants' outstanding growth and health over the years will reflect the value of the effort.

Double-digging simply means lifting a shovelful of topsoil out of the garden so that you can take a spading fork and loosen, without removing, the second layer of soil below the topsoil. As you double-dig, you can incorporate organic matter into the soil. You should add only small amounts of compost or chopped leaves to the lower layer of soil, because the rate of decay is much slower in the second 6 inches of soil than

Loosen the exposed subsoil by thrusting in a spading fork and twisting its tines back and forth. Don't turn the subsoil over or remove it from its place. For extra benefit from the double digging process, add a small amount of organic matter and work it in as you loosen the subsoil.

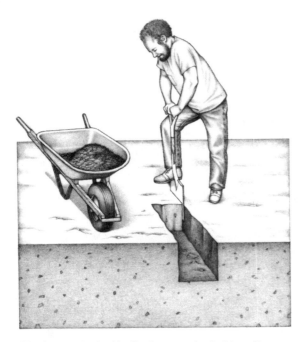

The first step in double-digging a garden bed is to dig out the top 1 foot of soil along one end of the bed. Reserve the soil in a wheelbarrow or on a groundcloth.

it is in the top 6 inches. Lavish most of the organic material on the topsoil as you dig and turn it.

The best way to double-dig an entire bed is to begin at one end of the bed and dig a 1-foot-wide trench. Pile the topsoil from that trench onto a ground cloth or into a garden cart. Next, loosen the subsoil in the trench by sticking your spading fork down as deeply as you can into it and twisting and wiggling the fork to loosen up the clumps. Also add a shovelful of organic matter.

Then, begin digging the topsoil from the next 1-foot section of the bed. Shovel this topsoil into the first trench, on top of the organic matter and loosened subsoil. As you do so, you can incorporate one or a few shovelfuls of organic matter into the topsoil. Move systematically down the bed, making consecutive

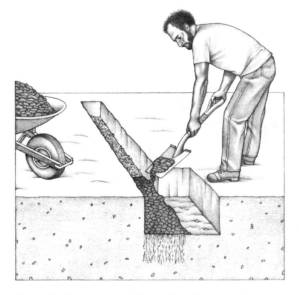

Repeat the first step, but this time shovel the topsoil onto the subsoil you just loosened. It's a good idea to shovel in some organic matter along with the topsoil as you work.

When you reach the end, use the reserved topsoil to cover the last area of exposed subsoil. Your bed is now ready for planting.

Loosen the exposed subsoil again, and repeat the shoveling and loosening process down the entire length of the bed.

trenches. Double-digging your beds will raise them 3 to 4 inches because this technique thoroughly loosens and aerates the soil. You can leave the sides of these raised beds in their natural state, or you can support them with decorative stones or landscape timbers, which help control erosion.

Green Manuring

A green manure crop is a crop that is grown and then incorporated into the soil to increase soil fertility and organic matter content. Common green manure crops are grassy crops such as oats or buckwheat, or legume crops like clover. Many gardeners plant a green manure crop in the fall, after finishing the harvest and clearing debris from the beds. Others make green manures part of a crop rotation, and plant green manures during the growing season. (For complete information about crop rotation, see "Rotate Crops" on page 146.)

If you plant a green manure crop in your vegetable beds, you will need to till or dig the crop into the soil before you plant your vegetable seeds or transplants. The best time to do that job is in early spring, about three to four weeks before you begin your vegetable garden, but only if you can do so without having to cultivate the soil when it is wet. If your soils tend to be wet in early spring, dig the green manure into the soil late in the fall and let it decompose over the winter.

"Selecting Green Manures," on page 74, will guide you in choosing the particular green manure crop that is best suited for your garden. Some green manures are legumes, crops whose roots form an association with soil-borne bacteria that can transform nitrogen from the atmosphere into nitrogen compounds that can be used by plants. If you select a legume, you'll get more of the benefits of this process, known as nitrogen fixation, if you also buy and apply an inoculant. The inoculant is a granulated mix that contains the appropriate symbiotic bacteria. (Some seed companies sell pre-inoculated seed.)

When you seed green manures, you can use a manually powered seeder that consists of a bag or reservoir for holding seed, connected to a crank-operated seed broadcaster. You can also try broadcasting seed by hand over small areas. If you are using a small amount of seed (less than 1 pound) per 1,000 square feet, you may want to mix the seed with fine sand before spreading to help ensure even distribution.

Mulching Permanent Plantings

Mulching is a multipurpose gardening technique. It helps prevent weed problems and reduces water loss from the soil. But these functions are secondary to the value of organic mulch as a soil amendment. A 4-inch layer of chopped leaves spread around a perennial bed in the fall will have completely disappeared by the following autumn. However, these leaves did not just evaporate. They began to decay where the leaves touched the soil surface and were slowly but steadily pulled down into the soil. The same thing happens with any organic mulch such as grass clippings, hay, or straw. Wood chips make an excellent mulch and also will disappear, but it will take two or three years.

Selecting Green Manures

One of the best ways to improve your soil is to grow green manure crops. Incorporating green manures into the soil increases organic matter content and improves tilth. The following list includes many of the more common green manure crops. You can often combine plantings of more than one species for best effect.

Crop	When to Sow	Rate per 1,000 Sq. Ft.	Cultural Requirements	Comments
LEGUMES				
Alfalfa	Spring	1–2 lb.	Needs good drainage and pH higher than 6.0	Significant nitrogen contribution. Perennial.
Alsike clover	Spring or late summer	½–1 lb.	Tolerates poor drainage and acid soils	Low-growing. Perennial.
Austrian peas	Late summer or fall	2–5 oz.	Prefer well-drained soils	Winter legume for warmer climates. Annual.
Crimson clover	Spring or fall	8–12 oz.	Likes neutral, well-drained soils	Tall clover with dense root system. Annual.
Hairy vetch	Late summer or fall	1–2 lb.	Will tolerate moderate drainage. Winter cover with rye	Good nitrogen fixer; may grow too vigorously in warmer climates. Annual.
Ladino clover	Early spring or fall	4–8 oz.	Needs well-drained soil	Best sown in fall. Plant with oats in spring. Biennial.
Red clover	Spring or late summer	4–8 oz.	Somewhat tolerant of acidity and poor drainage	Good phosphorus accumulation; grows quickly for incorporating during same season. Biennial.
White clover (Dutch)	Spring or late summer	4–8 oz.	Tolerates droughty soils	Good for undersowing in row crops as a "living mulch." Perennial.

Mulching is the best way to increase the organic matter content of the soil around existing plants such as trees, shrubs, and perennials. The general rule for trees and shrubs is to apply a 3- to 4-inch-deep mulch annually in a circle out to the dripline of the plant. Use the same approach for hedges. Place a 3- to 4-inch layer of organic mulch along both sides of the hedge out to the edge of the plants. Do not pile the mulch up against the trunk of woody plants. This provides a safe haven for rodents to feed on the wood, especially during the winter months. Also, don't pile mulch over the crowns of perennial plants—especially in winter—to avoid problems with crown rot and other diseases.

See "Organic Soil Amendments and

Crop	When to Sow	Rate per 1,000 Sq. Ft.	Cultural Requirements	Comments
White sweet clover	Spring or summer	½–1 lb.	Intolerant of acid soils and poor drainage	Extensive root mass accumulates phosphate from rock powders. Biennial.
Yellow sweet clover	Spring or summer	½–1 lb.	Intolerant of acid soils and poor drainage	Similar to white sweet clover, but less mass and faster growing. Biennial.
Soybeans	Spring or summer	2–3 lb.	Tolerate poor drainage	Inoculate for nitrogen fixation. Annual.
NONLEGUMES				
Annual ryegrass	Spring	1–2 lb.	Handles a wide range of soils	Good nurse crop. Annual.
Buckwheat	Spring or summer	2–3 lb.	Tolerates infertile, acid soils	Accumulates phosphorus. Annual.
Rapeseed	Spring or summer	6–8 oz.	Prefers moderately well-drained loam	Good cover for short growing periods in summer. Annual.
Spring oats	Spring or summer	2–3 lb.	Prefer well-drained, loamy soils. Tolerate some acidity	Quick-growing summer crop. Good nurse crop for clover. Annual.
Sudan grass (sorghum)	Spring or summer	1–2 lb.	Will handle somewhat poorly drained soils	Grows huge biomass in summer. Annual.
Winter rye	Late summer or fall	2–3 lb.	Prefers well-drained soil	Early growth in spring; allelopathic. Annual.

Mulches," on page 86, for a rundown on the composition and best uses of various organic mulches.

Top-dressing Lawns

Adding organic material to the soil under an existing lawn can be a challenge. One way to tackle it is to add a ½-inch layer of finished compost over the entire surface of the lawn in the spring and again in the fall. After a couple of years of that treatment, you can reduce the application to one treatment—a ¼-inch layer put down in the fall.

Make the spring application at least three weeks before your first mowing. If you cut the grass no shorter than 2 inches and leave the grass clippings on the lawn (they also provide a valuable source of organic matter for the underlying soil), you will not be able to see the compost at all a week after the first cut.

Dealing with Heavy Clay

If you're starting out with very heavy clay soil that has never been used for gardening and is clearly lacking in much humus or organic content, you will have to add considerable amounts of organic material and energy to make that soil as loose and friable as you can. Double-digging is your best option. Some gardeners will add sand along with the organic material to their heavy clay beds in which they expect to grow roots crops and flower bulbs. A lot of sand is required to make a significant difference, though. Adding small amounts of sand may actually cause your soil to harden, worsening its condition. To boost the sand component to the top 6 to 8 inches of the soil by 10 to 15 percent, you will need 3 to 5 tons per 1,000 square feet of garden. If you have a close and convenient source of sand, it may be worth the effort to spread and till in the sand. However, adding sand alone will not remedy problems with heavy clay. Using green manures and incorporating organic matter are the best long-term solutions.

Dealing with Drainage Problems

If your soil tests and observations have alerted you to a drainage problem in your yard, you have three options. Your first option could be to accept the wet spot and create a small bog garden. If you have other plans for the site, you'll have to find a way to improve drainage.

The drainage problem may be due to a hardpan somewhere in the top 2 feet of soil. If this is the case, you may be able to break up the compaction layer by double-digging. If the layer is deeper than you can reach by double-digging, you can try planting deep-rooted sweet clover in spring and allow it to grow in the wet area through to the following fall. The roots may penetrate the hardpan and naturally create better drainage.

Another way to sidestep a drainage problem is to create a raised bed in the wet area.

You'll have to bring in extra topsoil and build up the sides, essentially creating a layer of soil with good drainage for plants to grow in above the poorly drained area.

Lastly, you can install a drainage system. This is a project you may not want to tackle without professional help. See "The Chemical-Free Gardener's Library," on page 431, for references that explain the nuts and bolts of installing drainage systems.

Improving Biological Activity

Adding organic matter also tops the list of measures you can take to improve soil conditions for living organisms. Organic material stimulates the growth and reproductive capacity of the bacteria and other "micro-herd" members that help create a vital and productive soil. (See "The Biological Side of Soil," on page 78, for an explanation of the role of microorganisms in the soil.) If you have low biological activity in your soil, the first steps you should take are to increase your soil's organic matter content, using the techniques described in the previous section.

Adding Microbes

If you're a gardener who's converting a neglected or chemically treated site to organic methods, you may have soils with very low biological activity. Your soil may benefit from an augmentation of its existing microbial populations. Some organic fertilizer manufacturers offer products supplemented with bacterial cultures that give your soil and compost piles an extra biological boost. The cultures are in a dry, dormant, powdered form. After you spread this material over your soil or into a compost pile, the microbes become activated and biological activity accelerates. Keep in mind that you must add sufficient organic materials to provide a steady diet for the increased populations of soil microbes in order to get lasting benefit.

Reviving the Earthworm Population

If your earthworm count is low, don't despair. Once you provide more organic material to feed them, they will return. Earthworm egg casings can lay dormant as deep as 20 feet in the soil for as long as 20 years.

You can order earthworms from mail-order catalogs, but it's best to release them only into your compost heap, not your soils. The most common species sold, *Lumbricus rubellus* or red wiggler worms, are imported from Africa and are adapted to living in manure or very high organic matter soils. They most likely will not thrive in the average North American garden soil.

One of the many reasons not to use dry or granular, fast-acting chemical fertilizers in your garden is that they repel earthworms. As these fertilizers dissolve in soil water and leach down into the soil, they can force the earthworms to seek refuge someplace else. The earthworms are highly sensitive to changes in the physical and chemical environment and will avoid the salty conditions created by the chemical fertilizers. So, if you are making the transition from using chemical fertilizers to using organic soil amendments and fertilizers, have patience. As your soil reaches a healthy balance, you will see more earthworm activity.

Improving Mineral Content

I'm sure I sound like a broken record, but I repeat, one of the best ways to solve many mineral problems you might have in your soil is to add finished compost or other partially decayed organic material. The effect on the mineral conditions of the soil is not immediate, but over time, adding organic matter helps to balance mineral content and even to modify soil pH.

There are other soil amendments you can add to correct specific pH and mineral imbalances. In most cases, you should only add these amendments according to recommendations from soil tests or plant analyses. You must be precise about adding natural mineral supplements, or you can create an excess of a particular nutrient. The excess may damage plants or may interfere with uptake of some other nutrients. For details on the content, application methods, and application rates for the materials recommended in this section, see "Selecting Organic Fertilizers" on page 92.

Correcting an Acid Soil

When soil pH is below 6.0, certain soil nutrients become less soluble, and therefore less available to most plants in the landscape. The exceptions to this are acid-loving plants such as hollies, blueberries, and rhododendrons, which are adapted to absorb their required amounts of needed nutrients from acid soils. Phosphorus and other major nutrients become locked into complex compounds that don't readily break down or become available to most plants when the pH is less than 6.0.

Applying Lime

Limestones are minerals; they are the remains of primordial oceanic life, now mined out of quarries. Adding lime to the lawn and garden serves both to reduce the acidity (raise the pH) and to improve the soil structure and fertility. Limestone comes in several forms; the best one for home gardens is ground limestone.

There are two types of ground limestone: calcitic and dolomitic. Calcitic limestone releases calcium slowly in the soil. Dolomitic limestone slowly releases both calcium and magnesium. Choose the dolomitic type only if you know the soil has a magnesium deficiency. Otherwise, always use the calcitic limestone. Because ground limestone breaks down very slowly in the soil, you should apply it to the garden and lawn in the fall. That way you can assure its impact on the spring plants.

Lime not only increases pH, but also in-

The Biological Side of Soil

Although only a minute portion of the soil by weight and volume, the living organisms in soil play a vital role. Soil microorganisms power the decay cycle—nature's perfect system for recycling organic matter and maintaining healthy soils. Earthworms serve as natural "tillers" and soil conditioners. Many soil-dwelling insects are parasites and predators of insects that harm crop plants. And soil animals, including the much-maligned mole, also help improve soil aeration and eat some harmful insects.

Microorganisms are animals and plants too small to be seen with the naked eye. Some consist of a single cell, others are many-celled. They include nematodes, protozoa, fungi, bacteria, and actinomycetes (threadlike bacteria). These microorganisms (which I call the micro-herd) convert plant material into humus—a stable form of organic matter that serves as a food source for plants.

The Decay Cycle

In nature, when plants die, they are returned to the soil via the decay process. First, they are attacked by animals that feed on dead and dying tissues, including mites, beetles, millipedes, and earthworms. Bacteria and fungi also take part in the process under moist conditions. These organisms physically and chemically break the plant tissues down into simpler components. The waste products and, in their turn, the dead bodies of the soil-dwelling animals and microorganisms become part of the organic matter in the soil. As the process continues, complex compounds from the original tissues are chemically changed to simpler forms. Proteins are eventually broken down into simple nitrogen compounds that can be absorbed by plant roots. Minerals such as phosphorus, potassium, and calcium are also changed from more complex forms into soluble compounds that can enter root cells and be transported to plant tops for growth and development.

This death-to-life conversion process is ongoing and needs continuous fuel sources to work well. In natural environments such as forests, the ebb and flow of plant and animal life continually feeds the soil. In cultivated areas, farmers and gardeners must provide organic materials—green manure crops, composts, manure, mulches—to fuel the decay process. If synthetic chemical fertilizers rather than organic materials are used to provide plant nutrients,

creases the bacterial activity in the soil, thereby speeding up the decomposition of organic matter. Consequently, if you add lime but not organic material to your soil, you will get good results in the first season. In subsequent years, productivity will not reach its full potential unless you also add more organic material.

A rule of thumb for most soils that have tested as acidic (pH less than 6.0) is to apply 5 pounds per 100 square feet to raise the pH by one point. Generally, sandy soils will need less limestone to change pH; clay soils will need more. The best time to test soil pH is in mid- to late summer. That way, you can apply lime in the fall, and it will have time to act to correct pH before the next growing season. Retest the following summer to see if you need to repeat the liming process.

In most situations, it's easiest to apply lime with a small garden spreader. If you're just applying it to a small area, you can broadcast it by hand and rake it into the soil surface.

Once your soil reaches the proper pH level, you only need to retest every three or four years.

soil microorganisms die off because they have no food source. Plants will still grow, fed by the chemical fertilizers. However, soil organic matter plays many roles in the soil (see "Understanding Organic Matter" on page 70), and the loss of organic matter will affect soil structure and water-holding capacity as well as fertility.

Earthworms

Earthworms are probably the most important nonmicroscopic soil dwellers. Their favorite foods are dried leaves and other organic materials that gardeners want to incorporate into the soil. Worms drag these materials down into their burrows and digest them. One inch of organic matter laid on the surface of soil with a healthy earthworm population will be completely digested within a few months. Earthworms also work in the subsoil, and bring that mineral-rich soil closer to the garden's surface. Research shows that earthworms in 100 square feet of garden will bring from 4 to 8 pounds of soil to the surface each year.

Earthworms also excrete and spread their own manure, called castings. Their castings supply plants with nitrogen, phosphorus, potassium, and many micronutrients. In a 100-square-foot garden with a worm population of only five worms per cubic foot, earthworms provide more than 17 pounds (about $1/3$ pound per worm) of top-grade manure each year. A well-managed soil rich in humus might easily support 25 worms per cubic foot, which, in that same 100-square-foot garden, means at least 85 pounds of fertilizer!

Earthworms also secrete calcium carbonate, a compound that helps to moderate soil pH, so earthworm activity helps bring soils to a neutral pH over time. The rearrangement and loosening of the soil by earthworms enhances aeration, which allows more oxygen to penetrate the soil. This not only helps plants directly, but also enhances conditions for some beneficial soil micoorganisms. By their tunneling, earthworms create access to deeper soil levels for countless smaller organisms that contribute to soil health. Finally, in addition to aiding the flow of air and water through the soil, earthworm burrows provide vital channels for roots. For example, research has found that soybean roots will follow worm burrows to their full length—often 4 to 5 feet—and there can be as many as 1,200 burrows in a cubic yard of soil.

In high rainfall areas, pH will gradually decline over time, as calcium leaches downward through the soil.

Applying Wood Ashes

Wood ashes are a strong, fast-acting, alkaline material that can supply a great deal of calcium, potassium, and other elements per unit weight. They contain 20 to 50 percent calcium carbonate (a form of lime), depending on the type of wood. The highest percentages of calcium carbonate are found in hardwoods, especially young trees and twigs. Wood ashes also contain two components of a complete fertilizer, 3 to 7 percent potassium carbonate (potash) and 8 to 20 percent phosphorus pentoxide (phosphorus). In addition, they contain varying amounts of trace elements, including boron, copper, iron, magnesium, manganese, silicon, sodium, sulfur, and zinc.

Use wood ashes to adjust your pH situation in the short run only. Limit applications to 25 pounds per 1,000 square feet, and only apply them once every two or three years in any par-

More Can Be Worse

Many gardeners are convinced that if a little is good, more is better. But with many soil amendments and fertilizers, too much of a good thing can do more harm than good. Two common examples of this are overuse of dolomitic limestone and wood ashes.

Dolomitic limestone, which contains a high percentage of magnesium, is the most commonly available liming material. The reason it is so available is because it is denser and less dusty than calcitic limestone, and therefore, easier for manufacturers to work with and package. But, if it is the only lime you use, you will eventually overload your soil with magnesium and end up with a shortage of calcium. This mineral imbalance could reduce the health and yield of your plants; it also affects the soil's physical characteristics, making it harder to work.

Wood ashes are often overapplied because they are often free for the taking (you may even be producing your own if you have a wood stove). But wood ashes are relatively rich in potassium. When soil is overloaded with potassium, the soil's chemical balance is altered and calcium and magnesium become less available. So while you may correct your pH problem, you may end up with mineral deficiency problems instead.

ticular area. Overapplying wood ashes can create serious soil imbalances. See "More Can Be Worse," above, an explanation of the harmful side-effects of using wood ashes. Use limestone and organic material to solve a long-range pH problem.

You can spread wood ashes at any time of the year, although late winter or early spring is probably the best time. Mixed with water, wood ashes produce lye, which can burn plant tissue. Be careful to keep the ashes away from germinating seeds and seedling roots. Since you'll only be spreading small quantities of wood ashes over relatively large areas, mix the ashes with compost, greensand, or kelp in your spreader to get a large enough volume to ensure even coverage.

Applying Organic Matter

Over time, adding organic matter to your soil tends to balance nutrients, and this eventually will help to bring the pH into a neutral range.

Correcting an Alkaline Soil

If you live in the inland West or in an area where the soil is derived from limestone or marble, chances are you have alkaline, or basic, soil. Alkaline soils have a pH above 7.0. These soils contain substantial quantities of calcium, magnesium, and sodium carbonates. Irrigating with water that has a high pH can also cause soils to be alkaline. For most plants in the landscape, you will need to add materials that lower the pH level to the desired 6.0 to 7.0 range. Powdered sulfur and organic matter are two materials that will lower soil pH.

Applying Sulfur

You can add sulfur to your soil to adjust a high pH down to an appropriate level. Sulfur is a naturally occurring mineral that has been safely and widely used in the western United States as a soil amendment for many years. However, overuse of sulfur can weaken or kill plants and harm the soil balance.

To lower pH by one unit, spread 1 pound of sulfur per 100 square feet. You can broadcast the material and mix it into the top 3 to 4 inches of the soil. For established plantings such as rhododendrons that need acidic conditions, you can spread sulfur around the base of the plant (use an amount equivalent to 2 to 3 pounds per 100 square feet, and mix it into the soil. You can apply sulfur at any time of year that it's convenient.

Applying Organic Matter

Humus buffers soil alkalinity and acidity, meaning it allows for imbalances in soil pH. If your soil is too alkaline, add 2 to 3 inches of compost as a first step in bringing the pH down to a healthy level. After a few years, your soil's pH should be in the proper range.

One of the best organic materials for reducing soil pH is evergreen tree needles or leaf mold. The pH values of needles range from about 3.0 to 6.0. Spruce needles tend to be the most acidic, with pine and fir needles less so. When needles are incorporated into the soil, they create small, scattered sites where the pH is significantly more acidic than in the soil at large. Plant roots in contact with such sites can find favorable conditions for extracting nutrients. Thus, even though the overall pH has not been lowered much, plant growth can be improved.

You can also lower soil pH by using evergreen needles or chopped leaves as a mulch. As rain and irrigation water percolate through the mulch, some of the acids from the plant material are carried into the soil. That small, ongoing input of acid can help keep the soil from becoming more alkaline. The best time to gather is shortly after the brown needles are shed in the fall and early winter.

Correcting Mineral Imbalances

Your soil tests may have indicated that your soils are lacking a particular nutrient, such as phosphorus or potassium. There are many organic fertilizers that will help supply a particular mineral element. Here, we suggest products to use to help your plants recover from a deficiency problem and ways to correct your soil so the deficiency symptoms will not recur. For more information on the products mentioned, see "A Guide to Organic Soil Amendments and Fertilizers" on page 91.

Applying Nitrogen

If your plants' condition leads you to suspect that they are not getting enough nitrogen, immediately give them a foliar spray of diluted fish emulsion or some other organic liquid source of nitrogen. Apply weekly until the symptoms disappear.

Simultaneously, add some slow-release, nitrogen-rich fertilizers to the soil to further correct the deficiency. You can choose blood meal, fish meal, or a high-nitrogen bonemeal. Bonemeal is the best choice if your plants are also suffering from insufficient phosphorus uptake. Be wary of cottonseed meal, as it likely contains chemical pesticide residues.

Planting portions of your vegetable garden with legumes such as peas, beans, and soybeans will help build up soil nitrogen for use by crops planted in those beds in subsequent years. In the fall, plant a legume cover crop such as hairy vetch in the North and Austrian peas in the South. Plant the legume together with a small grain such as winter rye. Dig or till the crop under in spring to provide a good supply of nitrogen for the next growing season and afterwards. Be careful not to let cover crops grow too tall, or it will be very difficult to incorporate them into the soil.

If you overdo nitrogen fertilizing, the nitrogen level in your soil may get too high. The result will be plants with lush green foliage and little or no fruit. There is no immediate solution. Stop all fertilizing activity immediately and allow the natural leaching action of rain and irrigation to carry away the excess nitrogen over time.

Applying Phosphorus

Many garden soils don't need phosphorus applications, because appreciable amounts of this element are held in reserve. Too much phosphorus in the soil retards plants' abilities to take up micronutrients, specifically zinc, copper, and occasionally iron.

If your plants show phosphorus deficiency symptoms, use a foliar spray of fish or seaweed extracts. These extracts contain compounds that stimulate the enzyme systems of the plants, making them more efficient at absorbing the phosphate in the soil. Apply a dilute solution each week until the symptoms disappear.

Bonemeal is a good source of phosphorus.

You can apply a thin dusting of bonemeal over the root area of the affected plants to help eliminate the symptoms.

Your long-term solution to a phosphorus deficiency may be to adjust soil pH. Phosphorus is most available when soil pH is between 6.0 and 7.0. Very acid soil can cause phosphorus to combine chemically with other soil elements and therefore become less available for plant uptake. Adding compost to the soil can also make phosphorus more available, as the compost interacts chemically with some of the compounds that could otherwise bind up the phosphate ions.

You can also build up soil phosphorus by adding rock phosphate or colloidal phosphate to the compost pile in fall and then spreading the compost on your soil in the spring. The microbial activity in the compost pile transforms some of the rock powder to soluble form, so it can be immediately absorbed by young growing plants.

Moving now to the other side of the coin, too much phosphorus in the soil can bind up trace elements such as iron, manganese, and zinc and make these unavailable to your plants. This can easily occur when too much high-phosphate fertilizer has been applied. If you suspect you have problems with excess phosphorus, stop applications of any phosphorus-rich amendments to the soil for at least two years. Meanwhile, add nitrogen and potassium amendments to help create a better balance with the excessive phosphorus.

If you have excess phosphorus in your vegetable garden soil, you can try growing heavy phosphorus feeders, such as muskmelons, onions, and carrots.

Applying Potassium

A quick solution for a potassium deficiency is a weekly foliar spray with a kelp-derived material. Continue these treatments until the symptoms recede. A side-dressing of wood ashes can also help plants recover from potassium deficiency.

Long-term corrective treatments for a potassium deficiency include adding ground kelp, greensand, granite dust, finished compost, or aged manure. Apply wood ashes in large quantities only if you are working from information given to you from a soil test.

If your soil test or other symptoms indicate you have excessive potassium in your soil, there is little you can do to solve the problem quickly. Don't add wood ashes, manure, or other sources of potassium-rich amendments to the soil for at least two years. Add nitrogen and phosphorus amendments to bring these closer in balance with the excessive potassium.

In the vegetable garden, try growing potatoes, tomatoes, cabbage family plants, or carrots. These plants all remove large amounts of potassium from the soil. Remember to remove the nonedible portions from the garden at the end of the growing season, so they won't end up returning the potassium they've extracted back into the soil.

Applying Calcium

Calcium deficiency symptoms vary among the plants. The most sure route to identifying a problem is through a soil test. If test results indicate a deficiency of calcium, but your pH is in the proper range, apply gypsum to remedy the problem. The sulfate in the gypsum will counteract the calcium, with little change in soil pH.

Ground clam and oyster shells are another natural source of calcium. These contain 90 to 95 percent calcium carbonate and have roughly the same composition as limestone. They also contain many micronutrients. Limestone is usually richer in magnesium than shells, while shells are rich in iodine.

If you have collected shells yourself, you must grind the shells (not just break them) before applying them to the soil. Otherwise, the garden soil will be full of dangerous, sharp-edged fragments. Also, the more finely ground the material is, the more available it will be for uptake by plant roots.

Applying Magnesium

The best quick solution to a magnesium deficiency is a foliar spray of liquid kelp or seaweed extract every two weeks until the symptoms disappear. For a long-term solution, apply dolomitic limestone to the soil. Dolomitic limestone is a slow-release source of magnesium. You can create problems with an excess of magnesium, so it's best only to apply the quantity prescribed in soil test recommendations. If you suspect a magnesium deficiency, the safest remedy is to apply compost and a layer of organic mulch.

Well-mulched plants are not likely to show a magnesium deficiency, because organic material, such as leaves and chopped straw, breaks down slowly, adding magnesium along with the other nutrients.

If you need to increase your soil's magnesium level without increasing pH, use Epsom salts instead of dolomitic limestone. Langbeinite, commonly called Sul-Po-Mag or K-Mag, is a mined mineral that will increase both magnesium and potassium levels.

Applying Micronutrients

The need for a good soil test is especially important when dealing with micronutrient deficiencies. The amount needed to correct some of these deficiencies is very small—from 4 to 8 ounces per 1,000 square feet—and adding excess can cause toxicity symptoms in your plants.

Adding compost regularly is a safe approach to supplying micronutrients until you identify specific deficiencies through soil testing or foliar analysis. You can also apply kelp-based products to the soil, or use them in a foliar feeding program. For fruit trees, chelated mineral sprays are sometimes a good way to treat individual micronutrient deficiencies.

Pursue corrective liming of your soil to a pH between 6.0 and 6.8 because the acidity or alkalinity of the soil can restrict the availability of micronutrients. What was thought to be a problem of micronutrient deficiency or excess could well be rectified once you have established the proper conditions for good plant growth.

MAINTAINING A BALANCED SOIL

After you have solved all the problems identified in the assessment process, you are ready to maintain the soil to keep it active and vital year after year. This maintenance program is relatively simple, compared to the complexity of diagnosing and correcting soil imbalances. The basis of your soil maintenance program will be to continue adding quality organic material to the soil, but in smaller amounts. Once your soil is healthy, if you add organic material annually throughout your yard and garden and keep the soil covered by plants or organic mulch, you will likely not need to buy organic amendments or fertilizers.

If you're a gardener who suffers from never having enough time, and maybe have a dozen other things on which to spend a little extra money, you may be satisfied with sticking to a maintenance program and not worrying about feeding individual plants. Your plants will still be healthier than those of most of your neighbors. They will have fewer insect problems and seldom get diseases. They will do better getting through the heat and drought of summers, and you will get all the wonderful fruit and vegetables that you need.

Of course, a plant-feeding program with organic fertilizers will improve the performance and productivity of your plants. To get that superlative performance, you will have to spend money and a fair amount of your time to manage a plant-fertilizing program. This is a choice each gardener must make.

In a fertile, well-kept soil with approximately 5 percent organic matter and a near neutral pH, the gradual breakdown of organic materials combined with nitrogen fixation by legumes can provide as much as 3 pounds of actual nitrogen for every 1,000 square feet of yard and garden area each season. In other words, if you have a healthy, organically balanced soil, basic soil maintenance—adding organic matter and mulch—will give you results equivalent to spreading a 50-pound bag of 6 percent nitrogen fertilizer on every 1,000 square feet of your yard. That's why you should feed the soil first every year, and feed the plants if and when you can get to it.

Managing Mulch

During the soil-building years, you probably concentrated your attention on using soil amendments and fertilizers to get your soil back to a healthy balance. While mulching was an important step in that process, it was the finishing touch, so to speak.

Once you've made the transition to a soil-maintaining program, you can pay more attention to mulch. In many parts of the garden, adding mulch to healthy soil may be the only step needed to keep things in balance.

The advantages of using organic mulch to build and maintain the soil are ease and low cost. Laying mulch is easier than digging or tilling in organic matter; it requires little maintenance during the growing season and can often be acquired at no cost.

An organic mulch encourages microorganisms near the surface of the soil because it keeps the soil more consistently moist. Furthermore, the mulch itself gradually decomposes, providing an ongoing nutrient supplement to your plants. Some gardeners worry about the fact that the decomposing mulch ties up nitrogen in the top few inches of the soil, harming plant growth. This is not likely to be a problem

once your soil is balanced and has sufficient organic matter with plenty of available nitrogen. The amount that would be tied up due to the decomposition of the mulch would be a small fraction of the total available nitrogen.

A heavy organic mulch on beds and around trees and shrubs greatly reduces soil compaction. Bare soil tends to become compacted over time from the beating of the rain and the drying out of the soil particles in the blazing sun. Any mulch protects the surface of the soil from the impact of rain and sun, reducing this compacting process. Less compaction means healthier roots and a more active microlife below the surface of the soil.

A winter mulch under your shrubs and over your garden beds helps stabilize the temperature of the soil during cold weather. Mulch also prevents the alternate freezing and thawing fluctuations that occur in unprotected soil that can cause perennials and small shrubs to be lifted out of the soil. This fluctuation in soil temperature is also harmful to soil microorganisms. As the soil bacteria and fungi increase their numbers in the spring, the process can be assisted by protecting the soil from the cold. This layer of mulch cannot keep the soil from eventually freezing, but it does prevent the extreme temperature shifts that occur in the winter.

For details on what mulch to use where in your yard and garden, see "Organic Soil Amendments and Mulches" on page 86.

FEEDING YOUR PLANTS

Using organic fertilizers to quickly supply nutrients that may be lacking in your soils or to give your plants an extra boost is the final step in your system of organic soil management. This doesn't mean it will always be the last action you'll take, but it's secondary to the steps you'll take to build and maintain healthy soil.

If you are seeking maximum performance from your plants, you must address the individual needs of each flower, vegetable, tree, and shrub on your property. Some plants like lots of potassium and little nitrogen; others prefer the reverse ratio. You can use a plant-specific approach to fertilizing, giving each plant the amount of fertilizer it needs for best growth, applied when it needs it. For recommendations on fertilizing specific plants, see part 3, "Chemical-Free Garden Guides." There you'll find fertilizing recommendations for individual vegetable, flower, fruit, and ornamental plants.

A plant-specific fertilizing program will make use of the specialty organic fertilizers that are available from mail-order supply companies or at many well-stocked garden centers. For example, you can use blood meal, cottonseed meal, or feather meal as nitrogen sources. Bonemeal is a good source of phosphorus, and kelp or greensand are good for applying in specific instances when potassium is needed. "Selecting Organic Fertilizers," on page 92, gives a complete listing of organic fertilizer products, including average nutrient analysis and suggested application rates.

Using Dry Organic Fertilizers

Dry organic fertilizers can be amendments that supply a single nutrient (such as rock phosphate) or blended materials that supply several nutrients. Blended general-purpose organic fertilizers contain balanced amounts of nitrogen, phosphorus, and potassium, along with varying amounts of micronutrients. Read the label of the fertilizer to find out what nutrients are included in it. (See "How to Read a Bag of Fertilizer," for questions to consider when buying organic fertilizers and other organic gardening products.) Several preblended commercial organic fertilizers are available through mail-order supply houses and, increasingly, at garden centers. Or, you can make your own general-purpose fertilizer by mixing individual

---

How to Read a Bag of Fertilizer

Fertilizer manufacturers use a ratio of three numbers as a shorthand method of identifying how much of three major nutrients—nitrogen (N), phosphorus (P), and potassium (K)—are in their products. This NPK ratio (the letters are the standard scientific abbreviations for the three nutrients) represents the percent of each of the nutrients. So a 5-10-5 fertilizer contains 5 percent nitrogen, 10 percent phosphorus, and 5 percent potassium.

When buying fertilizers and other products labeled organic or natural, you need to look beyond the brand name and the NPK ratio to make sure you are getting a product that is truly derived from natural mineral or botanical sources. Some questions to ask yourself include:

🦋 Are the ingredients in the product listed on the label?

🦋 Are the ingredient names descriptive or mysterious?

🦋 Are all of the ingredients safe and natural?

🦋 Do the manufacturer and seller provide additional information about the product when asked?

🦋 Does the label state the particular problem the product will solve or the specific benefits it will provide?

Even some organic gardening products make fantastic claims for miraculous results. Be cautious. Don't expect magic in a good garden fertilizer or other product. It should simply be an aide to your gardening and a means to help or augment natural biological processes in your soil and garden.

---

amendments. See "Mix and Match," on page 89, for some suggestions on mixing amendments.

If you're a gardener who's making the switch from chemical to organic fertilizers, you may be

(continued on page 88)

Organic Soil Amendments and Mulches

You can choose from a wide range of materials to layer on or dig into your soils. Factors to consider in selecting soil amendments and mulches are the availability, cost, ease of handling, and pH range of the materials.

Compost. Finished compost is the best soil amendment. You can make it yourself or buy it commercially. Finished compost is well on its way to becoming stable humus. When mixed into the soil, it resists compaction and drains quickly, yet still retains an enormous amount of water. Compost will retain ten times its weight in water. It also serves as fodder for the "micro-herd," the soil microorganisms that break organic material down into nutrients in a form readily taken up by plant roots. Compost will vary a great deal in NPK content because of the variety of materials that can be used to make it. However, homemade compost is likely to have at least ½ pound each of nitrogen, phosphorus, and potassium in 100 pounds of finished product. See "Compost: Nature's Black Magic," on page 68, for more information on this important soil amendment.

Shredded leaves. If you don't have enough compost to feed all the soil in your yard and garden, chopped leaves are a good second choice. Leaves are cheap, readily available, and easy to use.

Be sure to chop or shred leaves before using them as a mulch or soil amendment. Whole leaves blow away easily when dry, and after wetting can form a crusted mat that keeps almost all moisture from seeping through to the soil underneath. If you incorporate whole leaves into the soil, they will take much longer to decay than chopped leaves. If you don't own a shredder, you can shred your leaves with a lawn mower. Run the mower repeatedly over a pile of leaves, criss-crossing the leaves until only small pieces remain.

Most leaves are acidic, but will not add enough acidity to significantly affect soil pH. Pine needles are even more acidic, and may reduce soil pH. Chopped leaves are also low in nitrogen, but you can add from 100 to 200 pounds of leaves to 1,000 square feet of garden without significantly tying up soil nitrogen.

Grass clippings. Grass clippings are frequently recommended as a good organic mulch for flower and vegetable beds. While technically true, why remove grass clippings from the lawn when they are the very best organic amendment for lawns? Leaving grass clippings on the lawn not only builds the humus content of the lawn soil, but also adds nitrogen, reducing lawn fertilizing needs by as much as 30 percent. If you mow frequently, the clippings will fall down among the grass plants and never show. The only times you should rake off grass clippings are if your lawn has a thatch accumulation problem, or if you have mown very tall grass. Dense clumps of long clippings could shade out portions of the turf.

If you do rake off lawn clippings, use them as mulch or add them to the compost pile. The nitrogen content of grass clippings is high, and almost immediately available. However, they will not last more than a few weeks as a mulch. Grass-clipping mulches work well around nitrogen-loving vegetable crops like spinach and lettuce. Because you can adjust the depth of this mulch so easily, you can spread a thin layer around plants while they are still quite young. Be sure to leave a little open space around each plant, because fresh grass clippings can give off enough heat as they rapidly decompose to burn vegetable and flower transplants. It's your choice whether to use grass clippings to help fertilize your lawn or to mulch your vegetables. If you're selective in your use of lawn clippings, you might be able to pull off both. Just remove a portion of your lawn clippings for mulching jobs, changing the area from which you take them at each mowing.

Aged manure. Aged manure is a wonderful soil amendment. It adds material well on its way to becoming humus and is a significant source of nutrients. Unfortunately, animal manure is not readily available to most home gardeners. If you can get manure, add it to soil only after it has aged for at least six months. Aged manure varies in its NPK ratio, depending on the animal source and on how much it has been leached by rains during aging. Some soil testing laboratories will analyze aged manure nutrient content. Testing will help you decide application rates and the need for other inputs, such as rock phosphate or greensand.

Hay and straw. Hay and straw are generally inexpensive sources of organic material. They are relatively low in nutrients, but will give soil a big boost in humus. They are available directly from farms or from any source that serves livestock owners, so check the telephone directory yellow pages under "Feed Dealers."

Hay usually carries seeds of weed plants that mature earlier than the grasses in the field where it was cut. Consequently, many chemical-free growers try *not* to use hay. A hay mulch also is a favorite habitat for rodents and slugs. If you've been having mouse or slug problems, think twice about using hay, or refine your techniques to minimize damage. For example, hay pushed close to a fruit tree seedling gives mice a perfect opportunity to nibble on the succulent bark through the winter when other food isn't available. Leave at least 2 feet of bare soil surface between a hay mulch and the tree stem. And while mulches do encourage ground beetles that prey on slugs, that benefit might not outweigh the damage in some situations. For example, if you mulch with hay directly under your tomato plants, either reconcile yourself to losses from slug damage or be certain to stake or support the plants so well that fruits are suspended well above the mulch.

Straw generally carries few weed seeds, since most of these seeds were removed in the same process that separated the grain seed from the straw. Straw mulch also holds up better over a growing season than a hay mulch.

Peat moss. Peat mosses, including sphagnum peat moss, are remains of aquatic plants that have been deposited in locations not favorable for their quick breakdown due to high water tables and/or extended periods of cold temperatures. The pH of peat moss is acidic, ranging from 3.0 to 4.5; the nitrogen content is low, and the water-absorbing capacity is very high. Peat moss is a useful soil amendment around acid-loving plants such as rhododendrons, azaleas, hemlock, pine, and spruce.

Peat humus or sedge peat, also known as reed peat or humus, can be used in the same manner as peat moss. Sedge peat or peat humus is dark brown to black and is relatively high in nitrogen (2.0 to 3.5 percent). It has a lower water-absorbing capacity than peat moss, and it will break down more quickly in the soil.

Sawdust. Use sawdust as a mulch or soil amendment only after it has aged. Some types of sawdust contain natural chemicals that can act as herbicides. If you put fresh sawdust on or in your soil, it may temporarily sterilize the soil. Fresh sawdust also needs nitrogen to break down, so it robs nitrogen from your plants, unless extra nitrogen is mixed in with it. Aged sawdust is very low in nitrogen. If you apply it to nitrogen-demanding crops such as vegetables or annual flowers, mix it with some manure, bloodmeal, or compost to supply nitrogen. If the compost has aged for 2 years or more and has turned black, you do not need to add nitrogen when you apply it. This aged material has little nutrient value, but will increase the organic matter content of the soil.

Wood chips. Bark and wood chips are often used as mulches. They work well to keep down weeds in established ornamental beds or plantings of perennial herbs. Like sawdust, these materials contain much more carbon than nitrogen. As soil microorganisms slowly digest these mulches, their populations swell. However, the microbes also need nitrogen to build their cells, so they may tie up soil nitrogen that plants need for optimum growth. Avoid this problem by spreading 1 inch of compost or well-aged manure before laying down wood chips or bark. Observe the plants carefully in succeeding seasons; you may need to water with a nitrogen-rich solution of manure tea or fish emulsion if the plants show signs of deficiency. Don't dig in bark or wood chips as a soil amendment: The materials are too large to be attacked by the "micro-herd."

Locally available materials. You may be able to find natural materials or manufacturing by-products in your area that serve as valuable soil amendments and mulches. Gardeners who live near the ocean may be able to collect seaweed. Rinse it well before adding it to your garden or compost pile. Other possible materials include apple pomace from a cider mill, soybean wastes from tofu making, cheese whey, nut shells, mushroom soil, and ground corn cobs. If you're getting an agricultural by-product, be sure to ask whether the source crops were treated with pesticides. The by-products could contain residues of these chemicals.

afraid that using organic amendments will be more complicated and less convenient than using premixed chemical fertilizers. Not so! Commercially formulated organic blended fertilizers can be just as convenient and effective as blended synthetic fertilizers. You don't need to custom-feed specific amendments to each of your plants unless it's an activity you enjoy. So, while some experts will spread a little blood meal around their tomatoes at planting, and then some bonemeal just when the blossoms are about to pop, most gardeners will be satisfied to make one or two applications of general-purpose organic fertilizer throughout the vegetable garden.

How to Apply Dry Fertilizers

You can apply dry and granular fertilizers three ways. The most common method is to broadcast the fertilizer, meaning to spread it evenly across an area, by hand or with a spreading tool. Generally, you should till, hoe, or rake the broadcast fertilizer into the top 4 to 6 inches of soil.

Another way to use dry fertilizers is to add small amounts to planting holes or rows as you plants seeds or transplants. The great advantage of dry organic fertilizers over dry synthetic fertilizers for this approach is that organic fertilizers are nonburning and will not harm delicate seedling roots.

You can also use dry fertilizers to boost plant growth by side-dressing, meaning spreading the fertilizers alongside the row during the growing season or around the dripline of trees or shrubs. It's best to work side-dressings of fertilizers into the top inch of the soil.

Fortunately, with a growing concern in America for the environment, there are more and more truly organic fertilizers coming on the market. Unfortunately, some companies are taking advantage of the increased concern for safety and abusing the word "organic." Like most everything else on the market, you really must read the label and determine the contents of the fertilizer to be sure it is what you want.

Using Liquid Organic Fertilizers

Another way to get very close to that absolute maximum performance from the plants in your landscape—the most and biggest blossoms, the brightest colors, the biggest fruit and vegetables—is to try using liquid fertilizer.

With this approach, all your plants get a light nutrient boost or snack every month or even every two weeks during the growing season. This is easy if you apply the fertilizer as a foliar spray and simply spray all your plants at the same time. Among farmers and orchardists, foliar feeding has become accepted as a useful, even vital, supplement to soil fertilization. It's also being used increasingly by gardeners and growers of ornamentals, from roses to houseplants.

Foliar feeding can supply nutrients when they are lacking or unavailable in the soil or when roots are stressed and cannot take them up well. It is especially appropriate for feeding fast-growing plants like vegetables. Growth of these plants often is limited because the roots cannot take up nutrients rapidly enough at key times.

Some foliar fertilizers such as kelp extracts are rich in micronutrients and growth hormones. These foliar sprays also appear to act as catalysts, increasing the plant's uptake of nutrients from the soil. You can make your own liquid fertilizer by brewing up compost or manure in water. See "Make Your Own Nutrient Tea," on page 90, for directions.

How to Apply Liquid Fertilizers

With flowering and fruiting plants, foliar sprays are most useful just before and during critical growth stages such as bloom, fruit setting, and maturing. With leaf crops, some suppliers recommend spraying every two weeks.

Mix and Match

If you want to mix your own general-purpose organic fertilizer, try combining individual amendments in the amounts shown here. Just pick one ingredient from each column. Because these amendments may vary in the amount of the nutrients they contain, this method won't give you a mixture with a precise NPK ratio. The ratio will be between 4-5-4 and 5-8-5. However, it will give a balanced supply of nutrients that will be steadily available to plants and will also encourage soil microorganisms to thrive.

Nitrogen (N)	Phosphorus (P)	Potassium (K)
2 parts blood meal	3 parts bonemeal	1 part kelp meal
3 parts fish meal	6 parts rock phosphate or colloidal phosphate	6 parts greensand

When using liquid fertilizers, always follow the label instructions for proper dilution and application methods. You can use a surfactant, such as coconut oil or a mild soap (¼ teaspoon per gallon of spray), to ensure better coverage of the leaves. Measure the surfactant carefully; if you use too much, it may penetrate the waxy covering of leaf surfaces and damage plants. A slightly acid spray mixture is the most effective, so check your spray pH. Use small amounts of vinegar to lower pH, baking soda to raise it. Aim for a pH of 6.0.

Any sprayer or mister will work, from hand-trigger units to knapsack sprayers. Set your sprayer to emit as fine a spray as possible. Never use a sprayer that has been used to apply herbicides. It is almost impossible to remove 100 percent of any herbicide residue from the tank, hose, and nozzle, and even a tiny bit can damage plants.

The best times to spray are early morning and early evening, when the liquids will be absorbed most quickly. Choose a day when no rain is forecast and temperatures aren't extreme. Cloudy days are good days for applying liquid fertilizers.

Spray until the liquid is dripping off the leaves. Be sure to concentrate the spray on the undersides of leaves. The pores in the leaf surface are more likely to be open on the leaf undersides, and it is through these openings that the fertilizers penetrate the leaves.

You can also water in liquid fertilizers around the root zone. This may be less efficient than a foliar spray. Although a liquid fertilizer is quickly absorbed by the roots of plants, there is still some loss, because some nutrients leach down past the roots.

You can also set up your drip irrigation system to carry liquid fertilizers to your plants. Kelp extract is a better product for this use, as fish emulsion can clog the irrigation emitters.

Using Growth Enhancers

Growth enhancers are materials that help plants absorb nutrients more effectively from the soil. The use of these materials is based on long-established practices. For centuries, farmers living near the ocean have used seaweed in various forms to improve the quality of their crops. They didn't understand exactly what was happening to the plants, but the seaweed made their crops more productive and more drought and insect resistant.

Now seaweed is sold as a liquid or powder concentrate of one or more species of kelp. Seaweed can also make plants more resistant to drought and diseases, and in some cases, increases a plant's insect resistance.

Seaweed is totally safe and provides some 60 trace elements that plants need in very small quantities. What makes it different from simple rock powders with many of those same trace elements is that it contains growth-promoting hormones and enzymes. These compounds are still not fully understood, but are clearly involved in improving a plant's growing conditions. Seaweed extracts do not leach easily and have a slow release rate. They are a great source of vitamins and beneficial enzymes, and their carbohydrates help plants absorb otherwise unavailable trace elements.

How to Apply Growth Enhancers

Follow the directions for spraying liquid fertilizers to apply growth enhancers as a foliar spray.

You can also apply seaweed directly to the soil either as a dried meal or as a liquid drench; soil application has the added benefit of stimulating soil bacteria. This in turn increases fertility through humus formation, aeration, and moisture retention. In this improved bacterial habitat, the nitrogen-fixing bacteria will be better able to fix more elements from plant residues and soil minerals.

A good general application rate for the dry form of kelp is 1 to 2 pounds of kelp meal per 100 square feet of garden applied each spring. You can apply the powder in a single application in the spring. When using liquid extract, apply it as a spray at least once a month for the first four or five months of the growing season.

If fresh seaweed is available, rinse it to remove the sea salt and apply it to your garden as a mulch, or compost it. Seaweed decays readily because it contains little cellulose. Furthermore, there's no need to worry about introducing weed seeds with seaweed mulch.

Using Chelated Trace Minerals

Chelation is a biochemical process that bonds metal ions to larger organic molecules. It occurs naturally in compost heaps and during humus formation. Chelated trace minerals sprays are products in which the trace metals are chemically bonded to organic molecules such as lignin (a component of wood). This bonding actually makes the minerals more available for uptake by plant roots and leaves.

These chelated trace minerals can be purchased in garden centers and from mail-order houses. While liquid kelp sprays are usually the most convenient and effective way for home gardeners to supply micronutrients for plants, chelated mineral sprays can be useful for specific micronutrient deficiencies. For example, if you have many apple trees and discover they are suffering from boron deficiency, a chelated boron spray may be the best solution to the problem.

A GUIDE TO ORGANIC SOIL AMENDMENTS AND FERTILIZERS

There's a wide array of organic substances and commercial products you can use to feed your soil and plants. Use this guide as a quick reference to find out what's in products, what their best uses are, and the best ways to apply them. Keep in mind that the commercial products listed here are not a comprehensive listing. Brand names come and go as companies bring new products on the market. When in doubt, ask for a product by its generic name: A knowledgeable salesperson will be able to help you find the commercial formulation you need.

Organic Matter

Organic matter is made up of partially decayed plant and animal remains. It is a storehouse of nutrients and has good water-holding capacity. As organic matter decomposes more fully, it is turned into humus. Humus is made up of the compounds that are most resistant to being broken down: fats, oils, waxes, and new compounds synthesized by soil organisms.

Compost

Compost is a mixture of organic materials that are actively or passively decomposing. Finished compost is material that has decomposed to the point that the original materials can no longer be distinguished.

Composition: Compost can be made from any raw organic material. Home gardeners usually make it from kitchen scraps, crop residues, yard wastes, green manure crops, and manure,

if it is available. The nutrient content will vary greatly depending on the original source of materials, how they are handled and the moisture content. The NPK ratio may range from 0.5-0.5-0.5 to 4-4-4. Commercial compost is most often made from manures and/or wastes from food-processing companies. Be sure that the material you buy is actually composted and not just dried and packaged.

Benefits/uses: Retains enormous amounts of water, up to ten times its own weight. Excellent nutrient source for microorganisms in the soil, which later release nutrients to your plants.

Application: Broadcast up to 2,000 pounds (approximately 1.5 cubic yards) per 1,000 square feet. May be applied to lawns, existing perennial plantings, garden crops, and potted plants.

Commercial products: Many brands of bagged compost

Cover Crops and Green Manures

Cover crops are crops grown to protect and enrich the soil and to control weeds. Green manures are cover crops that are grown specifically to be worked into the soil as a source of organic matter and available nutrients.

Composition: Many green manures are grass or small grain crops that extract particular nutrients from the soil. Others are legumes that grow in association with rhizobial bacteria to capture nitrogen from the air and make it available to plants. The most common are annual ryegrass, buckwheat, clovers, hairy vetch, and winter rye.

Benefits/uses: Adds organic matter and easily available nutrients to the soil.

Application: Plant in fall or early spring; inoculate legumes with the appropriate nitrogen-fixing bacteria. Mow and incorporate into soil four to six weeks before planting your next crop. Microbial activators can help these crops to break down more quickly. May also be cut and piled to be composted or used as mulch.

Selecting Organic Fertilizers

Use this table to select the appropriate fertilizers and application rates for your garden. The table lists the nitrogen-phosphorus-potassium (NPK) ratio, where relevant, as well as the content of other significant nutrients. It also lists the primary benefit of each fertilizer: Some supply particular nutrients, some help balance the content of soil minerals, others are primarily useful to enrich the soil with organic matter.

Application rates for low, medium, or adequate fertility soils are meant to be used in conjunction with an assessment of your soil by a soil testing laboratory, as well as your personal observations and the specific requirements of the crops you are growing.

Organic Amendment	Primary Benefit	Average Analysis	Average Application Rate per 1,000 Sq. Ft.	Comments
Alfalfa meal	Organic matter	5-1-2	Low: 50 lb. Medium: 35 lb. Adequate: 25 lb.	Contains triaconatol—a natural fatty acid growth stimulant—plus trace minerals.
Apple pomace	Organic matter	0.2-0-0.2	Low: 250 lb. Medium: 150 lb. Adequate: 100 lb.	Contains trace minerals.
Aragonite	Calcium	96% calcium carbonate	Low: 100 lb. Medium: 50 lb. Adequate: 25 lb.	Can replace limestone.
Bat guano (ancient)	Nitrogen	2-8-0	Low: 25 lb. Medium: 15 lb. Adequate: 10 lb.	Contains calcium.
Bat guano (fresh)	Nitrogen	10-3-1	Low: 30 lb. Medium: 20 lb. Adequate: 10 lb.	Contains calcium.
BioActivator	Organic matter	1 billion beneficial bacterial spores per gram	Low: 4 oz. Medium: 3 oz. Adequate: 2 oz.	Beneficial bacteria to inoculate composts and green manure crops.
Blood meal	Nitrogen	10-0-0	Low: 30 lb. Medium: 20 lb. Adequate: 10 lb.	
Bluegrass hay	Organic matter	1.8-0.6-1.8	Low: 250 lb. Medium: 150 lb. Adequate: 100 lb.	
Bonemeal (steamed)	Phosphate	1-11-0; 20% total phosphate; 24% calcium	Low: 30 lb. Medium: 20 lb. Adequate: 10 lb.	
Borax	Trace minerals	10% boron	Low: 5 oz. Medium: 4 oz. Adequate: 3 oz.	

Organic Amendment	Primary Benefit	Average Analysis	Average Application Rate per 1,000 Sq. Ft.	Comments
Calcitic limestone	Balancer, calcium	65–80% calcium carbonate; 3–15% magnesium carbonate	Low: 100 lb. Medium: 50 lb. Adequate: 25 lb.	
Cattle manure (dry)	Organic matter	2-2.3-2.4	Low: 200 lb. Medium: 150 lb. Adequate: 100 lb.	Should be composted or applied in the fall.
Coffee grounds	Nitrogen	2-0.3-0.2	Incorporate in compost	Acid-forming; needs limestone supplement.
Colloidal phosphate	Phosphate	0-2-2	Low: 60 lb. Medium: 25 lb. Adequate: 10 lb.	
Compost (dry commercial)	Organic matter	1-1-1	Low: 200 lb. Medium: 100 lb. Adequate: 50 lb.	
Compost (homemade)	Organic matter	0.5-0.5-0.5 to 4-4-4; 25% organic matter	Low: 2,000 lb. Medium: 1,000 lb. Adequate: 400 lb.	
Compost (mushroom)	Organic matter		Low: 350 lb. Medium: 250 lb. Adequate: 50 lb.	Ask supplier whether the material contains pesticide residues.
Corn stover (dry)	Organic matter	1.2-0.4-1.6	Low: 250 lb. Medium: 150 lb. Adequate: 100 lb.	
Corn stover (green)	Organic matter	0.3-0.1-0.3	Low: 1,000 lb. Medium: 600 lb. Adequate: 400 lb.	High in sugars when tilled or dug in while still green.
Cottonseed meal	Nitrogen	6-2-1	Low: 35 lb. Medium: 25 lb. Adequate: 10 lb.	May contain pesticide residues.
Cowpeas (dry)	Organic matter	3.1-0.6-2.3	Low: 200 lb. Medium: 150 lb. Adequate: 100 lb.	
Cowpeas (green)	Organic matter	0.4-0.1-0.4	Low: 800 lb. Medium: 600 lb. Adequate: 400 lb.	
Crab meal	Nitrogen	4-3-0.5	Low: 150 lb. Medium: 100 lb. Adequate: 50 lb.	Also useful to help control harmful nematodes.

(continued)

Selecting Organic Fertilizers—*Continued*

Organic Amendment	Primary Benefit	Average Analysis	Average Application Rate per 1,000 Sq. Ft.	Comments
Dolomitic limestone	Balancer, calcium, magnesium	51% calcium carbonate; 40% magnesium carbonate	Low: 100 lb. Medium: 50 lb. Adequate: 25 lb.	
Eggshells	Calcium	1.2-0.4-0.1	Low: 100 lb. Medium: 50 lb. Adequate: 25 lb.	Contain calcium plus trace minerals.
Epsom salts	Balancer, magnesium	10% magnesium; 13% sulfur	Low: 5 lb. Medium: 3 lb. Adequate: 1 lb.	
Feather meal	Nitrogen	11-0-0	Low: 30 lb. Medium: 20 lb. Adequate: 10 lb.	
Fescue hay	Organic matter	2.1-0.7-2.4	Low: 200 lb. Medium: 150 lb. Adequate: 100 lb.	
Fish emulsion	Nitrogen	4-1-1; 5% sulfur	Low: 2 oz. Medium: 1 oz. Adequate: 1 oz.	
Fish meal	Nitrogen	5-3-3	Low: 30 lb. Medium: 20 lb. Adequate: 10 lb.	
Flowers of sulfur	Balancer	99.5% sulfur	Low: 10 lb. Medium: 5 lb. Adequate: 2 lb.	
Granite meal	Potash	4% total potash; contains 67% silicas and 19 trace minerals	Low: 100 lb. Medium: 50 lb. Adequate: 25 lb.	
Grass clippings (green)	Organic matter	0.5-0.2-0.5	Low: 500 lb. Medium: 300 lb. Adequate: 200 lb.	
Greensand	Potash	7% total potash plus 32 trace minerals	Low: 100 lb. Medium: 50 lb. Adequate: 25 lb.	
Gypsum	Balancer, calcium	22% calcium; 17% sulfur	Low: 40 lb. Medium: 20 lb. Adequate: 5 lb.	Do not apply if pH is below 5.8.
Hairy vetch	Organic matter	2.8-0.8-2.3	Low: 200 lb. Medium: 150 lb. Adequate: 100 lb.	

Organic Amendment	Primary Benefit	Average Analysis	Average Application Rate per 1,000 Sq. Ft.	Comments
Hoof and horn meal	Nitrogen	12-2-0	Low: 30 lb. Medium: 20 lb. Adequate: 10 lb.	
Horse manure	Organic matter	1.7-0.7-1.8	Low: 200 lb. Medium: 150 lb. Adequate: 100 lb.	
Humates	Organic matter	Humic acids of variable composition	Low: 50 lb. Medium: 30 lb. Adequate: 15 lb.	
Kelp meal	Potash, trace minerals	1.5-0.5-2.5	Low: 20 lb. Medium: 10 lb. Adequate: 5 lb.	
Lespedeza hay	Organic matter	2.4-0.8-2.3	Low: 200 lb. Medium: 150 lb. Adequate: 100 lb.	
Oak leaves	Organic matter	0.8-9.4-0.1	Low: 250 lb. Medium: 150 lb. Adequate: 100 lb.	
Orchard grass hay	Organic matter	2.3-0.7-2.8	Low: 200 lb. Medium: 150 lb. Adequate: 100 lb.	
Oyster shells	Calcium	33.5% calcium	Low: 100 lb. Medium: 50 lb. Adequate: 25 lb.	
Peat moss	Organic matter	pH range 3.0–4.5	As needed	Use around acid-loving plants.
Poultry manure (dry)	Organic matter	4-4-2	Low: 100 lb. Medium: 50 lb. Adequate: 25 lb.	Should be composted or applied in the fall.
Red clover hay	Organic matter	2.8-0.6-2.3	Low: 200 lb. Medium: 150 lb. Adequate: 100 lb.	
Rock phosphate	Phosphate	0-3-0; 32% total phosphate; 32% calcium; contains 11 trace minerals	Low: 60 lb. Medium: 25 lb. Adequate: 10 lb.	
Sawdust	Organic matter	0.2-0-0.2	Low: 250 lb. Medium: 150 lb. Adequate: 100 lb.	Be sure sawdust is well-rotted before incorporating.

(continued)

Selecting Organic Fertilizers—*Continued*

Organic Amendment	Primary Benefit	Average Analysis	Average Application Rate per 1,000 Sq. Ft.	Comments
Sheep manure (dry)	Organic matter	4-1.4-3.5	Low: 100 lb. Medium: 50 lb. Adequate: 25 lb.	
Soybean meal	Nitrogen	7-0.5-2.3	Low: 50 lb. Medium: 25 lb. Adequate: 10 lb.	
Sul-Po-Mag	Potash, magnesium	0-0-22; 11% magnesium; 22% sulfur	Low: 10 lb. Medium: 7 lb. Adequate: 5 lb.	Do not use if applying dolomitic limestone; substitute greensand or other potassium source.
Sweet clover hay	Organic matter	2.2-0.6-2.2	Low: 200 lb. Medium: 150 lb. Adequate: 100 lb.	
Swine manure (dry)	Organic matter	2-1.8-1.8	Low: 200 lb. Medium: 150 lb. Adequate: 100 lb.	Should be composted or applied in the fall.
Timothy hay	Organic matter	1.8-0.7-2.8	Low: 200 lb. Medium: 150 lb. Adequate: 100 lb.	
Wheat bran	Organic matter	2.6-2.9-1.6	Low: 200 lb. Medium: 150 lb. Adequate: 100 lb.	
Wheat straw	Organic matter	0.7-0.2-1.2	Low: 250 lb. Medium: 150 lb. Adequate: 100 lb.	
White clover (green)	Organic matter	0.5-0.2-0.3	Low: 800 lb. Medium: 600 lb. Adequate: 400 lb.	
Wood ashes (leached)	Potash	0-1.2-2	Low: 20 lb. Medium: 10 lb. Adequate: 5 lb.	
Wood ashes (unleached)	Potash	0-1.5-8	Low: 10 lb. Medium: 5 lb. Adequate: 3 lb.	
Worm castings	Organic matter	0.5-0.5-0.3	Low: 250 lb. Medium: 100 lb. Adequate: 50 lb.	50% organic matter plus 11 trace minerals.

SOURCE: Reprinted with permission of Necessary Trading Company, New Castle, VA 24127.

Enzyme Products

Many enzyme products are brewery by-products. Many claims are made for the potential benefits of these products. Be cautious: Make sure product labels explain what the material contains as well as what it is supposed to accomplish.

Composition: Most enzyme products are produced by the activity of beneficial microbes. Exact ingredients are considered trade secrets.

Benefits/uses: These products can help the texture and water-holding capacity of your soil. Some are designed to help stabilize humus or stimulate natural processes surrounding the root zone of your plants.

Application: Since concentrations and ingredients vary greatly, follow the application instructions on the individual products.

Commercial products: Nitron; Roots

Food By-Products

These include kitchen scraps and wastes from vegetable processing plants or grocery stores.

Composition: Nutrients vary depending on the makeup of the materials. Food wastes from your kitchen such as coffee grounds contain nitrogen, while eggshells contain nitrogen and calcium. Avoid meat scraps, since these may attract rodents or other animals and often smell bad until they are thoroughly broken down. Vegetable processing wastes include apple and grape pomace (the leftovers after producing juice) and the skins, stems, and seeds from vegetables that are canned or frozen.

Benefits/uses: These materials are a good raw material for the compost pile. They may be available free for the taking. Try asking about picking up waste at your local stores or at processing plants if there are any in your local area.

Application: Make compost and apply at rates suggested for compost.

Humates

Humates are ancient organic plant life in the stages of being transformed into coal. They are mined for use as organic soil amendments. Humates are not currently sold for use by home gardeners, but will be more available for small-scale use in upcoming years.

Composition: Humates contain high levels of humic acids.

Benefits/uses: Help make phosphates available, especially in alkaline soils. Improves stability of soil humus.

Application: Broadcast 15 to 50 pounds per 1,000 square feet.

Manures

Manure is available in several forms. You can get it fresh from a farm or stable if you live in a rural area or from your own livestock. Garden centers offer bagged, dried, or composted manure.

Composition: Nutrient values vary greatly depending on the type of livestock, the bedding that is used, and how the manure was handled.

Benefits/uses: Manures are an excellent source of organic matter and nutrients. Composted manure is an excellent soil amendment for all parts of the yard and garden.

Application: Application rates vary depending on the variety of manure and its condition. Generally, you should compost fresh manure before applying it to your soil, and use the application rates given for compost. If you must apply fresh manure directly to your soil, wait at least 60 days after applying before planting food crops. The best time to apply raw manure is in the fall or winter shortly before planting a green manure crop.

Commercial products: Many brands of bagged dried manure

Microbial Inoculants

Microbial inoculants contain microorganisms that break down raw organic matter into more stable and usable plant foods.

Composition: Concentrated mixtures of naturally occurring bacteria and other beneficial microorganisms.

Benefits/uses: Increases the nutrients captured for your plants from your compost pile or green manure crop and speeds up the breakdown of organic matter into usable nutrients and humus.

Application: Apply at least 200 billion spores per ton of raw organic matter or 20 billion spores per 1,000 square feet of green manure crop.

Commercial products: BioActivator; Humus Alive!

Mushroom Compost

Mushroom compost is the spent bedding material in which mushrooms have been grown and harvested.

Composition: Mushroom compost from commercial mushroom production is generally made of horse manure and other organic material, such as wood chips. Use care if you choose this material; it may contain pesticides used on the mushroom crop.

Benefits/uses: May provide some nutrients as well as organic matter. Available directly from commercial mushroom producers, usually at low cost.

Application: Broadcast throughout growing areas at a rate up to 350 pounds per 1,000 square feet. Best applied in the fall after crops have been harvested.

Buyer Beware!

Many products that are sold for organic gardeners are by-products or waste materials. We can all feel proud of our efforts to use and re-use the things that other people would just throw away. But it is also important to be aware that some of the processes that produce the materials we want also produce stuff that we don't want. Please keep this issue in mind when you shop for fertilizers. A few examples are mentioned here.

Sewage sludge contains nutrients that cause harm when they are dumped in the environment (particularly water pollution). Capturing these nutrients for use as fertilizer is a good way to avoid this pollution. But sewage sludge also contains everything that anyone dumps down the drain—things like heavy metals, industrial chemicals, and pesticides. In general, we recommend that sludge products only be used on ornamentals and lawns, not on food crops.

Leather meal is a by-product of the tannery industry. It contains about 10 percent nitrogen, which is an important plant nutrient. Unfortunately, most tanneries use chromium in the tanning process. This chromium is found in significant concentrations, often 3 percent or higher, in the dried leather meal.

Cottonseed meal is produced from a crop that is treated with a lot of pesticides. Residues of these pesticides may be found in the dried product. Feed-grade cottonseed meal is monitored for pesticide residues and should be safer to use.

Mushroom compost is the spent bedding from commercial mushroom production. Mushrooms are often sprayed with pesticides, which may find their way into the compost. Be cautious when using spent mushroom bedding. Fully composting it again prior to application as a fertilizer will usually eliminate pesticide residue problems.

Organic Mulches

Mulches are materials layered on the soil surface to help protect soil from compaction, reduce water loss, keep down weeds, and add to soil fertility.

Composition: Many different materials can be used as mulches. These include grass clippings, green manure crops, hay, leaf mold, leaves, sawdust, straw, and wood chips. Home-owners can generate most of these materials on their own property, find them at local municipal composting operations, or buy them from area farmers or feed dealers.

Benefits/uses: Provide some nutrient benefits. However, their primary use (after weed suppression) is to increase the organic content of your soil as they slowly break down.

Application: Apply in layers as deep as 1 foot, depending on rainfall and the needs of your crops. Lay mulch after crops are showing and after the ground has warmed up well in the spring. Use caution when applying materials with a high carbon content such as sawdust, wood chips, or bark as a mulch on low organic content soils, since the microorganisms breaking them down will tie up nitrogen needed by your plants.

Peat Moss

Peat moss is a natural plant material harvested from peat bogs.

Composition: Dried peat has a very low pH (3.0 to 4.5).

Benefits/uses: Primarily a source of organic matter. Has excellent water-retentive properties. For use on acid-loving plants such as blueberries, rhododendrons, and azaleas. Peat humus or sedge peat also contains some nitrogen and has a higher pH, making it suitable for use on a wider variety of plants.

Application: Spread in a layer not more than 1 inch deep. Soak thoroughly with water and incorporate into the soil. Don't leave it on the soil surface as a mulch because it may crust over and prevent water from penetrating the soil.

Commercial products: Many brands of bagged peat moss

Worm Castings

You can generate your own worm castings by using composting worms to break down your kitchen and garden scraps or manure. Also harvested from the fishing worm industry.

Composition: Pure worm manure.

Benefits/uses: An excellent all-around soil amendment to increase humus content of your soil, improve water retention, and help potted plants or vegetable starts to remain healthy and strong.

Application: Add 5 to 10 percent to your potting mix for starts and potted houseplants, use up to 1 cup per transplant in the transplant hole to eliminate transplant shock, or broadcast up to 50 pounds per 1,000 square feet. May also be worked in around existing perennial plantings or placed in the row at planting time.

Commercial products: Biocast; Wiggle Worm Soil Builder

Soil Balancers

Soil balancers are corrective soil amendments. They provide minerals that are necessary for plant growth but also function to balance the proportion of these materials in the soil. Potassium, calcium, magnesium, and sulfur can interact chemically in the soil. If one of these materials is present in excess, it can block the other nutrients from being available for uptake by plant roots. In general, it is best to add balancers only in accordance with recommendations based on a soil test.

Soil-balancing products are generally sold by their generic names, not by brand names.

Aragonite

Aragonite is a mineral substance that is precipitated by sunlight passing through ocean water. It is mined from the ocean floor near Bermuda.

Composition: Aragonite is 96 percent calcium carbonate.

Benefits/uses: Liming material to raise soil pH.

Application: Broadcast at a rate of 50 pounds per 1,000 square feet to raise pH one unit.

Epsom Salts

Epsom salts are mined, processed magnesium sulfate.

Composition: Epsom salts contain 10 percent magnesium and 13 percent sulfur.

Benefits/uses: Provides rapidly available magnesium; can tie up excess calcium or potash.

Application: May be applied dry or dissolved in water and sprayed. Use sparingly at no more than 10 pounds per 1,000 square feet.

Flowers of Sulfur

Flowers of sulfur is mined sulfur. It is also sold as mineral sulfur. It combines chemically in the soil with potassium and other elements.

Composition: Flowers of sulfur is 92 percent sulfur.

Benefits/uses: Use in place of aluminum sulfate to lower soil pH. Especially useful for treating soil around acid-loving plants such as blueberries, rhododendrons, and azaleas.

Application: Ten pounds per 1,000 square feet will lower pH one unit. Use sparingly, only after testing soil. Generally apply in fall or winter.

Ground Limestone

Limestone is quarried and finely ground for use in adjusting soil pH. Standard dolomitic lime is generally high in magnesium. A high calcium lime is also available.

Composition: While exact composition varies, dolomitic lime contains about 50 percent calcium carbonate and 40 percent magnesium carbonate. Calcitic lime is about 72 percent calcium carbonate and 15 percent magnesium carbonate.

Benefits/uses: Raises soil pH. Calcitic lime can also help balance levels of calcium and magnesium for optimum growing conditions.

Application: Broadcast 50 pounds per 1,000 square feet to raise pH one unit on medium-weight soils. Heavier soils require more limestone to affect the pH.

Gypsum

Gypsum, also called land plaster, is calcium sulfate. Most sources are industrial by-products, not mined material. Mined gypsum is usually gray in color, while by-product gypsum is white. Organic gardeners may prefer to use naturally mined gypsum.

Composition: Gypsum contains about 23 percent available calcium and 18 percent sulfur.

Benefits/uses: Raises calcium or sulfur content of the soil without changing the pH. Helps correct excess magnesium or sodium content of soil. Helps loosen tight, clay soils.

Application: Broadcast up to 40 pounds per 1,000 square feet.

Oyster Shells

Finely ground oyster shells are a by-product of the seafood industry. It is sold by some mail-order companies and is available through feed stores as a chicken feed scratch.

Composition: Contains 31 to 36 percent calcium plus trace minerals.

Benefits/uses: An excellent supplement for your compost pile. May be used in place of other liming materials.

Application: Broadcast 50 pounds per 1,000 square feet; best applied in the fall.

Nitrogen Plant Foods

Fertilizer manufacturers use many of the materials listed in this section to blend their general-purpose organic fertilizers. If you buy blends, read labels carefully to determine that the materials in the product are truly organic. Some brands have been reviewed and approved by organic certification programs. About 20 states have set organic certification standards. Contact your local Cooperative Extension Service to find out if your state is one.

Alfalfa Meal

Alfalfa meal is alfalfa hay packaged as a ground or pelletized fertilizer.

Composition: Contains about 5 percent nitrogen.

Benefits/uses: Primarily a source of nitrogen and triacontanol, a plant growth promoter.

Application: Broadcast 25 to 50 pounds per 1,000 square feet before planting, or side-dress later in the season for crops needing additional nitrogen.

Blood Meal

Blood meal is dried blood, sometimes mixed with other materials to make it easier to spread. It is a by-product of the meat industry.

Composition: Blood meal contains 13 percent nitrogen.

Benefits/uses: Nitrogen fertilizer and animal pest repellent.

Application: Broadcast 10 to 30 pounds per 1,000 square feet before planting, or side-dress later in the season on crops requiring additional nitrogen.

Chilean Nitrate of Soda

Chilean nitrate of soda is a natural source of nitrogen nitrate mined in South America. It is a very strong and soluble nitrogen fertilizer.

Composition: Chilean nitrate of soda contains 16 percent nitrogen, 10 percent potassium, and 18 percent sodium.

Benefits/uses: Nitrogen fertilizer, not recommended for gardeners because of its high solubility and sodium content.

Application: Use very cautiously, if at all.

Cottonseed Meal

Cottonseed meal is the waste left after pressing cottonseed oil.

Composition: Ground cotton seeds. Use caution: Cotton crops are usually sprayed with large quantities of pesticides. Cottonseed meal from feed grade material is safer.

Benefits/uses: Particularly beneficial for acid-loving plants, such as blueberries, rhododendrons, and azaleas, as a nitrogen source and general fertilizer.

Application: Broadcast up to 35 pounds per 1,000 square feet or work into soil around existing perennial plantings.

Crab Meal and Seafood Meal

Crab and seafood meal are by-products of the seafood-processing industry. They are not as readily available in garden centers as fish meal, but are available through some mail-order supply companies.

Composition: Primarily the shells of crabs and shrimp.

Benefits/uses: Contains nitrogen and chitin. Chitin is valuable for texturizing the soil and has been shown to encourage the growth of organisms that inhibit harmful nematodes.

Application: Use 50 to 150 pounds per 1,000 square feet for nematode control. Additional nitrogen must be added for this treatment to be effective.

Commercial products: Bay Crab

Feather Meal

Feather meal is a by-product of the poultry industry.

Composition: Ground feathers from poultry factories. May contain some meat scraps.

Benefits/uses: Primarily a nitrogen source.

Application: Broadcast 10 to 30 pounds per 1,000 square feet.

Fish Emulsion

Fish emulsion is filtered and stabilized fish solubles, by-products of the fish protein concentrates used for animal feeds.

Composition: Fish emulsion has an NPK ratio of 4-1-1. It is usually treated with sulfuric or phosphoric acid to break down the solid material and make it more sprayable and to inhibit bacterial growth. Some processors have started to produce a spray-dried soluble fish powder that does not contain acid. It is more appropriate for the organic gardener and tends to be more economical to ship since the weight of the water has been removed. The spray-dried fish has an analysis of 12-0-1; 1 to 2 pounds is equivalent to 1 gallon of fish emulsion.

Benefits/uses: Foliar-applied nitrogen fertilizer. May also be used in irrigation systems.

Application: Mix 3 to 4 tablespoons of fish emulsion per gallon of water to spray up to 1,000 square feet. Mix 1 tablespoon soluble powder per gallon of water to spray 1,000 square feet.

Commercial products: Alaska; FoliaFish; Sea Mix (fish emulsion and liquid kelp)

Fish Meal

Fish meal is ground and dried fish parts. Some sources contain whole fish.

Composition: Average analysis is 5 to 8 percent nitrogen.

Benefits/uses: General-purpose fertilizer, primarily as a nitrogen source.

Application: Use as an early season starter fertilizer or as a side-dressing at 10 to 30 pounds per 1,000 feet of row.

Commercial products: High-Nitrogen Neptune

Guano

Guano is bird or bat excrement that has generally been deposited over a long period of time and has dried and aged.

Composition: Contains to 15 percent nitrogen, 10 percent phosphate, and sometimes a little potash. Also a good source of calcium.

Benefits/uses: High-analysis fertilizer for high-value plants.

Application: Side-dress, use as a starter for seedlings, or in potted plants.

Hoof and Horn Meal

Hoof and horn meal is a by-product of beef slaughterhouses.

Composition: Contains 12 percent nitrogen.

Benefits/uses: High-nitrogen fertilizer.

Application: Apply 10 to 30 pounds per 1,000 square feet broadcast or in the row at planting time.

Leather Meal or Tankage

Leather meal is ground leather scraps and leather waste, a by-product of tanneries.

Composition: Contains about 10 percent total nitrogen. Since most of this material comes from tanneries that use chromium, a heavy metal, in their processing, it usually contains unacceptably high chromium levels.

Benefits/uses: Nitrogen source.

Application: Not recommended.

Manure Teas

Manure tea is a solution of dissolved nutrients made by soaking manure in water.

Composition: Variable; will contain many of the soluble nutrients found in the manure.

Benefits/uses: The primary nutrient released by this process is nitrogen.

Application: Water plants well with plain water. Then dilute the manure tea concentrate to a pale tea color and water the soil around the plants. Avoid getting the solution on foliage.

Soybean Meal

Soybean meal is generally sold as animal feed; it is sometimes available as a by-product of soybean oil production.

Composition: Ground soybeans.

Benefits/uses: Nitrogen fertilizer. Good food for soil microorganisms.

Application: Broadcast 10 to 50 pounds per 1,000 square feet.

Phosphorus Plant Foods

Bonemeal

Bonemeal is finely ground bone. It is a by-product from animal slaughterhouses.

Composition: Contains 10 to 12 percent phosphate in available form, and up to 24 percent calcium. Some brands also contain up to 6 percent nitrogen.

Benefits/uses: For soils and plants that need available phosphorus. Particularly useful as a starter early in the season. Useful as a general fertilizer for flower bulbs.

Application: Apply 1 to 3 pounds per 100 feet of row in the row at planting. May also be broadcast and incorporated before planting.

Commercial products: Many brands of bagged bonemeal

Colloidal Phosphate

Colloidal phosphate is the clay that is washed out from between layers of rock phosphate as the phosphate is mined. It has a lower total phosphate content than rock phosphate, but more of the phosphate is in available form.

Composition: Contains about 16 percent total phosphate; about 2 percent in available form.

Benefits/uses: To build up the phosphate levels of your soil; very slowly available.

Application: Broadcast 50 pounds per 1,000 square feet over the entire garden every five years to maintain phosphate reserves. It is best to apply in the fall to maximize phosphate release by soil organisms.

Rock Phosphate

Rock phosphate is finely ground phosphate that is mined from many locations, including Florida, Idaho, and North Carolina.

Composition: Contains 32 percent total phosphate, 33 percent elemental calcium, and several trace minerals.

Benefits/uses: Source of phosphorus and calcium along with other trace minerals. Pro-

vides up to a ten-year reserve of phosphate.

Application: Broadcast 50 pounds per 1,000 square feet. The best application method is to add rock phosphate to the compost pile, as the composting process will help convert the phosphate to forms that are available for uptake by plant roots.

Potash Plant Foods

Granite Meal

Granite meal is ground from waste material from granite quarries.

Composition: Contains up to 5 percent total potash, high levels of silica, and many other trace minerals.

Benefits/uses: Use as a potash and mineral source where quick release of nutrients is not required. Especially valuable for pastures and hay fields.

Application: Broadcast 50 pounds per 1,000 square feet.

Greensand

Greensand is mined from deposits of minerals that were originally part of the ocean floor. They were raised up by geological processes to form part of the coast of the northeastern United States.

Composition: Contains about 7 percent total potash, along with iron and silica.

Benefits/uses: Source of potash and other minerals. Helps loosen clay soils and catalyzes the release of other minerals in the soil.

Application: Broadcast throughout your garden at a rate of 50 pounds per 1,000 square feet.

Potassium Sulfate

Potassium sulfate is a mined mineral. It is a highly soluble salt.

Composition: Analysis is 0-0-50.

Benefits/uses: Soluble source of potassium.

Application: Not recommended for garden use as it is highly soluble and can easily burn crops.

Sulfate of Potash-Magnesia or Langbeinite

Langbeinite is a mined mineral, but many sources of commercial sulfate of potash-magnesia products are actually industrial by-products.

Composition: Contains 22 percent soluble potash, 22 percent sulfur, and 11 percent magnesium.

Benefits/uses: Quick-release source of potassium. Use with caution because it is very soluble and can burn plants.

Application: Broadcast 5 to 10 pounds per 1,000 square feet or apply no more than 1 pound per 100 feet of row directly in the row at planting time.

Commercial products: K-Mag; Sul-Po-Mag

Wood Ashes

Ashes from wood fires, especially hardwood fires, are a source of minerals and will help raise soil pH.

Composition: Variable, depending on the type of wood burned. May contain many soluble nutrients. Ashes left to soak in the rain are safer to use in the garden, as some of the most soluble minerals will have leached out.

Benefits/uses: Source of potash and calcium.

Application: Broadcast no more than 20 pounds per 1,000 square feet every several years. Apply to a different location each year. Excesses of potash and calcium can result, requiring large applications of compost or the use of Epsom salts as a corrective.

Trace Mineral Sources

Borax

Borax is a mined mineral, hydrated sodium borate. It is also used as a cleaning agent, a water softener, and a preservative.

Composition: Approximately 10 percent boron.

Benefits/uses: Use only for where boron deficiencies have been determined by testing.

Application: Use no more than 3 to 5 ounces per 1,000 square feet. Apply cautiously; too much boron can be toxic to your plants.

Kelp Extracts

Kelp extracts are liquid or dry soluble concentrates extracted from *Ascophyllum nodosum* seaweeds. Their main use is as a plant growth stimulant.

Composition: Contains a large selection of trace minerals and potash. Also provides plant growth–promoting hormones.

Benefits/uses: Primarily a source of micronutrients and beneficial plant growth promoters. Also contains some potash. Excellent for foliar application to all growing plants. May also be used for watering or irrigation and as a rooting solution for transplants and cuttings.

Application: Mix 1 tablespoon of liquid or 1 teaspoon of soluble powder per gallon of spray solution to cover 500 square feet.

Commercial products: FoliaGro; Maxicrop; Sea Crop

Kelp Meal

Kelp meal products are generally made from dried and ground *Ascophyllum nodosum* seaweed harvested from the waters of the north Atlantic Ocean. They are used as long-term soil conditioners and plant food.

Composition: Contains a large selection of trace minerals and potash.

Benefits/uses: Potash and trace mineral source plus amino acids and vitamins. Helps the friability of the soil and stimulates the beneficial organisms in the soil.

Application: Broadcast 5 to 20 pounds per 1,000 square feet.

CHAPTER FIVE

Weed Control

By Miranda Smith

Weeds are a mixed blessing in any garden. Most gardeners, including organic gardeners, can rattle off the bad points of weeds without hesitation. Weeds compete with cultivated plants for precious supplies of light, nutrients, and water; they may harbor pests and diseases that readily spread to food crops and ornamentals; some are poisonous or allergenic; many seem nearly impossible to eradicate; and finally, almost everyone objects to spending time and energy getting rid of them.

Considering all that, chemical herbicides may seem like a panacea for gardeners. With a quick, easy spray, weed problems are gone. But there are hidden costs to using herbicides. They are toxic chemicals that may be health hazards to the people who apply them or to the people who are exposed to them when they walk, sit, or play on the lawn. They may persist in the environment and may have detrimental effects on beneficial soil organisms if they are applied to the soil or are washed in by rain.

Given the potential dangers of herbicides, the time and physical effort you devote to weeding could be one of the wisest investments you make in your garden. Organic gardeners combine a few basic strategies to create an effective weed control program without using synthetic herbicides.

❧ *Precise identification.* Planning a strategy to control weeds is most effective if you know exactly what type of weed you're fighting. Control methods differ for annual, biennial, or perennial weeds.

❧ *Cultural controls.* You can adjust your gardening practices to help avoid many weed problems. Using mulches to smother out weeds is one of the easiest and most effective techniques for weed control. It also provides the benefits of increasing soil fertility and reducing water loss from the soil. Using cover crops and green manures are other cultural practices that help with weed control.

🐛 *Physical controls.* Old-fashioned hoeing and hand pulling are two skills every organic gardener should refine so they become a pleasant pastime rather than a pain in the back. Power tools can also be used for weed control.

🐛 *Chemical controls.* Vinegar, salt, and one relatively new soap-based herbicide are the only organically acceptable chemical weed control methods. They are a last resort of limited use in your yard and garden.

Fortunately, weeds can be as helpful as they are troublesome. Sorrel may be a weed, but it's also a tasty and nutritious addition to a salad. Some weeds are good medicine, many are lovely ornamentals when properly confined, most contribute to soil and crop health. You can use weeds to help learn about the soil conditions in your garden and to attract insects that will prey on pests that are damaging your food crops.

As you learn to use chemical-free techniques for weed control, the benefits of having *some* weeds in your gardens may become more apparent. Eventually, depending upon the techniques and habits you develop, you could even come to regard them as allies that help promote good soil and plant health.

IDENTIFYING WEEDS

Before you rip out those weeds around your pepper or peony plants, take a good look at them. Do you know what species they are? Some garden weeds are justly famous plants: dandelions, quackgrass, ragweed. But you may identify many weeds simply because you know *you* didn't plant them. If so, take time to learn what species and type of weeds they are, so you can plan an efficient strategy for controlling them.

Annual Weeds

More than 80 percent of the weeds you'll find in your garden are annuals—plants that live and die in a single season and reproduce only by seed. These characteristics make them seem like vulnerable species. However, their survival is protected two ways. Most annual plants produce amazing numbers of seeds—hundreds of thousands in some cases—guaranteeing that at least a score or two will end up in favorable spots for germination and growth. Because of this, hand pulling plants before they set seed is usually the first, best method for keeping annual weed problems from worsening.

The second survival safeguard for annuals is seed dormancy, the ability of seeds to remain undeveloped but viable for as long as several years. This quality protects seeds from germinating in poor soil or unfavorable climatic conditions. (Seeds of perennial and biennial plants also exhibit dormancy; this quality is not the province of annuals alone.)

A plant will often produce both nondormant seeds and seeds that carry an inborn, or innate, dormancy. The innately dormant seeds will not germinate, even in favorable conditions, until the predetermined dormancy period ends. As examples of innate dormancy, think of columbine, pansy, and primrose. These flower seeds all need to be stratified—exposed to cold and/or alternating warm and cool periods—before they will grow.

Dormancy can also occur when conditions signal a poor growing environment. Soil oxygen and carbon dioxide levels, light availability, day length, temperature, and moisture are all crucial to seed germination. For example, many seeds, including coleus, impatiens, and lettuce, won't germinate unless they are exposed to light. This type of response is known as environmental dormancy.

Perennial Weeds

Perennials are plants that live at least three years. Most live much longer. Almost all perennials produce seeds but, unlike annuals, they also reproduce vegetatively, usually from nodes on underground stems and/or roots. Most gardeners would rank perennials, particularly woody ones, as the most annoying weeds. Some species, like poison ivy, send up vigorous new shoots as far as 20 feet from the parent plant.

Other perennials, even the small, herbaceous sort, can be tiresomely tenacious. If you hack off their tops, even removing what appears to be the growing crown, they're likely to re-gather their forces and sprout more plants. You've probably had that experience with dandelions—if you don't get the whole root, what was merely one plant turns into three or four! Generally, controlling stubborn perennial weeds without chemicals involves digging out plants, including rootstocks, sometimes for more than one season, and/or applying a heavy suppressive mulch.

Woody perennials are those with woody stems. Multiflora rose, poison ivy, and kudzu fall into this category. They have high reproductive capacities, and established plants are difficult to eradicate by digging. You'll learn to give top priority to eliminating them from your gardens with a relatively work-free mulching technique.

Biennial, Winter Annual, and Grass Weeds

Biennials live for two seasons. They grow only roots, stems, and leaves the first year and usually lie low to the ground in a rosette pattern. The second year, they produce upright stems that bear flowers and seeds. Common mullein and Queen-Anne's-lace are two common biennial weeds. For efficient control, it's best to treat biennials as perennials during the first year and annuals during the second.

Winter annuals behave similarly to biennials. They usually germinate between midsummer and early fall, forming only a base rosette of leaves. Early the following spring, they send up flower stalks and make seeds. Because they have such a jump on the season, they're usually the first plants to go to seed each year. Most winter annuals can change their behavior to suit local conditions. Some, such as winter cress, may act like annuals in the South but winter annuals in the North. Generally, control tactics for annuals also are successful for winter annuals.

Both annual and perennial grasses plague many gardeners. Grass seed may be spread mixed in hay mulches or can blow over from a lawn that was allowed to go to seed. Grasses are very difficult to pull. They either have rhizomes—reproductive underground stems—that creep through the soil or wide, fibrous root systems that cling tightly to it. You'll have to modify your usual weed control techniques somewhat when dealing with grasses.

Why Correct ID Matters

From the preceding discussion, you can understand why it's important to know whether the weeds in your yard are annual, biennial, or perennial. But can you tell just by observation to what category a particular weed belongs? The answer is no. While it may be obvious that some weeds are persistent perennials because of their vast, spreading root systems, others are not so obvious. For example, the weed commonly called sowthistle is actually *two* common weeds—one annual species, one perennial. They have somewhat different leaf shapes, and the annual has light yellow flowers, while the perennial has deep yellow flowers. However, if you make the mistake of treating perennial sowthistle as an annual, you may actually make your weed problem worse rather than better.

The best way to identify weeds is to get a good weed identification guide (see "The Chemical-Free Gardener's Library," on page 431, for suggested titles). The illustrations and descriptions in these books should have enough detail to help you identify your weeds. If you're stumped, take a specimen—uproot a whole weed,

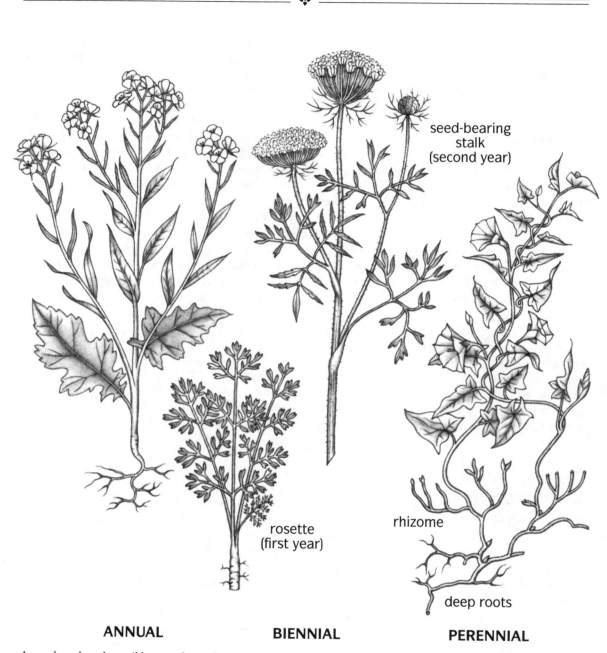

seed-bearing
stalk
(second year)

rosette
(first year)

rhizome

deep roots

ANNUAL **BIENNIAL** **PERENNIAL**

Annual weeds such as wild mustard grow for one season, set seed, and die. Biennial weeds such as Queen-Anne's-lace grow vegetatively for one season. The roots, and in some cases the foliage, survive the winter in a dormant state. During the second growing season, biennials flower, set seed, and die. Perennials persist for many seasons. Their roots, and sometimes their dormant stems, survive winter. They can spread by seed and by sprouts from spreading underground stems or roots.

don't just take in one or two leaves—to your local Cooperative Extension office for help.

Try to become familiar with the appearance of the common weeds in your garden as seedlings or young sprouts—the earlier you attack weeds, the better. For specific weed problems, once you've identified the weed in question, see "Weed Control Methods," on page 118, for suggested control strategies.

CULTURAL CONTROLS

Your best strategy in dealing with weeds, as with insects and disease, is prevention. However, unlike techniques for preventing insect and disease problems, keeping your crop plants healthy is not the key to preventing weeds. Watering and feeding crops inevitably improves conditions for weeds as well. The trick is to keep weeds from taking advantage of the bounty you provide for your food and ornamental plants.

You can prevent weed problems without using chemicals by keeping existing weeds from setting seed, mulching around your plants to smother out any weed seeds that germinate, or growing cover crops to form a dense living soil cover that will outcompete any weeds that try to sprout through.

Stopping Seed Formation

Soil contains millions of seeds. In England, researchers once moved the top few inches of a hectare (about 2½ acres) of land into a laboratory where they patiently counted all the seeds they could find. They reported finding 1.33 million seeds of prostrate knotweed, 1.73 million shepherd's purse seeds, and 3.21 million chickweed seeds.

Ridding your soil of weed seeds is as inconceivable as sweeping a beach clear of sand. However, if you don't like to spend time weeding, you'd be well advised to prevent resident weeds from adding to the seed banks in your soils.

Scout for Blooming Weeds

Vigilantly patrol the garden every few days, uprooting blooming weeds you may have missed while hoeing or tilling. Stray weeds are most apparent when they begin to bloom. You'll notice that some have been effectively camouflaged by neighboring crops or ornamentals. It could be coincidence, but grasses in the middle of a daylily patch often grow broader blades than they do in the lawn, and pigweed in potatoes may branch more laterally than it does in the corn rows.

Carry a bucket as you walk. You'll want to remove these plants from the garden in case some seeds have already formed or the plant is capable of putting its last bursts of dying energy into finishing seed formation. Stockpile flowering weeds in plastic bags or buckets until you're ready to build a hot compost pile. Weed seeds easily survive in compost piles unless temperatures reach 160°F or higher. You'll see evidence of their ability to survive in the green growing carpet that forms on the compost pile in early spring. If you don't build a hot compost pile, you can carefully cut off the seed stalks, throw them in the garbage, and add the remainder of the weed plants to your compost. For more details about composting, see "Compost: Nature's Black Magic" on page 68.

Some Weeds Are Worth Saving

You can combine your weed-hunting duty with monitoring the garden for signs of insect and disease problems. (See "The Best Garden Monitor," on page 206, for suggestions on how to effectively monitor your garden.) Don't confine yourself to hunting weeds in your cultivated areas. You should also look at nearby fencerows and neighboring fields from the weeder's perspective. A wild patch of dandelions, milkweed, assorted grasses, daisies, and Queen-Anne's-lace certainly makes a lovely view. However, it can also make a lot of seeds that could be carried or blown into your vegetable patches and flower gardens.

Before waging a no-holds-barred campaign against everything growing along fences or in neighboring fields, remember the beneficial functions of weeds. Weedy areas provide natural beauty, as well as food and habitats for birds, small animals, and insects that help control your garden pests. In the field just described, for example, the most serious potential weed is probably the dandelion. Milkweed seeds are distributed by the wind, but the plants are so easy to spot and pull. Also, young milkweed shoots are edible, and butterflies are attracted to its pleasantly fraganced blossom. Queen-Anne's-lace, like most tiny flowers, is a wonderful food for the small, beneficial wasps that prey on aphids and other six-legged garden adversaries. Unless you have had previous problems with infestations of carrot rust fly maggots, you probably don't want to eliminate this plant. After considering the weedy field in this way, you're likely to decide to save yourself trouble by mowing the area *only* during the weeks when dandelions are in flower.

Mulching to Smother Weeds

Mulches prevent many seeds from germinating because they create an unfavorable environment. Light levels under layers of mulch such as rotted hay or straw are so low that they can trigger seed dormancy. Those seeds that do germinate usually can't push their stems through the mulch so that leaves can unfold in sunlight. Without adequate light, the plants don't produce enough chlorophyll to enable further growth. Most of these plants sicken and die before you even notice them. The few that manage to stick their leaves into the light will be shallowly rooted and very easy to pull.

When to Apply Mulch

Your first mulching operation in early spring will be to cover the walkways in your vegetable garden. Wait until after you have applied compost or soil amendments and tilled or dug the garden, but no longer. Mulch all the pathways, even those near beds or rows you won't be planting until late spring. To be extra efficient, pile enough extra mulching material in the pathways so you'll have a ready supply at hand when your seedlings are large enough to be mulched.

In general, don't mulch seedlings until they are several inches tall. Mulches tend to hold moisture. If spring is rainy and cloudy or you live in an area where plants customarily fall prey to damping-off, root rot, or other cool-weather fungus diseases, the last thing you want to do is increase relative humidity levels around the young seedlings. An exception to this rule would be gardens in arid climates, where early mulching could be part of your overall water conservation method.

Fighting Weeds with Air

Believe it or not, ordinary air can be used to fight some weed problems. Certain weeds, including knotweed and plantain, thrive in compacted soil. Loosening the soil may make the growing environment less favorable for them.

If you have problems with weeds in an area with dense or compacted soil, first pull or dig out the existing weeds. Then aerate the soil by inserting the tines of a spading fork deeply and working the tool back and forth. Work in several inches of compost or other organic matter to help loosen the soil.

This practice should greatly reduce, or even eliminate, your problems with plantain and other weeds that grow well in compacted soils. Of course, be on the lookout for new weed species that will appreciate the improved soil conditions you've provided!

Also keep in mind that your weed control mulch will have some effect on soil temperatures. Light-colored mulch such as straw will reflect light and tend to keep soil temperatures cooler, while black plastic mulch will help soil warm sooner. You may want to use a light-colored mulch around lettuce and other crops that benefit from cool soil. If you're mulching tomatoes or peppers, use a dark mulch or hold off mulching until soil temperatures are high enough for good growth.

Keep topping up organic mulches as they wear thin during the growing season. By mid-July, you may need to renew many mulched areas to keep them effective against weeds. You can lay a side-dressing of organic fertilizer near those crops that need a boost as you renew the mulch.

If you mulch around trees and shrubs, apply the mulch early in spring. Remember that you may want to rake back the mulches in fall to avoid mouse damage to your plants.

Using Organic Mulches

Choosing, and finding, good mulching materials can be a challenge. Theoretically, anything can work as a mulch if it restricts light levels at the soil surface and prevents plants from growing through it to the open air.

Organic mulches, such as rotted hay, peanut shells, rice hulls, or lawn clippings, feed soil life and thus add nutrients and humus to the garden. Most of these materials are available at low or no cost. Using organic mulch is fundamental to organic soil improvement as well, so you'll likely be using mulches on many of your garden beds for that purpose. Organic mulches are described in detail in "Organic Soil Amendments and Mulches" on page 86.

Using Synthetic Mulches

Thin black or clear plastic films have become a favorite mulch, especially for nightshade family and squash family plants. Plastic captures and traps heat, raising the soil temperature enough to promote faster growth and give some protection against the plant stress that cool periods bring. Landscape fabrics are a good mulch for permanent plantings. These materials let air and moisture pass through and will keep down all but the most stubborn perennial weeds.

Plastic Mulch

Black plastic mulch also provides good weed control. Most weed seeds that germinate under the plastic can't get enough light to continue growing. (Weeds grow vigorously under clear plastic; gardeners who use clear plastic rely on herbicides to control weeds.) Quackgrass is one weed that can defeat plastic mulch. Because new shoots can rely on food supplies from a large plant network, some sprouts will find the strength to poke a hole through the plastic. If this happens in your garden, pull the shoots. Cover any resulting gaps in the plastic with a rock or some other mulch to prevent more sprouts from emerging.

Plastic mulch is usually sold in 2- or 3-foot-wide rolls. It's easiest to lay out if you have some help. Feed a broom handle or metal pipe through the center of the roll. Have two assistants stand at the end of your garden bed, holding the ends of the handle or pipe. Then you can easily pull off the plastic to the end of the bed, anchor the sides, and cut it to fit. There is also an attachment that will suspend the roll of plastic from a garden cart so you can do the job all alone.

Garden centers and mail-order catalogs also sell black plastic in precut sections, 3-by-25, -50, or -100 feet. These may be worth the expense for convenience or if you only have a small garden.

Once you have the plastic in place, you'll need to bury both edges of the mulch under a few inches of garden soil. This technique assures that the plastic will be stretched tightly over the bed and stay in place. Weeds often grow in the soil covering the edges. Since their roots travel laterally, they're easy to pull by hand. But, if you're like me, you'll probably find this job an extra chore. To avoid it, I also pull organic mulch from the walkways over the soil holding the plastic in place.

To plant transplants through the mulch, cut a single slit or two crossing slits in the plastic where you'll place each plant. Make the slits big enough so that you can get at the soil underneath and dig good holes for the young plants.

You can also plant large seeds, such as zucchini or other squashes, right under circular holes cut in tightly stretched and secured plastic. If you use this technique, plant extra seeds under each hole. Some of the seeds will move slightly and may come up too far away from the open air to make good growth. If they don't, and you are suddenly confronted with five squash plants where only two should grow, simply pull the weakest plants while they are still at the seed-leaf stage.

Puddling is almost certain with nonperforated plastic films. Every time it rains, water collects in spots where the underlying soil is slightly depressed. Don't wait for the water to evaporate; standing water invites fungal problems. Instead, poke a couple of small holes into the bottom of each puddle to let the water drain.

Whether you plant transplants or large seeds, your only weeding chore during the season for a plastic-mulched bed will be to hand pull any weeds that manage to poke through the holes where your crops are growing.

However, at the end of the season, you will face the task of removing all the plastic from your garden. This is because any plastic left in the garden will begin to shred during the winter, leaving your garden soil full of small pieces of plastic. After final harvesting, if your plastic is weighted with soil, scrape the soil off before you try to lift and roll it for winter storage. Otherwise, the plastic may tear, again leaving shreds in your garden.

You can combine black plastic mulch and floating row covers to create a virtually pest-proof environment for your crops. With black plastic preventing growth of most weeds, there is no need to pull back your row covers once they're in place. Use bricks or rocks to anchor both the plastic and row covers.

Landscape Fabrics

Landscape fabrics, also called geotextiles, are porous, synthetic materials frequently used by landscapers for controlling weeds in permanent ornamental plantings. Some garden centers and catalogs also sell small, precut pieces of landscape fabric, such as Typar, for home gardens. These are another convenient, but more expensive, option for chemical-free weed control.

Unlike black plastic, the fabrics allow water and moisture to pass through so that the soil's natural balance is less affected than it is by black plastic. Soluble fertilizers will pass through the fabrics, but solid fertilizer materials will not.

You can walk on landscape fabrics: They should not tear under your weight. In permanent plantings, you can cover the landscape fabrics with shredded bark or other decorative mulches and have weed control for several years. If you mulch on top of landscape fabric, you may have to pull occasional weeds that root in the mulch layer, and will periodically need to renew the mulch layer to maintain an attractive appearance.

Follow the planting instructions for black plastic when using landscape fabrics. You can keep landscape fabrics in place by covering the edges with soil, or by pinning them down with U-shaped pieces of wire.

There is a potential drawback to using landscape fabrics in a permanent planting, especially if you're a gardener who is prone to changing your mind. Recent studies show that in some cases, roots of trees and shrubs growing in soil covered by landscape fabric may grow up to the surface and into the fabric. In such a case, if a gardener decided to lift a plant, he could damage its roots and/or rip apart the landscape fabric in the process.

Mulching Perennial Weeds

Mulching is the easiest way to rid yourself of stubborn perennial weeds that seem impervious to all digging operations. A year, or possibly two, of heavy mulching kills spreading comfrey, hedge or field bindweed, Jerusalem artichoke, and even poison ivy. But a 6-inch layer of hay isn't likely to be adequate for these jobs.

In areas where perennial weeds are running rampant, mulch as early in spring as possible. Because your ultimate goal is not simply to rid yourself of the weed but also to bring the area into good productive capability, treat the soil well. Lime the area if it needs it. Apply some greensand or rock phosphate if trace elements or available phosphorus or potassium levels are low, and spread compost or manure. Because you won't be planting anything in the area for at least a year, even fresh manure can be used in a pinch. Then, lay down a thick layer of an organic mulch—hay, wood chips, shredded leaves, or whatever you have. Next, cover that mulch with a material that will prevent light from penetrating and shoots from emerging.

Weed Control Checklist

❧ Mulch pathways early to stop weed problems before they start.

❧ Mulch exposed soil to keep weeds from flourishing there.

❧ Plant a living mulch crop in the vegetable garden for weed control and soil improvement.

❧ Thoroughly dig out roots and tops of stubborn perennial weeds.

❧ Take weed patrol walks frequently to catch flowering weeds before they set seed.

❧ Learn how to use hoes and your hands efficiently for weed control.

❧ Plan a smothering attack on areas plagued by woody perennial weeds.

❧ Use organic herbicidal methods only in situations where they are the most effective, economical solution.

Black plastic does nicely, as does an old swimming pool liner or old carpeting. A 3- to 6-inch-thick layer of weighted newspapers can also do the trick. The best of all possible materials is probably sheet metal, such as old tin roofing, but this is not easily available to most home gardeners. If you're lucky enough to have access to some, use it.

Leave the mulch and heavy covering in place for the entire growing season. However, if your top covering is plastic, remove it as soon as fall sets in. You don't want to add weathered plastic to your soil surface. If you use a covering that won't fall apart over winter, leave it in place until spring.

After the ground thaws the following spring, remove the cover and pull back the remaining mulch. Probe under the soil surface to see if your adversaries' roots magically survived their year of darkness. In most cases, you'll find they have succumbed. You will be free to plant or transplant into the area without disturbing the underlying soil layers and thus, exposing new weed seeds to air and light. But if the roots aren't dead yet, re-cover the area as before. Two years under this kind of cover kills any rootstock, even kudzu or poison ivy.

Cover Crops

Cover crops are grass, legume, or grain crops grown to protect and enrich the soil. Cover crops suppress weed populations because they grow so quickly that newly germinating weed seeds can't compete. This characteristic is particularly true of early spring plantings of crops such as red and sweet clovers that germinate at slightly lower temperatures than the predominant weeds. Winter-hardy crops like Austrian pea or winter rye, which are sown in fall and left in place throughout the winter, also compete well. In spring, their well-established root systems enable them to quickly outgrow and shade out the seedling weeds.

Green manure crops are cover crops grown especially to be incorporated into the soil to improve fertility and add organic matter. You'll likely plant cover or green manure crops in your vegetable garden because of their beneficial effects on soil structure and fertility. For a complete rundown on how to select and plant green manure crops, see "Green Manuring" on page 72.

Planting Living Mulch

Some gardeners plant alsike or white clover between rows of young squash or corn to add nitrogen to the area and to avoid midseason weeding. The clover is called a living mulch because it is a growing crop, but serves all the functions of a standard mulch. Living mulches can be used between many row vegetable crops.

This system only works well if the mulch crop is seeded into a weed-free seedbed. After planting the main vegetable crop, keep areas between rows as well as between plants clear of weeds for about a month. Till or dig just before planting the mulch crop and pick out any exposed weed roots to prevent rerooting. Work carefully to avoid disturbing the root systems of your vegetable plants. Spread the mulch crop seed between the rows. It will grow throughout the summer. In the fall, it will die down at frost or can be tilled or dug in when you prepare the soil for winter cover.

Late-season plantings of broccoli and cauliflower can benefit from underseeding of a winter-hardy cover crop such as hairy vetch. To underseed means to plant one crop directly under a crop that is already growing.

To underseed a cover crop, let the vegetable crop get established for about one month, keeping the area weed-free. Then, broadcast the cover crop seed over the entire area, not just between the rows, when plants are 6 to 8 inches tall. By the time your vegetables are ready to harvest, you will be able to walk on the vetch without damaging it. Till in or dig in the vetch several weeks before planting the following spring. Don't let it flower or it could become a weed problem itself.

Cover Cropping Quackgrass

Quackgrass is a gardener's nemesis. It's one weed that seems nearly impossible to eradicate. However, there is a long-term control method that is truly effective, if you're willing to take the time and effort required.

Cover cropping with two buckwheat crops and one winter rye planting will kill quackgrass. This means sacrificing production from the area you attack for a full season, but you will solve your weed problem. You'll also contribute needed nutrients to the soil system and greatly improve your soil structure and tilth.

The process works because buckwheat forms such a dense leaf canopy that it prevents the quackgrass from manufacturing good nutrient supplies. Even with its wide network of storage roots and rhizomes, the grass becomes increasingly weak throughout the summer and fall. To top things off, the following spring, the decomposing winter rye releases chemicals that are toxic to quackgrass roots.

Start by tilling the quackgrass-plagued area in early spring, as soon as the soil is dry enough so that tilling won't make a hardpan or create clods. Walk the area after you've tilled, and pull and remove exposed roots and rhizomes.

Wait until the weather is settled and warm, after danger of frost is past, before planting the first buckwheat. You will probably need to till the area right before planting, again removing roots and rhizomes.

Seed the buckwheat heavily, about 3 pounds per 1,000 square feet. To be successful, the buckwheat must form such a dense leaf canopy that the quackgrass will be unable to get enough sunlight to grow well. Check the area at about the time the first true leaves are unfurling, and reseed any bare spots.

Till the buckwheat down when it begins to flower, and prepare the area for seeding again. Reseed with buckwheat at the same heavy rate as you did in spring.

In late summer or early fall, at least several weeks before first frost, till in the second buckwheat crop and let the area rest for about one week. Then seed winter rye at a rate of 3 pounds per 1,000 square feet. It will germinate and grow a few inches before dying down and going dormant for the winter months. The following spring, the rye will send up a luxuriant crop of fresh, green shoots. Till or dig in the rye at least two weeks before planting the garden. (Don't let the rye grow more than 16 inches tall or it will be almost impossible to till down.) The result should be rich, spongy soil—free of quackgrass rhizomes.

Oats are also used as an undersown or living mulch crop. Planted anytime from the middle to the end of summer, the crop will suppress weeds, but won't set seed itself. The oats will die down during winter, leaving a thick layer of mulch that will prevent soil erosion and suppress late-fall and early-spring weeds. Till or dig the oats shallowly into the soil two weeks before planting the following spring. Or, to really conserve your time and effort, hand pull the mulch back in spots and transplant established seedlings into it. It will retard weed growth until it decomposes, by which time your plants' leaf canopy will be shading the area.

PHYSICAL CONTROLS

Cultivating, hoeing, and hand pulling are the major physical control methods for weeds. If you're accustomed to using herbicides, all that sounds like a lot of work. And for the first few years, it certainly can be. However, you may find that you like hoeing and weeding more than you expected: Thinking about doing it may be worse than the actual doing. And in time, good techniques and some background knowledge can cut weeding time so much that you'll hardly notice the time or effort it takes.

Tilling

Tilling is usually the first order of business in spring. Many gardeners till the whole vegetable garden as soon as they can—up and down and back and forth. And all at the maximum depth the tines can reach. They may also use the tiller as a weed control device throughout the growing season. Pathways and areas between the rows are meat for their tines. However, there are drawbacks to frequent tilling. Even though you might appreciate the speed and ease with which your tiller chews up weeds, you could be better off doing some mulching, wheel hoeing, or hand hoeing rather than using the tiller for all your weed control work. See "Don't Dig In!" on page 73, for reasons why you should think twice before tilling.

Tilling also brings buried weed seeds closer to the soil surface, making it possible for them to germinate. You can't prevent this side effect, but it's wise to be aware of it. If tilling for weed control is the most practical method for your circumstances, remember to set the tines so that they only reach an inch or two into the soil. Tines set at this depth still kill or uproot annuals and first-year biennials—the majority of the weeds in your gardens.

Tilling Perennial Weeds

Perennials, with their long roots and underground reproductive systems, will usually survive tilling in the early part of the year. If they are becoming a serious problem in your garden, and you want to keep tilling instead of applying a smothering mulch, you have two options. You can combine tilling and digging, or you can let nature and the tiller work together to kill the

---

Never-Till Weeds

There are a few weeds—comfrey, dandelions, Jerusalem artichokes, and quackgrass—that you should not till under any circumstances. (The exception is tilling quackgrass when using cover crops to smother it out. See "Cover Cropping Quackgrass" on page 115.) All of these weeds can reproduce from tiny bits of the original rootstock. For every weed you till, you'll have two, three, four, or even more weeds to replace it.

Instead, dig these notorious garden thugs out by hand, sink barriers around them, or mulch heavily to smother them. Never try to till them unless you are willing to leave the ground fallow and till weekly for a full growing season or longer.

---

plant. Or you can do both.

If you dig, be prepared to dig again. A perennial weed like bindweed eradicated on the south side of a bed may reemerge on the north side within a couple of weeks. Dig it again and continue watching for new sprouts. Meanwhile, keep tilling at a shallow depth.

Perennials are weakest just after they bloom. The plants have put all their stored energy into the effort of reproduction. If a perennial weed in your garden blooms, give a cheer. It's the perfect opportunity to severely weaken that weed. Cut down or till all of the aboveground portions of the plant. Continue doing this at one- to two-week intervals for the rest of the season. If the plant manages to come up the next year, simple shallow tilling should finish it off.

Hoeing

Hoeing weeds actually can be a very pleasant job. The only requirements to make it so are good weather, refined skills, and the right tool.

Hoes are wonderful tools. They come in all shapes and sizes: some are heavy and broad, some are swan-necked and light, and some are as maneuverable and sharp as a razor blade. You will probably want to own several different types of hoes. See "Choose Your Weapon," below, for suggestions on the best hoes to use for weeding.

Choose Your Weapon

Your local garden center may stock a dozen different hoes. How do you know which to choose? Hoes have different shapes and designs related to the task for which they're created. Look for these hoes when you're going out to battle weeds.

Swan-neck hoe. Its gracefully curved neck positions the cutting blade to skim just below the surface. Perfect for light work around garden crops.

Oscillating hoe. This hoe is also called a hula or scuffle hoe. It has a hinged, double-edged blade that slides back and forth, barely disturbing the soil surface. This minimizes the number of new weed seeds brought to the surface as you hoe.

Collinear hoe. An unusual hoe designed by organic market gardener Eliot Coleman, with a narrow blade and angled handle. Use it for cutting off small weeds with minimal soil disturbance.

Eye hoe. This heavy-bladed hoe is also called a grub hoe. It is for hard chopping at tough, overgrown weeds.

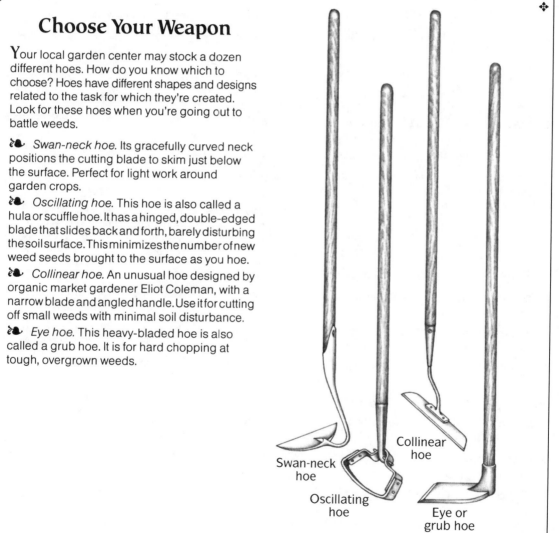

Swan-neck hoe

Oscillating hoe

Collinear hoe

Eye or grub hoe

Weed Control Methods

Once you've identified the weeds that are plaguing your garden, use this table to quickly learn what control methods will be most effective. Remember, it's always easier to tackle weed problems early in the season, before they outcompete your crops and before they set seed.

Common Name	Botanical Name	Family	Control Methods
ANNUAL WEEDS			
Bedstraw, catchweed	*Galium aparine*	Rubiaceae	Hoe or pull early in season before bloom. Scout hedgerows and field edges for this weed.
Beggarticks, devils	*Bidens frondosa*	Compositae	Hoe or pull before flowering. Mow in waste or wild areas.
Carpetweed	*Mollugo verticillata*	Aizoaceae	Hoe or pull as soon as you spot this weed. Do not let flowering plants remain on the soil surface.
Chickweed	*Stellaria media*	Caryophyllaceae	Hoe or pull. Also follow and pull trailing roots.
Cocklebur, heartleaf	*Xanthium strumarium*	Compositae	Hoe or pull. Mow in fields.
Corn cockle	*Agrostemma githago*	Caryophyllaceae	Hoe or pull. Use deep mulches to kill the seeds.
Dodder	*Cuscuta* spp.	Convolvulaceae	Pull both dodder and host plant. Remove from garden and compost nonflowering weeds at 160°F. Dispose of weeds with flowers.
Jimsonweed	*Datura stramonium*	Solanaceae	Pull.
Knotweed, prostrate	*Polygonum aviculare*	Polygonaceae	Hoe or pull below crown. Aerate soil and increase humus content.
Lamb's-quarters	*Chenopodium album*	Chenopodiaceae	Hoe when small. Mulch all trouble spots. Pull fall-germinating plants.
Lettuce, prickly	*Lactuca serriola*	Compositae	Hoe, cutting below crown. Do not allow to flower.
Mallow, common	*Malva neglecta*	Malvaceae	Hoe or pull.
Mayweed	*Anthemis cotula*	Compositae	Hoe or pull in early spring. Mow in waste or wild areas.
Morning-glory, tall	*Ipomoea purpurea*	Convolvulaceae	Hoe every seedling below crown. Mulch heavily.
Mustard, wild	*Brassica kaber*	Cruciferae	Hoe or pull. Mulch heavily. Watch for summer seedlings.
Nightshade, black	*Solanum nigrum*	Solanaceae	Pull as soon as you notice it.

Common Name	Botanical Name	Family	Control Methods
Pigweed, prostrate	*Amaranthus graecizans*	Amaranthaceae	Hoe or pull when young. Remove all pulled weeds from garden, because this weed reroots easily. Remove fall germinators.
Pigweed, redroot	*Amaranthus retroflexus*	Amaranthaceae	Hoe or pull when young. Remove all pulled weeds from garden, because this weed reroots easily. Remove fall germinators.
Purslane, common	*Portulaca oleracea*	Portulacaceae	Hoe or pull and enjoy in a salad.
Ragweed, common	*Ambrosia artemisiifolia*	Compositae	Hoe or pull before flowering. Mow in waste or wild areas.
Ragweed, giant	*Ambrosia trifida*	Compositae	Hoe or pull. Mow in waste or wild areas before the weeds flower.
Shepherd's purse	*Capsella bursa-pastoris*	Cruciferae	Hoe or pull. Be sure this weed does not set seed. Pull fall plants.
Sida, prickly	*Sida spinosa*	Malvaceae	Hoe or pull when small. Cut large plants below crown.
Smartweed, marshpepper	*Polygonum hydropiper*	Polygonaceae	Hoe or pull. Add humus to improve drainage.
Smartweed, Pennsylvania	*Polygonum pensylvanicum*	Polygonaceae	Hoe or pull. Add humus to improve drainage.
Sowthistle, annual	*Sonchus oleraceus*	Compositae	Hoe or pull. Use mulch to suppress new seedlings.
Spanishneedles	*Bidens bipinnata*	Compositae	Hoe or pull. Mow in waste or wild areas.
Spurge, spotted	*Euphorbia maculata*	Euphorbiaceae	Hoe or pull. Mulch. Watch for summer seedlings.
Velvetleaf	*Abutilon theophrasti*	Malvaceae	Hoe or pull before flowering. Do not let this weed set seed.
BIENNIAL WEEDS			
Burdock, common	*Arctium minus*	Compositae	Hoe below crown in first year. Dig out or cut flower stalk in second. Mulch problem spots deeply.
Cockle, white	*Lychnis alba*	Caryophyllaceae	Dig out rootstock. Mulch heavily in problem spots.
Henbit	*Lamium amplexicaule*	Labiatae	Dig, removing roots. Mulch heavily in problem spots.
Mullein, common	*Verbascum thapsus*	Scrophulariaceae	Hoe, cutting below crown.

(continued)

Weed Control Methods—*Continued*

Common Name	Botanical Name	Family	Control Methods
BIENNIAL WEEDS—*continued*			
Mullein, moth	*Verbascum blattaria*	Scrophulariaceae	Cut crown from root.
Poison hemlock	*Conium maculatum*	Umbelliferae	Dig taproot and remove from garden. Eliminate this lethal plant from garden.
Queen-Anne's-lace	*Daucus carota*	Umbelliferae	Dig taproot. Cut flower stalk.
Ragwort, tansy	*Senecio jacobaea*	Compositae	Dig root. Don't let this weed set seed. Aerate soil and increase humus content.
Teasel	*Dipsacus fullonum*	Dipsacaceae	Hoe below crown.
PERENNIAL WEEDS			
Bindweed, field	*Convolvulus arvensis*	Convolvulaceae	Dig and remove rootstock. Mulch area heavily.
Bindweed, hedge	*Calystegia sepium*	Convolvulaceae	Dig roots and all new sprouts. Mulch area heavily.
Chicory	*Cichorium intybus*	Compositae	Hoe below crown early in season.
Coltsfoot	*Tussilago farfara*	Compositae	Dig rootstock. Mulch heavily in problem spots.
Dandelion	*Taraxacum officinale*	Compositae	Dig taproot. Don't let this weed flower.
Dock, curly	*Rumex crispus*	Polygonaceae	Dig taproot when plant is young. Mulch heavily in problem spots.
Garlic, wild	*Allium vineale*	Liliaceae	Dig, removing bulbs. Mulch area.
Goldenrods	*Solidago* spp.	Compositae	Dig rootstock and each new sprout. Mulch area heavily.
Ground ivy	*Glechoma hederacea*	Labiatae	Pull all stems and roots when you spot this weed. Remove pulled weeds from garden since they reroot easily.
Heal-all	*Prunella vulgaris*	Labiatae	Dig rootstock and pull all runners. Remove all pulled weeds from garden, because this weed reroots easily.
Horsenettle	*Solanum carolinense*	Solanaceae	Dig rootstock and rhizomes. Mulch area heavily.
Ironweed, tall	*Vernonia altissima*	Compositae	Dig, removing rhizomes. Mulch area heavily.
Jerusalem artichoke	*Helianthus tuberosus*	Compositae	Dig roots and tubers. Mulch heavily.
Joepyeweed	*Eupatorium maculatum*	Compositae	Dig and remove roots from garden to prevent resprouting.
Loosestrife, purple	*Lythrum salicaria*	Lythraceae	Dig root system. Mulch area heavily.
Milkweed, common	*Asclepias syriaca*	Asclepiadaceae	Dig roots.

Common Name	Botanical Name	Family	Control Methods
Oxeye daisy	*Chrysanthemum leucanthemum*	Compositae	Dig rootstock. Mulch area heavily.
Plantain, broadleaf	*Plantago major*	Plantaginaceae	Dig roots. Aerate soil and increase humus content.
Pokeweed, common	*Phytolacca americana*	Phytolaccaceae	Hoe, cutting below crown. Repeat as needed.
Rocket, yellow	*Barbarea vulgaris*	Cruciferae	Hoe or pull and use in a salad.
St. Johnswort	*Hypericum perforatum*	Hypericaceae	Dig roots. Mulch heavily.
Sorrel, red	*Rumex acetosella*	Polygonaceae	Pull, lifting all rhizomes, and remove from garden.
Stinging nettle	*Urtica dioica*	Urticaceae	Dig, lifting rootstock. Protect hands when digging this weed.
Vervain, hoary	*Verbena stricta*	Verbenaceae	Dig roots. Aerate soil and increase humus content.
Woodsorrel, southern yellow	*Oxalis dillenii*	Oxalidaceae	Hoe or pull, removing from garden.
Yarrow	*Achillea millefolium*	Compositae	Dig rootstock. Do not let this weed set seed.

WOODY PERENNIAL WEEDS

Honeysuckle, Japanese	*Lonicera japonica*	Caprifoliaceae	Dig, lifting rhizomes. Mulch area deeply.
Kudzu vine	*Pueraria lobata*	Leguminosae	Dig all roots, repeatedly. Mulch area deeply.
Multiflora rose	*Rosa multiflora*	Rosaceae	Protect skin and dig roots. Mulch heavily for a season.
Poison ivy	*Toxicodendron radicans*	Anacardiaceae	Protect skin and dig rootstock repeatedly. Mulch area heavily.
Poison oak	*Toxicodendron toxicarium*	Anacardiaceae	Protect skin and dig, lifting stolons. Mulch area heavily.

WEED GRASSES

Bermudagrass	*Cynodon dactylon*	Gramineae	Dig rootstock and stolons. Mulch.
Crabgrass, smooth	*Digitaria ischaemum*	Gramineae	Dig crown. Remove stems.
Foxtail, yellow	*Setaria glauca*	Gramineae	Pull seedlings early. Dig plants.
Johnsongrass	*Sorghum halepense*	Gramineae	Dig, lifting rootstock. If serious, mulch for 1 or 2 seasons.
Quackgrass	*Agropyron repens*	Gramineae	Dig roots and rhizomes. Mulch.

How to Hoe

Hoeing is an excellent method for controlling annual weeds, which are killed when you cut their stems or growing crowns from the roots. If you keep up with the weeding, it should never be necessary to do more than quickly pass a well-sharpened hoe just under the soil surface. If done correctly, this job requires little or no strength, nor does it lead to an aching back.

The trick to pleasant hoeing is correct hand placement and posture. Experiment with the following technique and you may find you actually enjoy the few hours of hoeing you'll do. Most people instinctively grasp a hoe with their thumbs pointing down, probably because they think it gives them more pulling power. To further increase their strength, they lean forward, slightly bending their backs. After a couple of hours in this posture, hoeing is, literally, a pain.

When you hoe properly, you should feel rather like you're sweeping a floor. In fact, you may want to get out your kitchen broom, sweep a bit as practice, and then transfer your hands to the hoe handle. As with the broom, you should place your hands so that your thumbs point up. Skim the hoe blade through the top inch of soil, cutting a slice 6 to 8 inches long. Then position the hoe 3 to 4 inches back from the start of the first slice, and make another slice that overlaps the first one. In this way, you cultivate each part of the soil twice—once on the first cut, again on the second.

It will feel awkward at first, but you'll immediately notice that you're standing with your back straight, which will reduce the strain on it. Practice makes this technique feel natural and easy. For light surface hoeing, use your dominant hand at the top of the handle. If you want extra strength for deep work, reverse the hand placement.

Mechanized Hoeing

Weeds do sometimes get out of hand, even for the best of gardeners. If they're ignored for more than a week or so or when rainy, warm weather has pushed their growth, you're likely to find a snarly patch of tough, wiry stems when you get back out to the garden.

It *does* take strength to cut these fellows from their roots. But that doesn't mean that you should change the way you use your hoe. Instead, it means that you should change the tool. The wheel hoe—an oscillating or stationary hoe blade mounted on a wheel with two long handles—is an invaluable tool for anyone with a big garden, as well as for gardeners who sometimes let weeds go too long.

Using a wheel hoe correctly is simple: Relax and rock. If you try to push the blade of the wheel hoe through the soil, you're bound to end up frustrated and tired. The hoe attachment is designed for a scuffling motion. Push a little forward, then fall back. Try to develop a rocking motion rather than a pushing one. In this way, the momentum of the blade's action will do more than half the work.

To "rock" with a wheel hoe, hold the handles comfortably, and keep your elbows relaxed. Set the blade so it rests about an inch below the soil surface. Then extend your arms forward from the shoulder 6 to 8 inches, rocking the hoe forward. Next, draw your arms back 3 or 4 inches, reset the blade in the soil, and rock the wheel hoe forward again. You'll find your whole body gets in the rhythm, and you'll slowly move your feet forward as you make progress down the row. Most gardeners discover that after a little practice it seems much easier, faster, and more pleasant to use the wheel hoe rather than the tiller for routine cultivation.

Hand Pulling Weeds

Efficient hand weeding is a skill worth developing. It is the only way to effectively remove weeds growing close to your plants. It's also the gardening chore many people dread the most because they think it is time consuming and

Hold a hoe as you would a broom handle, with both thumbs pointing up. Don't chop at weeds; simply skim the hoe blade along, parallel to and just below the surface of the soil, left. *Try using a rocking motion when working with a wheel hoe. As with a hand hoe, the blade should cut through the soil parallel to and just below the soil surface,* right.

boring. Neither has to be true if you know some simple hand weeding tricks.

Weeding Row Crops

If your vegetable garden is planted in rows, you'll need to remove weeds growing on either side of a row, as well as weeds between plants in the row. It's most efficient to remove weeds on the sides of rows first, and then, before moving down the path, attack the in-row invaders.

Some gardeners like to hunker down on their haunches when pulling weeds, while others prefer resting on their knees. A kneeling

pad or kneepads make this posture more comfortable: You can make your own or buy items made especially for the garden—including weeding stools and pants with sewn-in kneepads—from garden centers or catalogs. While both these positions put some stress on your muscles, they are preferable to standing bent over at the waist, which can be harmful to your back.

The first trick is to get accustomed to weeding with both hands in sync. Practice by putting your hands in front of you at chest level. Keep your fingers relaxed, palms down, and elbows bent. Now, pinch your thumbs to the sides of your forefingers as you move your arms slightly up and outward, as if your hands were moving apart along the outline of a half-circle. In the garden, your hands will be on either side of the crop row, with your thumbs close to the base of the plants.

This technique allows you to work right up to the crop plants. It will be easy to catch weeds between your thumb and forefinger and throw them aside. Try to develop a rhythm and experiment to see whether your right or left arm should be stretched over the row. I find that I have more control by stretching my dominant arm.

After you've pulled weeds as far as you can reach alongside the rows, remove the weeds between plants in the row. For this job, your hands will move in an alternating, rather than a simultaneous, pattern. The fastest method I know is a pinching movement of the tip of the forefinger to the tip of my thumb.

To practice, put your hands out in front of you, with fingers relaxed and palms facing your body, one hand in front of the other. Now roll your hands, much like the motion when "... this old man goes rolling home" in the children's singing game.

Now, pinch your forefinger and thumb together as you reach the outermost edge of the imaginary circle your hands are tracing, and move your arms to the side as you roll your hands.

In the garden, you won't want to make the rolling action so extreme, and you certainly won't be able to keep this speed, because you'll need to discriminate between weeds and crops as you work. However, with practice, you will surprise yourself by how quickly you can clean up a row with this movement.

Weeding Beds and Borders

When you're pulling weeds in a flower border or in an intensively planted vegetable bed, you can still use a two-handed technique.

Clear out weeds around your desirable plants by pulling them up and out of the soil, working with two hands simultaneously. Use a pinching motion to remove weeds growing close to the base or amongst shoots. For perennials, use one hand to hold down the soil around the plant's crown while you prick out weeds with the other hand.

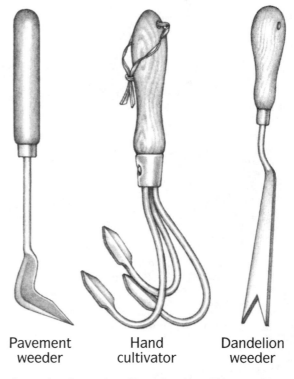

Pavement   Hand   Dandelion
weeder   cultivator   weeder

Just as there is a variety of hoes, there is a wide array of short-handled cutting and digging tools for helping with weeding chores. A hand cultivator with three or more tines is useful for disturbing the soil surface around close plantings to uproot young weed seedlings. A dandelion weeder is an excellent tool for uprooting weeds with long taproots. There are also special weeding trowels and tools for removing weeds in cracks between bricks or stone slabs in walkways.

Using String Trimmers

String trimmers are gasoline- or electric-powered tools that cut weeds with a length of synthetic string that whirls at a high speed. These tools are useful for cutting back weeds along walls, in hard-to-reach areas, or on steep slopes where you cannot use a tiller or mower.

String trimmers can only be used to cut back weed tops; they will not uproot weeds. They are only effective for controlling perennial weeds if you keep up a consistent attack, cutting back the weeds regularly throughout the growing season.

Also, use caution when weeding around permanent plantings like perennials and shrubs. A false move with your trimmer can damage foliage and bark.

Boiling Water

Boiling water kills annual weeds by literally burning the leaf tissue. Needless to say, it doesn't improve the health of worms or other beneficials close to the soil surface, but it certainly poses no long-term dangers. To try this approach, simply pour a pot of boiling water over the weeds you want to kill. Be very careful not to spill the water on your garden plants or on yourself.

Using boiling water against perennial weeds is a more time- and energy-consuming endeavor. To use boiling water to kill stubborn perennials, you'll have to expose their roots and all sites where new stems can sprout and grow. If you only kill the current batch of stems and leaves, most perennials are perfectly capable of sprouting new ones.

You can use boiling water as one element in a control program for poison ivy or other perennial weeds with stubborn root systems that are difficult to pull out of the ground. Begin by digging down to the root under each stem and follow it through the soil, making a trench as far around it as possible. Then pour several gallons of boiling water over the roots. Don't rebury the rootstock. Since you've gone to all the work of exposing the root complex, make it as difficult as possible for the plant to repair itself by growing new feeding roots. Simple exposure to drying by wind and bright sunshine will significantly weaken the plant, making it much easier to kill any stems that sprout after the first water campaign.

Solarization

You can also enlist the sun's heat to kill weed seeds in the top few inches of soil. Clear plastic spread tightly over the soil will help trap heat, raising the soil temperature to levels that will kill weed seeds, as well as microorganisms. This technique is also used to help solve problems with soil-borne plant pathogens. However, it can also kill earthworms and beneficial microorganisms, so it should only be used if you have a particularly weedy section in your garden, and only after other methods have proved unsuccessful. For instructions on how to prepare a bed for solarizing, see "Solarizing Soil" on page 152.

CHEMICAL CONTROLS

There are few choices for controlling weeds with chemicals that are acceptable for organic gardeners, even as a last resort. Unlike insecticides and fungicides, there are no naturally occurring substances, like sulfur, or plant-derived poisons, such as pyrethrin, that are widely useful for killing weeds. Two common substances that kill plants—vinegar and salt—can also have devastating effects on the soil's natural balance. One commercial organic, soap-based herbicide has recently come on the market, but its usefulness is limited to a narrow range of gardening practices.

Vinegar and Salt

The first rule for using vinegar or salt as an herbicide is never use either on land where you want anything to grow. For example, you might choose to spread these substances on the soil in an area where you plan to lay a brick path, or pour it between cracks in a patio. Both substances kill plants by changing the soil environment so drastically that plant roots cannot function.

Vinegar, a dilute acid, acidifies the soil, while salt interferes with a root's ability to absorb water and nutrients. Theoretically, you could use vinegar to solve a stubborn weed problem and subsequently apply enough lime to restore the soil pH to a normal range. However, balancing the pH in this way is tricky and gives you more work and headaches than a simple digging and mulching operation would.

Similarly, since salt can be washed from soil, you might assume that you could dump table salt over an offensive weed, wait for it to do its damage, and then flood the area so heavily that the salt just washes away. But most likely, it will end up further down in the subsoil, where it could interfere with growth of deep-rooted plants. The salt could also merely wash through the small waterways that connect one part of the garden with the rest. You can bet that it will take a long time and a great deal of water to wash all that salt out of the soil completely.

The second and final rule for using vinegar or salt to kill weeds is: Evaluate all your other options first. You'll likely find that it's not worth the possible harm to your yard or garden to use either of these substances as herbicides.

Soap-Based Herbicide

Gardeners who use insecticidal soap to kill insect pests know there are many precautions about possible plant damage from the spray. Taking this idea one step further has resulted in a commercial herbicide based on soap, Safer's SharpShooter. It kills leaves by damaging the surface leaf tissue. It works best on young or delicate foliage and affects any plant on which it is sprayed, beloved plant or undesirable weed. SharpShooter biodegrades into harmless substances within 48 hours and does not seriously harm populations of soil organisms. It is not registered for use on food crops. Most chemical-free growers confine its use to young weeds in ornamental beds.

BALANCING HARM AND BENEFITS

Gardeners' attitudes about weeds seem to fall into one of three categories. Some people are extremely rigorous; you almost never see a weed in their yards. Others are very sloppy. When they pick the vegetables for dinner, they have to pull a canopy of galinsoga or pigweed aside to find them. The third sort seem schizophrenic. They are rigorous in the beginning of the season but sloppy toward the end.

Being totally careless about weeding is not a good idea; you're only creating future problems for yourself if you allow perennials to take firm hold or weed seeds to stock the soil bank. But a guilt-ridden, compulsive attitude doesn't always serve you well either. It can transform the pleasure of taking care of a garden into a chore and a duty, and sooner or later, everyone rebels.

Fortunately, a middle-ground approach makes good gardening sense. If you, like me, are not naturally meticulous, your garden doesn't have to suffer for it as long as you follow some basic principles.

Researchers have demonstrated what good gardeners seem to know instinctively: Plants are most vulnerable to competition when they are young and small. Use the extra energy and excitement given by spring and early summer weather to keep your beds as clear of weeds as possible. Most crops require at least four to six weeks of life without competition to gain health and vigor.

The smaller the plant, the more important it is to give it the space it needs. In practical terms, this means you must keep the seedling carrots and direct-seeded lettuce as clean as possible for as long as you can. If you have a choice of weeding the broccoli or tomato transplants or the tiny carrots, choose the carrots. This also means that thinning to appropriate distances is crucial when plants are small.

And as for later in the season? Well, you might have done such a good initial weeding job that very few weeds remain, or have used enough mulch so that no weeds get through. But if you haven't, if some weeds remain, take heart from other research. According to studies, plants are often more healthy in a slightly weedy area than they are in a totally weed-free environment. This may be because damage from pest insects is decreased by weeds that serve as beneficial companions, attracting predators and parasites of the pest insects. For example, studies have shown that the presence of wild mustard among cabbage family crops increased the activity of parasitic wasps that attack cabbage-worms. Other studies showed that ragweed growing in corn or peach orchards provided an alternate food source for parasites of European corn borer and oriental fruit moths.

Because research of this nature is in its infancy, there are probably hundreds of beneficial weed/crop interactions that haven't been reported by scientists. Keep your eyes open, and you may notice many of them in your own yard and garden.

CHAPTER SIX

Disease Control

By Miranda Smith

Many gardeners may worry that without regular sprays of synthetic chemical fungicides, diseases will simply run rampant. But a little knowledge of how disease organisms attack plants and how they spread through the garden goes a long way. Organic gardeners use this understanding as a first line of defense and concentrate their efforts on *preventing* disease.

Even though preventive practices can seem like a lot of work in the beginning, they do get results. After a few years of using good, organic, preventive techniques, you will eliminate all but the strongest and most persistent of diseases. And even when these strike, you'll usually be able to exert enough control to save your plants or get a respectable harvest.

The organic approach to disease control is not all that different from the approach to controlling weeds. Organic gardeners rely first on cultural controls, such as choosing resistant plants, then on physical controls, such as cutting away diseased plant parts. Finally, there are chemical controls—the last resort to stop the progress of diseases in your garden. The elements of an organic disease management system include:

🙞 *Cultural controls.* These are used to prevent diseases from getting a foothold in the garden. They include choosing resistant cultivars, buying certified disease-free plants, maintaining a good soil nutrient balance, using good garden practices to maintain an optimum environment for plant growth, and practicing good garden sanitation to keep diseases from gaining ground in the garden. Crop rotation is another effective cultural control that will help keep you one step ahead of serious disease problems.

🙞 *Physical controls.* These are methods that physically destroy disease organisms or that block them from reaching plants. They include burning diseased plant parts or composting them in a hot compost pile, solarizing the soil, and using row covers to prevent insect vectors from transmitting disease.

🐛 *Chemical controls.* There are home-brewed sprays and environmentally safe, organic chemicals that can be used to fight disease once it occurs.

KNOW YOUR ENEMY

Disease prevention relies on a little background knowledge, especially since you're dealing with a largely invisible enemy. Plant diseases are caused by fungi, bacteria, and viruses (including viruslike organisms). These disease-causing organisms, or pathogens, create disease by using portions of the host plant as both home and food. Once pathogens begin to feed, they cause a variety of symptoms. By carefully examining your plants for these symptoms, you'll be able to get a good idea of what type of organism is causing the problem. (The symptom descriptions provided in part 3, "Chemical-Free Garden Guides," will also help you diagnose problems. For a list of more books on the subject, see "The Chemical-Free Gardener's Library" on page 431.)

Once you've identified the type of disease organism that has infected your plants, you'll be able to treat it—or at least prevent it in the future. In many cases, you won't be able to identify the disease organism by species. Symptoms of diseases may be so similar that the only way to identify the causal organism is by lab analysis of afflicted parts, a service your Cooperative Extension Service can provide. You can also take samples of a stricken plant to your local nursery for help in diagnosing the problem. (Be sure to ask for organic remedies.)

Fortunately, preventive measures are effective for all types of disease, and organic control measures for each broad group of disease organism generally help lessen the problems caused by all organisms in that group. Therefore, if you at least distinguish a fungal disease from a viral or bacterial one, you'll be able to choose the proper control steps to take.

Each of the three major types of disease-causing organisms have distinctive methods of attacking plants. To learn more about how the enemy operates so you can mount an effective defense of your garden, read the following profiles on fungi, bacteria, and viruses.

Fungi

Fungi are responsible for the greatest number of plant diseases, causing rotted tissue, moldy coatings, or spots on flowers, foliage, and stems. So-called fairy rings—ever-widening circles of yellowed grass that appear on lawns—also are caused by fungi. Despite the menace they pose, there are some good fungi, like the ones that transform garden debris into compost.

Common symptoms. Fungi can invade and rot stem bases, crowns of plants, foliage, flowers, or fruit. They can also cause blighted areas to appear, in which case plant parts wilt and die suddenly, but may only rot afterwards. Other symptoms of fungal diseases include: wilting; spots or blotches on leaves, flowers, fruit, or stems; galls (swelling); moldy or mildewed coating on plant parts; and blistered or curled leaves. Fungi also cause smuts, which are sooty masses on plant parts usually found on cereals and grasses; scabby areas on fruit or foliage; rust, characterized by powdery blisters—generally red-brown or yellowish—on leaves; and cankers, which are lesions on twigs or bark. If you suspect a fungal disease, use a hand lens to look at diseased plant parts very closely. You may be able to spot the fine, threadlike web (the hyphae) that makes up the body of most fungi or see clusters of tiny, spore-bearing stalks.

Important characteristics. Some fungi live only on material that is already dead (like the species involved in the composting process). Other fungi that live on dead material are capable of attacking living plants as well. They manage this by releasing toxins that kill plant cells in

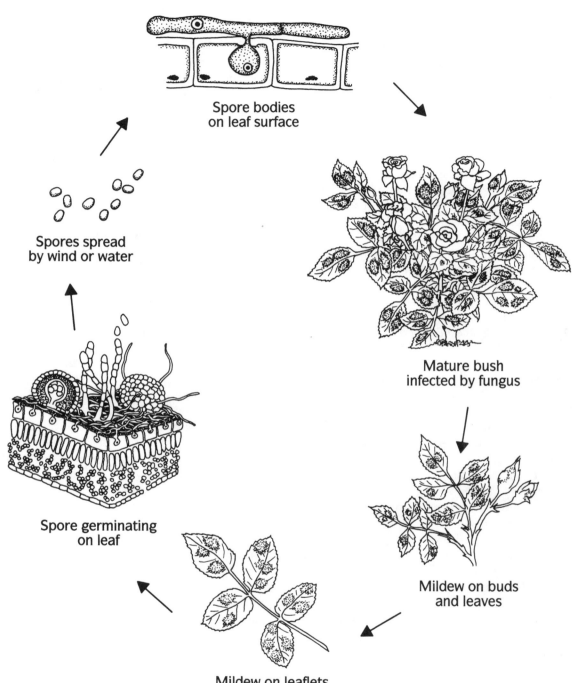

Spore bodies
on leaf surface

Spores spread
by wind or water

Mature bush
infected by fungus

Spore germinating
on leaf

Mildew on buds
and leaves

Mildew on leaflets

Powdery mildew is a common disease of many ornamentals and vegetable crops. There are many fungi that cause this disease; most can only infect one or a few plant species. However, all have similar life cycles to the fungus that causes powdery mildew in roses, shown above. A common symptom of the disease is a white powdery growth on the leaves. The white powder is the spore bodies and spores of the fungus. Wind and water carry the spores from infected leaves to healthy leaves. When environmental conditions are right, the spores germinate and penetrate the leaf cells, and then new fungal bodies grow and spread the fungus over the leaf.

advance of their spread through the plant. Other fungi survive equally well on living or dead material. They attack living plants during the growing season but dine just as happily on dead stalks, leaves, and roots. Many are attracted to bruised, damaged, or stressed plant tissue.

How fungi spread. Fungi reproduce by releasing spores. Some spores can germinate within a few minutes of being released from the growing fungus. Others remain dormant until environmental conditions, such as the amount and temperature of water on a leaf surface, signal good growing conditions. Some spores can wait as long as 20 years before germinating. Swimming spores live both above and below ground, moving through dew or soil water in response to chemical or electrical emissions from host plants. Wind-borne spores can travel on a breeze as light as a breath and can also be carried along by rain or mist. Some spores travel hundreds of miles each year, generally from south to north.

Prevention and control measures. Since most fungi germinate in high-moisture conditions, good soil drainage is crucial to control. Adding organic matter to improve soil drainage, double-digging beds, or planting in raised beds are all effective ways to improve soil drainage. Good air circulation is also important, because it helps reduce moisture on foliage, stems, flowers, and fruit. Space plants so they have ample access to light and enough space so air can circulate freely. Avoid working in the garden when foliage is wet to keep from spreading the spores from plant to plant. Try not to wet the leaves while watering, and water early in the day so leaves can dry before nightfall. Also try not to damage plants by digging into crowns or brushing into or tearing foliage; damaged plant tissue is an open invitation to fungi. For vegetables and other annual crops, rotations and composting garden debris are also important controls. When you spot the first sign of a fungal infection, remove all plants or plant parts that show

symptoms. If you have a newly built hot compost pile, one that will heat to 160°F, you can bury infected plant parts near its center to kill all traces of the fungus and avoid reinfecting the garden. Otherwise, dispose of infected plants in sealed bags in the trash, or burn them. If the fungi are ones that live or spread through the soil, like club root of cabbage family plants, dig and dispose of the infected soil as well.

Names of common fungal diseases. Alternaria blight, anthracnose, apple scab, black spot, brown rot, club root, damping-off, downy mildew, Fusarium wilt, gray mold, late blight, peach leaf curl, powdery mildew, root rot, rust, smut, southern blight, Verticillium wilt

Bacteria

Bacteria are one-celled organisms that can cause a variety of diseases in plants—many of them with symptoms similar to those caused by fungi. One symptom of bacterial diseases not often associated with fungal or viral diseases is easy to distinguish, even with eyes closed: a foul odor.

Common symptoms. Bacteria cause a variety of blights, characterized by plant parts that wilt and die, leaving blighted stem tips with leaves attached; after the blight occurs, rot may set in. They can also cause leaf spots and stem, crown, or fruit rots. Bacteria can also cause galls (swellings) and wilts. Unlike fungal rots, bacterial rots are often accompanied by a foul odor; afflicted parts may be filled with slimy, rotted tissue. Since they are single celled, bacteria don't produce the threadlike web of hyphae or the spore-bearing stalks characteristic of fungi.

Important characteristics. Bacteria overwinter on old plant debris, in hibernating insects, in cankers on living plants, and in the soil. They can remain viable for a few years without a host, but don't have the long dormancy of most fungi.

How bacteria spread. Bacteria can enter plants only through existing openings—they can't

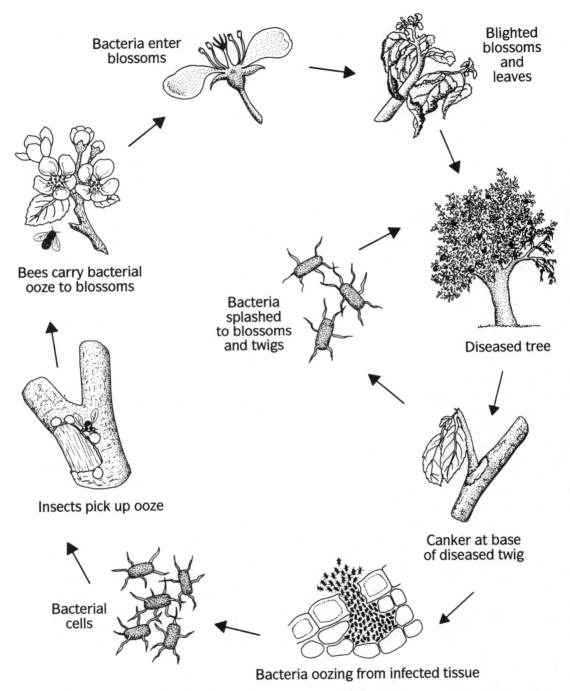

Bacteria enter blossoms

Blighted blossoms and leaves

Bees carry bacterial ooze to blossoms

Bacteria splashed to blossoms and twigs

Diseased tree

Insects pick up ooze

Canker at base of diseased twig

Bacterial cells

Bacteria oozing from infected tissue

Fire blight is a bacterial disease that affects pears, apples, and other fruit crops. The bacteria enter the plant through wounds in bark and through natural openings in flowers. They reproduce inside plant tissues, using nutrients from the plants to support their growth. Insects pick up bacterial cells on their bodies when they feed on infected plants and carry the bacteria to healthy plants. Splashing raindrops or irrigation water can also pick up bacterial cells and transfer them from one plant part to another.

make their own like fungi. But since plants have so many little natural holes in their leaf surfaces, this requirement doesn't slow bacteria down in the slightest. Even the smallest bruise on a stem or leaf makes a tiny dead spot, or extra doorway for bacteria. They can also enter through puncture wounds caused by insect feeding.

Prevention and control measures. Basic control of bacterial diseases is quite similar to fungal diseases. When you spot the first sign of a bacterial infection, remove all plants or parts of plants that show symptoms. If you have a newly built hot compost pile, one that will heat to 160°F, you can discard infected plant parts near its center to kill the bacteria. Otherwise, dispose of infected plants in the trash, or burn them. For soil-borne diseases, dig and dispose of the infected soil as well. Also, try not to damage plants by digging into crowns or brushing into or tearing foliage; damaged plant tissue provides an open invitation to bacterial diseases. For vegetables and other annuals, establish a rotation system to avoid planting susceptible plants in the same spot year after year.

Names of common bacterial diseases. Angular leaf spot, bacterial wilt, crown gall, fire blight, halo blight, potato scab, ring rot, soft rot

Viruses

Plant pathologists have identified more than 300 viruses and viruslike organisms that attack plants. Viral organisms are much smaller than bacterial cells. Although they cause a broad range of symptoms, they are spread in similar ways, and control measures for all virus diseases are similar. In some cases, symptoms of viral disease may closely resemble symptoms of nutrient deficiencies: Plant analysis is the only sure way to diagnose the problem.

Common symptoms. Viruses can cause stunting and abnormal growth patterns such as leaf cupping or twisting. Other symptoms include leaves that are mottled or streaked with yellow or have ring-shaped spots.

Important characteristics. Viruses are only active when inhabiting living hosts like your garden plants. They reproduce by stimulating their host cells to create more viruses. When the host dies, the virus becomes inactive. However, many dormant viruses can remain capable of infecting new hosts for as long as 50 years.

How viruses spread. Viruses are most frequently transmitted by insects, called vectors. The most notable virus vectors are aphids and leafhoppers. Some viruses are carried from one plant to another in an insect's saliva. These pathogens are particularly dependent upon sucking or chewing insects for transportation. Viruses may also be carried on an insect's feet and can also be spread mechanically, when they are picked up and moved around by a breeze, or even by the gardener's hand, clothing, or tools—especially pruning tools.

Prevention and control measures. Since many common viruses can remain dormant but capable of infection for long periods of time, digging and destroying an infected plant in your garden doesn't really do any good unless other infected host plants are removed from the area (this would include weeds and plants in the neighbor's yard). And unlike fungi and bacteria, a hot compost pile does not usually kill viruses. Remove virus-diseased plants from the garden (and surrounding areas) and bury them in a faraway spot, burn them, or put them out in sealed containers with your household trash.

Names of common viral diseases. Aster yellows, bean mosaic, cucumber mosaic, leafroll, tobacco mosaic virus, tobacco ring spot

Recognizing the Impostors

Not everything that goes wrong with a plant can be blamed on disease. Obviously, insects can cause diseaselike symptoms—an infestation of spider mites can cause yellowed, mottled foliage, and tunneling by borers can cause stem tips to wilt or die back. So when you inspect

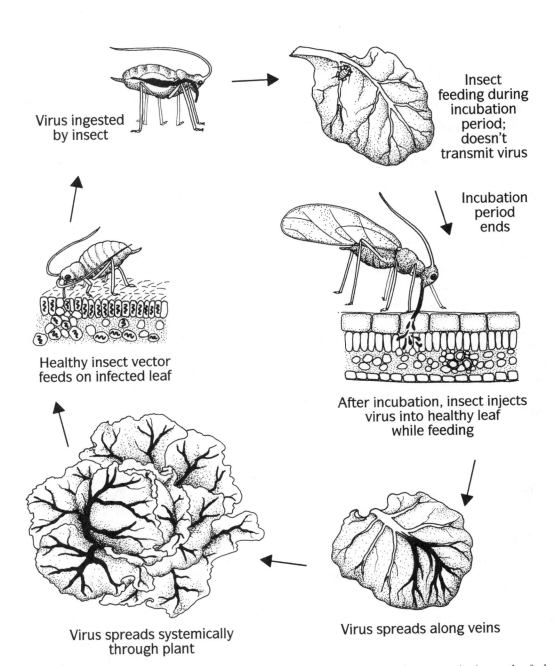

Virus ingested by insect

Insect feeding during incubation period; doesn't transmit virus

Incubation period ends

Healthy insect vector feeds on infected leaf

After incubation, insect injects virus into healthy leaf while feeding

Virus spreads systemically through plant

Virus spreads along veins

Mosaic is a common viral disease. It is usually transmitted by insects. Aphids can ingest lettuce mosaic virus as they feed on infected plants. After an incubation period, the virus can then pass out of the aphids into lettuce tissue through the insects' mouthparts.

afflicted plants, be sure to consider insects as a possible cause of the damage. Nematodes are small, eel-shaped worms, not visible to the naked eye, that can parasitize plants and cause disease-like symptoms. (There are also beneficial species of nematodes that help break down organic matter in the soil and insect-parasitic nematodes that can be used to control soil-dwelling insects.) Perhaps the most common of the plant-parasitic nematodes is the root-knot nematode. Aboveground symptoms of this pest include weakened plants that wilt in the sun, yellow or pale green leaves, and stunted fruit or flowers. For more information on nematodes and their control, see "A Knotty Problem" on page 136.

There are also cultural disorders brought on by environmental stresses such as nutrient deficiencies that can mimic diseases. See "Plant Symptoms of Mineral Imbalances," on page 64, for a summary of symptoms that may result from nutrient imbalances in the soil. Some disorders, such as blossom-end rot on tomatoes or tip-burn on lettuce, are caused by environmental stress in combination with a nutritional imbalance. Others, such as tomato sunscald or potato black heart, are a product of the environment alone.

There will always be environmental stresses —like weather—over which you have little or no control. But there are ways you can reduce or eliminate problems. For example, if your tomatoes or peppers have suffered from sunscald, you can choose cultivars with bigger leaves and site them where they'll get some afternoon shade. Placing them to the east of a row of pole beans or sunflowers could give shade in an open garden. See "Common Cultural Disorders," on page 138, for descriptions of and remedies for some of these cultural problems.

CULTURAL CONTROLS

Every day, in large and small ways, you can use cultural controls to stop diseases from ever becoming a critical problem in the garden. When you're browsing through seed catalogs, working the soil in the spring, watering and pruning, and cleaning up after a day in the garden, there are many simple things you can do to boost your garden's immunity to disease problems. As you read the following section, you will probably find lots of ideas that are easy to incorporate into your regular gardening routine.

Start with Built-In Defense

Make it a habit to look for plants that offer their own disease protection. These built-in defense systems include disease resistance and disease tolerance. Another smart tactic is to buy certified disease-free plants whenever possible.

Resistance

Resistance means that most of the individual plants of a particular cultivar resist infection by a particular plant pathogen. If spring breezes carry tobacco mosaic virus into your garden, as long as you have planted a resistant cultivar of tomato like 'Park's Better Bush', there probably will be no mosaic outbreak.

Resistance is often due to tiny differences in the chemical makeup of a particular cultivar or by structural differences such as thicker cuticles or leaf pores that open at the wrong time of day for the pathogen. For a more complete explanation of how resistant and tolerant cultivars manage to withstand disease and insect problems, see "How Resistance Works" on page 166.

Tolerance

A tolerant cultivar is one that is able to continue growing fairly successfully even when infected by a particular pathogen. For example, 'Jersey Giant' asparagus tolerates Fusarium crown and root rots, so if those diseases strike, you should still to able to enjoy tender asparagus stalks for dinner. (As an added bonus, this asparagus cultivar is also resistant to rust.) Sometimes

A Knotty Problem

Root-knot nematodes (*Meloidogyne* spp.) are a common soil-dwelling pest found throughout North America. They attack most cultivated plants and are especially problematic on carrots, lettuce, potatoes, and tomatoes. They also infest fruit trees. These microscopic, eel- or pear-shaped worms are round in cross-section, have no legs, and are not visible to the naked eye. Larvae are smaller versions of adults.

Nematode infection causes root swelling; infected roots have galls that are two to three times wider than the diameter of healthy roots. A series of infestations leave roots with a clubbed, or knotted, look. Infection occurs mostly in a zone from 2 to 10 inches below the soil surface. Infected roots are open to decay by fungi and other disease organisms. Above-ground, plants appear weak, wilt in the sun, and leaves turn yellow or pale green. Fruit or flowers are also stunted. Although plants rarely die, they don't yield a crop.

The life cycle of these pests begins when females inside a root-knot lay masses of eggs. When the larvae hatch, they move through the soil, searching for roots to infect. They invade fine roots and begin feeding. They undergo several molts until they reach a mature stage. Their feeding causes galls to form on the roots they have invaded. The entire life cycle takes three to four weeks in hot weather.

Your plan of attack for controlling nematodes should include:

❧ Avoiding spreading soil from nematode-infested areas to uninfested areas on seedlings, shoes, or dirty tools. Wash tools after using them in infected areas.

❧ Solarizing infested soil by covering wet soil with a thin sheet of clear plastic (use two layers in northern gardens) to trap heat for one to two months in summer. See "Solarization," on page 125, for more information on this technique.

❧ Replacing plants in infested beds with a cover crop of marigolds for a long-term suppressive effect. Studies show that root-knot larvae that penetrate marigold roots do not lay eggs. Also, marigold roots exude substances that deter feeding by nematodes for as long as three years after the marigold crop has been turned into the soil.

❧ Digging fresh green grass or other organic matter into nematode-infested soil to stimulate native nematode-trapping fungi.

❧ Trying a three-year crop rotation with nonsusceptible crops such as those in the grass family (Gramineae) or cabbage family (Cruciferae).

❧ Drenching the soil with neem, a botanical poison that is effective against nematodes as well as many insect pests. See "Neem," on page 224, for more information on this product.

❧ Applying chitin to the soil. Chitin is the plasticlike protein compound found in shellfish shells, insect exoskeletons, and nematode cuticles. When added to soil, it stimulates the growth and multiplication of a myriad of beneficial soil fungi that get their nourishment by decomposing chitin. These fungi also attack nematode eggs because they have chitin shells; the more fungi there are, the more eggs are absorbed by the strands of fungi as they wend their way through the soil. There does seem to be a somewhat selective effect, because the populations of beneficial nematodes (those that decompose dead plant materials and eat microbes) apparently increase in the presence of chitin. When chitin is broken down by soil organisms, nitrogen and potassium are freed for plants to use, so it also acts as a fertilizer.

You can use crushed lobster, crab, or shrimp shell wastes as a chitin source if they are available in your area. Five pounds will treat about 200 square feet of soil. Be sure to add a nitrogen source such as dried blood to support the growth flush in the fungal population; chitin alone will not be effective.

You can also purchase a commercial chitin product such as ClandoSan. The chitin in these products is also extracted from shrimp and crab shells. However, these products are not fully organic because the nitrogen source added is urea formaldehyde, a synthetic form of nitrogen fertilizer.

the plant is tolerant because it is hypersensitive to the pathogen. Cells adjacent to the invading organism die so quickly that the pathogen can't spread through the plant.

To help you with your plant selection, some of the resistant or tolerant cultivars of vegetable and fruit crops are listed in part 3, "Chemical-Free Garden Guides." Since plant breeders are continually introducing new and improved cultivars of popular garden plants, keep an eye out in catalogs and nurseries for new resistant and tolerant plants to try.

Certified Disease-Free Plants

Many ornamental and fruit-bearing plants sold by nurseries are labeled "certified disease-free." The certification is a guarantee that a plant pathologist has checked the crop to determine that it is not hosting disease pathogens. Strawberries and brambles, for example, are favorite hosts of several debilitating viruses. Although the damage done to the plant during the first couple years is minimal, damage increases as the pathogen builds populations over ensuing seasons. Plants that start off virus-free may very well become infected, because some pathogens are so widespread, but it will take longer for the pathogen to build up to levels that affect plant performance.

Making sure your soil is full of beneficial microorganisms and that the environment is appropriate will help enhance the plant's resistance. Good cultural practices, such as planting newly purchased strawberry plants in a different location every three or four years and removing old canes from brambles every year, add a second layer of protection.

Certified plants will cost a bit more because they are grown under controlled conditions to prevent infection. (For example, plants are grown under netting stretched over frames to exclude aphids, leafhoppers, and other sucking insects that can transmit virus diseases.) In addition to the great reduction in disease incidence that inspection provides, most nurseries selling certified stock will replace plants within the first year or two of their growth if disease symptoms appear.

Safeguarding Seeds

Seeds sold to home gardeners are not often certified as disease-free, although reputable seed houses do subject particular seeds to hot-water or chemical treatments to kill pathogens. If you grow your own seed for open-pollinated crops, save seed only from nondiseased plants. So many pathogens are seed-borne that it never pays to save seed from infected stock. Because it's so easy to overlook disease symptoms that were slight last year but could build to damaging levels this season, treat home-grown seed against pathogens. (Members of seed exchanges should also follow this practice to avoid importing pathogens.) See "Seed Dips," on page 140, for instructions on how to treat your seeds to kill disease pathogens.

Some plant pathogens that cause serious disease problems in the eastern United States are not present or will not thrive in western regions. Some of these pathogens can be seed-borne, so western-grown seed is less likely to be infected than eastern-grown seed. If you've had previous problems with diseases such as bean anthracnose or black leg of cabbage, try ordering seed from a producer in the western United States. That way, you'll have a better chance of at least getting a disease-free start with your crops.

Balance the Soil

Healthy soil is a crucial part of the garden's defense system against plant diseases. Just like humans, healthy plants resist or tolerate many more diseases than weakened ones. A healthy soil provides plants with just the conditions they need to obtain proper nutrition: a balanced supply of nutrients, slightly acid pH, good nutrient-holding and releasing qualities,

Common Cultural Disorders

Learning to distinguish cultural disorders, meaning those caused by poor environmental conditions (such as nutrient imbalances, unfavorable weather, or unhealthy soil), from true diseases can be tricky. The following table provides symptoms, causes, and remedies for common disorders. Bear in mind that most of the steps you can take to correct the problems will not save the current season's crop, but can remedy the situation so that crops in following seasons do not suffer from the same disorders.

Condition	Crop	Symptoms	Causes	Steps You Can Take
Black heart	Beets, turnips	Darkening in center; center may be hollow	Boron deficiency; sometimes potassium or phosphorus deficiency	Test the soil to identify what mineral is deficient and follow the recommendations for correcting the deficiency.
	Potatoes	Darkening in center; center may be hollow	Lack of oxygen	Add more organic matter to the soil to create pore spaces.
	Celery	Darkening in center; center may be hollow	Fluctuating soil moisture; calcium deficiency	Add more organic matter to the soil; stabilize moisture levels with soaker hoses and mulch. If a soil test reveals a calcium deficiency, add supplements in the form of natural ground limestone or bonemeal.
Blasting	All flowers	Buds or flowers drop prematurely	Soil too wet or dry; improperly stored bulbs	In soils that are chronically waterlogged, improve drainage by incorporating lots of organic matter. In dry soils, provide supplemental water and use mulch to help stabilize soil moisture levels.
	Onions	Leaf tips bleach, brown, and wither	Bright light after cloudy, wet conditions	No remedy for weather conditions.

and good moisture retention and aeration. Plants grown in such soils tend to be vigorous and therefore more resistant to disease attack.

An organic system for bringing your soils into balance is presented in chapter 4, Soil Improvement and Fertilizing. Refer to it to learn how to use organic soil amendments and fertilizers to produce healthy soil and plants.

Condition	Crop	Symptoms	Causes	Steps You Can Take
Blossom-end rot	Tomatoes, peppers, cucurbits	Dark, sunken area at blossom end of fruit	Dry conditions after wet; calcium deficiency	Water plants well to avoid dry soil conditions; remedy calcium deficiencies by applying calcitic limestone or bonemeal.
Cracked stem	Celery	Stem cracks	Boron deficiency	Test the soil to confirm boron deficiency and follow the recommendations for correcting the deficiency.
Hollow heart	Crucifers	Hollow stem	Boron deficiency	Test the soil to confirm boron deficiency and follow the recommendations for correcting the deficiency.
Sunscald	Tomatoes, peppers	White area appears and blisters before secondary rotting occurs	Excessive loss of foliage; heavy pruning or trellising of tomatoes	Use light cloth or a lath sunshade to shield heavily pruned plants from strong, midday sun. Take trellised plants down off supports and let them sprawl on the ground. Prune less vigorously next season.
Tipburn	Lettuce, potatoes	Leaf tips brown	Bright light after cloudy, wet conditions; potassium deficiency; calcium imbalance	No remedy for weather conditions. But to offset potassium deficiency, add well-rotted animal manures or seaweed fertilizers. To bring calcium levels into balance, add calcitic limestone or bonemeal.

Beware of Nutrient Imbalances

Soil nutrient imbalances affect the problems you encounter with plant diseases, because some pathogens are especially attracted to plants with a particular imbalance. For example, all of the Fusarium wilts are more prone to attack when potassium is low and nitrogen too abundant. On the other hand, southern blight attacks when

Seed Dips

Sterilizing dips can be made from common ingredients found in your kitchen cabinets. These dips may not be 100 percent reliable, but they certainly offer more protection than not cleaning seeds at all. Try either of the following dip recipes on seeds:

1 Tablespoon cider vinegar stirred into 1 quart water

½ cup household bleach added to 4½ cups water

Place seeds to be cleaned in the center of a large square of cheesecloth.

to leak out. Mix ingredients for either recipe in a glass bowl. Dunk the seed-filled bag two or three times into the sterilizing mixture.

Open the bag and remove seeds to dry on a layer of newspaper or paper towels. Make sure seeds are completely dry before storing.

Gather the edges of the cheesecloth together and secure with string or a rubber band. Make sure there are no openings for the seeds

nitrogen supplies are deficient. If symptoms of particular deficiencies or excesses are clear cut, you can add specific fertilizers to correct the problem. (See "Plant Symptoms of Mineral Imbalances," on page 64, for symptoms of nutrient deficiencies and excesses.) If you suspect a deficiency, test your soil, and follow the recommendations for remedying the problem. In the meantime, you can safely help to correct the deficiency by adding compost or composted manure to your soil to supply additional nutrients.

Provide the Optimum Environment

Appropriate environmental conditions are almost as important as healthy soils when it comes to disease prevention. You can't control the weather, of course, but your techniques can modify its effects. Here, too, proper soil conditions are crucial: Well-drained, well-aerated soil helps to keep soil oxygen levels high enough for healthy root growth during the warm, rainy

Hot-water treatment, or exposing seeds to hot water, can be an effective way to kill some seed-borne disease organisms. However, you must take pains to treat the seeds properly, or they may be damaged by excessive heat. Also, hot-water treatment will usually reduce germination percentage.

The technique is usually used for treating a large quantity of seeds. It requires heating several gallons of water to a specified temperature for a specified time. Don't try heating a small quantity of seed in a quart of water—the temperature of a small volume of water fluctuates too easily. At best, the treatment won't be effective, and at worst, you'll kill all the seed with excess heat.

If you try to hot-water treat seeds, pay close attention to the thermometer and clock, using the temperatures and times listed.

To treat seeds, fill a large pot with at least 10 gallons of water, and heat it to the proper temperature. Place the seeds in the center of a large square of cheesecloth, gather the edges together, and tie securely. Suspend the seeds in the water, keeping them well away from the bottom of the pot. Stir the water frequently during immersion. Use a good-quality dairy or candy thermometer to measure the water temperature, and make certain that the water is holding the correct temperature before adding the seeds. Time their immersion carefully. Once they've been treated, they should be planted immediately since they are well on the way to germination. (NOTE: Don't try to use your microwave for this heat treatment. You will not be able to monitor water temperature properly.)

Seed	Water Temp. (°F)	Time (min.)
Broccoli	122	20
Brussels sprouts	122	25
Cabbage	122	25
Cauliflower	122	20
Celery	118	30
Eggplant	122	25
Kale	122	20
Kohlrabi	122	20
Peppers	122	25
Tomatoes	122	25
Turnips	122	20

periods that favor many pathogenic fungi. Adding organic matter to the soil on a regular basis encourages good drainage and aeration. Below, you'll find other simple cultural techniques you can use to help create a healthy environment for your plants.

Mulching

Mulch is usually seen as a first-line defense against weeds and as a way to guard soil moisture reserves. But its role can also be expanded to include disease prevention. For example, a layer of mulch can help prevent some fungal diseases by preventing spores from splattering up from the soil onto foliage during rainstorms.

Different kinds of mulch have different characteristics that can be used to boost a plant's vigor, making it more resistant to disease. For example, heat-loving crops like cucumbers and melons benefit from black plastic mulch because it increases soil temperature. Crops that prefer cool growing conditions, such as cabbage, broccoli, and peas, benefit from a light-reflective mulch like hay, rice hulls, or peanut shells that can retain moisture and cool the soil. For more complete information on the types of mulches you can choose for your garden, see "Organic Soil Amendments and Mulches" on page 86.

When a disease strikes, think about the environmental conditions the plant has been living under and whether a mulch can help offset the ill effects. For example, if a planting of lettuce starts to rot near the bottom, close mulching with dry hay could help solve the problem by lifting the leaves off the moist soil surface. On the other hand, pulling mulch away from the crown of a plant that shows signs of rotting can help improve air circulation and reduce soil moisture, which might help reduce the spread of the disease.

Pruning and Trellising

Both of these techniques can be used to help fight disease in the garden. Pruning can be used to promote better air circulation, which helps eliminate the moist, humid conditions that encourage many fungal diseases. For example, thinning out overcrowded clumps of garden phlox by removing several of the stems at the base of the plant will improve air circulation, thus reducing the conditions that promote the fungi that cause powdery mildew. The same technique can be used for lilacs; remove crowded stems to open up the center of the plant and to allow air to circulate more freely. By providing plants with adequate growing room, you can also help improve air circulation.

Growing plants on trellises—or simply staking them so they remain upright, for that matter—also helps air circulation around the foliage. Trellising also exposes leaves to more sunlight, further reducing the chance that moisture will remain on the foliage. It also keeps fruit and foliage off the ground and away from fungi that may lurk in the soil. If you train tomatoes to grow on a pole or in cages you'll end up with fewer rotted tomatoes, since soil-borne fungi can't reach them.

Cucumbers, which are prone to Botrytis rot and other fungal diseases, will benefit from the air circulation provided by both these techniques. If plants are overcrowded, you can prune away extra leaves to allow more air and light to reach the plant. (Space plants more widely to eliminate the problem in future years.) Trellising will also allow air to move freely around the vines.

Watering Techniques

Good watering techniques are crucial in creating an environment that prevents disease. For example, if moisture-dependent fungi are attacking garden plants, it's better to water in the early morning than in the evening, because leaves will be able to dry more quickly, before nightfall. Watering frequently, but lightly, often increases problems with rot diseases. This technique promotes high relative humidity around the plants, creating just the conditions disease organisms prefer. For this reason, watering less frequently, but for longer periods so water reaches deep into the soil, decreases the likelihood that pathogens will be able to gain a foothold.

On the other hand, plants suffering under dry conditions are also more susceptible to disease, simply because they lack vigor. In areas where drought is a common problem, water-conserving soaker hoses or drip irrigation systems are a good investment. Again, long and thorough watering promotes greater plant health. As the soil gains organic matter from regular applications of compost, rotted manure, and other materials, drought will become less of a problem since soils with high humus levels hold more moisture. Be sure to couple good watering and soil-building techniques with the use of mulching for the best water-conserving strategy.

Crop Timing

When you plant is important to disease prevention primarily because of the environmental conditions under which plants grow. Cool, wet conditions promote many fungal diseases. Timing plantings so crops won't grow at the times of year when these conditions are most likely to occur can be an important preventive technique. For example, in northern climates, peas that mature in the late fall almost always contract the rotting fungal diseases that attack most vigorously when morning mists are dense and cool. Consequently, it's sensible to plant the main pea crop in the early spring when these fungi are not as active. If you've had lots of problems with root rot and damping-off attacking your seedlings and transplants in spring, try delaying your spring planting by a couple of weeks next year. This will allow the soil to heat up and dry out a bit more, which should allow plants to get off to a better start.

The timing of your crop can also help you prevent or lessen problems in future growing seasons with diseases that overwinter in the soil. For example, gardeners who normally lose most of their tomato crop at the end of the season to late blight might want to plant a faster-maturing cultivar and pull and compost plants before the disease has a chance to "reseed" in the soil.

Protective timing can sometimes be tricky. It's also a technique used for preventing insect damage, and what works to prevent diseases may not work to protect against insects. For example, in the North, early broccoli and cauliflower can fall victim to cabbage root fly maggots. By planting these crops for fall harvest, you can avoid cabbage maggot problems. But if you wait to plant too late in the season, you may find you have a different pest problem. Tarnished plant bugs seem particularly attracted to late-season cabbage family plants. As they feed, they often transmit black rot bacteria. So, you have averted problems with cabbage maggot, only to end up with rotted plants. It may take a combination of several techniques to successfully grow broccoli or cauliflower. You could plant in spring, using tar paper squares to keep out the cabbage root

flies. Or, you could plant late and cover your plants with floating row covers to prevent tarnished plant bugs from infecting your plants with disease organisms.

Keep the Garden Clean

"Clean" is not an adjective most people apply to their gardens. But chemical-free gardeners know that keeping the garden clean is an important disease-fighting technique. Gardeners who practice good garden sanitation not only have fewer problems with diseases, they'll also cut down on pest and weed problems as well. And while keeping a garden clean is a great deal easier than keeping a house clean, it does require some of the same attention to detail.

Do an Annual Cleanup

Inside the house, it's traditional for the major cleaning effort to come in the spring. Out in the vegetable garden, you should plan to concentrate your cleanup efforts in the fall. At the end of the growing season, routinely remove and compost all plant stalks. Lift plastic mulches and either dispose of them or save them for the following year. Even if you don't plan to use them for plants in the same family next season, form the habit of dipping plastic mulches in a 10 percent bleach solution (1 part bleach to 9 parts water or $1/2$ cup bleach added to $4^1/2$ cups water) and letting them air-dry before rolling and storing.

In the orchard, the time for the annual cleanup is late fall to early winter. You'll want to make an end-of-season inspection tour and pick up all fallen fruit, which may harbor diseases over the winter. Also, shake down any stray fruit and rake up fallen leaves for composting. Check your trees for damaged or dead limbs and prune them out. See "Pruning for Disease Control," on page 152, for complete instructions on how to prune diseased plant parts without spreading disease organisms in the process.

In the flower garden, rake mulch back from plant crowns in fall so they won't be exposed to the cold, damp conditions that promote crown rot. If you've had previous problems with diseases, it's a good idea to remove the mulch completely. Once the ground has frozen for winter, you can add new mulch to protect plants from frost heaving, but be sure to keep it away from the crowns of the plants. You may want to wait until late winter to cut back annuals, perennials, and ornamental grasses, because they can add ornamental interest throughout the winter. The seed heads of coneflowers and the billowy tan clumps of ornamental grasses are especially attractive. But don't leave diseased plant foliage in the garden: Remove and destroy it in fall. And be sure to cut back healthy ornamental foliage well before growth starts in spring.

Sterilize stakes and other supports by dipping them into the bleach solution as well. Give all tools a final cleaning by rinsing them in the bleach solution. After they're dry, wipe the metal parts with a cloth soaked in machinery oil to protect them from rusting over the winter.

Keep the *Gardener* Clean

Keep in mind that soil on shoes, tools, clothes, and hands can carry disease organisms from plant to plant or area to area. For this reason, it's a good idea to wait until the end of your gardening day to work in diseased portions of the garden. This way, you won't inadvertently carry pathogens from one place to another. Change clothes before moving from a diseased plant or area to a healthy one, and sterilize your hands and tools in a 10 percent bleach solution after working on diseased plants, or you could end up transmitting diseases from one part of the garden to another.

Cleaning your shoes can be tricky, but there are ways to manage. Rubber soles and tops or even rubber soles with quick-drying canvas tops are the easiest to sterilize. If you've been working in a part of the garden where diseases are a problem, scrape off any clinging soil into a bucket that will be dumped in the trash (*not* in the garden) or buried far away. Swish the shoes in the bleach solution, scrubbing off any soil with a brush if necessary. If you live in a humid climate, it may take more than overnight for your shoes to dry, so you'll need two pairs of gardening shoes.

The same caveat on washing your shoes applies to your clothing. If diseases are present in the garden, it is a good idea to wash your gardening outfit between wearings.

Clean Tools Regularly

It can be tempting, after a long afternoon spent tending the yard and garden, to simply toss the tools you've used into the shed and shut the door. But if you can muster the energy to wash and sterilize your tools after every use, you will be doing all the plants in your care a favor. Your tools may have come in contact with diseased plant material without you realizing it. If you don't clean them when you put them away (which is the best course of action for the health of your tools, too), clean them before you start to work the next time. This applies to tools you borrow from the neighbors as well; *always* sterilize a borrowed tool before using it in the garden.

To clean your tools, dip them into a bucket containing a 10 percent bleach solution. Wipe them off with a clean rag, let them dry thoroughly, and then apply a coat of light oil to all metal parts.

Inspect All Newcomers to the Garden

Beware of friends and neighbors bearing plants! Beneath the disguise of an innocent gift plant, there may be troublesome pathogens lurking. *Always* inspect new plants and seedlings before planting them in the garden. Look closely for signs of rot, damaged stems or leaves, fungal hyphae or spores, or leaf spots.

Disease Control Checklist

🐛 Grow your own transplants from seed (see "Disease-Free Seed Starting" on page 150) or buy from a reputable grower to ensure that you start out with disease-free plants.

🐛 Grow disease-resistant cultivars whenever possible.

🐛 Keep your soil healthy. Apply generous doses of compost and other organic materials to provide nutrients for your plants and also to promote beneficial organisms in the soil.

🐛 Water and fertilize to keep your plants growing vigorously.

🐛 Rotate crops in your vegetable garden to help keep populations of disease organisms from swelling.

🐛 Clean up dropped leaves around plants during the growing season and remove plant residues in the fall.

🐛 Don't work around plants when they are wet. Moist conditions favor the germination of fungal disease spores, which can be carried from plant to plant on your hands, clothes, shoes, and tools.

🐛 Water plants early in the day so foliage drys quickly.

🐛 Wash your tools after use and disinfect them with a 10 percent bleach solution (1 part bleach to 9 parts water). Disinfect pruning tools after every cut when pruning diseased plant tissues.

🐛 When disease problems threaten to reduce yields or kill plants, use sulfur and copper fungicides to help prevent their recurrence or spread.

Inspecting perennials for disease is sometimes difficult. Some symptoms are just too subtle to see without a microscope. However, if you buy only certified perennial stock from reputable nurseries, you have some assurance that the plant is disease-free. You can plant it where it is meant to live out its life and remove it if it does manifest disease symptoms. In the case of gift perennials or those dug from a friend's garden, you might want to plant those in a temporary site, away from the main garden beds, where you can observe them for any disease symptoms. Once you feel comfortable issuing them a clean bill of health, you can transplant them to their permanent location.

You have less risk of importing disease on purchased annuals, because most greenhouses buy good seed, plant in sterile media, control the environment carefully, and destroy flats of plants with disease problems.

Check Out the Neighborhood

Nearby wild areas, such as stream banks, and waste areas, such as vacant lots or construction sites, may be reservoirs of disease organisms that could migrate into your garden. Many common weeds belong to the same botanical families as some of your garden plants and may suffer from some of the same diseases. Walk through these areas routinely. Gather any diseased plants you find and dispose of them as you do diseased garden plants.

If you want to take extra precautions, refer to "Weed Control Methods," on page 118, to find out the families to which weeds belong. If you have had problems with disease on your cabbage family (Cruciferae) plants in the past, you may want to pay particular attention to removing weeds from that family, even if they don't show disease symptoms. If you need help identifying the weeds you see, check "The Chemical-Free Gardener's Library," on page 431, for the names of some good weed identification guides.

Rotate Crops

Rotating annual crops—changing their placement in the vegetable and flower garden each year—is a crucial element in your disease-prevention program and may help you fight diseases once they occur.

Understanding Rotation

To use rotation effectively, it's helpful to understand the terminology used to describe the relationships between plants. A plant species is the name given to a particular plant. For example, snap beans are *Phaseolus vulgaris.* Lima beans are closely related to snap beans. Limas belong to the same genus, *Phaseolus,* as snap beans, but are a different species, *P. limensis.* Beans are less closely related to peas, which belong to the genus *Pisum.* Beans and peas do belong to the same botanical family: Leguminosae, the legumes.

Disease organisms vary in their ability to infect different kinds of plants. Some species of fungi or bacteria may only infect a single species. Many can infect a few closely related species or several members of a plant family.

When you rotate crops, you change the type of plant growing in a particular spot in your garden. For example, suppose you plant cabbage in one bed in your vegetable garden. There may be some fungi in the soil in the bed that cause disease, perhaps club root. The fungi infect the cabbage, but due to your good garden management, the cabbages still grow fairly well and produce good heads. You may not even be aware that they are diseased. However, during the growing season, the fungal population is increasing. If you plant cabbage in the same spot next season, the fungi will be ready to launch a more powerful attack and may damage your cabbage so much that yields are reduced.

However, if part of your standard gardening practice is to not replant the same crop in the same area, the fungal population will have no plants to infect. With no food source, some of the fungi will die off. But fungal spores can wait in a dormant state for more than one year, so a three- to five-year rotation is needed to

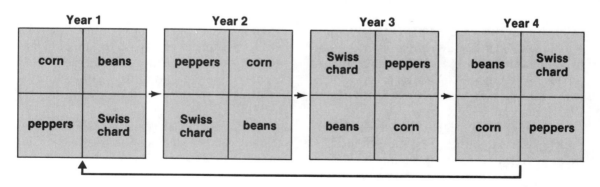

Rotating crops is like playing follow-the-leader. In the example above, think of beans as the "leader." In each succeeding year, corn grows in the bed where beans grew the year before. Peppers follow corn, and Swiss chard follows peppers. In your garden, rotation may be a more complicated game. If you grow several members of one crop family, you may not have sufficient space or variety of crops to do a full three- to five-year rotation.

really "starve out" the pathogen. Also, since many pathogens can infect several members of a plant family, you must concentrate on rotating *families* of crops, not just particular species. In the club root example, rotating cabbage is not enough. You must also be sure you don't replace the cabbage with other cabbage family crops: broccoli, cauliflower, brussels sprouts, or kohlrabi.

Rules of Rotation

There are two basic rotation rules to keep diseases from gaining a foothold in the garden.

Rotate plant families. Leave at least two, and preferably three or more, years between the time that members of the same plant family grow in the same ground. "Plant Families," below, lists the major plant families and the individual

Plant Families

Family Name	Members
Chenopodiaceae (goosefoot family)	Beets, chard, spinach
Compositae (daisy family)	Celtuce, chicory, dandelions, endive, lettuce, marigolds, sunflowers
Cruciferae (cabbage family or crucifers, or brassicas)	Alyssums, bok choy, broccoli, brussels sprouts, cabbage, cauliflower, collards, cress, kale, kohlrabi, many oriental greens, radishes, rutabagas, turnips
Cucurbitaceae (squash family or cucurbits)	Cucumbers, gourds, melons, pumpkins, squash
Gramineae (grass family)	Barley, corn, oats, rice, rye, wheat
Leguminosae (pea or bean family, legumes)	Alfalfa, beans, lupine, peanuts, peas, soybeans
Liliaceae (lily family or alliums)	Chives, garlic, leeks, onions, shallots
Polygonaceae (buckwheat family)	Buckwheat, sorrel
Rosaceae (rose family)	Bramble berries, strawberries
Solanaceae (nightshade family or solanaceous crops)	Eggplant, nicotiana, peppers, petunias, potatoes, tomatoes
Umbelliferae (parsley or carrot family)	Carrots, celeriac, celery, chervil, dill, parsley, parsnips

crops that belong to them. You can also check the family affiliations of the vegetables and flowers you are growing by referring to individual entries in part 3, "Chemical-Free Garden Guides."

Pay attention to nutritional needs along with disease prevention.   When planning rotations, keep in mind that some crops are heavy feeders, which means they take up significant amounts of nutrients from the soil as they grow. Others are light feeders, meaning they drain comparatively few nutrients as they grow. Avoid following one heavy nitrogen-user, corn for example, with another, say squash, unless you apply liberal quantities of compost or well-rotted manure between one season and the next.

Legume crops build soil nitrogen reserves. Using one of these nitrogen-supplying crops, such as peas or beans, before a nitrogen-user, helps reduce fertilizer needs. By staggering legumes, light feeders, and heavy feeders, you avoid draining the soil's nutrient levels. This has a dual benefit; it reduces the need for supplemental fertilizing, and it also boosts plant vigor, which encourages healthy growth and disease resistance. See "Feeding Habits in the Garden," on the opposite page, to see what crops fall into what category and how to plan rotations. Don't forget green manure crops in planning your rotation. Taking a bed out of production for a year to plant green manure can have the double benefit of improving soil quality and lessening disease problems.

Exceptions to the Rules

There are pathogens that can cross family boundaries to attack crops in several different families. This means that rotating plant families may not help to control these disease problems. For example, the bacterium *Pseudomonas marginalis* causes lettuce leaves to rot from the margins inward and may also cause butt rot, a soft rot of the stem tissue. This bacterium can also infect bean pods, cucumbers, peas, and potatoes (none of these crops belong to the same family as lettuce), causing various rot symptoms.

If you have a serious disease outbreak in your garden, your best course of action is to gather samples and get a precise identification of the pathogen involved. (See "Know Your Enemy," on page 129, for suggestions on how to identify pathogens.) You can then determine what other crops that pathogen might infect. If the pathogen only attacks one or a few species, using rotation to break the disease cycle is a good option. If the pathogen is one that can cross family lines, rotation may not be useful, unless you have a large vegetable garden and plant a wide variety of food and cover crops.

If the disease problems in your garden seem too complicated to solve with a rotation plan, rely on the other control methods outlined in this chapter to solve the problem. In any case, you can still use rotation as a helpful technique for preventing disease organisms from becoming a serious problem.

Other Good Gardening Practices

Good gardening practices contribute to plant health in many ways, even when it comes to disease prevention. Below, you'll find a checklist of other easy, commonsense cultural controls you can use to help keep diseases from becoming a problem in your garden. You may already be practicing some of these, while others may be new to you. It doesn't hurt to brush up on the basics, especially when the health of your garden is at stake.

Stay Away When It's Wet

Because so many fungi travel in water and germinate in a film of moisture, it's best to stay out of the garden when plants are wet. This caution extends even to morning mists and eve-

Feeding Habits in the Garden

As you plan your rotations, follow heavy feeders by light feeders the second season and by soil builders the third. Or, follow heavy feeders by soil builders and then by light feeders the third season. Try never to have heavy feeders following light feeders.

Heavy Feeders	Light Feeders	Soil Builders
Asparagus	Beets	Alfalfa
Broccoli	Carrots	Broad beans
Brussels sprouts	Garlic	Clover
Cabbage	Leeks	Lima beans
Cauliflower	Mustard	Peanuts
Celery	Onions	Peas
Collards	Parsnips	Snap beans
Corn	Peppers	Soybeans
Cucumbers	Potatoes	
Eggplant	Rutabagas	
Endive	Shallots	
Escarole	Sweet potatoes	
Kale	Swiss chard	
Kohlrabi	Turnips	
Lettuce		
Okra		
Parsley		
Pumpkins		
Radishes		
Rhubarb		
Spinach		
Squash, summer and winter		
Tomatoes		

ning dews. Make it a habit to wait until plants are dry before stepping so much as a foot into the flower or vegetable garden.

Spray the Right Way

Foliar spraying is an effective way to deliver nutrients to plants (see "Using Liquid Organic Fertilizers," on page 88, for a complete discussion of this technique), and the nutrient boost it gives plants can also encourage disease resistance. However, poor spraying practices can ultimately *cause* plant diseases.

Spray in early morning before plants are subjected to the harsh rays of the midday sun. Never spray at night in areas with high humidity. When the sun is at its highest, spray droplets on the leaves can act as tiny but powerful magnifying glasses. Tissue under the droplets literally burns, leaving little dead patches on the leaf or stem. Pathogens have no trouble finding an entryway through this damage.

Don't spray in the evening in areas with high humidity. The leaves will remain wet throughout the night, and many fungal spores germinate best in a thin film of water on the leaves. Leaves that are wet for long periods are thus more prone to disease problems.

Handle with Care

Rough handling can also create entryways for disease organisms. Plant tissues are so fragile that one leaf brushing against another can create a bruise. Don't touch your plants unless

you have to. If you want to check leaf texture or thickness by feeling a leaf, always touch an older, lower leaf rather than a new one on the top.

TLC for Seedlings

If you grow your own seedlings, make sure they get a healthy start in life. Seedling diseases such as damping-off can be controlled by using sterile seed-starting mix, making sure plants have good air circulation, and keeping soil moisture and humidity at moderate levels. See "Disease-Free Seed Starting," below, for suggestions on making your own seed-starting mix.

Raise seedlings in individual containers: soil blocks, peat pots, plastic pots, or any other

---

Disease-Free Seed Starting

If you want to ensure that your transplants are completely chemical-free, starting them yourself from seed may be a necessity. Most transplants sold at garden centers have been treated with chemical fertilizers and pesticides.

It's not difficult to avoid the diseases that commonly prey on new seedlings without using chemicals. Along with providing the proper environmental conditions, using a sterile seed-starting medium is essential. If you are making your own mixture, you can choose from such ingredients as vermiculite, perlite, and sphagnum moss. Vermiculite is a mica-based mineral that has been heated to make it expand to many times its original size. Perlite is a volcanic ash that has also been heated and "popped." Sphagnum is a type of moss that has been collected while still alive from acid bogs and then dried; milled sphagnum moss has been finely ground to allow easier spreading. Besides being relatively sterile, sphagnum moss also provides good moisture-holding capacity and helps control bacterial diseases in seedlings.

Because of its acidic nature, it is a good idea to add limestone to sphagnum moss to provide a more neutral soil environment.

Here are two recipes that you can use to make your own seed-starting medium. It's best to water your germinating seedlings with plain water, as some organic fertilizers may provide a medium for the growth of disease organisms. Once your transplants are established, you can transplant them to a mix that contains organic nutrients (see "Chemical-Free Transplants," on page 280 for recipes for these mixes). Or, feed them regularly with a balanced organic fertilizer, such as liquid seaweed extract, until you transplant them outdoors.

1 part sphagnum	1 part sphagnum
1 part vermiculite	1 part vermiculite
	1 part perlite

For either of the recipes above, add 1 tablespoon of lime for each 2 quarts of sphagnum you use.

---

type of container. Transplanting is less of a shock when seedlings are in separate containers. When transplanting seedlings grown massed in a flat or large container, you must pull the tangled, matted roots apart. This is physically damaging to the plant, no matter how careful you are. The broken roots are open doorways for many soil-borne diseases. If you do use flats, space the plants far enough apart so that root damage will be minimal at transplanting time.

PHYSICAL CONTROLS

Using cultural methods to keep plants growing vigorously and to avoid environmental conditions that favor disease is important but doesn't provide a guarantee that your garden will be disease-free. Once diseases strike, the next line of defense is using physical controls to remove the disease organisms from your garden. You can pick off leaves or flowers that show signs of diseases or cut away diseased portions of plants such as stem tips or entire stalks. In the case of root or crown rots and other soil-borne diseases, it's best to dig the entire plant—both roots and surrounding soil—and dispose of it. For some soil-borne diseases, you can use the sun's heat through a technique called solarization to kill pathogens. These techniques will help keep diseases from spreading within a single plant or from spreading through the garden.

Dispose of Diseases Properly

Keep an eye open for diseased plants every time you work in the garden. Carry a paper or plastic bag along with you, and put any diseased plant parts in the bag as soon as you remove them from the plant. Otherwise, spores may scatter from the diseased material as you carry it away for disposal, and you could inadvertently spread disease problems to healthy plants.

The proper way to dispose of diseased

Dealing with Damping-Off

Does this scene sound familiar? Your seeds have sprouted, and the tiny seedlings are growing and doing fine. But suddenly one day you find them keeled over, with rotted or girdled stems. The culprit? Damping-off.

Many of the fungi that cause what is commonly known as damping-off disease (the rotting and death of germinating seeds or tiny seedlings) can infect almost any plant. Using rotation to avoid damping-off is almost impossible. Instead, combat the disease with environmental management. For seeds sown directly in the garden, plant sparsely enough so that air circulation is good, cover light-loving seeds with vermiculite rather than soil in areas where damping-off has been a problem in previous years, and work to improve soil aeration and drainage. Indoors, sow seeds in sterile seed-sowing mix, covering them with mix or milled sphagnum moss (not sphagnum peat). Make sure soil moisture and humidity don't get too high. Good air circulation also helps reduce problems with damping-off.

plant parts depends on the nature of the disease. A freshly made, hot compost pile will heat up to 160°F or higher, which is sufficient to kill pathogenic fungi and bacteria. Be sure to put the diseased plant material in the center of the pile, where temperatures are highest. If you don't have a newly made hot compost pile, or if you use the slower, cold-composting method (see "Compost: Nature's Black Magic," on page 68, for a complete discussion of both methods), it's best to dispose of diseased plant material in the trash or bury it in an out-of-the-way spot. Viruses may not be killed even in a hot compost pile. If you suspect the diseased plant material is infected with a virus, either bury the prunings in an out-of-the-way area or put them in a sealed bag for disposal with the household trash.

Pruning for Disease Control

Pruning is an important cultural technique for preventing disease. Proper pruning helps trees and shrubs grow more vigorously by opening them up for good light penetration and air circulation.

Pruning is also important if disease strikes your fruit trees, bramble crops, or ornamental trees and shrubs. Removing diseased branches is one way to stop disease organisms from spreading through a woody plant. However, you'll need to take some extra precautions when pruning diseased trees or shrubs.

Be sure you prune enough tissue to stop the advance of a disease. Some disease organisms stay localized near the canker or other diseased area. For example, *Phomopsis* galls on ornamental shrubs are localized. Pruning away the gall should remove the pathogen. However, the fungus that causes dieback of rose advances past the canker without producing symptoms. You must prune what appears to be healthy tissue several inches away from the diseased area to ensure that you have removed all the diseased wood. As in any pruning situation, always be sure to prune a branch back properly to a healthy bud or to a main limb. Never leave a stub of bare wood, as it will die and become a likely site of entry for other disease or insect pests.

When pruning diseased tissue, you must sterilize your pruning tools between each cut. Carry along a bucket containing a 10 percent bleach solution (1 part bleach to 9 parts water). After each cut, dip the tool in the solution for 15 seconds. When you finish your pruning work, sterilize each of the tools you used for a final time, and then rinse them with clean water. Then coat all metal parts with a light oil.

Solarizing Soil

Soil solarization, covering the soil with clear plastic in midsummer, is an effective way to control soil-borne disease organisms. It also provides effective control for weeds and pathogenic nematodes. Since this technique depends on heat generated by the sun, it's a summertime activity in northern regions where cool, cloudy springs are the norm. Solarization works best in southern regions where both air temperatures and sun intensity are high.

Some studies also indicate that solarizing soil seems to have beneficial effects on plant growth, even beyond killing plant pathogens. What's not known is whether solarizing soil kills the beneficial nematodes and microorganisms along with the harmful ones. Solarization will kill all insects in the top layers of soil, including the ground beetles that prey on plant pests and the centipedes and other insects that are important in the decay cycle. So don't rush to solarize all your garden beds. Save this technique for times when you have a serious disease or weed problem that needs to be solved.

The best time to solarize is mid-June to mid-August in most parts of the country. Use 1- to 4-mil clear plastic. Black plastic won't heat subsurface soil enough to be effective. You'll likely have to leave the plastic in place for four weeks or more, depending on your climate and on the particular weather conditions during the time you solarize.

You can solarize plots as small as 2-by-3 feet. Begin by preparing the soil as you would for planting. Remove all weeds and crop residues, especially diseased plant material. (Plant tissue will insulate the disease pathogens from heat.) Turn under compost and other amendments, and then rake the surface smooth. Be sure to break up soil clods and remove surface stones, as they can hold the plastic away from the soil surface, creating air spaces that slow heating. After you finish preparing the soil, water it

To solarize a garden bed, stretch a sheet of clear plastic tightly over a smooth, moist soil surface and leave it in place for as long as several weeks. The heat that builds up in the covered soil will kill most soil-borne pathogens and weed seeds.

thoroughly. It takes less heat to kill organisms when the soil is wet, and moisture conducts heat deep into the soil. The best way to saturate the soil is to leave a sprinkler running on the plot for several hours.

Next, dig a trench several inches deep around the edge of the plot, then cover the plot with plastic. Be sure the edges of the plastic line the trench on all sides. Fill in the trench with soil, anchoring the plastic as tightly as possible with the soil as you go.

You can use a soil thermometer to check

the temperature of the soil. Just pull back a section of the plastic and insert the thermometer. You'll notice that the area in the middle of the solarized spot is warmer than those near the edges. Keep a record of the temperatures and after the soil has stabilized at its highest temperature, leave the plastic in place for about three more days. Refer to "Effects of Heat on Soil Life," on page 155, to check whether the temperatures your soil reaches are high enough to destroy the disease organisms or weed seeds that were causing problems.

After you finish solarizing, remove the plastic. If you wish to reuse, clean and dry it well before storing it. Since solarizing may have a detrimental effect on soil microorganisms that help make nutrients in organic matter available to plants, it's a good idea to feed solarized soil with a microbe-rich material such as compost or aged manure.

Row Covers

Floating row covers provide effective physical control against plant diseases by preventing insect feeding that can lead to disease infection. Insect damage can lead to disease problems because it creates wounds in plant tissue where fungi and bacteria can enter. Some insects, such as aphids and leafhoppers, can also be vectors that transmit disease organisms as they feed. See "Floating Row Covers," on page 196, for more information on row covers and how to use them in the garden.

CHEMICAL CONTROLS

Good garden management will generally keep disease from getting out of hand in your garden. However, there may be specific situations where disease problems become serious enough to ruin the harvest of a crop or even to threaten the life of a tree. Fruit crops, especially in certain parts of North America, are most prone to suffer from significant disease problems. If cultural and physical controls don't seem to be helping, there are organically acceptable chemical sprays you can use as a last resort.

This section contains directions for making sprays yourself, whenever that's possible. It also lists brand names of commercial products if the commercial products are commonly sold according to brand name. Remember, brand names may change throughout the years. Some sample product names are listed here, but the best way to ensure you get the product you want is to check the ingredients on the label.

Growth-Enhancing Sprays

There are a few sprays you can prepare from plant materials that help to lessen disease problems. These sprays are not fungicides or bactericides. Rather, they contain nutrients and hormones that help plants grow more vigorously, and so may help them to remain productive even when infected by a disease.

Stinging Nettle Spray

Stinging nettles, commonly viewed as troublesome weeds, can form the main ingredient in an effective growth enhancing spray. Known botanically as *Urtica dioica*, stinging nettles can be found throughout the eastern half of the United States, eastern Washington state, Idaho, Colorado, and into northern Texas. They also grow throughout southern Canada. These bristly plants grow from 2 to 6 feet tall and sport hairy leaves, which contain an acid that can sting and burn bare skin. When you forage for wild plants, be sure to wear pants, a long-sleeved shirt, and thick gloves. Try to collect healthy plants, as they will be the richest in growth-enhancing compounds. Look for plants growing in fertile, well-drained soil, in full sun. If you cannot collect your own, you can order a concentrate from some mail-order suppliers, particularly those specializing in biodynamic preparations.

Effects of Heat on Soil Life

Solarization kills organisms in the soil by raising soil temperature. This technique is an effective nonchemical way to kill many disease pathogens and weed seeds. However, it may also kill some beneficial organisms, such as ground beetles and other soil-dwelling insects that attack plant pests.

Temperature (°F)	Destroys
120	Nematodes, sclerotium rots
125	Damping-off (*Rhizoctonia solani*)
130	Botrytis gray mold
135	Fusarium yellows
140	Most plant pathogenic bacteria, fungi, earthworms, slugs, centipedes
150–160	Soil insects
160	Most plant viruses, all plant pathogenic bacteria
160–175	Most weed seeds
200–212	A few resistant plant viruses and weed seeds

Protection offered: Stinging nettle spray can help plants resist infection by many fungal diseases. On a plant with a mild case of Botrytis rot or powdery mildew, pick off infected areas and spray to help the plant resist further infection. During prolonged cool, wet periods, you can also spray as a preventive measure to strengthen the plants. Stinging nettle tea also repels aphids and gives plants a good dose of trace elements.

How to make: Gather 1 pound of plants or leaves. Crush the leaves and put them into a burlap bag or old pillowcase. Submerge the bag in a bucket containing 1 gallon of unchlorinated water. Cover the bucket, place it in a warm area, and let it sit for about one week.

When you open the bucket, be prepared: The odor will be strong. Strain the mixture through cheesecloth. Store any extra concentrate in glass jars, but don't keep it longer than one month.

How to use: To use, dilute the nettle concentrate by adding 5 parts unchlorinated water to 1 part concentrate. Depending on the seriousness of the disease problem, spray from once every two weeks to once a month.

Horsetail Spray

You don't need to visit a stable for the main ingredient of this spray. It's composed of dried horsetail, botanically known as *Equisetum arvense*. Dried horsetail is available from suppliers specializing in biodynamic garden supplies.

Protection offered: There is no scientific evidence to indicate how horsetail spray helps plants resist disease. In general, it is used as a preventive for fungal diseases.

How to make: In a glass or stainless steel pot, mix $1/8$ cup of dried leaves in 1 gallon of unchlorinated water. (If you have chlorinated tap water, either collect rainwater or let the tap water sit, uncovered, for two days so the chlorine will volatilize.) Bring to a boil, then let simmer for at least $1/2$ hour. Cool and strain through cheesecloth. Store extra concentrate in a glass container. This mixture keeps for a month.

How to use: Dilute the horsetail concentrate by adding 5 to 10 parts unchlorinated water to every 1 part concentrate. Spray infected plants once every week to two weeks. If you suspect that an outbreak of fungal diseases is imminent because of the prevailing weather conditions, begin a preventive spraying program even before you spot any symptoms.

Seaweed Spray

Often viewed as a supplemental source of nutrients, liquid seaweed can also help protect against disease problems in the garden. However, a word of warning is in order. Because fish emulsion is a good medium for fungal growth, don't use a concentrate that contains a mixture of seaweed and fish emulsion for disease control.

Protection offered: Liquid seaweed sprays can help many plants that are mildly diseased by generally promoting better growth and development. They do not have fungicidal or bactericidal activity. Try spraying a seaweed solution on diseased plants as one facet of your overall disease management strategy.

How to use: To use liquid seaweed as a fungus fighter in the garden, it must first be diluted. On plants that are sickly, dilute to half the rate recommended on the label and spray once a week. On fairly vigorous plants, follow the recommended dilution and spray only every two weeks or once a month. See "Kelp Extracts" and "Kelp Meal," on page 104, for more information on seaweed sprays.

Fungicides and Bactericides

You can make a fungicidal spray from baking soda or garlic, or use one of four sprays that have mineral elements as their active ingredients: sulfur, lime sulfur, copper, and bordeaux mix. Except for garlic oil spray, these sprays are too complex for the home gardener to prepare from scratch. It's best to buy them at garden centers or through mail-order suppliers. Commercial products named below are not a complete listing of available products (also remember that brand names may change). Carefully follow the mixing instructions and application rates recommended on the particular product you buy.

Recommending how frequently to apply a particular spray is also tricky business. As a chemical-free gardener, one of your goals is to keep the use of sprays—even these environmentally safe ones—to a bare minimum. There are a number of variables in the equation that give you the frequency of spraying. How severe are the disease symptoms? What are the temperature and relative humidity levels? A warm, wet spring or hot, humid summer can encourage the spread of fungi, so more frequent spraying may be necessary. Instead of spraying once every other week, as you would under dry conditions, you might need to up the frequency to once a week or once every couple days in especially wet weather. Start with the frequency rates recommended on the product you are using. Try to spray only when absolutely necessary, based on the particular combination of variables you are facing in your garden. And always remember that these sprays are caustic. Spraying too much and too often can end up harming the plants you are trying to protect as well as beneficial soil microbes and insects. For more tips on fashioning a fungicidal spray program, see "Planning *Your* Spray Program" on page 349.

Also, remember that these sprays can be harmful if they get on your skin or in your eyes. Follow all safety procedures you would for spraying any toxic substance. See "Spray Safely!"

on page 220, for a list of safety procedures to follow every time you spray.

Baking Soda

Old-fashioned baking soda has 101 uses, and one of them is controlling fungal disease.

Protection offered: Research has shown that an 0.5 percent solution of baking soda will help prevent roses from being damaged by black spot. It may also help prevent other fungus diseases. The mechanism of action of the baking soda solution is not known.

How to make: You can make a baking soda spray by dissolving 1 teaspoon of baking soda in 1 quart of water. Try adding a few drops of liquid soap or insecticidal soap to the solution to help it spread more evenly on the leaves.

How to use: Spray infected plants thoroughly, including the undersides of leaves.

Garlic Oil

While research shows that garlic has fungicidal and insecticidal properties, it is not a registered pesticide. However, you may find it effective for many purposes in the home garden.

Protection offered: You'll have to experiment with applying this spray for disease control; some reports indicate it is effective for combating mildews.

How to Make: For information on how to make and use garlic oils sprays, see "Garlic Oil Sprays" on page 216.

Sulfur

Farmers and gardeners have been using sulfur as a fungicide for thousands of years. It still has a place in a chemical-free gardener's judicious spraying program. Sulfur does not actually kill fungal spores. It prevents infestations because fungal spores cannot germinate in a sulfur film, and therefore cannot get a foothold on the plant. In order to be effective, the sulfur film must be on the leaf before the spores land. So in wet conditions, where the sulfur may be frequently washed away, and when spores may be produced in greater numbers, repeated sprays are necessary for good protection.

Protection offered: Sulfur sprays help protect many crops, including grapes, potatoes, strawberries, tomatoes, and tree fruits from outbreaks of brown rot, leaf spot, powdery mildew, and scab. It will also help reduce spider mite infestations on fruit trees.

How to use: Sulfur is sold as a powder or liquid. Powdered sulfur adheres well to plant surfaces and provides more even distribution. Liquid sulfur is less disruptive to beneficial insects and is easier to apply. Do not spray sulfur within two to three weeks of applying an oil spray, and do not spray when temperatures exceed 85°F.

Commercial products: Liquid sulfur or sulfur dust; Bonide Liquid Sulfur; Micronized Sulfur (powdered); Safer's Fungicide-Miticide; That Liquid Sulfur

Future Options for Fighting Fungi

Recent research indicates that two products not usually thought of as fungicides can help protect plants from fungal infections. Antitranspirants, such as Wilt-Pruf and Safer's Forever Green, are sprayed on trees and shrubs in fall to help protect them from winter damage. They also seem to help prevent spores that cause diseases such as powdery mildew from germinating and infecting plants.

Similarly, dormant-oil sprays used to smother overwintering insects and insect eggs on many trees and shrubs may also keep disease spores from infecting plants. (For more information on dormant oil, see "Dormant Oils" on page 212.) Both of these products are considered safe and acceptable for use by organic gardeners. Watch to see whether these products are eventually approved and registered for use as fungicides.

Lime Sulfur

Adding lime to sulfur enhances its effectiveness as a fungicide. The lime allows the sulfur to penetrate the leaf tissue, giving the sulfur the ability to kill recently germinated spores. It is more caustic than a plain sulfur spray and more likely to cause damage to plant tissue.

Protection offered: Lime sulfur sprays help control diseases, such as anthracnose, brown rot, leaf spot, mildew, and scab, as well as scale insects on dormant perennials, roses, foundation evergreens, and many fruit crops.

How to use: Wait two to three weeks after applying an oil spray before spraying lime sulfur. Never spray during periods when temperatures will exceed 85°F. You can rotate (alternate) sprays of sulfur and lime sulfur, so that you can have the benefit of lime sulfur's added fungicidal effectiveness, but reduce the possibility of leaf damage. Apply in early spring on dormant shrubs like lilacs and roses and evergreens such as juniper. On roses suffering from powdery mildew, apply when buds break in spring and again a week later. Spray raspberries infected with anthracnose or blight when the buds first show silver. Spray currants and gooseberries infected with anthracnose at bud break and again in 10 to 15 days.

Commercial products: Lime Sulfur

Copper

Copper sulfate is another chemical compound that will inhibit the germination and growth of fungal spores. It is also somewhat effective against bacterial spores. When mixed with other compounds, such as micronized sulfur, sodium carbonate, or hydroxide, copper can then penetrate the leaf tissue and will actually kill fungal and bacterial spores. However, the penetrating mixtures are also more likely to cause leaf damage.

Protection offered: Copper sprays help control anthracnose, bacterial leaf spot, black rot, blights, downy mildew, peach leaf curl, and Septoria leaf spot on fruit crops, nuts, and vegetable crops, especially peppers, potatoes, squash family crops, and tomatoes.

How to use: Copper is available in powdered or liquid form. Both are equally effective; choose the method of application that is preferable to you. Copper may be applied up to one day before harvest. Spray copper solutions in the early morning in very dry, bright weather so that they have a chance to dry. Otherwise, the solution may penetrate the leaf too far and kill the tissue. Use copper sprays rather than sulfur if you have sprayed dormant oil in the preceding two to three weeks.

Commercial products: Bonide Liquid Copper; Burgundy Mixture; Kocide; Top Cop; Top Cop with Sulfur

Bordeaux Mix

For centuries, grape growers in Europe relied on this mix of naturally occurring minerals to protect their crops from the ravages of fungal diseases. Modern-day gardeners can also take advantage of its disease-fighting powers. Keep in mind that bordeaux mix (copper sulfate and hydrated lime) is the most potent organic fungicide. You should always consider this the absolute last resort. *Never* apply it at rates higher than those recommended on the bottle.

Protection offered: Use bordeaux mix to fight anthracnose, black rot, blight, leaf spot, and mildew, on flowers, hardy ornamentals, small fruits, and shade trees.

How to use: Bordeaux mix is available in powdered form and may be dusted on plants or mixed with water to apply as a spray. For edible crops, be sure to use solutions at *half* the recommended dilution for trees and hardy ornamentals. If bordeaux is applied in cool, damp weather, plants may be injured. *Always read the dilution rates and follow them carefully.*

Commercial products: Bordeaux mix

CHAPTER SEVEN

Insect Control

By Linda A. Gilkeson

Controlling insect pests in your yard and garden organically will be one of your easier gardening tasks. There is a wide range of nonchemical control methods and products for combating insect problems. Interest in controlling pests without chemicals is on the upsurge, for farmers as well as home gardeners. Farmers are using sophisticated new products, and even computer systems, to help them battle insect pests with fewer or no pesticide applications.

In the home organic garden, you don't need a computer to manage pest problems. However, a systematic approach to dealing with pests will help prevent many problems from becoming serious enough to affect yields or damage plants.

You'll find organic pest management is a more casual system than the chemical-driven approach that relies on strict spray schedules for control. It involves blending natural methods and defenses into all your garden activities, beginning before you plant in spring and con-

tinuing throughout fall and winter. For example, it's possible to minimize damage by coordinating planting times to take advantage of weak points in the behavior or life cycles of pests. There are also physical barriers or traps you can use to stop pests from reaching your plants. It's also possible to have the native natural enemies of pests do much of your pest control work. In this chapter, you'll learn how to design and manage your gardens to encourage as many "good bugs" as possible.

The key to the system is to encourage your garden's natural resistance to pests and to work with the natural balance of beneficial and pest insects and organisms. When selecting a control method, start with the least intrusive step. Ask yourself what effect your control method will have on the rest of your garden. For example, watering frequently to keep plants healthy has little harmful effect anywhere in the garden. But spraying pyrethrin to control Colorado potato beetles may also kill many lady beetles or other beneficial insects that are near your potato plants.

Organic insect management is a blend of four types of control.

🐛 *Cultural controls.* These gardening practices emphasize keeping plants healthy, selecting well-adapted cultivars, and keeping the garden clean.

🐛 *Biological controls.* Encouraging and protecting populations of naturally occurring insect predators and parasites of insect pests is fundamental to organic pest management. They are your best allies in the garden. You can supplement their effect by releasing insectary-raised predators and parasites or by using microbial sprays to apply various diseases that infect pest insects.

🐛 *Physical controls.* Insect pests can be physically destroyed in order to stop the damage they do and avoid the dangers of using chemicals to kill them. These methods range from the primitive—handpicking and squashing bugs—to the complex—traps that lure insects in and then don't let them out.

🐛 *Chemical controls.* If pests get out of balance in your garden, overwhelming the capacity of other control methods to stop them, there are certain sprays and dusts that are acceptable for the home organic gardener to apply. These are derived from plant sources and are not as persistent in the environment as synthetic pesticides. However, they are toxins, and as such, should be used only as a last resort.

In this chapter, you'll find many specific examples of all four control categories. If you are a novice gardener, *don't panic!* Only a few species of pests are likely to bother a garden in any one area or at any one time. Insect populations often occur in cycles and are worse some years than others. For example, more Colorado potato beetles may survive after a mild winter, an unusually wet spring favors slugs, or a dry summer favors spider mites. I have gardened in many areas and climates across the continent.

In each area, only a few pests were recurring problems. For example, when I lived in one of Canada's prime potato-growing areas, Colorado potato beetles were a persistent pest. I also could count on slugs, cutworms in spring, and imported cabbageworms on cole crops. And while I always protected cabbage seedlings from root flies, the few pea weevils and corn earworms that arrived were too minor to need action.

When I lived in another, hotter area, I had to deal with imported cabbageworms, corn earworms, and tomato hornworms. In my present garden, carrot root flies are a number one problem, slugs are bad, cabbage aphids definitely require action, and beet leafminers are annoying for a few weeks. But, there are so few imported cabbageworms that I don't bother to control them. And to keep things in perspective, the worst damage to my gardens has always been from straying livestock, pets, or local wildlife. I battled for my city corn patch with cheeky squirrels, not corn borers.

In each of my gardens, I have been able to solve most pest problems without resorting to even the most innocuous sprays. Over the years, I've realized that it was my casual approach that kept pest numbers low: using permanent soil beds, lots of flowers and herbs, and a few stray weeds mixed in with the vegetables. You'll find that some simple measures, such as using cutworm collars or root fly barriers, are so easy and work so well, using them becomes routine. As you gain experience, chemical-free insect control will become a natural part of your garden schedule.

DIAGNOSING PEST PROBLEMS

Before you can use a pest control system, you need to know the identity of your pest. Insects are an incredibly diverse group of creatures, and you'll need to understand their hab-

Insect Life Cycles and Lifestyles

Life Cycles

Some insects have strange and complicated life cycles, but in general, they follow one of two main patterns:

Complete metamorphosis. So called because during a resting stage, the immature insect is transformed into an adult that looks entirely unlike the immature stage.

This life cycle begins with the egg. It hatches into a tiny, immature insect—a larva (plural is larvae). All young insects are larvae, some are also called by other names: A caterpillar is the larva of a moth or butterfly; a grub is a fat, C-shaped beetle larva; a maggot is a fly larva.

As the larvae grow, they shed their skins periodically until they reach maximum size. Then they are transformed into a resting stage, called a pupa. The pupa is a hardened shell that protects the developing adult inside. To protect themselves during pupation, some larvae spin a silken outer case, a cocoon (made by moths and some flies) or chrysalis (spun by butterflies). When the adult has developed fully, it emerges from the pupa. When the new adult first appears, it is soft, pliable, and light-colored. Over the next few hours, the wings expand as the insect pumps blood into its veins and the exoskeleton (the insect's hard outer covering) gradually hardens and darkens as chemical reactions take place.

Incomplete metamorphosis. So called because the development from immature to adult stage is gradual, without a pupal stage.

The insect starts life as an egg, which hatches into a larva that is often called a nymph. The nymphs shed their skins as they grow, becoming more like an adult with each molt. They get progressively larger, their bodies lengthen, and wing pads develop where future wings will be. The last molt is to the adult stage, with fully formed wings and reproductive organs.

Lifestyles

Insects also have a wide range of feeding habits; some insects are vegetarians, while others are meat-eaters.

Herbivores. Literally plant eaters, these are usually pests, because they chew or suck on leaves, stems, or roots for food. Usually, an individual insect must eat a relatively large amount of plant material to get enough protein and other nutrients to continue its development.

Parasites. Parasitic insects usually lay their eggs inside other insects. When the eggs hatch, the parasitic insect larva lives and grows inside the host insect until the host eventually dies. Then, the parasite goes through its pupal stage inside or attached to the outside of the dead host until the adult emerges. Entomologists like to call insect parasites parasitoids to distinguish them from insects such as lice or fleas that parasitize animals. A parasite larva usually kills one host as it develops, in contrast with a predator, which kills many.

Predators. Predators eat several and often hundreds of other insects during their life cycles. They are like lions, needing to kill many prey to feed themselves. In contrast, the larva of a parasite usually only kills one host insect in the course of its life cycle.

Predators are usually fast-moving insects with swift reflexes to enable them to catch other insects. Some insects, such as hover flies, aphid midges, and lacewings, are predators in the larval stage only, while others, such as lady beetles, are predators as both larvae and adults.

---

its and life cycles before you try to identify them. (For basic information on the forms and transformations of insects, see "Insect Life Cycles and Lifestyles" above). Insects undergo metamorphosis, a change in their form, one or more times in their lives. Perhaps the best-known example is the transformation of a caterpillar into a butterfly. In order to use control methods

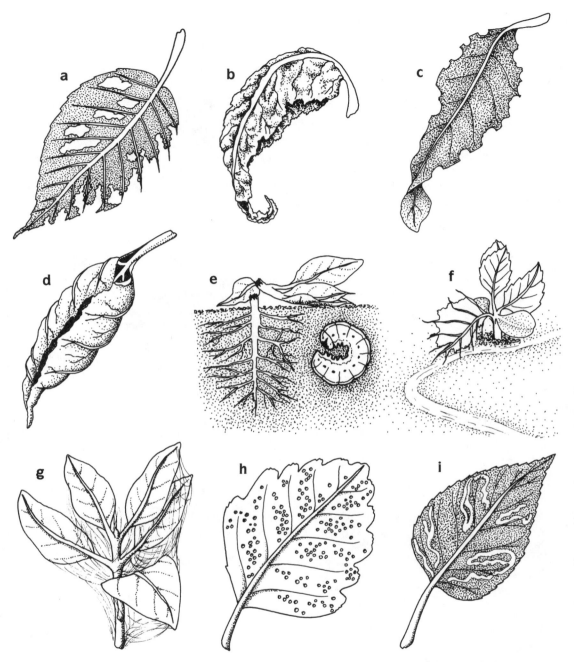

Beetles and caterpillars can chew large, ragged holes in leaves. Caterpillars sometimes leave deposits of dark green excrement on the leaves (a). Aphids, leafhoppers, and thrips suck sap from leaves. Their feeding can cause leaf curling, distortion, and twisting (b). Leaf weevils clip neat half circles from leaf margins. Larvae usually feed on roots (c). Leafrollers spin a fine web around one or many leaves, and feed inside the web (d). Cutworms crawl along the soil surface at night and chew through stems of seedlings (e). Slugs chew large, ragged holes in leaves. They feed at night, and may leave trails of silvery slime on plants or the soil surface (f). Spider mites spin a fine webbing from the undersides of leaves. Their feeding may cause leaves to develop white or yellow specks (g). Flea beetles chew many small holes in leaves, creating a shot-hole effect (h). Leafminers feed internally on leaf tissue; leaves may have twisting, silvery tunnels running through them (i).

most effectively, it helps to know the various forms your pest enemies take. If you can recognize pest insect eggs, for example, you can crush them, eliminating problems before they begin.

You'll have to find the insect pests in your garden before you can identify them. Sometimes it's as simple as finding a big beetle chewing on a leaf, but other pests require a little detective work on your part.

If you find damaged leaves, examine them closely. Check for slow-moving larvae or grubs. If you don't see the culprits, it could be because they feed at night or they escaped before you saw them or they have finished eating and left altogether. The latter situation is very common—gardeners often don't notice damage until after the perpetrator has left, usually to spin a cocoon somewhere. Caterpillars and beetle larvae eat the most during the last few days of their development; therefore, they do the greatest damage just before they stop feeding altogether. It is important to determine whether this is the case, so you'll know if you should apply a control. Look at the new growth on the plant: If it's undamaged, the pests likely have left. Also, fresh holes in leaves have a clean cut edge, whereas the margins of old holes dry out or turn brown.

If you suspect the pests are still there, compare the damage with symptoms in the illustration on the opposite page to help you decide what's attacking your plants. Once you have a lead on what to look for, you may be able to find one of the pests for identification.

Once you find the pest, try to identify it with the help of field guides (see "The Chemical-Free Gardener's Library," on page 431, for suggested titles). Your local Cooperative Extension Service office may also have guides to common pests in your region. Most of the pests you see will be common and identifiable, but if the specimen just doesn't fit the pictures, get some help from extension agents, university entomologists, or pest management services.

CULTURAL CONTROLS

Without doubt, the best time to take action against pests is before they become a problem, and using cultural controls helps prevent pests from getting a foothold. Many cultural controls are practices you probably already use in your garden. Others are easy to adopt by making simple changes in your schedule or methods.

Some examples of cultural controls include ensuring soil fertility, planting cultivars adapted to your local conditions, planting insect-resistant cultivars, using good sanitation practices, and cultivating and mulching to avoid pests. These preventive controls are generally inexpensive and easy and can help you avoid spending money and time later fighting pest infestations. They are the best first step toward chemical-free insect management.

Start with Healthy Plants

Your garden's first line of defense against pests is good health. Of course, plant health is fundamental to all of your gardening goals, not just to insect management, but healthy, vigorously growing plants have more reserves to draw from if they are damaged by insects. They're less likely to lose leaves or flowers or to show decreases in yield even when attacked by insects. They'll also recover faster than stressed or deficient plants would; they may also mount their own chemical defenses faster.

Fertile soil and adequate water are the keys to plant health, but if you plan on controlling insect pests organically, there are some aspects of fertilizing and watering that are especially important.

A Balanced Diet

From the pest control viewpoint, your goal should be a balanced diet for your plants. Before you pile manure on your vegetable garden, consider that overfertilizing with nitrogen can make your plants more susceptible to some pests. Leaves that have too much nitrogen in them are more attractive to sucking insects such as scales, mealybugs, and aphids, because the leaves are more nutritious for the insects. Corn fed too much nitrogen is more likely to be damaged by southwestern corn borers, partly because the cornstalks are softer and thus easier for the borers to penetrate.

In general, using a balanced organic fertilizer such as compost or well-rotted manure should keep your plants safe from excess nitrogen. The nitrogen in such organic fertilizers is released slowly and steadily, so plants can't take up the nitrogen all in a rush. Compost is also a source of vital micronutrients that will help improve plant health. A recent study at Cornell University found a significantly smaller pest population on collards grown with composted sludge and manure than on plants grown with highly soluble synthetic fertilizers. (This is another small example of the benefits of using organic rather than synthetic fertilizers.)

Water Therapy

Water stress harms plants in many ways, and water-stressed plants are especially vulnerable to damage from thrips and spider mites. In dry conditions, spider mites feed more in order to get the extra water they need to keep from dehydrating. Because they're feeding more, the mites increase their energy supply. This, coupled with high temperatures, leads them to lay more eggs, setting the stage for a pest population explosion. This is frequently a problem in home greenhouses and sunspaces. Prevent excessive feeding by misting frequently during dry weather to cool and humidify the air. Use a hose to soak the greenhouse floor, benches, and even walls (if they are waterproof) several times daily. Avoid splashing water on leaves of plants in the bright sun, especially delicate ornamentals such as fuchsias or begonias, because the leaves may be burned as the sun shines through the water droplets.

Aphids thrive on plants that are continually stressed from lack of water, so maintaining sufficient water in the soil is an important way to help control them. Dry soils also can leave plants vulnerable to attack if cracks open up around plant roots. For example, potato tuberworms do the worst damage to potatoes under such conditions because tubers are more exposed than in soils that are kept evenly moist.

A standard rule for watering is to be sure plants receive an inch of water weekly in hot weather, either from rain, irrigation, or a combination of the two. Perhaps a more practical rule is to water when plants begin to show the first sign of wilting during midday heat. I use the cucumber and squash vines in my garden as indicator plants because they seem to be the first to begin to droop. Water thoroughly to make sure the water penetrates deeply into the soil. This practice encourages plants to grow deep roots, making them less vulnerable in dry spells.

If you have shallow soil over rocks, it will take less water to soak the soil, and you'll have to water more often. These days, the need to conserve water is becoming a fact of life. Many gardeners rely on deep mulches and drip irrigation systems to reduce the amount of supplemental water they need to apply. Mulches are very effective in cooling soil and retaining water during the summer. In the spring, wait until soils have warmed and plants are well established before you mulch. As the weather gets warmer, you can keep adding mulch until it is 6 to 12 inches thick for maximum protection during hot weather.

Keep a Clean Garden

Garden sanitation is a basic principle of chemical-free gardening—one you should apply even before you bring plants into your garden. Carefully inspect all new plants, trees, or shrubs before you buy them to avoid bringing insect pests home to your garden or greenhouse. Thoroughly examine leaves, buds, bark, and roots (if possible) for insects, eggs, signs of insect damage, spider mites, or mite webbing. On bare-root nursery stock, you also can check for signs of girdling or boring in roots. Check the plants again just before you plant them.

Another simple and effective sanitation step is picking up dropped fruit, which may contain insects or eggs that will cause insect populations to snowball if you don't remove them promptly. During summer, you can reduce the local populations of codling moth, plum curculio, and apple maggots in your home apple orchard by picking up and using or destroying all dropped fruit daily. Fruit that can't be used should be buried deeply, fed to animals, burned, or put out in sealed containers for disposal. Don't put the fruit in a compost pile unless it is a freshly made pile, just beginning to heat up, that is likely to get very hot in the center (160°F). If you have such a pile, bury the infested fruit in the hottest part of the heat. See "Compost: Nature's Black Magic," on page 68, for directions on making a hot compost pile.

After the first of September, picking up fruit two or three times a month is sufficient. Unless you live in a commercial apple-growing area, where relatively high populations of pests are present because of the high concentration of trees, the scrupulous removal of dropped apples should be the only control you need to prevent the buildup of apple maggot populations in your orchard. Picking up dropped blueberries daily, especially those that drop early, also works to control blueberry fruit flies.

Sanitation also includes pruning twigs and branches that are damaged or infected by pests, such as borers or scale insects, to reduce the infestation on trees and shrubs. It is best to burn the prunings, or bury them at least 3 feet deep in the ground. Chipping the prunings will not necessarily kill insects.

Another sanitation step is to clean up piles of crop residues. Old potato piles or volunteer potatoes are sources of virus that can be spread by aphids; piles of rotting vegetation attract such pests as the sap beetles that attack sweet corn and raspberries in some areas. Remove roots of cabbage family plants as soon as they are harvested and burn them, compost them in the center of a hot compost pile, or dispose of them in sealed containers to reduce future cabbage root maggot populations.

Cultivating crop residues into the soil can kill pests immediately, can bury them so deeply they won't survive, or can expose them to killing cold or to birds and other predators. Cultivating crop residues will help suppress corn earworms, European corn borers, corn rootworms, wheat stem sawflies, and other pests.

A Beneficial Exception

While removing or digging in crop residues is usually a good practice, there are situations where leaving plant residues in or around your garden has beneficial side effects. Some detailed studies show that in some ecosystems, clean fields may be worse for beneficial insects that shelter in crop debris or overwinter on the bodies of their host pests than it is for the pests. These studies indicate that more pests may be parasitized by beneficial wasps or other insects in fields where weeds were left in the rows and that many beneficial species use crop residues as overwintering sites.

Clearly, whether to leave residues or cultivate cleanly depends on the pests and crops involved. On a garden scale, I recommend leaving protected zones—in mulches, under stones, and among weedy borders, for example—undisturbed because so many beneficial ground beetles and other insects live there. I do pull and completely dispose of crop residues I know are likely to be infested with pests. I compost other garden wastes and, when I lived in a cold region, I left a lot of old stems and stalks standing in the garden to hold the snow and provide winter protection.

Select Resistant Plants

Although breeding plants for resistance has been most successful in producing disease-resistant plants, there are some insect-resistant cultivars available. The potential value of insect-resistant plants was dramatically demonstrated in the 1880s, when the grape phylloxera (a small, aphidlike insect that attacks grape roots and stems) devastated vineyards in France. When it was found that native American grapes were resistant to phylloxera, the French wine grapes were grafted onto American rootstocks, literally saving the wine industry in France. Finding insect-resistant plants is not always possible, but when it is, it's a near-guarantee of success—without chemicals.

How Resistance Works

True resistance is a genetic characteristic of a plant and is not dependent on cultural practices, such as fertilizing or watering. Certain plants have physical or chemical characteristics that insects will avoid. For example, geranium leaves are covered with sticky or fuzzy hairs, and certain corn cultivars have tough stalks. Garlic leaves contain sulfur compounds that are repellent to pests; oak trees contain bitter-tasting tannins.

The ultimate in insect resistance is plants that naturally contain a chemical that is harmful or even fatal to pests. Geraniums, for example, contain a compound that paralyzes and often kills Japanese beetles when they feed on them.

Other plants are not truly resistant, but can grow leaves or roots fast enough to produce good yields even when they suffer a degree of pest damage that would reduce yields of other cultivars. These cultivars are termed insect-tolerant.

Using Resistance to Best Advantage

You may be able to bolster the survival chances of a less-resistant cultivar by planting it alongside a somewhat resistant one. For example,

Self-Defense Tactics

Some plants can mount their own chemical defenses in response to insect attacks. For example, scientific studies show that levels of toxic compounds called alkaloids increased tenfold in wild tobacco leaves after they were damaged by tobacco hornworms.

Other plants produce compounds called phytoalexins that repel pests or cause them to die or develop more slowly. For instance, after insects damage soybeans, the plants produce phytoalexins that are especially repellent to bean beetles. This effect is especially well-known in trees, including aspen, birch, willow, and some conifers. The latter respond to bark beetle attack by accumulating insecticidal and repellent chemicals at the site of the beetle attack. The genetic basis for plants' ability to produce their own "insecticides" is being studied by scientists who hope to use it in breeding programs for pest resistance.

a recent study found that taller cultivars of broccoli were significantly more attractive to cabbage aphids than short cultivars, and stands of mixed cultivars had fewer aphids generally than stands of a single cultivar. The resistance effect could disappear if only one cultivar were grown.

Environmental conditions can modify plant resistance. For example, onions grown in soils rich in organic matter can be twice as pungent as those grown in sandy soil. This extra pungency makes the onions more repellent to pests that don't like sulfur compounds. However, the extra sulfur could increase the attractiveness of onions to pests that are adapted to the sulfur compounds (such as onion maggots) and find their host plants by recognizing the sulfur compounds. The good news is that some beneficial wasps that parasitize onion pests also use the onion smell to find their prey and would also be more attracted to pungent onions as well.

The bottom line is that insect resistance is a complex area. The best bet for gardeners is to keep plants healthy: Their resistant characteristics will then be most powerful, and they will be able to recover more quickly from pest attack.

Time Plantings

Another cultural control is timing planting or harvesting to avoid peak populations of certain pests and thus avoid the most serious damage. This works best for pests that only have one generation a year, because once you miss the main period of pest activity, the rest of the growing season is pest-free. (See "Insect Life Cycles and Lifestyles," on page 161, for an explanation of insect generations.) It also can apply to some pests with two or three generations per year. For example, by planting carrots in June (in short and moderate season areas, earlier in long season areas), after the first generation of carrot rust fly has passed, you will avoid some potential damage. You can plant and harvest radishes early, before the first generation of cabbage root maggots appears. Hold off setting out cabbage transplants until after the first wave of root maggots; the plants will be well established before the second generation appears later in summer. The timing of insect emergence in spring varies with climate and insect species. Contact your local Cooperative Extension agent for information on approximate emergence times for pest insects in your area.

It isn't always easy to know when the peak generations of certain pests will occur. Although emergence times are roughly the same from year to year, an unusually early spring or one that is late and cold can make a big difference in emergence of overwintering pests. For pests that can be monitored with pheromone traps, you can tell by the weekly changes in numbers of males caught in the trap when the main generation of certain moths have passed. The directions supplied with specific pheromone traps will explain how to interpret the changes in numbers of the particular insect you are monitoring. See "Pheromone Traps," on page 204, to learn how and when to use these monitoring devices.

Mulch to Suppress Pests

Using mulch to suppress insect damage is a very specific control method. Reflective mulches such as aluminum-coated kraft-paper insulation (available at building supply stores) or aluminum foil can confuse aphids. Seemingly, the reflection of the blue sky from the mulch makes the insects lose track of what direction is up, so they do not land on the mulched plants. Studies on zucchini mulched with reflective material showed that the mulched plants had fewer problems with virus diseases that are transmitted by aphids, and consequently higher yields.

You can use a mulch of deep, loose material like straw or leaves (not hay, unless it is composted to kill seeds), at least 6 inches thick, to suppress Colorado potato beetles. When these pests first emerge after overwintering in the soil, they will only walk or climb to find food. After a first meal, they fly away to search for plants to eat. The mulch may interfere with the beetles' early efforts to find food, or they may avoid mulched areas because they are difficult to move through.

BIOLOGICAL CONTROLS

Biological control—using living organisms to control plant pests—is not a new idea. In fact, 1989 marked the 100th anniversary of this form of control in America. In 1889 in California, the U.S. Department of Agriculture released two Australian insect species, the vedalia lady beetle and a parasitic fly species, to control serious infestations of cottony cushion scale on citrus trees. The technique was successful, and cottony cushion scale has been only a minor pest on western citrus ever since.

Biological controls may be the most important and efficient control methods you use in your garden. Encouraging native predatory and parasitic insects and mites is cheap and simple. There are also now dozens of biological control agents for sale to home gardeners. If done properly, releasing an insect predator or parasite or a disease organism can establish nearly permanent control.

Conserving and Attracting Natural Enemies

There is an army of beneficial insects and mites of unimaginable variety in your garden, They vary from strangely shaped microscopic predatory mites to great darting black ground beetles. Some are predators: They eat insects that are pests in your garden. Others are parasites: They live in the bodies of pest insects, weakening and eventually killing them. You will probably never see many of these helpful creatures, yet you will notice their beneficial effects.

An important part of your organic insect control system is to encourage these natural enemies of pests to stay in your garden and do the pest control work for you. And oddly enough, one of the best ways to encourage beneficial insects and mites is to do a little less garden work! A garden tilled from edge to edge every season, with weedless rows of orderly vegetables, is a relatively barren habitat for beneficial insects, yet it gives pests a panorama of food. A garden with permanent beds and walkways, planted in a mixture of vegetables, flowers, and herbs with weeds and wild patches scattered throughout, provides all sorts of protected and semipermanent areas for a diverse community of beneficial species.

You may want to take the extra step of buying certain beneficial species and releasing them into your garden. This can be a tricky proposition, because some species are easier than others to maintain in the home garden. See "To Buy or Not to Buy," on page 173, for more information on beneficial bugs that make good buys for the home garden.

Protection

The most obvious way to protect beneficial insects is to avoid using toxic sprays or dusts. Even botanical poisons (which are considered acceptable for use in organic gardens) kill many kinds of insects—harmful and beneficial. Use these substances, including nicotine, pyrethrin, rotenone, ryania, sabadilla, and especially diatomaceous earth, with care and caution, and only when they are necessary to protect your plants. Apply them only on the plants being attacked. If you carelessly allow spray to hit weedy areas near your crop plants, you may wipe out the many beneficial insects that are hiding or feeding there.

Surprisingly, protecting beneficial insects from dust is also important. Insects constantly struggle to keep enough water in their bodies, because their bodies have so much surface area relative to volume. Dust from roads or cultivation can scratch the protective coating on insect bodies, causing more rapid water loss. Dust is more harmful to parasites and predators than it is to pests, because pests get plenty of moisture from the plants they eat, while the beneficials are eating insects—rather dry fare. Do anything you can to reduce dust in the garden or orchard, such as planting a protective hedge, planting ground covers to hold the soil, or building a windbreak fence.

Food

The adults of many beneficial insect species eat pollen and nectar: Only the immature stages are predators. Other beneficial species, such as minute pirate bugs, supplement their diets with pollen and plant juices, enabling them to survive when their target pests are scarce.

To Repel or to Attract?

The idea that planting certain plants around or near crop plants can reduce damage from pest insects has a long history. This notion--called companion planting—was generally assumed to work because the companion plants drove away the pests. There is evidence that some plants, such as southernwood and catnip, repel insects. However, most garden lore on repellent plants has not been substantiated by scientific study.

Some companion plants (including thyme and basil) repel insects when they are ground up and made into sprays that release volatile odors into the air. However, as whole plants growing undisturbed in your garden, they may not release enough of these volatile odors to repel pests.

But what about the countless gardeners who have noticed beneficial effects in their gardens when they try companion planting— are they deluding themselves? On the contrary, it is highly likely that companion planting *does* reduce pest populations, but not necessarily because the companion plants repel pests. Most plants recommended for companion planting are herbs and flowers that are specific-

ally attractive to native predators and parasites. Many of these beneficial species move so quickly or are so small and inconspicuous that you don't realize they are there. Once they are lured into your garden by your companion plantings, they attack pests. The only effect you *see* is a reduction in pest damage.

The attraction of many companion plants is their supply of pollen and nectar—necessary food for many native parasites and predators, especially for the egg-laying females. Companion plants also provide a source of alternate diets to sustain predators during winter, early spring, or at times when pests are not present on your crops. An astonishing example is goldenrod, which in northern Florida was found to support more than 75 different species of aphid predators. The predators were feeding on a nonpest aphid (there really is such a thing!) in the goldenrod, and so were present and ready to eat other aphids when they appeared in nearby crops. Companion plants also shield beneficial insects from hot sun and drying winds and are a refuge when the garden is being cut, cultivated, or sprayed.

Entice adult biocontrols to stay around your garden by planting companion plants that are rich in pollen and nectar. The beneficials are attracted to the nectar plants, and while in the area, they search for suitable hosts or prey for their offspring. Choose small-flowered species. Many beneficial insects, particularly the parasitic wasps, are extremely small and can drown in the pools of nectar in large flowers. They are most attracted to plants with very small flowers such as the carrot family, Umbelliferae, which includes dill, caraway, fennel, lovage, and parsley. Small-flowered weeds like Queen-Anne's-lace (also in the carrot family), corn spurry, lamb's-

quarters, nettles, and wild mustard also attract beneficial insects. Many mint family members such as catnip, hyssop, lemon balm, rosemary, and thyme are important nectar plants. Plants in the daisy family, Compositae, such as coneflowers, daisies, and yarrow are excellent sources of pollen and nectar. Goldenrod, another daisy family member, is a superb host plant for beneficial insects. Some plants, such as peaches, also provide another source of food from tiny glands on their leaves or stems that ooze sweet sap that many insects love; lesser burdock has fine "food hairs" on the leaves that parasitic wasps bite off and eat.

(continued on page 172)

Suggested Companion Plants

Companion planting is a mixture of folklore and science. More and more research studies are showing the helpful effects of certain species. The attractant and repellent plants listed here are all documented examples of helpful companion plants. Use it as a guide, and experiment with your own combinations. Some companion plants can be interplanted with your crops or flowers. Others may compete too vigorously if planted directly in the garden, and should be planted separately in borders or hedgerows.

Companion Plant	Where Grown	Attracts	Repels
Angelica (*Angelica archangelica*)	Border	Lacewings, lady beetles, parasitic wasps	
Anise (*Pimpinella anisum*)	Interplant	Parasitic wasps	Slightly repels imported cabbageworm
Asters (*Aster* spp.)	Border	Honeybees, ichneumonid wasps	
Borage (*Borago officinalis*)	Border	Honeybees	
Caraway (*Carum carvi*)	Border	Parasitic wasps	
Catnip (*Nepeta cataria*)	Border	Bees, imported cabbageworms, parasitic wasps	Green peach aphids, flea beetles, squash bugs, cucumber beetles
Corn spurry (*Spergula arvensis*)	Interplant	Predators and parasites of cabbage pests	Caterpillars, aphids, rootworms
Dandelion (*Taraxacum officinale*)	Border	Pollen for lady beetles, lacewings, other predators	Colorado potato beetles
Dill (*Anethum graveolens*)	Interplant, border	Aphid predators and parasites	
Fennel (*Foeniculum vulgare*)	Interplant	Hover flies, parasitic wasps, tachinid flies	
Goldenrods (*Solidago* spp.)	Border	Honeybees, lacewings, minute pirate bugs, soldier beetles, spiders, other predators, and many parasites	
Hawthorns (*Crataegus* spp.)	Border	Winter host of parasite of diamondback moth	
Ivies (*Hedera* spp.)	Border	Hover flies, tachinid flies	
Marigolds (*Tagetes* spp.)	Interplant, border	Hover flies	Root nematodes, Mexican bean beetles, aphids, Colorado potato beetles

Companion Plant	Where Grown	Attracts	Repels
Mustards (*Brassica* spp.)	Interplant, border	Flowers attract parasites, especially of cabbageworms	Aphids from neighboring brussels sprouts, collards
Nasturtium (*Tropaeolum majus*)	Interplant		Slightly repels Colorado potato beetles
Queen-Anne's-lace (*Daucus carota* var. *carota*)	Border	Many parasitic wasps and flies, hover flies, Japanese beetle parasites, lady beetles, minute pirate bugs	
Radish (*Raphanus sativus*)	Interplant		Striped cucumber beetles
Rye (*Secale cereale*)	Interplant	Rove beetles	Root-knot nematodes
Scorpion weeds (*Phacelia* spp.)	Interplant, border	Honeybees, numerous parasitic wasps, tachinid flies	
Southernwood (*Artemisia abrotanum*)	Border		Moths, flea beetles from cabbage
Spiny amaranth (*Amaranthus spinosus*)	Interplant	Black cutworms	
Stinging nettle (*Urtica dioica*)	Border	Numerous predators, parasites; alternate hosts of aphid predators	
Sunflower (*Helianthus annuus*)	Border	Lacewings, other predators, parasitic wasps	
Sweet clover (*Melilotus alba*)	Interplant, border	Honeybees, tachinid fly parasites of many caterpillars	
Tansy (*Tanacetum vulgare*)	Border	Imported cabbageworms	Slightly repels green peach aphids, squash bugs, Colorado potato beetles
Tomato (*Lycopersicon esculentum*)	Interplant		Flea beetles on cabbage
White clover (*Trifolium repens*)	Interplant, border	Parasites of aphids and cabbageworms; shelters ground beetles, spiders	Cabbage root flies
Wormwood (*Artemisia* spp.)	Border		Flea beetles on cabbage
Yarrows (*Achillea* spp.)	Border	Hover flies, lady beetles, parasitic wasps	

Plant buckwheat or sweet clover around the garden and encourage a variety of weeds and flowers in and around your garden to provide food all season from early spring to late fall for native beneficial insects. See "Suggested Companion Plants," on page 170, for more suggestions on what to plant to attract beneficials.

Water

Just like other animals, beneficial insects need water. Some get enough liquid from their prey or by supplementing their diets with a drink of plant sap, but most rely on dew or raindrops for water.

You can make a simple "insect bath" for your garden from an old birdbath or other shallow container. Fill the container to the top with rocks or large gravel to make dry islands where the insects can land. You can also float a piece of plywood in a bucket of water to make a watering site for beneficials, including the honeybees that pollinate your crops. Cut the plywood to cover nearly the entire surface of the water, so the insects won't fall in and drown. They will drink at the edges or from water that collects across the surface ridges in the plywood. You'll be amazed at the number and variety of insects that visit for a drink on a hot summer day!

Shelter

For beneficial insects, shelter is not just protection from wind and weather extremes, it is also shelter for their populations when a cultivated area like your garden is being disturbed by tilling, harvesting, or spraying. The more permanent stable zones there are nearby, the less the beneficial insects are affected by disturbances in your gardens.

Shelter also is a place for beneficial species to find extra food. For example, *Anagrus epos,* a very effective parasitic wasp that controls grape leafhopper in California, gets an early start in the season by living on nonpest leafhoppers in blackberry bushes around the vineyards. Some

You can make an insect bath to entice beneficial insects to your garden by filling a shallow container with rocks and water (top). Or, you can float a circular piece of plywood in a bucket (bottom).

predators and parasites spend part of the year feeding on species that are not pests; this makes it possible for them to maintain a large population that is ready to attack when the pest species shows up.

Hedgerows are one of the best shelters for beneficial species. Flowering shrubs and bushes with a mixture of flowering plants and weeds in an undisturbed, year-round hedge or border sustain many predators and parasites. Permanent pathways and borders around vegetable beds shelter the numerous beneficial ground beetles, rove beetles, and millipedes in your garden. These permanent patches give the soil-dwellers hiding places and overwintering spots when the garden beds are bare and inhospitable. Stone mulched pathways, sod or clover, or thick mulches of organic materials or newspaper all give the ground-living predators a stable home. Although it might seem that such mulches would encourage slugs, the reverse is actually true, because many ground beetles and their larvae eat slug eggs. By attracting and building up their populations in the permanent walkways, you will create a hungry crew ready to stage slug-eating raids further afield among the garden crops.

Cover crops in orchards and berry patches provide both shelter and food to beneficial insects. Studies in California showed that orchards with cover crops generally had lower infestations of aphids, codling moths, and leafhoppers and a greater number and variety of predatory soil-dwelling species than orchards with cultivated soil.

To Buy or Not to Buy

Today, there is a fascinating selection of predators and parasites for sale from insectaries. The most recent guide to beneficial organisms for sale in North America lists 54 species of biocontrol agents. They include insect-parasitic nematodes, predatory mites, and insects that control everything from aphids, gypsy moths, and scales to whiteflies, Colorado potato beetles, and bollworms. At first glance, it might seem there's a biocontrol agent to solve any pest problem you have, but it isn't as simple as that (or as the suppliers might have you believe). It's important to know just what these insects are likely to do and whether they really will be effective in a home garden. Lady beetles and preying mantids have been sold to home gardeners for years, but have they been worth the investment?

As a general rule, buying and releasing biocontrols for the home garden only is effective in situations that meet the following conditions:

1. *You are sure you've identified the pest species correctly.* Many biocontrol agents, particularly parasitic wasps, attack only one or a few related species, so it's critical to get the pest identification right.

2. *The pest you want to control stays in relatively local populations.* If the pest you're fighting migrates into your yard all season, a small release of biocontrol agents would have little chance of controlling the population. For example, aphids build up large local populations, and it is feasible to release biocontrol agents in the garden to control them. However, gypsy moths are a regional problem: If parasites are to have any effect, they must be released over large areas in a community-wide program. Other examples of localized pests are leafminers, mealybugs, scales, spider mites, and whiteflies.

3. *The pest does not have enough natural enemies already present to control it.* If your garden has native species that control the pest, protecting and encouraging the natives is by far the most economical and ecologically sound solution. Sometimes pests (for example, aphids) appear in damaging numbers so early in the spring that native predators are not yet present in sufficient numbers to suppress them. In that case, a very early release of purchased biocontrols may be useful to supplement the activity of the native populations.

4. *Your predator releases will not be wiped out by spray drift from neighboring properties.* If you have neighbors that spray toxic pesticides frequently, the spray drift is likely to kill your purchases before they have a chance to reduce pest populations. You will be better off using other kinds of nontoxic controls—and talking to your neighbor about pest control alternatives.

Unwise Buys in Bugs

After you've determined that your pest problem could be effectively controlled by a parasite or predator, you'll need to shop for a beneficial insect to release. While every gardener's situation is unique, there are general reasons why some widely known beneficial insects are well

(continued on page 177)

Is It Friend or Foe?

You must be able to identify the insects in your garden if you're going to take an active hand in balancing their populations with a combination of traps, purchased biological controls, and sprays. Many insects look pretty much the same to most people, yet they may be different species with completely different roles. For example, hover flies, whose larvae are valuable aphid predators, look a lot like wasps. Rove beetles, important ground-dwelling predators, are often mistaken for earwigs.

Very few of the species you see in your garden are pests (it's estimated that less than 1 percent of all insect species are pests). If you don't know what a bug is, leave it alone, because chances are it's one of the good guys. Beneficial insects are often found at the scene of the crime because they're after the pests, too. They're attracted to the odor of the pest and sometimes by the smell of damaged leaves, which tells them where to start searching for their prey.

It's especially important to identify the insects caught in sticky and pheromone traps, because a pile of dead insects is no assurance that harmful insects are being eliminated. Killing significant numbers of beneficial bugs is needlessly destructive and makes pest control even more difficult. Correct identification is also important when you are using traps as monitoring tools to time sprays or releases of bio-control agents.

This said, there are several sources of information to help you identify the insects in your yard and garden. First, get a good insect guide with color photographs (a number are listed in "The Chemical-Free Gardener's Library" on page 431). Be sure to read descriptions carefully, including the size and recorded distribution area to see if a species is likely to live in your area. When identifying an insect, pay special attention to details such as antennae, legs, and mouthparts. Don't go by color alone unless the insect has a very distinctive pattern. Local Cooperative Extension offices and state land grant universities often publish excellent guides to local crop pests, which are very useful.

Unfortunately, there are very few guides that show beneficial species. The illustrations on these pages show several common beneficial insects. If you're not certain whether an insect is friend or foe, take or send the specimen, well-protected in a closed vial (not loose in an envelope or squashed in a plastic bag!) to a local extension agent, university entomologist, diagnostic laboratory, or local garden center.

The following is a rundown of some of the beneficial species you may find in your gardens:

Flies: Believe it or not, there are numerous beneficial flies: pollinators, predators, and parasites. Some, such as the big, bristly, dark gray tachinid flies, lay their eggs or larvae directly on caterpillars and other pests. These are very important wild predators because female tachinids often lay thousands of eggs each. Others flies, such as the tiny, delicate aphid midge, lay their eggs on leaves among aphid colonies so that when the eggs hatch, the tiny, voracious, orange maggots are near their food supply. Flies have only one pair of wings, instead of two pairs like other insects, hence the scientific name of the group, Diptera, which literally means "two-wings." There are many beelike flies and flies with yellow and black stripes that look like wasps. Count the wings to tell the difference: Flies have two wings; wasps have four.

Tachinid fly

True bugs: There really is a group of insects called true bugs, to distinguish them from the generic term "bugs" used for any insect. True bugs generally have somewhat leathery forewings held crossed one over the other flat against the body, each with a membranous section at the tip; their second pair of wings (the hindwings) are membranous and folded under the forewings. True bugs also have a characteristic triangular shape on the top of their thoraxes (the middle body section, behind the head). They have sharp needlelike beaks for sucking their food. The pests in this group pierce plant tissue to drink sap; the predatory species pierce their prey to drink blood. Most beneficial true bugs are general predators of a variety of soft-bodied insects, such as aphids, beetle larvae, leafhopper nymphs, small caterpillars, spider mites, and thrips. While they don't always confine themselves to pests (and they can be pretty cannibalistic when they are hungry), they are extremely important predators of pests in agricultural systems. Some predatory bugs, like assassin bugs, ambush bugs, minute pirate bugs, or spined soldier bugs, live up to their names, but there are others, like damsel bugs or flower bugs, whose names belie their ferocity.

Beetles: Everyone recognizes the common orange lady beetles with black spots, but there are many other beneficial species in the lady beetle family. And this family is just one of many families of beetles, each containing hundreds of species of hardy beneficial predators. Beetles are most easily recognized by their extremely hard forewings that serve as rigid wing covers for the membranous underwings. Some, such as certain species of weevils, have fused wing covers and can't fly. All beetles have chewing mouthparts. Most are medium-size to large insects ranging from $\frac{1}{8}$ inch to more than 1 inch long. Ground beetles are large, blue-black, swift predators of snail and slug eggs, root maggots, root weevil grubs, cutworms, and small potato beetle larvae. Some, like the fiery searcher, run up trees to capture armyworms or tent caterpillars. Rove beetles are important predators and parasites of pests that spend at least part of their life cycles in the soil. Some rove beetles climb plants at night to eat aphids,

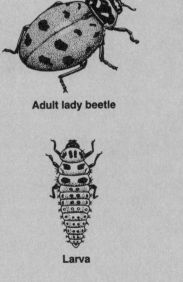

Adult lady beetle

Larva

Spined soldier bug

(continued)

Is It Friend or Foe?—*Continued*

and others parasitize cabbage root maggots. With their slightly elongated bodies and short, stubby top wings, rove beetles look more like earwigs than beetles.

Other important groups of beetles are the small, hemispherical hister beetles, the ferocious, iridescently colored tiger beetles, the familiar fireflies that eat slug and snail eggs and insect larvae, as well as the leathery winged soldier beetles that eat aphids and caterpillars.

Wasps: Although you probably immediately think of the yellow jacket wasps that wield a painful sting, there are other families of wasps (including ants, bees, and sawflies). Most wasps have thin waists between their thoraxes and abdomens; their wings are clear and membranous. Yellow jackets and mud-dauber wasps are excellent predators that feed caterpillars, flies, and grubs to their offspring.

The parasitic wasps are the most important group of native biological control insects. There are many different families of parasitic wasps, but most are in three main families: chalcids, braconids, and ichneumonids. They range in size from minute *Trichogramma* wasps, as small as the point of a pencil, to some huge, inky black ichneumonids with bodies 1½ inches long, trailing several inches of threadlike ovipositor (this looks like a stinger, but it is perfectly harmless). Parasitic wasps inject their eggs inside a host insect, and the larvae grow by absorbing liquid nourishment through their skins. Some, such as the aphid parasites, use the mummified shell of the aphid to protect their own pupae. Larvae of other wasp species wiggle out and spin a cocoon outside the dead host. You may have seen dead caterpillars with small white cocoons clustered on them or rigid mummified aphids on leaves; these are all the handiwork of parasitic wasps.

Lacewings: The brown or green, alligator-like larvae of several species of native lacewings (also called golden-eyed flies or antlions) prey on a variety of small, soft insects, including aphids, moths eggs, leafhoppers, scale insects, thrips, and small caterpillars. The adults are delicate, green or brown insects (1 inch long) and have relatively large, transparent wings marked with a characteristic network of veins.

Predatory mites: Mites and their relatives, the spiders, are not insects; they are arachnids. Adult mites and spiders have eight legs, whereas insects have six legs. Predatory mites are extremely small (less than ¹/₅₀ inch long) but are very important predators. They have sucking mouthparts to pierce their prey and generally move very quickly. They control many kinds of plant-feeding mites, such as spider mites, cyclamen mites, or rust mites. Some species are effective predators of thrips and fungus gnats. The best-known predatory mites, those in the family Phytoseiidae, mostly live in foliage, eating leaf-feeding pests. Other important predatory mites live in the top layer of the soil, feeding on everything from fungi to fly larvae.

Spiders: Unfortunately, many people are horrified by spiders, which are some of the best predators around (the few truly poisonous species are extremely rare). We are most familiar with the relatively large, wingless, eight-legged creatures that spin webs, but there are many other kinds of spiders. Some species spin thick silk funnels, some hide in burrows and snatch insects that wander too close, others leap on their prey using a silk thread as a dragline. The more spiders you can tolerate in your garden, the better, because they consume large numbers of insects.

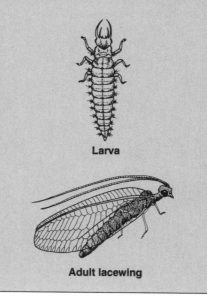

Larva

Adult lacewing

worth encouraging, but not worth buying to release in the home garden.

Lady Beetles

Convergent lady beetles (*Hippodamia convergens*), the species sold, are so named because they spend much of the year clustered in large groups. They eat very little, living off their stored fat. In winter, these beetle clusters move to mountainous areas to overwinter. In early spring, they become very active, fly long distances, feed voraciously on aphids, and lay their eggs. In late spring, they return to their resting state.

Collectors scoop up resting lady beetles while they are clustered; they are not reared in insectaries. So when you put them out in your garden in spring, their instinct is to wake up and migrate. They will only feed and reproduce on-site if they are prevented from leaving, as they would be if released in a greenhouse. In fact, the greenhouse is the one place where purchased lady beetles are a good investment for the home gardener. If you release lady beetles in your greenhouse, be sure the vents are screened. An order of 1,000 beetles should be plenty for most home greenhouses.

Home gardeners may think their lady beetle release was a success because they see lady beetles in their garden after they release purchased beetles. However, native lady beetles are also migrating at this time and finding aphid colonies: The beetles in their garden are more likely to be migrating wild beetles than purchased ones. A hint: If you can buy lady beetles that have been collected in the spring, when they are ready to start feeding, they are much more likely to stay in the garden and eat aphids.

Praying Mantids

Egg cases of the Chinese praying mantid (*Tenodera aridifolia sinensis*) are widely available through garden suppliers, but they are another questionable buy for the home garden. Mantids are fascinating insects—amazing and entertaining to watch, they make interesting pets—but they eat any insect they can catch, including each other. I have seen them eat lacewings, which are native aphid predators, and butterflies that stray too close to flowers hiding the mantid. Also, praying mantids have only one generation each year, and so cannot increase their numbers in response to increasing pest populations as many other predators do. Another drawback is that about 90 percent of the young mantids die shortly after they hatch if there is not enough prey readily available.

Decollate Snails

Predatory decollate snails (*Rumina decollata*) eat brown garden snails, decaying vegetable matter, and, if those food sources are scarce, living seedlings and transplants. Therefore, once the brown snails are gone, this predator can become a very serious pest in its own right, particularly because there are no predators that eat decollate snails. These snails are used very successfully in commercial citrus groves in California where they do no harm to established trees and provide excellent control of the brown snails. California gardeners may see these snails available for sale from beneficials suppliers, but they are not a wise choice for the home garden.

Better Buys in Bugs

Many of the popular biocontrol agents have been developed for use in the greenhouse industry; therefore, more of them will be useful in home greenhouses or on houseplants than in the garden. However, when pests such as spider mites or whiteflies occur in a garden or orchard, biocontrol agents can certainly be used successfully.

Whitefly Parasitic Wasp

Encarsia formosa, a minute parasitic wasp, is usually sold as pupae glued to cards that you can hang on plants. The tiny adults (the size of a pencil point) emerge within one week and lay

Buyer's Guide to Beneficial Bugs

Insectaries and some garden supply catalogs offer an ever-increasing selection of beneficial insects and mites. The beneficial species listed here control many common pest insects, but some only provide good control if released on a commercial or community-wide scale. Species that are effective when released in the home garden are marked with a symbol for the garden ✬; those that provide good control of pests in home greenhouses are marked with a symbol for a greenhouse 🏠. Asterisks indicate that the species looks promising for the home garden and/or greenhouse, but has not been fully tested.

Pests Controlled	Beneficial Species	Common Name	Where Effective
Aphids	*Aphidoletes aphidimyza*	Predatory midge	✬ 🏠
	Aphidius matricariae	Parasitic wasp	✬ 🏠
Colorado potato beetles	*Edovum puttleri*	Parasitic wasp	✬ *
	Podisus maculiventris	Spined soldier bug	✬ *
Fungus gnats	*Geolaelaps* spp.	Predatory mites	🏠
Grape leafhoppers	*Anagrus epos*	Parasitic wasp	
Gypsy moths	*Cotesia melanoscela*	Parasitic wasp	
	Glyptapanteles flavicoxis	Parasitic wasp	
	Meteorus pulchricornis	Parasitic wasp	
Leafminers	*Dacnusa sibirica*	Parasitic wasp	🏠
	Diglyphus isaea	Parasitic wasp	🏠
Mealybugs	*Cryptolaemus montrouzieri*	Australian lady beetle	🏠
	Leptomastix dactylopii	Parasitic wasp	🏠
	Leptomastidea abnormis	Parasitic wasp	🏠
	Anagyrus pseudococci	Parasitic wasp	🏠
Mexican bean beetles	*Podisus maculiventris*	Spined soldier bug	✬ *
	Pediobius foveolatus	Parasitic wasp	✬ *
Mites, European red	*Metaseiulus occidentalis*	Predatory mite	✬ 🏠

their eggs in developing whitefly scales.

Protection offered: *E. formosa* parasitizes both the greenhouse whitefly and sweet potato whitefly, a pest that has spread throughout the continent on a wide range of host plants.

How to use: *Encarsia* wasps are most active and successful in warm, bright conditions, so it is better to use them in spring and summer; for whitefly problems in fall and winter, unless you keep your greenhouse quite warm (over

Pests Controlled	Beneficial Species	Common Name	Where Effective
Mites, spider	*Phytoseiulus persimilis*	Predatory mite	🌱 🏠
	Phytoseiulus longipes	Predatory mite	🌱 🏠
	Amblyseius californicus	Predatory mite	🌱 🏠
Moth eggs	*Trichogramma* spp.	Parasitic wasps	🌱*
Navel orangeworms	*Goniozus legneri*	Parasitic wasp	
	Pentalitomastix spp.	Parasitic wasps	
Scale, black	*Metaphycus helvolus*	Parasitic wasp	🌱 🏠
Scale, red	*Aphytis melinus*	Parasitic wasp	🌱 🏠
	Compreriella bifasciata	Parasitic wasp	🌱 🏠
Scale, soft brown	*Chilocorus nigritus*	Lady beetle	🌱 🏠
	Lindorus lopthantae	Lady beetle	🌱 🏠
Thrips, greenhouse	*Thripobius semileuteus*	Parasitic wasp	🏠*
Thrips, western flower	*Amblyseius cucumeris*	Predatory mite	🌱 🏠
Whiteflies	*Encarsia formosa*	Parasitic wasp	🌱 🏠
	Delphastus spp.	Lady beetles	🌱* 🏠*
GENERAL PREDATORS:			
Aphids, mealybugs, scale	*Hippodamia convergens*	Convergent ladybug	🏠
Aphids, small caterpillars, thrips	*Chrysoperla carnea* (*Chrysopa carnea*)	Green lacewing	🏠
Aphids, small caterpillars, thrips	*Chrysoperla rufilabrus* (*Chrysopa rufilabrus*)	Brown lacewing	🌱 🏠
Aphids, small caterpillars, spider mites, tarnished plant bugs, thrips	*Orius tristicolor*	Minute pirate bug	🌱* 🏠*
Many common pest insects	*Tenodera* spp.	Praying mantid	

70°F at night), try other whitefly controls (see "35 Common Garden Pests," on page 230, for other control measures for whitefly). Order *Encarsia* when the *very first* whitefly appears. If you don't notice a whitefly problem until there are many adults resting in the tops of your plants, spray with pyrethrum or insecticidal soap to lower the population before releasing parasites. Release at least five parasites per plant or one or two parasites per square foot. For a 200- to

500-square-foot greenhouse, or the same area of a garden, a minimum order of 1,000 parasites should be enough if you catch the whitefly early. Space cards evenly throughout the greenhouse or garden. A second release two weeks later is usually necessary. Yellow sticky traps, an effective control for whitefly, are compatible with use of *Encarsia* because the wasps are not particularly attracted to yellow.

Spider Mite Predatory Mites

These mites are all tiny predators (less than $^1/_{50}$ inch long) that eat various species of spider mites. All of these predator species can be used in a garden during the summer, but some won't be hardy enough to overwinter in the colder areas of the country.

Protection offered: *Phytoseiulus persimilis* is the most widely sold species for spider mite control. However, if your greenhouse or garden is very hot in summer (consistently over 90°F) you might have better results with *Amblyseius californicus, Phytoseiulus longipes,* or the high-temperature strain of *P. persimilis,* which is more tolerant of hot conditions. *Metaseiulus occidentalis* is an excellent hardy predator for European red mite in apple orchards and berry patches as far north as the Canadian apple-growing regions. Once established, it should only need to be re-released after a severe winter or other disruption to the population.

How to use: The predators are usually sold mixed with a granular material, such as bran, vermiculite, or ground corn cobs, or mixed with pieces of leaves. It's easy to shake the granules or leaf pieces, with mites riding along, onto leaves where spider mite damage exists. A minimum order of 1,000 predators should clean up spider mites in a home greenhouse or garden (200 to 500 square feet). When your order arrives, distribute the granules or leaf pieces evenly over the affected plants. The mites are so small you may not be able to spot them in the mixture, but rest assured they will travel between your plants as necessary to find spider mites to eat. Try to keep humidity up and temperatures down in the areas around your plants by misting regularly with a hose to encourage the predators.

For fruit trees, if European red mite numbers are low and you just want to establish a predator population for future years, release 50 to 100 per tree; if you want to control an outbreak during the same season, release 1,000 per tree.

Aphid Predatory Midge

The aphid midge (*Aphidoletes aphidimyza*) is an excellent native aphid predator. The midges are sold as pupae; when the small ($^1/_{16}$-inch-long), gray, long-legged flies emerge, they lay eggs near aphid colonies. After two or three days, tiny, bright orange larvae emerge and attack aphids, feeding for four to six days until they are about $^1/_8$ inch long. Then they drop to the ground to pupate for two weeks.

Protection offered: Equally useful in greenhouse, garden, or orchard, larvae of this midge eat all kinds of aphids.

How to use: I have found that as few as 3 midges per apple tree, released in the spring, as soon as aphids appear, are adequate to control apple aphids for the rest of the season because they get an early start that is later supplemented by efforts of the local aphid predators. Releasing 3 to 5 midges per infested plant in a greenhouse or garden is usually sufficient. A minimum order of 250 should be enough for most home gardens, greenhouses, or orchards. A second release two weeks later is a good idea. The midges are not likely to succeed in hot, dry, or windy areas unless the garden is well sheltered and moisture is available from irrigation or other water sources.

Scale Predators and Parasites

The shiny black lady beetles *Chilocorus nigritus* and *Lindorus lopthantae* are voracious predators of soft scales. Females lay eggs in small

How to Handle Beneficial Bugs

If you order insect predators or parasites, be prepared to take action quickly when they arrive. They are living critters and can't be left in the package long. Keep these points in mind:

1. When the beneficials are delivered—don't open the package! They may have escaped from the inner wrapping. If you open the container in your kitchen or living room, you may end up with a houseful of bugs. *Read the directions* on the label for handling and releasing: Every species is unique and must be treated differently.

2. Release the beneficials in your garden as soon as you can after they arrive. Shipping and being confined in the packaging are stressful for the insects. Don't keep them in the packaging more than 24 hours.

3. If you can't release them in your garden right away, keep them cool. For most beneficials, the door of your refrigerator (where the temperature is about 45°F) is suitable, but a few need warmer storage. Follow storage directions printed on the packaging.

4. When you're ready to release the beneficials, take the package to the exact spot in your garden where you want to release them. Release some of the beneficials right on or near the infested plants and the rest as evenly as possible throughout the rest of the surrounding area.

5. Try to get a good look at the beneficials as you release them. You don't want to mistakenly kill them later on, thinking they may be pests. You can preserve a few for future reference by dropping them in a small vial of rubbing alcohol.

6. If you think the package is empty, don't panic. Look with your magnifying glass. Some beneficials, like predatory mites, are too small to see with the naked eye. Others may come mixed with a bran, sawdust, or vermiculite carrier. The easy-to-see carrier helps you know whether you're distributing the insects evenly.

---

clusters under bark or dead scales; the larvae, which look like small brown alligators with black spines, attack scales. Their life cycle takes four to five weeks. Several species of parasitic wasps also attack scales.

Protection offered: The predatory lady beetles control soft scales on houseplants, ornamental figs, and citrus trees. The parasitic wasps help control scales on houseplants or in greenhouses. The parasites are particular about the species of scale, so exact pest identification is important. Use *Metaphycus helvolus* on hemispherical scale and black scale; *Aphytis melinus* or *Comperiellas bifasciate* on California red scale and oleander scale.

How to use: Scale infestations usually occur on only a few plants in the house or small greenhouse. The most efficient way to use predators is to cage them on the infested plants for a few weeks. You can make a simple cage out of a large square of lightweight, sheer curtain material. Just drape it over the plants and fasten it loosely at the base of the pot with string. You can put supports around delicate plants to hold the screening away from the foliage.

For predatory lady beetles, try a minimum order (usually several hundred) distributed over infested plants. For control with wasps, order five to ten parasites per infested plant and repeat the same release in two or three weeks.

Mealybug Predator and Parasites

The mealybug destroyer, *Cryptolaemus montrouzieri*, also called the Australian lady beetle, is a black-and-coral beetle that is an excellent predator of several species of mealybugs. However, demand has outstripped supply worldwide in the last few years, making them virtually unobtainable. Several companies are making special efforts to produce more beetles, so supply problems should ease in the future. There are also parasitic wasps that control mealybugs.

Protection offered: Three parasitic wasps are also sold separately or in a mixture for mealybug control: *Leptomastidea abnormis* kills citrus mealybugs only, *Leptomastix dactylopii* controls citrus and long-tailed mealybug, and *Anagyrus pseudococci* gets citrus, long-tailed, and obscure mealybugs.

How to use: The minimum order of Australian lady beetles (two to five beetles per infested plant) is enough for most gardeners. The beetle larvae are covered with white fluff, similar to the mealybugs they eat, so watch for them moving around among the stationary mealybugs. They leave behind some of the white cottony residues from dead mealybugs: You can wash this residue off leaves later.

Parasites work well as a follow-up biocontrol after Australian lady beetles have eaten the bulk of the mealybugs. Release five to ten parasites per infested plant or one per 5 square feet a few weeks after releasing the predators. If you aren't sure what species of mealybug is damaging your plants, order the mixture and apply it at double the suggested rate.

Lacewings

Lacewings (*Chrysopa carnea* and *Chrysoperla rufilabrus*) are a good buy for home gardeners because they are hardy and will become established in most areas. They eat small, soft-bodied pests. The adults are ½-inch, delicate, beautiful insects with large, netted wings, whereas the larvae are small, alligator-like crawlers with large, curved mandibles for capturing their prey.

Protection offered: Lacewing larvae eat aphids, mealybugs, and small caterpillars, and in some cases, have been effective controls for thrips.

How to use: Lacewing larvae are cannibalistic, so distribute the eggs widely throughout the garden when you get them. Buy the smallest order you can, and apply one to three eggs per plant. Usually one release in the home garden or orchard is sufficient to establish a local population. If you have a severe aphid problem, reduce the population by spraying plants with a strong water spray, and then put out ten eggs per plant to establish a sufficiently large lacewing population. Try to order *C. rufilabrus*, because it seems to give the best control.

Trichogramma Wasps

Minute parasitic wasps from the genus *Trichogramma* have been studied for nearly a century and widely available for controlling pests for many years. These wasps are less than $\frac{1}{50}$ inch long. They lay their eggs in the eggs of more than 200 species of moths and butterflies whose larvae eat leaves.

The problem for the home gardener has been a lack of information on precisely when releasing *Trichogramma* is effective. Also, the quality of wasps sold has not always been adequate. *Trichogramma* species are not interchangeable; you must buy the species that parasitizes the type of caterpillars you want to control. However, insectaries frequently do not tell you what species they sell. In some cases, insectaries have even accidentally mixed up species during the rearing process.

Too often, *Trichogramma* wasps have been sold as a cure-all for many pests, including beetles, that they have not been shown to control. As a result, *Trichogramma* has a dubious reputation. I have noticed that suppliers are trying harder to explain when the use of these wasps is appropriate and how to release them successfully.

Protection offered: Mass releases of various species of *Trichogramma* over large areas have successfully controlled orchard, corn, cotton, forestry, and field crop pests. *Trichogramma* is one of the most widely applied biological control agents in commercial agriculture, but whether it is useful on a small, garden-scale program is still not known. One large-scale pesticide company plans to start research and rearing of *Trichogramma* wasps, so we should see more types of these wasps available in the future.

How to use: If you want to experiment with *Trichogramma,* make sure the wasps are present when the target pest eggs are being laid. Professional pest managers use pheromone traps to find out when peak flights of pest moths occur in the area. For the home gardener, buying traps and *Trichogramma* may be too costly. The best course is to release wasps every five to seven days for one month during the period moths are present. Most suppliers ship the parasite pupae glued to small cards. After the cards are set out in the garden, the adult wasps emerge from the pupae and fly off to find moth eggs for egg-laying sites. The suggested release rate is 5,000 to 7,000 wasps (generally that amount is on one card) per 2,000 square feet of garden. For home orchards, release 5,000 to 7,000 parasites per two to three trees. If trees are under heavy caterpillar attack, release at least 5,000 per tree. To control European corn borer, release *T. evanescens* or *T. nibilale.* For orchard or tree pests, release *T. minutum.*

New Bugs with Promise

Research on beneficial insects for home garden and agricultural use is very active, and many new insect predators and parasites should be developed for commercial sale in the next several years. Two valuable insects for home gardeners, commercially available in 1991 or 1992, are minute pirate bugs and spined soldier bugs.

Minute Pirate Bug

These quick, black-and-white-patterned, ¼-inch true bugs (*Orius tristicolor*) are native to most of North America. Both adults and the wingless yellow or brown nymphs are excellent native predators of rust mites, spider mites, thrips, and small, soft insects such as aphids, leafhoppers, and small caterpillars. Their life cycles take three to four weeks to complete. Large populations will build up in areas where there are plants with lots of pollen, such as goldenrod, wild carrot, and yarrow. Methods for mass-producing this predator are currently being developed. Once it is widely available, this native species is likely to be worth establishing in home gardens and orchards, especially in areas where flower thrips cause serious damage to flowers and fruit. Buy the smallest order (or try releasing two to five bugs per infested plant) and distribute them widely throughout the garden.

Spined Soldier Bug

This predatory bug (*Podisus maculiventris*) attacks soft pests such as the larvae of Colorado potato beetles and Mexican bean beetles. Soldier bugs are just beginning to be used in home gardens. Their use looks very promising, but is still experimental. If you want to experiment, try releasing five per square yard of bean or potato patch. In three weeks, there should be a decline in pest larvae. Take a close look at the soldier bugs before you release them, and be sure you can identify them: They look very similar to stink bugs, a common garden pest.

Microbial Insecticides

Like other animals, insects suffer from a variety of diseases caused by bacteria, fungi, nematodes, protozoa, and viruses. These naturally occurring insect diseases have been studied for many years as potential pest control agents; several are available for use in the home garden.

One of the first concerns you may have about using insect diseases is whether humans or other animals can catch the diseases. After all, malaria is really a disease of both humans and mosquitoes. Regulatory agencies have been extremely careful about the potential risks of insect diseases—so much so that registration of microbial insecticides has been considerably delayed by the extensive testing required, and only a few such products are now registered for use in North America. One of these, the bacterium *Bacillus thuringiensis*, has been sold commercially for decades. With sales in 1988 of more than $35 million, it is worth nearly 1 percent of the global pesticide trade. It has never been known to live in any kind of organism other than certain insect larvae. Ironically, this very specificity—the wonderful advantage to using these insect diseases to control pests—is a disadvantage to manufacturing companies that may not want to spend the time and money required to test a product with such a limited market.

Most insect diseases, with the exception of parasitic nematodes, take a relatively long time to infect their hosts. The insect must eat viruses, bacteria, and protozoa to become infected, whereas fungi penetrate the surface of the insect once it comes into contact with the fungal spores. Insect-parasitic nematodes actively search through the soil for pests to infect. In some cases, after a disease organism is sprayed on a pest population, one insect infects another, providing control long after the first spray. A good example is the bacterial milky disease spores (*Bacillus popilliae*), which continue to attack Japanese beetle grubs in the soil, in some cases also spreading to new areas, more than 45 years after the soil was originally inoculated.

One problem with using insect diseases as pesticides is the difficulty in knowing whether they are working or not. Because they rarely kill immediately, it is easy to assume the spray didn't work. The key is to continue monitoring the success of your spray program, even a couple of weeks or months after spraying, by checking for sick or peculiar-looking insects. Diseased insects may have opaque pink or chalky white blood (normal insect blood is green or yellowish) or cottony or fuzzy growths on their bodies. They may move sluggishly or act strangely—sitting exposed on top of plants or hanging upside down from twigs.

In the following listings, some brand names of commercial products are listed. Keep in mind that brand names may change with time. Ask for the microbial pesticide by its generic name if you're not certain about a brand name; a knowledgeable salesperson will be able to help. In many cases, you'll be more likely to find these products in mail-order catalogs than at garden centers.

Bacillus thuringiensis (BT)

I first read about the bacterial insect disease, *Bacillus thuringiensis,* or BT, nearly 20 years ago in an *Organic Gardening and Farming* magazine article on new products. Although my local Department of Agriculture representative had never heard of it, he made a special effort to find a source and was able to give me a few tablespoons to try out in my garden. I was so impressed with the results on imported cabbageworms eating my cabbage that I have depended on BT for control of such caterpillars. Today BT is the most widely used biological control agent in the world.

BT belongs to a group of bacteria that form spores with thick, protective walls that enable them to survive for a short time in the environment. It is also a crystal-forming bacterium, that is, it produces a diamond-shaped crystal of toxic material inside the spore. After an insect eats the spores, the toxic crystals dissolve in its stomach juices, which immediately paralyzes the gut and causes the insect to stop eating. The spores also germinate and multiply in the insect's blood, causing acute blood poisoning. As the BT cells multiply, they also produce yet another toxin, thuringiensin (for information on development of this toxin as an insecticide see "Thuringiensin" on page 229). The insect usually dies from the combined effects of starvation, poisoning, and

Don't Stress Your Microbials

Don't be fooled by appearances when you buy microbial insecticides. While the container may look similar to packaging for insecticidal chemicals, what you've bought is a box of microscopic animals that may die if not properly handled. For instance, it's not a good idea to leave your box of microbes sitting in the car on a hot day while you finish shopping. Generally, microbial products last longest when kept under cool, dry conditions in the original container. They don't keep at all once the water is added to make a spray, because the water activates the dormant organisms.

Also remember that environmental factors can shorten or prolong the life of microbes after spraying. Exposure to the ultraviolet light in sunlight can drastically shorten the life of the spores. Some organisms, such as *Nosema* protozoa, last only 8 to 12 hours in direct sunlight; viruses generally last less than three days. Unprotected *Bacillus thuringiensis* (BT) spores last less than a day. Thorough coverage of the lower surfaces of leaves improves effectiveness because the organisms will last longer in the shade of the leaf underside.

Temperatures higher than 90°F also shorten the lives of microbial sprays. Spray in the evening on hot summer days as the air starts to cool. The microbes then have the longest possible period of time at lower temperatures, without sunlight, to be picked up by a host insect.

Exposure to high, drying winds shortens the lifespan of microbial spores. Winds also disperse the microbes and blow them onto the ground. This is not necessarily bad, because the soil is a natural storehouse for several insect diseases, but it does put them out of reach of leaf-eating pests that you want to control. Heavy rains will also wash the microorganisms into the soil, but moderate rainfall is helpful—the splashing raindrops will spread the disease to other plants.

---

bacterial infection. Unfortunately, BT does not live in the environment for very long; therefore, it can't be relied on to continue spreading in pest populations.

BT is not toxic to humans and other mammals. It is specific to certain groups of insects—mainly caterpillars, although some flies and beetles are susceptible to some varieties of BT—and has no effect at all on other groups of pest or beneficial insects. But keep in mind that caterpillars are the larvae of butterflies, and BT infects a broad range of species. If you are a butterfly-lover, be very careful when and how you spray BT in your yard and garden. Since BT doesn't last long in the environment, if you spray it specifically on plants that are infested with pest caterpillars, you will likely not cause great harm to the larvae of your butterfly friends.

But don't let the spray drift to uninfected plants, or to weedy or waste areas where the caterpillars you want to preserve may be feeding.

Because of the concentration of research on this bacterium, there are now more than 1,100 strains isolated. The varieties you are most likely to use are *Bacillus thuringiensis* var. *kurstaki* (BTK), *Bacillus thuringiensis* var. *israelensis* (BTI), and *Bacillus thuringiensis* var. *san diego* (BTSD).

Along with research on different strains of BT, there has been a great deal of work on various additives that increase the effectiveness and longevity of BT in the environment. Some BT products contain ultraviolet inhibitors that help protect the spores from deteriorating in sunlight before caterpillars have a chance to eat them.

Protection offered: The most widely sold variety is BTK (strain HD-1), which controls a wide range of caterpillars, including cabbage looper, diamondback moth, imported cabbageworm, spruce budworm, and tomato hornworm. Another strain of BTK, NRD-12, shows promise for controlling beet armyworm and is more effective than HD-1 against gypsy moth, spruce budworm, and tobacco budworm. BTI is now sold widely for control of mosquitoes, black flies, and stable flies. BTSD is active against Colorado potato beetle larvae, boll weevils, and elm leaf beetles and has some effect on black vine weevils. It does not affect insects susceptible to the other BT varieties.

How to use: Most BT products are sold as wettable powders or liquid concentrates that are mixed with water to make a spray (follow dilution directions on label). The unmixed products keep well up to two years if stored in a cool, dry place. Do not store the diluted spray mixture. You can also buy a granular BT product that you sprinkle on tips of corn ears or into silks to control European corn borer. Apply BT sprays when caterpillars or larvae are just big enough to begin eating holes through leaves and thus will eat enough spores to infect themselves. Thorough coverage of leaf undersides is important because spores will last longest there, where they are protected from sun. Spraying in the evening will also help prolong spore life. BT can be mixed with other insecticides, soap sprays,

BT Varieties and Victims

The three widely available varieties of BT (*Bacillus thuringiensis*) are listed here along with the pest insects they control. V indicates variable results as a control method; H indicates applying a higher concentration than the label rate is necessary for effective control; G indicates good control; X indicates excellent control.

BTK (*Bacillus thuringiensis* var. *kurstaki*)

Alfalfa caterpillar (X)	Fall webworm (G)
Armyworms (G)	Grape leaffolder (G)
Bagworms (X)	Grapeleaf skeletonizer (G)
Beet armyworm (G)	
Cabbage looper (G)	Green cloverworm (G)
Cankerworms (X)	Gypsy moth (H)
Codling moth (V)	Hornworms (G)
Corn earworm/tomato fruitworm (V)	Imported cabbageworm (X)
Cutworms (G)	Inchworm (G)
Diamondback moth (X)	Io moth (G)
Douglas-fir moths (G)	Jack pine budworm (G)
European corn borer (G)	Leafrollers (G)
	Melonworm (G)

Mimosa webworm (G)	Sod webworm (G)
Oleander hawk moth (G)	Spanworms (X)
Orangedog (G)	Spruce budworms (H)
Peachtree borer (V)	Tent caterpillars (X)
Pickleworm (G)	Tobacco budworm (G)
Pine butterfly (G)	Tobacco hornworm (G)
Redhumped caterpillar (G)	Variegated cutworm (G)
Saddleback caterpillar (G)	Walnut caterpillar (G)
Saltmarsh caterpillar (G)	Western spruce budworm (G)

BTSD (*Bacillus thuringiensis* var. *san diego*)

Black vine weevil (V)	Elm leaf beetle (G)
Boll weevil (G)	
Colorado potato beetle (G)	

BTI (*Bacillus thuringiensis* var. *israelensis*)

Black flies (G)	Mosquitoes (G)
Fungus gnats (G)	

or horticultural oils to increase effectiveness.

Although it was thought impossible at one time, some insects, such as flies and stored products moths, have become resistant to BT. Therefore, as with any pesticide, time your sprays to have the most effect against the pest populations and only use sprays when they are needed, not as a preventive measure.

Commercial products: BTK (HD-1): Bactur; Bugtime; Caterpillar Attack; Caterpillar Killer; Dipel; Dipel Granular; Thuricide
BTK (NRD-12): Javelin
BTI: Bactimos; Gnatrol; Mosquito Attack; Teknar; Vectobac
BTSD: Colorado Potato Beetle Attack; M-One

Milky Disease Spores

Milky disease spores are the oldest commercial insect disease product on the market. The bacteria that cause milky disease (also called milky spore disease) are the most important enemies of Japanese beetles in North America. First discovered in 1933 in New Jersey, milky disease bacteria were widely applied by the U.S. Department of Agriculture between 1939 and 1951 and have been used ever since to control the grubs of Japanese beetles.

Two bacteria cause milky disease: *Bacillus popilliae* and *B. lentimorbus*. Both are spore-forming bacteria that survive for years in the soil. Japanese beetle grubs eat the spores while feeding on grass roots. Infected grubs are filled with an opaque, milky white liquid that is chock-full of bacterial spores. *B. lentimorbus* mostly attacks the youngest stages of the grubs, while *B. popilliae* mainly attacks older larvae. The two species usually are combined in commercial products.

As infected grubs move through the soil, they spread the disease to uninfected areas. Some areas still have diseased larvae appearing 45 years after spores were applied to the sod. This disease seems to be specific for Japanese beetles and a few closely related species, and after such a long history of use, there are no concerns about safety for other nontarget organisms.

Protection offered: The disease controls Japanese beetles, June beetles, and May beetles in the grub stage.

How to use: Areas of sod and lawn, especially in new housing developments or areas that have not been in grass before, should be treated once with milky disease spores. The spores are sold as a dust you can apply any time of year, except when the ground is frozen. The disease will have the most impact on Japanese beetle populations if it is applied on a community-wide basis because beetles can fly into your yard from as far as $1/8$ mile away. Spreading spores on your lawn only will control the grubs, but you will still see migrant beetles on your plants.

The disease is most effective where soil temperatures exceed 70°F during the summer. It is not as effective north of New York City and throughout central Pennsylvania (40°N latitude) and the upper Midwest as it is further south.

Use 7 to 10 pounds of spore dust per acre or about 10 ounces per 2,500 square feet, applying the dust in spots roughly 4 feet apart. This is about one level teaspoon of powder per spot. About 20 ounces treats 5,000 feet of lawn and 1 pound treats about 225 spots.

You can make an old-fashioned, and still very useful, applicator from a 1-pound coffee can or other large tin and a broom handle. First, punch holes in the bottom of the can with a 10 penny nail (this size is important: it determines how much powder is released). Then bolt the side of the can to the broom handle (or other round stick or dowel) so that the bottom of the can is 4 inches from one end of the handle.

Fill the can three-quarters full with milky disease dust. To apply the dust, sharply tap the end of the stick against the lawn. One rap will release the right amount of powder for each treatment spot. Try to apply the dust just before a rain, or water the area lightly after you apply the dust to carry the powder down to the grass roots.

A granular formulation of milky disease is also available. It can be applied with a broadcast seeder or fertilizer spreader. Use about 4 pounds per 2,500 square feet. Water it afterwards for best results.

Commercial products: Doom; Grub Attack; Grub Killer; Japidemic

Viral Diseases

The insect disease viruses belong to the group known as baculoviruses, which are adapted exclusively to infect insects and mites and have never been known to infect other kinds of animals or plants. Viral diseases break out naturally in crowded insect populations. It seems that some viruses are always present, but latent, and under stress conditions, they spread through the population. Their devastating effect on crowded cultures of silkworms has been known since the 1500s. Baculoviruses should be a top priority for research in biological control because of their safety to humans and other nontarget organisms and to the environment.

Most of the insect disease viruses infect caterpillars, and a few attack sawflies and flies. Of the more than 450 viruses known so far, the majority are from two main groups: the granulosis viruses (GVs) and the nuclear polyhedrosis viruses (NPVs)—don't worry about their jaw-breaking names, even researchers who study them call them by their initials. Both of these viruses form a capsule that protects them in the environment until they are eaten by an insect. After the insect eats a leaf with the virus on it, the capsule dissolves inside the insect's gut, releasing the particles, which then infect the stomach cells and spread to other organs. The victims stops eating a few hours after eating the virus, but it may live for three to nine more days. When the insect dies, its body is full of a liquid containing millions of virus capsules. The slightest disturbance will cause its body to burst open, re-

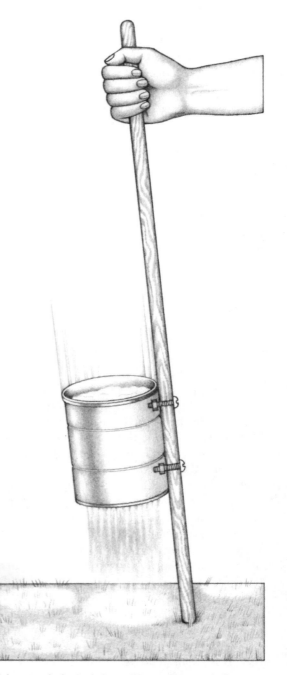

A homemade duster fashioned from a broom handle and coffee can is useful for spreading milky disease spores on your lawn to control Japanese beetle grubs.

leasing the capsules onto the surrounding leaves.

Studies show that predatory and parasitic insects are not harmed by the viruses that kill their prey. Predatory bugs and lacewings that feed on infected armyworms even excrete enough live virus particles to infect other armyworms feeding nearby.

Protection offered: The commercial status of virus products is still very shaky. Between 1960 and 1975, 17 different virus preparations were produced commercially or were prepared for marketing in the United States, but only a few are available. These are for control of cotton bollworm, codling moth, tobacco budworm, and possibly in the near future, for control of imported cabbageworm.

The United States and Canadian forest services hold registrations for five viruses used against forest pests (mostly for gypsy moths and sawflies); these viruses are not available to the public. Decyde (for codling moths) was marketed for a short time and then withdrawn.

A cooperative group of researchers and apple growers in California has renewed efforts to make codling moth GV available by organizing the production of the virus. This is a valuable service because the virus seems to be highly effective at controlling codling moth, a key pest in apples. Experiments have shown that three applications protected 97 percent of the apple crop. It also controls closely related pests like fruit tree leafroller and oriental fruit moth.

How to use: Viruses remain infective less than a day in full sunlight, so time sprays carefully. Apply them once or twice weekly during the pest's main egg-laying period so the virus can infect young caterpillars and other larvae just after they hatch (check with your local Cooperative Extension agent for information on dates for this period in your area). Good spray coverage on leaf undersides is important because virus particles will last longest in the shade. In hot, dry weather, spray in the evening to prolong the life of the virus.

Commercial products: Elcar (for cotton bollworm and tobacco budworm); Codling moth NPV (limited registration in California, Washington, and Oregon)

Fungal Diseases

Fungal diseases of insects are common, especially in dense populations of caterpillars, aphids, and flies. Fungi produce strands of mold, the mycelium, that can gradually penetrate an insect's protective cuticle both by mechanical force and by secreting chemicals that dissolve the cuticle. The mycelium moves on to infect the blood and internal organs; it is usually a slow death.

Hundreds of fungal diseases have been recorded in insects, although few have been studied for commercial potential. Probably the most widely known is *Beauveria bassiana,* first recorded in the early 1800s as a silkworm disease. It is known to infect more than 175 species, not all of them pests. It is a common disease in insects that spend part of their life cycles in the soil. Under the right conditions, it gives good, long-lasting control of Colorado potato beetles in the soil, especially where they overwinter. *Beauveria* products have been planned and tested but, although they are used extensively in other countries, they are not available in North America.

A fungal disease that has been tested in North America, but not registered for use, is *Verticillium lecanii.* Various strains of this fungus provide control for aphids, thrips, or whiteflies.

By 1992, you may see either of the two fungi on the market in this country. Others that are under investigation or are close to being registered for use in North America are *Lagenidium,* a very promising control for mosquitoes, *Coelomomyces,* currently being tested on aquatic pests, such as mosquitoes, and *Paecilomyces,* for use against whiteflies and related pests. New, very effective strains of this fungus have been discovered by researchers in Florida and Texas who are currently seeking patents. Others you might want to know about are *Metarrhizium,* which attacks over 200 species, mostly soil-dwellers such as wireworms, and *Entomophthera,* which attacks a wide variety of insects.

Protozoan Diseases

Protozoa are tiny, one-celled animals (their name literally means "first animals") that are either free-living in the environment or parasitic and living inside other animals. The important protozoa for biological control are a group that form spores; this is the usual stage that is transmitted from one insect to another. A pest must eat the spores to be infected. The spores then germinate in its gut, and the infection spreads. When an insect catches a protozoan disease, it is affected slowly. While not all infected insects die, survivors become chronically ill; they are slow and sluggish, don't reproduce well, and may be abnormally sensitive to insecticides and high temperatures. Protozoa are likely to be most useful as a means of lowering pest numbers through chronic effects of disease because they continue to act over several generations once established in an area.

Protection offered: The protozoan *Vairimorpha necatrix,* which attacks various caterpillars, is being studied for its value. One protozoan product, *Nosema locustae,* is now available commercially for control of a wide range of grasshopper species and Mormon crickets.

How to use: *Nosema* products are sold as spores mixed in bran bait that attracts the hoppers to eat it. They are effective when used as a community-wide control, spread over large areas of a local district (the bait can be spread by an airplane).

In your yard, broadcast the bait on lawns and garden beds in early summer when you see immature grasshoppers (less than ¾ inch long). Use about 1 pound per acre. If your property is smaller than 1 acre, it is not worth applying *Nosema,* because grasshoppers cover so much territory they are not likely to become infected.

If you have problems with grasshoppers in a small yard, try to get several of your neighbors to broadcast *Nosema* as a cooperative effort. You can expect some carryover effect into the next season because infected grasshoppers that don't die continue to lay infected eggs. However, you should reapply yearly as long as your grasshopper problem persists.

Commercial products: Grasshopper Attack; Grasshopper Control, NOLO-Bait

Insect Parasitic Nematodes

Nematodes (also called eelworms) are narrow, hollow worms with pointed heads and tails. Some beneficial nematodes break down organic matter and can be found in compost piles. Other nematodes are pests that attack plant roots or are parasitic types that kill insects. Most of these species are too small to see with the unaided eye.

Some parasitic nematodes have been studied for commercial development as biological controls of common pests. The two most important groups of parasitic nematodes are *Heterorhabditis heliothidis* (HH) with its related species, and *Neoaplectana carpocapsae* (NC), which also goes by the name of *Steinernema carpocapsae* (=*feltiae*).

The life cycles of both groups are similar: Eggs hatch into juvenile nematodes that shed their skins several times as they grow to the adult stage. The third time the juvenile molts its skin, it enters a resistant stage, with an extra-protective skin that enables it to live in the environment for an extended time (months in some cases). This is the stage that seeks out insects by homing in on their breathing and body heat and then enters through the insect's mouth, breathing tubes, or other body openings.

The nematodes release bacteria carried in their bodies into the insect's body. These bacteria multiply, providing food for the nematodes. At summer soil temperatures, an infected insect usually dies within one or two days from massive blood poisoning, making nematodes the fastest-acting microbial biological control. Any target insects that are not immediately killed may become sterile or exhibit odd behavior that makes them vulnerable to predators. An insect infected with HH may appear reddish. If infected with NC, it will be chalky white or gray. The nematodes continue to feed inside the insect until they are too crowded, then the resistant third stage juveniles leave the corpses to seek other prey.

A wide range of pests have been infected by nematodes in laboratory experiments, but considerably fewer have been successfully controlled in field conditions. This is because nematodes need moist conditions to be most effective and, like other microbial biocontrol products, die very quickly when exposed to direct sunlight. Generally, nematodes are unsuccessful in warm, dry soils or against foliage pests. Nematodes are best used to control soil pests or those that live in protected, hidden environments—like borers that live under tree bark—where controls such as sprays, dusts, or predatory insects are least effective.

Protection offered: HH nematodes provide control for black vine weevils, corn rootworm larvae, cucumber beetle larvae, fungus gnat larvae, masked chafers, mole crickets, and wireworms. NC nematodes have been successful against carpenterworms, currant borers, earwigs, navel orangeworms, onion maggots, pillbugs, seed corn maggots, sod webworms, sowbugs, and strawberry root weevils.

Both types of nematodes have shown promise against cabbage root maggots, chafers, codling moth larvae, Colorado potato beetle larvae (when they crawl into the soil to pupate), cutworms, fall armyworms, Japanese beetle grubs, and June bug grubs.

How to use: Nematodes are usually sold in a semidehydrated state, as a powder, or embedded in a sponge which is soaked in water to make a solution of nematodes. One company sells them in a handy container with the dehydrated nematodes inside so that all you do is add cool water and shake well.

You can apply nematodes with a watering can or sprayer, but you should agitate the tank or container frequently while spraying to keep the nematodes in the solution. They are not harmed when sprayed through standard spray equipment with large nozzles, and NC nematodes can even withstand being sprayed through pressurized sprayers or mist blowers. You can squirt them into borer holes using a clean oilcan or syringe, and they have been successfully released through trickle irrigation systems. To modify trickle irrigation systems, insert a 1-quart plastic jar containing the nematode solution into the drip line just after the header hose. You will need to make a hole in the bottom of the jar and glue in a hose fitting compatible with the irrigation system.

For soil pests, you will need to apply about 35,000 nematodes per square foot or about 15,000 per plant. One million nematodes will treat soil pests in a row area 3-by-55 feet (165 square feet). To control pests in sod, spray nematodes evenly over the grass with a watering can or sprayer or pour them directly onto the grass: Use 100,000 to 500,000 nematodes per square yard. Apply the nematodes just before a heavy rainstorm, or water well after application, using at least $1/2$ inch of water to wash the nematodes down to the soil. The nematodes need several weeks to disperse through the soil and find the pests. It may take more than six weeks before you will know whether treatments have been effective.

Nematodes control various borers. For carpenterworms, squirt a mixture of nematodes and water into the holes bored into trees (about 17,000 nematodes per squirt from an oilcan when mixed according to label directions). Use a syringe to inject nematodes into squash vines to control squash borers. Syringes are usually marked in cubic centimeters (cc). There are about 5,000 nematodes in 2 cc of the nematode/

water mixture. You can also inject nematodes into holes bored inside the tips of corn ears, onto the silks, to control corn earworms.

Promising results have been seen against overwintering codling moths on apple trees when nematodes were sprayed onto the tree bark or were soaked into absorbent tree bands, which infected the larvae when they took refuge there. To make a tree band, line a 2-foot-wide strip of plastic or nylon cloth with terry cloth, an old towel, or plastic sponge material (like the spongy material used to wrap fragile items for shipping). Wrap the band around the tree with the cloth or sponge to the outside, and tie a string around the middle of the band so that the top section falls over the string. Soak the absorbent cloth with the water mixture of nematodes once or twice weekly.

Commercial products: BioSafe; Grub Eaters; Phero Tech; Scanmask; Seek

Bug-Killing Microbes

Using naturally occurring disease pathogens to kill insect pests is a strong area of research and development for the 1990s. Many of the pathogens listed below are commercially available; others will become available as the decade progresses. Check with your organic gardening supplier to see if the specific pathogens you'd like to use are on the market.

Bacteria

Bacillus thuringiensis var. *israelensis* (BTI)—black flies, mosquitoes
Bacillus thuringiensis var. *kurstaki* (BTK)—caterpillar pests
Bacillus thuringiensis var. *san diego* (BTSD)—Colorado potato beetle
Bacillus popilliae—Japanese beetle

Baculoviruses

Nuclear polyhedrosis virus (NPV)—armyworms, cabbage loopers, cotton bollworm, gypsy moths, soybean looper, tobacco budworm, velvetbean caterpillar
Granulosis virus (GV)—cabbage butterfly, codling moth, oriental fruit moth, potato tuberworm

Protozoa

Nosema locustae—grasshoppers, Mormon crickets
Vairimorpha necatrix—caterpillars

Fungi

Beauveria bassiana—many species that have soil-dwelling stages
Coelomomyces spp.—aquatic insects
Entomophthora spp.—many insect species
Lagenidium giganteum—mosquitoes
Metarrhizium anisopliae—soil pests, wireworm
Nomuraea rileyi—soybean caterpillars
Paecilomyces farinosus—whiteflies
Verticillium lecanii—aphids, thrips, whitefly

Nematodes

Steinernema bibionis—many soil pests and borers
Steinernema carpocapsae (=*feltiae*)—many soil pests and borers
Heterorhabditis glaseri—many soil pests and borers
Heterorhabditis bacteriophora—many soil pests and borers
Heterorhabditis heliothidis—many soil pests and borers

PHYSICAL CONTROLS

After using cultural measures to avoid possible insect damage and making your garden a refuge for insect predators and parasites, it's time to take up watch for the arrival of the bad guys. There are many simple devices you can make or buy to help you monitor the populations of pest insects in your garden. Some of these devices also serve as effective control measures in themselves.

When insects appear, your first steps in organic control should include several measures that prevent damage by physically keeping insects off of your plants. The equipment you need for these control methods ranges from the most basic tools—your fingers—to insect traps that are the product of sophisticated scientific research on insect biology and behavior.

I am a great advocate of these controls because I have consistently found that the majority of home garden insect problems can be solved with some form of physical control. They are practical, effective, and generally long-lasting. Floating row covers, tree bands, and plant collars will give you season-long control with minimal maintenance. Other physical controls, such as copper slug barriers, provide years of control.

The most important reason to rely on physical controls is their simplicity and effectiveness. Generally, once these controls are put in place, they provide season-long control. And as a preventive control, they help you avoid situations in which using a poison dust or spray would be the only effective control measure.

Handpicking

Although not for the squeamish, picking pests off by hand is less trouble in some cases than spraying or other measures. It is certainly a method with no side effects on nontarget insects!

Equip yourself with a pail of soapy water when you set out in the garden to handpick. You can pick up individual insects with your fingers and drop them into the water to kill them. If you are repelled by the thought of handling certain pests—like huge green tomato hornworms—you can break off the leaflet with the caterpillar on it and drop it in the bucket. Handpicking is an effective way to reduce damage from spinach leafminers that infest spinach, chard, and beet greens. If you pick and destroy the "mined" parts of leaves from the first brood early in the season, the next generation of leafminers will be substantially reduced. Egg masses of gypsy moths and tussock moths can be scraped off tree bark. As the silks dry up on your sweet corn, you can check the tip of each ear for corn earworms, small white or greenish caterpillars, and dig them out before they do much damage. It is a daunting task to handpick Mexican bean beetles or Colorado potato beetles, but it can be done. (You can even enlist the aid of the littlest gardeners in your family, who often are not squeamish about handling bugs, and pay them by the cupful.) While the beetles and larvae of these two insects are distinctive, the eggs of both look like lady beetle eggs; if there are any lady beetles about, be cautious about destroying clusters of upright yellow eggs.

Shaking

A variation of handpicking that is particularly effective for beetle pests is shaking or jarring the insects out of the foliage. This works especially well early in the morning when it is cool and insects are sluggish. Spread a plastic or cloth sheet along the garden row or under shrubs, trees, or flowers and sharply tap or shake the plants. This is a good way to catch Japanese beetles, Colorado potato beetles, and plum curculios. Drop the pests that fall onto the cloth into a pail of soapy water to finish them off. You can also use this method to catch black vine weevils on rhododendrons and other ornamentals. These pests feed at night, so plan your bug-stalking foray for after dark.

A handheld beating tray made of a square yard of canvas or plastic stretched on a light wooden frame is helpful for this technique. To make the tray, sew four small triangular pieces of material at the four corners of your canvas or plastic. Cut two sturdy wooden dowels or 1×2s to fit and fasten them together in the middle with a bolt and wing nut. Insert the ends of these crosspieces into the corner pockets to make a rigid tray.

Hold the tray under the branch with one hand while tapping the branch with the padded stick. This is an effective way to monitor orchard pests. Use moderation: If you break the branches off your trees or bushes, the insect problem will become of secondary importance.

Detasseling

Detasseling corn by hand to control European corn borers has proven useful in reducing damage. Removing and destroying tassels kills the borers that are feeding on the tassels, and also removes the pollen source—a major part of the larval diet. You must remove the tassels when they are young, before they have shed their pollen. Because of this, it's important to use cultivars that you know from experience are reliable pollinators. Remove the tassels from all the plants in three out of four rows of corn, leaving a quarter of the corn with the flowers intact to ensure good pollination. You should

Tapping tree or shrub branches with a padded stick will dislodge plum curculios. Use a canvas tray to catch the insects as they fall, and then dump them into a pail of soapy water to kill them.

use this method in combination with other controls, such as BT sprays, parasitic nematodes, and placing droplets of mineral oil in the tips of the ears.

Vacuuming

The high-tech version of handpicking is vacuuming. Commercial strawberry producers use a machine called a "Bug-Vac" to remove tarnished plant bugs. The gentle suction from this machine removes the pests but not the beneficial predator mites, which cling tightly to leaves. While you can't take your vacuum cleaner out to your garden to suck up pests, you can successfully vacuum whiteflies off plants in a home greenhouse. Whiteflies usually rest on the undersides of top leaves of plants. Use an ordinary home vacuum cleaner or a handheld vacuum unit to clean whiteflies off leaves twice a week. Use care so you don't damage the foliage as you vacuum. This method is particularly useful if you have released parasitic wasps to control the whiteflies (see "Whitefly Parasitic Wasp," on page 177, for instructions on how to release parasitic wasps), because the wasps rest in the middle and lower parts of plants. By carefully vacuuming just the whiteflies at the top of the plant, you can help achieve a balance between pest and parasite populations sooner.

Water Sprays

Water sprays are another simple, cheap, nontoxic control method. A water spray kills mostly by physically damaging insects and, unlike chemical sprays, pests can't develop resistance to it. Water is a good control for aphids and spider mites. Water is as effective as most other sprays against aphids because their bodies are delicate. The force of a stiff spray of water knocks aphids off plants and bushes, killing and injuring many of them. Use a strong jet of water from a hose nozzle, powerful enough to wash aphids or mites away without damaging

any foliage. Be sure to spray the undersides of the leaves, as well. Repeat sprays as often as necessary to keep aphids and mites under control. Avoid splashing cold water on delicate ornamentals, such as fuchsias. If the weather is hot and sunny, spray in the early morning or at dusk to avoid leaving droplets on leaves, which could cause foliage to burn.

Insect Control Checklist

🐛 Use insect-resistant or -tolerant plants when available.

🐛 Grow your own transplants or buy plants from a reputable producer to avoid importing insect pests into your garden.

🐛 Keep your plants healthy so they can better withstand insect damage, and clear away dropped fruit and infested plant residues to reduce overwintering sites for pests.

🐛 Take frequent monitoring walks to check for signs of insect damage in your yard and garden.

🐛 Plant nectar crops and put out an insect bath to encourage the beneficial insects that prey on the pests in your garden.

🐛 Use two safe, inexpensive control methods—handpicking insect pests and washing them off plants with a strong spray of water—whenever practical.

🐛 Buy and release beneficials such as lacewings when pest populations are on the rise.

🐛 Put out barriers such as mulches, collars, row covers, and tree bands to keep pests from reaching your plants.

🐛 Use microbial insecticides, horticultural oil, and homemade repellent sprays and dusts to fight many common garden pests.

🐛 Spray or dust with botanical poisons only as a last resort when large populations of insect pests invade your garden.

Barriers

Using barriers to prevent pests from reaching plants is one of the simplest, oldest, and most effective ways to prevent damage. Most of the methods for protecting plants with barriers are familiar to organic gardeners. However, there are recent technical improvements in materials that make barriers more effective than ever before.

Floating Row Covers

Floating row covers don't really float. They are lengths of synthetic fabric that are so lightweight they appear to float when draped over your plants. The covers look like the white interfacing used in clothing and are made of spunbonded polypropylene or extruded plastic. They let in more than 80 percent of the sunlight that shines on them, and rain and irrigation water can pass through them. Leaving these covers on makes it possible to have season-long pest control and to thwart some species that are particularly trying for organic gardeners. They are most useful for food crops, as you aren't likely to want to cover your ornamental plants.

Floating row covers were invented to improve plant growth and extend the growing season. The microclimate under a cover is warmer and more humid during the day than the surrounding air. Minimum night temperatures are also higher, and there is less difference between day and night temperatures because heat loss at night is slowed. In coastal and short-season areas, plants may benefit from the heat-retaining properties of the row cover all season. In regions with hot summers, high temperatures under the cover may be partly offset by reduced evaporation, but you may have to remove the cover when it gets really hot.

The covers do break down in the sunlight, but should last at least 20 weeks. I have used mine for two seasons (and am saving them for a third). I patch small rips with duct tape or any plastic tape suitable for outdoor use, taping on both sides of the fabric so tape will be sticking to tape. In southern gardens with long, hot summers, row covers may last only one season.

Preserve your covers by removing them from the garden promptly after use, rinsing them with water to remove soil and dust, allowing them to dry thoroughly, and storing them away from sunlight.

You can also use good-quality cheesecloth, fine nylon mesh, organdy or sheer curtain material tacked onto bamboo hoops or wooden lath frames to screen insects away from plants. Because these fabrics block more light than polypropylene does, they are best suited for protecting seedlings. They should be removed once the danger of pest damage has passed or when the plants have become large enough to withstand some minor pest damage.

Protection offered: Floating row covers provide excellent protection for seedlings of all kinds from pests of all kinds (even seed-stealing birds). They will protect cabbage family seedlings from such difficult pests as flea beetles, cabbage root maggots, and the leaf-eating caterpillars. In my area, where carrot rust flies are a big problem, I swear by row covers to protect carrots, which grow large and sweet under cover. Row covers protect green beans from Mexican bean beetles and potato leafhoppers, shelter early asparagus spears from asparagus beetles, and keep Colorado potato beetles away from tomatoes, eggplant, and potatoes.

How to use: Begin by making sure you don't trap pests under the cover: Examine your plants thoroughly to make sure they're bug-free. Drape the covers over your plants, and bury the edges of the fabric with soil, allowing enough slack for plant growth. Spun-bonded polypropylene covers don't need to be supported by frames, even over seedlings. However, you may find it easier to take the covers on and off (so you can weed, thin, and harvest) if the cloth is tacked over lightweight frames or stretched over hoops of bamboo or aluminum tubing.

Leave a skirt of material several inches wide around the frame to bury in the soil. Beware of sharp corners on frames that can tear the material.

To stop carrot rust fly damage, leave covers on until carrots are pulled, because there is usually a late summer brood of flies. If these flies lay eggs on the carrots before they are pulled, the maggots will tunnel and grow in the carrots even after harvest. For crops such as beans or cabbage, row covers can be removed when the plants are big enough to withstand some insect damage. If you cover plants that need to be pollinated by insects, such as squash or melons, either remove the covers when the plants start to flower, or hand-pollinate them and leave the covers in place.

Commercial products: Agronet; Kimberley Farms Floating Row Covers; Miracle Mulch; Reemay

Cutworm Collars

Cutworm collars are stiff cylinders made of paper, cardboard, or plastic that encircle transplant stems at soil level. Putting collars around transplants at planting time should be a routine practice in early spring if cutworms are likely to be a problem in your area. Cutworms rest in the soil during the day and crawl along the soil at night, searching for plant stems to chew. The collars block the cutworms, completely preventing injury.

Protection offered: Collars protect against most species of cutworms, but they're not effective for climbing cutworms. Filling the collars with wood ashes or diatomaceous earth helps prevent root maggot flies from laying eggs near stem bases.

How to make: You can cut cutworm collars from a paper towel or toilet paper roll and slip them over the top of small seedlings. Or, curve a strip of lightweight cardboard around a seedling stem and clip it in place with staples or paper clips. Make the collars 2 to 3 inches wide and 1½ to 2 inches in diameter.

How to use: As you plant seedlings, encircle the stems with the collars. Push the collars into the soil so that about half the collar is below the soil surface. Paper collars disintegrate eventually, but by the time they do, your plants should be large enough that cutworms will not do significant damage.

Tree Bands

Barriers around tree trunks can be used to prevent pests from crawling up the trunk, so they're an effective control for insects that can't fly. Tree bands can be coated with sticky materials to make them into traps.

Protection offered: Tree bands are excellent barriers for older gypsy moth larvae, because they migrate daily from the treetop down the trunk to hide in leaf litter during the day, then climb back up at night to feed. Barriers are also useful on apple trees to intercept codling moth larvae looking for a place to spin cocoons, and on citrus to stop snails, ants, and beetles.

How to make: Estimate or measure the circumference of the tree trunks you plan to barricade. Cut 8- to 12-inch-wide strips of cotton cloth or burlap of the appropriate length for each tree. Be sure strips are long enough to overlap at the ends when wrapped around the tree.

How to use: As soon as trees leaf out in spring, tie bands of cotton cloth or burlap to tree trunks with a string around the middle of the cloth. Pull the top section of cloth down over the string so the cloth makes a dead end for pests trying to climb the trunk. If used for gypsy moth larvae, check daily in late afternoon and destroy the larvae. For codling moth larvae, removing the pests once weekly is sufficient.

You can also use corrugated paper or cardboard to form tree bands by wrapping several layers of it around the trunk, with the exposed ridges facing the tree. Tie with string. The larvae will seek shelter in the spaces between the paper and the bark. Remove the bands weekly and destroy the larvae. Continue this practice throughout the summer. You can reuse the bands until they wear out from handling and exposure to weather.

You can buy silicone-coated, flexible tape that is too slippery for ants and beetles to cross. Simply wrap this tape around the trunk to form an impassable barrier. On rough-barked trees, put a band of sticky compound like Tangle-Trap or Bug Gum along the inside edges of the top and bottom of the tape to prevent insects from crawling up or down through crannies between the tape and bark. Put an extra band of the adhesive along the outside top to stop insects that do manage to cross the slippery tape.

Snail-repellent tapes are also available to wrap around trunks. These have a sticky backing and are coated with cayenne pepper and salt to repel snails.

Commercial products: Repel'M III; Slick 'N' Stick; Snail Tape

Copper Barriers

Copper is very toxic to slugs and snails, and copper strips wrapped around tree trunks or stems of shrubs make a highly effective slug and snail repellent. Some scientific studies indicate that copper is effective because slugs and snails actually get an electric shock when they touch it. It's theorized that the slugs' slimy coating interacts chemically with the copper, creating an electric current. Using copper strips as a permanent edging for borders or beds is an effective but expensive way to keep slugs and snails off flowers and vegetables.

How to use: Estimate or measure the circumference of the stem or trunk of the plant. Use a copper strip that is longer than the circumference, so you can enlarge the strip as the plant gets bigger. Punch holes in the ends of the strips. Fasten the copper strip securely around the trunk or stem by feeding a piece of wire through the holes and twisting it tight. Remove suckers, water sprouts, and nearby weeds that might provide alternate routes for the snails and slugs to reach your plants.

To make a copper barrier around a flower or vegetable bed, bury a 3- to 4-inch-wide copper strip around the edge of the bed or border, with 2 to 3 inches of the copper exposed. Then

Slugs and snails will not cross a copper barrier. You can keep snails from climbing citrus trees by fastening a copper strip around the trunk (left). A copper border strip will save strawberries, vegetables, or flowering plants in a garden bed from slug and snail damage (right).

bend the top $\frac{1}{2}$ inch of the strip outward at a right angle to form a lip. Check the enclosed area and get rid of any slugs or snails that are already inside. Once they are removed, the bed or border should stay slug-free.

To protect plants on greenhouse benches, staple copper strips directly to the sides of wooden benches and around wooden legs. Or staple strips to wooden blocks mounted between bench supports and the top. Make sure the benches don't touch the greenhouse wall or glazing, because slugs can climb them to reach your benches as well. Protect plants grown at floor level with strips of copper as you would a bed or border.

Commercial products: Snail-Barr

Ant Barriers

Ants feed on aphid secretions. In fact, ants will actually carry aphids onto plants to set up a food source, then tend them and protect them from predators. Ant barriers on legs of greenhouse tables prevent ants from climbing up to seedlings.

How to make: Cut a hole that corresponds in size and shape to a cross-section of each table leg through the center of an aluminum pie plate .

How to use: Slide an inverted pie plate up each table leg. Fold each pie plate downward to form a cup and coat the inside of the cupped plate with a sticky compound like Tanglefoot. Be sure the crack between the pie plate and the table leg is sealed with caulking or Tanglefoot. Renew the sticky compounds when necessary; if the greenhouse isn't too dusty, the sticky surfaces may last as long as one year. You can leave these traps in place permanently to guard against ants.

Dehydrating Dusts

Insects have complex internal systems that minimize water loss when they breathe and a waxy or oily cuticle that prevents water loss through body surfaces. Any dust or powder that scratches this waxy coating destroys the insect's water balance and can kill the insect. These materials can be used as barriers because insects will try to avoid them. Slugs and snails also prefer to avoid dust and powder barriers but will cross them if they get hungry enough.

Protection offered: Dusts work well against cabbage root flies and, if renewed frequently, will reduce carrot rust flies. When painted on tree trunks, dehydrating dusts repel ants and may help deter adult forms of borers from laying eggs on the bark. Dehydrating barriers also have some effect on slugs.

How to make: To make a dehydrating dust paint, mix $\frac{1}{4}$ pound diatomaceous earth with 1 teaspoon of pure soap, like Ivory liquid, and enough water to make a thick slurry. Applying this paint to the lower trunk gives double protection; it shields the bark from the sun as well as discourages pests.

How to use: Spread a circle of dry wood ashes, diatomaceous earth, talc, or lime around any plants being attacked. Cover the area out to the dripline, or at least within a 6-inch radius of the stem. To deter cabbage root flies from laying eggs around the stems of cabbage family plants, heap a cone of diatomaceous earth or other dust around the stems at the soil line. Dust barriers are most effective when they're dry, so reapply after it rains or after you water the garden.

Root Fly Barriers

Paper or tar paper squares laid around the stems of cabbage family plants prevent female root flies from laying their eggs near roots (eggs hatch into maggots that burrow into roots).

Protection offered: If placed carefully, these squares protect cabbage family plants from cabbage root flies.

How to make: Cut a 6- to 8-inch square of tar paper or other heavy paper. Tar paper, available from your local lumber yard, works particularly well because it also repels the flies.

How to use: Plant seedlings through an

X-shaped slit in the center of a paper square. Make sure the paper fits as closely as possible to the stem so the female flies can't find any opening in which to lay eggs. Anchor the paper barrier flat against the soil surface with pebbles or a little soil. Leave the barriers in place all season because there are several generations of maggot flies throughout the growing season.

Traps

The way insects sense their surroundings and find their food plants or mates is quite complex. (See "How Do Insects Find Their Food [Your Garden]?" on the opposite page.) The most effective traps mimic the environmental cues that are important to the insects. Traps generally consist of an attractive component or lure (usually a color, odor, or shape) and a trapping component (usually sticky glue, water, or other liquid).

Traps are used in two ways: to trap enough individual insects to prevent significant crop damage or to monitor the emergence or arrival of a pest species.

When you're using traps to control pests directly, judge the effectiveness of the trapping program by its success in decreasing damage to your plants, not just by the body count in the trap. Even if your trap is filled with pests, if your plants are showing damage, you should try other control measures. If trapping alone is not succeeding in bringing the numbers of insects below damaging levels, it's possible that that particular pest population is very large in that season or the trap is attracting insects from outside the area to your garden.

Although monitoring traps do not prevent damage, they are useful because they help you time a spray treatment for maximum effect on the target pests while causing minimum harm to beneficial organisms. Monitoring also allows you to time releases of biological control agents that must be released at a precise point in the pest's life cycle to be effective.

Visual Traps

Some insects have "favorite" colors that cue them to the location of their host plants. These insects can be fooled by a trap board or strip painted with that color and covered with sticky glue. The color will attract the insects; when they alight, their feet and wings stick, and they die quickly. This trap is useful for gardeners because they can check how many and what type of insects are killed in the trap. Visual traps are easy and inexpensive to make.

Yellow Sticky Traps

Many insect species are attracted to yellow. The most commonly used insect trap is a bright yellow sheet of cardboard, plywood, or plastic coated with a sticky compound. To be effective, the color must be bright yellow.

Protection offered: Onion flies, cabbage root flies, carrot rust flies, aphids, and imported cabbageworms will land on yellow sticky traps. In the greenhouse, yellow traps will attract whiteflies, fungus gnats, aphids, and some thrips. Outdoors, in areas where imported cabbageworm is not a serious pest, traps may be the only control method you need to use to prevent damage (the traps attract the adult females, a white butterfly, when they are ready to lay eggs). You may find some winged aphids in the traps, but don't rely on these traps to control aphids. The wingless (nonflying) forms are the ones attacking your plants.

How to make: Paint cardboard, plywood, or other rigid material with white primer, then with two coats of bright yellow paint (Federal Safety Yellow No. 659 from Rustoleum Company and Saturn Yellow from Day-Glo Colors are two that work well). Long, narrow, rectangular or oval shapes make the best attractants, so a painted 1-quart milk carton is a good trap.

Once the trap is the appropriate shade of yellow, it's ready for the sticky coating. To catch small, light-bodied insects such as whiteflies,

How Do Insects Find Their Food (Your Garden)?

Insects have powerful senses of taste and smell, but the way they detect aromas and tastes is very different from how humans experience these senses. Insects have fine sensory hairs, sensory pegs, and other structures scattered all over their body surfaces. For example, male honeybees have more than 30,000 receptors on their antennae alone. Some of these receptors sense taste and smell; others sense sound, light, movement, even magnetism and gravity. Taste and smell receptors can be located anywhere on the body, not just the head. For example, houseflies and some butterflies sense sweetness with receptors located on their feet. The precision of insect chemical detection is hard to believe—insects can recognize a single molecule of an odor wafting in the air.

Insects do not see the same colors we do—they tend to see yellow, green, blue, and ultraviolet wavelengths, which is why black (ultraviolet) lights are used in light traps. Very few can detect red colors (one exception seems to be apple maggot flies). Insects with very primitive eyes (called ocelli), such as maggots and caterpillars, find vertical dark shapes to climb by swaying their bodies back and forth to move their ocelli. Eyes of predators, such as dragonflies and praying mantids, are very highly developed. They judge distance and size of their prey very accurately and are very efficient at seeing the slightest movement.

Chemical receptors that are equivalent to our senses of taste and smell are usually the most important to plant-feeding insects. They search for chemical compounds that they recognize as belonging to their food plants and can tell the type of plant and whether the leaf is suitable for food. For many plant-eating insects, it is thought that odors tempt the female to hover in an area and begin searching, then color or other cues take over and entice her to land and try things out. In some species, such as the diamondback moth, the reproductive state of the female moth affects her response to plant cues. She becomes more and more interested in the "smell" of cabbage plants as the time nears for egg laying. Insects that parasitize other insects also search out their prey by "smell"; they can even tell if another parasite has already laid an egg in that particular pest. Generally, predators and parasitic insects have more acute senses than plant-eating species, which helps them react quickly to the odor and movement of their prey.

Most traps make use of insects' chemical receptors, although detection of shapes also appears to be important to some species. A trap's size and shape, its height above the ground, and the kind of background are all important visual cues that influence its attractiveness.

paint traps with Tangle-Trap diluted with paint thinner (1 part Tangle-Trap to 2 parts thinner) or use Stiky Stuff, STP oil treatment, or the brush-on formula of Tangle-Trap without dilution. To catch heavier insects like cabbage butterflies, use Tangle-Trap or Stickem Special without dilution (use a spatula, putty knife, or kitchen knife to apply it). Heavy insects can escape from traps coated with the lighter materials. When you are handling the glue, watch out! It is extremely sticky and messy to work with. It's a good idea to leave one corner of the trap untreated as a fingerhold. You can reuse plywood traps many times: Just scrape the glue and insects off the wood or wipe them away with baby oil and re-treat it.

You can make a simple wire guard to enclose the trap so your hair and sleeves won't get caught in the glue while you are working near the traps. If you are trapping small insects, hang the trap inside a cylinder of ½-inch plastic netting to protect you and keep other nontarget insects from gumming up the trap.

How to use: To catch garden pests, place the traps on stakes around the garden at average plant height, among or close to the foliage.

In greenhouses, suspend traps from trellis wires near the tops of plants to catch whiteflies and thrips. Hang them near ground level to catch fungus gnats. If you put out one trap per plant in a greenhouse, they may be the sole control measure needed for whiteflies and fungus gnats. In your house, place a trap on a stake in each houseplant pot to control fungus gnats.

Small insects eventually dissolve in the glue so traps remain effective for several months indoors. After a couple of weeks outdoors, however, the glue loses its stickiness and will not catch small insects. Replace disposable traps or renew the glue on homemade traps.

Commercial products: BioLure; Olson Peel-off Squares; Trapstix; Whitefly Attack

Blue Sticky Traps

Thrips are attracted to yellow sticky traps, but in some light conditions, they seem more attracted to blue sticky traps. Some commercial growers now use blue sticky traps to monitor thrips, particularly western flower thrips and onion thrips.

Protection offered: You can use blue sticky traps to monitor thrips populations, but not to control thrips. The blue traps do not attract aphid-parasitic wasps that are caught on yellow traps when they are used in a greenhouse. You can experiment with blue sticky traps, but in the home garden, yellow sticky traps are generally more efficient, as they attract and trap other pest insects as well.

How to make: Follow the instructions for making yellow sticky traps (see above), but paint the traps a bright, medium blue shade, such as cobalt blue or royal blue.

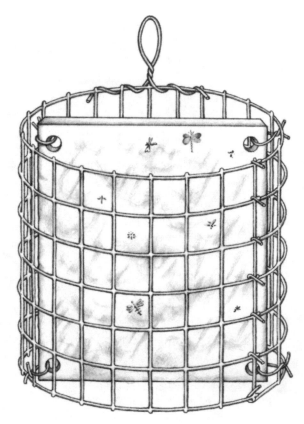

Yellow sticky traps are effective for trapping aphids and other insect pests. However, they can be a nuisance in your garden, as your hair and clothes may get stuck as you work near them. You can avoid this sticky situation by making wire cages around the traps.

How to use: Use these traps as you would yellow sticky traps (see above).

Commercial products: Olson Blue Stiky Strips; Phero Tech Chromacard

Apple Maggot Traps

Apple maggot adults are small flies with dark patterns on their clear wings. These flies lay their eggs in apples and are visually attracted to apple-sized red balls, especially if they smell like apples. Commercial apple maggot traps are red spheres coated with sticky compounds that entrap the flies that mistakenly land on them.

Protection offered: Using apple maggot traps is an easy way to deal with these vexing pests. These traps are also excellent for monitoring the emergence of apple maggot flies to determine the most effective time to spray.

How to make: Coat any apple-sized red ball with about ½ ounce of diluted Tangle-Trap (1 part Tangle-Trap to 2 parts paint thinner) or use Stiky Stuff or the brush-on formula of Tangle-Trap. Old croquet balls painted red work well, as do rubber or plastic balls. You can put an eye screw in a wooden ball and attach a support wire, and tie or glue string to rubber or plastic balls. Renew the sticky surface of the balls every two weeks by scraping off the accumulated insects and applying new glue. In dusty locations, traps will need more frequent renewing.

You can also buy apple-scented lures that you can attach to the wire or string just above the red ball. Some studies show that traps with lures are from two to ten times more effective than traps alone. However, some researchers think the lures attract other closely related species of flies that gum up the trap without improving the catch of apple maggots. Some brands of lures are more long-lasting than others.

How to use: For small orchards of 10 to 15 trees, set out one trap for every dwarf tree, two or three traps for every semi-dwarf, and up to six for a full-size tree. These trap-to-tree ratios should give excellent control. Hang traps starting in mid-June and leave them in place until the apples are picked.

To trap apple maggots in a large orchard, place one trap every 100 feet along the perimeter trees in an orchard block. Also use one or two traps per acre within the block and put a trap in every wild, abandoned apple and crab-apple tree within 400 yards of the orchard.

Commercial products: Ladd apple maggot traps with synthetic apple odor bait; BioLure trap with attractant dispenser card attached (also attracts blueberry maggot and walnut husk fly)

Cherry Fruit Fly Traps

While apple maggot flies are partial to the color red, cherry fruit flies go for the color yellow. To trap these pests, you need a variation on the yellow sticky trap, baited with ammonia.

Protection offered: Use these traps to control cherry fruit flies and also as a monitor to time sprays of botanical poisons if you have severe problems with this pest.

How to make: Paint a 10-by-6-inch piece of plywood bright yellow (Federal Safety Yellow No. 659 from Rustoleum Company or Saturn Yellow from Day-Glo Colors are two colors that work well), and then coat with about ½ ounce of diluted Tanglefoot (1 part Tanglefoot to 2 parts paint thinner) or undiluted Stiky Stuff or the brush-on version of Tangle-Trap. Below it, hang a small, screen-covered jar filled with a mixture of household ammonia and water, 1 part each, or a commercial apple maggot lure. Instead of a flat piece of plywood, you can paint the bell-shaped top half of a plastic soft drink bottle. In one study, this bottle trap was found superior to commercial designs for controlling Western cherry fruit flies.

How to use: For a small orchard, use at least four traps. Hang them 6 to 8 feet high among the leaves, preferably on the south side of the trees. Renew the bait weekly and check that the glue is still sticky. When it loses its stickiness, scrape off the accumulated insects and apply more glue.

Water Traps

Bright yellow pans or basins filled with water with a small amount of liquid soap added are attractive to winged aphids and cabbage root flies. Adding soap breaks the surface tension of the water, so insects will be less likely to float on the water's surface. The yellow color attracts the pests, who try to alight and are drowned.

Protection offered: Water traps are useful to monitor aphids in commercial applications, and for cabbage root flies in the home garden.

How to make: Paint the inside of a heavy plastic basin or metal pan bright yellow (Federal Safety Yellow No. 659 from Rustoleum Company and Saturn Yellow from Day-Glo Colors are two that work well). Add $1/2$ inch or more of water and a few drops of liquid soap to the pan.

How to use: Set out the traps anywhere in the garden. Just be sure the trap is exposed enough that insects will see it and be able to fly into it. Put the trap on a box or stand if plants are growing densely. Monitor this type of trap carefully to make sure you are not catching any tiny beneficial parasitic wasps in the water. These extremely valuable natural enemies are not particularly attracted to yellow, unless there is a tint of green in it, but they like to land on horizontal surfaces. They are clumsy when they come in for a landing so are often killed in pans of water. If you are trapping beneficial insects, your garden is better off without water traps.

Light Traps

Light traps use ultraviolet light (blacklight) to attract insects to their death by electrocution.

Protection offered: These "bug zappers" are indiscriminate and kill beneficial insects as well as troublesome pests. They may make your pest problem worse in the long run by seriously reducing the number of helpful insects that are a part of the natural checks-and-balances system in your garden. These traps can play a useful role inside buildings such as dairy barns to catch flies, but they should almost never be used outdoors. One exception is limited use of light traps at night near fruit trees to kill codling moths.

How to use: To trap codling moths with a light trap, rig one trap near your fruit trees. Use an automatic timer to activate the light from 11:00 P.M. to 3:00 A.M. This will result in effective killing of the codling moths without killing too many beneficial insects.

Commercial products: Several brands of light traps

Pheromone Traps

Insects respond to chemical cues from other members of the same species. These chemicals are called pheromones. The most widely studied are the sex pheromones of moths. Female moths emit the pheromones to attract males. The males can detect incredibly low concentrations of female pheromones, and in experiments with marked moths, males were attracted from as far away as 5 miles.

Commercial quantities of sex pheromones are available for more than 40 moth species; sex pheromones are also available to improve the efficiency of traps for houseflies and Japanese beetles. Pheromones are dispensed from lures designed to release the chemical slowly into the air. There are a variety of designs for lures, from rubber membranes that look like big pencil erasers, to small flat or domed packets that sandwich the pheromones between plastic membranes. There are also lures made of long, hollow, plastic straws filled with pheromones.

Through advances in the technology of plastic membranes, pheromones are now dispensed evenly over a much longer period (four to six months) than was possible a few years ago. The lures are used inside traps that usually have a sticky area to catch the males as they come close to investigate. The most common pheromone traps are made of sturdy waterproofed cardboard, with sticky glue on one side. The traps are folded, with the glue side inside, into tentlike shapes that keep the rain and dust off the glue. The lure hangs inside the cardboard shape to attract the males inside to the sticky surface.

The greatest advantage to using sex pheromones in traps is that most attract only one insect species, so they won't attract beneficial insects or other nonpests. This greater selectivity also makes it easier to count and identify the trapped insects.

Pheromone traps are most commonly used in monitoring, to time pesticide applications (particularly important when using sprays with

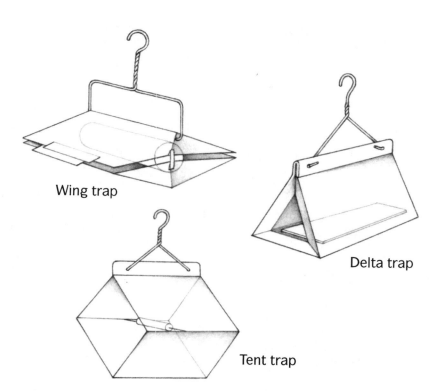

Wing trap

Delta trap

Tent trap

Pheromone traps have a hidden lure that contains a chemical that attracts a particular insect species. Insects following the chemical cue fly into the trap and cannot escape. Most pheromone traps will not trap enough insects to give adequate control. Use them to monitor for pest insects, so that you can best plan the release time of beneficial insects or other control measures.

short residual activity, such as ryania and rotenone), or to time release of biological control insects, such as *Trichogramma* wasps, which are moth egg parasites and thus must be released when host eggs are being laid. Monitoring traps are also used as a follow-up to determine if a control method was successful.

Protection offered: Pheromone traps have been used as a successful control against moth species that mate only once, such as codling moths. The traps lure so many males that not all females can mate successfully, ultimately reducing the local population.

Pheromones are not foolproof. Moths of a given species from different geographical regions may not respond to the same pheromone blend. (For example, different pheromone blends are sold for European corn borer in Iowa and in New York.) Sometimes, response to the pheromone differs from year to year in the same area. See "Sex and the Single Moth," on page 207, for a complete listing of pheromones you can use to monitor garden pests.

How to make: Once you have obtained pheromone dispensers from a commercial supplier, you can incorporate them into a homemade trap. Suspend the lure above a sticky card or an open container of water with a few drops

The Best Garden Monitor

What's the best monitor of all for garden pests? You are! Unlike commercial growers who have hundreds of acres planted or greenhouses filled with thousands of plants, most home gardeners have the potential to examine all the plants in their gardens on a daily basis. Your own eyes can be more effective tools than fancy pheromone traps are.

Here's how to be an effective garden monitor.

1. Tour your yard early in the day, when it's cool. Insects are less active then and will be easier to spot sitting on or under plants.

2. Take a hand magnifying lens with you. (Buy one with a chain you can hang around your neck so you won't misplace it.) The added detail you'll see can help with identifying pests—and telling the pests from the beneficials.

3. Check all parts of your plants. Lift up leaves and look for pests on the undersides. Some fungal diseases, like downy mildew, first show signs on leaf undersides. Check around the base of stems, where borers may have tunneled into your plants.

4. Carry a small notebook. Jot down notes to transfer later to the cultivar comparison records and weather diary in your garden workbook.

5. Check soil moisture periodically as you tour the garden. This can give you an early cue whether any of your plants need supplemental water.

6. Bring along a pair of pruning shears and a plastic or paper bag. That way you're always prepared to spot-prune diseased leaves or stems and safely remove them from the garden. You can also pull flowering weeds and put them in the bag for disposal.

7. Tuck a couple of empty pill vials in your pocket. That way, you can scoop up any unknown insects for later identification.

---

of liquid soap squirted into it. A simple and effective trap designed for tomato fruitworms would work well for other species with a change of pheromones: take a 1-quart, plastic, ice-cream or yogurt container and cut three large holes in the sides of the top half. If the lid isn't opaque, paint it white. This is important to shade the lure, which you fasten to the inside of the lid with tape, wire, or string. Fill the bottom half of the container, up to the level of the holes, with soapy water or a half-and-half mix of water and antifreeze. Use duct tape or some other heavy-duty tape to mount the trap on a sturdy stake.

How to use: Most pheromones available are for fruit tree pests, so you'll be hanging them in trees. For monitoring, hang traps from tree branches about 6 feet off the ground. Don't use the lowest branch. Hang one to six traps per acre (follow directions on the trap package, as placement varies with species). One trap is usually enough in most home gardens or orchards. Hang traps two to three weeks before the expected emergence of the pest (check with your local Cooperative Extension agents for information on pest emergence dates in your area). If you're uncertain when to hang traps, a general rule is to have them out by the time buds begin to open.

For trapping to control pests directly, use one or two traps per dwarf tree, and two traps per full-size tree, for each target species. In small home orchards (up to 5,000 square feet), use three traps (one at either end and one in the middle). For large home orchards (more than 5,000 square feet), use five traps, placing one at each corner of the garden and one in the middle. Situate traps for different species at least 10 feet apart in a garden. In trees, hang traps for different species as far from each other as possible within the tree. If there are wild areas, abandoned orchards, or weedy fields within 1/4 mile of your yard, place traps downwind of these areas, if possible, to catch new males that migrate from wild plant species to your garden.

You will need to check the traps daily, every few days, or weekly, depending on the type of trap you use. Be sure to check the package directions to determine how frequently to check. If only a few moths are in the trap, pick them off the glue with a sharp twig and leave the trap in place. When traps are full, replace disposable ones, and follow the supplier's recommendations for renewing pheromone lures in reusable types. Some traps last four to six months and need not be renewed all season. If you buy lures separately, leave them in the package and store them in a cool, dry place until they're needed. BioLure lures can be stored for a few months, unopened, in the freezer.

Commercial products: BioLure traps; Pherocon traps; Phero Tech traps; Scentry traps

Baited Traps

Some effective traps use simple baits made of common foods to attract insects. The odors remind the insects of their favorite food plants or of a good place to lay eggs so that the larvae will have food when they hatch. Baits can be liquid, such as fermenting fruit to attract Japanese beetles or beer to attract slugs. Solid baits could be potatoes, which attract wireworms, or sprouting onions, which attract maggot flies. Liquid baits work by drowning the pests they attract. Insects attracted to solid baits are killed when you destroy the trap food itself. These traps are inexpensive and easy to make yourself.

Sex and the Single Moth

More than 40 insect pheromones are being produced commercially, but many of these are not available for home gardeners. In the following list, pheromones marked with an asterisk are those sold in small quantities for gardeners. Others on this list may become available in small amounts as demand warrants; check with an organic garden supplier regarding availability if you are interested in any of these pheromones.

Alfalfa looper
Almond moth
Angoumois grain
  moth
Apple maggot
Artichoke plume moth
Blueberry maggot
Boll weevil
Cabbage looper*

Cherry fruit fly
Codling moth*
Corn earworm
  (Tomato fruitworm)*
European corn borer
  (3 different geographical races)
European pine shoot
  moth

Fall armyworm
Fruit flies (*Rhagoletis* species)
Fruittree leafroller
Grape berry moth
Gypsy moth*
Housefly
Indianmeal moth
Japanese beetle
Mediterranean fruit
  fly
Melon fly
Obliquebanded leaf-
  roller
Omnivorous leaftier*
Orange tortrix
Oriental fruit fly

Oriental fruit moth
Pink bollworm
Potato tuberworm
Raisin moth
Redbanded leafroller
Rice stalk borer
Soybean looper
Spruce budworm
  (eastern and
  western)
Threelined leafroller
Tobacco budworm*
Tomato pinworm
Tufted apple bud moth
Walnut husk fly
Western pine shoot
  borer

Japanese Beetle Traps

Traps baited with floral and fruit scents attract female Japanese beetles. Most traps are made of some type of baffle with a bait container attached, hung above a funnel that leads to a collection container. The attracted beetles fly into the baffle and slide down the funnel into the container, which you can remove to dispose of the beetles. To increase catches of both sexes, commercial traps often add sex pheromones to attract males.

Protection offered: Critics of the traps say they attract more beetles to the area, so one or two traps, placed in the middle of a garden, may end up attracting more beetles to feed on plants. In one study, traps caught massive numbers of adult beetles, but the number of beetle grubs in the soil around the area of the traps did not decrease. Other studies, however, have shown that mass-trapping of Japanese beetles is effective as a control when large numbers of traps are used throughout a community. Certainly, traps should be considered as only a part of a complete Japanese beetle control program, which integrates such control methods as applying milky disease spores to lawns to attack grubs (see "Milky Disease Spores" on page 187) and shaking beetles from plants in the early morning (see "Handpicking" on page 193).

How to make: Cut a wide opening in the top of a 1-gallon plastic jug (leave the handle in place for carrying) and fill it one-third full with fermented wine or sugar and water, pieces of mashed fruit, and some yeast to enhance fermentation (see "Japanese Beetle Treats" for a recipe). Strain out beetles each evening.

How to use: Set traps 1 to 3 feet above the ground in open, sunny areas in the spring, away from foliage and 10 to 25 feet downwind from favorite food plants (these may include most of the plants in your garden). To trap beetles over large areas, place a trap every 150 to 200 feet around the entire area needing protection. Traps should be emptied frequently, daily if necessary, since dead beetles are repellent to the live ones flying in. (The smell of decomposing beetles would repel anything!) Because of the unpleasant odor, you'll probably want to bury the dead bugs or throw them in the trash.

Commercial products: Bag-a-Bug; Beetle Bagger; BioLure traps; Safer traps

Slug and Snail Traps

Slugs and snails are attracted to fermenting, yeasty odors, hence the popular stale beer slug trap. Any fermenting material will do—yeast and water, beer, or spoiled yogurt. The slugs and snails climb into the container of liquid and are drowned.

Protection offered: While these traps will catch many slugs and snails, they may not afford your garden sufficient protection if you have large populations of these pests.

Japanese Beetle Treats

When Japanese beetles invade your garden, you can fight back with homemade traps. Use a plastic gallon jug with the top portion cut off as a container and fill it with the following bait. Beetles will find it irresistible. They'll fly in and never fly out.

1 pint water

1 banana, mashed (any type of fruit except citrus can be substituted)

½ cup sugar, honey, or other sweetener

½ cup wine, if available

¼ teaspoon baking yeast

Keep this mixture in a warm place until it starts to ferment and then serve up a feast for the beetles!

How to make: You can make an easy-to-use trap from a 1-gallon plastic milk jug by cutting a 1-inch hole in each side, an inch from the bottom.

How to use: Bury the jug so the holes are at ground level and pour in the bait. When the trap is full, just lift it from the hole, pour out the bait and dead pests, rinse, and refill.

Another option is to put bait materials into pans set into the soil with the lip flush with the soil surface. Set out the traps as soon as slug damage appears, or as soon as you plant if your past experience leads you to expect slug problems.

Commercial products: Slug Bar; Slug Saloon

Wireworm Traps

Wireworms are larvae of click beetles. Wireworms bore into seeds, underground tubers, and plant roots. Gardens in newly turned sod may have large numbers of wireworms in the soil during the spring.

Protection offered: Wireworm traps are very effective and completely harmless to beneficial insects. But, using wireworm traps requires considerable time and effort, unless you are only trying to control wireworms in a small patch of garden.

How to make: Cut potatoes in half, and cut out the eyes. Poke a short stick through each piece to serve as a handle.

How to use: Put the traps out as soon as the ground warms in spring, preferably before planting your garden. Use as many traps as you have the patience and potatoes to make. Bury the traps about 1 inch below the soil surface. Remove them after one or two days and kill the wireworms by destroying the potatoes or shaking the wireworms out of the potatoes into soapy water.

Onion Maggot Traps

Damage from the larvae of these small flies is worst on seedling onions. A single maggot can kill several seedlings, although large bulbs tolerate more larvae.

Protection offered: This trap uses the susceptible plant itself as a decoy to keep the onion maggot flies from attacking the crop, and can be highly effective in the home garden.

How to use: Plant cull onions—onions that have sprouted in storage—about 2 inches deep between the rows where you've sown seeds for your main crop of onions. The bulbs will grow much faster than the seedlings and attract the egg-laying flies. Two weeks after the bulbs sprout, pull them out and destroy them to prevent the next generation of onion maggots from developing. This trap works best when used along with repellents such as ginger or hot pepper sprinkled on the seed rows to repel flies (see " 'Hot' Dusts" on page 218).

Other Traps

A few miscellaneous traps don't fit into the categories of pheromones or baits. They use simple techniques to protect trees from climbing pests and rid lawns of destructive chinch bugs.

Sticky Tree Bands

These traps are similar to tree bands (see page 197), but they will actually kill the pest insects, while tree bands may just stop the insects from getting to your plants. Once a pest insect touches the sticky surface on a sticky tree band, it is immobilized and will eventually die of dehydration or starvation.

Protection offered: Sticky bands on tree trunks are used to keep ants out of citrus trees and to keep gypsy moths and some pest beetles out of ornamental and fruit trees.

How to make: Using a 1-inch paintbrush or spatula, paint a 3-inch band of sticky compound all the way around the trunk on a mature tree. The sticky substance spreads better if kept warm. Don't use solvents to dilute it because they may damage bark. Check the stickiness every few weeks and reapply if necessary. On young trees, wrap a width of fabric tightly around the trunk (stretchy polyester or rough burlap works well because it grips the bark) and cover with a sheet of plastic food wrap. Apply the sticky compound to the plastic. When the glue needs to be renewed, simply replace the plastic.

How to use: Do not apply sticky compounds *directly* to trunks of young trees, especially in hot, sunny weather, because the material may injure the bark. Compounds such as Tanglefoot or Stickem are considered safe to apply to mature trees.

Commercial products: Stickem; Stiky Stuff; Tanglefoot

Chinch Bug Traps

Chinch bugs chew on stems and leaves of lawn grasses. To monitor or control chinch bugs in the lawn, you can drive them out of the sod with soapy water and into a trap cloth for counting and disposal.

Protection offered: This type of trapping works best for small areas. If you have a large lawn that is infested with chinch bugs, dusting with sabadilla may provide more effective control.

How to make: Mix 1 ounce of liquid dishwashing soap in 2 gallons of water.

How to use: Pour the mixture over 1 square yard of lawn. For large areas, you can use the garden hose with a siphon mixer attachment (available at garden centers) to spray the soapy water. Lay a large piece of white cloth, preferably flannel, over the treated area for 15 to 20 minutes, then pick it up. The bugs are driven out of the sod by the soapy soaking and catch their feet in the flannel. Count them and then kill them by rinsing them off the flannel in a bucket of soapy water. If there are fewer than 10 to 15 bugs per square foot, there is probably no need to try to reduce the chinch bug population, especially if you use good management practices to keep the lawn growing vigorously. It's good to rinse the soap off the treated grass by watering well after you take up the flannel.

Trap Crops

You can use plants that are more attractive to a pest than the crop you want to protect as trap crops planted in or between your garden rows. Pull the trap plants when they become infested and destroy them. This is most successful with pests that have only a few generations in a summer or for crops that only need protection for a critical period in the season.

Protection offered: The dilemma when using trap crops is that they may attract more pests to the area than would have appeared otherwise. And if they're not pulled at the right time, the trap crops can provide more food for future generations of pests. Also, trap plants attract beneficial insects that feed on the pests. You may destroy important beneficial insects when you destroy the trap plants. Since most adult predators and parasites move fast, they should escape harm, but immature stages of these beneficials are usually less mobile and will be caught along with the bad bugs.

How to use: There are many ways to use trap crops. For example, an early planting of squash attracts pickleworms that might destroy melons; destroy the squash vines before larvae are fully developed.

Dill or lovage are said to lure tomato hornworms away from tomatoes; the worms are easy to see and to pick off the trap crop.

Mexican bean beetles are more attracted to green beans than to soybeans, so green beans can be planted between rows of soybeans as a trap crop.

Nasturtiums will attract flea beetles away from cabbage seedlings until the plants are large enough to withstand attack.

Soil Solarization

In hot weather, a clear plastic film laid over the soil will trap enough heat to pasteurize the top 6 to 12 inches of soil. This process, called solarization, is an effective way to kill disease organisms and weed seeds in the soil. Solarization also kills soil-living stages of many insects and mites. However, earthworms and beneficial microorganisms and insects may be destroyed, too, so it's best to save this treatment for situations in which you face a severe pest infestation. It's not necessary to repeat this treatment every year, as the beneficial effects seem to last for several seasons. For more information on this technique, see "Solarizing Soil" on page 152.

CHEMICAL CONTROLS

Despite our best efforts to keep our gardens healthy and naturally balanced, a pest insect species occasionally will invade in force. What can organic gardeners do when insects are decimating their broccoli transplants or threatening the survival of a shrub?

In these cases, there are insecticidal sprays and dusts considered acceptable for the organic garden. Most of these sprays and dusts are chemicals—whatever their origin or degree of toxicity. As such, they are the last resort and should be used only when all other options have failed.

Why are these sprays acceptable while synthetic, petrochemical-based sprays are not? Two primary reasons are that they are less likely to poison nontarget organisms and less likely to accumulate in the environment than are synthetic insecticides. "Organic" sprays have short residual periods, meaning that residues of the sprays cannot be detected on crops shortly after spraying; some are considered to leave no residue at all. Toxic compounds in the sprays break down into harmless compounds quickly in the environment compared to the much longer period of toxicity for conventional pesticides. This means that there is less risk to other organisms that you don't want to harm and that these products won't accumulate in the soil or ground-water or become concentrated in the food chain. Some of the sprays listed in this section, such as insecticidal soap or horticultural oils, don't have any residual period, because they only kill the insects directly hit by the spray.

Something you will notice about the sprays and dusts in this section is the variety of ways these products affect insects. Some are directly toxic when eaten, while others kill by suffocation or by dehydration. This means that you must know how each type of spray works and what pests are susceptible in order to use them correctly.

It's also important to realize that resistance can develop when *any* pesticide is overused, even those discussed here. A pesticide-resistant pest population evolves over time when all of the individuals most susceptible to the poison are killed off, leaving only the tougher ones to breed. More of their offspring survive the next spray and eventually a population appears that can no longer be killed with that chemical. This happens when the same pesticides are used repeatedly, especially those that kill by poisoning as opposed to those that kill by some physical effect, such as dehydration (diatomaceous earth) or suffocation (dormant oil). To avoid encouraging the development of resistant pests, use insecticides sparingly, time them to have the maximum effect on pests, and don't use the same one over and over again. Be sure you take proper precautions to protect your own health and safety when you use insecticidal sprays or dusts. (See "Spray Safely!" on page 220.)

Horticultural Oils

Petroleum oil sprays have been used on plants to kill overwintering eggs and adults of fruit tree pests since at least 1787. The sprays consist of 1 to 3 percent oil mixed in water—only a thin layer of oil is needed to kill susceptible insects. Oil sprays are contact insecticides, that is, they must come in direct contact with the insect or mite. How oils kill insects is not completely understood. Among the possible effects are suffocation, disturbing the insect's water balance, dissolving egg coverings, and interfering with enzyme activity. Newly hatched insects suffocate within a day of application as their breathing tubes are blocked and the corrosive and toxic action of the oil takes effect. So far, there is no evidence for development of resistance to oil sprays after more than 50 years of use. Some species and developmental stages of insects are more sensitive to oils than others. Oil sprays are not poisonous to people.

Horticultural oils all contain the same ingredients—oil, water, and an emulsifier, such as soap—but they differ in the degree of refinement of the oil. The more viscous, less refined oils are termed dormant oils. These are applied in spring before growth starts or in fall after leaves drop. Summer oils are more refined and can be used while leaves are still on the tree. Supreme oils are the highest-quality oils, useful at any time of year.

Dormant Oils

There are several advantages to using dormant oils: They extend the time period during which pests can be controlled; dormant oils kill insects before hatching, so they provide a way to completely avoid damage; and it's easier to completely cover a plant with spray because trees are leafless.

Protection offered: The most important group of insects controlled by oils are scales; all life stages are killed. Dormant oils also kill mealybugs, thrips, pear psylla nymphs, and aphid and mite eggs. Oil also kills most exposed insect eggs, with the exception of pear psylla eggs and most moth eggs. Dormant oils will eliminate eggs of codling moth, oriental fruit moth, and fruit tree leafroller.

How to use: Dormant oils must be mixed with water and an emulsifier before spraying. Oil will not dissolve in water, but will form a

mixture called an emulsion: tiny droplets of oil suspended evenly in the water. Follow label directions carefully to create an emulsion, and measure carefully. There is a precise relationship between oil dosage and insect mortality; emulsifiers influence the effectiveness of these sprays by determining the amount of oil deposited on the plant. To be effective, you must have thorough coverage without overspraying. You will need from 4 to 10 quarts of spray per fruit tree.

Try to spray on a calm day; wind causes the oil to be distributed unevenly. Spray when no rain is forecast for 24 hours and temperatures will remain above freezing. If it rains before the oil spray dries, the oil will be diluted, and therefore less effective. It's okay to spray wet bark, and once the spray has dried, rain has no effect. If the oil spray freezes, the emulsion will break, and the oil will stick to the bark when it thaws. Keep agitating the mixture while spraying to maintain the emulsion, and do not use a spray if it doesn't emulsify properly when mixed. (Mixed spray should be a uniform cloudy liquid). Lime sulfur sprays for disease control can be mixed with dormant oil sprays. (See "Multipurpose Controls," on page 222, for more information on mixing lime sulfur and oil.)

Commercial products: Later's Dormant Spray; Volck Dormant Oil

Summer Oils

Superior and supreme horticultural oils can be used on a variety of fruit, nut, ornamental, and shade trees (almonds, apples, apricots, cherries, citrus, figs, grapes, nectarines, peaches, pears, plums, olives, and walnuts) to control growing season pests. In Hawaii, oils are registered for use on guava, macadamia nuts, papaya, and passion fruit.

Protection offered: Summer oils are most commonly used to control mealybugs, rust mites, scales, spider mites, and aphid eggs. In Canada, there is a minor use registration for oils on greenhouse cucumbers and tomatoes to control whitefly (it controls adults and has some effect on larvae and eggs) and on field-grown rutabagas against green peach aphids.

How to use: Summer oils are usually sold as a concentrate that must be diluted with water. Oil will not dissolve in water, but will form a mixture called an emulsion: tiny droplets of oil suspended evenly in the water. Measure ingredients and follow label directions carefully when mixing the spray. If the spray mix you use has excess oil in it, it can cause plant injury.

Apply successive sprays at least six weeks apart, and avoid using on trees weakened by disease, drought, drying winds, or high-nitrogen applications. Don't apply oil if daytime temperatures are likely to exceed 85°F, or night temperatures are expected to fall below freezing. Don't use oil sprays when the soil is dry or air humidity is low (less than 30 percent relative humidity), because these conditions increase the chances of spray injury. If possible, spray right after trees are irrigated. Don't use oils on ferns or conifers (it will wash the color out of blue spruce) and never use oils within a month before or after sprays containing sulfur. It is risky to use oil sprays on Japanese maple, beech, and black walnut trees. If you must do so, use a diluted spray and apply it carefully. On these trees, it is a good idea to spray a small section first to check for leaf injury.

On citrus trees, summer oil can be used from petal fall in spring through September to control scale insects. Before spraying, check with local Cooperative Extension agents for the best timing of sprays for your area and your cultivars. On lemons, oils are usually applied in April and May; for other citrus, oils are used in late summer or fall (navel oranges are very susceptible to damage from oil so do not spray them after September 1). Avoid treating citrus trees while mature fruit is present because fruit may drop or the color and quality may suffer.

A 1-percent emulsion of supreme oil can be used on greenhouse cucumbers and tomatoes, and on rutabagas. Spray plants until the leaves are well coated and the spray liquid starts to drip from the leaves. Apply at weekly intervals as needed. At temperatures above 77°F, there may be some damage to young leaves. Concentrations of 2 percent or higher will cause significant damage. A 3-day period between last spray and harvest is required for greenhouse crops; leave 21 days before harvest on rutabagas. Spray in early morning or in the evening to avoid direct sunlight. Wait 24 hours before using other sprays.

Commercial products: Omni Supreme Spray; Scalecide; Sunspray Ultra-Fine Spray

Diatomaceous Earth

Thirty million years ago, the tiny silica shells of one-celled algae, or diatoms, rained down on the sea floors, building up into deep, chalky deposits of diatomite. When these fossilized remains are mined and milled to break the shells into needlelike shards of silica, they become an insecticidal powder known as diatomaceous earth (DE). The first patents on DE were issued in the late 1800s, but commercial formulations were not brought onto the market until the 1950s.

To a gardener, diatomaceous earth looks and feels like a fine talcum powder, but to an insect it is a lethal dust that both scratches and absorbs the wax layer on the bug's surface, leaving it to die from dehydration. The more opportunity the insect has to get the powder on it, the faster it will dry out. Of course, with this type of mechanical insecticidal action, diatomaceous earth is not specific to certain pests. It will eventually kill any insect, although fuzzy ones, like bees, may not be greatly affected, and those with a greasy coating, like cockroaches, must be repeatedly exposed to large amounts to be damaged. The dust does not break down with time in the environment, so it remains insecticidal until it is washed away by rain or turned into the soil by cultivation. It is nontoxic to mammals.

Diatomaceous earth comes in swimming pool filter grade and "natural" grades. Pool filter grades are chemically treated and partially melted to form crystalline silica, a respiratory health hazard to mammals. The natural grades are ground and bagged and usually contain 97 percent noncrystalline (amorphous) silica, which our bodies are able to dissolve. This is the only type that should be used in insect control.

Protection offered: Diatomaceous earth is an excellent product for use in stored grain and seeds and for flea and louse control on animals. Its usefulness in the garden is offset by the danger it poses to beneficial insects and mites. With care, diatomaceous earth can be used to control cabbage root flies and thrips and to repel slugs and snails in the garden. It is also useful to control fungus gnats on houseplants.

How to use: Only use natural grade diatomaceous earth and then only in specific problem areas. Do not dust it widely over crops. Apply it around the stems of cabbage family plants to protect them from cabbage root fly. Also spread it around seedlings of many types of plants to protect them from sowbugs and pillbugs. For stubborn cases of thrips damage, dust just the undersides of affected leaves (never blossoms) and in a circle around the soil beneath the plant. Apply the dust when plants are wet from dew or after being watered, because the powder is very light and blows away easily. Diatomaceous earth can also be made into a paint to protect tree trunks by mixing it with pure soap and water to make a thick slurry (see "Dehydrating Dusts," on page 199, for directions for tree paint). Wear a cotton dust mask when applying the dust to avoid irritating mucous membranes.

Commercial products: Fossil Flower; Insectigone; Perma-Guard; Shield Garden Dust (diatomaceous earth and pyrethrins)

Insecticidal Soaps

Soapy water has a long track record as an insecticide; fish and whale oil soap sprays were common more than 100 years ago, and early gardening books recommended sprays made with laundry soap. Since then, several commercial insecticidal soaps have come on the market. The great advantage of soaps is that they are not toxic to people, birds, and other animals. Soaps are the salts of fatty acids, which are common in all living things. Soap is formed when fatty acids are mixed with water and a base, such as sodium hydroxide (also known as caustic soda or lye) in laundry soaps or potassium hydroxide in some insecticidal soaps. Soap has varying insecticidal effects against certain groups of insects, depending on the kind and proportions of fatty acids and base used. Soaps kill insects on contact by paralyzing them, disrupting membranes, and affecting their growth and development. Beetles are less susceptible to soap, so lady beetles are relatively safe, but soap sprays do kill their larvae.

Several studies found home-mixed soap sprays just as effective as commercial insecticidal soaps for killing insects. The advantages of using commercial insecticidal soaps are that they are less toxic to plants and they are legally registered as pesticides. The fatty acid content of laundry and dish soaps is variable, and some have additives, such as whiteners, perfumes, and colors, that may harm plants.

Plants with thin cuticles, such as beans, Chinese cabbage, cucumbers, ferns, gardenias, Japanese maples, nasturtiums, and young peas, are easily damaged by soap sprays. Tomatoes and potatoes are less susceptible to damage, and cabbages seem virtually impervious, although lowered yields have been reported after heavy use of soaps.

Protection offered: Soaps are generally recommended for control of soft-bodied insects such as aphids, mealybugs, scales, thrips, whiteflies, and also mites. I do not usually recommend using soaps as a primary means of controlling aphids, however, because even the commercial brands kill only 60 to 80 percent of aphids. It takes only one to two weeks for remaining aphids to rebound to pre-spray levels, so repeated sprays are required. Also, natural enemies of aphids are killed by soap sprays.

How to make: You can use household soaps, such as Ivory Snow, Ivory Liquid, or Shaklee's Basic H to make an insecticidal soap solution. However, the effectiveness of these home mixes may be more variable than those of commercial insecticidal soaps.

You can also make your own soap with olive oil and lye. To make olive oil soap, measure 3 tablespoons of water (soft water or rainwater) into a glass, enamel, or stainless steel bowl. Carefully add 4 tablespoons of lye, stirring until the lye dissolves. This mixture will get hot. Use caution: Lye will burn skin. If any lye gets on your skin, immediately wash it off. Once lye is dissolved, slowly pour in 1 cup of oil, stirring constantly. Continue to stir for 5 minutes. Pour the soap into a plastic or glass container. It will harden as it cools. This recipe produces 1¼ cups of solid soap. To make an insecticidal spray solution, mix 1 scant teaspoon of concentrate in 1 cup soft water (or 1 part soap in 50 parts water).

How to use: When mixing soap solutions, start with from 1 teaspoon to 1 tablespoon of soap per gallon of water. Try doubling the concentration if plants are undamaged and insect control is not satisfactory. All soaps, whether homemade or commercial, will damage plants if used repeatedly or mixed at high concentrations.

A good rule is to use no more than three successive sprays on any particular plant. Because soaps are contact insecticides, spray both upper

Is It Safe?

The effectiveness of insecticidal soaps is linked to the "hardness" of your tap water. In hard water, minerals such as calcium, magnesium, and iron combine chemically with the fatty acids in insecticidal soap. Not only does this reduce the soap's insecticidal activity, it can also cause increased leaf injury.

You can perform a simple test to find out whether insecticidal soaps will be effective and safe for your plants when mixed with your tap water. Add 3 tablespoons of insecticidal soap concentrate to a quart of water in a glass jar. Close, mix thoroughly, and allow to stand for 15 minutes. If the mix remains uniform, light, and milky, the soap spray will be very effective. If a scum develops on the surface, the spray will be less effective. If a scum forms and milky curds appear floating in the water, then you should try a different water source or not use insecticidal soap sprays.

and undersides of leaves thoroughly to maximize contact with insects. To avoid leaf damage, spray soap on overcast days or in the evening, especially in greenhouses. Test plants for injury before spraying an entire bed. To be safe, you can wash soap off plants with clear water a few hours after spraying.

Soaps can be mixed with other insecticidal sprays, such as *Bacillus thuringiensis,* horticultural oils, pyrethrins, and rotenone.

Commercial products: Acco Highway Soap Spray; Ringer's Aphid-Mite Attack; Safer Insecticidal Soap; Savona

Home Preparations

Safe and cheap: That sums up the case for using homemade preparations for controlling garden pests. These sprays are often as effective as more powerful commercial products. And using homemade sprays allows you to make just as much as you need, when you need it, from common ingredients, rather than paying for a packaged product that must be fetched from the store and probably contains more than you can use anyway.

Alcohol Sprays

The idea of using rubbing alcohol as a spray for plant pests has been around for years. Some people swear by it, while others swear at it for causing leaf burning.

Protection offered: People that have used alcohol sprays say they work on aphids, mealybugs, scale insects, thrips, and whiteflies. Alcohol sprays have been used successfully on houseplants and tropical foliage plants. Most of these have heavy, waxy cuticles that are not easily harmed. Alcohol sprays can damage African violets and apple trees.

How to make: Use only 70 percent isopropyl alcohol (rubbing alcohol); mix 1 to 2 cups alcohol per quart of water. Using undiluted alcohol as a spray is very risky for plants. You can also mix up an insecticidal soap spray according to the dilution rate on the label but substitute alcohol for half of the water required.

How to use: Since alcohol can damage plants, always test your spray mix on a few leaves or plants first. If the spray kills the pests and no leaf damage shows within the next two or three days, go ahead and spray further, using exactly the same ingredients and proportions you tested.

Tomato Leaf Sprays

Plants belonging to the nightshade family, such as tomatoes, potatoes, and tobacco, have significant amounts of toxic compounds called alkaloids in their leaves. These toxins are water soluble and can be soaked from chopped leaves and made into homemade sprays. Their toxicity,

however, may account for only part of their effectiveness. The sprays may also attract natural pest enemies that follow the powerful chemicals in these plants as cues in searching for prey. (For directions on making a tobacco leaf spray see "Nicotine" on page 225.)

Protection offered: Tomato leaf sprays have been used to protect plants from aphids. Also, spraying tomato leaf spray on corn may reduce corn earworm damage. The corn earworm is also called the tomato fruitworm, as it also attacks tomato plants. A scientific study has shown that corn plants sprayed with tomato leaf spray attracted significantly more *Trichogramma* wasps to parasitize the corn earworm eggs than did unsprayed plants.

How to make: Soak 1 to 2 cups of chopped or mashed tomato leaves in 2 cups of water overnight. Strain through cheesecloth or fine mesh, add about 2 more cups of water to the strained liquid, and spray. For aphid control, be sure to thoroughly cover the leaf undersides, especially of lower leaves and growing tips of plants where aphids congregate.

How to use: Spray plants thoroughly, particularly undersides of lower leaves and growing tips where aphids congregate. While this spray is not poisonous to humans on contact, use care in handling, especially if you are allergic to nightshade family plants.

Garlic Oil Sprays

Organic gardeners have long been familiar with the repellent or toxic effect of garlic on pests. When it is combined with mineral oil and pure soap, as it is in the recipe that follows, devised at the Henry Doubleday Research Association in England, it becomes an effective insecticide. Some studies also suggest that a garlic oil spray has fungicidal properties.

Protection offered: Good results, with quick kill, have been noted against aphids, cabbage loopers, earwigs, June bugs, leafhoppers, squash bugs, and whiteflies. The spray does not appear to harm adult lady beetles, and some gardeners have found that it doesn't work against Colorado potato beetles, grape leaf skeletonizers, grasshoppers, red ants, or sowbugs.

How to make: Soak 3 ounces of finely minced garlic cloves in 2 teaspoons of mineral oil for at least 24 hours. Slowly add 1 pint of water that has ¼ ounce of liquid soap or commercial insecticidal soap mixed into it. Stir thoroughly and strain into a glass jar for storage. Use at a rate of 1 to 2 tablespoons of mixture to a pint of water. If this is effective, try a more dilute solution in order to use as little as possible.

How to use: Spray plants carefully to ensure thorough coverage. To check for possible leaf damage to sensitive ornamentals from the oil and soap in the spray, do a test spray on a few leaves or plants first. If no leaf damage shows up in two or three days, go ahead and spray more.

Rodale's All-Purpose Spray

This spray uses the repellent effects of garlic, onion, and hot pepper along with the insecticidal properties of soap to make an all-purpose garden spray. As with any spray containing soap, test spray plants with delicate leaves, such as beans and some flowers, to check for leaf injury before spraying widely.

Protection offered: Try this spray against any leaf-eating pests and make a note of what pests are successfully controlled.

How to make: Chop, grind, or liquefy one garlic bulb and one small onion. Add 1 teaspoon of powdered cayenne pepper and mix with 1 quart of water. Steep 1 hour, strain through cheesecloth, and then add 1 tablespoon of nondetergent liquid soap to the strained liquid. Mix well and use.

How to use: Spray plants thoroughly, being sure to cover the undersides of leaves where many pests are found. When spraying, be care-ful not to get the mixture in your eyes or nose, because it would cause painful burning. The spray can be stored up to one week in a refrigerator, tightly covered.

Herbal Sprays

Many organic gardeners are familiar with using sprays made from aromatic herbs to repel pests from garden plants. Several recent studies confirm the repellent effect of such sprays. The essential oils of sage and thyme and the alcohol extracts of such herbs as hyssop, rosemary, sage, thyme, and white clover can be used in this manner. They have been shown to reduce the number of eggs laid and the amount of feeding damage to cabbage by caterpillars of diamond-back moths and large white butterflies. Sprays made from tansy have demonstrated a repellent effect on imported cabbageworm on cabbage, reducing the number of eggs laid on the plants. Teas made from wormwood or nasturtiums are reputed to repel aphids from fruit trees, and sprays made from ground or blended catnip, chives, feverfew, marigolds, or rue have also been used by gardeners against pests that feed on leaves.

Protection offered: Try herbal sprays against any leaf-eating pests and make a note of what works for future reference.

How to make: In general, herbal sprays are made by mashing or blending 1 to 2 cups of fresh leaves with 2 to 4 cups of water and leaving them to soak overnight. Or you can make an herbal tea by pouring the same amount of boiling water over 2 to 4 cups fresh or 1 to 2 cups dry leaves and leaving them to steep until cool. Strain the water through cheesecloth before spraying and dilute further with 2 to 4 cups of water. Add a very small amount of nondetergent liquid soap (¼ teaspoon in 1 to 2 quarts of water) to help the spray stick to leaves and spread better.

You also can buy commercial essential herbal oils and dilute with water to make a spray. Experiment with proportions, starting with a few drops of oil per cup of water.

How to use: Spray plants thoroughly, especially undersides of leaves, and repeat at weekly intervals if necessary.

"Hot" Dusts

Black pepper, chili pepper, dill, ginger, paprika, and red pepper all contain capsaicin, a compound shown to repel insects. Synthetic capsaicin is also available for field use. Researchers have found that as little as $1/25$ ounce of capsaicin sprinkled around an onion plant reduced the number of onion maggot eggs laid around the plant by 75 percent, compared to a control plant.

Protection offered: Capsaicin-containing dusts repel onion maggots from seedlings, as well as other root maggot flies from cabbage family plants and carrots. Pepper dusts around the base of plants help repel ants, which is desirable in a garden where ants often protect and maintain aphid colonies on plants.

How to make: It can be rather expensive to buy enough packaged pepper dusts to sprinkle throughout your garden. However, if you grow and dry your own red peppers, chili peppers, or dill, you can make lots of dust at low cost. Use a mortar and pestle to grind the peppers or dill weed, including the seeds, to dust. Be careful handling the hot peppers because they irritate sensitive skin. It is very painful if you accidentally rub your eyes after handling peppers.

How to use: Sprinkle along seeded rows of onions, cabbage, or carrots in a band at least 6 inches wider than the row or planting bed. A fine sprinkling will suffice, but the more dust you use, the better the effect. Renew after a heavy rain or irrigation. To protect plants from ants, sprinkle around the base of plants in an area as wide as the widest leaves.

"Bug Juice"

In the 1960s, the idea of catching pest insects and making them into a spray surfaced. Many people found that it worked to reduce pest problems in their crops. But in 1972, the Environmental Protection Agency warned people to stop using bug-juice sprays because they could be harmful to humans and animals (the insects could contain disease organisms that could infect mammals and other animals) and because they were not registered as a pesticide.

There are three explanations of how "bug juice" works against pests. One is that it's likely that some of the pests you collect are diseased. By grinding this up and spreading it, you spread the disease in areas where other pests are likely to eat it. Many caterpillar populations contain latent diseases, especially viruses, that are always present but don't break out until the caterpillars are under stress from overcrowding or other unfavorable environmental conditions. And one diseased insect can harbor enough disease organisms to cover your entire garden and more with the disease.

A second explanation is that the odor of the crushed pests sprayed on the plants attracts more predators and parasites of that pest. Thirdly, there may also be a repellent effect on the pests themselves from the odor of dead insects or from alarm pheromones—compounds secreted by the insects as a warning signal to others of their species—given off by the mashed bugs. For example, the odor of dead beetles in a Japanese beetle trap acts as a repellent to other Japanese beetles.

Protection offered: Bug-juice sprays have been used on a variety of pests with success. The best targets are fairly large pests that appear in large numbers, such as cabbage loopers, Colorado potato beetles, and Mexican bean beetles. Very small, fast, or rare insects are too difficult to catch. (Imagine trying to catch enough leafhoppers or flea beetles to make into a spray!) When collecting bugs, be sure that you are catching pests; sometimes beneficial insects, such a lady beetles and syrphid fly larvae, appear in large numbers and might be mistaken for pests.

How to make: Collect about ¹/₂ cup of pest insects, particularly any that look sick. Sick insects could be an off-color or be acting abnormally (moving sluggishly, sitting on top leaves of plants, hanging upside down from stems). It is a good idea to wear gloves when handling insects, especially if you are allergy prone. Put the insects in a blender with about 2 cups of water and liquefy. Don't use a kitchen blender that you use for food preparation—it's important not to risk contaminating food because some naturally occurring insect diseases may not be specific only to insects. Some, like entomopox disease, are similar to human disease organisms. If you don't have an old blender, you can use a mortar and pestle to mash the insects.

Strain the blended mixture through cheesecloth or a fine sieve and dilute ¹/₄ cup of this concentrate with 1 to 2 cups of water in a sprayer. The leftovers can be frozen for a year or more.

How to use: Use the spray against the same pests you collect: In other words, don't try to use a Colorado potato beetle spray to control aphids. Spray plants thoroughly on both sides of the leaves. It's particularly important to spray leaf undersides, where sunlight won't act to destroy disease organisms as quickly as it will on the upper-leaf surfaces. Although effects of some bug-juice sprays are reported to last as long as two months, they probably work best if applied frequently (once or twice a week). Disease organisms are likely to lose their viability in a few days in the environment, and repellent or attractant smells also aren't likely to last.

Wear a filter mask, long-sleeved shirt, rubber gloves, and long pants when mixing and spraying bug juice to avoid skin contact with the spray. Wash any sprayed produce thoroughly before eating it.

Botanical Pesticides

Botanical pesticides come from plant material. The active ingredients in these sprays are extracted directly from flowers, leaves, bark, or roots. Most of these potent toxins kill any insect that eats them, and so are not very selective. Most even have poisonous effects on fish, birds, humans, and other animals.

However, in contrast to most petrochemical-based products, botanical pesticides don't last long in the environment. They break down to harmless compounds, usually within days. Because of this, these sprays must be applied at just the right time, and sometimes applied repeatedly to control heavy infestations of certain pests.

Handle botanical pesticides with particular caution. See "Spray Safely!" on page 220, for important guidelines on how to handle the toxic materials discussed in this section. Be sure to read the labels on commercial products and use them exactly according to the directions.

Pyrethrin

The dried, powdered flowers of the pyrethrum daisy, *Tanacetum* (=*Chrysanthemum*) *cinerariifolium* and *T. coccineum*, were used as early as 1880 to control mosquitoes. The popularity of pyrethrum insecticides waned when synthetic insecticides were introduced, but they are now enjoying a commercial comeback. Many new products formulated with natural pyrethrins are available. Pyrethrins are the insecticidal chemicals extracted from the pyrethrum daisy. Do *not* confuse them with pyrethroids, the term for a new class of synthetic pesticides.

Pyrethrins, which are mainly concentrated in the seeds of the flower head, are a contact insecticide, meaning the insect only has to touch

Spray Safely!

Although the sprays and dusts organic gardeners use when pests get out of control are much safer for the environment than petrochemical-based pesticides, some are very toxic to humans, birds, fish, or plants at the time they are sprayed. Soaps are about as safe a pesticide as you can get, yet even they will injure plants if improperly used. Another important case in point is rotenone: Used for many years by organic gardeners, the fresh spray is more toxic (in terms of the dose necessary to kill a group of laboratory rats) than such synthetic chemicals as carbaryl, malathion, or methoxychlor. Pyrethrins are just as toxic.

Of course, after being sprayed, most botanicals break down within days into harmless compounds and do not accumulate in the food chain, but it is important to remember that just because a pesticide is of botanical origin, it is not necessarily harmless to people.

To be sure that you are safe when you're handling botanical pesticides, always follow these rules:

1. Always keep the products in the original container. The package contains the name and active ingredients, along with mixing and application information. It also lists pests for which the product is registered and often gives antidote information in case of poisoning.

2. Store containers, tightly closed, in a cool, dry place, away from the reach of children and pets (a locked or closed high cupboard is ideal), and away from anywhere food is prepared or stored.

3. Mix and use exactly according to directions and measure amounts accurately. When mixing wettable powders into water, be especially careful to avoid breathing dust, because the powder contains concentrated pesticide.

4. Wear protective clothing and equipment while handling, mixing, and applying pesticides. Wear coveralls or long pants and a long-sleeved shirt, shoes (rubber boots are best) and socks, and gloves (use rubber or polyethylene gloves, not cloth or leather, which absorb sprays). Use a face mask to protect yourself from dusts and spray droplets—for most botanicals a tight-fitting disposable dust mask is adequate. If the label says to avoid breathing vapor or mist (such as on some ryania and sabadilla products), you should use a proper cartridge or cannister respirator. Use goggles if you will be exposed to the spray for a prolonged period. The most common route for pesticide poisoning is absorption through the skin, particularly the eyes, which absorb pesticides easily and rapidly.

5. Wash skin and clothing thoroughly after spraying. Dispose of empty product containers in sanitary landfills or, if allowed by state regulations, burn containers. (If you burn them, be sure to stay out of the smoke!).

6. Don't go into treated areas until sprays have dried or dust has settled.

the substance to be affected. Pyrethrins have a quick knockdown effect on insects: Flying insects are paralyzed, whereas resting insects seem to be excited at first, then become paralyzed. Pyrethrins can be applied up to one day before harvest because they are quickly destroyed by light and heat and are not persistent in the environment.

Pyrethrins will kill lady beetles but do not appear to be very harmful to bees. They are toxic to fish and to the aquatic insects and other small animals that fish eat. Pyrethrins do not seem to be toxic to birds or mammals. Most commercial products have piperonyl butoxide (PBO) added to enhance toxicity. PBO is a synthetically produced chemical substance. Questions about the side effects and safety of PBO have arisen, so it seems wise to use caution when handling products with this ingredient.

Protection offered: Pyrethrins are registered for flowers, fruits, and vegetables, including greenhouse crops. They are effective on many chewing and sucking insects, including most aphids, cabbage loopers, celery leaftiers, codling moths, Colorado potato beetles, leafhoppers, Mexican bean beetles, spider mites, stink bugs, several species of thrips, tomato pinworms, and whiteflies. They are especially good against flies, gnats, mosquitoes, and stored products pests. Flea beetles are not affected, nor are imported cabbageworms, diamondback moths, pear psylla, and tarnished plant bugs.

How to make: If you grow your own pyrethrum daisies, you'll have the main ingredient for a make-it-yourself spray. Just be sure to grow the correct species (*T. cinerariifolium* or *T. coccineum*).

The concentration of pyrethrins is at its peak when the flowers are at full bloom—from the time the first row of florets on the central disk opens to the time all the florets are open. Pick flowers in full bloom and hang them in a sheltered, dark spot to dry. Once the flowers have dried thoroughly, grind them to a fine powder, using a mortar and pestle, old blender, or small hammer mill. Mix with water and add a few drops of liquid soap. Store in a glass jar and keep the lid tightly closed, because the mixture loses activity if left open. You'll have to experiment with the amount of water to add, because the concentration of pyrethrins in the flowers is an unknown variable. If the spray you make doesn't seem to kill insects, use less water the next time to make a more concentrated spray.

You can also extract the pyrethrins in alcohol. Put as many crushed flower heads as you can in a cup and soak overnight with $1/8$ cup isopropyl alcohol. Strain the mixture through cheesecloth and discard the flower material. Store the alcohol extract in a tightly sealed jar. When you need to use the pyrethrins, add 3 quarts of water to the extract to make a spray.

Beware if you are a hay fever sufferer, especially if you are allergic to ragweed. You may have an allergic reaction to pyrethrum flowers (this is not a problem with the extracted pyrethrins, only the flower heads). Also, keep in mind that pyrethrins stay potent longer in whole flowers than in ground flowers, so don't grind the flowers before storing. Store whole flower heads in a sealed, lightproof container under cool conditions.

How to use: Pyrethrins are available as premixed sprays, liquid concentrates, or wettable powders. Pyrethrins are more effective at lower temperatures, so for best results, apply in early evening when temperatures are lower. Spray both the upper and lower surfaces of the leaves, because spray must directly contact the insects' bodies to be effective. Spray twice at a 2-hour interval for better control of insects such as thrips that hide in leaf sheaths and crevices. The first spray will excite them and bring them out of hiding, the second will kill them. Some products warn against use on young plants or new growth. Never use pyrethrin products around waterways and ponds.

Commercial products: Entire (soap and pyrethrins, no PBO); Pyrenone (6 percent pyrethrins, contains PBO); Red Arrow (rotenone and pyrethrins, no PBO); Safer Yard and Garden Insect Control (pyrethrins and insecticidal soap, no PBO); Shield Garden Dust (with pyrethrins and diatomaceous earth); Shultz Instant Insecticide (pyrethrins with PBO); Trounce (soap and pyrethrins, no PBO)

Rotenone

Rotenone is derived from roots of South American legumes of the *Lonchocarpus* genus. Amazonian Indians used it for centuries to kill fish for mass harvesting, but it was not used on crops until 1848.

Rotenone occurs in more than 65 species of plants; however, most commercial supplies come from Peruvian cubé, Malaysian derris, or

Multipurpose Controls

There are two common organic pest control products that pack a double punch—oil and lime sulfur spray and garden dusts. These products contain both insecticidal and fungicidal substances and help control a broad range of insect and disease pests. Home gardeners find multipurpose controls an easy solution to pest problems, because they can apply one of these products without having to diagnose the specific insect or disease that has invaded their garden. The price paid for the convenience is the death of many beneficial insects and a higher level use of chemicals. Because of this, you might want to think of multipurpose controls as the last of your last resorts.

Organic garden dusts combine botanical insecticides such as rotenone and pyrethrin with fungicides such as copper or sulfur. You can apply garden dust by shaking it on plants directly from the container. Or, you can mix it with water according to the product label directions. Garden dusts are approved for use in the vegetable and flower garden to control chewing beetles such as striped cucumber beetle and Mexican bean beetle, flea beetles, leafhoppers, and squash vine borer. The dusts also help prevent the spread of fungal diseases including anthracnose, early blight, late blight, and powdery mildew.

Oil and lime sulfur can be mixed and sprayed on fruit trees, roses, and some ornamental shrubs and trees, but only when they are dormant. The dormant oil helps control scales and spider mites, while the lime sulfur helps prevent the spread of many fungus diseases. Don't try to mimic the action of this spray by making separate sprays of dormant oil and lime sulfur. If these two materials are combined at full strength, they will burn foliage. The multipurpose formulation contains lower concentrations of the active ingredients than are found in the single-ingredient formulations.

Brazilian tembo plants. It is a broad-spectrum, slow-acting, nerve poison that paralyzes insects. Most products contain 1 to 2 percent of active ingredients, but one formula with 5 percent rotenone is advertised as the "organic gardener's answer to broad-spectrum chemical pesticides." That comparison may be quite true, but the question is whether such a pesticide is needed in a home garden.

Rotenone is not very soluble in water, doesn't damage plants, and is unstable in sunlight, air, and water. Applications lose their effect on insects in a week. Rotenone was once a favorite of organic gardeners because of its supposed short life in the environment. However, new information shows that rotenone persists longer in the environment and is more toxic than was originally thought. There is some evidence that it causes growth abnormalities in laboratory animals.

A recent research study found that residues from rotenone dust on tomatoes and lettuce lasted nearly twice as long as the wettable powder formulation and that some residue remained in tomato sauce even after it was boiled. Although there are no records of human poisonings, rotenone may cause skin irritation, facial numbness, and respiratory problems in humans allergic to the compound. Rotenone is very toxic to fish, birds, and pigs.

Some rotenone products contain piperonyl butoxide (PBO), a synthetic substance that increases the rotenone's effectiveness. Some safety questions about PBO have arisen, so use caution if you select these products.

Protection offered: Rotenone is highly effective for controlling flea beetles and also works well against aphids, Colorado potato beetles, cucumber beetles, leafhoppers, plant bugs, spider mites, whiteflies, and other chewing insects. The spray leaves a white residue that is unsightly on ornamentals, especially those with textured leaves.

How to use: When applying rotenone, use good protective equipment (face mask, rubber gloves). The wettable powder form, which is mixed into a spray with water (the package will say wettable powder or WP), is preferable to the dust formulation, because a less active ingredient is needed to get good coverage and there is less likelihood of inhaling the dust. Mix wettable powders carefully to prevent dust from flying up. Don't try to mix dust formulations into water: The dusts are nearly impossible to dissolve. Spray plants thoroughly, especially the undersides of leaves where many species of pests hide. Although some sources state that bees are not affected, others recommend protecting bees by spraying at dusk, after bees have returned to the hive. Never use rotenone near waterways or ponds.

When you buy rotenone, make sure the package comes from a fresh stock in the store and buy only enough for one season; rotenone loses its potency quickly, and old dust is ineffective.

Commercial products: Atox; Deritox; Prentox; Pyrellin (pyrethrins, rotenone, and other cubé resins)

Ryania

The roots, leaves, and stems of the South American shrub *Ryania speciosa* yield ryanodyne, the active ingredient in this botanical insecticide. Ryania is more stable to light and air than rotenone or pyrethrum and has a longer residual effect than either. It is a contact and stomach poison and doesn't always kill insects outright. Instead, they become paralyzed and stop feeding. Ryania is not toxic to plants and has relatively low toxicity for mammals. Ryania is very water soluble and is quickly diluted by rain or heavy

dew (and thus becomes less effective). The dust can be stored at least three years, and some gardeners report good results with powder stored for five years. Keep the powder in a cool, dry, dark place.

Protection offered: Ryania is effective against codling moths in apple orchards and on other caterpillars, including cabbage loopers, corn earworms, European corn borers, imported cabbageworms, tomato fruitworms, and caterpillars of oriental fruit moths and diamondback moths. It also controls many chewing and sucking insects, such as aphids, Colorado potato beetles, Japanese beetles, Mexican bean beetles, milkweed bugs, and squash bugs.

How to use: For control of codling moths, apply sprays 10 to 14 days apart, starting when petals begin to fall. For corn borers and corn earworms, use dust and apply it to the ears at 5-day intervals. For cabbage loopers, diamondback moths, and imported cabbageworms, apply sprays 10 to 14 days apart beginning when caterpillars hatch and start to feed. For control of citrus and onion thrips, see "Sweet Poison" on page 224.

Spray thoroughly, especially on leaf undersides where eggs and caterpillars are most likely found. For thrips control, make sure spray reaches crevices of leaf sheaths and buds where the thrips hide.

Commercial products: Ryan 50; Ryania dust; Triple Plus (a mixture of pyrethrins, rotenone, and ryanodyne)

Sabadilla

Another Central and South American plant with insecticidal activity is a lily family member *Schoenocaulon officinale,* the source of sabadilla. The insecticidal compound comes from the powdered ripe seeds and has been used as louse powder for centuries. Sabadilla is unstable in light and loses its effect soon after it is applied. Sabadilla is a toxic product not to be treated lightly. Human poisoning symptoms include retching, muscle spasms, slowed heart rate, and lowered blood pressure; dust and seeds can irritate mucous membranes and bring on bouts of sneezing. The effects are slow to disappear, and there is evidence that small doses may have cumulative effects. Sabadilla is toxic to honeybees, but does not seem to harm predators and parasites such as lady beetles, predatory mites, and armored scale parasites.

Protection offered: Sabadilla dust has mostly been used in the citrus industry in California for control of citrus thrips (especially good with sugar added as bait, see "Sweet Poison" above). Although not used widely, sabadilla will kill many other insects, including aphids, armyworms, blister beetles, cabbage loopers, chinch bugs, codling moths, European corn borers, grasshoppers, harlequin bugs, imported cabbageworms, squash bugs, stink bugs, tarnished plant bugs, and webworms.

How to use: Sabadilla is sold in dust form (usually in a lime or sulfur carrier) and as a wettable powder for mixing a water spray. When handling sabadilla products, protect yourself with a face mask, goggles, gloves, and protective clothing. Start spraying as soon as pests appear, or as soon as eggs hatch, so larvae are able to eat the leaves and therefore eat the spray to poison themselves. Spray plants thoroughly, making sure undersides of leaves are well covered, at 10- to 14-day intervals. For thrips control, it is especially important to make sure sprays reach crevices in leaves, between leaf sheaths, and into rough patches on twigs or stems.

Commercial products: Red Devil dust; Veratran D (for citrus thrips)

Neem

The insecticidal properties of the neem tree (*Azadirachta indica*) have been used in India for centuries to protect stored grains, but it is only in the last few years that its enormous potential in pest control products has been realized in developed countries. Research is currently going on throughout the world on formulating and using neem extracts.

Neem is a shade tree native to the Indian subcontinent, grown widely throughout the world in warm and tropical zones. Experimental plantings are now growing well in Florida and California. Another tree, the chinaberry (*Melia azadarach*), also has similar insecticidal properties. Although not as effective as neem, it is slightly hardier and grows widely in the southern and southeastern United States.

The insecticidal ingredients in neem are most concentrated in the oil from the seed kernels, which can be extracted by water, alcohols, or petroleum ether. Neem oil has a variety of effects on insects and mites: It is toxic; it acts as a repellent or feeding deterrent; it stops or disrupts growth; and it sterilizes some species. Although much more research needs to be done, neem appears to be somewhat selective in its effects on beneficial insect species, having little effect on the parasitic wasps and one species of predatory mite that have been studied. Interestingly, one study found a beneficial effect on the growth of earthworms from a neem soil drench. Toxicity to humans and other mammals seems to be very low; in India, it is used in toothpaste, soap, cosmetics, and pharmaceuticals. The pressed cake left over after oil is extracted is used for cattle feed.

Protection offered: More than 123 insect species, three mite species, and five nematode species are affected by neem extracts. Among this group are such difficult pests as Colorado potato beetles, corn earworms, flea beetles, gypsy moths, Mexican bean beetles, oriental fruit flies, root-knot nematodes, serpentine leafminers, spotted cucumber beetles, and two-spotted spider mites. One commercial formulation, Margosan-O, is registered in the United States to control aphids, caterpillar pests, chinch bugs, gypsy moths, leafminers, mealybugs, thrips, and whiteflies, but only on ornamentals. The manufacturer plans to expand the Environmental Protection Agency registration to include food crops and household insect pests.

How to make: Southern gardeners can make a water extract from neem seeds if they can get them, or from chinaberry seeds, which are more common than neem, but less toxic to insects and more toxic to humans. To extract insecticidal compounds from the seeds, wrap 1 pound of depulped, cleaned, dried seeds in a cloth bag, crush them, and suspend the bag overnight in a bucket containing 1 pint of water. After 12 hours, remove the bag and squeeze out the liquid. Discard the crushed seeds. Add $\frac{1}{8}$ teaspoon dishwashing liquid or commercial insecticidal soap to the liquid extract. Dilute 1 part of this concentrated insecticidal solution with 17 parts water to make a spray.

Another way to extract the insecticide is to shred 1 pound of whole neem or chinaberry fruit in an old blender or food processor (add a small amount of water before processing). After shredding, add enough water to cover all the pulp and let sit overnight. The next day, strain and discard the pulp and add water to the strained liquid to make 4 or 5 quarts of spray mixture. Add $\frac{1}{16}$ teaspoon dishwashing liquid or insecticidal soap to improve spray coverage. The mix should remain effective for three or four days if stored in a dark place.

Be sure to keep the chinaberries and extracts out of the reach of children. Ingesting as few as four or five berries can cause poisoning.

How to use: Sprays can be used on foliage or as a soil drench to control soil stages of pests, such as leafminers and thrips. Spray foliage in the early morning or late afternoon, so leaves will stay wet with spray longer for maximum effectiveness.

Commercial products: Margosan-O

Nicotine

One of the top three insecticides in the 1880s, nicotine in several forms is still widely used. Nicotine comes from the tobacco plant and is extremely toxic to insects (and humans!). Tobacco dust (0.5 percent nicotine) made from ground stems and leaves is commercially available, as are products made with nicotine sulphate, the extremely toxic compound extracted from tobacco leaves. The great advantage of homemade nicotine tea is that it is very short-lived, retaining its toxicity for only a few hours after spraying. It is relatively nonhazardous to bees and lady beetles because of its short persistence.

Protection offered: Nicotine is effective against ground and soil pests, especially root aphids and fungus gnats, and on many leaf-chewing insects, such as aphids, immature scales, leafhoppers, thrips, leafminers, pear psylla, and asparagus beetle larvae.

How to make: You can brew your own batch of nicotine tea by soaking tobacco leaves or cigarette butts in water to make a spray. Soak 1 cup of dried, crushed tobacco leaves, or an equivalent amount of cigarette butts, in 1 gallon of warm water with $\frac{1}{4}$ teaspoon pure soap added.

Strain the mixture through cheesecloth after it has soaked for ½ hour. The solution will keep for several weeks if stored in a tightly closed container.

How to use: Be extremely careful when handling nicotine sulphate preparations. The liquid concentrate is very toxic. Mix according to label directions. Use good skin protection, especially gloves, goggles, and protective clothing. For soil pests, pour the spray mixture onto the soil in the area of the stem base and root zone. For leaf pests, spray leaves thoroughly, especially the undersides. Nicotine can be absorbed by plant leaves and remain there for several weeks. To be safe, use nicotine spray only on young plants and only up to one month before harvest. It's probably safest not to spray nicotine on eggplant, peppers, or tomatoes. While most tobacco cultivars now grown are resistant to tobacco mosaic virus, nicotine sprays could contain the pathogen, which will infect nightshade family crops.

Commercial products: Tobacco dust; nicotine sulphate

Quassia

Quassia, a Latin American tree, is related to the *Ailanthus* (tree of heaven). It yields a mild insecticide from bark chips and shavings that is one of the safest botanical insecticides (it is used medicinally by herbalists). Quassia does not affect lady beetles and honeybees.

Protection offered: Quassia controls aphids, caterpillars, Colorado potato beetle larvae, sawflies, and several species of flies.

How to make: You can buy quassia chips in natural food stores. To make a spray, crush, grind, or chop ¼ cup of bark chips and add them to 1 to 2 quarts of boiling water. Allow the mixture to cool, strain, and use the liquid to spray pest insects. Or, steep the bark chips overnight in 1 to 2 quarts cool water, then strain and spray the liquid.

How to use: Spray plants thoroughly and ensure good coverage on the undersides of leaves. Spray frequently (as often as twice a week) to control pests once they start feeding on leaves.

NEW AND UPCOMING CONTROLS

New and unusual pest control products are being developed to meet the demand from growers and consumers alike for safer alternatives to conventional pesticides. Some of the products we describe here are not yet available to gardeners, but are likely to be on the market in the near future.

Citrus Oils

In 1984, an entomologist at the University of Georgia discovered that orange peels contain compounds that killed fire ants, which led to research on the insecticidal compounds in citrus. Since then, these compounds have been identified as the citrus limonoids—compounds concentrated in the seeds and oil glands on citrus peels. These compounds can be extracted in quantity from citrus industry wastes. Citrus limonoids kill insects and deter pests from feeding on leaves. The toxic effects on insects include causing them to regurgitate, become sluggish, and stop eating. Because limonoids affect leaf-eating pests, they seem to be safe for honeybees and predatory insects.

Two limonoid compounds have been developed commercially and are now sold widely in flea control products for pets. Registration for use on food crops has been slower in coming, but there is now at least one such product on the market, and more will certainly follow.

Protection offered: Limonoid compounds on leaves has been shown to effectively reduce feeding damage from Colorado potato beetle larvae by 65 percent. On corn, limonoids caused a 20 to 50 percent reduction in feeding from fall armyworm and a 95 percent reduction in corn earworm damage. Limonoids are also effective against spider mites and aphids. So far, the limonoids seem to have little effect on spruce budworms, tobacco caterpillars, and naturally enough, on citrus pests such as scales and citrus mites that are adapted to cope with the toxic citrus compounds.

How to use: Prepare the spray according to the directions on the label. Spray to cover leaves thoroughly, especially on the undersides where many pests feed. Treat at one- to two-week intervals to maintain the repellent effect as leaves grow and rain washes away the compounds.

Commercial products: Aphid-Mite Attack (contains a combination of citrus compounds and insecticidal soap)

Insect Growth Regulators

The internal workings of an insect, like those of any other animal, are regulated by hormones. When the first insect hormones, the juvenile hormones, were extracted in the 1950s, researchers found they could be used to interrupt insects' developmental processes. Affected insects usually died, or could not reproduce. This led to excited speculation about using hormones for controlling insect pests, particularly because it was thought unlikely that insects could develop resistance to their own natural hormones.

Practical difficulties arose because producing sufficient material for field use was neither cheap nor simple. Once this obstacle was overcome, the problem remained that juvenile hormones are only effective at a certain stage of an insect's development. For this reason, timing applications to coincide with just the right stage is tricky in the field. Nonetheless, one juvenile hormone, methoprene, is now on the market and is considered one of the safest materials ever used in pest control.

Other insect growth regulators (IGRs) interfere with the production of chitin in the exoskeleton, the hard outer coating of insect bodies. Chitin is a flexible compound, chemically somewhat like a hard plastic. If the synthesis of chitin is disturbed, the insect cannot accomplish its molt to the adult stage and usually dies. These IGRs must be eaten to be effective, and therefore are not as likely to affect nontarget insects, such as beneficial predators and parasitic wasps.

Protection offered: Kinoprene, which was off the market for five years, is an excellent aphid control. Methoprene is used to control mosquitoes, fungus gnats in mushroom houses, blackflies, some midges, fleas, and cattle flies (but not house flies). Similar IGRs have shown promise against some termites, and one has been registered for, and used successfully on, more than 130,000 acres in Texas against red imported fire ants.

Diflubenzuron is one of the most studied of IGRs and shows promise against eggs and larvae of codling moths, Colorado potato beetle larvae, armyworms, and whitefly larvae.

How to use: To control aphids (with Kinoprene) or fungus gnats (with Methoprene) on houseplants or greenhouse plants, follow the mixing directions on the container and spray thoroughly to get good coverage on both sides of the leaves.

Commercial products: Altosid; Diflubenzuron (not commercially available); Enstar Methoprene

Mating Disruption with Pheromones

Entomologists have long toyed with methods to disrupt the mating of insect pest species of moths by flooding an area with female sex pheromones. It is an effective technique because the pheromone so confuses the males that they spend much time and energy following the tantalizing odors around the orchard or garden, never finding a mate. The females remain unmated, fail to lay eggs, so pest populations are reduced. The development of twist-tie and cloth-patch dispensers for pheromones has made it possible to put out many sources of pheromone simply and cheaply.

Protection offered: Promising results have been achieved against codling moths, corn earworms, gypsy moths, oriental fruit moths, tomato pinworms, and several species of grape berry moths. Twist-tie and patch dispensers for oriental fruit moth are now available for use. Other types of mating disruption products for home gardeners should become available in the future.

How to use: Simply attach the twist-ties to branches of trees or shrubs, to trellises, or to fences, and leave in place.

Commercial products: Checkmate; Isomate-M

Abamectin

Streptomyces bacteria are familiar to us as important producers of antibiotics used in medicine. More than ten years ago, widespread research started on the avermectins, including abamectins and ivermectins, naturally occurring antibiotics produced by the bacterium *Streptomyces avermitilis.*

The avermectins have been tested against nearly 100 species of insects and mites and found to be toxic in some degree to almost all of them. The toxin affects them in several ways: by paralyzing the insects, disturbing their water balance, disrupting molting, and preventing feeding and reproducing. Death is usually very slow, taking from 1 day to as long as 30 days. Generally, these antibiotics have low toxicity to vertebrates; the avermectins are widely fed to livestock to control parasitic worms and stable and horn flies. Abamectin is used on plant pests, generally with good results, and is also effective against pest nematodes. These compounds do affect beneficial insects and mites, however, particu-

larly if they eat prey that has been poisoned by abamectin. In one study, it was found that abamectin on leaves quickly lost its toxicity to beneficial predator mites while remaining toxic to their spider mite prey. However, the predators died or laid fewer eggs after eating spider mites treated with abamectin.

Protection offered: Abamectin is only registered to control spider mites and leafminers on flower and ornamental foliage crops. In fact, it is about the only registered pesticide that does control chrysanthemum leafminer. It is also available as a fire ant bait. Studies on other pests show that it is particularly effective on beet armyworms, cabbage loopers, corn earworms, diamondback moths, fall armyworms, fruit flies, gypsy moth larvae, houseflies, tobacco hornworms, tomato leafminers, and some leafrollers. However, it has not yet been registered for use against these pests.

How to use: Spray both upper and lower surfaces of leaves thoroughly to ensure good coverage.

Commercial products: Avid

Starch Spray

Using starch to control insects is an old-fashioned remedy on the verge of making a commercial appearance in a new form. Organic gardeners have used flour sprinkled on plants or mixed in water to make a spray for many years. Starch spray is completely nontoxic to plants, animals, and people. It isn't toxic to insects either: It kills them by physically trapping their legs and wings in the gluey starch and suffocating them.

A new product made from dextrin (a type of gummy sugar) extracted from potato starch is currently being tested for the commercial market. It should be available to gardeners in the near future.

Protection offered: Potato starch dextrin sprays have been shown to control aphids, spider mites, thrips, and whiteflies. Oddly enough, it has also controlled powdery mildew on cucumbers. This spray should be useful against a wider variety of pests and plant diseases as well. Flour dusts and flour sprays are often recommended to control imported cabbageworms and cabbage loopers on cole crops.

How to make: You can make your own potato starch spray by mixing 2 to 4 tablespoons of potato flour (available from natural food stores) in 1 quart of water and adding 2 to 3 drops of liquid, nondetergent soap.

How to use: The commercial product should be mixed with water according to label directions. Spray to cover leaves thoroughly, especially on leaf undersides. You can make a more concentrated spray, if necessary, to improve the effect on aphids and thrips without harming the plant. If there is a residue left on leaves, especially of ornamentals, you can wash it away with water a few days after spraying.

Commercial products: Hugtite (not available in the United States in 1991)

Thuringiensin

One of the toxins produced by *Bacillus thuringiensis* (BT) is called thuringiensin. It has been isolated from the food medium used to grow the bacteria and is now being studied for its potential as a pesticide. Because it is a by-product of microbial activity, it will require registration as a separate insecticide, especially since there are some questions about its safety to mammals. Thuringiensin is mainly active against larvae, killing both by contact and when eaten. It shows promising activity against such hard-to-control species as beet armyworm, Colorado potato beetle larvae, tarnished plant bugs, and two-spotted spider mites. It is not as selective as BT sprays. Although thuringiensin does not seem to be toxic on contact to beneficial insects, it has been shown to harm the beneficials when they eat poisoned larvae. Testing of one thuringiensin product is being pursued for commercial sale.

35 Common Garden Pests

This table describes the appearance and life cycles of 35 of the most common pests of North American gardens. It also lists the regions in which the pests occur, the damage they cause, and the plants they attack.

Some entries in the table describe a specific species of pest, such as European corn borer, while others describe a group of species, such as aphids. Control methods listed for the group entries may not apply for every species in that group or for every host plant. For example,

neem is one control substance listed for aphids; however, neem has not yet been registered for use on food crops. Refer to the label on the container or other information supplied with pest control products for specific listings of their registered uses.

Several control methods are given for each pest. For difficult species such as codling moth or Colorado potato beetles, you probably will need to use a combination of methods.

Insect Pests

Aphids
Acyrthosiphon pisum
and many other species

| 1/8"

Wingless adult

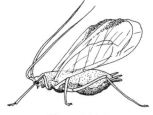

Winged adult

Description: Tiny, pear-shaped, 1/32–1/8-in. insects with long antennae and 2 tubes projecting backwards from their abdomens. Green to black, reddish brown, or dusty gray. Usually found in crowded colonies on leaf undersides and/or in growing tips; winged forms appear when colonies overcrowded. Found throughout North America.

Hosts: Most fruit and vegetable crops; many flowers and ornamentals.

Damage: Aphids suck plant sap, causing leaf and bud distortion and blossom and leaf drop. Their feeding may spread virus diseases. Sticky honeydew excreted on leaves and fruit supports growth of sooty molds.

Life cycle: Eggs overwinter, hatch in early spring into females that give birth to live nymphs; nymphs mature within a week and bear more nymphs. Males appear in fall and mate with females, who then lay overwintering eggs. Some species are put onto plants by ants, who protect them from predators.

Controls: Wash aphids from plants with a strong spray of water; encourage native predators and parasites; spray with homemade garlic or tomato leaf sprays; use dormant oil sprays on fruit trees; release aphid midges, lacewings, lady beetles (in greenhouse only); spray with alcohol, citrus oil, insecticidal soap, or neem; dust boric acid on soil around plants to control ants; as a last resort, spray pyrethrin, nicotine, or rotenone.

Apple maggot
Rhagoletis pomonella

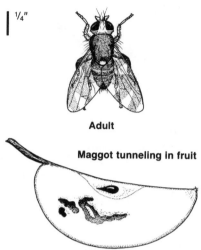

¼"

Adult

Maggot tunneling in fruit

Description: Adults: black, ¼-in. fruit flies with yellow legs and transparent wings patterned with dark crosswise bands. Larvae: white maggots. Found in eastern U.S. and Canada, also in northern California.

Hosts: Apple, blueberry, plum; related flies attack cherry, peach, and walnut.

Damage: Larvae tunnel through fruit, which drops early; early cultivars usually most damaged.

Life cycle: Adults start emerging mid-June to July, lay eggs in punctures in fruit skin. Eggs hatch within a week, larvae tunnel in fruit until fruit drops. Mature larvae leave fruit and pupate in soil to overwinter; 1 generation per year. Some pupae remain dormant several years.

Controls: Pick up, destroy fallen fruit daily until September; after that, twice a month; from mid-June until harvest hang apple maggot traps in trees (1 per dwarf tree, 6 per full-size tree); encourage predators of the pupae (ground beetles and rove beetles) by planting white clover ground cover in orchards.

Armyworms
Spodoptera frugiperda
and similar species

2"

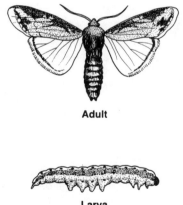

Adult

Larva

Description: Adults: pale gray-brown moths, forewings with white dot in center (wingspan 1½–2 in.). Larvae: young larvae smooth, pale green; full grown larvae up to 1½ in., greenish brown with white stripes along the sides and dark or light stripes down the backs. Eggs: greenish white, laid in masses along lower leaves. Found east of the Rockies, occasionally New Mexico, Arizona, California; also southern Canada. Beet armyworm is common in southern U.S.

Hosts: Corn and other field crops. Related species attack many garden crops.

Damage: Larvae feed together in large groups at night, hiding during the day under stones, soil, or in the center leaves of plants. When food supply is exhausted, they move en masse to neighboring crops. Older larvae can devour whole plants overnight. Crop damage around the sides of a garden or field indicates an invasion by armyworms.

Life cycle: Half-grown larvae, sometimes pupae, overwinter in soil or litter around roots, resuming feeding in early spring, then pupating for 2 weeks. Adult moths are active and lay eggs only at night. Two to 3 generations per year; larvae of June generation do the most damage.

Controls: Encourage native parasitic wasps and flies; spray BTK (*Bacillus thuringiensis* var. *kurstaki*) to kill larvae; spray summer oil in July to kill eggs if larvae were a problem in spring or if many adult moths are present.

(continued)

Blister beetles

Epicauta vittata
and other beetles
in Meloidae family

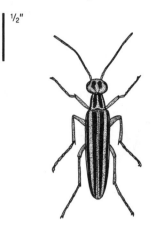

½"

Description: Adults: metallic, black, blue, purplish, or brown, ¼–¾-in. beetles with soft, elongated bodies, long legs, and narrow necks; heads are often larger than the thoraxes; beetles cling to plants when disturbed. Larvae: youngest larvae are tiny, narrow, and elongate with large heads; later stages are progressively fatter grubs with smaller heads; last stage nearly legless. Eggs: cylindrical, laid in grasshopper egg burrows in soil. Found throughout North America.

Hosts: Adults feed on many flowers, shrubs, and vegetables. Larvae of most species eat grasshopper eggs.

Damage: Large numbers of adults feeding on flowers and foliage rapidly defoliate plants. Larvae are often beneficial.

Life cycle: Beetles lay eggs in midsummer in grasshopper egg burrows; larvae feed on grasshopper eggs for a month. Larvae then overwinter in the resting state, may remain inactive up to 2 years. Larvae pupate in spring, adults emerge in early summer. Most species with 1 generation per year, correlated with grasshopper life cycles; some species have 3-year life cycles.

Controls: Except in areas where severe crop damage occurs, benefit of control is debatable because larvae are effective grasshopper predators. Knock adults from plants into a pail of soapy water. Wear gloves, as contact with crushed beetles causes burns and blisters on skin; protect plants with floating row covers or screens, especially during midsummer when beetles are present; as a last resort, spray with pyrethrin or rotenone.

Boring beetles

Chrysobothris femorata
and similar species

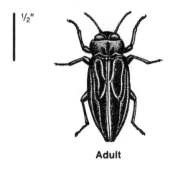

½"

Adult

Larva

Description: Adults: slightly flattened, metallic brown or dark gray, ¼–½-in. beetles with irregular sculpturing on wing covers. Larvae: legless, pale yellow or white grubs with brown, retracted heads; one very wide segment just behind the head (up to 1¼ in.). Eggs: wrinkled, yellow disks laid in cracks in bark. Found throughout North America.

Hosts: Nearly all deciduous fruit and shade trees. One species attacks jack and red pine.

Damage: Larvae bore into sapwood of young trees, bark of older trees, forming galleries filled with crumbly castings, usually on the sunny side of trunks. Attacked patches of bark exude gummy sap, turn dark and die; if bark dies entirely around the trunk, the tree will die. In the West, oak is the primary host; in the East, maples and fruit trees are most seriously attacked.

Life cycle: Grubs overwinter in chambers 1 in. deep in wood and pupate in the spring. Adults emerge in summer and lay eggs in bark crevices of weakened or stressed trees. When eggs hatch, grubs burrow into bark, feeding as deep as 2 in. in tunnels under bark for the rest of summer; usually unable to complete development on healthy trees. One generation per year.

Controls: Maintain healthy, vigorous trees and avoid injury to bark; remove injured limbs as soon as damage occurs; protect trunks of newly transplanted trees for first 2 years with white paint or by wrapping trunks; dig out borer larvae, scrape away damaged bark, and paint with wound paint.

Cabbage looper
Trichoplusia ni

1½"

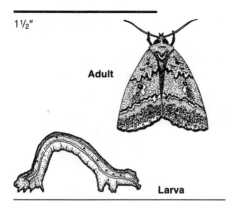

Adult

Larva

Description: Adults: large gray moths with a silver spot in the middle of each forewing (1½-in. wingspan). Larvae: green inchworms with 2 white lines down their backs, one along each side; they move by looping their bodies. Found in most of U.S. and in southern Canada.

Hosts: Cabbage family preferred; also beets, celery, lettuce, peas, spinach, tomatoes.

Damage: Larvae eat large holes in leaves; may destroy plants.

Life cycle: Moths emerge in May, lay eggs on leaves. Larvae feed 3–4 weeks, then pupate in cocoons attached to stems or leaves. Three to 4 generations per year.

Controls: Handpick several times a week; attract native parasitic wasps with flowering weeds and herbs between plants; spray with BTK (*Bacillus thuringiensis* var. *kurstaki*) or garlic oil; spray with abamectin (when available), pyrethrin, or sabadilla.

Cabbage maggot
Delia radicum
(= *Hylemya brassicae*)

¼"

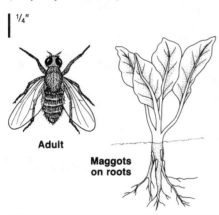

Adult

Maggots on roots

Description: Adults: gray, ¼-in. flies with long legs. Larvae: white, tapering maggots. Found throughout North America.

Hosts: Cabbage family crops.

Damage: Maggots tunnel in roots, ruining root crops, allowing disease organisms to enter, and stunting or killing plants. First sign of injury is usually temporary wilting.

Life cycle: Adults emerge from overwintering pupae from late March on and lay eggs in soil beside roots. Larvae tunnel in roots 3–4 weeks, then pupate in soil for 2–3 weeks. Two to 4 generations per year in most areas.

Controls: Cover seedlings with floating row covers, edges buried in soil; set out transplants through slits in tar paper squares or black plastic mulch; burn or destroy all cabbage family plant roots at harvest; apply parasitic nematodes to soil around roots; where populations usually low, mound wood ash, diatomaceous earth, or hot dusts (dill, ginger, red pepper) around stems; renew frequently.

Carrot rust fly
Psila rosae

¼"

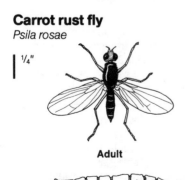

Adult

Maggot

Description: Adults: shiny, metallic, greenish black, ¼-in. flies with yellow heads and legs. Larvae: white, tapering maggots. Found throughout North America.

Hosts: Carrot family crops.

Damage: Maggots eat root hairs and tunnel into roots, allowing root rots to enter and stunting or killing plants. Maggots continue to destroy harvested root crops in storage.

Life cycle: Adults emerge mid-April to May, laying eggs in soil close to plants. Larvae burrow in roots for 3–4 weeks, then pupate. Two to 3 generations per year.

Controls: Cover carrot beds with floating row covers immediately after seeding. Bury edges of covers, leave covered until harvest; apply parasitic nematodes to soil.

(continued)

Codling moth
Cydia (=Laspeyresia) pomonella

3/4"

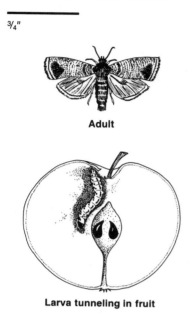

Adult

Larva tunneling in fruit

Description: Adults: gray-brown moths; forewings with fine, white lines and brown tips; hindwings brown with pale fringes (3/4-in. wingspan). Larvae: pink or creamy white caterpillars; brown heads. Eggs: flattened white eggs laid on leaves, twigs, and fruit. Found throughout North America.

Hosts: Apple, apricot, cherry, peach, pear, plum.

Damage: Larvae tunnel through fruit to the center, ruining fruit.

Life cycle: Overwintering larvae pupate in spring; adults emerge about the time apple trees bloom. Females lay eggs on fruit, larvae burrow into fruit core, usually from blossom end. After 3–5 weeks, larvae leave fruit to pupate under tree bark or in ground litter. Two to 3 generations per year, 5–8 weeks apart.

Controls: Sow or encourage cover crop to support native predators and parasites, especially ground beetles that eat cocoons; collect and destroy larvae from corrugated cardboard tree bands; scrape away loose bark and overwintering cocoons before warm spring weather and apply dormant oil spray; use pheromone traps to determine when main flight of moths occurs and release *Trichogramma* wasps to coincide with egg-laying period; apply codling moth granulosis virus 1–2 times weekly during main egg production season (only registered in California, Washington, Oregon); spray parasitic nematodes into absorbent tree bands several times weekly from June to the beginning of August; if you expect severe codling moth problems, spray with ryania starting when 75 percent of petals fall, followed by 3 sprays at 1–2 week intervals.

Colorado potato beetle
Leptinotarsa decemlineata

5/16"

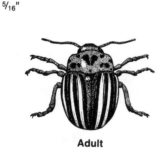

Adult

Larva

Description: Adults: 5/16-in., yellowish orange beetles with 10 black, lengthwise stripes on wing covers; thoraxes yellow with black spots. Larvae: dark orange, humpbacked grubs with black spots along sides. Eggs: bright yellow, oval; laid on end in clusters. Found throughout North America.

Hosts: Nightshade family plants, including petunias.

Damage: Beetles and larvae defoliate plants, reducing yields or killing young plants.

Life cycle: Overwintering adults emerge from soil about the time potato plants emerge in spring. After feeding, females lay eggs on leaves. Eggs hatch in 4–9 days. Larvae feed for 2–3 weeks, then pupate in soil. Adults emerge in 5–10 days for second generation. A third generation occurs in parts of southern U.S.

Controls: Control early season adults by shaking them from plants onto ground cloth early in the morning, also by handpicking; attract native parasites and predators with pollen and nectar flowers, ground beetles with deep straw mulches; cover plants with floating row covers until midseason; try a release of spined soldier bugs; in southern states, try a release of parasitic wasps *Edovum puttleri* to attack second generation larvae; apply parasitic nematodes to soil to attack larvae as they prepare to pupate; use double strength sprays of BTSD (*Bacillus thuringiensis* var. *san diego*) to control larvae; as a last resort, spray weekly with pyrethrin, rotenone, or neem.

Corn earworm, tomato fruitworm

Helicoverpa (=Heliothis) zea

1½"

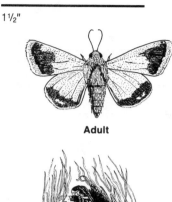

Adult

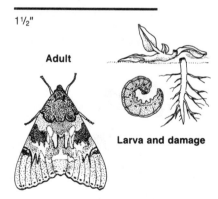

Larva and damage

Description: Adults: large, light tan moths (1½–2-in. wingspan). Larvae: light yellow, green, pink, or brown, 1½–2-in. caterpillars with white and dark stripes along sides, yellow heads, black legs. Eggs: white, ribbed, round. Found throughout North America. Not hardy in Canada, but will migrate from U.S. in spring.

Hosts: Corn (early and late plantings most affected), tomatoes, many flowers.

Damage: Larvae eat buds and chew large holes in leaves. In corn, larvae feed on fresh silks, then move down the ears eating kernels, leaving trails of castings. Larvae burrow into ripe tomatoes.

Life cycle: Adults emerge in early spring, can fly long distances. Females lay eggs on leaves or tips of corn ears; eggs hatch in 3 days. Larvae feed for 2–4 weeks, pupate in soil. Adults emerge 10–25 days later. One to 4 generations per year.

Controls: Plant tight-husked corn cultivars, like Illini hybrids; after silks start to dry, spray BTK (*Bacillus thuringiensis* var. *kurstaki*) into the tips of ears or apply granular BTK; attract native parasitic wasps; squirt parasitic nematodes into tips of ears; squirt mineral oil on tips of ears; open corn husks and remove larvae; release lacewings or minute pirate bugs; mix pyrethrin or rotenone with a molasses bait (3 parts water to 1 part molasses) and paint it in a band around corn stalks above soil to kill emerging adults; use pheromone traps to monitor appearance in large plantings; as a last resort, spray abamectin (when available), neem, or ryania.

Cutworms

several *Euxoa* and *Agrotis* species

1½"

Adult

Larva and damage

Description: Adults: brown or gray moths (1½-in. wingspan). Larvae: fat, gray or dull brown, 1-in. caterpillars with shiny heads. Found throughout North America.

Hosts: Most early vegetable and flower seedlings and transplants.

Damage: Caterpillars rest curled beside plant stems below soil surface during the day. At night, they feed on stems at soil line. Transplants are cut off, seedlings may be completely eaten. Most damaging in May and June, especially in gardens in recently turned sod.

Life cycle: Overwintered pupae or eggs emerge on first warm spring days. Adults lay eggs on grass or soil surface early May to early June. Eggs hatch in 5–7 days, larvae feed on grass and other plants for 3–5 weeks, then pupate in soil. Adults emerge late August to early September. One generation per year, most areas; late second generation may damage crops in warm fall weather.

Controls: Use cutworm collars on all spring transplants; scatter moist bran mixed with molasses and BTK (*Bacillus thuringiensis* var. *kurstaki*) over soil a week before planting to kill some larvae; apply solution of parasitic nematodes to soil.

(continued)

European corn borer

Ostrinia nubilalis

1"

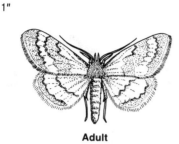

Adult

Larva

Description: Adults: female moths pale yellowish brown, with darker zigzag patterns across wings; males darker colored (1-in. wingspan). Larvae: flesh-colored, 1-in. caterpillars with small, brown spots. Eggs: masses of 15–20 white, overlapping eggs laid on the undersides of leaves. Found in north and central U.S. and in central and eastern Canada.

Hosts: Beans, corn, onions, peppers, potatoes, small grains, tomatoes, many other crops.

Damage: Young larvae feed on leaves, corn tassels, and beneath husks. Older larvae burrow in corn stalks and ears; stalks may break.

Life cycle: Larvae overwinter in plant stems left in fields, pupate in early spring. Adults emerge in June. Eggs laid late June to mid-July, hatch in 1 week; larvae feed for 3–4 weeks. One to 3 generations per year.

Controls: Grow resistant cultivars and cultivars with strong stalks; remove and destroy tassels from ⅔ of corn plants before pollen sheds to eliminate many young larvae; spray BTK (*Bacillus thuringiensis* var. *kurstaki*) thoroughly on leaf undersides and into tips of ears after silks wilt, or apply granular BTK in tips of ears. Rotate crops (only effective for large plantings); when available, try releases of *Trichogramma nubilale* or *T. evanescens* when eggs are present in large plantings; leave flowering weeds between plants to attract native parasitic flies and wasps. Clean up, turn under corn residues as soon as harvested if infestations severe, otherwise leave stalks in the garden to protect predators. As a last resort, spray with pyrethrin, ryania, or sabadilla.

Flea beetles

several *Phyllotreta* and *Epitrix* spp.

⅛"

Description: Adults: black, brown, or bronze beetles with large hind legs; jump like fleas when disturbed; ⅛ in. or smaller. Larvae: thin, white, legless grubs with brown heads; soil dwellers. Found throughout North America.

Hosts: Most vegetable crops.

Damage: Adults chew many small, round holes in leaves (shot-hole effect), most damaging to seedlings; larger plants not usually seriously damaged. Larvae feed on plant roots.

Life cycle: Adults overwinter in soil or in leaf litter along hedgerows. Eggs laid on or near roots in spring. Adults die off in June or early July, larvae continue feeding on roots and pupate in soil. One to 2 generations per year, depending on species. Adults of species with second generation emerge late July to August.

Controls: Where spring populations are high, cover seedlings with floating row covers until plants are well grown and adult beetles die off (July); apply solution of parasitic nematodes to soil to control larvae; interplant to provide shade, which they avoid; plant late in the season to avoid problem; as a last resort, spray with neem, pyrethrin, rotenone, or sabadilla.

Imported cabbageworm
Pieris rapae

1½"

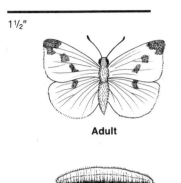

Adult

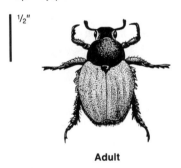

Larva

Description: Adults: white butterflies, forewings with black tips and 2–3 spots (1½–2-in. wingspan). Larvae: velvety, medium green caterpillars with fine yellow-orange stripe down their backs (grow to 1½ in.). Eggs: conical, yellow with ridges, laid on the undersides of leaves. Found throughout North America.

Hosts: Cabbage family plants.

Damage: Larvae eat large, ragged holes in leaves and cabbage heads, soiling leaves with dark green excrement.

Life cycle: Butterflies appear in early spring from overwintering pupae and lay eggs. Larvae eat for 2–3 weeks, then pupate in trash on soil. Adults emerge in 1–2 weeks. Three to 5 generations per year, overlapping so larvae present all season.

Controls: Cover plants with floating row cover all season; handpick larvae in light infestations; use yellow sticky traps to catch female butterflies; spray larvae with BTK (*Bacillus thuringiensis* var. *kurstaki*); as last resort, use sabadilla.

Japanese beetle
Popillia japonica

½"

Adult

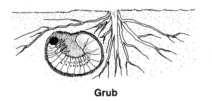

Grub

Description: Adults: metallic blue-green, ½-in. beetles with bronze wing covers, legs rather long compared to many beetles, fine hairs all over their bodies. Larvae: dirty white, fat, ¾-in. grubs with brown heads. Eggs: white, laid in sod. Found in all states east of the Mississippi River.

Hosts: Many food crops and garden plants.

Damage: Adults eat flowers and skeletonize leaves; heavy infestations may completely defoliate plant. Larvae feed on roots of lawn and garden plants.

Life cycle: Overwintering larvae deep in soil move toward surface in spring to feed, pupate early summer; adults emerge and feed midsummer to fall, laying eggs in late summer. Eggs hatch into larvae that overwinter. One generation every 1–2 years.

Controls: Shake beetles from plants in early morning onto ground cloth, then destroy; cover vegetable crops with floating row covers; apply milky disease spores to sod to control grubs; plant species or cultivars of plants unattractive to adults; plant to attract native species of parasitic wasps and flies; set out traps throughout the entire community to reduce adult populations; apply parasitic nematodes to soil to control grubs; spray with rotenone as a last resort.

(continued)

Lace bugs

Stephanitis pyrioides
and other members of
Tingidae family

1/8"

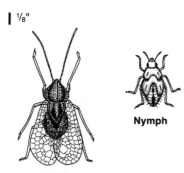

Adult   **Nymph**

Description: Adults: oval or rectangular, 1/8-in. bugs with distinct, lacelike pattern on wings and heads; unusually wide, flattened, winglike hoods over thoraxes. Larvae: smaller, darker bugs, covered with spines. Eggs: inserted in plant tissue, along underside midrib; frequently with hard, conelike cap projecting from leaf. Found throughout North America.

Hosts: Many flowers, ornamental trees and shrubs, vegetables.

Damage: Adults and nymphs suck plant juices on the undersides of leaves, resulting in speckled white or gray blotched appearance on leaf surfaces; spots of excrement on undersides.

Life cycle: Most overwinter in egg stage, some as adults under bark of trees. Eggs hatch into nymphs that feed on plant juices on undersides of leaves, molting to adults over several weeks. Three or more generations per year.

Controls: Spray summer oil (not on chrysanthemum flowers); spray pyrethrin or rotenone as a last resort.

Leafhoppers

over 2,000 species,
Cicadellidae family

1/8"

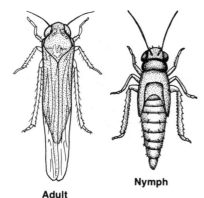

Adult   **Nymph**

Description: Adults: wedge-shaped, slender, 1/8–1/2-in. bugs with wings folded over their bodies, forward point on head very pronounced in some species, some with bright bands of color across wings, all jump rapidly into flight when disturbed. Larvae: wingless, pale nymphs, shape similar to adults; hop rapidly when disturbed. Eggs: minute, laid in veins and stems of plants. Found throughout North America.

Hosts: Most fruits and vegetables, some flowers and weeds.

Damage: Both adults and nymphs suck juice from stems and undersides of leaves. While feeding, they inject a toxic saliva that distorts and stunts plant growth and causes tipburn and yellowed, curled leaves. Fruit may be spotted with insect excrement and honeydew. They also spread virus diseases.

Life cycle: Adults become active early in spring, laying eggs when leaves begin to appear on trees. Some species migrate north to Canada during summer and back south in fall. Eggs are laid in plant tissue, hatching in 10–14 days. Nymphs develop for several weeks before molting to adults. Most species have 2–5 generations per year, overwintering as eggs or adults.

Controls: Use water or soap sprays frequently to wash nymphs from plants; conserve, attract natural enemies (big-eyed flies, parasitic wasps); brush plants with hands and watch for leafhoppers. If you can count more than 25 leafhoppers per 50 leaves, spray with pyrethrin, rotenone, or sabadilla.

Leafminers

several *Liriomyza*
and *Pegomya* species

less than 1/8"

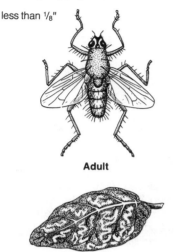

Adult

Mines in leaves

Description: Adults: black or black-and-yellow flies, usually less than 1/8 in., rarely seen. Larvae: pale green, stubby, translucent maggots, found in tunnels in leaves. Eggs: white, cylindrical, laid side-by-side in clusters on the undersides of leaves. Several species found throughout North America.

Hosts: Beans, beets, cabbage, chard, lettuce, peppers, tomatoes, many ornamentals.

Damage: Larvae tunnel between the leaf surfaces, feeding on leaf tissue and leaving round or winding mines, often destroying seedlings. On large, well-grown vegetables, more a nuisance than serious pest; serious pest of ornamentals.

Life cycle: Adults emerge from overwintered cocoons in early spring and lay eggs on leaves. Larvae tunnel into leaves beneath surface for 1–3 weeks, then drop to soil to pupate for 2–4 weeks. Two to 3 generations per year, more in greenhouses.

Controls: Cover seedlings with floating row covers, remove when plants are well-established; pick and destroy leaves with mines, remove clusters of eggs; remove nearby dock or lamb's-quarters, which are alternate hosts for beet leafminer; encourage native parasites with nectar plants; spray with abamectin (when available), neem, or nicotine.

Leafrollers

Archips argyrospila
and related species

1/2"

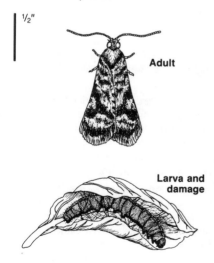

Adult

Larva and damage

Description: Adults: golden brown mottled, 1/2-in. moths. Larvae: green caterpillars with brown heads and fine spines on their bodies (up to 1 in.); usually found in webbing or rolled leaves at tips of branches. Eggs: light yellowish brown, laid in masses of 30–100 on tree branches and trunks, covered with a brown protective coating. Found throughout North America, worst damage is to apples in northern U.S. and Canada.

Hosts: Most fruit and ornamental trees; roses.

Damage: Larvae spin webs at branch tips, pulling leaves together and feeding on enclosed buds, leaves, and developing fruit.

Life cycle: Eggs overwinter on tree bark, hatch in early spring; larvae feed 1 month, spin webs, and pupate within the rolled leaves or in a cocoon on bark. Adults emerge in late June or July (northern U.S.) and lay eggs that overwinter. One generation per year.

Controls: Apply dormant oil sprays just before buds break in spring to kill egg masses; check branches of young or dwarf trees weekly and remove caterpillars; encourage native parasitic wasps such as *Trichogramma;* when larvae start feeding, before protected from sprays by rolled leaves, apply BTK (*Bacillus thuringiensis* var. *kurstaki*) sprays or pyrethrin or rotenone.

(continued)

Mexican bean beetle
Epilachna varivestis

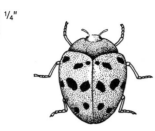

¼"

Adult

Larvae and damage

Description: Adults: oval, yellowish brown, ¼-in. beetles with 16 black spots on their wing covers; markings less distinct on overwintered adults. Larvae: fat, dark yellowish orange, ⅓-in. grubs with long, branched spines. Eggs: yellow, laid on end in clusters on undersides of leaves. Found in most states east of the Mississippi River; also parts of Texas, Arizona, Utah, Colorado, and Nebraska.

Hosts: Cowpeas, lima beans, snap beans, soybeans.

Damage: Both larvae and adults chew on leaves from beneath, leaving characteristic lacy appearance; may severely defoliate and kill plants; most abundant in weed-free fields.

Life cycle: Adults overwinter in leaf litter in nearby fields or woods; in spring, adults fly to beans to lay eggs. Eggs hatch in 5–14 days. Larvae feed 2–4 weeks, then pupate on leaves. One to 3 generations per year.

Controls: Cover plants with floating row covers, at least until plants are well-grown; encourage native predators that attack larvae by allowing flowering weeds and by planting herbs; avoid main beetle populations by planting early bearing bush beans; handpick beetles and larvae from small bean patches; plant soybeans as a trap crop, destroy after infested with larvae; till under plant remains as soon as harvest is complete; release parasitic wasp *Pediobius foveolatus* to control second generation larvae when weather is warm (not effective in cool spring weather); try release of spined soldier bugs for earlier season control; spray weekly with pyrethrin, sabadilla, rotenone, or neem.

Oriental fruit moth
Grapholita molesta

½"

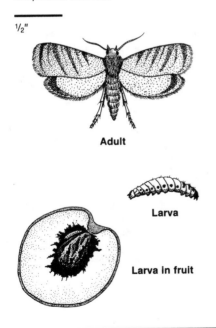

Adult

Larva

Larva in fruit

Description: Adults: dark gray moths with dark brown, mottled forewings (½-in. wingspan). Larvae: off-white to pinkish gray with brown heads (up to ½-in.). Eggs: flat, white, laid on twigs, undersides of leaves. Found in eastern U.S., Pacific Northwest states, Ontario.

Hosts: Most fruit trees, some ornamental trees.

Damage: Early season larvae bore into young twigs, causing them to wilt and die; midsummer generation larvae bore into developing fruit, leaving masses of gummy material mixed with castings on fruit; late-summer generations enter stem end of maturing fruit and bore into pit, ruining fruit.

Life cycle: Larvae in cocoons overwinter attached to bark of trees, on weeds, or in soil around trees, pupating in early spring. Adults emerge early May to mid-June, females lay eggs on leaves and twigs. Eggs hatch in 10–14 days; larvae feed 2–3 weeks, then pupate. Second brood appears mid-July, third brood end of August in northern U.S. Three to 4 generations in the North, 6–7 in the southern states.

Controls: Where climate permits, plant early cultivars of peaches and apricots to be harvested before late-summer broods bore into fruit; cultivate soil around trees at least 4 in. deep before trees bloom to kill overwintering larvae; attract, protect native parasitic wasps and flies; use mating disruption with pheromone patches, apply pheromone patches to lower limbs of trees (about 1 patch per 4 trees); spray summer oil to kill eggs, and larvae.

Plum curculio
Conotrachelus nenuphar

3/16"

Adults and damage

Larva

Description: Adults: dark brownish gray, hard-shelled, 3/16-in. weevils with long snouts, sculpturing on wing covers, and white hairs on their bodies. Larvae: plump, white, 1/3-in. grubs with brown heads. Eggs: round, white, laid under crescent-shaped cut in fruit skin. Found in eastern North America.

Hosts: Most tree fruit crops; blueberries.

Damage: Feeding and egg-laying by adults damages fruit skins; larvae tunnel in fruit, usually feeding near pit, causing premature fruit drop or rotting.

Life cycle: Adults prefer to overwinter in nearby wooded areas, but will survive in orchard debris. In spring, they move to trees when leaves and blossoms appear, attack fruit when it appears from June to August. Eggs in fruit hatch in 5–10 days, larvae feed 2–3 weeks. When fruit drops, larvae leave to pupate in soil. Adults emerge late July to late October, feed on ripe or fallen fruit until overwintering. One to 2 generations per year.

Controls: Sharply tap tree branches with a soft mallet to knock beetles onto a ground cloth, then destroy; in each tree, hang large, green apple sprayed with an apple fragrance perfume as a decoy after petal fall; frequently remove and destroy all fallen fruit, especially small early drops; let chickens into the orchard to feed on dropped fruits; in areas where severe infestations are likely, check developing fruit for egg scars every 4–5 days, starting as soon as blossoms set, when first egg scar is seen, apply Triple Plus (pyrethrin-ryania-rotenone mix), repeat in 7–10 days.

Sawflies
Calirua cerasi
and other members of
Tenthredinidae family

1/4"

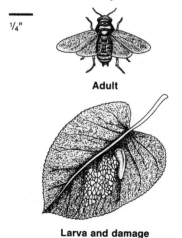

Adult

Larva and damage

Description: Adults: stout-bodied, dark, 1/8–1/2-in. insects with a dark spot along the margins of the forewings. Larvae: variable, often green with prominent white spots along their bodies. Eggs: laid in or on plants. Found throughout North America.

Hosts: Many fruits; some ornamental trees.

Damage: Larvae bore or mine in fruit, leaving brown, crumbly material on the surface; feeding causes berries to drop prematurely. On larch and other needle trees, larvae feed on foliage, stripping needles on upper branches.

Life cycle: Pupae overwinter in cocoons in soil, adults emerge in spring and lay eggs on host plants. Young larvae mine foliage or burrow into fruit to the core, exiting later through the characteristic hole in the side. They drop to the soil to pupate for winter. One generation per year.

Controls: Usually a minor pest in most areas. Remove host weeds around fruit trees; spread ground cover around trees to catch larvae as they drop to the ground to pupate, and collect and destroy them daily; spray summer oil on larch; spray larvae with insecticidal soap or with rotenone, if the infestation is severe, starting as soon as petals begin to drop and again in 2 weeks.

(continued)

Scales

over 200 species,
Coccoidea superfamily

1/100–1/10"

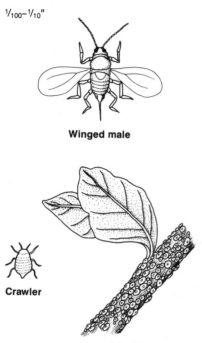

Winged male

Crawler

**Infestation
of female scales**

Description: Adults: females look like hard or soft bumps on stems, leaves, fruit, some so small they look like gray ash, always without legs, wings, or appendages (1/100–1/10 inch); males are minute flying insects with yellow wings. Larvae: mobile crawlers like minute mealybugs, with threadlike mouthparts. Eggs: masses laid inside edge of female scale, some species give birth to live young. Found throughout North America.

Hosts: Many fruits, indoor plants, ornamental shrubs and trees.

Damage: All stages suck plant sap, weakening plants, which become yellow, drop leaves, and eventually die if infestation is severe. Large quantities of honeydew excreted onto foliage, fruit.

Life cycle: Females lay as many as 2,000 eggs or give birth to several live young per day. Mobile nymphs crawl around on plants, feeding for a short time before molting. Female nymphs lose their legs and antennae during molt to adult scales; males molt to tiny, flylike insects. One to 5 generations per year, depending on climate and species (more generations on indoor plants).

Controls: Prune and dispose of infested branches and twigs; encourage and attract numerous native biological controls; scrub scales gently from twigs with a soft brush and soapy water, rinse well; try rubbing alcohol sprays; on houseplants, use pure water or soap sprays to dislodge crawlers and remove honeydew; release *Chilocorus nigritus* and *Lindorus lophanthae* (lady beetles) for soft scale species; release *Metaphycus helvolus* (parasitic wasp) for soft brown scale, *Aphytis melinus* (parasitic wasp) for California red scale and oleander scale; on fruit and ornamental trees, apply dormant oil sprays before buds break in early spring; during summer apply summer oil (but not on citrus after July or on holly); as a last resort, spray pyrethrin or rotenone.

Squash bug

Anasa tristis

5/8"

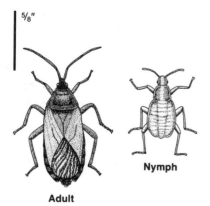

Nymph

Adult

Description: Adults: black or brownish, 5/8-in. bugs covered with fine, dark hairs, margins around their abdomens are striped with yellowish orange; give off disagreeable odor in defense. Larvae: Pale green nymphs, changing to dark thoraxes and abdomens, usually covered with white powder. Eggs: Elliptical, shiny yellow, turning to brown; laid on the undersides of leaves, usually in groups.

Hosts: Gourd family crops.

Damage: Both adults and nymphs suck plant juices, causing leaves and shoots to blacken and die; fruit on attacked plants prevented from forming.

Life cycle: Adults overwinter under garden litter, vines, or boards; females lay eggs in spring; nymphs take all season to develop, molting 5 times before maturity. One generation per year.

Controls: Maintain healthy plant growth; handpick all stages from the undersides of leaves; protect and encourage native parasitic flies; cover with floating row covers (hand pollinate flowers to set fruit); spray rotenone or sabadilla as a last resort.

Striped cucumber beetle
Acalymma vittatum

1/4"

Description: Adults: yellow, 1/4-in. beetles with black heads and 3 wide black stripes on their wing covers. Larvae: slender, white, 1/4-in. grubs. Eggs: round, orange, laid in soil. Found in U.S. as far west as Colorado and New Mexico; in Canada, west to Saskatchewan. Similar species abundant west of the Rockies.

Hosts: Squash family crops, beans, corn, peas, blossoms of many plants.

Damage: Adults swarm on seedlings, feeding on leaves, young shoots, often killing plant; they also attack stems and flowers of older plants and eat holes in fruit; feeding can transmit wilt and mosaic viruses. Larvae feed on roots of cucurbits only, killing or stunting plants.

Life cycle: Adults overwinter in dense grass or under leaves, emerging in April to early June. They eat weed pollen for 2 weeks before moving to crop plants and lay eggs in soil at the base of cucurbits. Eggs hatch after 10 days. Larvae burrow into soil, feed on roots for 2–6 weeks, and pupate in early August. Adults emerge in 2 weeks to feed on blossoms and maturing fruit. One to 2 generations per year.

Controls: Cover seedlings or plants with screen or floating row covers (hand pollination becomes necessary); apply parasitic nematodes to soil to control larvae; put down a deep straw mulch, which seems to prevent adults from walking between plants; spray with sabadilla or rotenone.

Tarnished plant bug
Lygus lineolaris

1/4"

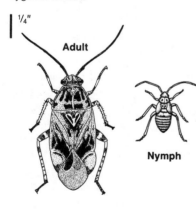

Adult

Nymph

Description: Adults: oval, 1/4-in. bugs, light green to brown with yellow, reddish, or black mottling; forewings with black-tipped yellow triangle; move very quickly. Larvae: small, yellow-green nymphs, like miniature adults without wings. Eggs: Curved, elongate, laid in leaves, stems. Found throughout North America.

Hosts: Many flowers, fruits, vegetables.

Damage: Adults and nymphs suck plant juices. Their saliva causes shoot and fruit distortions, bud drop, wilting, stunting, tip dieback.

Life cycle: Adults overwinter under bark or in leaf litter, emerge in early spring to feed on weeds and fruit buds. They lay eggs in leaf tissue; eggs hatch in 10 days. Nymphs feed for 3–4 weeks before final molt. Two to 5 generations per year, overlapping so all stages present most of season.

Controls: Cover plants with floating row covers; encourage native predatory bugs and beetles by planting ground covers and pollen plants; release minute pirate bugs; spray rotenone or sabadilla as a last resort.

(continued)

Thrips

Thrips tabaci and several
other species

1/50–1/25"

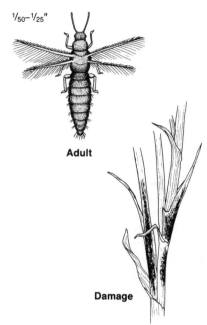

Adult

Damage

Description: Adults: minute, elongate, fast-moving, 1/50–1/25-in., yellow, brown, or black insects with small, narrow, fringed wings. Larvae: nymphs resemble small adults without wings, usually light green or yellow with red eyes. Eggs: not visible, laid in plant tissue. Found throughout North America.

Hosts: Many flowers, fruits, vegetables.

Damage: Adults and nymphs suck sap from plant tissue, leaving silvery spots or streaks on leaves; severe infestations stunt plants, serious crop losses from species feeding in flowers, causing tattered flowers, deformed fruit.

Life cycle: In northern areas, adults and nymphs overwinter in sod, debris, cracks in bark, and become active in early spring; in the South or in greenhouses, thrips may continue to reproduce slowly during winter. Eggs are laid in plant tissue; hatch in 3–5 days. Nymphs feed for 1–3 weeks and then pupate, some species in soil, others on leaves. Adults emerge in 1–2 weeks. Five to 15 generations per year outdoors, more in greenhouses.

Controls: Apply dormant oil sprays to fruit trees; encourage native predators (pirate bugs, lacewings, lady beetles); for onion or western flower thrips, release predatory mite *Amblyseius cucumeris* (100 per plant); hang up blue sticky traps (yellow also works) to catch adults moving into crop; try releases of minute pirate bugs (1–5 per plant); as a last resort, spray with alcohol, insecticidal soap, neem, nicotine, pyrethrin, ryania, sabadilla, or apply diatomaceous earth, just on the undersides of leaves and on soil around affected plants.

Webworms

Several members of Arctiidae and
Pyralidae families

1"

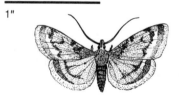

Adult

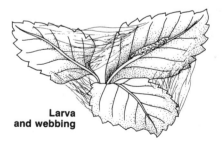

**Larva
and webbing**

Description: Adults: white to brown, 1-in. moths with pale yellow or brown markings on wings. Larvae: pale green to nearly black, 3/4-in. caterpillars with a dark or light stripe down their backs and three dark spots on the sides of each body segment; young larvae drop on silken thread when disturbed. Eggs: pale, pearly green, often laid in rows on undersides of leaves. Found throughout U.S. and southern Canada.

Hosts: Most fruit and shade trees; many vegetable crops.

Damage: Caterpillars spin a light webbing around leaves, feeding under the web, on undersides of leaves, eating holes until only a dry leaf "skeleton" remains.

Life cycle: Pupae or larvae overwinter in cocoons in the soil, completing pupation in the spring. Adult moths emerge from late spring to mid-summer and lay eggs that hatch in a week. Caterpillars spin webs and feed for a month before pupating. Two to 3 generations per year in most areas.

Controls: Remove host weeds in garden vicinity; knock caterpillars off leaves into a pail of soapy water (they drop readily when disturbed); remove and destroy webs by burning or immersion in soapy water; spray BTK (*Bacillus thuringiensis* var. *kurstaki*), only effective if it reaches leaves where larvae feed; pyrethrin or rotenone sprays as last resort.

Weevils

Listroderes difficilis
and similar species

1/4"

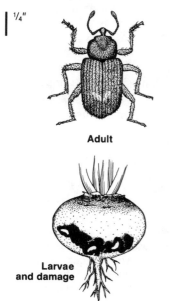

Adult

**Larvae
and damage**

Description: Adults: small, hard-shelled, 1/4–3/8-in. beetles with characteristic snouts with elbowed antennae attached near end; dull gray or brown, flightless due to fused wing covers. Larvae: plump, legless, milky white or pinkish grubs, usually with brown heads. Eggs: minute, round, laid in soil around plants. Found throughout North America.

Hosts: Many fruit, ornamental, and vegetable plants; conifer seedlings.

Damage: Adults feed at night, notching neat half-circles from leaf margins or consuming needles of conifers; damage usually not severe unless adults feed on seedlings, cutting them off at soil line. Worst damage is from larvae feeding on roots and burrowing in crowns of plants.

Life cycle: Adult females (males rare or unknown) lay eggs in soil near roots; eggs hatch in 2 weeks. Larvae feed on roots through summer and fall, then overwinter in soil and resume feeding in spring. They pupate in late spring and adults emerge in June. Adults from previous year also overwinter in trash and weeds near fields, becoming active mid-April and laying eggs in May. One to 2 generations per year.

Controls: Destroy overwintering sites, piles of garden trash around strawberry patches, vegetable beds; practice 3-year rotation between plantings of susceptible crops; drench soil around plant roots with parasitic nematodes to control larvae (works well if soil is kept moist); apply pyrethrin or rotenone leaf sprays at night to kill adults, as soon as first notch is seen in a leaf, to prevent adults from laying eggs.

Whiteflies

*Trialeurodes vaporariorum,
Bemisia tabaci,* other species

1/20"

Adult

Flies on leaves

Description: Adults: mothlike, 1/20-in. insects with powdery white wings; most rest on the undersides of top leaves of plants. Larvae: flattened, legless, transluscent, 1/30-in. scales found on the undersides of lower leaves. Eggs: gray or yellow, pinpoint cones, often laid in semicircles on leaf undersides. Found throughout North America in greenhouses; overwintering in areas with winters above freezing, including Gulf states, Florida, southern California, west coastal areas.

Hosts: Citrus crops, as well as many greenhouse foliage plants, ornamentals, vegetables.

Damage: Nymphs and adults suck plant juices, weakening plants. Sooty mold grows on honeydew excreted on leaves and fruit. Feeding spreads virus diseases.

Life cycle: Females lay eggs, which hatch in 2 days into mobile scales. These molt to a legless nymphal stage and continue to feed on undersides of leaves until they pupate in place on the leaf. The life cycle takes 20–30 days at 65–75°F, less time at warmer temperatures. Numerous overlapping generations occur per year, continuing all winter in greenhouses and warm climates.

Controls: Use yellow sticky traps to catch adults; in greenhouses, vacuum adults weekly from tips of plants; release parasitic wasp *Encarsia formosa* at the rate of 5 per plant as soon as first whitefly is seen and again in 2 weeks. In warm regions, encourage numerous native or introduced parasitic wasps and predatory beetles. For severe problems, control larvae with weekly sprays of alcohol, garlic oil, insecticidal soap, pyrethrins, or rotenone on the undersides of leaves.

(continued)

Wireworms

Limonius agonus and
many other species

1½"

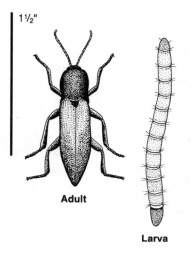

Adult

Larva

Description: Adults: brown, gray, or black, elongate, flattened, 1½-in. click beetles, some with a pair of eyespots on thoraxes. Larvae: slender, cylindrical, 1–1½ in., grubs with jointed appearance; shiny, tough, smooth skin, yellow to reddish brown. Found throughout North America.

Hosts: Gladiolus and other flower corms, most vegetable crops.

Damage: Larvae bore into sown seeds or roots, stunting or killing plants; boring in tubers and bulbs ruins them for storage or sale and hastens decay; problem worst in newly turned sod, continues for several years.

Life cycle: Overwintered adults lay eggs in plant roots in early spring; larvae hatch in 3–10 days, spend 2–6 years feeding on roots. They feed near soil surface when the soil is cool in spring and fall, and move deeper as soils warm in summer and again in late fall to overwinter. Mature larvae pupate in late summer. One generation every 2–6 years; usually all stages present in infested field.

Controls: Cultivate thoroughly once per week for 4–6 weeks in fall to destroy many larvae; allow chickens to run on infested ground as long as possible to scratch up larvae; set out traps made from buried pieces of raw potato as soon as ground can be worked; check every 1–2 days and destroy larvae; delay planting tubers and corms until soil is very warm; apply solution of parasitic nematodes to soil.

European red mite

Panonychus ulmi

$\frac{1}{75}$"

Description: Adults: minute, 8 legged, $\frac{1}{75}$ in., reddish or carmine colored, with prominent bristles in rows down their bodies. Nymphs: similar to adults; smaller, lighter color. Eggs: round, pearly pink to dark red, laid in cracks in bark in fall, undersides of leaves in summer. Found throughout North America.

Hosts: Most fruit crops.

Damage: Feeding on plant juices causes yellow speckled foliage in light infestations; severe infestations cause bronzing of leaves, leaf drop, stunted growth, weak fruit buds, poor-quality fruit.

Life cycle: Eggs overwinter in cracks in bark or twigs, branches, and trunks. Eggs hatch about the time plum blossoms are in full bloom and apples buds show pink. Nymphs move to leaves to feed, maturing in 7–10 days. Numerous overlapping generations per year, with all stages present during summer.

Controls: Spray dormant oil before trees break dormancy to kill overwintering eggs in bark crevices; release predatory mite *Metaseiulus occidentalis* (*Typhlodromus occidentalis*); spray with abamectin, citrus oils, insecticidal soap, neem, or pyrethrin as a last resort.

Slugs

Limax maximus
and many other species

from $\frac{1}{8}$" to 8"

Adult

Damaged leaf

Description: Adults: gray, tan, brown, olive green or black, some species have spots or variegated patterns; soft-bodied, muscular, plump mollusks without external shells; move on a large flat foot, leaving trails of mucus; newly hatched garden slugs are $\frac{1}{8}$ in., adult spotted banana slugs can be 5–8 in. Eggs: clear, oval, laid in masses under stones, debris. Garden slugs found throughout North America; banana slugs in high-rainfall areas on both coasts of North America.

Hosts: Virtually any plant, especially young or tender foliage, although they prefer decaying plant material.

Damage: All species rasp large holes in leaves, stems, and bulbs; may demolish seedlings. Fine trails of mucus on leaves or nearby soil is sometimes visible. Most damaging in cool, wet years or regions.

Life cycle: Adults lay eggs in clusters in moist soil or under rocks. Eggs hatch in 2–4 weeks. Tiny slugs continue to grow for 5 months to 2 years before reaching sexual maturity.

Controls: Repel slugs with copper strips around trunks of trees and shrubs; push 4–8-in. copper strips into soil as edging for garden beds, or tack along perimeter or around legs of greenhouse benches; use traps of overturned clay pots with one edge lifted slightly, pieces of board or plastic, cabbage leaves or raw potatoes laid flat on soil. Check and destroy slugs in traps daily until few are caught; continue to check weekly. Set out traps of shallow pans filled with stale beer or any fermenting liquid, buried with the lip flush with the soil surface; maintain permanent walkways of clover, sod, or stone mulches to protect predatory ground beetles; protect seedling rows with wide bands of cinders, wood ashes, diatomaceous earth, and cedar sawdust renewed frequently.

(continued)

Two-spotted spider mite
Tetranychus urticae

$1/75$–$1/50$"

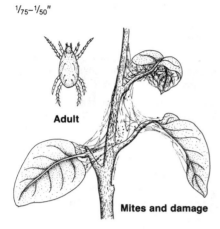

Adult

Mites and damage

Description: Adults: minute, 8 legged, greenish gray, $1/75$–$1/50$ in., with fine hairs over their bodies; overwintering adults are orange; fine webbing on the undersides of leaves and on branch tips are characteristic. Nymphs: similar to adults, smaller, paler color. Eggs: translucent, round, laid on webbing. Found throughout North America, especially in greenhouses, field crops in warm regions.

Hosts: Many food crops and ornamentals.

Damage: Mites suck juice from cells on the undersides of leaves, weakening plants, causing leaves to drop. The first sign of damage is yellow speckled areas on leaves, fine webbing present underneath; in severe infestations, leaves turn yellow or nearly white with brown edges, fine webbing covers leaves and growing tips.

Life cycle: Overwintered adults move from garden debris onto crop in early spring to lay eggs, which hatch in 2–3 days. Nymphs develop to adult in 7–10 days. Many generations per season.

Controls: For a few plants, spray daily with water to raise humidity; release predatory mite *Phytoseiulus persimilis* in greenhouses and on strawberry and vegetable beds (1,000 per 500 sq. ft. or 2 per small plant), concentrating releases on infested leaves; in hot conditions (above 90°F) use *Amblyseius californicus, Phytoseiulus longipes,* or the heat-adapted strain of *P. persimilis*; for severe infestations, spray weekly with abamectin, citrus oils, insecticidal soap, neem, pyrethrin, or rotenone.

Part Three

Chemical-Free Garden Guides

CHAPTER EIGHT

Vegetables

By Anna Carr

Your vegetable garden is probably the easiest part of your yard to manage organically. Since you start fresh each season, it's relatively simple to use fall-planted green manures and yearly applications of compost to enrich the soil. With a little thought, you can plan a rotation among your rows and beds to help prevent disease and interplant crops to reduce insect problems.

The following encyclopedia of vegetable crops lists guidelines for fertilizing plants and also provides information on the insects and diseases that may attack each crop. Crops are listed alphabetically by common name. (The botanical name and family of each crop follows the common name.) To troubleshoot a problem in your garden, start by looking up the affected crop. Skim the entry until you find the symptoms that match those on your plants. If the symptoms are a disease problem, you'll find the name of the disease, a full description of the symptoms, and prevention and control measures.

If the symptoms are caused by insects, in some cases, you'll find the name of the insect, description, and complete control measures. In most cases, however, you'll find only the name of the pest responsible along with two or three of the most reliable control measures. If you'd like more information about that insect or how to control it, see "35 Common Garden Pests" on page 230. There you'll find comprehensive information on the pest, its life cycle and host plants, and how to control it. If you're not familiar with any of the recommended insect and disease control measures, refer to chapters 6 and 7 for detailed explanations on when and how to use control methods and products.

As you scan the entries, you may wonder how anyone manages to garden organically, given all the insects and disease organisms waiting out there. Remember that any individual garden probably will be troubled by only a few pests.

It's a good idea to read over the entries on all the vegetables you grow for valuable tips on preventing problems before they arise. Most entries include tables listing insect- and disease-resistant cultivars. (If none are listed, it's because resistant cultivars of that crop aren't currently available). Sources of seeds or plants for each cultivar listed in the tables are keyed by number. See "Sources," on page 426, for the names and addresses of the suppliers that correspond to the numbers in the listings.

Asparagus

Asparagus officinalis
Liliaceae

Fertilizing

Mulch heavily in very early spring with 8 in. or more of rich compost or rotted manure. Apply a balanced organic fertilizer every 2 years once plants are established.

Insect Control

Defoliated Plants; Misshapen Young Spears

Both asparagus beetles and spotted asparagus beetles feed on plants and young stalks, causing defoliation and misshapen spears.

Asparagus beetles are metallic blue-black, 1/4-in. beetles with 4 white spots and red margins on the wing covers and reddish thoraxes. The beetles and their gray, fleshy larvae feed on young stalks, leaves, and stems. Clean up beds in fall to destroy overwintering sites. Handpick the beetles, and encourage lady beetles and parasitic wasps. For serious infestations, use pyrethrin or pyrethrin/rotenone spray or dust. Also use these methods for adult spotted asparagus beetles. These are orange-red, 1/3-in. beetles with 12 black spots on their wings. Orange larvae feed only on berries; control larvae by shaking berries onto a sheet and destroying them.

Disease Control

Brown Discoloration on Crowns or Spears

Asparagus stalks suffering from crown rot will turn brown from near the soil surface to about 6 in. into the soil. Plants suffering from Fusarium wilt will have wilted, stunted, brownish spears. Prevent these fungal diseases by planting disease-free crowns and keeping soil pH above 6.0. Keep infested plants as productive as possible by providing adequate water and nutrients. Mildly infested plants will continue to produce; harvest moderately to avoid stressing plants. Remove any severely infested plants.

Reddish Brown Masses on Stems

Spears infected by rust fungi develop reddish brown spots on stems; spears later turn yellow, weaken, and die. Prevent by planting rust-resistant cultivars. Clean up old stems and stubble in fall to eliminate overwintering rust fungus spores.

Resistant Asparagus Cultivars

Cultivar	Resists (R)/Tolerates (T)
'Greenwich'	**R:** Fusarium yellows; Source-widely available
'Jersey Giant'	**R:** rust; **T:** Fusarium yellows; Sources-4, 16, 18, 19, 23
'Martha Washington'	**R:** rust; **T:** Fusarium yellows; Source-widely available
'Mary Washington'	**R:** rust; Source-widely available
'Viking KB3'	**R:** rust; **T:** Fusarium yellows; Source-33
'Waltham'	**R:** rust; Sources-9, 11

Bean, lima

Phaseolus lunatus
Leguminosae

Fertilizing

Lima bean is a heavier feeder than other beans. Use plenty of rich compost to supply a steady amount of nutrients. If plants seem to need a boost, side-dress with balanced organic fertilizer at flowering time. Use the proper bacterial inoculant (available through seed catalogs or at garden centers) to promote nitrogen fixation.

Insect Control

See "35 Common Garden Pests," on page 230, for additional information and control measures for the insect problems listed below.

Yellowed, Stunted Plants

Aphids suck sap from leaves and stems causing foliage to curl, pucker, and turn yellow. Leaves and buds may become stunted. Encourage natural predators and parasites; release aphid midges or lacewings. Spray with water or insecticidal soap if aphids appear on plants. If aphids persist, use pyrethrin or pyrethrin/rotenone spray or dust.

Adult and nymph leafhoppers also suck plant sap, causing yellowed foliage and stunting. Protect bush limas from leafhoppers by covering the plants with floating row covers. If exposed plants become infested, use frequent water or soap sprays to wash off nymphs. Spray with pyrethrin or sabadilla as a last resort.

Damage to Buds, Young Plants, and Pods

Corn earworms eat flower buds and damage young plants, resulting in stunted growth. They may also eat leaves and bore into pods. Handpick earworms; spray or apply granular BTK (*Bacillus thuringiensis* var. *kurstaki*). Encourage parasitic wasps and other predators for biological control.

Lima bean pod borers are white to greenish or reddish, 1-in. caterpillars that chew through pods and eat seeds. They are easily controlled by handpicking and careful garden cleanup.

Seedling Stems Severed

At night, cutworms eat through seedling stems at or below the soil surface. Apply a solution of parasitic nematodes or BTK soil pellets mixed with a molasses/bran bait to the soil surface 1 week before planting. Cultivate the garden well to destroy the adult moths' egg-laying sites.

Holes in Leaves

Tiny holes in leaves. Adult flea beetles chew many tiny holes in leaves. Protect bush limas from flea beetles by covering the plants with floating row covers. Use parasitic nematodes to control larvae in the soil. Apply pyrethrin, sabadilla, or rotenone as a last resort.

Skeletonized leaves. Mexican bean beetles and their larvae chew on leaf tissue, leaving a dry leaf "skeleton" behind. They may also damage stems and pods. Use floating row covers to protect young plants. Planting early helps avoid major infestations. Handpick the beetles and rub the orange eggs off leaves. If you spot bean beetles in large bean plantings, release parasitic wasps or predatory spined soldier bugs. As a last resort, apply pyrethrin or rotenone dust or spray. Destroy or till under plant remains as soon as harvest is complete.

Disease Control

Small, Reddish Brown Spots on Plants

Bacterial spot appears as small, reddish brown spots on leaves, stems, and pods. Rotate crops and use clean seed to avoid infection. Also, avoid planting lima beans near trees and shrubs, as many common species are alternate hosts.

White, Cottony Patches on Pods

Symptoms of downy mildew include purple lesions on pods, flowers, and young shoots; fuzzy, white mold may grow on leaf undersides. Upper surfaces of older leaves may have pale yellow-green areas. Plants die rapidly. Use a 3-year rotation and choose western-grown seed of resistant cultivars to avoid this fungal disease. Treat with a soda-and-soap spray (1 tsp. baking soda, 1 tsp. liquid detergent, 1 qt. water) as soon as symptoms appear.

Resistant Lima Bean Cultivars

Cultivar	Resists (R)/Tolerates (T)
'Eastland'	**R:** downy mildew; Sources-12, 26, 33
'Nemagreen'	**R:** nematodes; Source-13

Bean, snap

Phaseolus vulgaris
Leguminosae

Fertilizing

Avoid excessive nitrogen. In rich soils, the only feeding that may improve yield is a top-dressing of compost or a dose of wood ashes and bonemeal at flowering time. Use the proper bacterial inoculant (available through seed catalogs or at garden centers) to promote nitrogen fixation.

Insect Control

See "35 Common Garden Pests," on page 230, for additional information and control measures for the insect problems listed below.

Yellowed, Stunted Plants

Aphids suck sap from leaves and stems, causing foliage to curl, pucker, and turn yellow. Leaves and buds may become stunted. Avoid excessive nitrogen fertilization as a preventive measure. Release aphid midges or lacewings to control infestations. Spray with insecticidal soap or pyrethrin if the problem persists.

Adult and nymph leafhoppers also suck plant sap, causing yellowed foliage and stunting. Protect snap beans from these pests by covering the plants with floating row covers. If exposed plants become infested, use frequent water or soap sprays to wash off nymphs. As a last resort, spray with sabadilla or pyrethrin.

Seedling Stems Severed

At night, cutworms eat through seedling stems at or below the soil surface. Apply a solution of parasitic nematodes or BTK (*Bacillus thuringiensis* var. *kurstaki*) soil pellets mixed with a molasses/bran bait to the soil surface 1 week before planting. Cultivate the garden well to destroy the adult moths' egg-laying sites.

Holes in Leaves

Tiny holes in leaves. Adult flea beetles chew many tiny holes in leaves. To avoid, intercrop beans with unrelated vegetables or flowers or use floating row covers. Apply pyrethrin, rotenone, or sabadilla as a last resort.

Skeletonized leaves. Mexican bean beetles and their larvae chew on leaf tissue, leaving a dry leaf "skeleton" behind. They may also damage stems and pods. Use floating row covers to protect young plants. Planting early helps avoid major infestations. Handpick the beetles and rub the orange eggs off the leaves. If you spot bean beetles in large bean plantings, release parasitic wasps or predatory spined soldier bugs. Destroy or till under plant remains as soon as harvest is complete. As a last resort, apply pyrethrin or rotenone dust or spray.

Disease Control

Control of serious bean diseases is difficult. Use resistant cultivars to keep problems from developing. Never pick or handle beans when wet, to avoid spreading bacterial or fungal spores present in water films on leaves.

Black, Sunken Spots on Pods

Anthracnose is a fungal disease that appears as brown streaking on leaves and stems and black, sunken cankers on pods. Avoid the disease by rotating crops, destroying crop residues, and purchasing western-grown seed. Once anthracnose appears, pull and destroy infected plants. Sterilize any tools that have come in contact with diseased plants. Spraying with copper-based fungicide gives some protection to uninfected beans.

Large Brown Blotches on Leaves

Infection by bacterial blight causes large brown blotches surrounded by yellow halos on leaves, water-soaked spots on pods, and discolored seed. The bacteria overwinter on bean stems and can be spread by wind. Plant western-grown seed and use a 2- to 3-year rotation to avoid the disease.

Mottled, Elongated Leaves

Crinkled, mottled leaves and rough, misshapen pods are symptoms of common bean mosaic. This and other viral diseases may be carried by aphids, so aphid control is an important preventive measure. Pull and destroy any infected plants.

Reddish Orange to Brown Spore Masses on Leaf Undersides

Fungal rust appears as small, reddish orange to brown spore masses, primarily on the undersides of leaves. Leaves quickly yellow, dry up, and drop. If the disease has been a problem in your garden, dust susceptible pole bean cultivars with sulfur as a preventive. Also, treat bean poles with a lime sulfur dip (1 part lime sulfur to 10 parts water) before reusing them.

Seeds Do Not Germinate

Avoid fungal seed rot, which can kill seeds or germinating seedlings, by waiting until the soil is sufficiently warm for planting.

Resistant Snap Bean Cultivars

Cultivar	Resists (R)/Tolerates (T)
'Goldcrop'	**R:** curly top, mosaics; Source-widely available
'Kentucky Wonder'	**R:** rusts; Source-widely available
'Lake Largo'	**R:** mosaics, some rusts; Source-16
'Provider'	**R:** downy mildew, mosaics; **T:** powdery mildew; Source-widely available
'Roma II'	**R:** mosaics; Source-widely available
'Royal Burgundy'	**R:** Mexican bean beetle; Source-widely available
'Stringless Black Valentine'	**R:** Mexican bean beetle; Source-18
'Sungold'	**R:** mosaics, some rusts; Sources-12, 19, 33
'Tendercrop'	**R:** mosaics; Source-widely available
'Top Crop'	**R:** mosaics; Source-widely available

Beet

Beta vulgaris
Chenopodiaceae

Fertilizing

A rich soil needs no amendments during the season. Beets thrive on organic matter and do best with a neutral soil pH.

Insect Control

Lay down floating row covers at planting time and leave in place all season to protect plants from all flying pests. See "35 Common Garden Pests," on page 230, for additional information and control measures for the insect problems listed below.

Stunted, Yellowed Plants

Aphids suck sap from leaves, causing foliage to curl, pucker, and turn yellow. Leaves may become stunted. Encourage natural predators or release aphid midges or lacewings. Spray insecticidal soap or pyrethrin as a last resort.

Adult and nymph leafhoppers also suck plant sap, causing yellowed foliage and stunting. Encourage natural predators. If plants become infested, use frequent water or soap sprays to wash off nymphs. As a last resort, spray with pyrethrin or sabadilla.

Chewed Leaves

Chewed leaves. Blister beetles feed in groups on foliage and may cause total defoliation. Wear gloves when handpicking blister beetles. Spray or dust with pyrethrin or rotenone for severe infestations.

Chewed, curled leaves. Beet webworm larvae chew leaves and form shelters by curling leaves and tying them with webs. Handpick larvae. Use BTK (*Bacillus thuringiensis* var. *kurstaki*) sprays for serious infestations.

Tiny Holes in Leaves

Adult flea beetles chew many tiny holes in leaves. Apply parasitic nematodes to destroy soil-dwelling larvae. As a last resort, spray with sabadilla.

White or Brown Tunnels in Leaves

Leafminer larvae feed internally in leaves, leaving white or brown tunnels. Leaves may turn yellow and look blistered. Set up yellow sticky traps to catch adult leafminers, and remove and destroy leaves infested by larvae. Encourage native parasites by planting nectar plants. As a last resort, spray with rotenone just as larvae hatch and before they are protected inside tunnels.

Disease Control
Crinkled Leaves; Hairy Roots

Curly top is a viral disease characterized by stunted, crinkled leaves and hairy, woody roots. Remove and burn infected plants. Control leafhoppers, which can transmit the virus.

Seedlings Die

Fungal damping-off or root rot is common in cool, wet soils. Seedlings appear water-soaked at or just below the soil line and frequently die. Plants that survive may form roots that have black, dry portions. Improve soil drainage and thin seedlings to avoid problems.

Black Spots inside Roots

Plants that have black, dead spots inside the roots and red, distorted inner leaves may be suffering from boron deficiency. For more information on this problem, see "Elementary Nutrition" on page 262.

Tan to Brown Spots on Leaves

Fungal leaf spots are characterized by small, round, tan to brown spots on leaves and petioles. Older spots turn gray with brown borders. Use a 3-year crop rotation to control. Watering early in the day and providing adequate nutrients minimize damage from this disease.

Resistant Beet Cultivars

Cultivar	Resists (R)/Tolerates (T)
'Big Red Hybrid'	**T:** Cercospora leaf spot; Sources-16, 33
'Red Ace Hybrid'	**R:** Cercospora leaf spot; Source-widely available

Broccoli

Brassica oleracea, Botrytis group
Cruciferae

See "Cabbage" below.

Brussels sprouts

Brassica oleracea, Gemmifera group
Cruciferae

See "Cabbage" below.

Cabbage

Brassica oleracea, Capitata group
Cruciferae

Fertilizing

Cabbage-family crops grow best in rich, moist soil that is high in organic matter. Apply fish emulsion, seaweed, or other liquid fertilizers every 2–3 weeks, or side-dress head-forming crops with balanced organic fertilizers just as heads begin to form. Avoid excessive nitrogen. Broccoli, brussels sprouts, and cabbage will respond more to supplemental fertilizers than will cauliflower, Chinese cabbage, and kale.

Insect Control

To protect against all flying pests, cover plants with floating row covers as soon as they are set out. See "35 Common Garden Pests," on page 230, for additional information and control measures for the insect problems listed below.

Stunted, Yellowed Plants

Feeding by aphids can cause cabbage leaves to be cupped or puckered and turn yellow. Leaves and buds may become stunted. Interplanting with unrelated flowers or vegetables results in fewer aphids. Control aphids by spraying young seedlings with a forceful water spray or with insecticidal soap. Bring in and encourage lacewings and/or aphid midges. As a last resort, spray with pyrethrin or pyrethrin/rotenone.

Holes in Leaves

Tiny holes in leaves. Flea beetles chew tiny holes in leaves. Parasitic nematodes will control soil-dwelling larvae. Spray rotenone as a last resort.

Small, ragged holes in leaves. Cabbage loopers leave small, ragged holes in leaves. Spray with BTK (*Bacillus thuringiensis* var. *kurstaki*) 10 days after moths appear and every 7–10 days after that, as needed. Apply pyrethrin or sabadilla as a last resort.

Large, ragged holes in leaves. Imported cabbageworms, slugs, and snails chew large holes in leaves. Handpick imported cabbageworms and rub their white eggs off the leaves; apply BTK weekly as needed. As a last resort, apply ryania or sabadilla.

Use traps and organic baits to catch slugs and snails. Top-dress around plants with diatomaceous earth or wood ashes for added protection.

Wilting

Wilted plants. Cabbage maggots damage plant roots, causing plants to wilt. Cover plants with floating row covers at planting time. If you don't use covers, plant through small slits in black plastic or through a tar paper square. Apply parasitic nematodes for serious maggot infestations.

Wilted leaves with white spots. Thrips suck plant sap, causing tiny white spots to appear on leaves. Severely infested plants may wilt and die. Trap thrips with sticky blue traps. Apply insecticidal soap as soon as they appear.

Wilted leaves with black spots. Harlequin bugs are shield-shaped, 1/4-in., black insects with red, orange, or yellow markings. The bugs suck sap from plants, causing leaves to wilt and develop black spots. Use sabadilla dust every week as needed for control.

Seedling Stems Severed

At night, cutworms chew young plant stems near the soil level, damaging the plants or completely severing the tops. Prevent cutworm damage by preparing soil well ahead of planting and by destroying all weeds. Apply a solution of parasitic nematodes around transplants or put cutworm collars around their stems.

White or Brown Tunnels in Leaves

Leafminer larvae feed internally in leaves, leaving white or brown tunnels. Leaves may turn yellow and look blistered. Remove infested leaves and clean up garden trash to keep leafminers under control.

Disease Control

Many disease organisms that attack cabbage family members can remain in the soil for several years. Once they've struck, carefully remove and destroy infected plants, roots and all. Solarize the soil or wait 3 years before planting any cabbage family crops in the infected ground. As a general preventive measure, always remove both tops and roots of cabbage family plants from the garden when harvesting.

Elementary Nutrition

Your tomato crop looks beautiful—glowing red fruit is peeking out over the leaves, just waiting to be eaten. But when you reach in to pick the fruit, you find that what looked from afar like a perfect tomato has a blackened, soft underside. What disease is it? In this case and others, the problem is due not to disease but to a nutrient deficiency. The tomato has developed blossom-end rot because of a calcium deficiency, sometimes brought on by an uneven water supply.

Vegetable crops need a balanced supply of nutrients to stay healthy. Besides using nitrogen, potassium, and phosphorus, your crops need calcium, magnesium, sulfur, chlorine, iron, copper, zinc, manganese, boron, and molybdenum. If your plants are not getting all the nutrients they need, the only clue you may get is weaker growth or a poorer yield than you would expect. Often, though, a nutrient-deficient plant may show diseaselike symptoms, such as stunted growth or brown tips or black spots on leaves. And in some cases, an oversupply of a nutrient, such as nitrogen, can cause abnormal growth. If you spot symptoms that look like disease, always rule out nutrient imbalances before you treat your plants for a disease. (See "Recognizing the Impostors," on page 133, for more information about nutrient imbalances.) While nutrient deficiencies are not difficult to correct, they are even easier to avoid. Following a regular soil testing program will alert you to potential problems and help you correct deficiencies before they harm your crops.

Boron

Boron is the minor element that most commonly limits yields in the vegetable garden. While all plants need some boron, many root crops and cabbage family plants have a relatively greater demand for this micronutrient. Boron deficiency is most commonly found in light-textured soils that are low in organic matter. If you have acid soil, you may notice that growth problems due to lack of boron crop up after you add lime to raise pH. Because the subsoil is lower in boron than the surface soil, plants more often show a deficiency during periods of drought, when their roots penetrate more deeply in search of water.

If your soil is boron deficient, your plants will grow slowly and may appear to have a bushy or "boxy" shape as the growing tips die and the plants branch out along the stem. Young leaves may turn black and the fruit will often darken and crack. You may see the following growth problems.

🌢 *Cracked stem of celery.* Young plants grow slowly. Leaf tips die back and leaves are distorted. Brown spots and cracks appear on the leaf stalk crosswise to the ribs.

🌢 *Black heart of turnip.* Plants show very slow growth, dieback, and leaf distortion. The inside of the turnip shows gray spots that change to brown or black.

🌢 *Internal black spot of beet.* Inner leaves are red and distorted. The roots will contain black tissue that is dead and hard. This internal damage will often happen before the tops show symptoms.

🌢 *Browning of cauliflower.* A slight brownish discoloration will gradually spread over the head; the head will taste bitter. The inside of the stem will turn brown and crack.

If you catch the symptoms early, you may be able to save your crop by applying a foliar spray of liquid kelp or seaweed extract every two weeks until the symptoms disappear. You should also have your soil analyzed by a soil laboratory. If boron is lacking, you will get a recommendation as to what type and how much of a correcting agent should be added. Granite dust, rock phosphate, or dried chicken

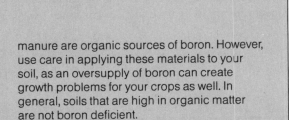

manure are organic sources of boron. However, use care in applying these materials to your soil, as an oversupply of boron can create growth problems for your crops as well. In general, soils that are high in organic matter are not boron deficient.

Calcium

Calcium is another nutrient that your vegetables need to grow and fruit well. It is used by the plant to produce cell walls and aids in proper root development. Plants that are calcium deficient are stunted and have poor root systems. The leaves will be normal in size but new leaves may curl upward at the tips. You may also notice these problems:

🦠 *Blossom-end rot.* This is a common problem of tomatoes and peppers. The first symptom is a water-soaked spot or bruise on the end of the fruit. As the fruit grows, the spot will darken and the end of the fruit will become flattened, black, and leathery. This problem is often related to rapid changes in soil moisture, extreme temperature changes, and root damage due to close cultivation. Some cultivars are less prone to blossom-end rot.

🦠 *Black heart of celery.* This problem usually appears after the plants are about half-grown. New leaf tips die back, and the brown areas may spread down the inner stalks, blackening the center. A bi-weekly spray of kelp or seaweed extract may help if you catch the symptoms early enough.

While you can't control the weather, there are a few things you can do to minimize calcium deficiency problems. First, try to maintain constant soil moisture by adding compost to the soil, mulching to retain moisture, and watering when necessary. Cultivate shallowly to avoid root damage. Check your soil pH and add calcitic limestone if your soil is acid.

Discolored Areas on Leaves

Brown or grayish patches on leaves. Black leg is a fungal disease that can kill young seedlings or plants or destroy the root system of older plants. Infected leaves show brown or grayish patches scattered with tiny black dots. Prevent black leg by purchasing western-grown, disease-free seed or by soaking other seed in hot water.

Yellow, wedge-shaped areas on leaves. Yellow, wedge-shaped areas with blackened veins on leaves and lopsided or nonexistent heads are symptoms of bacterial black rot. Prevent black rot by purchasing western-grown, disease-free seed or by soaking other seed in hot water.

Poor Crop Development

Plants infected with club root fungus have stunted yellowish tops; roots have abnormal swellings. Prevent club root by working lime into the bed to raise the pH to 7.2 or above and by improving soil drainage. Also, start out right by buying healthy seedlings or use sterile growing medium for starting your own.

Pale Leaf Spots; White Mold on Leaf Undersides

Downy mildew symptoms include light spots on leaves that turn papery, white mildew on the undersides of leaves, and blackened areas on cabbage and cauliflower heads. To prevent this fungal disease, eliminate weeds, thin plantings for better air circulation, and water from below. Spray infected plants with a soda-and-soap spray (1 tsp. baking soda, 1 tsp. liquid detergent, 1 qt. water) or copper-based fungicide.

Yellowed Leaves

Fusarium yellows is caused by a fungus that may be brought in on infected transplants. Symptoms include yellow-green leaves that later show a distinct yellowing on one side of the midrib. Stems may twist, leaves may drop prematurely, and any heads produced will be small. Since stress encourages the disease, water well during dry periods and avoid excessive nitrogen, but make sure there is adequate potassium. Many cultivars are resistant to Fusarium yellows.

Resistant Cabbage Family Cultivars

Cultivar	Resists (R)/Tolerates (T)
'Alpha Paloma' (cauliflower)	**T:** cabbage root maggot; Source-34
'Blues' (Chinese cabbage)	**R:** Alternaria, downy mildew, soft rot, viruses; Source-15
'Bravo' (cabbage)	**R:** Fusarium yellows; **T:** black rot; Source-12
'China Pride' (Chinese cabbage)	**T:** bacterial soft rot, downy mildew, tip burn; Source-33
'Citation' (broccoli)	**T:** downy mildew; Source-12
'Cloud Nine' (cauliflower)	**T:** mildew; Source-33
'Danish Ballhead' (cabbage)	**T:** cabbage looper, imported cabbageworm, thrips; Source-widely available
'De Cicco' (broccoli)	**R:** striped flea beetle; Sources-15, 30
'Early Jersey Wakefield' (cabbage)	**R:** Fusarium yellows, Mexican bean beetle, striped flea beetle; **T:** cabbage looper, imported cabbageworm, thrips; Source-widely available
'Emperor' (broccoli)	**R:** hollow stem; **T:** black rot, downy mildew; Sources-15, 26, 33
'Grand Slam Hybrid' (cabbage)	**R:** black rot, black speck, Fusarium yellows; Source-18
'Green Dwarf #36' (broccoli)	**R:** black rot, downy mildew, hollow stem; Source–26
'Hancock Hybrid' (cabbage)	**R:** black rot, Fusarium yellows, tip burn; Source-16
'Mariner' (broccoli)	**T:** bacterial leaf spot, black rot, downy mildew, hollow stem; Source-33
'Multikeeper' (cabbage)	**T:** black rot, black speck, Fusarium yellows, splitting, thrips, tip burn; Source-33
'Premium Crop' (broccoli)	**R:** Fusarium yellows; Source-widely available
'Red Acre' (cabbage)	**R:** white cabbage butterfly; **T:** cabbage looper, imported cabbageworm; Sources-8, 9, 11, 12, 30
'Red Danish' (cabbage)	**R:** white cabbage butterfly; **T:** Fusarium yellows, thrips; Source-33
'Rosalind Hybrid' (broccoli)	**R:** cabbage butterfly (purple); Source-35
'Sicilian Purple' (cauliflower)	**R:** cabbage butterfly; Source-23
'Struckton' (cabbage)	**T:** Fusarium yellows, thrips; Source-33
'Super Snowball A' (cauliflower)	**R:** striped flea beetle; Sources-8, 9, 18
'White Rock' (cauliflower)	**T:** cabbage root maggot; Sources-33, 34

Cabbage, Chinese

Brassica rapa, Pekinensis group
Cruciferae

See "Cabbage" on page 260.

Carrot

Daucus carota var. *sativus*
Umbelliferae

Fertilizing

Prepare the soil deeply and enrich it with plenty of organic matter. Carrots will not grow well in poorly drained soil. Apply balanced organic fertilizer at midseason to ensure rapid, steady growth. Avoid excessive nitrogen, which causes woody roots.

Insect Control

See "35 Common Garden Pests," on page 230, for additional information and control measures for the insect problems listed below.

Rotted or Dwarfed Plants

Carrot rust fly maggots feed on roots, causing dwarfism. Soft rot bacteria may invade the wounds, causing the whole plant to rot. Apply a solution of parasitic nematodes to control soil-dwelling maggots or pupae, and cover plants with floating row covers to keep future generations from infesting plants. Sprinkle rock phosphate around uncovered plants to deter adults from laying eggs. Harvest uncovered crops early to avoid injury from a second generation of flies.

Weak or Dying Plants

Plants weaken. Adult and nymph forms of leafhoppers suck sap from leaves, causing plants to weaken. Use floating row covers to keep out these insects; spray with water, insecticidal soap, or pyrethrin if pests have already infested plants.

Plants wilt and die. Wireworm larvae chew on roots, causing plants to wilt and die. Control the pests with parasitic nematodes, and keep the soil well watered. Cultivate deeply and repeatedly in fall to destroy overwintering forms.

Defoliated Plants

Adult vegetable weevils and their larvae eat leaves and roots, feeding at night. They may defoliate carrot plants or cut stems off at soil level. Practice a 3-year rotation between susceptible crops. Careful garden cleanup and deep cultivation help to control weevils; row covers keep them out. Apply parasitic nematodes to the soil early in the season and at midseason to eliminate the second generation.

Disease Control

Yellowed Leaves; Witches'-Broom Forms

Control leafhoppers to prevent the spread of aster yellows, a viruslike disease. The disease appears as yellowing of young leaves, followed by formation of a witches'-broom of new shoots. Roots are stunted and of poor quality. Pull and burn infected weeds, particularly perennials, which act as overwintering reservoir hosts for the disease organism.

Streaked and Spotted Foliage

Infection by bacterial blight causes irregular brown spots on leaves and brown streaks on petioles. If it occurs, rogue infected plants, improve air circulation, and water early in the day so leaves dry before nightfall. Practice a 3-year rotation with unrelated crops or solarize the soil before planting in infected ground. Use preventive sprays of copper-based fungicide in problem areas.

Dark Spots on Leaves

Infection by Alternaria leaf blight fungus causes dark brown or black spots to form along leaf edges. Spots can increase in number and size, eventually killing leaflets. Also, petioles can be girdled by lesions. Use a rotation of at least 2 years to help lessen problems with Alternaria, or plant resistant cultivars.

Rotted Roots

Till deeply to prevent fungal root rot, characterized by rotting or moldy areas on roots. If root rot has been a problem previously, fertilize with calcium within a month of planting, since a deficiency may aggravate symptoms. Remove infested plants immediately. A 3-year rotation is important to reduce soil fungus populations.

Resistant Carrot Cultivars

Cultivar	Resists (R)/Tolerates (T)
'Huron'	**T:** Alternaria, leaf spot; Source-33
'Orange Sherbet'	**T:** blight; Source-33
'Orlando Gold Hybrid'	**R:** Alternaria; Sources-9, 16, 27, 33
'Seminole'	**T:** Alternaria, leaf spot; Source-33
'Spartan Premium 80'	**T:** leaf blight, rusty root; Source-33

Cauliflower

Brassica oleracea, Botrytis group
Cruciferae

See "Cabbage" on page 260.

Celery

Apium graveolens var. *dulce*
Umbelliferae

Fertilizing

Celery is a heavy nitrogen feeder. Rich soil with plenty of organic matter produces the best-quality plants. Apply balanced organic fertilizer shortly after setting out transplants. Spray with fish emulsion, seaweed, or other high-nitrogen, nonburning organic fertilizer every 2 weeks.

Insect Control

For season-long protection against all flying insects, cover plants with floating row covers as soon as they are set out. See "35 Common Garden Pests," on page 230, for additional information and control measures for the insect problems listed below.

Yellowed, Stunted Plants

Aphids suck sap from leaves and stems, causing foliage to curl, pucker, and turn yellow. Leaves and stems may become stunted. Repel aphids with reflective mulch; encourage or release natural predators such as lacewings. As a last resort, spray with insecticidal soap or pyrethrin.

Adult and nymph leafhoppers also suck plant sap, causing yellowed foliage and stunting. Encourage natural predators. Spray with water or insecticidal soap every few days. For serious infestations, apply pyrethrin or sabadilla.

Dwarfed or Rotted Plants

Carrot rust fly maggots feed on roots, causing dwarfing. Soft rot bacteria may invade the wounds, causing the whole plant to rot. Parasitic nematodes control soil-dwelling maggots or pupae, and floating row covers keep future generations from infesting plants.

Disease Control

New Leaf Tips Die; Brown or Black Area Forms in Center of Plants

Plants suffering from calcium deficiency may develop black heart. New leaf tips die back; brown or black areas form and spread down the inner stalks to the center of the plant. For more information on this nutrient deficiency, see "Elementary Nutrition" on page 262.

Brown Cracks on Stalks

Plants suffering from boron deficiency will grow slowly. Cracks will appear in the stalks, crosswise to the ribs. Leaves may be distorted. For more information on cracked stem of celery, see "Elementary Nutrition" on page 262.

Yellow Plant Parts

Small yellow or gray spots on leaves; stunted growth. Early blight is a fungal disease that appears as spreading yellow spots on seedling leaves that subsequently turn gray and dry; the spots may be covered with a gray mold in wet weather. Sunken lesions may form on stalks, and plant growth may be stunted. Prevent early blight by soaking seed in hot water. If early blight symptoms appear, spray healthy plants with copper-based fungicide to prevent disease from spreading.

Yellow leaves; reddish stalks. Avoid Fusarium yellows, a fungal disease that causes yellowing of leaves and reddish discoloration of stalk tissues, by growing resistant cultivars. If the disease does occur, remove infected plants; solarize the soil or wait 3 years before replanting celery or celeriac. Green-stemmed cultivars generally are more resistant to Fusarium yellows than golden-stemmed cultivars.

Yellow leaves; flattened petioles.   Aphids infect plants with viral mosaic, which appears as yellowed leaves and flattened petiole growth; control aphids to prevent the disease.

Yellowed, stunted plants.   Reduce nematode populations, which can cause stunted, yellowed growth, by increasing the organic matter content of the soil; solarize infested soil or apply a chitin product to further control them.

Water-Soaked or Rotted Stems

Pink rot, stem rot, or other fungal rots may cause damping-off of seedlings, water-soaked spots on stalks, and breakdown of entire stems. If rots appear, improve drainage and air circulation. Replace the top 1–2 in. of heavy soil with clean sand. Pull and destroy severely infected plants. Spraying mildly infected plants with garlic, horsetail, copper, or sulfur sprays may help them tolerate the disease.

Resistant Celery Cultivars

Cultivar	Resists (R)/Tolerates (T)
'Golden Self-Blanching'	**T:** blight; Source-widely available
'Starlet'	**T:** Fusarium yellows; Source-33
'Summit'	**T:** Fusarium yellows; Source-33
'Utah 52–70 R Improved'	**R:** black heart, western mosaic; Sources-4, 18, 26, 34
'Ventura'	**T:** Fusarium yellows; Sources-15, 33

Corn

Zea mays var. *rugosa*
Gramineae

Fertilizing

Corn is a very heavy feeder. Feed with balanced organic fertilizer when plants are knee high, and again when silk is visible at the tips of young ears.

Insect Control

See "35 Common Garden Pests," on page 230, for additional information and control measures for the insect problems listed below.

Curled, Puckered, and Yellowed Foliage

Aphids suck sap from leaves, tassels, ears, and stalks, causing foliage to curl, pucker, and turn yellow. Plant growth may become stunted. If aphids get out of hand early in the season, spray plants with insecticidal soap as needed.

Damaged Ears

Damaged ears; stunted growth.   Damaged buds on young plants are early signs of corn earworms. Plant growth may be stunted. Ears may be destroyed from the tip down. Plant tight-husked cultivars to prevent earworm problems. For large plantings, use pheromone traps to monitor adult moths. Kill moths before they lay eggs by spraying with ryania or neem. To control larvae, spray or apply granular BTK (*Bacillus thuringiensis* var. *kurstaki*) in the tips of the ears every 4–5 days after the silks start to dry. After the silks wilt, put a drop or two of mineral oil on the tip of each ear, or squirt parasitic nematodes into the tips of the ears. (This kills larvae without interfering with the flavor or quality of the corn.)

Bored ears and stalks; chewed leaves; wilted plants. European corn borers chew corn leaves and tassels and bore into ears and stalks. A sawdustlike trail may be evident around stalks, and plants may wilt. To avoid this pest, plant as early as weather allows. Spray ryania to kill the adult moths before they can lay eggs, and also, to kill larvae as they hatch and begin feeding. Drop BTK granules in the whorled leaves of plants in early summer to stop the first generation of caterpillars. Spray BTK on leaf undersides and silks after the silks wilt. As a last resort, spray with pyrethrin to control borers. Reduce future borer problems by breaking off stalks within 1 in. of the ground at harvest time and by rotating crops (if you have a large garden).

Bored ears; chewed leaves and stalks. Feeding at night, fall armyworm larvae bore into corn ears and chew stalks and leaves. Fall armyworms attack most often in cool, wet weather; spray young plants with BTK every 7 days while larvae are active. Parasitic nematodes control armyworms in the soil.

Chewed silks and tassels; skeletonized leaves. Japanese beetles feed on corn silks and tassels and may chew areas in leaves, leaving a dry leaf "skeleton." For long-term control of Japanese beetles, apply parasitic nematodes or milky spore disease to the garden soil and surrounding sod. Handpick adult beetles. Spray with ryania or rotenone as a last resort.

Tunneled ears and stalks; girdled stalks. Southwestern corn borer larvae are white with faint spots, about 1½-in. long. They feed on leaves, stalks, and ears, forming tunnels and sometimes girdling stems and causing stalks to break. The adults are white or pale yellow, ¾-in. moths. Borer damage is more serious when soil is high in nitrogen and low in phosphorus; adjust fertility to reduce problems. If borers have already attacked, squirt mineral oil into the tips of the ears 4–5 days after the silks wilt.

Tiny Holes in Leaves

Adult flea beetles chew many tiny holes in leaves. These insects may spread bacterial wilt diseases. If you've had past problems with such diseases on your corn plants, apply pyrethrin or rotenone dust or spray to control flea beetles from planting until midsummer.

Disease Control
Yellow Lesions on Leaves

Northern blight is characterized by yellow or tan lesions that spread and can eventually kill leaves; southern blight causes yellow flecking of leaves, or larger lesions with yellowish borders, and also blackening of silks. The fungi that cause northern and southern corn leaf blights remain in the soil for 3 years. If blight has infected your corn, rotate crops or solarize the soil before replanting.

Stunted Plants

Stunted plants; mottled leaves; poor seed set. Maize dwarf mosaic is a virus that causes leaf mottling and stunting, with poor or no seed set. Aphids transport this disease from infected Johnsongrass and other weeds. Control aphids to avoid mosaic problems.

Stunted or yellow plants or knots on roots. Nematodes may cause stunted plant growth, yellowing, and knotted roots. Reduce nematode populations by solarizing the soil or treating with a chitin product before planting. Rotating crops and increasing the organic matter content also help to diminish nematode populations.

Brown, Raised Spots on Leaves

Fungal rust appears as circular, brown, raised areas on leaves that later burst, releasing brown or black spores. Water early in the day and maintain good air circulation to avoid rust infection. Apply garlic or sulfur sprays as necessary to keep disease from spreading.

Grayish White Galls on Plants

Carefully remove and destroy fungal smut galls—firm or spongy, grayish white growths that form on leaves, stalks, or ears—before they burst. Infection at seedling stage leads to stunted, malformed plants. To prevent recurrence or avoid smut altogether, keep plants well watered, control borers, and clean up garden debris.

Wilted, Pale, Streaked Leaves

Flea beetles spread Stewart's wilt and other bacterial wilts; wilt symptoms include pale, streaked leaves and exudation of a yellow, sticky substance from cut stems. Control flea beetles from planting time until midsummer to avoid wilts.

Resistant Corn Cultivars

Cultivar	Resists (R)/Tolerates (T)
'Bunker Hill'	**T:** corn earworm, maize dwarf mosaic, northern leaf blight, Stewart's wilt; Source-33
'Flavor King'	**T:** bird damage, corn earworm, rust; Source-33
'Honey and Cream'	**T:** corn earworm; Sources-4, 11, 19, 20, 27
'Silver Queen'	**T:** leaf blight, Stewart's wilt; Source-widely available
'Stylepak'	**T:** smut, Stewart's wilt; Source-33
'Summer Pearl'	**T:** rust, Stewart's wilt; Source-33
'Viking'	**R:** smut; Sources-9, 11
'Sweetie 82'	**T:** corn earworm, rust; Sources-4, 16, 18

Cucumber

Cucumis sativus
Cucurbitaceae

Fertilizing

Cucumber is a heavy feeder. Supply plenty of phosphorus. Side-dress with blended organic fertilizer that is high in phosphorus after fruit sets or spray with seaweed or fish emulsion every 3 weeks.

Insect Control

Floating row covers will protect plants from many flying insect pests. Remove covers once plants flower unless you hand pollinate. The best way to hand pollinate is to use an artist's paintbrush to spread pollen from male stamens to female stigmas. See "35 Common Garden Pests," on page 230, for additional information and control measures for the insect problems listed below.

Yellowed, Stunted Plants

Aphids suck sap from leaves, fruit, and stems, causing foliage to curl, pucker, and turn yellow. Leaves and buds may become stunted. Lay a reflective mulch under plants to keep aphids away. Use a forceful spray of water to dislodge aphids from young plants. Spray with insecticidal soap, as needed, to reduce persistent aphid populations.

Chewed Plant Parts; Plants Die from Disease

Striped cucumber beetle adults and larvae damage plants by chewing leaves, stems, and fruit and by spreading disease organisms that can quickly kill plants. Use floating row covers to protect young plants against striped and spotted cucumber beetles. Parasitic nematodes offer some measure of control against these beetles. Spraying pyrethrin or rotenone is a potent last-line defense.

Wilted Plant Parts

Wilted, dried-up leaves. Squash bug adults and nymphs suck plant sap, causing leaves to wilt, dry, and turn black. Protect plants with row covers. Destroy egg masses, usually found on leaf undersides. Use boards as traps; collect and destroy bugs that gather underneath. As a last resort, spray sabadilla or rotenone.

Sudden wilting of plants. Squash vine borer moths are 1–1½-in. orange-and-black, clear-winged moths that lay eggs along stems.

The white, brown-headed larvae hatch and tunnel into stems, and their feeding may cause plants to suddenly wilt. Plant extra seeds or plants in anticipation that some will be lost to borer damage. Use floating row covers or wrap the stem bases with nylon stocking to prevent moths from laying eggs there. If stalks are attacked, slit the stems and remove borers. Or inject borer-infested stems with BTK (*Bacillus thuringiensis* var. *kurstaki*) or parasitic nematodes.

Disease Control

In general, if you've had previous problems with cucumber diseases, remember that your best hope for getting good yields is to plant resistant cultivars.

Spots on Leaves

Concentric leaf spots; dark spots on fruit. Alternaria leaf blight is carried over on diseased plant refuse. Infection by this fungus causes small leaf spots that later enlarge and form concentric rings, as well as dark spots on fruit. Cut and destroy infected leaves and fruit before spores mature. Copper-based fungicide gives some protection. Crop rotation helps prevent or lessen blight damage.

Water-soaked spots on leaves; irregular leaf holes. Leaves infected by angular leaf spot bacteria will show water-soaked areas that turn gray and die, leaving irregular holes. Clip and destroy infected leaves and stems. Avoid handling wet plants, to keep from spreading the disease. Follow a 4-year rotation schedule to break the cycle of infection. Use a preventive spray of copper-based fungicide if past experience leads you to expect an outbreak.

Leaves Become Brown

Anthracnose commonly occurs during a wet growing season; infection by the fungus causes small, wet-looking, dark spots on leaves that merge. Leaves turn brown and may die;

fruit may blacken and drop. Pull and destroy severely infected plants and avoid handling wet plants, to keep the disease from spreading. Spraying with copper-based fungicide may offer a degree of prevention.

Plants Wilt Quickly

Plants suffering from bacterial wilt may wilt even when still green; a white, sticky substance may ooze from a cut stem. Protect plants from cucumber beetles, which may introduce this disease. Pull and destroy any infected plants.

Clean up weeds and debris in fall and use an annual rotation to sidestep wilt problems.

Mottled Leaves; Stunted Growth

Cucumber mosaic is incurable. The virus causes yellow spots and curling of young leaves, followed by mottling on leaves; older leaves turn brown and die. Fruit may become light colored and warty, and plants may be stunted. Control aphids that carry the virus, pull and destroy infected plants, and eliminate perennial weeds around the garden.

Resistant Cucumber Cultivars

Cultivar	Resists (R)/Tolerates (T)
'Liberty'	**R:** angular leaf spot, downy mildew, mosaic, powdery mildew, scab; Source-widely available
'Marketmore 80'	**R:** mosaics, powdery mildew, scab; **T:** downy mildew, spotted cucumber beetle; Source-widely available
'Park's Whopper' improved hybrid	**R:** angular leaf spot, anthracnose, cucumber mosaic, scab; **T:** downy mildew, powdery mildew; Source-26
'Poinsett 76'	**R:** angular leaf spot, anthracnose, downy mildew, powdery mildew, scab; **T:** spotted cucumber beetle; Sources-16, 30
'Seneca Comet Hybrid'	**T:** angular leaf spot, anthracnose, cucumber mosaic, downy mildew, scab; Source-12
'Seneca Trailblazer' (monoecious)	**T:** angular leaf spot, cucumber mosaic virus, downy mildew, powdery mildew, scab; Sources-12, 33
'Supersett'	**T:** angular leaf spot, anthracnose, downy mildew, mosaics, powdery mildew, scab; Sources-15, 33
'Sweet Slice Hybrid'	**T:** anthracnose, downy mildew, mosaic, powdery mildew, scab, target leaf spot; Source-widely available
'Victory'	**T:** anthracnose, cucumber mosaic, downy mildew, powdery mildew, scab; Source-33
'Wisconsin SMR 58'	**R:** black spot, mosaics, scab; **T:** spotted cucumber beetle; Source-widely available

White Spots on Leaf Undersides

Powdery mildew is a fungal disease characterized by a white powdery growth on leaf undersides that spreads to cover entire leaf surfaces. Leaves may wither and die, and fruit will be poor quality. Spray plants weekly with a baking soda solution (1 tsp. baking soda in 1 qt. water) if powdery mildew threatens. Don't spray with sulfur fungicide, because it may damage plant tissue. Clean up plant debris in fall to avoid problems the following spring.

Sunken Green Spots on Cucumbers

Scab fungi can cause lesions on vines, leaves, and fruit; fruit may ooze sap and become moldy. To reduce problems with scab, improve air circulation and water early in the day to allow leaves to dry before evening. Use row covers and plastic mulch during spring and fall to maintain temperatures high enough for vigorous growth. Rotate crops and choose a resistant cultivar if scab has been a problem.

Eggplant

Solanum melongena var. esculentum
Solanaceae

Fertilizing

Spray plants with liquid kelp every few weeks to encourage good growth.

Insect Control

See "35 Common Garden Pests," on page 230, for additional information and control measures for the insect problems listed below.

Defoliated Plants; Skeletonized Leaves

Colorado potato beetles and their larvae eat leaves, leaving behind dry leaf "skeletons" or defoliating plants. Handpick adult beetles and larvae and rub orange eggs off the leaves. Apply BTSD (*Bacillus thuringiensis* var. *san diego*) to control larvae. Parasitic nematodes destroy soil-dwelling stages. As a last resort, use ryania or rotenone to kill adults.

Tiny Holes in Leaves

Adult flea beetles chew many tiny holes in leaves, while their larvae feed on underground plant parts. Use floating row covers to protect plants from these insects, especially during the first month of growth. For serious infestations, spray with rotenone.

Dry, Stippled Yellow, or Distorted Leaves

Spider mites feed on plant sap, causing pale yellow spots on leaves as well as leaf discoloration and distortion. Insecticidal soap sprays or just a forceful stream of water works well against spider mites; increase watering and import predatory mites if large populations are anticipated.

Disease Control

Brown Leaf Spots with Concentric Rings

Alternaria blight is a fungus disease that can cause damping-off of seedlings. If older plants become infected, circular brown spots that contain concentric rings form on leaves; brown or black sunken spots appear on fruit. Plants may eventually drop all leaves and die. Help plants resist blight by providing adequate nutrition and good air circulation. Pull and destroy severely infected plants. Also, spray plants with copper-based fungicide as a preventive measure if blight has been a problem previously.

Yellowed or Withered Leaves

Infection by Verticillium wilt causes lower leaves to turn yellowish and wilt. Symptoms usually appear after fruit set. Fruit from plants infected with the fungus will be small and may have dark internal streaks. The fungus is easily transmitted by tools or even water. Prevent the disease by waiting until temperatures are sufficiently warm before setting out seedlings and by practicing a 4-year rotation. Pull and burn any infected plants.

Resistant Eggplant Cultivars

Cultivar	Resists (R)/Tolerates (T)
'Blacknite'	**T:** tobacco mosaic; Source-33
'Classy Chassis'	**T:** tobacco mosaic; Source-33
'Dusky Hybrid'	**T:** tobacco mosaic; Source-widely available

Kale

Brassica oleracea, Acephala group
Cruciferae

See "Cabbage" on page 260.

Lettuce

Lactuca sativa
Compositae

Fertilizing

Plants need plenty of organic matter and lots of moisture for rapid growth. For the sweetest, most tender lettuce, supply plenty of nitrogen and potassium. Feed every 2 weeks with fish emulsion or liquid kelp if growth seems slow. Calcium is vital, especially for heading types; work bonemeal into the soil to supply calcium.

Insect Control

See "35 Common Garden Pests," on page 230, for additional information and control measures for the insect problems listed below.

Yellowed, Stunted Plants

Aphids suck sap from leaves, causing them to curl, pucker, and turn yellow. Plants may become stunted. Keep aphids away with reflective mulch. Dislodge aphids on plants with a strong stream of water. Import and encourage lacewings and other predators. Use insecticidal soap or pyrethrin as a last resort.

Adult and nymph leafhoppers suck sap from leaves, causing plants to become yellow and stunted. Keep out leafhoppers by covering plants with floating row covers from seeding to harvest. Spray uncovered plants with water or insecticidal soap in the morning, as often as necessary. As a last resort, spray with pyrethrin or sabadilla.

Seedling Stems Severed

Cutworms chew through stems of seedlings or transplants at or below the soil surface. Apply a solution of parasitic nematodes or BTK (*Bacillus thuringiensis* var. *kurstaki*) soil pellets mixed with a molasses/bran bait to soil surface 1 week before planting. Put cutworm collars around transplants.

Ragged Holes in Leaves; Bored Heads

Small, ragged holes in leaves; bored heads. Cabbage loopers chew small, ragged holes in leaves and later bore into developing heads of lettuce. Handpick cabbage loopers or spray weekly with BTK. As a last resort, dust with sabadilla.

Ragged holes in leaves; green excrement; bored, mushy heads. Imported cabbageworms chew ragged holes in leaves, leave bits of green excrement, and eventually bore into heads, causing them to become mushy. Handpick these pests or spray BTK weekly. As a last resort, dust with sabadilla.

Large, ragged holes in leaves. Slugs and snails chew large, ragged holes in leaves, leaving trails of slime on leaves and on the soil surface. Use organic baits and traps to control slugs and snails. Mulching with thistle leaves and stems or

---

Soil Care for the Vegetable Garden

A typical vegetable garden needs an annual supply of about 2 pounds of nitrogen per 1,000 square feet, 0.7 pound of phosphorus per 1,000 square feet, and 2.8 pounds of potassium per 1,000 square feet. Here are some guidelines for seasonal soil care that will help satisfy these requirements.

Spring

Use a tiller or hand tool to work 1 inch of compost, well-rotted manure, or other organic material into the top 6 inches of soil. Dig carefully around existing plants like rhubarb or overwintering spinach to avoid damaging their roots. You can also add a blended organic fertilizer: The rate at which you apply it will depend on your individual soil's condition.

Summer

Cover the entire garden surface around the plants with 3 to 4 inches of organic mulch from May or early June until the end of the growing season.

Fall

If your soil needs pH adjustment, fall is the best time to add the appropriate amendment. Remove the organic mulch to the compost pile and leave the soil bare until it freezes solid. Then add 3 to 4 inches of organic mulch for the winter. An alternative is to plant a green manure crop, which can be dug or tilled in the spring in place of compost or well-rotted manure.

dusting soil and plants with diatomaceous earth or other rough material may further prevent slug damage.

Armyworm caterpillars also chew large, ragged holes in leaves. Handpick armyworms or spray BTK at weekly intervals, as needed.

White or Brown Tunnels in Leaves

Leafminer larvae feed internally in leaves, leaving white or brown tunnels. Leaves may turn yellow and look blistered. Floating row covers keep out leafminers. The best defense is to remove and destroy infested leaves. Rotenone is effective as a last resort if applied just as larvae hatch, but before they burrow into leaves.

Poor Development; Wilted Plants

Wireworm larvae chew on roots, causing poor growth or wilting. Set out traps made from raw potatoes. Apply parasitic nematodes to soil to control.

Disease Control

Grow resistant cultivars to avoid problems with diseases faced in past seasons. Don't overwater, as it can create conditions that foster disease. Strengthen plants with periodic sprays of liquid kelp.

Slimy Heads

Gray mold is caused by a fungus that grows up through the lettuce head, transforming it into a slimy, rotten mass. Avoid infection by maintaining good air circulation and soil drainage and by removing old leaves that rest on the soil surface. Clean up debris. Spray weekly with a baking soda spray (1 tsp. baking soda in 1 qt. water) during cool, wet weather to help prevent the disease.

White Mold on Leaves

White mold on leaf undersides; yellow areas on leaves. Downy mildew appears as light green or yellow areas on leaves, with a white mold on leaf undersides. To prevent this fungus disease, water at ground level (not from overhead) and give plants plenty of space. Eliminate nearby weeds, especially in the fall when disease is most likely to occur. Pull and burn mildewed plants and replant infected soil with an unrelated crop. Carefully clean up all plant refuse in fall. Spray with copper sulfate only as a last resort.

Powdery dust on upper leaf surfaces; curled leaves. Powdery mildew is a fungal disease that appears as a powdery dusting on upper leaf surfaces; affected leaves eventually curl, turn brown, and die. To control this disease, thin plants so leaves don't touch, and remove old leaves that rest on the ground. If powdery mildew has been a problem in your garden, try a preventive treatment with sulfur spray or dust.

Seedlings Die

Damping-off can injure or kill young seedlings. Stems turn mushy near the soil line and may collapse. Start seeds in flats of sterile planting mix to help prevent infection by the fungus. Thin plantings and provide adequate air circulation to further reduce likelihood of problems.

Rust-Colored Spots on Leaves

Bottom rot can cause the bottom portion or the entire lettuce head to turn rust colored and eventually decompose. Start seeds in flats of sterile planting mix to help prevent infection by the fungus. Thin plantings and provide adequate air circulation to further reduce likelihood of problems.

Mottled, Browned, and Stunted Leaves

Infection by mosaic viruses causes leaf mottling, browning, and severe stunting. To avoid, plant certified disease-free seed and keep aphids away from plants. There is no cure for mosaic; pull and destroy infected plants.

Resistant Lettuce Cultivars

Cultivar	Resists (R)/Tolerates (T)
'Canasta' (French crisp)	**R:** bottom rot, tip burn; Source-15
'Erthel' (cos)	**R:** mildew, mosaic; Source-35
'Green Lake' (head)	**T:** bolting, rib blight, root rot, tip burn; Source-33
'Ithaca' (head)	**R:** blight, brown rib, downy mildew, tip burn; Sources-9, 11, 12, 18, 19, 33
'Montello' (head)	**R:** root rot; **T:** grey mold, mosaic, rib blight, tip burn; Source-16
'Nancy' (butterhead)	**R:** many mildews and mosaics; Source-15
'Parris Island Cos' (romaine or cos)	**T:** mosaic, tip burn; Source-widely available
'Salad Bibb' (butterhead)	**R:** broad bean wilt, downy mildew, lettuce mosaic; Source-12
'Salad Crisp' (head)	**T:** cucumber mosaic; Source-33

Melon

Cucumis melo
Cucurbitaceae

Fertilizing

Neutral to slightly alkaline soil promotes best growth. No fertilizing is necessary on rich, well-prepared soil. Avoid excessive nitrogen, even on less-than-adequate soil, but provide plenty of phosphorus.

Insect Control

Use row covers to protect young plants from many insect pests, but remove them when blossoms form unless you plan on hand pollinating. See "35 Common Garden Pests," on page 230, for additional information and control measures for the insect problems listed below.

Defoliated Plants; Chewed Fruit

Adult blister beetles defoliate plants and feed on fruit. Wear gloves when handpicking blister beetles. Cover plants in midsummer with floating row covers. Apply pyrethrin or rotenone as a last resort if the population grows.

Chewed Plant Parts; Plants Die from Disease

Adult striped cucumber beetles chew leaves and flowers; larvae feed on underground stems and roots. Adults transmit mosaic and other diseases that can kill the plants. Cover plants with floating row covers. Handpick beetles and egg clusters on exposed plants. Clean up garden litter to remove beetle habitats. Start plants indoors so they are strong and well established by the time cucumber beetles emerge. Apply parasitic nematodes around plant bases. Pyrethrin, sabadilla, or rotenone are effective controls for severe infestations.

Wilted Plants

Sudden wilting of plants. Squash vine borer moths are 1-1½-in., orange-and-black, clear-winged moths that lay eggs along stems. The white, brown-headed larvae hatch and tunnel into stems, and their feeding may cause plants to suddenly wilt. Stagger plantings to help ensure that some vines will escape injury. Wrap stem bases with nylon stocking to prevent moths from laying eggs on plants; spray with BTK (*Bacillus thuringiensis* var. *kurstaki*) every week when vines begin to run. If borers do show up, slit open infested stems and remove the larvae. Or, inject BTK or parasitic nematodes into the infested vine.

Wilted, dried-up, blackened leaves. Adult and nymph squash bugs suck juices from leaves, causing leaves to wilt, dry up, and turn black. Trap and handpick squash bugs, carefully removing their eggs also. Spray with sabadilla or rotenone, if necessary, for serious infestations.

Plants wilt and die. Wireworms chew the roots of plants, causing them to wilt and die. Parasitic nematodes control these pests; for minor wireworm problems, simply rest the growing melons on a board or upside-down can, and catch and destroy wireworms hiding beneath.

Disease Control

Several diseases that affect melons are more prevalent when the soil is cold and wet; northern gardeners should use row covers and plastic mulch to boost soil temperatures when growing melons.

Spots on Leaves

Leaf spots with concentric rings; dark spots on fruit. Alternaria leaf blight is a fungal disease that causes small leaf spots that later enlarge and form concentric rings. Dark spots also appear on fruit. Create optimum growing conditions and rotate crops to avoid this disease. Cut off and destroy infected plant parts. Clean up debris in the fall to keep the blight from recurring; spray emerging seedlings with copper-based fungicide as a preventive measure if the disease has been a problem previously.

Water-soaked spots on leaves; black, sunken spots on fruit. Anthracnose appears as small, dark, water-soaked spots on leaves that later turn brown, coalesce, and kill leaves. Black, sunken spots appear on fruit. Remove and destroy infected plants. Clean up all plant debris. Avoid handling wet plants, as this can spread the fungus.

Yellow spots on leaves; downy, purple spots on leaf undersides. Downy mildew appears as angular yellow spots on leaves. Lower leaf surfaces will be covered with a faint purple fungus in wet weather. Leaves die, and fruit may be dwarfed and have poor flavor. Downy mildew is likely to occur where cucumber beetles are present and air circulation is poor. Avoid working around wet plants. Remove and burn infected leaves and fruit. Soda-and-soap sprays (1 tsp. baking soda, 1 tsp. liquid detergent, 1 qt. water) give some protection and may even halt the spread of mildew. Use a 3-year rotation or solarize the soil before replanting susceptible plants in infected ground.

Mottled green or yellow leaves. Infection by mosaic viruses causes leaves to curl and become mottled; older leaves turn brown and die. Plants may become stunted. Control aphids and cucumber beetles to prevent infection. Remove and destroy infected crops and weeds, particularly perennial ones.

Limp Leaves

Plants infected with bacterial wilt will turn limp even when still green, and a white, sticky substance may ooze from a cut stem. Cucumber beetles may spread this disease. Promptly uproot any infected plants. Remove and destroy the diseased plants, but not if they are intertwined with healthy ones that could be injured in the process.

White, Powdery Growth on Leaves

Powdery mildew is a fungal disease that first appears as a white, powdery growth on leaf undersides; the white growth eventually expands to cover most of both upper and lower leaf surfaces. Fruit may be sunburned and of poor quality. Control powdery mildew with a baking soda solution (1 tsp. baking soda in 1 qt. water), but don't use sulfur, because it can damage plant tissue. Trellis plants where possible and promote good air circulation. Avoid working around wet plants.

Resistant Melon Cultivars

Cultivar	Resists (R)/Tolerates (T)
'Can/Am Express' (muskmelon)	**T:** downy mildew, Fusarium yellows, powdery mildew; Source-33
'Edisto 47' (muskmelon)	**R:** Alternaria leaf spot, downy mildew, powdery mildew; Source-30
'Hale's Best Jumbo' (muskmelon)	**R:** cucumber beetles, powdery mildew; Sources-9, 11, 13, 18, 20
'Hearts of Gold' (muskmelon)	**R:** spotted cucumber beetle, striped cucumber beetle; Sources-4, 20
'Honeyloupe' (muskmelon)	**R:** southern blight, Verticillium; Source-33
'Morning Dew' (honeydew)	**T:** downy mildew, Fusarium wilt, powdery mildew; Source-12
'Pulsar' (muskmelon)	**R:** Fusarium wilt, powdery mildew; Sources-12, 15, 18, 19, 27
'Quick Sweet' (muskmelon)	**T:** downy mildew, Fusarium yellows, powdery mildew; Source-33
'Saticoy Hybrid' (muskmelon)	**T:** fruit spot, Fusarium wilt, powdery mildew; Source-widely available
'Starship' (muskmelon)	**R:** Fusarium wilt; **T:** powdery mildew; Source-12
'Tam Honeydew Improved' (honeydew)	**R:** downy mildew, powdery mildew; Source-13

Okra

Abelmoschus esculentus
Malvaceae

Fertilizing

Avoid heavy doses of nitrogen; plants will benefit from a dose of fish emulsion or liquid kelp just after flowering.

Insect Control

See "35 Common Garden Pests," on page 230, for additional information and control measures for the insect problems listed below.

Chemical-Free Transplants

If you've opted to stop using synthetic chemicals in your garden, think twice about buying vegetable or flower transplants at your local garden center. Most commercially produced transplants have been fed with synthetic fertilizers and may have been treated with chemical pesticides. Why not raise your own transplants so you can be sure your plants are completely organic? You'll need an indoor or protected area with sufficient light and heat to produce sturdy plants. (Refer to "The Chemical-Free Gardener's Library," on page 431, for titles of books about seed starting and transplanting procedures.)

Your soil mix is key to producing healthy, disease-free transplants. First, see the discussion on "Disease-Free Seed Starting," on page 150, for directions for making your own organic seed-starting mix. This is a sterile mixture that will help you prevent fungal diseases from killing off young seedlings. Once your seedlings have their true leaves, they can be transplanted into a richer mix. These mixes supply the nutrients plants need without relying on supplemental use of liquid chemical fertilizers. Try one of these formulas to make a balanced soil mix for transplants.

1 part screened, finished compost or leaf mold and 1 part vermiculite or perlite.

1 part finished compost or leaf mold; 1 part commercial potting soil; and 1 part of either sharp sand, perlite, or vermiculite, or a mixture of all three.

1 part of commercial potting soil, compost, or leaf mold; 1 part sphagnum moss or peat moss; and 1 part perlite or sharp sand.

1 part compost or leaf mold; 2 parts potting soil; and 1 part compost or well-rotted, sifted manure makes an especially rich potting mix.

Plain garden soil is generally not suitable for seed-starting or for raising seedlings. It will pack down and crust over in containers and also contains insects, weed seeds, and harmful fungi. If you plan to use soil or compost that is not from a hot, active pile as an ingredient in a mixture, pasteurize it first. Exposure to temperatures from 160° to 180°F for 30 minutes will kill most insects, weed seeds, and pathogenic bacteria and fungi in soil. It's important to monitor the temperature, as excessively high temperatures will destroy most of the beneficial organisms, deplete the organic matter, and release toxic salts into the soil. Try one of the following methods (heating soil will create quite a smell, so if you are concerned about the odor lingering in your house, you might want to use the outdoor methods).

🐛 *Conventional oven.* Fill a clean, shallow pan with moist soil. Cover the pan with aluminum foil, insert a meat thermometer into the soil, and place the pan in an oven heated to 200°F. Start timing when the temperature reaches 140°F and continue heating for 30 minutes. Remember that the temperature of the soil should not exceed 180°F.

🐛 *Microwave oven.* Be sure your soil is moist and free of stones and metallic particles. Put it in a polypropylene baking bag or in a microwave-safe mixing bowl. In either case, the container should not be tightly sealed. At low power (30 to 40 percent), it may require 10 to 15 minutes of operation. At full power, it will take about 2½ minutes for a 2-pound batch. If you see any sparks, stop the process immediately; this indicates that metallic particles are present in the soil. In this case, use another method.

🐛 *Outdoor barbeque grill.* Fill a clean, shallow pan with soil. Set the pan over the fire of an outdoor barbecue grill. Insert a meat thermometer into the soil. When the soil reaches 140°F, begin timing, and keep soil over the heat for 30 minutes. If the soil temperature threatens to exceed 180°F, add a small amount of cool water to the soil to moderate the temperature.

Let the soil cool before using or storing in a covered container. If your first batch of pasteurized soil still has disease or weed problems, you can try increasing the duration of the treatment or using a slightly higher temperature.

Yellowed, Stunted Plants

Aphids suck sap from leaves, fruit, and stems, causing foliage to curl, pucker, and turn yellow. Leaves and buds may become stunted. Use reflective mulch to deter aphids. If necessary, apply insecticidal soap or pyrethrin to thwart a heavy infestation.

Holes in Leaves

Holes in buds and leaves; stunted growth. Corn earworms chew holes in buds and leaves of young plants, causing stunting. Handpick corn earworms. Release lacewings or minute pirate bugs, and encourage natural predators. Use weekly sprays of BTK (*Bacillus thuringiensis* var. *kurstaki*) for further control.

Ragged holes in leaves; green excrement; bored fruit. Imported cabbageworms chew ragged holes in leaves, leave green excrement, and bore into the plant. Handpick worms. Use weekly sprays of BTK for further control. As a last resort, apply ryania or sabadilla.

Seedling Stems Severed

Cutworms chew through stems of seedlings or transplants at or below the soil surface. Apply a solution of parasitic nematodes or BTK soil pellets mixed with a molasses/bran bait to the soil surface 1 week before planting. Further protect young seedlings with collars.

Pods Drop Prematurely; Misshapen Pods

Green stink bugs are $1/2$-in., light green bugs; nymphs are round and bluish gray with red marks. Adults and nymphs suck sap mainly from pods and flowers, causing premature pod drop and misshaped pods. Handpick the bugs. For serious infestations, spray plants with pyrethrin or pyrethrin/rotenone.

Skeletonized Leaves; Chewed Flowers

Japanese beetles chew leaves, leaving a dry leaf "skeleton" behind, and also chew flowers.

Protect plants with floating row covers to keep out adult Japanese beetles. For lasting control, use milky disease spores or parasitic nematodes to eliminate grubs in the soil. For severe infestations, spray with ryania or rotenone.

Dry, Stippled Yellow, or Distorted Leaves

Spider mites feed on plant sap, causing tiny pale spots. They also inject toxins that cause leaf discoloration and distortion. Insecticidal soap sprays or just a forceful stream of water work well against spider mites; increase watering and import predatory mites if large populations are anticipated.

Disease Control
Wilting, Rolled Leaves

Early symptoms of Fusarium wilt include yellowing and stunting. Leaves later roll up and wilt; plants may die. The disease often occurs in areas where soils are infested with root-knot nematodes. There is no cure or resistant cultivar. Preventive measures include increasing soil organic matter and rotating okra with corn, mustard, or collards, which do not host nematodes. In addition, solarize the soil, plant a marigold cover crop, or apply a chitin source to reduce nematode infestation before planting. Fusarium fungi remain in the soil for 10 years; use as long a rotation as possible to reduce chances of infection. Clean up plant residues immediately after harvest to reduce chances of infection the following season.

Stem Base Rots

Southern blight first causes a soft rot at the soil line, and the fungal mold spreads over the rotted area and soil surface around the stem. Destroy diseased plants immediately; also remove the top inch of soil around the stem. Treat uninfected plants with garlic or sulfur spray as a preventive measure. Separate okra plantings from nightshade family plants, peanuts, and melons. Increase organic matter and provide plenty of nitrogen. Solarize the soil or use a 4-year rotation with corn or cereal crops. Covering growing beds with black plastic may help prevent the disease.

Wilted Plants

Wilted leaves and stems are early symptoms of Verticillium wilt. Later, leaf edges curl and leaves turn yellow; whole plants may die. A long rotation helps reduce incidence of the fungus. Avoid planting okra where nightshade family crops, cucumbers, or beans have recently been. Avoid setting out plants until temperatures are sufficiently warm. Destroy infected plant debris in the fall.

Onion

Allium cepa
Amaryllidaceae

Fertilizing

Good drainage and plenty of organic matter are necessary for healthy, vigorous growth. Feed every 2–3 weeks with fish emulsion or liquid kelp or side-dress with dried blood or other high-nitrogen fertilizer. For bulbing types, stop fertilizing once bulbs begin to swell.

Insect Control

See "35 Common Garden Pests," on page 230, for additional information and control measures for the insect problems listed below.

Yellowed, Stunted Plants

Aphids suck sap from leaves and stems, causing foliage to curl, pucker, and turn yellow. Leaves may become stunted. Onion sets have fewer problems with aphids than seed-grown plants have. Reflective mulches will help deter the pests; use insecticidal soap or pyrethrin sprays as needed to reduce a heavy infestation.

Seedling Stems Severed

Cutworms chew through stems of seedlings at or below the soil surface. Apply a solu-
tion of parasitic nematodes or BTK (*Bacillus thuringiensis* var. *kurstaki*) soil pellets mixed with a molasses/bran bait to the soil surface 1 week before planting. Diatomaceous earth or wood ashes mixed into the soil also give some control.

Yellowed, Dying Plants

Onion maggots are white, $1/3$-in., blunt-ended larvae that tunnel into onion bulbs, mostly in spring. Damage may cause plants to turn yellow and die. Control maggots already in the soil by applying parasitic nematodes at planting time. Floating row covers keep out egg-laying adults, which are gray or brown, $1/4$-in. flies with large wings. Use cull onions in rows of seeds as a trap crop. Sprinkle hot pepper or ginger along seedling rows. Remove and destroy any infested plants.

Whitened, Withered Foliage

Onion thrips, both adult and nymph forms, suck plant sap, causing many tiny white spots to appear on leaves. Their feeding eventually causes plants to wilt and die. Onion thrips are a more serious problem when soil is dry and the garden is weedy. Blue sticky traps offer some protection. Release minute pirate bugs or predatory mites. Spray plants with insecticidal soap, nicotine, or pyrethrin, if necessary.

Wilted Plants; Poor Development of Plants

Wireworms chew on plant parts underground, causing wilting and poor development. Avoid problems with wireworms by not planting onions in soil that was recently covered with sod. If these pests do appear, parasitic nematodes can help eliminate them.

Disease Control

Using resistant onion cultivars is critical since none of the following diseases can be cured.

Soft, Brown Tissue at Neck of Bulbs

Neck rot strikes injured or diseased bulbs. The fungus causes tissues at the neck to become soft, brown, and sunken, and later to form a hard, black crust. Avoid cultivation near bulbs and dig carefully to avoid damaging them.

Leaf Spots

Yellow or gray spots on leaves. Downy mildew is a fungal disease that appears first on stems and older leaves as yellow or gray, elongated spots that later become covered with purple, furry mold; leaves eventually collapse. Plant onion sets instead of seeds, as onions grown from seed are more susceptible. If the disease crops up, destroy all plant refuse and use a 3-year rotation or solarize the soil to prevent a recurrence. Don't handle wet plants. Remove severely infected plants and spray healthy ones with a soda-and-soap spray (1 tsp. baking soda, 1 tsp. liquid detergent, 1 qt. water) or copper-based fungicide to prevent spread of disease. (Apply copper with care, as it can damage leaf tissue.)

White or purple lesions on leaves. Purple blotch is a fungal disease that appears on leaves as small, sunken, white lesions that enlarge and turn purple. The lesions can girdle leaves and stems; bulbs may show a yellow or red decayed area, usually only in the outer scales. Purple blotch occurs where air circulation is poor. Prevent the disease by thinning plants, watering early in the day so leaves dry out before night, and cleaning up thoroughly in the fall. Apply a preventive spray of copper-based fungicide if the disease has been a problem in past seasons.

Dark streaks on seedling stem bases. Seedlings infected with smut have streaks at the bases of new leaves; streaked areas are filled with brown material. New leaves may bend or twist abnormally, and plants are stunted. Bulbs have raised, black lesions at the base of scales. Excessive nitrogen fertilizing and overwatering tend to encourage smut fungus. Onions grown from seed are more susceptible than those grown from sets. Don't plant any seedlings from a flat that contains infected plants. Wait to mulch soil until it has warmed thoroughly. Use a 3-year rotation as a further preventive measure. Pull and destroy infected plants.

Tops Wilted; Stunted Growth

If pink root fungus strikes, causing roots to turn various colors and then shrivel, wait 4 years before replanting susceptible crops (including carrots, cauliflower, cucumbers, lima beans, peas, spinach, and nightshade family crops) or solarize the soil before planting.

Small Green or Black Dots on Bulbs

Smudge, a fungal disease characterized by small green or black dots on outer scales of bulbs, may occur if crops aren't rotated or debris isn't cleaned up in fall. Avoid problems in storage onions by curing bulbs as quickly as possible after digging. Yellow and red onion types are resistant.

Resistant Onion Cultivars

Cultivar	Resists (R)/Tolerates (T)
'Crystal Wax Pickling'	**R:** pink root; Sources-4, 26
'Early White Supreme Hybrid'	**R:** pink root; Source-26
'Egyptian Tree'	**R:** maggots; Source-widely available
'Evergreen Hardy White'	**T:** pink root, smut, thrips; Source-30
'Hybrid Big Mac'	**R:** pink root; Source-11
'Long White Summer Bunching'	**T:** Fusarium yellows, pink root; Source-33
'Northern Oak'	**T:** Fusarium yellows, pink root; Source-33
'Tokyo Long White' (bunching onion)	**R:** botrytis leaf blight, pink root, smut, thrips; Sources-12, 33
'Valiant'	**T:** Fusarium yellows; Sources-27, 33

Pea

Pisum sativum
Leguminosae

Fertilizing

Peas are light feeders, but need adequate phosphorus. No fertilizing is necessary in soil prepared well with manure and bonemeal. Use the proper bacterial inoculant (available through seed catalogs or at garden centers) to promote nitrogen fixation.

Insect Control

See "35 Common Garden Pests," on page 230, for additional information and control measures for the insect problems listed below.

Yellowed, Stunted Plants

Aphids suck sap from leaves, fruit, and stems, causing foliage to curl, pucker, and turn yellow. Leaves and buds may become stunted. Use reflective mulch to repel aphids. Release and encourage lacewings. Use insecticidal soap or pyrethrin sprays if the aphid problem escalates.

Defoliated Plants; Chewed Fruit

Adult blister beetles defoliate plants and feed on pods. Wear gloves to handpick these pests. For serious infestations, spray with pyrethrin or rotenone.

Chewed Plant Parts; Plants Die from Disease

Adult spotted cucumber beetles are greenish yellow with 11 black spots on their wing covers. The beetles chew leaves and flowers. The tiny white larvae feed on underground stems and roots. Adults transmit mosaic and other diseases that can kill the plants. Apply parasitic nematodes to soil to control larvae. As a last resort, use pyrethrin or rotenone spray or dust.

Holes in Blossoms

Pea weevils are brown, $1/5$-in. beetles that are spotted black and white. They feed at night, chewing holes in blossoms. The thick-bodied white larvae feed on seeds inside the pods. Plant early to avoid these pests. Spray or dust with rotenone before first bloom and again after pods appear. Use an annual rotation and clean up garden debris to break the cycle of infestations.

Disease Control

Good drainage and a long crop rotation will help prevent most pea diseases.

Purplish Stems

Bacterial blight symptoms include purplish stems, decay of young pods, yellowish leaflets, and cracked or oozing lesions on larger pods. Avoid the disease by planting western-grown seed.

Stunted, Yellow Leaves

Infection by Fusarium wilt fungi causes dwarfing and yellowing of leaves. Cut stems show yellow discoloration. Plants may wilt and die. Avoid Fusarium wilt problems by careful clean-up immediately after harvest. Fusarium fungi remain in the soil for 10 years; use as long a rotation as possible to reduce chances of infection. Plant seed as early as possible and incorporate plenty of humus into the soil.

Mosaic viruses cause various symptoms including stunting, rosetting, chlorosis, and downward rolling of leaves. Aphids carry mosaic and other virus diseases. Protect young plants from aphid damage and conscientiously pull leguminous weeds to avoid the disease.

White, Powdery Mold on Leaves, Stems, and Pods

Powdery mildew appears as a white powdery mold on stems, leaves, and pods. Vines are dwarfed and can eventually die. To prevent mildew problems, thin plants to encourage good air circulation, and water from below to avoid wetting leaves. If you spot powdery mildew symptoms, spray all vines with garlic, horsetail,

Resistant Pea Cultivars

Cultivar	Resists (R)/Tolerates (T)
'Green Arrow'	**R:** downy mildew, Fusarium wilt, leaf curl; Source-widely available
'Knight'	**R:** downy mildew, Fusarium wilt, pea enation mosaic, powdery mildew; Sources-12, 15, 18, 27
'Maestro'	**T:** bean yellow mosaic, common wilt, pea enation mosaic, powdery mildew; Source-widely available
'Olympia'	**T:** bean mosaic, pea enation mosaic, powdery mildew; Sources-8, 33
'Oregon Sugar Pod II'	**R:** Fusarium wilt, pea enation mosaic, powdery mildew; Source-widely available
'Petit Pois Giroy'	**R:** Fusarium wilt, top yellows; Source-26

or sulfur spray to help plants resist further infection. Many cultivars are resistant.

Brown Lower Stems

Root rot fungi cause water-soaked areas or brown lesions on lower stems and roots, poor growth, stunting, and wilting in warm weather. The disease frequently occurs when the soil is cool, wet, and poorly drained. To avoid root rots, start seeds indoors in peat pots and wait until soil is frostless before setting out. Provide good fertility and drainage for strong, rapid growth.

Pepper

Capsicum annuum, Grossum group
Solanaceae

Fertilizing

Apply fish emulsion or liquid seaweed every 3 weeks from transplanting. Good fertility and adequate, steady moisture are critical for healthy harvests.

Insect Control

See "35 Common Garden Pests," on page 230, for additional information and control measures for the insect problems listed below.

Yellowed, Stunted Plants

Aphids suck sap from leaves, stems, and blossoms, causing foliage to curl, pucker, and turn yellow. Leaves and buds may become stunted. Use reflective mulch to keep aphids away from young plants. Import and encourage lacewings and other predators. Spray with insecticidal soap or pyrethrin if further protection is necessary.

Maggots in Fruit

Pepper maggot flies are ¹/₃-in., yellow-striped flies that lay eggs on fruit. Eggs hatch into slender white maggots that feed inside fruit. Floating row covers keep out pepper maggot flies. If flies reach fruit and lay eggs, remove the peppers before the maggots inside have a chance to mature.

Holes in Leaves

Shotgunlike holes in leaves. European corn borer larvae chew shotgunlike holes in leaves and bore into stems and fruit. Handpick these pests before they enter stems and fruit, or spray with BTK (*Bacillus thuringiensis* var. *kurstaki*). Apply ryania or sabadilla as a last resort.

Tiny holes in leaves. Flea beetles chew many tiny holes in leaves. Use floating row covers to keep flea beetles away from plants. If flea beetles attack unprotected plants, spray with rotenone.

White or Brown Tunnels in Leaves

Leafminer larvae tunnel through leaves. Row covers keep these pests away. On uncovered plants, pick off and destroy any leaves that become infested. As a last resort, spray with rotenone just as larvae hatch and before they are protected inside tunnels.

Misshapen and Discolored Fruit

Pepper weevil larvae feed on buds or fruit, causing the plant tissue to become misshapen or discolored. Pepper weevils overwinter in garden debris. Destroy infested fruit and clean up carefully in fall to protect next year's garden. Dust or spray fruit with rotenone if necessary.

Disease Control

Black or Yellow Sunken Spots on Fruit

Anthracnose symptoms include damping-off of seedlings, dying back of shoots, leaf spots, and yellow, sunken spots on ripe fruits, followed by fruit rot. Use a 3-year rotation with unrelated plants and use fresh seed to avoid this fungus. If it does strike your plants, remove and destroy infected fruit. Don't handle wet plants. Use copper-based fungicide as a preventive if anthracnose has been a problem in past seasons.

Drooping Lower Leaves; Rotted Roots

Fusarium wilt symptoms include drooping lower leaves, young shoot dieback, stem girdling, and root rot. The fungal disease may be a problem if the soil is poorly drained or if root-knot nematodes are present. Solarize the soil, rotate crops, and apply a chitin source to control nematodes and end the disease cycle.

Yellow Leaves

Yellow older leaves. Verticillium wilt is a fungal disease that appears as wilting and yellowing leaves, followed by a gradual drying up of the whole plant. Rotate crops and carefully clean up garden debris to prevent this disease. Pull and destroy diseased plants.

Mottled green and yellow leaves. Aphids carry mosaic viruses that can cause yellow mosaic or chlorosis on leaves, distortion, and stunting. The disease is unlikely to be a problem if aphids are kept away from plants. Remove all nightshade family weeds and wild cucumbers around the garden, and keep peppers away from cucumbers, potatoes, and tomatoes. These plants all host mosaic viruses. Smokers should wash their hands with detergent before handling plants. If mosaic symptoms appear, pull and destroy any infected plants. Many types of peppers are resistant to tobacco mosaic.

Lower Stem Soft; White Mold

Southern blight first causes a soft rot at the soil line, and the fungal mold spreads over the rotted area and soil surface around the stem. Help prevent the disease by increasing organic matter and providing plenty of nitrogen. Remove infected plants and the top inch of infected soil around stem bases. Covering growing beds with black plastic may help prevent the disease.

Resistant Pepper Cultivars

Cultivar	Resists (R)/Tolerates (T)
'Bell Tower'	**R:** tobacco mosaic; **T:** potato virus Y; Sources-15, 33
'Giant Szegedi'	**T:** Verticillium; Source-33
'Orobelle Hybrid'	**R:** potato virus Y, tobacco mosaic; Sources-15, 18, 26

Potato

Fertilizing

Fortify the soil with rotted manure, compost, and rock fertilizers well in advance of planting. Avoid excessive nitrogen. Apply a booster of high-phosphorus blended organic fertilizer after 1 month of growth.

Insect Control

See "35 Common Garden Pests," on page 230, for additional information and control measures for the insect problems listed below.

Yellowed, Stunted Plants

Aphids suck sap from leaves, stems, and blossoms, causing foliage to curl, pucker, and turn yellow. Leaves and buds may become stunted. Wash aphids off plants with a strong water spray. Import and encourage lacewings and aphid midges. Use insecticidal soap or treat with rotenone as necessary to deal with a heavy infestation.

Adult and nymph forms of leafhoppers suck sap from leaves, buds, and stems, causing plants to become yellowed and stunted. Use floating row covers to protect against leafhoppers. Remove all nightshade family weeds and don't plant near tomatoes or peppers; these plants are all hosts to leafhoppers. Spray frequently with water or insecticidal soap. Use pyrethrin or sabadilla to control a massive invasion.

Defoliated Plants

Adult blister beetles feed on foliage. Wear gloves to handpick blister beetles; apply pyrethrin or rotenone if beetle population soars.

Colorado potato beetles and their larvae feed on leaves and stems, sometimes leaving dry leaf "skeletons" behind. Row covers keep adult Colorado potato beetles away. Handpick adults and grubs; destroy eggs. Try releasing spined soldier bugs. Spraying with BTSD (*Bacillus thuringiensis* var. *san diego*) is the best control for grubs. Spray or dust adults with rotenone/pyrethrin if necessary.

Seedling Stems Severed

Cutworms feed at night severing stems at or below the soil line. Apply a solution of parasitic nematodes or BTK (*Bacillus thuringiensis* var. *kurstaki*) soil pellets mixed with a molasses/bran bait to soil surface 1 week before planting.

Tiny Holes in Leaves

Flea beetles chew many tiny holes in leaves. Use floating row covers to keep flea beetles off plants. Parasitic nematodes control soil-dwelling larvae. For heavy infestations, spray with rotenone.

Wilting

Plants wilt suddenly. White grubs are curved white larvae with brown heads and 3 pairs of legs. White grubs feed on potato roots and tubers; the resulting damage may cause the plant to wilt suddenly. These pests are most plentiful in new gardens. Wait several years before planting potatoes in ground recently covered with sod, or use parasitic nematodes to eliminate the pests before planting.

Wilted plants; poor development of plants. Wireworms feed on potato roots and tubers, causing wilting and poor development. They are most plentiful in new gardens. Wait several years before planting potatoes in areas that were covered with sod, or use parasitic nematodes to eliminate the pests before planting.

Disease Control

Leaf Spots

Dark concentric rings on older leaves. Early blight symptoms include dark spots developing in concentric rings on leaves, puckered skin, and shallow lesions on tubers. Prevent the fungus by planting certified seed, improving air circulation, rotating crops, and cleaning up carefully in fall. Applying copper-based fungicide or bordeaux mixture may be necessary to control this disease. Cut away blighted foliage as soon as the disease symptoms appear, and begin spraying with the fungicide. Some growers report success with garlic sprays applied every few days (this works as both preventive measure and cure).

Brownish black spots on leaves. Late blight is a fungal disease that appears as brownish black spots on leaf edges or tips, brown streaks on stems, and sunken spots or blotches on tubers. Preventive measures for late blight include planting certified seed, improving air circulation, rotating crops, and cleaning up carefully in fall. To reduce late blight problems in storage, reduce watering and fertilizing as plants near maturity: wait 2 weeks after tops die before harvesting, so tubers will cure and toughen properly. Copper fungicide or bordeaux mix may be necessary to control this disease. Cut away blighted foliage as soon as disease symptoms appear, and begin spraying with the fungicide. Some growers report success with garlic sprays applied every few days (this works as both preventive measure and cure).

Yellow Leaves

Yellow leaves; stunted plants. Symptoms of root-knot nematodes include stunting, yellowing, and knots on roots. If root-knot nematodes are a problem, solarize the soil, grow a marigold cover crop, or use a chitin source to reduce the number of pests before planting. Build up soil humus content as an ongoing preventive measure.

Yellow older leaves. Verticillium wilt is a fungal disease that appears as wilting and yellowing leaves, followed by a gradual drying up of the whole plant. Rotate crops and carefully clean up garden debris to prevent this disease. Pull and destroy diseased plants.

Russeting; Rough Spots on Tubers

Skin russeting and rough, corky spots on tubers are symptoms of scab. This fungal disease is a sign of high soil pH and inadequate watering. Keep pH below 6.0 and maintain even water supply to prevent scab. Use only well-rotted manure when preparing soil, since fresh manure may contain the fungus. A good first-line defense is to choose resistant cultivars.

Resistant Potato Cultivars

Cultivar	Resists (R)/Tolerates (T)
'Beltville'	**R:** nematodes, scab, Verticillium wilt; Source-11
'Kennebec'	**R:** early blight, late blight, tobacco mosaic; Sources-4, 9, 11, 13, 16, 18, 20
'Krantz'	**R:** early blight, late blight, scab; Source-26
'Rhinered'	**R:** scab, Verticillium wilt; Source-16
'Russet Burbank'	**R:** scab; Sources-9, 16, 18

Pumpkin

Cucurbita pepo var. *pepo*
Cucurbitaceae

See "Squash" on page 293.

Radish

Raphanus sativus
Cruciferae

Fertilizing

Radish is a light feeder. Compost-enriched soil is adequate.

Insect Control

See "35 Common Garden Pests," on page 230, for additional information and control measures for the insect problems listed below.

Tiny Holes in Leaves

Flea beetles chew many tiny holes in leaves. They won't be a problem if the soil has been treated with parasitic nematodes and if floating row covers are used to keep out future generations. Use rotenone to control severe infestations on uncovered plants.

Yellowed Seedlings; Wilted Plants

Cabbage maggots tunnel into stem and roots. Symptoms include yellowing and stunting of young plants, wilting, and brown tunnels in stem bases. Row covers keep out cabbage maggot flies. Mound wood ashes or diatomaceous earth around unprotected seedlings to deter the flies from laying eggs. Apply parasitic nematodes to soil.

Resistant Radish Cultivars

Cultivar	Resists (R)/Tolerates (T)
'Fancy Red II'	**R:** Fusarium yellows; **T:** black root, scurf; Source-12
'Red Devil B'	**T:** Fusarium yellows, scurf; Source-33
'Red King'	**R:** club root, Fusarium yellows; Source-12
'Red Pak'	**T:** Fusarium yellows, Rhizoctonia, pithiness, scurf; Sources-15, 33
'Saxafire'	**T:** club root; Source-33

The Problem-Free Vegetables

There are a few vegetable crops that are tailor-made for chemical-free gardening. Just be sure they are properly fed and watered, and you likely won't have to give them a second thought.

Garlic

Allium sativum   Amaryllidaceae

Garlic is a heavy nitrogen feeder. Side-dress fall-planted garlic with balanced organic fertilizer in spring. Insects rarely attack garlic. In fact, garlic is frequently cited as a good companion plant to repel insect pests. Be sure soil is well drained to avoid disease problems.

Horseradish

Armoracia rusticana   Cruciferae

This spicy root crop is a tenacious grower. If you plant it, be careful to dig out all roots at harvest time, or it may become a weed problem in the garden. Horseradish generally needs no supplemental fertilizer. The only pest problem you may encounter with horseradish is thrips. If their feeding threatens plant health, spray with insecticidal soap or pyrethrin.

Leeks

Allium ampeloprasum, Porrum group
Amaryllidaceae

Leeks are heavy feeders. Fertilize every 1 to 2 weeks with liquid kelp, fish emulsion, or other fast-release organic fertilizer. Leeks are seldom bothered by insects and will have few disease problems as long as soil drainage is good and plants have adequate air circulation.

Rhubarb

Rheum rhabarbarum   Polygonaceae

Rhubarb is a perennial vegetable. Mulch rhubarb crowns well in late fall with well-rotted manure and straw or other rich compost. These vigorous plants are rarely troubled by insects. You can easily handpick any Japanese beetles that appear on the plants. The crowns may become infected by rot fungi, which will cause leaves to yellow and collapse. Remove and destroy affected plants, and spray neighboring healthy stalks with bordeaux mix to prevent spread. You'll see few disease problems as long as you keep stalks thinned to promote good air circulation and clean up thoroughly around crowns in fall.

Disease Control

Bluish Black Discoloration on Roots

Black root is a fungal disease that appears as bluish black discoloration of roots that can extend inward in streaks. Plant and harvest radishes before hot weather to avoid this disease.

Enlarged, Distorted Roots

Club root fungus causes abnormal enlargement and distortion of roots. Pull and destroy infected plants. To prevent a recurrence, rotate radishes with unrelated crops or solarize soil before planting radishes or any other crucifers in the same spot.

Seedlings Die

Damping-off fungus causes water-soaked lesions on the stem near the soil; seedlings may die. Those that survive will have small, rotted roots. Be sure soil is well drained and plants are thinned for good air circulation to prevent this disease.

Spinach

Spinacia oleracea
Chenopodiaceae

Fertilizing

Spinach is a heavy feeder. Prepare soil with plenty of organic matter. Apply balanced, high-nitrogen fertilizer such as blood meal or kelp meal at midseason or use dilute foliar fertilizer every 1–2 weeks. Apply lime as needed so pH ranges from 6.0–7.0.

Insect Control

See "35 Common Garden Pests," on page 230, for additional information and control measures for the insect problems listed below.

Yellowed, Stunted Plants

Aphids suck sap from leaves and stems, causing foliage to curl, pucker, and turn yellow. Leaves may become stunted. Use reflective mulch to repel these pests, or protect plants with floating row covers. Interplant with unrelated crops. Import lacewings and other beneficials if aphid populations swell. Spray plants with insecticidal soap for further control.

Tiny Holes in Leaves

Flea beetles chew many tiny holes in leaves. Plants grown under floating row covers won't be bothered by flea beetles, especially if parasitic nematodes have been introduced to soil. Prepare soil deeply and interplant to discourage pests. Apply rotenone dust or spray, if necessary, to control a serious infestation.

White or Brown Tunnels in Leaves

Leafminer larvae tunnel through leaves and may cause leaves to become yellow, curled, or blistered. Row covers will keep out leafminers. Cut away and destroy parts of leaves infested by leafminers before the insects mature.

Disease Control

Yellow Plant Parts

Yellow, curled leaves. Spinach blight appears as mottling of young leaves, followed by yellowing, curling, and death. Plants affected early are stunted. The virus is carried by aphids. Plant resistant cultivars, destroy surrounding weeds, and control aphids to keep plants free of disease.

Yellow leaf spots. Downy mildew is a fungal disease that appears as yellowish areas on leaves with a gray or purple mold on leaf undersides. Prevent it by following a 3-year rotation scheme using adequate spacing and by not working around wet plants. Spray with a soda-and-soap spray (1 tsp. baking soda, 1 tsp. liquid detergent, 1 qt. water) or copper-based fungicide as a preventive if the disease has been a problem previously. Choose resistant cultivars to avoid problems with downy mildew.

Yellow plants. Fusarium wilt symptoms include gradual wilting and yellowing, starting on the oldest leaves; combined with dry conditions, it can kill plants. Delay fall planting or plant a very early spring crop to avoid the warm soil temperatures that promote the wilt fungus. Fusarium fungi remain in the soil for 10 years; use as long a rotation as possible to reduce chances of infection.

White Pustules on Undersides of Leaves

White rust fungus overwinters in decayed plant matter. It causes white pustules to form on petioles and leaf undersides. Leaves covered with pustules will turn brown and die. To break the disease cycle, clean thoroughly in the fall and follow a 3-year rotation. Spray with sulfur or copper-based fungicide as a preventive if white rust has been a problem previously.

Resistant Spinach Cultivars

Cultivar	Resists (R)/Tolerates (T)
'Giant Nobel Hybrid'	**R:** downy mildew; **T:** tip burn; Sources-4, 9
'Indian Summer'	**T:** downy mildew, mosaic; Source-15
'Melody Hybrid'	**R:** blight, downy mildew, mosaic; Source-widely available
'Vienna Hybrid'	**R:** blight, downy mildew, mosaic; Sources-26, 33

Squash

Cucurbita spp.
Cucurbitaceae

Fertilizing

Soil should be rich in phosphorus. No added fertilizing is needed in rich garden soil, but if growth slows or plants are stressed, apply foliar spray of liquid kelp or manure tea every week as needed until plants resume good growth.

Insect Control

See "35 Common Garden Pests," on page 230, for additional information and control measures for the insect problems listed below.

Yellowed, Stunted Plants

Aphids suck sap from leaves, stems, and blossoms, causing foliage to curl, pucker, and turn yellow. Leaves and buds may become stunted. Use reflective mulch to deter aphids. Encourage and release natural predators such as lacewings. Apply insecticidal soap as necessary to control a heavy infestation.

Leaves Stippled, Yellow, and Dry

Spider mites suck sap from plants, causing leaves to become stippled, yellow, and dry. Fine webs may appear on plants. Frequent applications of insecticidal soap control these pests.

Wilting

Wilted, dried-up leaves. Adult and nymph squash bugs suck sap from leaves, causing them to wilt, blacken, and dry. Handpick eggs as well as nymph and adult squash bugs. Clean up garden debris in fall to eliminate overwintering sites. Row covers offer good protection for small plants. Spray with rotenone or sabadilla, if necessary, to bring squash bugs under control.

Sudden wilting of plant. Squash vine borer moths are 1–1½-in., orange-and-black, clear-winged moths that lay eggs along stems. The white, brown-headed larvae hatch and tunnel into stems, and their feeding may cause plants to suddenly wilt. Wrap a nylon stocking around the stem base to prevent egg laying. Stagger plantings to ensure continued harvest. If borers do succeed in penetrating vines, inject BTK (*Bacillus thuringiensis* var. *kurstaki*) or parasitic nematodes into infested vines. Or, slit the vine and remove the borer.

Plants Die of Disease

Both larval and adult forms of cucumber beetles feed on plants, but the major threat is through transmitted diseases. Control cucumber beetles by destroying crop residues in fall and deeply tilling the soil in spring. During the growing season, protect plants with floating row covers from planting to flowering. Interplant summer squash with corn or beans to confuse beetles. Apply parasitic nematodes to soil around plants. Treat badly infested plants with sabadilla or rotenone as a last resort.

Disease Control

Concentric Rings on Leaves

Alternaria leaf blight symptoms include leaf spots that enlarge, forming concentric rings, and eventually cause the leaf to curl and shrivel. The fungus is a serious threat to weakened or stressed plants growing in poor soil or bearing too many squash. Copper sprays may help control the disease. Rotate crops and clean up plant debris and weeds thoroughly in fall.

Gradual Wilting

Bacterial wilt occasionally affects pumpkins and winter squash, causing gradual wilting of leaves and shoots while they are still green. Another sign of bacterial wilt is a white sap that exudes from a cut stem. Control cucumber beetles to prevent the disease. Carefully uproot infected plants, but if they're intertwined with healthy plants, don't try to remove them.

Powdery Spots on Undersides of Leaves

Powdery mildew is a fungal disease that first appears as a powdery growth on leaf undersides. The mildew spreads to cover most of the leaf surfaces; leaves wither and die. If it occurs very early in the season, replant. If mature plants are stricken, spray weekly with a solution of baking soda and water (1 tsp. baking soda in 1 qt. water).

Dark, Oozing Spots on Squash

Fungal scab causes dark, oozing lesions to form on leaves, stems, and fruit; it can be a problem when soil is cold and wet. Improve air circulation and practice 3-year rotation with unrelated crops to avoid the disease. Remove severely infected plants and spray with sulfur to protect others.

Resistant Squash Cultivars

Cultivar	Resists (R)/Tolerates (T)
'Bennings Green Tint' (summer)	**T:** serpentine leaf miner, spotted cucumber beetle, striped cucumber beetle; Sources-9, 11, 34
'Blue Hubbard' (winter)	**R:** spotted cucumber beetle; **T:** serpentine leaf miner; Source-widely available
'Early Butternut Hybrid' (winter)	**R:** cucumber beetle; Source-widely available
'Multipik'(summer)	**T:** powdery mildew; Source-12
'Seneca Zucchini' (summer)	**T:** mosaic, spotted cucumber beetle; Sources-18, 23, 33
'Sweet Mama Hybrid' (buttercup)	**R:** Fusarium yellows, squash borer; Source -widely available
'Table King' (bush acorn)	**R:** cucumber beetle; Source-widely available
'Zucchini Select' (summer)	**T:** downy mildew, powdery mildew; Source-33

Sweet potato

Ipomoea batatas
Convolvulaceae

Fertilizing

Plants will benefit from an application of bonemeal or other good potassium fertilizer. Don't supply too much nitrogen.

Insect Control

See "35 Common Garden Pests," on page 230, for additional information and control measures for the insect problems listed below.

Plants Chewed

Plants parts chewed. Fall armyworms eat leaves, stems, and buds. Handpick and apply BTK (*Bacillus thuringiensis* var. *kurstaki*) on the foliage or apply parasitic nematodes to soil around plants to kill the larvae as they hatch from eggs.

Holes in leaves; pitted potatoes. Sweetpotato weevil larvae bore into stems, roots, and tubers. Adults chew leaves, vines, and roots. Control sweetpotato weevils with parasitic nematodes, and mound up soil around stems to make it more difficult for larvae to reach roots.

Shallow Channels on Leaf Surfaces

Sweetpotato flea beetles cut into the surfaces of leaves as they feed, but do not fully puncture the leaves. Their feeding can seriously damage leaves. Larvae feed just under the skin of the roots. Control larvae with applications of parasitic nematodes to the soil. Cover young plants with floating row covers, to avoid leaf damage, or plant resistant cultivars.

Wilted Plants; Poor Development

Wireworm larvae chew on roots, causing poor growth or wilting. Set out traps made from raw potatoes and apply parasitic nematodes to the soil to control.

Weakened Plants; Yellow Leaves

Adult and nymph whiteflies suck sap from leaves, buds, and stems, causing yellowed leaves and poor growth. Honeydew may also be present. Set up yellow sticky traps to catch whiteflies. Spray with insecticidal soap or pyrethrin, especially on leaf undersides, to combat heavy infestations.

Disease Control

Keeping the soil slightly acid helps reduce many disease problems.

Rotted Roots

Fusarium rots can cause rotting of part or all of the root in storage; the fungus can gain entry if sweet potatoes are injured during harvesting. Dig carefully when potatoes reach the right size; don't wait for cold weather.

Resistant Sweet Potato Cultivars

Cultivar	Resists (R)/Tolerates (T)
'Centennial'	**R:** wilt; **T:** southern potato wireworm, sweetpotato flea beetle; Sources-4, 9, 11, 13, 16, 20, 26
'Jewell'	**R:** sweetpotato flea beetle; Source-9, 11, 16

Tomato

Lycopersicon esculentum
Solanaceae

Fertilizing

In poor-quality soils, side-dress with high-phosphorus blended organic fertilizer at blossoming.

Insect Control

See "35 Common Garden Pests," on page 230, for additional information and control measures for the insect problems listed below.

Yellowed, Stunted Plants

Aphids suck sap from leaves, stems, and blossoms, causing foliage to curl, pucker, and turn yellow. Leaves and buds may become stunted. Use reflective mulch to repel aphids. Use insecticidal soap, if necessary, to keep pest numbers down.

Defoliated Plants; Skeletonized Leaves

Colorado potato beetles and their larvae feed on leaves and stems, leaving behind dry leaf "skeletons" or defoliating plants. Handpick the beetles and grubs. Spray grubs with double-strength BTSD (*Bacillus thuringiensis* var. *san diego*). Release spined soldier bugs. For heavy infestations, spray with pyrethrin/rotenone.

Seedling Stems Severed

Cutworms feed at night, severing stems at or below the soil line. Collars or other barriers protect plants from these pests. If soil is badly infested, treat it with BTK (*Bacillus thuringiensis* var. *kurstaki*) soil granules mixed with a molasses/bran bait or with parasitic nematodes before planting.

Chewed Leaves

Tiny holes in leaves. Flea beetles chew many tiny holes in leaves. Use row covers to protect young transplants from these pests, or wait and set out plants after pest population naturally peaks. Plant eggplant nearby as a decoy plant. Apply pyrethrin/rotenone, if necessary, to control a heavy infestation.

Holes in leaves. Tomato hornworms are large green caterpillars with 7 or 8 diagonal white stripes and a black horn projecting from the rear; adults are large, grayish or brown moths with white zigzag stripes on the rear wings. Larvae chew holes in leaves and leave dark droppings on leaves. Handpick. Encourage native parasitic wasps. Spray with BTK every few days for severe infestation. Cultivate the top 6 in. of the soil in fall to kill pupae.

Small, ragged holes in leaves. Cabbage looper larvae chew ragged holes in leaves. Control by spraying with BTK. Use pyrethrin or sabadilla as a last resort.

Deformed Fruit

Deformed fruit; distorted seeds. Green stink bugs are 1/2-in., light green, speckled, true bugs. Adult and nymphs suck sap from leaves, fruit, and flowers, causing deformed fruit and distorted seeds. They hide out in weedy areas; cultivate well and eliminate nearby weeds to give them fewer places to hide. Handpick or treat infested plants with pyrethrin or pyrethrin/rotenone.

Deformed fruit; silver spots or streaks on leaves. Adult and nymph stages of thrips feed on plant tissue, causing silvery spots or streaks to appear on leaves. Plants may be stunted, and fruit may be deformed. Trap thrips with blue sticky traps. Insecticidal soap works if the infestation isn't too severe; otherwise, spray with pyrethrin.

Weakened Plants

Weakened plants; mottled foliage. Adult and nymph leafhoppers suck sap from leaves, buds, and stems, causing plants to weaken. Row covers protect young plants during outbreaks of leafhoppers. Spray frequently with water or insecticidal soap. Pyrethrin or sabadilla are effective against severe infestations.

Weakened plants; yellowed leaves. Adult and nymph whiteflies suck sap from leaves, buds, and stems, causing yellowed leaves and poor growth. Plants may die. Don't buy transplants infested with whiteflies. If whiteflies do appear in the garden, spray with insecticidal soap or pyrethrin, especially on leaf undersides.

Disease Control

Use a 4-year rotation, practice good weed control, and cultivate in fall to minimize problems with many tomato diseases. Plant disease-resistant cultivars when possible.

Water-Soaked Spots on Fruit

Anthracnose is a fungal disease that appears as slightly sunken, water-soaked spots on fruit. Remove and destroy plants infected with this disease. Pick up and destroy rotting fruit. Good preventive measures include buying healthy transplants, making sure soil is well drained, and not touching wet plants.

Blossom End of Fruit Darkens

Fruit suffering from a calcium deficiency will develop blossom-end rot. The blossom end of the fruit will turn dark; later it will become sunken, black, and leathery. For more information on blossom-end rot, see "Elementary Nutrition" on page 262.

Leaf Spots

Dark spots on older leaves; stem rot. Early blight symptoms include seedling damping-off, circular brown spots with concentric rings, defoliation, cracked fruit, and cankers on fruit stems and branches. Control this fungal disease by burning crop residue and eliminating weeds, particularly nightshades and horse nettle. Destroy severely infected plants and don't save their seeds. Use copper fungicides as part of a preventive program.

Water-soaked patches on older leaves. Late blight symptoms include pale green or brown, water-soaked patches on leaves, a downy white mold around spots on leaf undersides, shriveling and death of foliage, and greenish brown greasy spots on fruits. Control this fungal disease by burning crop residue and eliminating weeds, particularly nightshades and horse nettle. Destroy severely infected plants and don't save their seeds. Apply copper fungicides as part of a preventive program.

Water-soaked spots on leaves. Septoria leaf spot appears as small yellowish areas on leaves that become brown or grayish; black mold may develop in the discolored areas. A 4-year rotation helps prevent this fungal disease. For further prevention, eliminate nightshade family weeds and clean up plant debris thoroughly in fall. Apply a copper-based fungicide only if the disease threatens the crop.

Powdery covering on upper leaves; yellow spots on lower leaves. Powdery mildew is a fungal disease that appears as a powdery covering on the upper surfaces of leaves and as light or bright yellow spots on lower leaves. It doesn't usually reduce yields, but it may invite sunscald problems. Discourage mildew by creating good air circulation by suckering and staking plants. Water from below to avoid wetting foliage. Garlic or horsetail sprays may help prevent the disease.

Orange dots on leaves; rings on fruit. Spotted wilt virus symptoms include small orange flecks on leaves, death of older leaves, dwarfing, and concentric rings of yellow alternating with green or red on fruit. The virus is transmitted by thrips; control the pests to prevent the disease.

Yellow Leaves

Yellow leaves; wilting. Fusarium wilt causes lower leaves to yellow and die, and cut stems will show brownish liquid inside. Fruit usually decays and falls off plants. Too much nitrogen and low potassium levels may encourage this fungus. Many Fusarium-resistant cultivars are available.

Yellow leaves; stunted plants. Root-knot nematodes attack roots, causing stunting, yellow leaves, low yields, and root knots. Increasing soil organic matter helps diminish root-knot nematode problems. Solarizing the soil or treating it with a chitin product also provides control. Many cultivars are nematode tolerant.

Yellow leaf margins. Verticillium wilt appears as yellowing on leaf margins that progresses to destroy whole leaves, beginning with older leaves. Plant resistant cultivars whenever possible. This fungal disease is more prevalent when temperatures are cool. Wait to mulch plants until after the soil has warmed. In northern regions, use cloches or row covers to protect transplants if temperatures fall. Remove and burn infected plants, and sterilize tools.

Malformed Leaves on Young Plants

Tobacco mosaic virus symptoms include puckering or bunching of young leaves, plant stunting, mottled leaves, reduced yield, and mottled fruit. Smokers should wash their hands before gardening in order to avoid infecting plants with this virus. Dip seedlings, roots and all, in milk before setting out and occasionally spray growing plants with milk as a preventive step. Clean up the garden and eliminate weeds, especially those in the nightshade family. Remove and destroy infected plants and those immediately around them.

Moldy Stems

Southern blight first causes a soft rot of the stem at the soil line, and the fungal mold spreads over the rotted area and the soil around the stem. Increase soil humus content and available nitrogen to avoid this disease. Remove and destroy infected plants as soon as the disease appears. Till deeply, burying the topsoil at least 4 inches, to avoid future problems. Covering growing beds with black plastic may help prevent the disease.

Resistant Tomato Cultivars

Cultivar	Resists (R)/Tolerates (T)
'Burpee's Supersteak Hybrid'	**T:** Fusarium wilt, root-knot nematodes, Verticillium wilt; Source-widely available
'Celebrity Hybrid'	**R:** Fusarium wilt, nematodes, septoria leaf spot, tobacco mosaic, Verticillium; Source-widely available
'Del Oro'	**R:** Alternaria stem canker, Fusarium wilt, nematodes, Verticillium; Source-12
'Early Girl Hybrid'	**R:** leafminers, Verticillium; Sources-4, 9, 11, 13, 19, 23
'First Lady Hybrid'	**R:** cracking, Fusarium yellows, nematodes, tobacco mosaic, Verticillium; Source-widely available
'Floramerica'	**R:** blossom-end rot and 15 diseases; Source-widely available
'Quick Pick'	**R:** crown wilt, Fusarium wilt, nematodes, tobacco mosaic, Verticillium wilt; Sources-13, 26
'Sweet Million' (cherry)	**R:** Fusarium wilt, nematodes, septoria leaf spot, tobacco mosaic; Sources-26, 27, 33

Turnip

Brassica rapa, Rapifera group
Cruciferae

Fertilizing

Turnips are light feeders. No additional fertilizing is needed in average garden soil, but a side-dressing of bonemeal or other phosphorus fertilizer improves yields. Avoid excessive nitrogen.

Insect Control

Use floating row covers to keep out all flying pests. See "35 Common Garden Pests," on page 230, for additional information and control measures for the insect problems listed below.

Yellowed, Stunted Plants

Aphids suck sap from leaves, causing foliage to curl, pucker, and turn yellow. Leaves may become stunted. Reflective mulch discourages aphids. Use pyrethrin or insecticidal soap as needed for further control.

Holes in Leaves

Small, ragged holes in leaves. Cabbage loopers chew small, ragged holes in leaves. Handpick cabbage loopers and other caterpillar pests, or apply BTK (*Bacillus thuringiensis* var. *kurstaki*). Sabadilla or pyrethrin/rotenone are also effective when facing a massive invasion.

Tiny holes in leaves. Flea beetles chew many tiny holes in leaves. To break the pest cycle, deeply prepare the soil. Protect plants with floating row covers. Apply rotenone as a last resort.

Large, ragged holes in leaves. Slugs chew large, ragged holes in leaves and leave slimy trails. Use organic baits and traps to control these pests. Diatomaceous earth or wood ashes sprinkled around plants also provide some control.

Wilting

Plants wilt during heat of day. Cabbage maggot larvae tunnel through roots and stems, causing stunting, wilting, and disease invasion. Cover plants with floating row covers or heap wood ashes or diatomaceous earth around stems to deter adults from laying eggs. Apply parasitic nematodes to the soil to control maggots.

Wilted leaves with black spots. Harlequin bugs are shield-shaped, ¼-in., black bugs with red, orange, or yellow markings. They cause white or black spots on leaves, which later wilt. Handpick these pests and remove the eggs. Use sabadilla as a last resort.

Disease Control

Slow Growth; Gray, Brown, or Black Spots inside Roots

Plants suffering from black heart, caused by boron deficiency, may grow slowly and have distorted leaves. Gray spots, which later turn brown or black, form inside roots. For more information on black heart, see "Elementary Nutrition" on page 262.

Leaf Spots

Gray or yellow leaf spots. Anthracnose causes small gray or yellow leaf spots and dry, sunken areas on roots. Plant in early spring so plants mature before the soil is warm to avoid this fungal disease. Remove and destroy infected plants.

Yellow, wedge-shaped areas on leaves. Black rot is a bacterial disease characterized by wilting or blackening of leaf margins, spreading to cause large yellow splotches on leaves; roots may show dark or rotting portions. The bacteria are carried on seed; use western-grown seeds treated in hot water. As further protection, clean up debris, and follow a 3-year rotation with unrelated crops.

Black spots on leaves; distorted leaves; stunting. Aphids carry turnip mosaic and other viruses. Symptoms include black spots on leaves, stunting, leaf mottling, and distortion. There is no cure for these diseases. Control aphids to prevent problems with viral diseases.

Poor Crop Development

Infection by the club root fungus causes wilting and poor development of plant tops; roots will become enlarged and misshapen and develop club-shaped swellings. Prevent club root by working lime into the bed to raise the pH to 7.2 or above, improving soil drainage, and avoiding overfertilizing with potassium. Practice a long crop rotation (the fungus persists in soil for 7 years), and remove all crop residues, including roots of cabbage family plants from the garden at harvest.

White Mold on Leaf Undersides

Downy mildew is a fungal disease that appears as white mold on leaf undersides, followed by yellowing and death of leaves; roots may crack and be discolored. Appearance of mildew may indicate poor air circulation; thin plants to provide more breathing room. Avoid handling plants when they are wet, to prevent the spread of the disease. Cleaning up debris is a good control and prevention step.

Resistant Turnip Cultivars

Cultivar	Resists (R)/Tolerates (T)
'Crawford Turnips'	**T:** downy mildew; Source-13
'Scarlet Queen Hybrid'	**R:** downy mildew; Source-26
'Seven Top'	**T:** striped flea beetle; Sources-13, 18, 30

Watermelon

Citrullus lanatus
Cucurbitaceae

Fertilizing

No fertilizing needed in rich, well-prepared garden soil. Avoid excessive nitrogen.

Insect Control

Floating row covers protect young plants from flying insects. See "35 Common Garden Pests," on page 230, for additional information and control measures for the insect problems listed below.

Yellowed, Stunted Plants

Aphids suck sap from leaves, stems, and blossoms, causing foliage to curl, pucker, and turn yellow. Leaves and buds may become stunted. Use reflective mulch to repel aphids. For heavy infestations, spray with insecticidal soap.

Plants Die from Disease

Both larval and adult forms of cucumber beetles feed on plants, but the major threat they pose is through transmitting disease. Cover plants with floating row covers. Apply parasitic nematodes around stem bases. As a last resort, spray with pyrethrin, sabadilla, or pyrethrin/rotenone.

Disease Control

Leaf Spots

Spots or rings on leaves; dark spots on fruit. Alternaria leaf blight is a fungal disease that appears as small leaf spots that later enlarge and form concentric rings; dark spots also form on fruit. Follow a 3-year rotation plan to avoid Alternaria blight.

Black spots on leaves and fruit. Anthracnose is a fungal disease that causes small dark spots on leaves and fruit. Severely diseased plants may lose leaves and fruit. Follow a 3-year rotation and use preventive sprays of copper-based fungicide if anthracnose has been a problem in past seasons.

Wilted Plants; Brown Discoloration of Stems

Fusarium wilt symptoms include seedling damping-off, sudden wilting of older plants, and formation of white or pink mold on dead stems during wet conditions. Fusarium fungi remain in the soil for 10 years; use as long a rotation as possible to reduce chances of infection.

Rough, Mottled Leaves; Stunted Plants

Plants infected with mosaic develop rough, mottled leaf surfaces and may be stunted and yellowed. Aphids carry this disease; control aphids and squash family weeds (which serve as alternate hosts to aphids and mosaic) to reduce chances of infection.

Resistant Watermelon Cultivars

Cultivar	Resists (R)/Tolerates (T)
'Bush Baby II Hybrid'	**R:** anthracnose, Fusarium wilt; Source-26
'Bush Jubilee'	**R:** anthracnose, Fusarium wilt; Sources-12, 18, 20, 26
'Charleston Gray'	**T:** anthracnose, Fusarium wilt; Source-widely available
'Crimson Sweet'	**R:** spotted cucumber beetle; Source-widely available
'Paradise Hybrid'	**T:** anthracnose, Fusarium wilt; Source-12
'Royal Charleston Hybrid'	**R:** anthracnose, Fusarium wilt; Source-16
'Sweet Favorite Hybrid'	**T:** anthracnose, Fusarium wilt; Source-widely available

CHAPTER NINE

Flowers

By Anna Carr

Whether growing annuals, perennials, or bulbs, the best way to start the move toward chemical-free gardening is to learn everything you can about your site. Examine your soil. Is it heavy clay, sandy and light, or rich and loamy? Generally, most flowers will thrive in well-drained soil that is rich in organic matter. Whatever your soil type, adding organic matter such as compost is wise. It improves drainage and tilth and increases water- and nutrient-holding capacity. Especially with long-lived perennials and hardy bulbs time spent improving the soil when you plant is time well spent. For information on how to improve the soil, see chapter 4.

Try to plant your flowers in areas that most closely match the cultural conditions they require. Plant sun-loving marigolds or peonies in a bed or border that receives 5 or more hours of sun per day. Shade-loving hostas will thrive in an area under trees or on the north side of your house. By selecting plants that are well matched to the conditions your garden offers, you'll be well on your way to having a garden full of healthy flowers. And healthy plants are better able to withstand attacks by insects and diseases.

It's also a good idea to consider the common pests and diseases that may attack a plant when you select a site—don't plant perennials commonly afflicted by powdery mildew where air circulation is poor. Keep flowers that harbor virus diseases away from vegetables so that your food plants aren't infected.

The following encyclopedia of annuals, perennials, and bulbs lists guidelines for fertilizing plants and provides information on the insects and diseases that may attack them. To troubleshoot a problem, look up the affected crop. Skim the entry until you find the symptoms that match those on your plants. If the symptoms are a disease problem, you'll find the name of the disease, a full description of the symptoms, and prevention and control measures. If the symptoms are caused by insects, in some cases, you'll find the name of the insect, description, and complete control measures. In most cases, however, you'll find the name of the pest responsible, along with only two or three of the most reliable control measures. If you'd like more information about that insect or how to control it, see "35 Common Garden Pests" on page 230. There, you'll find comprehensive information on the pest, its life cycle and host plants, and how to control it. If you're not familiar with any of the recommended insect and disease control measures, refer to chapters 6 and 7 for detailed explanations on when and how to use control methods and products.

In many cases, the entries that follow list the stronger botanical poisons for controlling insects. Before using, decide if spraying or dusting with poisons is necessary. In the case of annual flowers, pulling up and discarding afflicted plants may be the best course of action. Losing a few plants is a small price to pay to protect the environment—and those important beneficial insects that keep balance in our gardens. Cultural controls—cutting away infected plant parts, handpicking insects, and providing well-drained soil—are the safest alternatives.

Finally, you'll notice that the plants are listed in alphabetical order by their botanical names rather than by common names. (The common name of each flower follows the botanical name.) This eliminates any confusion; botanical names are the same the world over. In many cases, you won't even notice the difference: Botanical names have long served as common names. Examples include ageratum, canna, dahlia, iris, and zinnia. But, a few common flowers have botanical names that differ from their common ones. Marigold is *Tagetes;* daylily is *Hemerocallis.* If you don't find the flower you're looking for, look for its common name in the index on page 438.

Ageratum houstonianum

Ageratum

Fertilizing

Apply balanced organic fertilizer once during the season for vigorous growth and blooming.

Insect Control

See "35 Common Garden Pests," on page 230, for additional information and control measures for the insect problems listed below.

Weakened Plants; Leaves Yellowed

Whitefly nymphs and adults suck sap from leaves, buds, and stems, causing leaves to yellow and the plant to weaken. Check plants carefully for these pests before purchasing. Set up yellow sticky traps to monitor the pests. Destroy infested plants to prevent the pests from spreading. Or, spray with insecticidal soap, especially the undersides of leaves. Spray pyrethrin as a last resort to combat infestations.

Tiny Yellow Dots on Leaves; Webby Foliage

Spider mites suck sap from leaves, causing yellow stipples on leaves. The mites inject toxins as they feed, causing leaf distortion and discoloration. They also cover leaves, stems, and flowers with fine webbing. Spray all surfaces of leaves with a strong jet of water every other day to control these pests. If this fails, apply abamectin, insecticidal soap, or pyrethrin/rotenone. Pull and destroy severely infested plants.

Large, Ragged Holes in Leaves

Slugs and snails chew large, ragged holes in leaves, stems, and flowers, feeding from the bottom up. They may leave trails of slime on plants or on the soil surface. Slugs hide under boards, rocks, clippings, and debris; clean up the garden to eliminate hiding places. Put out beer traps early in the season before populations build. Surround plantings with barriers of diatomaceous earth or copper sheeting.

Disease Control

White Powdery Covering on Leaves

Powdery mildew appears as a white or ash gray powdery covering on leaves. As the fungus spreads, leaves become distorted and may drop off. Avoid ongoing powdery mildew problems by cleaning up refuse in fall and destroying severely infected plants. Be sure plants have plenty of air circulation; space them 8–12 in. apart. Water from below to keep foliage dry. Spray with sulfur or garlic if the disease does occur.

Leaves Yellow and Wilt; Plants Topple Over

Soil-borne fungi can cause root rot on ageratum. Afflicted plants turn yellow and wilt. There is no cure once it occurs; dig and destroy infected plants. Preventive measures are effective: Be sure plants have well-drained soil; add lots of organic matter to promote better drainage.

Alcea rosea

Hollyhock

Fertilizing

In less fertile soils, feed plants every month with high-phosphorus blended organic fertilizer. Plants especially need a boost at blossom time.

Insect Control

See "35 Common Garden Pests," on page 230, for additional information and control measures for the insect problems listed below.

Leaves Skeletonized; Flowers Eaten

Japanese beetles chew leaves, leaving a dry leaf "skeleton" behind. They also chew flowers. Their larvae feed on roots. Handpick Japanese beetles. For serious infestations, use neem extract or rotenone. For long-term control, apply milky disease spores to the bordering lawn to eliminate grubs.

Tiny Yellow Dots on Leaves; Webby Foliage

Spider mites suck sap from leaves, causing yellow stipples on leaves. The mites inject toxins as they feed, causing leaf distortion and discoloration. They also cover leaves, stems, and flowers with fine webbing. Spray all surfaces of leaves with a strong jet of water every other day to control these pests. If this fails, apply abamectin, insecticidal soap, or pyrethrin/rotenone. Pull and destroy severely infested plants.

Flowers and Leaves Deformed or Marked with Spots

Tarnished plant bugs suck sap from plants and release a toxin that can deform leaves and shoots. Flowers may become dwarfed and the buds deformed. Control by handpicking; for serious infestations, spray with rotenone. Discourage overwintering adults by cleaning up weeds and debris in spring and fall.

Cupped Leaf Edges; Brown, Dried-Out Blotches on Leaves

Leafhoppers suck sap from leaves, buds, and stems, causing leaves to become mottled or distorted and to eventually drop off. Encourage natural predators such as big-eyed flies and parasitic wasps. Treat an infestation of leafhoppers first with insecticidal soap; if the problem remains or grows worse, treat with sabadilla or pyrethrin/rotenone.

Disease Control

Brown Spots with Black Margins on Leaves

Anthracnose appears as dark brown blotches or spots with black outlines on leaves and stems.

Flowers may be deformed. To avoid spreading this disease, don't work around wet plants. Pick off diseased plant parts; destroy severely infected plants. If anthracnose has been a problem previously, apply preventive sprays of copper fungicide or bordeaux mix.

Leaves Pale Above; Powdery, Orange-Red Blisters Beneath

Rust is a fungal disease that causes pale areas to appear on upper leaf surfaces, with corresponding orange-red blisters on leaf undersides. Provide good air circulation around plants; avoid wetting foliage when watering. Cut off and destroy leaves infected with rust; cut plants back to the ground in fall, and destroy or discard leaves and stems. Dust or spray leaves with sulfur beginning early in the season to prevent rust or to treat a mild infection.

Antirrhinum majus

Snapdragon

Fertilizing

Snapdragon is a heavy feeder. Apply high-phosphorus blended organic fertilizer at midseason. Spray with dilute fish emulsion or seaweed spray every 3–4 weeks throughout the season.

Insect Control

See "35 Common Garden Pests," on page 230, for additional information and control measures for the insect problems listed below.

Yellowed Leaves; Stunted Plants

Aphids suck sap from leaves, stems, and blossoms, causing foliage to curl, pucker, and turn yellow. Leaves and buds may become stunted. Encourage natural predators and parasites; release aphid midges or lacewings. Spray with water or insecticidal soap. Destroy seriously infested plants or use pyrethrin or pyrethrin/rotenone spray or dust.

Buying Healthy Flowers

To get your flower garden off to a good start and minimize future problems with pests and diseases, take time to inspect annuals, perennials, and bulbs carefully when you purchase them. If you're ordering by mail, order from a reputable dealer, open shipments as soon as you receive them, and inspect them carefully. Healthy, unstressed plants will perform best in your garden and are better prepared to ward off pests and diseases. Here are some pointers to remember when selecting flowers.

Annuals. Deep green leaves and bushy, compact growth are signs of healthy, unstressed plants. Annuals that have been kept in pots or flats too long may show the following symptoms: loss of lower leaves, yellowed foliage, thick masses of roots circling the pot, and soil that is quick to dry out. By the time these symptoms occur, they are likely suffering from stress. Annuals grown in sterile potting mixes such as peat-perlite, which don't provide necessary plant nutrients, will also develop yellowed leaves and scraggly growth if they're not fertilized regularly.

Although annual bedding plants in full flower are pretty, they're not necessarily the best buy, because they take longer to establish in the garden than plants that haven't started flowering. The first few weeks annuals spend in your garden should be devoted to growing roots, which will lead to a season-long show, not supporting flowers, however pretty.

Hot sidewalks in front of discount stores or supermarkets aren't the best environment for bedding plants. Plants displayed under these conditions are often under severe stress because of heat and drought, which will damage roots.

Finally, always look carefully for signs of insect infestation or disease. Don't buy plants that show evidence of aphids, spider mites, whiteflies, or other pests. Disease symptoms to look for include rotted lesions on the stems or leaves and yellowed or spotted foliage.

Bulbs. Healthy bulbs are solid, firm, and have their paperlike bulb sheaths intact. Don't buy bulbs that have scrapes, cuts, blackened rotted spots, or mold. Avoid bulbs that have withered flesh or softened or rotted-looking bases. Lily bulbs should have a few healthy, fleshy roots attached to the base.

Perennials. Pot-grown perennials from a local nursery should have healthy-looking shoots and good, thick growth. They should also have well-developed root systems; the root ball should hold together when the plant is tipped out of its pot. Look for signs of insect infestation as well as leaf spot, rotted stems, and other symptoms of disease. Beware of plants that have been hastily potted up for sale—plants treated in this manner will have leaves askew and the soil surface will often look freshly dug.

If you're ordering by mail from a company you haven't tried before, start with a small order to judge the quality and size of the plants they supply. Always look for a money-back guarantee. Don't be swayed by pretty catalogs with lots of colorful pictures—small nurseries with less fancy catalogs sometimes have bigger, healthier plants for the same price. When your order arrives, read the care instructions that accompany it carefully, and follow the recommendations provided by the nursery. Again, be sure to inspect the plants carefully for signs of insects or disease.

Tiny Yellow Dots on Leaves; Webby Foliage

Spider mites suck sap from leaves, causing yellow stipples on leaves. The mites inject toxins as they feed, causing leaf distortion and discoloration. They also cover leaves, stems, and flowers with fine webbing. Spray all surfaces of leaves with a strong jet of water every other day to control these pests. If this fails, apply abamectin, insecticidal soap, or pyrethrin/rotenone. Pull and destroy severely infested plants.

Disease Control

Pale Areas or Spots with Brown Margins on Leaves

Anthracnose appears as pale blotches with brown outlines on leaves and stems. Blight, another fungal disease, causes cream or tan spots on leaves and stems. Flowers may be deformed; stems may be girdled, causing wilt. Use disease-free seed and practice good garden sanitation. Don't work around wet plants. Avoid wetting foliage when watering; space plants to ensure good air circulation. Pick off diseased plant parts; dig and destroy severely infected plants. If fungal diseases are a particular problem in your area, apply preventive sprays of copper fungicide or bordeaux mix.

Stem Bases Turn Black; Leaves Yellow and Wilt; Plants Topple Over

Several fungi cause stem and root rots on snapdragons. Afflicted plants turn yellow; black spores may appear on stems. There is no cure for crown rot once it occurs; dig and destroy infected plants. Preventive measures are effective: Be sure plants have well-drained soil; add lots of organic matter to promote better drainage. Avoid damaging crowns when digging in the garden. Keep winter mulch away from crowns.

If the problem is serious, solarize the soil before replanting in the same spot.

Gray or White Mold on Flowers and Foliage

Gray mold rots blossoms and foliage, causing moldy gray or brown areas. Afflicted plant parts wilt; plants may topple over. Be sure plants have good air circulation, plenty of sun, and well-drained soil. Water plants from below and avoid overcrowding. Pick and destroy diseased flowers and leaves; dig and destroy severely infected plants. If gray mold is a particular problem, apply preventive sprays of sulfur or copper fungicides.

Brown Blisters on Leaves; Plants Wilt Quickly

Rust is a fungal disease that causes brown blisters with yellow margins on leaves, stems, and flowers. Plants may flower poorly or suddenly wilt and die. Be sure plants have plenty of air circulation; avoid wetting foliage when watering. Cut off and destroy leaves infected with rust; cut plants back to the ground in fall and destroy or discard leaves and stems. If you anticipate rust problems, spray with sulfur every 10 days beginning in early spring, continuing as needed.

Aquilegia spp. Columbine

Fertilizing

Top-dress plants with plenty of rich compost or leaf mold every spring. Apply balanced organic fertilizer at midseason.

Insect Control

See "35 Common Garden Pests," on page 230, for additional information and control measures for the insect problems listed below.

Yellowed Foliage; Stunted Plants

Aphids suck sap from leaves, stems, and blossoms, causing foliage to curl, pucker, and turn yellow. Leaves and buds may become stunted.

Don't overfertilize with nitrogen; the resulting succulent growth encourages aphids. Encourage natural predators and parasites; release aphid midges or lacewings. Spray with water or insecticidal soap. Destroy seriously infested plants or use pyrethrin or pyrethrin/rotenone spray or dust.

Leaves Marked with Serpentine Tan or Brown Tunnels

Leafminer larvae tunnel through leaves, feeding on plant tissue. Leaves may turn brown and collapse. Remove and destroy leaves infested with the pests as they are discovered; cut back plants to the ground and clean up garden debris in fall to prevent pests from overwintering. Larvae can sometimes be prevented from entering the leaves by spraying weekly with insecticidal soap as soon as the first tunnel appears.

Disease Control
Stem Bases Turn Black; Leaves Yellow and Wilt; Plants Topple Over

Several fungi cause crown and root rots on columbine. Afflicted plants turn yellow; black spores may appear on stems. There is no cure for crown rot once it occurs; dig and destroy infected plants. Preventive measures are effective: Be sure plants have well-drained soil; add lots of organic matter to promote better drainage. Avoid damaging crowns when digging in the garden. Keep winter mulch away from crowns. If the problem is serious, solarize the soil before replanting in the same spot.

Begonia × tuberhybrida

Tuberous begonia

Fertilizing

Fertilize every 2 weeks with a weak seaweed or manure solution. Stop fertilizing if buds begin to drop or plant gets too leggy.

Insect Control

See "35 Common Garden Pests," on page 230, for additional information and control measures for the insect problems listed below.

Deformed Flowers; Leaves and Petals Flecked with White

Thrips feed on buds, stem tips, and flowers. Flowers may appear discolored, flecked with white, or deformed. Flower buds may turn brown and die. These pests are difficult to control, for they burrow into plant tissue. Cut away and destroy severely infested plant parts. Use blue sticky traps to monitor populations and trap pests. Regular applications of insecticidal soap may provide some control once pests are spotted on traps, but test soaps on a small part of a plant first since some cultivars are damaged by soaps. Dust tubers with pyrethrin to control in storage.

Disease Control
Brown Spots on Leaves

Both bacteria and fungi cause leaf spots on tuberous begonia foliage. Bacterial leaf spot is characterized by small, brown, blisterlike spots with transparent yellow margins; the spots become slimy. Infection by fungi causes brown, black, or transparent spots. Leaves may fall off; in serious cases, the whole plant may rot. Cultural controls work well; pick off and destroy infected foliage, be sure plants have good air circulation, and avoid wetting the foliage when watering. If necessary, treat diseased foliage with 3–4 sprays at 10-day intervals of copper-based fungicide or bordeaux mix.

White Powdery Covering on Leaves

Powdery mildew appears as a white or ash gray powdery covering on leaves. As the fungus spreads, leaves become distorted and may drop off. Avoid ongoing powdery mildew problems by cleaning up refuse in fall and destroying severely infected plants. Be sure plants have plenty of air circulation. Water from below to keep foliage dry. Spray with sulfur or garlic if the disease does occur.

Stem Bases Turn Black; Stems and Tubers Rot; Plants Topple Over

Tuberous begonias are subject to a fungal disease that rots stems and tubers. There is no cure once the disease occurs; dig and destroy infected plants. Don't overcrowd plants, to ensure good air circulation; avoid wetting foliage when watering; and be sure soil remains moist but is well drained. Don't top-dress plants with fresh manure or unfinished compost. If the problem is serious, solarize the soil before replanting in the same spot.

Calendula officinalis

Pot marigold

Fertilizing

Pot marigold is a light feeder. Spray weak plants with a dilute seaweed solution or other balanced organic fertilizer to improve vigor.

Insect Control

See "35 Common Garden Pests," on page 230, for additional information and control measures for the insect problems listed below.

Yellowed Leaves; Stunted Plants

Aphids suck sap from leaves, stems, and blossoms, causing foliage to curl, pucker, and turn yellow. Leaves and buds may become stunted. Don't overfertilize with nitrogen; the resulting succulent growth encourages aphids. Encour-

age natural predators and parasites; release aphid midges or lacewings. Spray with water or insecticidal soap. Destroy seriously infested plants or use pyrethrin or pyrethrin/rotenone spray or dust.

Holes in Leaves

Defoliated plants. Adult blister beetles will feed heavily on plant tissue, often defoliating one plant before moving on to the next. Wear gloves to handpick blister beetles. Apply pyrethrin or rotenone for serious infestations.

Large holes in leaves. Imported cabbageworms chew large holes in leaves and stems. Spray or dust with BTK (*Bacillus thuringiensis* var. *kurstaki*) if handpicking doesn't keep these pests in check.

Stems Break Off; Leaves Wilt; Small Holes in Stems

Common stalk borers are long, slender caterpillars with a dark brown or purple band around their bodies and several brown or purple lengthwise stripes; the stripes fade as the caterpillars grow. Adults are grayish brown moths. Caterpillars bore into and tunnel through stalks. Remove and destroy stems infested with common stalk borers or try inserting straight pins into the stalks to destroy the tiny pests within. Clean up weeds in and around the garden, and cut stalks to the ground in fall and destroy. BTK sprays are only effective before the young borers enter stems. If borers have been a problem in your garden, spray weekly for 6 weeks beginning in early summer.

Disease Control

Leaves Greenish Yellow or Curled and Deformed; Shoots Spindly or Stunted

Pot marigold is host to several virus diseases. Symptoms include spindly, stunted growth, yellowed foliage, and leaves marked with ring spots, mottling, and pale or dead areas. Aphids and leafhoppers spread virus diseases, so by controlling the pests, you control the disease. There is no cure once plants are infected; pull and destroy ones that show symptoms.

White Powdery Covering on Leaves

Powdery mildew appears as a white or ash gray powdery covering on leaves. As the fungus spreads, leaves become distorted and may drop off. Avoid ongoing powdery mildew problems by cleaning up refuse in fall and destroying severely infected plants. Be sure plants have plenty of air circulation. Water from below to keep foliage dry. Spray with sulfur or garlic if the disease does occur.

Brown Spots on Leaves

Several fungi cause leaf spots on this species. Spots are small at first, but enlarge and run together into large blotches. Don't overcrowd plants, to ensure good air circulation; avoid working with plants when foliage is wet; and pick off and destroy infected plant parts as soon as you spot them. Dig and destroy severely infected plants. If leaf spots are a repeated problem, spray regularly with sulfur or bordeaux mix.

Callistephus chinensis

Annual aster

Fertilizing

No additional feeding is needed as long as the soil is fairly fertile. However, monthly sprays with seaweed may improve the plants' vigor and help them fend off pests and diseases.

Insect Control

See "35 Common Garden Pests," on page 230, for additional information and control measures for the insect problems listed below.

Holes in Leaves and Flowers

Several species of beetles chew holes in flowers and leaves, including black blister beetles and Japanese beetles. Larvae feed on roots. Control these pests by handpicking (be sure to wear gloves if you suspect black blister beetles). For serious infestations, spray with pyrethrin/rotenone. For long-term control, apply milky disease spores to lawn areas to kill Japanese beetle larvae.

Leaves Discolored, Distorted

Feeding by aster leafhoppers causes white or yellow mottling on leaves, and leaves eventually fall off. Leafhoppers can spread aster yellows disease. Encourage natural predators such as big-eyed flies and parasitic wasps. Treat an infestation of leafhoppers first with insecticidal soap; if the problem remains or grows worse, treat with sabadilla or pyrethrin/ rotenone.

Yellowed Leaves; Stunted Plants

Aphids suck sap from leaves, stems, and blossoms, causing foliage to curl, pucker, and turn yellow. Leaves and buds may become stunted. Encourage natural predators and parasites; release aphid midges or lacewings. Spray with water or insecticidal soap. Destroy seriously infested plants or use pyrethrin or pyrethrin/rotenone spray or dust.

Stems Break Off; Leaves Wilt; Small Holes in Stems

Common stalk borers are long, slender caterpillars with a dark brown or purple band around their bodies and several brown or purple lengthwise stripes; the stripes fade as the caterpillars grow. Adults are grayish brown moths. Caterpillars bore into and tunnel through stalks. Remove and destroy stems infested with common stalk borers or try inserting straight pins into the stalks to destroy the tiny pests within. Clean up weeds in and around the garden, and cut stalks to the ground in fall and destroy. BTK

(*Bacillus thuringiensis* var. *kurstaki*) sprays are only effective before the young borers enter stems. If borers have been a problem in your garden, spray weekly for 6 weeks beginning in early summer.

Flowers and Leaves Deformed or Marked with Spots

Tarnished plant bugs suck sap from plants and release a toxin that can deform leaves and shoots. Flowers may become dwarfed and buds deformed. Control by handpicking; for serious infestations spray with rotenone. Discourage overwintering adults by cleaning up weeds and debris in spring and fall.

Disease Control

Foliage and Flowers Greenish Yellow; Plants Sprout Many Spindly Shoots

Plants suffering from aster yellows turn greenish yellow. They sprout many stunted, spindly shoots, giving the appearance of a witches'-broom. Flowers may have some green petals. There is no control for aster yellows; dig and destroy infected plants as soon as you spot them. Prevent spread of the virus by controlling sucking pests such as leafhoppers and aphids.

Wilting or Stunted Plants; Drooping Blooms

Plants infected by Fusarium fungi wilt and die. Older plants may become stunted or distorted. Flowers may droop suddenly. Stems may be black around base with a covering of pink spores. Don't grow asters in the same soil year after year; rotate plants. If rotation isn't possible, solarize the soil and improve drainage. Dig and destroy plants showing signs of infection. Wilt-resistant cultivars are available.

Leaves Pale Above; Yellow-Orange Blisters Beneath

Rust is a fungal disease that causes pale areas to appear on upper leaf surfaces, with corresponding yellow-orange blisters on leaf undersides. Be sure plants have plenty of air circulation; avoid wetting foliage when watering. Cut off and destroy leaves infected with rust; cut

plants back to the ground in fall, and destroy or discard leaves and stems. Dust or spray leaves with sulfur beginning early in the season to prevent rust or to treat a mild infection.

Canna ×
generalis

Canna

Fertilizing

Top-dress with rich compost in midsummer.

Insect Control

See "35 Common Garden Pests," on page 230, for additional information and control measures for the insect problems listed below.

Holes in Leaves

Holes in leaves or chewed leaf edges. Several caterpillars eat canna leaves and flower buds. Handpick these pests or dust plants with BTK (*Bacillus thuringiensis* var. *kurstaki*) if plants are heavily infested. Use pyrethrin/rotenone spray if other controls fail.

Leaves chewed and stuck or rolled together with silk. Leafrollers protect themselves when feeding by rolling terminal leaves into tubes and binding them with strands or webs of silk. Leafrollers can usually be controlled by handpicking or spraying with BTK as needed.

Holes in leaves and flowers. Japanese beetles chew holes in petals, buds, and leaves. Monitor these pests in spring and midsummer and control by handpicking. For serious infestations, use pyrethrin/rotenone. For long-term control, dust your lawn with milky disease spores to control larvae.

Disease Control
Water-Soaked Streaks on Leaves; Flower Buds and Stalks Rot

Bacterial bud rot causes water-soaked streaks and white, yellow, or black spots on leaves. Flower buds turn black and die, and stalks rot. Avoid problems with bacterial bud rot by purchasing high-quality, disease-free rhizomes and maintaining good drainage and air circulation around plants. If rot does set in, pull and destroy infected plants.

Leaves Greenish Yellow or Curled and Deformed; Shoots Spindly or Stunted

Cannas are host to several virus diseases. Symptoms include spindly, stunted growth, yellowed foliage, and leaves marked with ring spots, mottling, and pale or dead areas. Aphids and leafhoppers spread virus diseases, so by controlling the pests, you control the disease. There is no cure once plants are infected; pull and destroy ones that show symptoms.

Chrysanthemum spp.

Fertilizing

Chrysanthemum is a heavy feeder. Top-dress with rich compost and organic high-phosphorus blended fertilizer in spring and again at midseason. Or feed every 2 weeks with seaweed spray or manure tea.

Insect Control

See "35 Common Garden Pests," on page 230, for additional information and control measures for the insect problems listed below.

Yellowed Leaves; Stunted Plants

Aphids suck sap from leaves, stems, and blossoms, causing foliage to curl, pucker, and turn yellow. Leaves and buds may become stunted. Don't overfertilize with nitrogen; the resulting succulent growth encourages aphids. Encourage natural predators and parasites; release aphid midges or lacewings. Spray with water or insecticidal soap. Destroy seriously infested plants or use pyrethrin or pyrethrin/rotenone spray or dust.

Leaves Marred by Serpentine Tan or Brown Tunnels

Leafminer larvae tunnel through leaves, feeding on plant tissue. Leaves may turn brown and collapse. Remove and destroy leaves infested with the pests as they are discovered; cut back plants to the ground and clean up garden debris in fall to prevent pests from overwintering. Larvae can sometimes be prevented from entering the leaves by spraying weekly with insecticidal soap as soon as the first tunnel appears.

Tiny Galls on Foliage

Chrysanthemum gall midges are gnatlike, 1/8-in. flies with long legs and antennae. Their larvae enter leaves and cause tiny pimplelike galls to form on the leaves; leaves may become distorted. Remove and destroy infested leaves as they are discovered; cut back plants to the ground and clean up garden debris in fall to prevent pests from overwintering. For serious infestations, spray with insecticidal soap 3 times, 5 days apart as soon as you spot the first gall. This will kill emerging larvae, eggs, and adults.

Stems Break Off; Leaves Wilt; Small Holes in Stems

Common stalk borers are long, slender caterpillars with a dark brown or purple band around their bodies and several brown or purple lengthwise stripes; the stripes fade as the caterpillars grow. Adults are grayish brown moths. Caterpillars bore into and tunnel through stalks. Remove and destroy stems infested with stalk borers or try inserting straight pins into the stalks to destroy the tiny pests within. Clean up weeds in and around the garden, and cut stalks to the ground in fall and destroy. BTK (*Bacillus thuringiensis* var. *kurstaki*) sprays are only effective before the young borers enter stems. If borers have been a problem in your garden, spray weekly for 6 weeks beginning in early summer.

Flowers and Leaves Deformed or Marked with Spots

Tarnished plant bugs suck sap from plants and release a toxin that can deform leaves and shoots. Flowers may become dwarfed and buds deformed. Control by handpicking; for serious infestations, spray with rotenone. Discourage overwintering adults by cleaning up weeds and debris in spring and fall.

Pale Leaves; Damaged Stems

Chrysanthemum lace bugs feed on stems and the undersides of leaves. Leaves turn pale, stems are damaged, and resinous dark droppings are left on leaf undersides. Check lower leaves for lace bugs in late spring and mid-summer. Knock off any you find with a forceful spray of water, or treat tops and undersides of leaves with insectidal soap.

Yellow-Brown Spots or Blotches on Leaves

Foliar nematodes are tiny, slender, unsegmented roundworms that enter leaf pores or wounds and feed on plants internally. Yellow-brown spots may appear on leaves; leaves may eventually turn brittle and fall off. Flowers may also be affected. Keep foliar nematodes in check by removing brown leaves and the pair of leaves directly above them; don't wet foliage, as that helps spread the tiny pests.

Disease Control

Foliage and Flowers Greenish Yellow; Plants Sprout Many Spindly Shoots

Plants suffering from aster yellows turn greenish yellow. They sprout many stunted, spindly shoots, giving the appearance of a witches'-broom. Flowers may have some green petals. There is no control for aster yellows; dig and destroy infected plants as soon as you spot them. Prevent the virus from spreading by controlling sucking pests such as leafhoppers and aphids.

Yellow, Brown, or Black Spots on Leaves

Several fungi cause yellow, brown, or black spots on leaves. As spots enlarge, entire leaves may wither. Cultural controls work well: Pick off and destroy infected foliage, be sure plants have good air circulation, and avoid wetting the foliage when watering. Dig and destroy seriously infected plants. Clean up garden debris regularly, cut plants to the ground at the end of the growing season. If leaf spot is a problem in your area, use preventive sulfur sprays.

Leaves Pale Above with Orange-Red Blisters Beneath

Rust is a fungal disease that causes pale areas to appear on upper leaf surfaces, with corresponding orange-red blisters on leaf undersides. Be sure that plants have plenty of air circulation; avoid wetting the foliage when watering. Cut off and destroy leaves infected with rust; cut plants back to the ground in fall, and destroy or discard leaves and stems. Dust or spray leaves with sulfur beginning early in the season to prevent rust or to treat a mild infection.

Clematis spp.

Clematis

Fertilizing

Apply balanced organic fertilizer in early spring as needed.

Insect Control

See "35 Common Garden Pests," on page 230, for additional information and control measures for the insect problems listed below.

Flowers and Foliage Eaten

Blister beetles feed in groups on flowers and foliage and may cause total defoliation. Wear gloves when handpicking. For serious infestations, spray with pyrethrin or rotenone.

Stunted Plants Lack Vigor; Dead Stems

Clematis borers are dull white, $^2/_3$-in. larvae of moths that have purple to black forewings and transparent back wings with dark margins. Larvae bore through clematis roots and crowns, causing stunted, vigorless plants; stems may wilt and die. Cut or dig out infested roots and stems, use a pin to kill larvae in stems, or inject borer-infested stems with BTK (*Bacillus thuringiensis* var. *kurstaki*) or parasitic nematodes. Rotenone sprayed on plant bases kills larvae before they enter stems.

Disease Control

White Powdery Covering on Leaves

Powdery mildew appears as a white or ash gray powdery covering on leaves. As the fungus spreads, leaves become distorted and may drop off. Avoid ongoing powdery mildew problems by cleaning up refuse in fall. Be sure plants have plenty of air circulation. Water from below to keep foliage dry. Spray with sulfur or garlic if the disease does occur.

Rotted Stem Sections; Shoots Wilt; Spots on Leaves

Stem rot causes rotting of tissues near the soil line, girdling the stem and causing wilting and death. Rot fungi and other fungi also cause spots on foliage. Cultural controls work well: Improve air circulation by thinning and supporting vines on trellises. Remove and destroy spotted leaves and cut away infected stems when you see them. Avoid heavy mulch around crowns of plants. Cut out infected stems, then spray plants and drench the ground with sulfur fungicide.

Coleus × hybridus   Coleus

Fertilizing

Feed monthly with seaweed spray or other weak organic liquid fertilizer.

Insect Control

See "35 Common Garden Pests," on page 230, for additional information and control measures for the insect problems listed below.

Weakened Plants; Leaves Yellowed

Whitefly nymphs and adults suck sap from leaves, buds, and stems, causing leaves to yellow and plants to weaken. Check plants carefully for these pests before purchasing. Set up yellow sticky traps to monitor the pests. Destroy infested plants to prevent the pests from spreading throughout the garden. Or, spray with insecticidal soap, especially the undersides of leaves. Use pyrethrin as a last resort to combat infestations.

Holes in Leaves

Chewed leaves, flowers, and buds. Yellow woollybear caterpillars are covered with yellow, reddish, or white, long hair and are 1–1½ in. Adults are white moths with a small black dot on each wing and have 1½-in. wingspans. The caterpillars feed on leaves, flowers, and buds. Handpick these pests as they appear in early and late summer. Check for eggs on leaves and clean up garden debris to remove breeding places. BTK (*Bacillus thuringiensis* var. *kurstaki*) sprays will control young caterpillars.

Large, ragged holes in leaves. Slugs and snails chew large, ragged holes in leaves, stems, and flowers, feeding from the bottom up. They may leave trails of slime on plants or on the soil surface. Slugs hide under boards, rocks, clippings, and debris; clean up the garden to eliminate hiding places. Put out beer traps early in the season before populations build. Surround plantings with barriers of diatomaceous earth or copper sheeting.

Disease Control

Leaves Greenish Yellow or Curled and Deformed; Shoots Spindly or Stunted

Infection by coleus mosaic virus may cause leaves to become puckered, crinkled, or distorted, with spots or rings. Symptoms may vary on different cultivars. Aphids and leafhoppers spread virus diseases, so by controlling the pests, you control the disease. There is no cure once plants are infected; pull and destroy ones that show symptoms.

Dahlia spp.

Dahlia

Fertilizing

Dahlia is a heavy feeder. Plant in very rich soil and fertilize in midsummer with a handful each of steamed bonemeal, rotted manure, and a balanced organic fertilizer. Apply foliar spray such as kelp, if necessary, later in the season, but avoid excessive nitrogen.

Insect Control

See "35 Common Garden Pests," on page 230, for additional information and control measures for the insect problems listed below.

White or Yellow Speckles on Leaves; Dried-Out Blotches on Leaves

Leafhoppers suck sap from leaves, buds, and stems, causing leaves to become mottled with white or yellow specks. Brown, dried-out blotches follow, and leaves become distorted and eventually drop off. Leafhoppers can spread aster yellows disease. Encourage natural predators such as big-eyed flies and parasitic wasps. Treat an infestation of leafhoppers first with insecticidal soap; if the problem remains or grows worse, treat with sabadilla or pyrethrin/rotenone.

Leaf Spots

Tiny yellow dots on leaves; webby foliage. Spider mites suck sap from leaves, causing yellow stipples on leaves. The mites inject toxins as they feed, causing leaf distortion and discoloration. They also cover leaves, stems, and flowers with fine webbing. Spray all surfaces of leaves with a strong jet of water every other day to control these pests. If this fails, apply abamectin, insecticidal soap, or pyrethrin/rotenone. Pull and destroy severely infested plants.

Deformed flowers; leaves and petals flecked with white. Thrips feed on buds, stem tips, and flowers. Flowers may appear discolored, flecked with white, or deformed. Flower buds may turn brown and die. These pests are difficult to control, for they burrow into plant tissue. Cut away and destroy severely infested plant parts. Use blue sticky traps to monitor populations and trap pests. Regular applications of insecticidal soap may provide some control once

pests are spotted on traps. Dust tuberous roots with pyrethrin to control in storage.

Stems Break Off; Leaves Wilt; Small Holes in Stems

Dahlias are attacked by several species of borers. These are long, slender caterpillars that bore into and tunnel through stalks. Adults are moths. Remove and destroy stems infested with borers or try inserting straight pins into the stalks to destroy the tiny pests within. Clean up weeds in and around the garden, and cut stalks to the ground in fall and destroy. BTK (*Bacillus thuringiensis* var. *kurstaki*) sprays are only effec-

Soil Care for the Flower Garden

Compost and mulch are the best foods for the flower garden. The trick is to time applications to best meet the different requirements of annual and perennial types.

Spring

When planting annuals or perennials, work in compost and 1 cup of worm castings or low-analysis blended organic fertilizer around each plant. (Wait until fall to feed established perennials.) If you're preparing a whole bed, work in as much as 1/2-inch layer of compost or 10 pounds of an organic fertilizer blend. Wait three weeks after planting to cultivate and mulch. This allows the soil to warm up, which speeds the activity of beneficial soil microorganisms. Use 3 to 4 inches of clean organic matter such as wood chips, bark, cocoa shells, or peanut hulls or 2 inches of rich compost to mulch around your flowers.

Summer

Foliar feed your flowering plants at least 3 times during the season with fish and kelp extracts. Mist gently in early morning or evening.

Be sure to cover leaves completely with spray, especially leaf undersides.

Test your soil pH now to prepare for fall fertilization. Most flowers like a pH near neutral (7.0).

Be sure to keep flowers well-watered, as water is more critical than fertilizer. You can mix in kelp, fish, or compost tea with your irrigation water.

Fall

Fall is the best time to fertilize most established perennials. If your perennials are mulched, pull back the mulch so you can work the fertilizer into the soil. Apply kelp meal at the rate of 1/2 pound per 100 square feet, and no more than 5 pounds per 100 square feet of a 3-4-3 or similar analysis blended organic fertilizer. Don't overfeed established perennials. They have more extensive root systems than annual flowers and so have greater capacity to collect minerals from the soil. An overfed perennial may spread too much and overgrow its intended site.

tive before the young borers enter stems. If borers have been a problem in your garden, spray weekly for 6 weeks beginning in early summer.

Disease Control

Gray Mold on Flowers and Foliage; Flowers Turn Brown and Rot

Gray mold rots blossoms, young shoots, and foliage, causing moldy gray or brown blighted areas. Afflicted plant parts wilt. Be sure plants have good air circulation, plenty of sun, and well-drained soil. Water plants from below and avoid overcrowding. Pick and destroy diseased flowers and leaves; dig and destroy severely infected plants. If gray mold is a particular problem, spray regularly with bordeaux mix.

White Powdery Covering on Leaves

Powdery mildew appears as a white or ash gray powdery covering on leaves. As the fungus spreads, leaves become distorted and may drop off. Avoid ongoing powdery mildew problems by cleaning up refuse in fall and destroying severely infected plants. Be sure plants have plenty of air circulation. Water from below to keep foliage dry. Spray with sulfur or garlic if the disease does occur.

Plants Wilt

Dahlias are attacked by soil-dwelling fungi that cause the plants to either wilt suddenly or die. White mold may cover lower stems; black streaks are noticeable when stems are cut. Preventive measures are effective: Be sure plants have good air circulation, plenty of sun, and well-drained soil. Don't overcrowd plants, and keep mulch away from stems. Dig and destroy afflicted plants or cut away afflicted stems. Apply copper fungicide if necessary.

Stunted, Yellowed Plants; Knots on Roots

Root-knot nematodes infest dahlias, causing stunted plants and galls or knots on roots. Add plenty of organic matter to planting beds to discourage these pests. When digging roots for overwintering in fall, clean off the soil and soak them for 30 minutes in hot water (120°F); or destroy infested roots.

Leaves Greenish Yellow or Curled and Deformed; Shoots Spindly or Stunted

Dahlias are host to several virus diseases. Symptoms include spindly, stunted growth, yellowed foliage, and leaves marked with ring spots, mottling, and pale or dead areas. Aphids and leafhoppers spread virus diseases, so by controlling the pests, you control the disease. There is no cure once plants are infected; pull and destroy ones that show symptoms.

Delphinium spp.   Delphinium

Fertilizing

Delphinium is a heavy feeder. Fertilize with a high-phosphorus blended organic fertilizer and compost every spring. Add just a topdressing of wood ashes and bonemeal after blooming. Avoid excessive nitrogen.

Insect Control

See "35 Common Garden Pests," on page 230, for additional information and control measures for the insect problems listed below.

Yellowed Leaves; Stunted Plants

Aphids suck sap from leaves, stems, and blossoms, causing foliage to curl, pucker, and turn yellow. Leaves and buds may be stunted. Don't overfertilize with nitrogen; the resulting succulent growth encourages aphids. Encourage natural predators and parasites; release aphid midges or lacewings. Spray with water or insecticidal soap. Destroy seriously infested plants or use pyrethrin or pyrethrin/rotenone spray or dust.

Tiny Dots on Leaves; Webby Foliage

Spider mites suck sap from leaves, causing yellow stipples on leaves. The mites inject toxins as they feed, causing leaf distortion and discoloration. They also cover leaves, stems, and flowers with fine webbing. Spray all surfaces of leaves with a strong jet of water every other day to control these pests. Keep plants well watered. If this fails, apply abamectin, insecticidal soap, or pyrethrin/rotenone. Pull and destroy severely infested plants.

Stems Break Off; Leaves Wilt; Small Holes in Stems

Common stalk borers are long, slender caterpillars with a dark brown or purple band around their bodies and several brown or purple lengthwise stripes; the stripes fade as the caterpillars grow. Adults are grayish brown moths. Caterpillars bore into and tunnel through stalks. Remove and destroy infested stems, or try inserting straight pins into the stalks to destroy the tiny pests. Clean up weeds in and around the garden, and cut stalks to the ground in fall and destroy. BTK (*Bacillus thuringiensis* var. *kurstaki*) sprays are only effective before the young borers enter stems. If borers have been a problem, spray weekly for 6 weeks beginning in early summer.

Seedlings Severed at Base

Cutworms feed at night, severing stems at or below the soil line. Apply a solution of parasitic nematodes or BTK soil pellets mixed with a molasses/bran bait to the soil surface 1 week before planting. An easy way to protect young plants is with paper collars.

Leaves Covered with Tan to Brown Blotches; Foliage Appears Blighted

Larkspur leafminer larvae tunnel through leaves, feeding on plant tissue. Large areas of leaves will turn brown or tan; foliage will appear discolored and diseased. Remove and destroy leaves infested with the pests as they are discovered; cut back plants to the ground and clean up garden debris in fall to prevent pests from overwintering. Larvae can sometimes be prevented from entering the leaves by spraying weekly with insecticidal soap as soon as the first tunnel appears.

Disease Control

Yellow, Brown, or Black Spots on Leaves

Several fungi cause yellow, brown, or black spots on leaves. As spots enlarge, entire leaves may wither. Cultural controls work well: Pick off and destroy infected foliage, be sure plants have good air circulation, and avoid wetting the foliage when watering. Dig and destroy seriously infected plants. Clean up garden debris regularly, cut plants to the ground at the end of the growing season. If leaf spot is a problem in your area, use preventive sulfur sprays.

Plants Rot at Base

Stem bases turn black; leaves wilt; plants topple over. Both bacteria and fungi cause crown rot on delphiniums. Afflicted plants may wilt suddenly or turn yellow and wilt slowly. Stems may turn black from the base upward; leaves may turn brown. Crown rot typically occurs in poorly drained soil. There is no cure for crown rot once it occurs; dig and destroy infected plants. Preventive measures are effective: Be sure plants have well-drained soil; add lots of organic matter to promote better drainage. Avoid damaging crowns when digging in the garden. Keep winter mulch away from crowns. If the problem is serious, solarize the soil before replanting in the same spot. Grow delphiniums as biennials, rotating with unrelated plants every 2 years.

Water-soaked lesions on stems near soil line. Symptoms of damping-off include rotted roots and water-soaked lesions at the base of seedling stems. Afflicted seedlings topple over and die. Use a sterile, well-drained, potting medium to prevent this fungal disease. Maintain good air circulation.

White Powdery Covering on Leaves

Powdery mildew appears as a white or ash gray powdery covering on leaves. As the fungus spreads, leaves become distorted and may drop off. Avoid ongoing powdery mildew problems by cleaning up refuse in fall and destroying severely infected plants. Be sure plants have plenty of air circulation. Water from below to keep foliage dry. Spray with sulfur or garlic if the disease does occur.

Leaves Greenish Yellow or Curled and Deformed; Shoots Spindly or Stunted

Delphiniums are host to several virus diseases. Symptoms include spindly, stunted growth, yellowed foliage, and leaves marked with ring spots, mottling, and pale or dead areas. Aphids and leafhoppers spread virus diseases, so by controlling the pests, you control the disease. There is no cure once plants are infected; pull and destroy ones that show symptoms.

Dianthus spp.

Dianthus, pinks

Fertilizing

Dianthus is not a heavy feeder, but a monthly dose of high-phosphorus blended organic fertilizer promotes the best flower production.

Insect Control

See "35 Common Garden Pests," on page 230, for additional information and control measures for the insect problems listed below.

Yellowed Leaves; Stunted Plants

Aphids suck sap from leaves, stems, and blossoms, causing foliage to curl, pucker, and turn yellow. Leaves and buds may become stunted. Don't overfertilize with nitrogen; the resulting succulent growth encourages aphids. Encourage natural predators and parasites; release aphid midges or lacewings. Spray with water or insecticidal soap. Destroy seriously infested plants or use pyrethrin or pyrethrin/rotenone spray or dust.

Tiny Yellow Dots on Leaves; Webby Foliage

Spider mites suck sap from leaves, causing yellow stipples on leaves. The mites inject toxins as they feed, causing leaf distortion and discoloration. They also cover leaves, stems, and flowers with fine webbing. Spray all surfaces of leaves with a strong jet of water every other day to control these pests. Keep plants well watered. If this fails, apply abamectin, insecticidal soap, or pyrethrin/rotenone. Pull and destroy severely infested plants.

Disease Control

Stem Bases Turn Black; Leaves Wilt; Plants Topple Over

Dianthus is afflicted by a variety of diseases that cause the stems to rot and plants to wilt and topple over. Afflicted plants may wilt suddenly or turn yellow and wilt slowly. Stems may turn black from the base upward; leaves may turn brown. Dig and destroy infected plants. Preventive measures are effective: Be sure plants have well-drained soil, add lots of organic matter to promote better drainage, don't overcrowd plants, avoid damaging crowns when digging in the garden, and keep winter mulch away from crowns. If the problem is serious, solarize the soil before replanting in the same spot.

Leaves Greenish Yellow or Curled and Deformed; Shoots Spindly or Stunted

Dianthus is host to several virus diseases. Symptoms include spindly, stunted growth, yellowed foliage, and leaves marked with ring spots, mottling, and pale or dead areas. Aphids and leafhoppers spread virus diseases, so by controlling the pests, you control the disease. There is no cure once plants are infected; pull and destroy ones that show symptoms.

Gladiolus spp.

Gladiolus

Fertilizing

Glads are heavy phosphorus feeders. Apply colloidal phosphate in fall or at spring planting time. Avoid feeding nitrogen and potassium.

Insect Control

See "35 Common Garden Pests," on page 230, for additional information and control measures for the insect problems listed below.

Yellowed, Stunted Plants

Aphids suck sap from leaves, stems, and blossoms, causing foliage to curl, pucker, and turn yellow. Leaves and buds may become stunted. Encourage natural predators and parasites; release aphid midges or lacewings. Spray with water or insecticidal soap. Destroy seriously infested plants or use pyrethrin or pyrethrin/rotenone spray or dust.

Deformed Flowers; Leaves and Petals Flecked with White

Thrips feed on buds, stem tips, flowers, and corms. Flowers may appear discolored, flecked with white, or deformed. Buds may turn brown and die. Infested corms become dark, sticky, and rough. These pests are difficult to control, for they burrow into plant tissue. Cut away and destroy severely infested plant parts. Use blue sticky traps to monitor populations and trap pests. Regular applications of insecticidal soap may provide some control once pests are spotted on traps. Dust tubers with pyrethrin to control thrips in storage. Or soak them in a Lysol solution (1½ Tbsp. in 1 gal. water) for several hours before planting.

Flowers and Leaves Deformed or Marked with Spots

Tarnished plant bugs suck sap from plants and release a toxin that can deform leaves and shoots. Flowers may become dwarfed and buds deformed. Control by handpicking; for serious infestations, spray with rotenone. Discourage overwintering adults by cleaning up weeds and debris in spring and fall.

Disease Control

Leaf Spots

Dark, water-soaked leaf spots. Bacterial blight appears on leaves as water-soaked, dark green blotches that later turn brown; leaves may die. Leaf surfaces may be slimy. Grow plants in well-drained soil; blight is especially a problem in wet weather. Cut off leaves showing signs of this disease; discard severely infected plants.

Reddish brown spots on leaves; pale to brown spots on corms. Scab is a bacterial disease that causes reddish brown spots to form on leaves; brown spots form on flowers. Plants rot at base; leaves and stems fall over. Corms have pale spots that turn dark brown and eventually have sunken centers with scabby margins. Dig and destroy infested plants and do not replant corms in infested soil; do not plant corms that show evidence of the disease.

Rotted Corms; Distorted or Yellowed Leaves

Several fungi cause corms to rot during winter storage. Infected plants may have pale, water-soaked spots, brown to reddish brown spots, sunken areas, or scabs on corms. Stalks may curl or bend; leaves turn yellow and die. Grow glads in well-drained soil and with good air circulation. Lift and destroy plants that show signs of disease. Inspect stored corms several times during the winter and discard any that look infected. Take care not to damage corms during digging; dig during dry weather; cure corms for 2–3 weeks at 80–85°F after digging, then store at 35–40°F. Do not replant in infected soil. Or, solarize the soil before replanting in the same spot. If you spot early signs of disease, spray foliage with bordeaux mix.

Leaves Greenish Yellow or Curled and Deformed; Shoots Spindly or Stunted

Gladiolus is host to several virus diseases. Symptoms include spindly, stunted growth, yellowed foliage, and leaves marked with ring spots, mottling, and pale or dead areas. Aphids and leafhoppers spread virus diseases, so by controlling the pests, you control the disease. There is no cure once plants are infected; pull and destroy ones that show symptoms.

Gypsophila spp.   Baby's-breath

Fertilizing

Top-dress perennial species with rich compost and fertilize with high-phosphorus blended organic fertilizer in spring and midsummer.

Insect Control

See "35 Common Garden Pests," on page 230, for additional information and control measures for the insect problem listed below.

Cupped Leaf Edges; Brown, Dried-Out Blotches on Leaves

Leafhoppers suck sap from leaves, buds, and stems, causing leaves to become mottled or distorted and to eventually drop off. Leafhoppers can spread aster yellows disease. Encourage natural predators such as big-eyed flies and parasitic wasps. Treat an infestation of leafhoppers first with insecticidal soap; if the problem remains or grows worse, treat with sabadilla or pyrethrin/rotenone.

Disease Control

Foliage and Flowers Greenish Yellow; Plants Sprout Many Spindly Shoots

Plants suffering from aster yellows turn greenish yellow. They sprout many stunted, spindly shoots, giving the appearance of a witches'-broom. Flowers may have some green petals. There is no control for aster yellows; dig and destroy infected plants as soon as you spot them. Prevent spread of the virus by controlling sucking pests such as leafhoppers and aphids.

Stem Bases Turn Black; Leaves Yellow and Wilt; Plants Topple Over

Stem rot causes afflicted plants to turn yellow; black spores may appear on stems. Cut away infected plant parts; dig and destroy infected plants. Preventive measures are effective: Be sure plants have well-drained soil; add lots of organic matter to promote better drainage. Avoid damaging crowns when digging in the garden. Keep winter mulch away from crowns. If the problem is serious, solarize the soil before replanting in the same spot.

Hemerocallis spp.   Daylily

Fertilizing

Daylily is not a heavy feeder. It requires no fertilization, although an annual topdressing with compost will improve performance.

Insect Control

See "35 Common Garden Pests," on page 230, for additional information and control measures for the insect problems listed below.

Flower Buds Die; Corky Lesions on Stems

Flower thrips feed on buds, stem tips, and flowers. Blooms are distorted, stalks may not develop. Stems may have corky lesions. Pick off and destroy badly infested buds or other plant parts. These pests are difficult to control because they burrow into plant tissue. Use blue sticky traps to monitor populations and trap pests. Regular applications of insecticidal soap may provide some control once pests are spotted on traps.

Disease Control

Disease problems are rare as long as the soil is well drained and plants have good air circulation. Leaf spot occasionally occurs, but can be controlled by picking infected foliage and discarding it.

Hosta spp.

Hosta, Funkia

Fertilizing

Hosta is not a heavy feeder. It requires no fertilization, although an annual topdressing with compost will improve performance.

Insect Control

See "35 Common Garden Pests," on page 230, for additional information and control measures for the insect problem listed below.

Large, Ragged Holes in Leaves

Slugs and snails chew large, ragged holes in leaves, stems, and flowers, feeding from the bottom up. They may leave trails of slime on plants or on the soil surface. Slugs hide under boards, rocks, clippings, and debris; clean up the garden to eliminate hiding places. Put out beer traps early in the season before populations build. Surround plantings with barriers of diatomaceous earth or copper sheeting.

Disease Control

Stem Bases Turn Black; Leaves Yellow and Wilt; Plants Topple Over

Fungi can cause crown rots on hostas. Afflicted plants turn yellow; black spores may appear on stems. There is no cure for crown rot once it occurs; dig and destroy infected plants. Preventive measures are effective: Be sure plants have well-drained soil; add lots of organic matter to promote better drainage. Avoid damaging crowns when digging in the garden. Keep winter mulch away from crowns.

Hyacinthus orientalis

Hyacinth

Fertilizing

Hyacinth is a heavy feeder. Top-dress with rich compost every spring and feed with a high-phosphorus organic fertilizer. Repeat phosphorus feeding in fall.

Insect Control

Yellowed or Distorted Foliage; Decayed Bulbs

Stunted, yellowed, or deformed leaves and flowers, or lack of leaves and flowers are symptoms of infestation by bulb mites. These tiny whitish mites feed in groups. Infested bulbs have corky, brown spots that become powdery. When purchasing bulbs, inspect them carefully for damage or signs of infestation. Bulb mites are attracted to damaged or rotting bulbs. Dig and destroy infested bulbs; solarize the soil before planting in previously infested ground.

Plants with Swollen Spots on Leaves; Plants Fail to Grow in Spring

Bulb and stem nematodes are small roundworms that feed on bulb scales and are barely visible to the naked eye. Infested bulbs have yellow-green, swollen spots on foliage; severely infested plants fail to grow or flower in spring. Dig and destroy infested bulbs, which will have dark rings or blotches when cut and examined in cross-section. Buy healthy looking, undamaged bulbs, and plant hyacinths in well-drained soil to discourage this pest.

Disease Control
Yellowed Leaves; Gray Mold on Bulbs

Hyacinths are subject to a variety of rots that cause foliage to turn yellow or brown and wither. Flowers and foliage may be covered by gray mold, especially in cold, wet weather; bulbs may rot. These diseases are difficult to control once they occur. Dig and destroy infected bulbs. Solarize the soil before replanting the same area with new, healthy bulbs. To avoid rot, plant hyacinths in well-drained soil.

Flower Stalks Water-Soaked; Stripes on Leaves

Yellow rot first appears as yellow, water-soaked stripes on leaves and flower stalks that eventually turn brown. Bulbs eventually rot; cut leaves and bulbs have yellow slime. Yellow rot, caused by bacteria, can't be safely cured; dig and destroy infected bulbs. Solarize the soil before replanting the same area with new, healthy bulbs.

Impatiens spp.

Impatiens

Fertilizing

No additional feeding is necessary as long as the soil is rich in organic matter. Apply liquid seaweed or other foliar spray if necessary to perk up plants at midsummer.

Insect Control

See "35 Common Garden Pests," on page 230, for additional information and control measures for the insect problem listed below.

Yellowed, Stunted Plants

Aphids suck sap from leaves, stems, and blossoms, causing foliage to curl, pucker, and turn yellow. Leaves and buds may become stunted. Don't overfertilize with nitrogen; the resulting succulent growth encourages aphids. Encourage natural predators and parasites; release aphid midges or lacewings. Spray with water or insecticidal soap. (Test insecticidal soap on a small part of an impatiens plant before spraying because the soap can damage foliage.) Destroy seriously infested plants or use pyrethrin or pyrethrin/rotenone spray or dust.

Disease Control
Water-Soaked Lesions on Stems Near Soil Line

Seedlings that have water-soaked, blackened areas at the base of the stems near the soil line have a fungal disease called damping-off.

Plants fall over, often while still green. Older plants may have brown lesions on stems. Use a sterile, well-drained soil medium and provide good air circulation to prevent damping-off or other soil-borne diseases when starting seeds in flats. Avoid excessive humidity and keep plants a bit on the dry side.

Iris spp.

Iris

Fertilizing

Most species need no fertilizing as long as the growing bed was prepared well at planting time. Some gardeners work bonemeal or wood ashes in around bearded iris in spring or after blooming. Japanese and bearded irises benefit from leaf mold or well-rotted manure, but shouldn't be limed.

Insect Control

See "35 Common Garden Pests," on page 230, for additional information and control measures for the insect problems listed below.

Yellowed, Stunted Plants

Aphids suck sap from leaves, stems, and blossoms, causing foliage to curl, pucker, and turn yellow. Leaves and buds may become stunted. Encourage natural predators and parasites; release aphid midges or lacewings. Spray with water or insecticidal soap. For serious infestations, use pyrethrin or pyrethrin/rotenone spray or dust.

Irregular Tunnels in Leaves; Rhizomes Damaged

Iris borers are pinkish white, $1^1/_2$- to 2-in. larvae with brown heads that tunnel through lower leaves and eventually into rhizomes. Adults are night-flying, gray-brown moths with 1- to 2-in. wingspans. The larvae tunnel into the base of the foliage, causing water-soaked spots; plants wilt; rhizomes and flowers rot. Borer damage leaves plants vulnerable to bacterial soft rot.

Cultural controls are helpful: Cut stalks and leaves at the base of the plants in fall and discard to prevent borers from overwintering there. In spring, look for borers in leaves just above the soil; pinch them in their tunnels to crush them before they enter rhizomes. Dig infested plants; cut away and discard all infested or diseased rhizomes after flowering. Replant only healthy rhizomes. In spring, dust the base of plants with pyrethrin to kill emerging larvae.

Flower Buds Die; Petals Distorted

Several species of thrips infest iris. They feed on inner folds of leaves, causing stunted growth and russet or sooty areas on leaves. Tops of plants eventually turn brown and die. Flowers may appear discolored, flecked with white, or deformed. These pests are difficult to control, for they burrow into plant tissue. Don't purchase sickly looking irises that may be infested. Cut away and destroy severely infested plant parts. Use blue sticky traps to monitor populations and trap pests. Regular applications of insecticidal soap may provide some control once pests are spotted in traps.

Disease Control
Leaf Spots

Water-soaked streaks on leaves; rotted rhizomes. Bacterial soft rot is a serious problem for German irises. Infection causes water-soaked streaks on leaves; leaves may turn yellow and wilt. Infection travels downward to rhizomes, which rot and have a foul odor. Healthy leaves will topple. Bacterial soft rot tends to occur after borer infestations. Destroy infected rhizomes and leaves. Control borers to lessen the chances of the disease.

Dark green or gray-brown spots on leaves. Both bacteria and fungi cause leaf spots on iris foliage. Bacterial leaf spot is characterized by translucent, dark green spots; fungal leaf spot by gray spots with brown edges. Pick off and destroy infected foliage; cut back foliage to the ground in fall and destroy. If necessary, treat with regular applications of bordeaux mix.

Stems Rot at Base

Overcrowded plants can develop fungal crown rot. Leaves of afflicted plants turn brown at the base, foliage turns yellow, and black spores may appear on stems. White or brown mold may be present. Rhizomes may also rot. Dig and divide iris clumps every few years to avoid overcrowding. Be sure plants have well-drained soil; add lots of organic matter to promote better drainage. Avoid damaging crowns when digging in the garden. Keep winter mulch away from crowns.

Powdery, Orange-Red Blisters on Both Sides of Leaves

Infection by rust fungi causes orange-red blisters on both sides of iris leaves. Be sure plants have plenty of air circulation; avoid wetting foliage when watering. Cut off and destroy leaves infected with rust; cut plants back to the ground in fall, and destroy or discard leaves and stems. Dust or spray leaves with sulfur beginning early in the season to prevent rust or to treat a mild infection.

Lilium spp.

Lily

Fertilizing

Lily is a light feeder. Fertilize lightly with high-phosphorus, high-potassium organic fertilizer in early spring and again before blooming. Avoid excessive nitrogen.

Insect Control

See "35 Common Garden Pests," on page 230, for additional information and control measures for the insect problems listed below.

Yellowed Leaves

Yellowed leaves; stunted plants. Aphids suck sap from leaves, stems, and blossoms, causing foliage to curl, pucker, and turn yellow. Leaves and buds may become stunted. Aphids are rarely serious on lilies, but they do transmit virus diseases. Encourage natural predators and parasites; release aphid midges or lacewings. Spray with water or insecticidal soap. Destroy seriously infested plants or use pyrethrin or pyrethrin/rotenone spray or dust.

Yellowed or decayed leaves; decayed bulbs. Lilies that produce stunted, yellowed, or deformed leaves and flowers, or that do not develop at all, may be infested with bulb mites, which are tiny whitish mites that feed in groups. Infested bulbs have corky, brown spots that become powdery. When purchasing bulbs, inspect them carefully for damage or signs of infestation.

Bulb mites are attracted to damaged or rotting bulbs. Dig and destroy infested bulbs; solarize the soil before planting in previously infested ground.

Disease Control

Avoid disease problems with lilies by inspecting bulbs carefully when you buy them. Handle them carefully until planting time to avoid bruising them, and plant in well-drained soil.

Leaf Spots or Blemishes

Water-soaked streaks on leaves; rotted bulbs. Bacterial soft rot may appear as water-soaked streaks on leaves; leaves may turn yellow and wilt. Infection travels downward to bulbs, which rot and smell bad. Healthy leaves will topple. If bacterial soft rot occurs, lift and destroy infected plants. To prevent problems in the future, plant lilies in well-drained soil, avoid damaging bulbs when planting or digging near them, and improve air circulation.

Shoots wilt and die suddenly; flower buds rot; gray mold on plants. Gray mold is a fungus disease that causes emerging shoots to suddenly wilt and die. Shoots may be covered with mold, or yellow or reddish brown spots may develop on leaves; spots may run together and whole leaves may die. Flowers, buds, and stems may rot. Flowers may be deformed and turn brown. Pick and destroy infected leaves; dig and destroy severely infected plants. Spray remaining plants with a copper fungicide weekly until the disease is under control. Clean up garden refuse in the fall.

Mottled leaves; stunted stems. Lilies are susceptible to a variety of virus diseases that may cause yellowed, mottled, or streaked leaves and stunted stems. Flowers may be discolored. Aphids and leafhoppers spread virus diseases, so by controlling the pests, you control the disease. There is no cure once plants are infected; pull and destroy ones that show symptoms.

Understanding Crown Rot

Crown rot is a serious disease that can attack nearly any type of flower. Caused by both bacteria and fungi, afflicted plants wilt suddenly or turn yellow and wilt slowly. Stems turn black at the base, and the roots rot. Plants afflicted with bacterial crown rot will have masses of slimy, foul-smelling ooze. If you suspect fungal crown rot, look closely for tiny fruiting bodies of the fungi or gray or black mold on plant parts. Crown rot is often the culprit when plants fail to appear in spring.

Although there is no cure for crown rot once it occurs—you need to dig afflicted plants and discard them, together with the soil in which they've been growing—cultural controls work well. When planting perennials, make sure that the soil is well drained and has plenty of organic matter. It's a good idea to mark plantings of hardy bulbs and perennials—especially those that appear late in the spring or that die down after flowering. That way, you'll avoid digging into or damaging them during parts of the season when they're not in bloom.

Keep mulch away from the crowns of plants during winter to reduce moisture and prevent rot during this season. Leaf mulch around perennials is especially a problem during winter because the leaves mat down on top of plants, smothering them and encouraging the damp conditions that lead to fungal attack. Chopped leaves make a fine mulch, but keep them away from the crowns.

Leaves pale above; dusty blisters beneath. Infection by rust fungus causes pale areas to appear on upper leaf surfaces, with corresponding dusty blisters on leaf undersides. Provide good air circulation around foliage; avoid wetting foliage when watering. Cut off and destroy leaves infected with rust; cut plants back to the ground in fall, and destroy or discard leaves and stems. Dust or spray leaves with sulfur beginning early in season to prevent rust or to treat a mild infection.

Narcissus spp.   Daffodil

Fertilizing

If desired, apply high-phosphorus and high-potassium blended organic fertilizer in early spring. Work in bonemeal with a light top-dressing of wood ashes and finished compost every fall.

Insect Control

Bulbs Softened; Plants Fail to Appear in Spring

Narcissus bulb flies are hairy, yellow-and-black flies that look like small bumblebees. Lesser bulb flies are blackish green, $1/3$-in. flies. Maggots are white to yellowish, $1/2$–$3/4$-in. larvae that bore into bulbs, causing the bulbs to soften and exposing bulbs to attack by disease organisms. Inspect bulbs carefully at purchase or planting time: Look for entry holes, softness, or signs of rot. Destroy bulbs infested with these pests. Narcissus bulb flies attack healthy bulbs, whereas lesser bulb flies attack already weakened plants. If bulb flies are a problem in your area, try covering plants with floating row covers during the egg-laying period. Dust plants weekly with pyrethrin/rotenone if the pests have been a problem in past years.

Yellowed or Decayed Leaves; Decayed Bulbs

Daffodils that produce stunted, yellowed, or deformed leaves and flowers, or that do not develop at all, may be infested with bulb mites, which are tiny whitish mites that feed in groups. Infested bulbs have corky, brown spots that become powdery. When purchasing bulbs, or storing them for forcing, inspect them carefully for damage or signs of infestation. Bulb mites are attracted to damaged or rotting bulbs. Dig and destroy infested bulbs; solarize the soil before planting in previously infested ground.

Disease Control

If you buy healthy, undamaged bulbs from a reputable dealer; handle them with care at planting time; and plant in well-drained soil, disease is unlikely to be a problem.

Stunted Plants; Deformed Flowers

Infection by Fusarium basal rot causes the base of the bulb to turn soft and brown. The rot spreads up through the bulb. Infected plants are stunted and have few flowers. Dig and destroy bulbs that show signs of disease. Take care not to scrape or damage bulbs at planting time; fungi most often infect bulbs through wounds.

White or Brown Streaks on Leaves; Foliage Wilt

Plants suffering from viral decline will develop white or brown streaks on the leaves late in their growing season. Foliage may wilt and topple over. There is no cure for decline. Pull out diseased plants. Control aphids, which spread the disease. Plant only large, healthy-looking bulbs.

Plants Fail to Grow and/or Flower; Swollen Spots on Leaves

Nematodes are tiny, slender, unsegmented roundworms that enter pores or wounds and feed on plants internally. Infected leaves are deformed with yellow-green spots and small, swollen areas. Bulbs develop dark internal circles and may fail to grow or bloom in spring. In the fall, lift and destroy badly infected bulbs; also clean up and destroy foliage from these bulbs. Soak mildly infested ones in a hot water bath (110°F) for 3 hours, then plunge them immediately into cold water. Let them dry and store them in a cool, dark place until fall when they can be replanted. Solarize nematode-infested soil or treat with a chitin source. Increase soil humus content as a long-range preventive measure.

Paeonia spp.

Peony

Fertilizing

Every year, fertilize with high-phosphorus blended organic fertilizer after blooming. Where plants are growing in rich topsoil, a handful of bonemeal and some limestone or wood ashes may be enough. Feed tree peonies with well-rotted manure and bonemeal in early spring and late summer.

Insect Control

Peonies are seldom seriously bothered by insects; to prevent problems, cut stems to the ground and discard them each fall. Ants feed on a sugary solution on flowers and buds, but do no damage to plants. See "35 Common Garden Pests," on page 230, for additional information and control measures for the insect problem listed below.

Flower Buds Die or Petals Are Distorted

Flower thrips feed on buds, stem tips, and flowers, causing distortion or white, brown, or red flecks. Flower buds may turn brown and die. These pests are difficult to control, for they burrow into plant tissue. Cut away and destroy severely infested plant parts. Use blue sticky traps to monitor populations and trap pests. Regular applications of insecticidal soap may provide some control once pests are spotted on traps.

Disease Control

To prevent serious disease problems, plant peonies in well-drained soil rich in organic matter. Cut stems to the ground each fall and discard.

Stem Lesions

Anthracnose appears as sunken lesions with pink blisters on stems. Plants may die. Cultural controls such as regular fall cleanup and thinning stems to improve air circulation are effective. Spray with copper fungicide to control anthracnose if cultural controls don't do the trick.

Wilting

Shoots wilt and collapse; gray mold near crown. Several fungi cause blights or stem and crown rots in peonies. Infection by botrytis blight causes shoots to wilt suddenly and topple over. Stem bases are blackened and rotted; gray mold may be present near soil. Buds may wither and blacken. Flowers and leaves may turn brown and develop mold. Cultural controls are effective. Remove and destroy infected plant parts as soon as symptoms appear. Don't put manure near plant crowns; remove mulch near crowns in spring to allow soil to dry out. Avoid overwatering and plant peonies in well-drained soil; each fall, cut away stems to below ground level and discard or burn them. If the problem is persistent, scrape away the top 2 in. of soil around plants and replace with clean sand. In spring, spray young shoots and soil with bordeaux mix, and repeat treatment in 2 weeks.

Plants stunted; yellow or spotted leaves; galls on roots. Infection by root-knot nematodes causes plants to wilt, become stunted, and have yellowed or bronzed foliage. Roots may be poorly developed with tiny galls on them. If soil is infested with nematodes, remove plants, solarize the soil, and replant with nematode-free stock, or apply a chitin source. Increase soil organic matter as a long-term prevention measure.

Papaver orientale

Oriental poppy

Fertilizing

Oriental poppy is a light feeder. Plants growing in deep, rich loam do not need any feeding.

Insect Control

See "35 Common Garden Pests," on page 230, for additional information and control measures for the insect problem listed below.

Yellowed Leaves; Stunted Plants

Aphids suck sap from leaves, stems, and blossoms, causing foliage to curl, pucker, and turn yellow. Leaves and buds may become stunted. Encourage natural predators and parasites; release aphid midges or lacewings. Spray with water or insecticidal soap. Destroy seriously infested plants or use pyrethrin or pyrethrin/rotenone spray or dust.

Disease Control

Water-Soaked Spots on Foliage; Foliage and Flowers Turn Black

Bacterial blight appears as blackened, water-soaked spots on leaves, stems, and flowers. Infected plants turn brown and lose leaves; girdled stems die. Dig and destroy infected plants, along with the soil in which they are growing. Solarize infected soil before replanting. Avoid bacterial blight by using disease-free seed. As a preventive, water early in the day so leaves dry quickly.

White or Gray Powdery Spots on Leaves; Blighted Seedlings

Downy mildew appears as white or gray powdery spots on both sides of leaves. As the fungus spreads, stems become distorted and die; flowers fail to open. The disease blights seedlings as well. Clean up refuse in fall and destroy severely infected plants. Be sure plants have plenty of air circulation; plant in well-drained soil. Plant only disease-free seeds. Water from below to keep foliage dry. Spray with sulfur or copper fungicide if the disease does occur.

Leaves Greenish Yellow or Curled and Deformed; Shoots Spindly or Stunted

Poppies can host several virus diseases. Symptoms include spindly, stunted growth, yellowed foliage, and leaves marked with ring spots, mottling, and pale or dead areas. Aphids and leafhoppers spread virus diseases, so by controlling the pests, you control the disease. There is no cure once plants are infected; pull and destroy ones that show symptoms.

Pelargonium spp.

Geranium

Fertilizing

Geranium is not a heavy feeder. A top-dressing with rich compost when planting out in the garden is enough to give plants a good start.

Insect Control

See "35 Common Garden Pests," on page 230, for additional information and control measures for the insect problems listed below.

Yellowed or Spotted Foliage

Yellowed, stunted plants. Aphids suck sap from leaves, stems, and blossoms, causing foliage to curl, pucker, and turn yellow. Leaves and buds may become stunted. Don't overfertilize with nitrogen; the resulting succulent growth encourages aphids. Encourage natural predators and parasites; release aphid midges or lacewings. Spray with water or insecticidal soap. Destroy seriously infested plants or use pyrethrin or pyrethrin/rotenone spray or dust.

Tiny yellow dots on leaves; webby foliage. Spider mites suck sap, causing yellow stipples on leaves. The mites inject toxins as they feed, causing leaf distortion and discoloration. They also cover leaves, stems, and flowers with fine webbing. Inspect greenhouse-grown plants before purchase. Spray all surfaces of leaves with a strong jet of water every other day to control these pests. If this fails, apply abamectin, insecticidal soap, or pyrethrin/rotenone. Pull and destroy severely infested plants.

Weakened Plants; Leaves Yellowed

Whitefly nymphs and adults suck sap from leaves, buds, and stems, causing leaves to yellow and plants to weaken. Check plants carefully for these pests before purchasing. Set up yellow sticky traps to monitor the pests. Destroy infested plants to prevent the pests from spreading throughout the garden. Or, spray with insecticidal soap, especially the undersides of leaves. Use pyrethrin as a last resort to combat infestations.

Disease Control
Leaves Covered with Spots or Blotches

Geraniums, especially greenhouse-grown ones, are afflicted by bacteria and fungi that cause leaf spots. Bacterial leaf spot causes leaves to develop small, brown, sunken spots that may merge, causing leaves to turn yellow or brown; leaves may fall off or hang on plant. Stems are pale gray outside, black inside. Roots may be black. Fungal leaf spots may appear as black or brown spots, sometimes with concentric rings. Leaves may turn black and fall off. Bacterial and fungal leaf spots tend to occur where plants are overcrowded or don't receive enough light. Inspect plants at purchase for signs of disease; don't overwinter infected specimens. Cultural controls are effective: Avoid overcrowding, to be sure plants have plenty of light and air; remove and destroy infected leaves. Destroy badly infected plants; treat remaining plants with a copper fungicide or bordeaux mixture.

Rotted Stem Sections; Shoots Wilt; Spots on Leaves

Stem rot is a fungus disease that causes stems to rot at the base near the soil, moving up the stem, and eventually causing foliage to wilt and die. It is especially a problem on geranium cuttings. Cultural controls work well: Take cuttings from healthy plants only; root in a sterile medium. Inspect plants carefully for signs of disease at purchase. Cut away and destroy infected stems or seriously diseased plants.

Petunia × *hybrida*

Petunia

Fertilizing

Petunia is not a heavy feeder, but for large, plentiful blossoms, fertilize at midseason with a balanced organic fertilizer.

Insect Control

See "35 Common Garden Pests," on page 230, for additional information and control measures for the insect problems listed below.

Holes in Leaves and Flowers

A variety of beetles chew holes in petunia leaves and flowers. Flea beetles chew many tiny holes; Colorado potato beetles and cucumber beetles chew larger, ragged holes. Handpick larger beetles. If pests persist, apply insecticidal soap or sabadilla dust in early morning. For long-term Japanese beetle control, dust your lawn with milky disease spores to eliminate grubs.

Disease Control
Rotted Stems; Shoots Wilt

Several fungi cause stem rot on petunias. Afflicted stems rot at the base near the soil; foliage eventually wilts and dies. Cultural controls work well: Inspect plants carefully for signs of disease at purchase; plant petunias in well-drained soil. Cut away and destroy infected stems or seriously diseased plants.

Leaves Greenish Yellow or Curled and Deformed; Shoots Spindly or Stunted

Petunias are host to several virus diseases, including beet curly top, tobacco and cucumber mosaic, tomato spotted wilt, and aster yellows. Symptoms include spindly, stunted or deformed growth, yellowed foliage, and leaves marked with ring spots, mottling, and pale or dead areas.

Aphids and leafhoppers spread virus diseases, so by controlling the pests, you control the disease. There is no cure once plants are infected; pull and destroy ones that show symptoms. Wash your hands and tools with detergent after handling. Don't smoke near plants, to avoid introducing mosaic to the garden.

Phlox spp.

Phlox

Fertilizing

Feed in spring and midsummer with a balanced organic fertilizer. Plants benefit from a little extra potassium; top-dress with a handful of wood ashes and finish with a good mulch of compost or rotted manure.

Insect Control

See "35 Common Garden Pests," on page 230, for additional information and control measures for the insect problems listed below.

Leaf Spots

White or light green leaf spots. Phlox plant bugs are yellow-green, ¼-in. bugs with 4 black stripes. Young bugs are red or orange. Both young bugs and adults suck sap from upper surfaces of new leaves and buds, causing light green or whitish spots. Growth may be deformed or dwarfed. Handpick bugs. Pyrethrin sprays kill phlox plant bugs, but thorough annual cleanup is necessary to break the cycle of infestation. Remove and discard or burn all stems in fall.

Tiny yellow dots on leaves; webby foliage. Spider mites suck sap from leaves, causing yellow stipples on leaves. The mites inject toxins as they feed, causing leaf distortion and discoloration. They also cover leaves, stems, and flowers with fine webbing. Spray all surfaces of leaves with a strong jet of water every other day to control these pests. If this fails, apply abamectin, insecticidal soap, or pyrethrin/rotenone. Cut and destroy severely infested stems.

Disease Control

Deformed Leaves; Swollen or Deformed Stems; Stunted Plants

Plants infested with bulb and stem nematodes have leaves that are crinkled and wrinkled or thin and threadlike. Shoot tips are distorted; stems are swollen. Plants are stunted, fail to flower, and may die. These nematodes swim on the film of water covering plants or are carried on garden tools, animals, and gardeners from plant to plant. There is no cure once plants are infected; dig and destroy them. Do not grow phlox in infected soil in subsequent years. A thorough annual cleanup will help control these pests.

Brown Spots on Leaves

Several fungi cause leaf spots on phlox. Spots are small at first, but enlarge and run together, forming large blotches. Don't over-crowd plants, to ensure good air circulation; avoid working with plants when foliage is wet; and pick off and destroy infected plant parts as soon as you spot them. Dig and destroy severely infected plants. If leaf spots are a repeated problem, spray regularly with sulfur or bordeaux mix.

White Powdery Covering on Leaves

Powdery mildew appears as a white or ash gray powdery covering on leaves. As the fungus spreads, leaves become distorted and may drop off. To prevent powdery mildew, spray with sulfur fungicide approximately every 10 days if weather is warm and wet. Avoid ongoing powdery mildew problems by cleaning up refuse in fall and destroying severely infected plants. Be sure plants have plenty of air circulation; thin stems so air can flow freely. Water from below to keep foliage dry.

Rosa spp.

Rose

See "*Rosa* spp." on page 402.

Salvia spp.

Salvia

Fertilizing

Perennial and annual salvias do best in soils with low fertility. Avoid excessive nitrogen.

Insect Control

See "35 Common Garden Pests," on page 230, for additional information and control measures for the insect problems listed below.

Yellowed Leaves; Stunted Plants

Aphids suck sap from leaves, stems, and blossoms, causing foliage to curl, pucker, and turn yellow. Leaves and buds may become stunted. Encourage natural predators and parasites; re-lease aphid midges or lacewings. Spray with water or insecticidal soap. Destroy seriously infested plants or use pyrethrin or pyrethrin/rotenone spray or dust.

Tiny Yellow Dots on Leaves; Webby Foliage

Spider mites suck sap from leaves, causing yellow stipples on leaves. The mites inject toxins as they feed, causing leaf distortion and discoloration. They also cover leaves, stems, and flowers with fine webbing. Spray all surfaces of leaves with a strong jet of water every other day to control these pests. If this fails, apply abamectin, insecticidal soap, or pyrethrin/rotenone. Pull and destroy severely infested plants.

Disease Control

Salvias are seldom seriously affected by diseases. Leaf spot and rust occasionally occur, but rarely are serious problems.

Water-Soaked Lesions on Stems Near Soil Line

Infection by damping-off fungi can cause water-soaked lesions to appear on seedling stem bases; roots may rot. Afflicted seedlings topple over and die. Use a sterile, well-drained potting medium to prevent this disease. Maintain good air circulation around seedlings.

Tagetes spp.   Marigold

Fertilizing

Marigold is not a heavy feeder. Avoid excessive nitrogen.

Insect Control

See "35 Common Garden Pests," on page 230, for additional information and control measures for the insect problems listed below.

Leaves Skeletonized; Flowers Eaten

Japanese beetles chew leaves, leaving a dry leaf "skeleton" behind. They also chew flowers. Their larvae feed on roots. Handpick Japanese beetles. For serious infestations, use neem extract or rotenone. For long-term control, apply milky disease spores to the bordering lawn to eliminate grubs.

Tiny Yellow Dots on Leaves; Webby Foliage

Spider mites suck sap from leaves, causing yellow stipples on leaves. The mites inject toxins as they feed, causing leaf distortion and discoloration. They also cover leaves, stems, and flowers with fine webbing. Spray all surfaces of leaves with a strong jet of water every other day to control these pests. If this fails, apply abamectin, insecticidal soap, or pyrethrin/rotenone. Pull and destroy severely infested plants.

Disease Control

Marigolds are seldom seriously bothered by disease provided they have full sun and well-drained soil.

Stems Turn Black at Base; Plants Wilt

Both bacteria and fungi can cause plants to rot at the base and wilt. Afflicted plants may wilt suddenly or turn yellow and wilt slowly. Stems may turn black from the base upward; leaves may turn brown. Dig and destroy infected plants. Preventive measures are effective: Be sure plants have well-drained soil; add lots of organic matter to promote better drainage. If the problem is serious, solarize the soil before replanting in the same spot.

Foliage and Flowers Greenish Yellow; Plants Sprout Many Spindly Shoots

Plants suffering from aster yellows turn greenish yellow. They sprout many stunted, spindly shoots, giving the appearance of a witches'-broom. Flowers may have some green petals. There is no control for aster yellows; dig and destroy plants as soon as you spot them. Prevent the virus by controlling sucking pests such as leafhoppers and aphids.

Tropaeolum majus Nasturtium

Fertilizing

Nasturtium is not a heavy feeder. Avoid excessive nitrogen.

Insect Control

See "35 Common Garden Pests," on page 230, for additional information and control measures for the insect problems listed below.

Stunted or Deformed Leaves or Flowers

Yellowed leaves; stunted plants. Aphids suck sap from leaves, stems, and blossoms, causing foliage to curl, pucker, and turn yellow. Leaves and buds may become stunted. Aphids are a common problem, but don't usually threaten the plant's health. Encourage natural predators and parasites; release aphid midges or lacewings. Spray with water or insecticidal soap. Destroy seriously infested plants or use pyrethrin or pyrethrin/rotenone spray or dust.

Flowers and leaves deformed or marked with spots. Tarnished plant bugs suck sap from plants and release a toxin that can deform leaves and shoots. Flowers may become dwarfed and buds deformed. Control by handpicking; for serious infestations, spray with rotenone. Discourage overwintering adults by cleaning up weeds and debris in spring and fall.

Holes in Leaves

Small, ragged holes in leaves; plants defoliated. Cabbage loopers and imported cabbageworms can chew nasturtium leaves and completely defoliate plants. Handpick loopers or spray with BTK (*Bacillus thuringiensis* var. *kurstaki*) 10 days after moths appear, and every 7–10 days after that as needed. Use pyrethrin or sabadilla as a last resort.

Tiny holes in leaves. Flea beetles chew tiny holes in leaves. Parasitic nematodes will control soil-dwelling larvae. Spray with rotenone as a last resort.

Disease Control

Plants Turn Yellow and Wilt; Stems Rot at Soil Line

Plants suffering from bacterial wilt turn yellow, wilt, and die. Stems look water-soaked and have dark streaks. Roots blacken and rot, and flowers may not form. Gray liquid may ooze from cut stems. There is no cure for bacterial wilt, which also occurs on eggplant, peppers, and tomatoes. Dig and destroy infected plants and solarize the soil before growing any susceptible crops in that bed.

Leaves Covered with Spots or Blotches

Fungi and bacteria may cause leaf spot. Leaves may develop brown, black, yellow, red, or gray spots. Spots may enlarge and kill entire leaves. Pick and destroy infected leaves as soon as spots appear; dig and destroy severely infected plants. Avoid wetting leaves when watering; be sure plants have good air circulation. Sulfur spray provides some protection if applied as soon as the disease appears. If the infection is serious, don't grow nasturtiums for 1 year.

Tulipa spp.

Tulip

Fertilizing

Top-dress with well-rotted manure or rich compost and bonemeal (1 cup per sq. yd.) every spring, about 1 month before blooming.

Insect Control

See "35 Common Garden Pests," on page 230, for additional information and control measures for the insect problems listed below.

Leaves Yellow

Yellowed leaves; stunted plants. Tulip bulb aphids infest both the bulbs and aboveground portions of the plant. They suck sap from leaves, stems, and blossoms, causing foliage to curl, pucker, and turn yellow. Leaves and buds may become stunted. Inspect bulbs carefully when you purchase them; on bulbs, aphids are gray with a waxy coating and cluster under the bulb coat. Destroy seriously infested bulbs or dust with pyrethrin or pyrethrin/rotenone.

Foliage yellowed or distorted; bulbs decayed. Bulb mites are white, have 8 legs, and are $1/50$–$1/25$ in. Feeding causes stunted, yellowed, or deformed leaves; flowers are deformed or do not develop. Bulbs have corky, brown spots that become powdery. Destroy bulbs heavily infested with bulb mites. Dip lightly infested ones in hot water (122°F) for 3–4 minutes. Solarize infested soil before replanting.

Disease Control

Inspect bulbs carefully when you purchase them. Don't buy bulbs with cut marks, black or brown rotted spots, or moldy areas. Papery bulb sheath should be intact; it provides protection against fungi. Handle bulbs carefully during storage and at planting time. Bulbs exposed to temperatures over 70°F during storage will produce small, distorted flowers or fail to flower altogether. Plant in well-drained soil.

Streaked or Spotted Foliage; Rotted Flowers

Also known as fire, botrytis blight is a serious disease of tulips. Red-brown spots that later turn gray appear on leaves or flowers. Plants may be stunted or turn pale yellow-green. Flowers may be deformed; stems may rot. Bulbs and lower stems have black or dark brown spots. Gray mold may be present. Dig and destroy plants infected with botrytis blight, being careful to remove the entire bulb. To prevent other tulips from becoming infected, water early in the day so foliage has a chance to dry before evening. Trim off leaves as soon as they turn yellow, and remove spent blossoms. For further protection, apply bordeaux mix as soon as shoots appear in spring, and again 7 days later.

Plants Stunted; Yellow or Spotted Leaves; Galls on Roots

Infection by nematodes causes plants to wilt, become stunted, have swollen stems, or have yellowed or bronzed foliage. Roots may be poorly developed with tiny galls on them. Bulb scales may turn brown. Control nematodes by solarizing the soil or treating with a chitin source. If bulbs become infested, dig them up and discard them. Increase soil organic matter as a long-term preventive measure.

Verbena × *hybrida* Verbena

Fertilizing

Apply an organic high-phosphorus blended fertilizer in midsummer, and spray with seaweed or other organic foliar fertilizer if necessary to keep plants at peak performance.

Insect Control

See "35 Common Garden Pests," on page 230, for additional information and control measures for the insect problems listed below.

Yellow or Distorted Leaves

Yellowed, stunted plants. Aphids suck sap from leaves, stems, and blossoms, causing foliage to curl, pucker, and turn yellow. Leaves and buds may become stunted. Encourage natural predators and parasites; release aphid midges or lacewings. Spray with water or insecticidal soap. Destroy seriously infested plants or use pyrethrin or pyrethrin/rotenone spray or dust.

Tiny yellow dots on leaves; webby foliage. Spider mites suck sap from leaves, causing yellow stipples on leaves. The mites inject toxins as they feed, causing leaf distortion and discoloration. They also cover leaves, stems, and flowers with fine webbing. Spray all surfaces of leaves with a strong jet of water every other day to control these pests. If this fails, apply abamectin, insecticidal soap, or pyrethrin/rotenone. Pull and destroy severely infested plants.

Weakened plants; leaves yellowed. Whitefly nymphs and adults suck sap from leaves, buds, and stems, causing leaves to yellow and plants to weaken. Check plants carefully for these pests before purchasing. Set up yellow sticky traps to monitor the pests. Destroy infested plants to prevent the pests from spreading throughout the garden. Or, spray with insecticidal soap, especially the undersides of leaves. Use pyrethrin as a last resort to combat infestations.

Leaves Covered with Tan to Brown Blotches

Leafminer larvae tunnel through leaves, feeding on plant tissue. Large areas of leaves will turn brown or tan; foliage will appear discolored and diseased. Remove and destroy leaves infested with the pests as they are discovered; cut back plants to the ground and clean up garden debris in fall to prevent pests from overwintering. Larvae can sometimes be prevented from entering the leaves by spraying weekly with insecticidal soap as soon as the first tunnel appears.

Leaves Stuck or Rolled Together with Silk

Leafrollers protect themselves when feeding by rolling terminal leaves into tubes and binding them with strands or webs of silk. Handpick leafrollers or use weekly sprays of BTK (*Bacillus thuringiensis* var. *kurstaki*).

Chewed Leaves

Yellow woollybear caterpillars are covered with yellow, reddish, or white long hair and are 1–1½ in. long. Adults are white moths with a small black dot on each wing and have 1½-in. wingspans. The caterpillars feed on leaves. Handpick yellow woollybear caterpillars or use weekly sprays of BTK.

Disease Control

Leaves Yellow and Wilt

Infection by bacterial wilt causes leaves to yellow, wilt, and die. Cut stems will reveal dark areas. Pull and destroy plants infected with this disease. Rotate crops or solarize the soil before replanting in that bed.

Viola spp.

Pansy

Fertilizing

Feed with a balanced organic fertilizer in midsummer to encourage a second round of flowering later in the season. Don't overfeed with nitrogen.

Insect Control

See "35 Common Garden Pests," on page 230, for additional information and control measures for the insect problems listed below.

Yellowed or Distorted Leaves

Yellowed, stunted plants. Aphids suck sap from leaves, stems, and blossoms, causing foliage to curl, pucker, and turn yellow. Leaves and buds may become stunted. Don't overfertilize with nitrogen; the resulting succulent growth encourages aphids. Encourage natural predators and parasites; release aphid midges or lacewings. Spray with water or insecticidal soap. Destroy seriously infested plants or use pyrethrin or pyrethrin/rotenone spray or dust.

Leaves stippled with tiny yellow dots; webby foliage. Spider mites suck sap from leaves, causing them to become stippled. The mites inject toxins as they feed, causing leaf distortion and discoloration. They also cover leaves, stems, and flowers with fine webbing. Spray all surfaces of leaves with a strong jet of water every other day to control these pests. If this fails, apply abamectin, insecticidal soap, or pyrethrin/rotenone. Pull and destroy severely infested plants.

Chewed or Skeletonized Leaves

Several pests chew holes in pansy and violet foliage, including greenhouse leaftier, 3/8-in., light green caterpillars that fasten leaves together with silk and leave ragged, chewed edges. Violet sawfly larvae are blue-black, 1/2-in. larvae that skeletonize leaves. Sawfly larvae are primarily active at night. Control both pests by handpicking. For serious infestations, use BTK (*Bacillus thuringiensis* var. *kurstaki*) for leaftiers; insecticidal soap for sawfly larvae.

Disease Control

Leaf Blotches

Leaves have brown blotches with black margins. Anthracnose appears as brown blotches outlined in black on leaves. Flowers are deformed or spotted; plants may die. Pick off diseased plant parts; destroy severely infected plants. To avoid spreading this disease, don't work around wet plants. Be sure plants have good air circulation, and water early in the day so the foliage dries off quickly. Spray remaining plants with copper fungicide. If anthracnose is a particular problem in your area, spray regularly with a copper fungicide or bordeaux mix.

Leaves covered with dark spots or blotches. Infection by leaf spot may cause brown, black, or transparent spots on leaves. The spots may enlarge and kill leaves. Don't overcrowd plants; don't work around wet plants; and pick off and destroy infected plant parts. Dig and destroy severely infected plants. If leaf spots are a repeated problem, spray regularly with sulfur, fungicidal soap, or bordeaux mix.

Yellow blisters on leaves; pale green spots beneath. Rust appears as yellow blisters on upper leaf surfaces, with corresponding pale green areas on lower leaf surfaces. Stems may also be infected. Be sure plants have plenty of air circulation; avoid wetting foliage when watering. Pull and destroy severely infected plants; spray remaining plants with fungicidal soap or sulfur. Cut plants back to the ground in fall and destroy or discard leaves and stems.

Rotted Roots; Wilting

Root rot causes rotting roots and lower leaves. Webby mold may be present on lower stems. Upper plant parts may wilt and fall over.

Zinnia spp.

Fertilizing

Zinnia is a light feeder. Avoid excessive nitrogen.

Insect Control

See "35 Common Garden Pests," on page 230, for additional information and control measures for the insect problems listed below.

Leaves Skeletonized; Flowers Eaten

Japanese beetles chew leaves, leaving a dry leaf "skeleton" behind. They also chew flowers. Their larvae feed on roots. Handpick Japanese beetles. For serious infestations, use neem extract or rotenone. For long-term control, dust your lawn with milky disease spores to eliminate grubs.

Tiny Yellow Dots on Leaves; Webby Foliage

Spider mites suck sap from leaves, causing yellow stipples. They inject toxins, causing leaf distortion and discoloration. They also cover leaves, stems, and flowers with fine webbing. Spray leaf surfaces with a strong jet of water every other day to control these pests. If this fails, apply abamectin, insecticidal soap, or pyrethrin/rotenone. Pull and destroy severely infested plants.

Flowers and Leaves Deformed or Marked with Spots

Tarnished plant bugs suck sap from plants and release a toxin that can deform leaves and shoots. Flowers may become dwarfed and buds deformed. Control by handpicking; for serious

Using fresh manure may cause fungal root rot. Plant pansies in well-drained soil. Dig and destroy infected plants, and solarize the soil before replanting.

Zinnia

infestations, spray with rotenone. Discourage overwintering adults by cleaning up weeds and debris in spring and fall.

Disease Control
Leaves Yellow and Wilt; Plants Topple Over

Soil-borne fungi can cause root rot on zinnias. Afflicted plants turn yellow and wilt. There is no cure once it occurs; dig and destroy infected plants. Preventive measures are effective: Be sure plants have well-drained soil; add lots of organic matter to promote better drainage.

Red-Brown Spots on Flowers; Brown Cankers on Stems

Plants infected by blight fungi develop small, red-brown spots on flowers. Dark brown cankers appear on stems. Pick and destroy infected flowers; dig out and destroy severely infected plants. If blight has been a past problem, use a preventive spray of sulfur or bordeaux mix.

White Powdery Covering on Leaves

Powdery mildew appears as a white or ash gray powdery covering on leaves. As the fungus spreads, leaves distort and may drop off. Avoid ongoing mildew problems by cleaning up refuse in fall and destroying severely infected plants. Be sure plants have plenty of air circulation. Water from below to keep foliage dry. Spray with sulfur or garlic if the disease occurs. Mildew-resistant cultivars are available.

CHAPTER TEN

Fruits

By Joseph Smillie

The old saying that an ounce of prevention is worth a pound of cure is especially true when you are growing fruit. It's commonly thought that gardeners can't raise fruit trees successfully without relying on synthetic chemicals for insect and disease control. Many commercial fruit growers offer the same argument, but more and more organic fruit producers are proving them wrong. And whether your orchard, vineyard, or berry patch consists of a few plants or several acres of them, the principles of caring for them are the same.

Your first step toward growing fruit without synthetic chemicals is to develop a management program that includes an overall preventive strategy and appropriate curative tactics. Don't let those big words intimidate you. While experience is the best of all possible teachers, even a beginner can manage a home orchard effectively.

You will have more opportunity to develop a preventive strategy if you are planning new fruit plantings. If you are working with existing trees or bushes, you may have to focus more on curative measures than on prevention.

In planning your fruit-growing strategy, try to anticipate problems, and design in features that will avert or help control expected pests and diseases. For example, you can eliminate apple scab by selecting scab-resistant cultivars, control pest mites by nurturing predator mites, reduce bitter pit problems by balancing soil levels of boron and calcium, and curb many insect pests by leaving some grassy areas wild and planting certain wildflowers to feed parasitic wasps. A healthy, mineral-balanced soil and a diverse habitat of various sod crops, shrubs, and trees will help fruit-bearing plants to be more resistant or tolerant of pests and diseases.

In spite of good planning, intensive preparation, and wise cultivar selection, you probably will have some pest and disease problems. Fruit just tastes too good to be left alone. If you're an ecologically minded gardener, you probably don't mind sharing some of the bounty with nature, but you must suppress most diseases and many pest problems, or they can multiply and destroy the crop and even the plants.

The following encyclopedia of fruits and berries lists guidelines for fertilizing plants. Since fruit crops are plantings that remain in your yard for many years, you must think about their nutrient needs both at planting and throughout many seasons of production. To best know your trees' nutrient needs, you'll need to test your soil, do foliar analysis, and watch for deficiency symptoms. For more in-depth information on soil improvement and fertilizer products see chapter 4.

The entries also provide information on insects and diseases that might affect your plantings, listed by symptom. (The botanical name and family of each crop follows the common name.) To troubleshoot a problem in your garden, start by looking up the affected crop.

Skim the entry until you find the symptoms that match those on your plants. If the symptoms are a disease problem, you'll find the name of the disease, a full description of the symptoms, and prevention and control measures. If the symptoms are caused by insects, in some cases, you'll find the name of the insect, description, and complete control measures. In most cases, you'll find the name of the pest responsible, along with only two or three of the most reliable control measures. If you'd like more information about that insect or how to control it, see "35 Common Garden Pests" on page 230. There, you'll find comprehensive information on the pest, its life cycle and host plants, and how to control it. If you're not familiar with any of the recommended insect and disease control measures, refer to chapters 6 and 7 for detailed explanations on when and how to use control methods and products.

Apple

Fertilizing

Apply 4–6 in. of rich compost annually. Add supplemental nitrogen with a foliar application of fish emulsion before bloom, but avoid excess nitrogen, which can aggravate insect pest problems. Apple trees are heavy potassium feeders. If soil test results show potassium deficiency, but high magnesium, use potassium sulfate. If magnesium is also deficient, use Sul-Po-Mag to supply potassium. If trees show signs of boron deficiency, use a foliar boron spray. Spray trees every 2 weeks with liquid seaweed or chelated foliar mineral sprays to supply trace minerals.

Malus pumila
Rosaceae

Insect Control

See "35 Common Garden Pests," on page 230, for additional information and control measures for the insect problems listed below.

Foliage Curls, Puckers, and Turns Yellow

Aphids suck sap from leaves and buds, causing foliage to curl, pucker, and turn yellow. Leaves and buds may be stunted. Ants introduce aphid infestations. Control ants with a premixed commercial boron sugar spray. Encourage native predators, including lady beetles and lacewings, and release aphid midges. For serious infestation, spray with insecticidal soap.

Getting a Smart Start

If you're starting fresh with raising backyard fruit, you have the best shot at planning ahead to prevent pest problems. You can choose the best possible site, select pest-resistant cultivars, and carefully prepare the soil.

The site: The most important element of a fruit-growing site is air and water drainage. A slope is usually ideal, as it allows air to flow away from the plant tops and water to drain from the soil around roots. This helps prevent a heavy, wet atmosphere that favors disease, water-logged soils that impede root function, and spring frosts that can kill fruit blossoms.

The cultivars: Choosing cultivars that resist or tolerate diseases prevalent in your area is essential if you hope to garden without chemicals. Some diseases are so powerful and persistent that if you plant a susceptible cultivar, the best you can hope for is a yearly spray battle with no hope of reprieve. Resistant cultivars are listed for each type of fruit included in this chapter. New cultivars are released each year. Check with your Cooperative Extension Service or current gardening publications for listings of the most recently developed disease-resistant fruits.

The soil: Compost is particularly important for fruit production. Fruit growers use compost as a nutritive mulch for feeder roots of fruit trees and bushes that grow near the soil surface. Composted animal manure is the best source of slow-release nitrogen for fruits, and compost usually supplies sufficient trace minerals for most fruits.

Many backyard growers plant new trees in existing sod. However, if you are planting in a tilled area, you'll be well rewarded if you take time the year before you plant to till and enrich the soil and plant a green manure crop.

When planting fruit trees, take extra care to prepare adequate planting holes. Add 1 cup of bonemeal to the back fill to supply phosphorus. Apply about a 6-inch layer of rich compost out to the dripline of the tree. This mulch supplies nutrients and also prevents surrounding sod from encroaching too heavily and competing with your trees.

If aphids have been a problem in previous seasons, use a dormant oil spray to smother egg masses.

Tunnels in Fruit

Apple maggot flies lay eggs just beneath the skin of the apples, and the larvae tunnel into the fruit. Pick up and destroy fallen fruit. Hang 1 red ball coated with a sticky substance or 1 commercial apple maggot fly trap at eye level in each dwarf tree (6 per full-size tree) 1 month after petal fall to trap the flies. Spraying BTK (*Bacillus thuringiensis* var. *kurstaki*) mixed with a commercial feeding attractant or with skim milk will help control larvae.

Codling moth larvae also tunnel into fruit and eat apple flesh. Wrap trees with cloth strips in fall; remove and burn in spring to destroy overwintering cocoons. Use corrugated cardboard tree bands during the growing season to trap larvae. Use pheromone traps to monitor for main flight of moths and release *Trichogramma* wasps to coincide with the egg-laying period. Gardeners in California, Oregon, and Washington can apply codling moth granulosis virus once or twice a week during the main egg-production season. Set up a black light trap near the trees, using a timer to activate the light from 11:00 P.M. to 3:00 A.M. (this kills the adult moths, but very few other insects). For severe infestations, spray with ryania mixed with a feeding attractant, starting when 75 percent of petals have fallen, and follow up with 3 sprays at 1–2-week intervals.

Webs in Trees

Webs in branches. Fall webworms feed on leaves and produce large webs on branches. Tent caterpillars—hairy, black caterpillars with narrow brown and yellow lines and blue spots along their sides—also feed on leaves and produce webs. Remove and destroy webs. Spray with BTK, being sure to cover leaves where caterpillars are feeding.

Small webs on branch tips. Leafrollers pull leaves together and spin webs, feeding inside on buds, leaves, and developing fruit. Damaged fruit shows deep, brown scars. Apply dormant oil just before bud break to kill egg masses. Handpick caterpillars. Apply BTK when larvae start feeding but are not yet protected by webs.

Misshapen Fruit with Indented Areas or Cavities

Green fruitworms are green, 1-in. caterpillars with white or yellow lengthwise stripes. They chew on new leaves and flower buds and bore into young apples, forming indented areas or cavities. Spray with BTK beginning at petal fall.

Defoliated Trees

Gypsy moth caterpillars have gray, hairy bodies with rows of blue and red spots along the sides of the back; they grow to 2½ in. They feed on leaves, defoliating trees. Scrape brown or yellow egg masses off trunks into a bucket of soapy water. Spray with BTK in spring. Wrap tree trunks with burlap skirts in June to trap the insects.

Leaves Stippled Yellow

European red mites and other spider mites suck juices from plant cells, causing yellowed speckling on foliage. Pest mites are usually controlled by predator mites. If your trees have mite problems, spraying with insecticidal soap will give temporary control. Release predator mites (*Metaseiulus occidentalis*) to re-establish the natural balance.

Fruit Drops; Fruit Has Cuts in Skin

Adult plum curculios feed on and lay eggs in developing fruit, reducing fruit quality. The larvae feed internally in fruit. Monitor for plum curculio by hanging a large green apple, such as a Granny Smith, sprinkled with an apple fragrance perfume in trees after petal fall, and watch to see if egg-laying scars appear on these apple lures. Every 4–5 days, beginning at blossom set, shake the trees in the early morning to dislodge beetles onto sheets spread under the tree. Destroy all infested fruit during the season. If you raise chickens, fence them in around your trees to feed on dropped fruit. If you will be away from home for an extended period during the summer, which would make the periodic shaking program impossible, plan to apply 2 sprays of Triple Plus (pyrethrin-rotenone-ryania mix) 7–10 days apart when you first notice signs of the pest.

Leaves Yellow; Trees Weakened

San Jose and oystershell scale suck sap from leaves, fruit, and wood, weakening and possibly killing branches or entire trees. Spray with dormant oil before bud break, and prune out branches that are completely covered with scales. Release scale parasites 2 weeks after spraying.

Deformed Fruit

Tarnished plant bugs feed on blossoms, buds, and developing fruit; heavy feeding can cause deformed fruit. Encourage native predators and release minute pirate bugs. Spray with rotenone or sabadilla as a last resort.

Disease Control

Olive Green Spots on Leaf Undersides; Corky Spots on Fruit

Apple scab symptoms first appear as olive green spots on the undersides of young leaves.

Spots later appear on the upper leaf surfaces and blossoms. Leaves may curl and crack. Spots develop on fruit, and later form corky "scabs." When planting new trees, always select scab-resistant or scab-tolerant cultivars. If you have susceptible cultivars, plan a preventive spray program. Your program will include 5–15 sprays during the growing season, depending on the temperature and humidity levels. If the weather is warm and wet, spray weekly from green tip until blossoms begin to open.

Pale Yellow Spots on Leaves

Cedar apple rust can infect many apple cultivars in areas where its alternate hosts, members of the genus *Juniperus,* are prevalent. Symptoms of the fungus include yellowish spots on leaves that turn orange, and spots may appear on fruit as well. Remove alternate hosts (which include red cedar) growing within 300 yards.

Apply copper-based fungicide to help lessen damage from the disease.

Withered, Blackened Blossoms; Blackened, Curved Twigs

Fire blight is a bacterial disease spread by rain and insects during bloom. It is very difficult to control once it is established. Monitor blossoms for the tell-tale sign of an amber ooze. Later, the fruit spur or twigs will turn black and wilt into a cane-handle shape that readily identifies the disease. Prune out all infected twigs, cutting at least 6 in. of healthy tissue below the infected area as well. Disinfect tools in a household bleach solution (1 part bleach to 9 parts water) after each cut; burn all prunings or put out for disposal in sealed containers. Spraying bordeaux mix can be an effective preventive control.

Resistant Apple Cultivars

Cultivar	Resists (R)/Tolerates (T)
'Freedom'	**R:** scab; **T:** fire blight, powdery mildew, woolly apple aphid; Source-widely available
'Jonafree'	**R:** scab; **T:** cedar apple rust, fire blight; Sources-9, 11, 16, 28, 32
'Liberty'	**R:** cedar apple rust, scab; **T:** fire blight, powdery mildew; Source-widely available
'Macfree'	**R:** scab; **T:** cedar apple rust, fire blight; Sources-2, 3, 15
'Nova Easygro'	**R:** cedar apple rust, scab; **T:** fire blight; Sources-2, 22
'Prima'	**R:** scab; **T:** powdery mildew; Sources-14, 25, 28, 32
'Priscilla'	**R:** cedar apple rust, scab; **T:** fire blight; Source-31
'Redfree'	**R:** scab; **T:** cedar apple rust, powdery mildew; Source-28

Blueberry

Fertilizing

Blueberries need light, well-drained soil with a high organic matter level and pH between 4.8 and 5.6. Blueberries are very light feeders with a modest nitrogen requirement. Apply a thick sawdust mulch annually. Side-dress with acidic fish fertilizer if nitrogen is needed. To avoid iron deficiency, apply a foliar chelated iron spray once a year.

Insect Control

See "35 Common Garden Pests," on page 230, for additional information and control measures for the insect problems listed below.

Worms in Berries

The blueberry maggot fly is very similar to the apple maggot fly. Flies lay eggs on the blueberries, and the larvae tunnel into the fruit. Pick up and destroy infested fruit. Control blueberry maggot fly with sprays of ryania mixed with a feeding attractant.

Fruit Drops; Fruit Has Cuts in Skin

Adult plum curculios feed on and lay eggs in developing berries, reducing berry quality. The larvae feed internally in berries. Monitor by hanging a large green apple, such as a Granny Smith, sprinkled with an apple fragrance perfume in bushes after petal fall. Every 4–5 days, beginning at blossom set, shake bushes in the early morning to dislodge beetles onto sheets spread under the tree. Destroy all infested berries during the season. If you'll be away for an extended period during the summer, making the periodic shaking program impossible, plan to apply 2 sprays of Triple Plus (pyrethrin-rotenone-ryania mix) 7–10 days apart when you first notice signs of the pest.

Leaves Yellow; Bushes Weakened

San Jose and oystershell scale suck sap from leaves, fruit, and wood, weakening and possibly killing branches or entire bushes. Spray with dormant oil before bud break, and prune out branches that are completely covered with scales. Release scale parasites 2 weeks after spraying.

Disease Control

Spraying with copper and sulfur fungicides can temporarily suppress many diseases. However, planting disease-resistant cultivars and pruning out and destroying disease-infested plant parts are the only effective strategies for disease control in blueberries. Rabbiteye blueberries seem to be more resistant than highbush types to diseases, such as canker, and are not as bothered by pests. They are also heat and drought tolerant; they will grow in long-season areas.

Cankers on Stems

Bacterial stem canker appears as reddish brown or black cankers on stems. Prune infected stems, disinfecting tools in a household bleach solution (1 part bleach to 9 parts water) after each cut. If plants are severely infested, dig them out and destroy them.

Galls on Stems

Cane galls are rough, warty growths on stems. Crown gall can appear as galls on both stems and roots. Remove infected plant parts, disinfecting tools and your hands in a household bleach solution to prevent the diseases from spreading. Burn diseased plant parts or dispose of them in sealed containers.

Berries Shrivel before Ripening

Infection by mummy berry fungus causes blueberries to dry up and drop off the bush before they ripen. Maintain good air circulation by pruning to help prevent mummy berry. Pick off and destroy infected fruit. Rake up all dropped fruit, leaves, and debris to prevent the disease from spreading.

White Mold on Leaves

Powdery mildew appears as a white mold on upper leaf surfaces. Remove and destroy infected plant parts. Disinfect tools in a household bleach solution after each cut. Sulfur sprays may give some control.

Resistant Blueberry Cultivars

Cultivar	Resists (R)/Tolerates (T)
'Berkeley'	**T:** cracking, powdery mildew; Source-widely available
'Bluejay'	**T:** cracking, mummy berry; Sources-6, 9, 21, 29
'Elliott'	**T:** cracking, mummy berry; Source-widely available
'Patriot'	**T:** root rot; Sources-11, 16, 21
'Spartan'	**T:** mummy berry; Sources-25, 28

Bramble fruit

Rubus spp.
Rosaceae

Fertilizing

Bramble fruits, which include red and black raspberries, blackberries, and loganberries, are not heavy feeders, but they do best in soils that are well-drained and high in organic matter. Supply organic matter by applying a good-quality compost mulch in the planting year and 8 in. annually of partially broken down organic matter, such as old leaves or straw or partially decomposed wood chips.

Insect Control

See "35 Common Garden Pests," on page 230, for additional information and control measures for the insect problems listed below.

Tiny White Spots on Leaves

Bramble leafhopper adults and nymphs suck the sap from leaves, causing tiny white spots or mottled areas to appear. Fruit may not develop or ripen well. Native parasitic wasps generally keep leafhoppers under control. In case of severe infestation, spray with water or insecticidal soap.

Shoot Tips Wilt

Raspberry cane borer beetles lay eggs near tips of shoots and then girdle the shoots above and below the egg-laying site, causing the shoot tip to wilt and die. The larvae overwinter in the cane, and the following season bore downward through the cane to the crown. Prune wilted tips a few inches below the girdling injury. Burn or otherwise destroy the cuttings.

Raspberry cane maggots are white, tapered larvae that also feed inside the canes and cause shoot tips to wilt. Also control them by pruning off and destroying wilted tips.

Canes Wilt and Die

Raspberry crown borer moths are black, wasplike insects with clear wings and yellow bands on their bodies. Female moths lay eggs on foliage in late summer, and larvae crawl to base of canes and chew out cavities to overwinter. The following season, they feed in crowns and roots and may ruin canes. Cut infested canes off below the soil line and destroy them. Also destroy rust-colored egg masses on leaves in late summer.

Worms in Berries

Raspberry fruitworm adults are tiny, light brown beetles that feed on leaves and blossoms.

Planning *Your* Spray Program

Spray recommendations usually include an application schedule. For example: Spray sulfur or copper fungicide every 7 to 10 days from the time symptoms appear until 20 days before harvest. However, the majority of spray recommendations in this book *don't* include such clear-cut directions. Why? Because organic gardeners seek to minimize their use of sprays. They analyze the severity of the disease and their local weather conditions and only spray when it is most necessary and effective. This is more complicated than following a set schedule, but results in use of fewer sprays.

Temperature and relative humidity are two prime factors to consider in deciding when to spray. Fungi and bacteria grow better and spread more rapidly in warm, wet weather. So during a warm, rainy spring, you would need to spray more often than during a dry spring. In the humid eastern states, this might mean spraying weekly, or even every few days if frequent hard rains are washing the sprays off your trees.

Keep in mind that organic sprays—which are based on fungicidal properties of the elements sulfur and copper—are caustic. If you spray too much, you can harm leaf tissue, soil microorganisms, and beneficial insects.

If you are certain that some of your fruit plantings are suffering from disease, begin by identifying the disease involved. Many do not respond at all to sprays. Check the recommendations in this chapter. If a spray is listed, remember that they are more effective as preventives than as cures. If it's June, and you see disease symptoms on a peach or pear tree, you may have to accept that for this growing season, you'll have some damage to your tree and crop. However, next spring, you can begin a spray program that will help prevent the disease from recurring.

If you decide to spray, your local Cooperative Extension Service office can help with recommendations on when to spray in your local area. And don't hesitate to ask for recommendations for copper or sulfur fungicides if their first recommendation is for a synthetic fungicide. Copper and sulfur sprays have been used for decades to control disease in fruit crops and are still two of the most effective materials used by commercial fruit producers. For comparisons of copper and sulfur fungicide products, including tips on which ones to use when, see "Fungicides and Bactericides" on page 156.

The light yellow, $1/3$-in. larvae penetrate buds and small fruit. Spray with rotenone and/or pyrethrin sprays at bud stage and just before blossom. Cultivate the soil around canes in late summer to expose pupae.

Chewed Leaves

Raspberry sawflies lay eggs on leaves, and the larvae eat leaf tissue. Heavy damage may result in crop loss. Handpick larvae. Spray with BTK (*Bacillus thuringiensis* var. *kurstaki*), or as a last resort, with pyrethrin or rotenone.

Disease Control

Brambles are susceptible to many diseases that have no cure. Selecting proven local disease- and virus-resistant cultivars, and removing and destroying all diseased and nonbearing canes are the only economically and ecologically sound strategies. Spraying with copper or sulfur fungicides will give short-term control only.

Reddish Brown Spots on New Canes

Anthracnose infection appears as small, reddish brown or purple spots on new canes. As canes grow, the spots enlarge and turn into sunken cankers; small yellow or purple spots also appear on leaves. Spraying with copper-based fungicide every 7–10 days may give some control, but you will likely need to prune out and destroy infested canes.

Spur blight fungi also cause reddish brown patches to appear on canes, usually in late summer. Leaves show large brown blotches and may drop. Many buds on infected canes will

Resistant Bramble Cultivars

Cultivar	Resists (R)/Tolerates (T)
'Amity' (red raspberry)	**R:** large raspberry aphid (causes mosaic), root rot, spur blight; **T:** mildew; Source-24
'Autumn Bliss' (red raspberry)	**R:** large raspberry aphid (causes mosaic); Source-24
'Black Hawk' (black raspberry)	**R:** anthracnose; Source-widely available
'Chilliwack' (red raspberry)	**R:** root rot, large raspberry aphid (causes mosaic); Sources-24, 25, 28
'Darrow' (blackberry)	**T:** orange rust; Source-widely available
'Dirksen'(black raspberry)	**T:** anthracnose, leaf spot, mildew; Sources-6, 9, 13
'Haida' (red raspberry)	**R:** large raspberry aphid (causes mosaic), spur blight; Source-24
'Jewel'(black raspberry)	**R:** anthracnose; Source-widely available
'Newburgh' (red raspberry)	**R:** root rot; **T:** anthracnose, mosaic, spur blight; Source-widely available
'Prestige' (red raspberry)	**R:** large raspberry aphid (causes mosaic), powdery mildew, spur blight; Source-24
'Royalty' (purple raspberry)	**R:** large raspberry aphid (causes mosaic), leaf curl; **T:** raspberry fruitworm; Source-widely available
'Southland' (red raspberry)	**R:** anthracnose, leaf spot, mildew; Sources-24, 32
'Success' (purple raspberry)	**R:** spur blight; Source-24

die. Fruiting spurs may die before fruit sets. Remove and destroy infected canes.

Small, Tightly Curled Leaves

Infection by leaf curl virus results in small, dark green, tightly curled leaves. The disease cannot be cured. Remove and destroy infected and surrounding plants.

Mottled, Puckered Leaves

Plants infected with mosaic virus have bright yellow mottling on leaves, and leaves appear puckered. Infected stands will be weak and less productive. Control aphids, which spread the virus. Remove and destroy infected and surrounding plants.

Yellow Spots on Leaves

Rust fungi cause yellow spots to appear on leaves, with corresponding yellow or black blisters forming on leaf undersides. Remove infected canes. Copper or sulfur fungicide sprays may have some effect.

Leaves Appear Striped

Canes infected with Verticillium wilt have yellow or reddish brown patches between the veins, making them appear striped. Affected leaves roll up and wither, starting from the base of the cane. Canes show blue or purple streaks and whole canes may die. Remove and destroy infected and surrounding plants.

Cherry

Prunus avium (sweet cherry)
P. cerasus (sour cherry)
Rosaceae

Fertilizing

Put down 4–6 in. of compost or composted manure annually. Mix 1 cup of potassium sulfate or Sul-Po-Mag with mulch to supply potassium. Use a foliar spray of zinc if soil tests or leaf analysis indicate deficiency or if deficiency symptoms appear on leaves.

Insect Control

Sweet cherries are generally more susceptible to insect problems than are sour cherries. See "35 Common Garden Pests," on page 230, for additional information and control measures for the insect problems listed below.

Foliage Curls, Puckers, and Turns Yellow

Aphids suck sap from leaves and buds, causing foliage to curl, pucker, and turn yellow.

Leaves and buds may be stunted. Ants introduce aphid infestations. Control ants with a premixed commercial boron sugar spray. Encourage native predators, including lady beetles and lacewings, and release aphid midges. For serious infestation, spray with insecticidal soap. If aphids have been a problem in previous seasons, use a dormant oil spray to smother egg masses.

Small, Misshapen Fruit

Cherry fruit flies, close relatives of the apple maggot fly, are small flies with dark-banded wings. They lay eggs in developing cherries and the white, tapered, $1/_3$-in. maggots eat the cherry flesh. Control by removing all infested fruit and cultivating in spring to destroy pupae that overwinter in the soil. Hang yellow sticky traps baited with ammonia or apple maggot fly lure in trees to trap flies.

Holes in Fruit Skin; Tunnels in Fruit

Codling moth larvae tunnel into cherries. Wrap trees with cloth strips in fall; remove and burn in spring to destroy overwintering cocoons. Use corrugated cardboard tree bands during the growing season to trap larvae. Use phero- mone traps to monitor for main flight of moths and release *Trichogramma* wasps to coincide with the egg-laying period. Gardeners in California, Oregon, and Washington can apply codling moth granulosis virus once or twice a week during the main egg-production season. Set up a black light trap near the trees, using a timer to activate the light from 11:00 P.M. to 3:00 A.M. (this kills the adult moths, but very few other insects). For severe infestations, spray with ryania mixed with a feeding attractant, starting when 75 percent of petals have fallen, and follow up with 3 sprays at 1–2 week intervals.

Leaves Stippled Yellow

European red mites and other spider mites suck juices from plant cells, causing yellowed speckling on foliage. Pest mites are usually con- trolled by predator mites. If your trees have mite problems, spraying with insecticidal soap will give temporary control. Release predator mites (*Metaseiulus occidentalis*) to re-establish the natural balance.

Holes in Trunk; Sawdust and Gummy Sap near Holes

Peachtree borers are clear-winged blue moths with yellow or orange markings. The moths lay eggs on tree trunks or other objects near trees. The larvae, which are white with brown heads, burrow into trees near the base of the trunk, both above and below ground level. Their tunneling can weaken and even kill trees. Keep bases of trees clear to control and monitor tree borers. Probe in holes with a sharpened end of a coat hanger to kill larvae.

Skeletonized Leaves

The sluglike larvae of pear sawflies eat leaf tissue, leaving behind a dry leaf "skeleton." Remove host weeds around trees. Dusting leaves with wood ashes may deter larvae. Use caution: Wood ashes may damage leaf tissues. Spray larvae with insecticidal soap or pyrethrin/diatomaceous earth as a last resort.

Deformed Leaves and Blossoms; Scarred Fruit

Pear thrips pierce developing buds and leaves and suck sap, causing disfigured leaves and blossoms. They also attack young fruit, caus- ing scabbing and russeting. Predatory mites usu- ally control this insect. If thrips become a problem, spray with insecticidal soap every 3 days for 2 weeks. This should lower pest populations enough so that predators will then provide effec- tive control.

Fruit Drops; Fruit Has Cuts in Skin

Adult plum curculios feed on and lay eggs in developing fruit, reducing fruit quality. The larvae feed internally in fruit. Monitor for plum curculio by hanging a large green apple, such as a Granny Smith, sprinkled with an apple fra- grance perfume in trees after petal fall. Every 4–5 days, beginning at blossom set, shake the trees in the early morning to dislodge beetles onto sheets spread under the tree. Destroy all infested fruit during the season. If you raise chickens, fence them in around your trees to feed on dropped fruit. If you will be away from home for an extended period during the sum- mer, which would make the periodic shaking program impossible, plan to apply 2 sprays of Triple Plus (pyrethrin-rotenone-ryania mix) 7–10 days apart when you first notice signs of the pest.

Disease Control

Sweet cherries are generally more suscep- tible to disease problems than are sour cherries.

Resistant Cherry Cultivars

Cultivar	Resists (R)/Tolerates (T)
'Hedelfingen' (sweet)	**T:** bacterial canker, leaf spot; Source-widely available
'North Star' (sour)	**T:** brown rot, cracking; Source-widely available
'Sam' (sweet)	**R:** cracking; Source-widely available
'Van' (sweet)	**R:** cracking; **T:** Cytospora canker; Source-widely available
'Windsor' (sweet)	**T:** brown rot, Cytospora canker; Source-widely available

Cherry trees can be infected by several virus diseases. These diseases cannot be cured. Avoid them by planting only certified virus-free stock. Pruning dead and diseased limbs is also an essential general practice to limit disease problems. Pruning back and even topping cherry trees in decline will often stimulate healthy new growth.

Black Swellings on Limbs

Black knot is a fungus disease that appears as a cancerous, black growth on twigs and branches. Prune infected limbs 1 ft. back from the edge of the diseased area. Disinfect tools in a household bleach solution (1 part bleach to 9 parts water) after each cut. Burn prunings immediately or put in sealed containers for disposal. Remove all nearby wild plum or cherry trees. If the problem persists, apply 2 sprays of lime-sulfur, 7 days apart, before bud break in spring.

Blossoms Turn Brown and Die

The first symptoms of fungal brown rot are browning and collapse of blossoms. Cankers form on twigs; growing tips may die back. Final symptoms are brown spots on fruit that spread until the entire fruit rots and shrivels. Pick and destroy any mummified fruit, and prune away dead twigs. Apply bordeaux mix spray at red bud stage and "popcorn" bud stage (when buds appear about 50 percent white).

Yellowing of New Growth

Cytospora canker appears as wilting or yellowing of new shoots and leaves. Infected growth later turns brown; cankers form at the base of a bud in late winter. Keep watch for canker symptoms year-round, and prune and destroy any diseased tissues by burning or placing them in sealed containers for removal with your household garbage.

Small Purple Spots on Leaves

Leaves infected by leaf spot fungi show small red or purple leaf spots. The infected tissue may dry up and fall out, leaving many small holes in the leaves, or entire leaves may drop off. If leaf spot is a problem in your region, use a preventive copper or sulfur fungicide spray.

Grape

Vitis spp.
Vitaceae

Fertilizing

Grapes are heavy feeders and require a high level of most nutrients. Grapes grow best when soil pH is between 5.6 and 5.8. Phosphorus uptake is hampered at this low pH; supply phosphorus by tilling in green manure crops fed with colloidal phosphate. Monitor potassium needs by soil testing or leaf analysis; supply potassium by applying Sul-Po-Mag. Grapes respond well to weekly sprays of seaweed extract. If leaf analysis shows a zinc deficiency, apply a chelated zinc foliar spray.

Since grapes are often planted on slopes prone to erosion, require regular cultivation, and can live up to 50 years, it is important to continue to incorporate organic matter into the soil by applying mulch or growing and tilling in green manure crops around your vines.

Insect Control

Webbing on Blossoms and Berries

The grape berry moth is a brown moth with a 1/2-in. wingspan that lays eggs on grape stems, blossoms, and berries. The green or gray-green, slightly hairy larvae feed on blossoms and small berries, leaving silken threads behind that form webbed clusters. Control the caterpillar larvae of the grape berry moth with BTK (*Bacillus thuringiensis* var. *kurstaki*) sprays, or by releasing *Trichogramma* wasps. Time sprays and releases by monitoring with pheromone traps.

Cottony Masses on Foliage and Berries

Grape mealybugs look like white cottony growths on plants. The insects, inside their protective covering, feed on plant sap and secrete a sticky honeydew on which a sooty fungus may develop. Encourage native predators and parasites, including lady beetles.

Weakened Vines

The grape root borer is the larvae of a wasplike brown moth. The borers tunnel in the roots, often girdling them and ruining the vine. If you suspect grape root borers have invaded your vines, look for the cocoons near the soil surface in June. Prevent them from spreading by mounding 1 ft. of soil around trunks to keep adult moths from emerging.

Tiny White Spots on Leaves; Leaves Turn Brown and Drop

Leafhoppers damage grapevines by sucking sap from the leaves, causing tiny white spots on leaves. When infestations are heavy, leaves may turn yellow or brown and fall, and yields are poor. Plant cover crops and flowers, and leave adjacent areas wild to encourage beneficial parasites and predators. As a last resort, spray with pyrethrin or rotenone.

Chewed Leaves and Blossoms

Rose chafer beetles are 1/2-in., long-legged, tan beetles that feed on leaves, flowers, and berries. The larvae feed on roots of grasses and weeds. They usually do not cause serious damage. In years when they are very abundant, control with sprays of pyrethrin, rotenone, or diatomaceous earth if necessary.

Disease Control

Grapes demand excellent air drainage to prevent frost damage and to reduce the intensity of mildew, rot, and other diseases. If any of the following disease problems arise on your vines, plan a preventive spray program with sulfur or bordeaux mix to minimize problems in subsequent growing seasons.

In general, muscadine grapes are resistant to diseases prevalent in the South, including Pierce's disease. Also, even though European vinifera grape vines are less hardy and tend to be more susceptible to diseases in the United States, when grown in California and similar climates, a home gardener will probably encounter few problems with them.

Always check with your local Cooperative Extension agent to see what grape diseases are prevalent in your area. A cultivar that is susceptible to a particular disease may still be grown in your area with no problem if that disease does not occur there. For example, California usually doesn't have a problem with downy mildew or black rot, but may have powdery mildew, botrytis, and Pierce's disease. Eastern areas will have more problems with diseases in general, including powdery and downy mildews, botrytis, and phomopsis. Southern areas should select cultivars resistant to Pierce's disease.

Gray Spots on Leaves

Anthracnose appears as irregular gray spots on leaves that may dry up and fall out, leaving many small holes in the leaves. Spots may also appear on berries. Prune out and destroy diseased twigs, disinfecting tools in a household bleach solution (1 part bleach to 9 parts water) after each cut.

Reddish Brown Spots on Leaves

Grape vines suffering from black rot will develop circular, reddish brown spots on leaves. Tiny, black, raised dots may appear in the spots. Fruit will shrivel before it ripens. Pick off all infected fruit. Rake up and discard mulch around the vines and apply fresh mulch. If you have had past problems with black rot, apply preventive sprays of copper fungicide.

Pale Areas on Leaves; White Mildew on Leaf Undersides

Symptoms of downy mildew include purple lesions on pods, flowers, and young shoots; fuzzy, white mold may grow on leaf undersides.

Resistant Grape Cultivars

Cultivar	Resists (R)/Tolerates (T)
'Canadice' (American seedless)	**R:** crown gall, downy mildew, powdery mildew; **T:** botrytis, leaf scorch; Source-widely available
'Cayuga White' (American hybrid)	**R:** botrytis, cracking, eutypa, powdery mildew; **T:** black rot, downy mildew, leaf scorch; Sources-10, 22
'Concord' (American)	**R:** botrytis, crown gall, downy mildew, leaf scorch; **T:** powdery mildew; Source-widely available
'De Chaunac' (French hybrid)	**R:** black rot, botrytis; **T:** crown gall, downy mildew, phomopsis; Sources-10, 22
'Edelweiss' (American)	**R:** black rot, botrytis, downy mildew, powdery mildew; Sources-8, 10, 11, 16
'Foch' (French hybrid)	**R:** black rot, botrytis, downy mildew; **T:** powdery mildew; Source-widely available
'Fredonia' (American)	**R:** black rot, botrytis; **T:** brown rot, powdery mildew; Source-widely available
'Mars' (American seedless)	**R:** anthracnose, black rot, botrytis, cracking, downy mildew, powdery mildew; **T:** phomopsis; Source-widely available
'Reliance' (American seedless)	**T:** anthracnose; Source-widely available
'Steuben' (American)	**R:** botrytis, downy mildew, powdery mildew; Source-widely available
'Swenson Red' (American hybrid)	**R:** black rot; **T:** botrytis, powdery mildew; Source-widely available

The BIG Pests

Many backyard fruit growers discover that insect and disease pests are small problems compared to a few larger pests: birds, rabbits, woodchucks, and deer. Birds may completely strip fruit from bushes and cherry trees, while feeding by deer and woodchucks can damage or kill young trees.

Commercial fruit growers use propane cannons and inflated hawk kites to scare birds, but home gardeners can keep birds away from their fruit by covering bushes or trees with clear plastic film, fine-mesh nylon netting, or floating row covers. Covering fruit trees to keep birds away is easiest if you grow dwarf types.

Wrap the trunks of young trees with white plastic tree wraps in fall to prevent rabbits or mice from chewing on bark in the winter. Be sure to remove the tree wrap in summer to allow the bark to dry.

Fencing your trees or bushes is the most effective way to keep deer from feeding on your fruit crops. However, you may have some success if you hang bars of deodorant soap on trees and bushes. The soap bars are a more effective repellent when wet, so you may want to hand spray them with water in the evenings during autumn or hunting season, when deer are more likely to be foraging near your home. Other repellents that some gardeners have found effective include human hair and dried blood. Hinder is an organic animal repellent made from ammonium salts of fatty acids. It is available through mail-order catalogs.

Leaves may curl and drop off. Remove and destroy infected leaves.

Leaves Turn Brown; Tips Die Back

Pierce's disease is caused by a bacterium and is most prevalent in the South. Infected leaves turn brown, although leaf veins may remain green. Tips die back in late summer; fruit shrivels, and roots may die. There is no effective control method. If you live in an area where Pierce's disease is a problem, be sure to plant resistant cultivars.

White Powdery Covering on Leaves, Flowers, and Fruit

Infection by powdery mildew fungi causes a white powdery covering to appear on young shoots, leaves, flowers, and fruit. Thin vines regularly to maintain good air circulation.

Nectarine

Prunus persica var. *nucipersica*

See "Peach" on the opposite page.

Peach

Prunus persica
Rosaceae

Fertilizing

Peach trees are heavy feeders, especially when their limited root systems have to compete with sod. Add 1 cup of bonemeal or colloidal phosphate to each hole when planting new trees. Apply 4–6 in. of rich, composted manure annually. If soil test results show a potassium deficiency, but high magnesium, use potassium sulfate. If magnesium is also deficient, use Sul-Po-Mag to supply potassium. Spray trees every 2 weeks during growing season with liquid seaweed or chelated foliar mineral sprays to supply trace minerals.

Insect Control

See "35 Common Garden Pests," on page 230, for additional information and control measures for the insect problems listed below.

Foliage Curls, Puckers, and Turns Yellow

Aphids suck sap from leaves and buds, causing foliage to curl, pucker, and turn yellow. Leaves and buds may be stunted. Ants introduce aphid infestations. Control ants with a premixed commercial boron sugar spray. Encourage native predators, including lady beetles and lacewings, and release aphid midges. For serious infestation, spray with insecticidal soap. If aphids have been a problem in previous seasons, use a dormant oil spray to smother egg masses.

Leaves Stippled Yellow

European red mites and other spider mites suck juices from plant cells, causing yellowed speckling on foliage. Pest mites are usually controlled by predator mites. If your trees have mite problems, spraying with insecticidal soap will give temporary control. Release predator mites (*Metaseiulus occidentalis*) to re-establish the natural balance.

Wilted Shoot Tips; Gummy Holes in Fruit

Oriental fruit moth larvae first burrow into the tips of new shoots; later broods feed inside fruit. Avoid problems by planting early maturing cultivars for harvest before late broods damage fruit. Put out mating disruptives, such as Isomate twist ties, or a few pheromone monitor lure caps to keep males and females from mating. Release *Trichogramma* and braconid wasps as an alternative or supplemental control measure.

Peach twig borers are small, red-brown caterpillars that also bore into twigs and fruits. The adult moths have gray, fringed wings and are about ¼ in. long. Release parasitic wasps or spray with BTK (*Bacillus thuringiensis* var. *kurstaki*) to control.

Holes in Trunk; Sawdust and Sap near Holes

Peachtree borers are clear-winged blue moths with yellow or orange markings. The moths lay eggs on tree trunks or other objects near trees. The larvae, which are white with brown heads, burrow into trees near the base of the trunk, both above and below ground level. Their tunneling can weaken and even kill trees. Keep bases of trees clear to control and monitor tree borers. Probe in holes with the sharpened end of a coat hanger to kill larvae. Use pheromone traps to monitor moths; spray with pyrethrin or rotenone when infestation reaches critical level (follow instructions with trap).

Fruit Drops; Fruit Has Cuts in Skin

Adult plum curculios feed on and lay eggs in developing fruit, reducing fruit quality. The larvae feed internally in fruit. Monitor for plum curculio by hanging a large green apple, such as a Granny Smith, sprinkled with an apple fragrance perfume in trees after petal fall. Every 4–5 days, beginning at blossom set, shake the trees in the early morning to dislodge beetles onto sheets spread under the tree. Destroy all infested fruit during the season. If you raise chickens, fence them in around your trees to feed on dropped fruit. If you will be away from home for an extended period during the summer, which would make the periodic shaking program impossible, plan to apply 2 sprays of Triple Plus (pyrethrin-rotenone-ryania mix) 7–10 days apart when you first notice signs of the pest.

Leaves Yellow; Trees Weakened

San Jose and oystershell scale suck sap from leaves, fruit, and wood, weakening and possibly killing branches or entire trees. Spray with dormant oil before bud break, and prune out branches that are completely covered with scales. Release scale parasites 2 weeks after spraying.

Deformed Fruit

Tarnished plant bugs feed on blossoms, buds, and developing fruit; heavy feeding can cause deformed fruit. Encourage native predators and release minute pirate bugs. Spray with rotenone or sabadilla as a last resort.

Disease Control

Never plant peach trees on an old peach orchard site because of the strong possibility of residual viruses and nematodes in the soil.

Pale Green Spots on Leaves

Symptoms of bacterial leaf spot include small, round, pale green spots on leaves that turn light brown, small sunken spots on fruit, and fruit cracking. Prune and destroy infected parts. Spray bordeaux mix or copper sulfate to control.

Blossoms Turn Brown and Die

The first symptoms of fungal brown rot are browning and collapse of blossoms. Cankers form on twigs; growing tips may die back. Final

---

Pruning Primer

Proper pruning is an important technique in disease control and prevention in the orchard or berry patch. Here are some general tips to remember when you're pruning for this purpose.

🌿 You can prune dead or diseased plant parts at any time of year. Many gardeners carry a pair of pruning shears with them every time they check their trees, bushes, and vines. Pruning diseased tissue prevents spread of disease organisms to healthy tissue: The sooner it's done, the better.

🌿 Use proper technique whenever you prune. Always prune back to healthy buds when you cut away diseased tissue. Don't leave stubs sticking out from the trunk. However, remember not to cut into the branch collar; it's part of the tree's built-in mechanism for stopping the spread of disease.

🌿 Disinfect your tools or hands as you work. Disease spores can cling to your tools or hands and be spread to healthy tissue. Use a household bleach solution (1 part bleach to 9 parts water) as a disinfectant.

For titles of books that explain all the ins and outs of pruning fruit plantings for best production, see "The Chemical-Free Gardener's Library" on page 431.

symptoms are brown spots on fruit that spread until the entire fruit rots and shrivels. Pick and destroy any mummified fruit, and prune away dead twigs. Spray lime-sulfur during prebloom and flowable sulfur after blossoming for control.

Yellowing of New Shoots

Yellowing and wilting of new shoots and leaves are symptoms of cytospora canker. The new growth later turns brown, and gummy cankers form at bud bases during late winter. Cut branches infected with the fungus and burn them or put them in sealed containers for disposal. If canker symptoms appear, use preventive sprays with flowable sulfur in seasons that follow.

Blistering, Curling of New Leaves

New leaves infected with peach leaf curl fungi blister and become distorted, curl up, turn red, wither, and drop. Remove and destroy infected leaves as symptoms appear. Spray with bordeaux mix or other copper-based fungicide as soon as leaf tissue starts showing in subsequent seasons.

White, Velvety Mold on New Growth

Powdery mildew fungi overwinter in leaf and flower buds. When new growth occurs, it is stunted, distorted, and covered with white, velvety mildew. Plant resistant cultivars. Preventive sprays of flowable sulfur may give some protection.

Dark Green Spots on Fruit

Small, dark green spots on immature fruit that turn brown as fruit matures are symptoms of scab. Remove infected fruit and clean up fallen leaves and fruit. If scab has been a past problem, plan a preventive spray program. It will include 5–15 sprays during the growing season, depending on the temperature and humidity levels. If the weather is warm and wet, spray weekly from the time when flower buds first show green until blossoms begin to open.

Resistant Peach and Nectarine Cultivars

Cultivar	Resists (R)/Tolerates (T)
'Frost' (peach)	**R:** leaf curl; **T:** split pit; Sources-25, 28
'Harbelle' (peach)	**R:** bacterial spot, brown rot, cytospora canker; **T:** browning; Source-22
'Harbrite' (peach)	**R:** brown rot; **T:** bacterial spot; Sources-7, 22
'Harken' (peach)	**R:** brown rot; **T:** bacterial spot, browning; Sources-5, 14, 22, 25, 28
'Harko' (nectarine)	**T:** brown rot; Sources-25, 28
'Madison' (peach)	**R:** bacterial spot, cytospora canker; Source-widely available
'Mericrest' (nectarine)	**T:** bacterial spot, brown rot, cytospora canker; Sources-9, 11, 21, 32
'Newhaven' (peach)	**R:** bacterial spot, browning; **T:** brown rot; Sources-2, 7, 14
'Q-18' (peach)	**R:** leaf curl; Source-28
'Redhaven' (peach)	**T:** bacterial spot, browning, leaf curl; Source-widely available

Pear

Pyrus communis
Rosaceae

Fertilizing

Pears grow well on a wide variety of soils. Pears are not especially heavy feeders and seem able to satisfy their mineral needs from most soils if you supply an annual nutritive compost mulch. Do not overfertilize with nitrogen because the succulent growth is more susceptible to fire blight. If boron deficiency symptoms appear, correct with a foliar boron spray. Pears do well in a permanent sod of grasses and legumes, especially if they are mulched.

Insect Control

See "35 Common Garden Pests," on page 230, for additional information and control measures for the insect problems listed below.

Foliage Curls, Puckers, and Turns Yellow

Aphids suck sap from leaves and buds, causing foliage to curl, pucker, and turn yellow. Leaves and buds may be stunted. Ants introduce aphid infestations. Control ants with a premixed commercial boron sugar spray. Encourage native predators, including lady beetles and lacewings, and release aphid midges. For serious infestation, spray with insecticidal soap. If aphids have been a problem in previous seasons, use a dormant oil spray to smother egg masses.

Holes in Fruit Skins; Tunnels in Fruit

Codling moth larvae eat pear flesh, tunneling into the fruit. Wrap trees with cloth strips in fall; remove and burn in spring to destroy overwintering cocoons. Use corrugated cardboard tree bands during the growing season to trap larvae. Use pheromone traps to monitor for main flight of moths and release *Trichogramma* wasps to coincide with the egg-laying period. Gardeners in California, Oregon, and Washington can apply codling moth granulosis virus once or twice a week during the main egg-production season. Set up a black light trap near the trees, and use a timer to activate the light from 11:00 P.M. to 3:00 A.M. (this kills the adult moths, but very few other insects). For severe infestations, spray with ryania mixed with a feeding attractant, starting when 75 percent of the petals have fallen, and follow up with 3 sprays at 1–2-week intervals.

Leaves Stippled Yellow

European red mites and other spider mites suck juices from plant cells, causing yellowed speckling on foliage. Pest mites are usually controlled by predator mites. If your trees have mite problems, spraying with insecticidal soap will give temporary control. Release predator mites (*Metaseiulus occidentalis*) to re-establish the natural balance.

Wilted Shoot Tips; Gummy Holes in Fruit

Oriental fruit moth larvae first burrow into the tips of new shoots; late broods feed inside fruit. Avoid problems by planting early maturing cultivars for harvest before late broods damage fruit. Put out mating disruptives, such as Isomate twist ties, or a few pheromone monitor lure caps to keep males and females from mating. Release *Trichogramma* and braconid wasps as an alternative or supplemental control measure.

Leaves Yellow; Black Soot on Leaves

Pear psylla are tiny red-brown insects with membranous wings. Nymphs are yellow or green and have flattened bodies. Adults and nymphs suck sap from foliage and fruit and excrete a sticky honeydew in which black mold may grow. Pear psylla can also transmit virus diseases. Encourage natural predators, including lady beetles. If psylla becomes a problem, spray with insecticidal soap every 3–4 days during the growing season until the insect is gone. Spray light horticultural oil in fall and dormant oil in early spring.

Skeletonized Leaves

The sluglike larvae of pear sawflies eat leaf tissue, leaving behind a dry leaf "skeleton." Remove host weeds around trees. Dusting leaves with wood ashes may deter larvae. Use caution: Wood ashes may damage leaf tissues. Spray larvae with insecticidal soap or pyrethrin/diatomaceous earth as a last resort.

Deformed Leaves and Blossoms; Scarred Fruit

Pear thrips pierce developing buds and leaves and suck sap, causing disfigured leaves and blossoms. They also attack young fruit, causing scabbing and russeting. Predatory mites usually control this insect. If thrips become a problem, spray with insecticidal soap every 3 days for 2 weeks. This should lower pest populations enough so that predators will then provide effective control.

Disease Control

Be sure to remove all dead and diseased wood, but do not prune pears excessively.

Olive Green Spots on Leaf Undersides; Corky Spots on Fruit

Apple scab symptoms first appear as olive green spots on the undersides of young leaves. Spots later appear on the upper leaf surfaces and blossoms. Leaves may curl and crack. Spots develop on fruit and later form corky "scabs." If scab symptoms appear, plan a preventive spray program for subsequent seasons. Your program will include 5–15 sprays during the growing season, depending on the temperature and humidity levels. If the weather is warm and wet, spray weekly from the time when flower buds first show green until blossoms begin to open.

Pale Yellow Spots on Leaves

Cedar apple rust can infect many pear cultivars in areas where its alternate hosts, members of the genus *Juniperus,* are prevalent. Symptoms of the fungus include yellowish spots on leaves that turn orange, and spots may appear on fruit as well. If your trees have this disease, remove alternate hosts (which include red cedar) within 300 yards. Apply copper-based fungicide to help lessen damage from the disease.

Resistant Pear Cultivars

Cultivar	Resists (R)/Tolerates (T)
'Harrow Delight'	**R:** fire blight; Sources-2, 3, 22, 28, 32
'Kieffer'	**T:** codling moth, fire blight; Source-widely available
'Magness'	**T:** codling moth, fire blight; Source-widely available
'Moonglow'	**T:** codling moth, fire blight; Source-widely available
'Orient'	**T:** codling moth, fire blight; Source-widely available
'Pineapple'	**R:** fire blight; Sources-7, 11, 13
'Seckel'	**T:** codling moth, fire blight; Source-widely available

Withered, Blackened Blossoms; Blackened, Curved Twigs

Fire blight is a bacterial disease spread by rain and insects during bloom. It is very difficult to control once it is established. Monitor blossoms for the tell-tale sign of an amber ooze. Later, the fruit spur or twigs will turn black and wilt into a cane-handle shape that readily iden- tifies the disease. Prune out all infected twigs, cutting off at least 6 in. of healthy tissue below the infected areas as well. Disinfect tools in a household bleach solution (1 part bleach to 9 parts water) after each cut; burn all prunings or put them out for disposal in sealed containers. Spraying with bordeaux mix can be an effective preventive control.

Plum

Prunus domestica (European plum)
P. salicina (Japanese plum)
Rosaceae

Fertilizing

Plum trees are not heavy feeders and sur- vive in many conditions unsuitable to other fruit trees. European cultivars will even tolerate heavy clay soil, as long as the water drainage is good. Plum trees may need supplemental potas- sium in heavy crop years. To be safe, add 1 cup per tree of potassium sulfate or Sul-Po-Mag to the annual compost mulch.

Insect Control

See "35 Common Garden Pests," on page 230, for additional information and control mea- sures for the insect problems listed below.

Foliage Curls, Puckers, and Turns Yellow

Aphids suck sap from leaves and buds, causing foliage to curl, pucker, and turn yellow. Leaves and buds may be stunted. Ants intro- duce aphid infestations. Control ants with a premixed commercial boron sugar spray. Encour- age native predators, including lady beetles and lacewings, and release aphid midges. For seri- ous infestation, spray with insecticidal soap. If aphids have been a problem in previous seasons, use a dormant oil spray to smother egg masses.

Worms in Fruit

Apple maggot flies lay eggs just beneath the skin of the plums, and the larvae tunnel into the fruit. Pick up and destroy fallen fruit. Hang 1 red ball coated with a sticky substance or 1 commercial apple maggot fly trap at eye level in each dwarf tree (6 per full-size tree) 1 month after petal fall to trap the flies. Spraying BTK (*Bacillus thuringiensis* var. *kurstaki*) mixed with a commercial feeding attractant or with skim milk will help control larvae.

Leaves Stippled Yellow

European red mites and other spider mites suck juices from plant cells, causing yellowed speckling on foliage. Pest mites are usually con- trolled by predator mites. If your trees have mite problems, spraying with insecticidal soap will give temporary control. Release predator mites (*Metaseiulus occidentalis*) to re-establish the natural balance.

Deformed Leaves and Blossoms; Scarred Fruit

Pear thrips pierce developing buds and leaves and suck sap, causing disfigured leaves and blossoms. They also attack young fruit, causing scabbing and russeting. Predatory mites usually control this insect. If thrips become a problem, spray with insecticidal soap every 3 days for 2 weeks. This should lower pest populations enough so that predators will then provide effective control.

Fruit Drops; Fruit Has Cuts in Skin

Adult plum curculios feed on and lay eggs in developing fruit, reducing fruit quality. The larvae feed internally in fruit. Monitor for plum curculio by hanging a large green apple, such as a Granny Smith, sprinkled with an apple fragrance perfume in trees after petal fall. Every 4–5 days, beginning at blossom set, shake the trees in the early morning to dislodge beetles onto sheets spread under the tree. Destroy all infested fruit during the season. If you raise chickens, fence them in around your trees to feed on dropped fruit. If you will be away from home for an extended period during the summer, which would make the periodic shaking program impossible, plan to apply 2 sprays of Triple Plus (pyrethrin-rotenone-ryania mix) 7–10 days apart when you first notice signs of the pest.

Disease Control
Black Swellings on Limbs

Black knot is a fungus disease that appears as a cancerous, black growth on twigs and branches. Prune infected limbs 1 ft. back from the edge of the diseased area. Disinfect tools in a household bleach solution (1 part bleach to 9 parts water) after each cut. Burn prunings immediately or put them in sealed containers for disposal. Remove all nearby wild plum or cherry trees. If the problem persists, apply 2 sprays of lime-sulfur, 7 days apart, before bud break in spring.

Yellowing of New Shoots

Yellowing and wilting of new shoots and leaves are symptoms of cytospora canker. The new growth later turns brown, and gummy cankers form at bud bases during late winter. Cut branches infected with the fungus and burn them or put them in sealed containers for disposal. Use preventive sprays of flowable sulfur in subsequent seasons.

Resistant Plum Cultivars

Cultivar	Resists (R)/Tolerates (T)
'Au-Amber' (Japanese)	**R:** bacterial canker, bacterial fruit and leaf spot, plum leaf scald; Sources-7, 14
'Au-Producer' (Japanese)	**R:** bacterial canker, bacterial spot; **T:** black knot, leaf scald; Sources-7, 14
'Au-Roadside' (Japanese)	**R:** bacterial canker, bacterial spot, black knot, leaf scald; Sources-2, 7, 14
'Crimson' (Japanese)	**R:** bacterial canker, bacterial spot, black knot; Sources-7, 13, 14
'Homeside' (Japanese)	**T:** bacterial canker, bacterial spot, black knot, leaf scald; Source-7
'Oneida' (European)	**T:** bacterial spot; Source-22
'President' (European)	**R:** bacterial spot; **T:** bacterial canker, black knot; Source-5
'Robusto' (Japanese)	**T:** bacterial canker, bacterial spot, leaf scald; Source-14

Strawberry

Fragaria × ananassa
Rosaceae

Fertilizing

Strawberries do best on rich soils with a pH around 6.5, but they can tolerate poorer soils with a much lower pH. Before planting, enrich soil with compost. Add about 2 Tbsp. of bonemeal to the planting furrow beneath each plant at planting. Apply 6 in. of quality compost annually in fall. Use a winter covering mulch over plants to prevent freezing injury.

Insect Control

See "35 Common Garden Pests," on page 230, for additional information and control measures for the insect problems listed below.

Dwarfed Berries with Sunken Areas

Tarnished plant bugs suck sap from fruit buds and blossoms, causing dwarfed berries with sunken areas. Cover plants with floating row covers. Encourage native predators and release minute pirate bugs. Spray with rotenone or sabadilla as a last resort.

Leaves Folded or Rolled Together

Strawberry leafroller larvae fold or roll leaves together with webbing and feed within, causing leaves to turn brown and die. Apply dormant oil just before bud break to smother egg masses. Handpick larvae. Spray with BTK (*Bacillus thuringiensis* var. *kurstaki*) when larvae start to feed but before they are protected inside rolled leaves.

Holes in Blossoms; Stunted Plants

The strawberry root weevil feeds on leaves and blossoms; larvae feed on roots, causing stunting. Rotate planting areas to avoid problems with this pest. As a last resort, spray weevils with pyrethrin.

Sudden Wilting of Plant

White grubs are fat, whitish larvae of Japanese beetles and other beetles. The grubs feed on roots, causing wilting of seemingly healthy plants. Apply parasitic nematodes or milky disease spores (for Japanese beetle grubs) to control grubs.

Stunted, Dying Plants

Strawberry crown borer beetles are flightless, dark brown beetles with 3 dark spots on each wing cover. The curved, white, dark-headed larvae tunnel into and eat through the plant crowns. They may hollow out so much of the crown that growth stops or the plant dies. Deep cultivation in fall may expose and destroy many hibernating beetles. Rotate new plantings.

Disease Control

Carefully remove mulch in spring and keep berries well-weeded to minimize disease problems. Using a black plastic mulch can reduce disease problems, because humidity levels around the plants will be lower. Choose cultivars carefully: Cultivars that are resistant to a given disease in one region may be susceptible to it in another. Buy only locally proven disease-resistant, virus-free plants.

Discolored Petals

Symptoms of botrytis fruit rot include discolored petals and wilted fruit stems. Small, water-soaked spots may appear on berries. Remove and destroy infested plants. Provide good ventilation. Spraying with sulfur fungicide in subsequent seasons may help prevent recurrence.

White Powdery Covering on Leaves

Powdery mildew symptoms include upward curling of leaf edges and a white powdery fungus on leaves. Remove and destroy infected leaves. Disinfect your hands and tools after each cut by dipping them in a household bleach solution (1 part bleach to 9 parts water). Thin plants to improve air circulation. Spraying with sulfur is somewhat helpful.

Stunted Plants; Reddish Brown Roots

Red stele is a fungal disease that causes a reddish brown discoloration of the root core and the loss of small feeder roots. Plants are stunted and wilted. There is no control method. Remove and destroy infected and surrounding plants. If red stele has been a problem in the past, plant new beds with resistant cultivars.

Wilted, Dry Leaf Margins

Verticillium wilt symptoms include dry, wilted leaf margins, slow growth, and black streaks on leaf stalks and runners. There is no effective control for this fungus disease. Always be sure to purchase certified disease-free stock. Pull and destroy infected plants. If you've had past problems with Verticillium wilt, select resistant cultivars for new plantings.

Resistant Strawberry Cultivars

Cultivar	Resists (R)/Tolerates (T)
'Allstar'	**R:** red stele; **T:** leaf scorch, Verticillium wilt; Source-widely available
'Delite'	**R:** red stele, Verticillium wilt; **T:** leaf blight, leaf scorch, leaf spot, root-knot nematode; Source-widely available
'Earliglow'	**R:** red stele; **T:** botrytis, leaf scorch, Verticillium wilt; Source-widely available
'Guardian'	**R:** red stele, Verticillium wilt; **T:** leaf scorch, leaf spot; Source-widely available
'Lateglow'	**R:** red stele, Verticillium wilt; **T:** leaf scorch, leaf spot, root rot; Source-widely available
'Redchief'	**R:** red stele; **T:** leaf scorch, powdery mildew, Verticillium wilt; Source-widely available
'Scott'	**R:** red stele; **T:** leaf scorch, powdery mildew, Verticillium wilt; Source-widely available
'Surecrop'	**R:** red stele, Verticillium wilt; **T:** leaf scorch, leaf spot; Source-widely available
'Tribute'	**R:** red stele; **T:** leaf blight, powdery mildew, Verticillium wilt; Source-widely available
'Tristar'	**R:** red stele; **T:** powdery mildew, Verticillium wilt; Source-widely available

CHAPTER ELEVEN

Trees and Shrubs

By Anna Carr

Trees and shrubs are surely the largest and most costly plants in any landscape. As with any other type of plant, the best way to choose a tree or shrub that will remain healthy and happy in your garden is to learn everything you can about your site and the conditions that exist there naturally. If you hope to care for permanent plantings such as trees and shrubs without using synthetic chemicals, it's vital to plant species that are naturally well-adapted to your site. For example, although it's relatively easy to change the soil pH to satisfy the demands of an annual crop of vegetables, adjusting the soil conditions for a long-lived tree or shrub means a long-term annual commitment. Plants that are well suited to the soil, light, water, and exposure in which they are planted will have fewer problems in the long run than ones that aren't.

Matching the tree to the site also means selecting plants that are the right size at maturity for your landscape. A large sycamore or oak planted along a street under electric wires or alongside a small patio may look fine when newly planted, but it's a disaster waiting to happen. The frequent, severe pruning such plants will require to keep them in bounds will ruin the shape of the tree. It will also leave it weakened and open to attack by insects and disease. Shallow-rooted trees such as maples and beeches planted in a lawn suffer a similar fate: Lawn mowers and foot traffic repeatedly damage roots and compact soil, leaving plants open to attack. In fact, it's best not to plant grass right up to the trunk of any tree, because it's just too easy to ram it with a lawn mower or damage the trunk with a string trimmer. Although it may take months or years for such damage to become evident, it will eventually endanger a plant's health. Instead, surround your trees with low-growing, low-maintenance ground covers; they'll be happier and you'll have less of a job trimming around them.

There are several ways to choose the best plant or plants for your site. You can look for plants that are growing well in a neighbor's garden. But, beware of species that are planted too frequently. If everyone in your neighborhood has planted the same species of tree, it's altogether possible that a disease or insect pest could march through the neighborhood and attack or kill them all. Protect your investment by doing a bit of research and selecting your trees and shrubs carefully. Ask a local nursery owner for suggestions, look for plants you admire at a local park or arboretum, consult your local Cooperative Extension Service, or ask a tree expert at a local botanical garden what they might suggest.

The following encyclopedia of trees and shrubs lists guidelines for fertilizing plants and also provides information on the insects and diseases that may attack them. To troubleshoot a problem in your garden, start by looking up the affected plant. Skim the entry until you find the symptoms that match those on your plants. If the symptoms are a disease problem, you'll find the name of the disease, a full description of the symptoms, and prevention and control measures. If the symptoms are caused by insects, in some cases, you'll find the name of the insect,

a description, and complete control measures. In most cases, you'll find the name of the pest responsible, along with only two or three of the most reliable control measures. If you'd like more information about that insect or how to control it, see "35 Common Garden Pests" on page 230. There, you'll find comprehensive information on the pest, its life cycle and host plants, and how to control it. If you're not familiar with any of the recommended insect and disease control measures, refer to chapters 6 and 7 for detailed explanations on when and how to use control methods and products. In most cases, you'll only be able to treat young, newly planted trees, but controlling pests and diseases will help them get off to a good start. The encyclopedia entries will also give you a good idea of problems to be aware of when selecting trees and shrubs.

The encyclopedia is organized in alphabetical order by botanical name (the common name of each tree follows the botanical name). This eliminates any confusion; botanical names are the same the world over. If you don't know the botanical name for a tree or shrub, look for its common name in the index on page 438.

Acer spp.

Maple

Fertilizing

Most species respond to annual late winter feeding with balanced organic fertilizer.

Insect Control

See "35 Common Garden Pests," on page 230, for additional information and control measures for the insect problems listed below.

Foliage Curls, Puckers, and Turns Yellow

Aphids suck sap from leaves, stems, and blossoms, causing foliage to curl, pucker, and turn yellow. Leaves and buds may become stunted. Aphids produce honeydew, which will drip from tree branches and encourage the growth of sooty mold. Prevent problems by giving trees plenty

Tree Stress: Symptoms and Solutions

What can you do if your tree is gradually dying and you don't know why? Try giving your tree a checkup—it may show signs of stress overload. Just like people, trees can have problems with stress, although they have different ways of showing it. If your tree shows one or more of the following symptoms, it may be "stressed out."

- Slow growth
- Sparse, distorted, or yellowing leaves
- Brown leaf edges
- Early fall color and/or leaf drop
- Bud, twig, or branch dieback

In some cases, these symptoms are caused by insects or diseases. Look closely at the tree for evidence of insect infestation. If you can't see any obvious signs, you may want to take a sample of the plant part showing symptoms to your extension agent or to a local plant clinic. If there isn't a specific disease or insect causing your problem, your plant may be suffering from the syndrome called tree decline.

Decline is a general term that refers to a progressive loss of vigor not caused by any specific disease or disorder. It's usually the result of one or more stress factors affecting a plant over a number of years, although it may also be caused by a single stressful event (such as a severe injury).

Trees are subject to many types of stress, which may or may not be apparent. Some problems, such as defoliation by insects, are easy to see. But it may take the eye of a trained observer to diagnose nutrient deficiencies, salt damage, and water stress. Root-zone problems such as soil compaction (leading to poor root development) or the severing of roots during excavations may also be less than obvious. Other causes of stress include lawn mower damage, scraping or filling around tree roots, and air pollution.

Although there's no single explanation of why decline occurs, development of the syndrome often follows a general sequence. Initially, stress factors leave the tree unable to respond to its environment, lowering its resistance to disease and insect pests. If the original problem isn't corrected, and an additional stress factor occurs, the combined effects may cause further distress symptoms and could lead to death. For example, if a late frost damages a tree's leaves, it should produce new leaves and continue to grow normally. However, if insects defoliate the tree in the same year, it may not have the energy to leaf out again and will die. The ability to deal with stress varies from plant to plant. Some plants may be especially prone to certain problems; others, such as older trees, are usually less resilient.

---

of room, encouraging native populations of beneficial insects, and not feeding excessively. If a strong jet of water doesn't control aphids, try insecticidal soap or summer oil sprays, except on Japanese maple, on which you should use pyrethrin/rotenone.

Holes in Trunks or Limbs; Bark Darkens; Limbs Die or Break Off

A variety of borers tunnel into maple trunks and limbs. Tunnel entrances may be surrounded by gummy sap. Bark darkens and dies. Infested limbs may die; they are the first to break off in severe weather. Serious infestations may kill the tree. Borers are most likely to attack trees already weakened by fungal diseases or stress. If possible, prune out damaged wood and burn or destroy it to stop the infestation cycle. Also gather and burn or discard fallen twigs, which may be infested. Increase fertility and watering to build the tree's overall health and vigor. Where pruning isn't an option, kill the borers in their tun-

If your tree is suffering and you can't trace the cause to a specific disease or insect, review the list of stress factors to see if any apply in your situation. A soil test can tell you if your tree needs to be fed. It is easy to remedy a nutrient deficiency or lack of water, and the tree should recover if it has not developed other problems in the meantime. Other factors, such as mechanical root damage or exposure to de-icing salts may not be avoidable. Preventing stress is the easiest way to keep your trees healthy. Use the following guidelines to keep your trees from becoming stressed out.

❧ **Use plants adapted to your site.** If a tree is not fully hardy in your area, it will probably not grow as well as it should. Many trees are adaptable to a variety of soil and light conditions, but make sure that you meet any conditions that they specifically require.

❧ **Use plants that are resistant to diseases and insects.** Plant trees that are naturally resistant or less susceptible to attack by insects and diseases. Maples, oaks, and dogwoods are common trees that are often affected by decline. See "The Trouble-Free Trees and Shrubs," on page 388, for some suggestions, or ask your nursery owner for local recommendations.

❧ **Keep in mind the space you have available.** Besides looking awkward, a large tree in a small yard may interfere with power lines and require major pruning regularly, which can open it up to attack by diseases or insects. Planting a tree too close to the street may subject it to root-zone problems such as construction damage or to soil compaction from foot traffic.

❧ **Avoid scraping and filling around tree roots.** This is a special problem on new construction sites. Dumping topsoil over tree roots to change the surrounding grade cuts off vital oxygen and water supplies to the trees. If you have a tree that you particularly want to save, you may want to alert the construction company of your intention. You should also fence off the desirable trees to keep loose fill and heavy trucks away from the drip line. If the damage has already been done, removing some of the added soil and aerating the roots may be necessary.

❧ **Use tree guards on young plants.** Wrapping or covering the trunk is the easiest way to avoid damage from animals, lawn mowers, or string trimmers.

❧ **Use good cultural practices.** Proper planting techniques will get your new trees off to a good start. Mulching and regular watering can also help young trees. Fertilizing when necessary will avoid stress due to nutrient deficiencies.

nels with a flexible wire, or inject parasitic nematodes into the entry holes, then plug the holes with putty.

Holes in Leaves, Flowers, or Fruit

Boxelder bugs are brownish black, $1/2$-in. bugs with red markings. Nymphs are bright red. These bugs chew holes in leaves, flowers, or fruit. Boxelder bugs gather on bark and branches in fall; spray with summer oil or insecticidal soap when pests first appear. Don't spray oil or insecticidal soap on Japanese maples, as it may cause foliar damage.

Tiny, Wartlike Growths on Leaves; Leaves Distorted

Several different mites cause galls on maple leaves. Infested leaves have wartlike lumps or small projections that resemble pencil points. Galls may be green, red, purple, or pink. Severely infested leaves are distorted. Although unsightly, galls do not seriously threaten tree health. Spray with dormant oil just before leaf buds open in spring. A dormant spray of lime sulfur is also effective.

Plants Weaken; Cottony Masses on Leaves or Twigs

Both maple phenacoccus scale and cottony maple scale look like cottony masses on leaves and twigs. These pests suck sap from stems and leaves, causing plants to weaken. Leaves may turn yellow and drop. Many native beneficial insects feed on scales. Apply dormant oil spray to control scales in late winter or early spring. Spray insecticidal soap or summer oil in spring when buds burst to control immature scale, called crawlers; repeat in midsummer. Don't spray insecticidal soap or summer oil on Japanese maples, as it may damage foliage.

Disease Control

Sunken Spots or Blotches on Leaves

Anthracnose is a fungal disease that causes brown spots or blotches on leaves; spots run together and give leaves a scorched appearance. Feed and water infected trees to help them fight the disease. Clean up infected foliage in fall. Spray trees with bordeaux mix when the problem occurs.

Seeping Lesions on Branches and/or Trunk

Several fungi cause cankers on maples. Cankers, from which sap oozes, appear at the base of the trunk or on twigs and branches. Cankers can girdle and kill branches or the entire tree. Other symptoms include wilting, dieback, and a thinning crown. Infected inner bark is red-brown. Preventive measures are useful: Plant maples in well-drained soil rich in organic matter; avoid damaging the trunk with lawn mowers and other equipment; treat injuries promptly if they occur; and keep trees healthy and well watered. Remove and destroy branches killed by cankers. If possible, cut out infected tissue on the trunk and carve away 2 in. of healthy bark from the perimeter of the infected area. Heavily infected trees should be cut and burned.

Sudden Wilting of One Part of Tree

Verticillium wilt causes leaves on a single branch or one side of the tree to wilt suddenly. Leaves on infected plants may be yellowish or small; infected trees may die suddenly or slowly. The fungi that cause the disease are soil-borne. Cut and burn diseased branches. Feed the sick tree with a high-nitrogen fertilizer such as blood meal to promote growth; the tree will seal off infected areas. Dig a narrow 36–40-in.-deep trench between infected and healthy maple trees to cut any root grafts, and then immediately backfill the trench. If the entire tree is diseased, remove the tree along with its root system. Don't plant another maple in the infected soil. Good fertility and thorough watering help trees resist infection.

Albizia julibrissin   Mimosa

Fertilizing

Feed balanced organic fertilizer in late fall or spring as needed.

Insect Control

See "35 Common Garden Pests," on page 230, for additional information and control measures for the insect problems listed below.

Leaves Yellowed

Psyllids are small, jumping insects resembling tiny cicadas with whitish, waxy filaments. They suck sap, causing leaves to discolor and cup, and plants to weaken. Sooty mold may accumulate on the honeydew they secrete. Unless there are more than 25 psyllids per tip, no control is necessary; if populations warrant, spray with insecticidal soap.

Webs on Branches; Leaves Skeletonized

Webworms feed at the tips of branches under the protection of webs. Leaves in webs are tied together with silk and skeletonized.

Control webworms with a strong spray of BTK (*Bacillus thuringiensis* var. *kurstaki*) as soon as webs appear; repeat every week until feeding stops.

Disease Control
Leaves Wilt and Shrivel; Branches Die

Mimosa wilt is a fungal disease with no cure. The leaves on branches of afficted trees wilt and shrivel, but may remain green or yellow-green for a time. The leaves eventually fall and branches die. Remove and burn infected trees. Don't plant mimosas if you live in an area where the disease is prevalent. Wilt-resistant cultivars have been introduced.

Alnus spp.

Alder

Fertilizing

Feed balanced organic fertilizer in late fall or spring as needed.

Insect Control

See "35 Common Garden Pests," on page 230, for additional information and control measures for the insect problems listed below.

Leaves Yellowed; Plants Weakened

Yellowed, stunted plants. Aphids suck sap from leaves, stems, and blossoms, causing foliage to curl, pucker, and turn yellow. Leaves and buds may become stunted. Aphids produce honeydew, which will drip from tree branches and encourage the growth of sooty mold. Encourage populations of native beneficial insects and avoid feeding excessively. Control aphid infestations with high-pressure water sprays or insecticidal soap as necessary; dormant oil before budbreak in spring smothers aphid eggs.

Plants weaken; bumps on twigs. Scales suck sap from stems, twigs, and leaves, causing plants to weaken. Leaves may turn yellow and drop. Adult scales look like many whitish to dark brown bumps on stems. When natural enemies don't control scales, treat with dormant oil spray in late winter or spring for several consecutive years. Use insecticidal soap to control immature scales, called crawlers, in early spring.

Mottled leaves. Adult and nymph lace bugs suck sap from leaves, leaving brown excrement on leaf undersides. Upper surfaces of leaves become pale and mottled. Control serious lace bug infestations with insecticidal soap.

Holes in Trunk; Bark Darkens

Flatheaded borer larvae tunnel into wood of trunks. Tunnel entrances may be surrounded by gummy sap. Bark darkens and dies. In severe instances, trees may be killed. Flatheaded borers attack weak trees that aren't receiving enough

(continued on page 374)

Disease Look-Alikes

Diagnosing insects and disease problems on trees and shrubs is not easy, especially on mature trees. When you're searching for the cause of discolored foliage, dying branch tips, or other symptoms, don't overlook the fact that many environmental factors can affect a tree's health. You can often adjust environmental factors to provide a tree with the best conditions possible. By being aware of potential problems, you can help your trees deal with those factors that can't be avoided.

Salt injury. Salt is extremely harmful to plants and comes from many sources. Trees that grow near the ocean are often subjected to blowing salt spray. Strong winds can carry the salt for long distances, damaging the leaves of plants far inland. Trees can also be damaged by the salt applied to streets and sidewalks to melt ice and snow. De-icing salt can hurt trees in two ways: Salt spray blown up from passing cars can damage foliage, and salt-laden melt-water can produce toxic conditions around the roots. Even your pets could be harming your trees! This condition, known as dog injury, happens when soluble salts from urine enter the soil and burn the roots.

Symptoms of salt injury include brown leaf edges, early leaf drop, shoot dieback, and possibly death. If the damage occurs in winter, salt can destroy buds and delay spring leafing-out. Obviously, there is no way to control damage from ocean salt, but there are trees and shrubs that grow well in seaside gardens—ask your local extension agent or nursery owner for recommendations. Protect trees along roads by erecting a barrier to deflect salt spray from cars. Use sand or sawdust instead of salt to improve traction on slippery sidewalks. If dog injury is your problem, either screen off the area or have a talk with your dog. When planting trees or shrubs along streets and walkways, consider using salt-tolerant species, such as red oak and white ash, and avoid intolerant species like beech, hemlock, white pine, and sugar maple.

Nutrient deficiency. These symptoms vary widely, depending on what is lacking, but they often include leaf yellowing and stunted growth. (For more information, see "Plant Symp-toms of Mineral Imbalances" on page 64.) Some trees are more susceptible to certain deficiencies than others. For example, eastern pin oaks, river birch, and construction-damaged trees are prone to iron deficiency. A soil test can tell you what nutrients are lacking, and it will recommend the type and amount of correcting agent to add. Overall, trees growing in soils that are high in organic matter are less likely to lack nutrients.

Water deficiency. Drought conditions are, of course, the most common cause of water stress. In some cases, though, trees can be harmed by a lack of water even if there is abundant rainfall. If the tree is surrounded by impervious substances such as pavement, water won't be able to enter the soil. Tree roots that are cut or damaged may not be able to transmit water to the leaves. Or, a steep grade around a tree may encourage water to run off before it's absorbed by the soil.

Water deficiency symptoms include leaf scorch (browning of leaf edges), leaf wilting, and sparse foliage. Stem wilting, early fruit and leaf drop, and the death of twigs and branches may be followed by the death of the whole tree. If you can provide water before the tree is too far gone, it should eventually recover. Punching holes in the root area with a soil auger will help water get to the roots more quickly. When you water, also remember that slow soakings, several times a week, if necessary, are better than one sudden flooding.

Winter injury. This problem is generally caused by rapid temperature changes or late spring freezes, but seldom by excessive cold alone. Evergreens such as boxwood, fir, holly, laurel, pine, rhododendrons, and spruce are especially susceptible. Unlike deciduous plants, which lose their leaves in winter, evergreens lose water through the pores in their leaf surfaces all year. Water loss increases when plants are subjected to drying winds. Sudden warm spells when the ground is still frozen can also be a problem. The leaves will respond to the warmth by opening their pores, but the roots will only be able to draw limited water from the frozen ground. When the roots cannot keep up with the demand, the leaves will turn brown, wilt, and die. Terminal buds will become brittle and snap easily when bent.

If your plants already show these symptoms, there is not much you can do besides pruning out the dead wood in the spring. Preventing the damage is the best course of action. Any practice that promotes good root growth will help the plant meet its water needs. A heavy mulch will prevent deep freezing and facilitate water absorption by the roots. Soaking the soil around your evergreens before freezing weather sets in will make water available to the roots when they need it. Spraying the leaves of evergreens with an antitranspirant such as Wilt-Pruf will cut down on water loss and minimize winter injury. You should also avoid placing susceptible plants where they will be exposed to wind. Protect established plants by setting up a burlap cloth shelter in late fall or by planting an evergreen windbreak.

Girdling roots. Under normal conditions, tree roots grow away from the trunk, spreading out in search of water and nutrients. But sometimes, a root wraps around the trunk or another root, strangling it and causing a slow decline and possibly death of the tree. An afflicted tree may have leaves that are smaller than normal or show early fall color. Often, only one branch or side of an afflicted tree will show symptoms. Aboveground, a girdled root will look like a thick coil wrapped around the trunk at ground level. If you can see that your trunk has a girdling root, carefully remove it with a saw, axe, or chisel. In the case of below-ground girdling roots, you probably won't recognize the cause of the problem until it's too late.

One common cause of girdling roots is trees that are kept in a container too long. You may want to check the root system of a container-grown plant before you buy it. If there are many roots circling around the base of the pot, they may continue to grow that way when the tree is planted. When setting out a container-grown tree, any roots that are growing on the outside of the root ball can be cut with a knife or teased out with your fingers to encourage lateral growth. Dig a proper-size planting hole, too—don't cram the roots into a tiny area. If the tree is planted along a foundation or street, the roots will grow out until they hit a barrier and may double back on themselves in search of more favorable conditions.

Lawn mower and string trimmer injury. These tools pose a significant hazard to young trees and to older trees with thin bark. When a lawn mower hits into a tree, it can cut a thin horizontal groove into the bark near ground level. If this happens once or twice the plant will probably recover, but hitting the trunk repeatedly during the lawn-mowing season may kill the tree. Lawn mower blades can also damage surface roots. String trimmer damage is another common affliction. These machines are small and seem well suited to cutting grass in inaccessible areas, like around tree trunks. However, don't use them to trim grass around unprotected trees. Using these trimmers carelessly can strip the bark from the base of the trunk and lead to the death of the tree. Even if the damage itself is not enough to kill the plant, it provides easy access for disease organisms. If you are not willing to trim around trees by hand, consider putting plastic guards around the base of your trees to protect tender bark.

Other problems. There are additional factors that can damage your trees, and, unfortunately, many are uncontrollable. A sudden yellowing and dieback of your tree may indicate a broken or leaking gas main. Lightning can also destroy your trees. Damage may not be visible immediately, but the tree may die several months later due to internal burns. Herbicide damage can be caused by spray drift from neighboring properties. Air pollution can also cause damage, especially if you live in an urban or industrial area.

A sick-looking tree may be affected by its surroundings and not by disease or insects. But, you should be aware that a tree weakened by environmental stress is more susceptible to these factors, so treating for a pest problem may not "cure" the tree if it is still being adversely affected by its environment. While keeping your trees healthy may seem difficult, remember that trees are tough, adaptable plants. By being aware of potential problems and common symptoms, you can protect your trees and help them grow to their potential.

water or nutrients. Prune in late fall or early winter so wounds can heal before beetles become active. If possible, prune out damaged wood and burn or destroy it to stop the infestation cycle.

Plants Defoliated, Tents in Branch Crotches

Tent caterpillars hide in silken tents that they spin in branch crotches. Eastern tent caterpillars are hairy, black, 2-in. caterpillars with narrow brown and yellow lines and blue spots along their sides. Western tent caterpillars are orange-brown with blue dots on their backs and sides. On dry days, the caterpillars emerge from their nests to feed. The caterpillars chew on leaves, typically leaving only a dry leaf "skeleton."

They return to their tents during cool, wet weather and in the evening. Prune and destroy nests during these times. Apply BTK (*Bacillus thuringiensis* var. *kurstaki*) in early summer when eggs are first hatching.

Disease Control

Seeping Lesions on Branches; Dieback

Several fungi cause cankers, which can girdle and kill twigs and branches. Afflicted branches may wilt and die. Keep trees healthy and well watered. Remove and destroy branches killed by cankers. Heavily infected trees should be cut and burned.

Betula spp.

Birch

Fertilizing

Apply balanced organic fertilizer every other fall or early spring as necessary.

Insect Control

See "35 Common Garden Pests," on page 230, for additional information and control measures for the insect problems listed below.

Yellow Foliage

Foliage curls, puckers, and turns yellow. Aphids suck sap from leaves, stems, and blossoms, causing foliage to curl, pucker, and turn yellow. Leaves and buds may become stunted.

Foliage may be covered by honeydew, which encourages sooty mold. Aphids may indicate too much nitrogen fertilizer or excessive pruning, which creates lots of succulent new growth. Encourage populations of native beneficial insects. Spray with a strong jet of water or with insecticidal soap. Apply dormant oil in late winter before budbreak to smother overwintering eggs.

Yellowed foliage; lumpy bark. Bronze birch borer larvae bore winding tunnels under the bark of the trunk, eventually girdling the trunk. The trunk swells around tunnels, creating lumps under the bark. Leaves may be yellowed and sparse. Heavily infested plants will eventually die. Plant birches in moist soil rich in organic matter; provide good fertility and water deeply to help the tree withstand damage. If possible, prune out damaged wood and burn or destroy it to stop the infection cycle. River birch (*Betula nigra*) and monarch birch (*B. maximowicziana*) are resistant to bronze birch borers.

Plants weaken; bumps on twigs. Scales suck sap from stems, twigs, and leaves, causing plants to weaken. Leaves may turn yellow and drop. Adult scales look like many whitish to dark brown bumps on stems. Spray lime sulfur or dormant oil just before bud break to control scales.

Leaves Covered with Tan to Brown Blotches; Serpentine Tunnels in Leaves

Birch leafminer larvae tunnel through leaves, feeding on plant tissue. Leaves may turn brown and collapse. Leafminers may cause leaves to fall prematurely. Although new leaves usually regrow, the damage stresses the tree. Use summer oil, neem extract, or rotenone, if necessary, to control severe infestations. Use yellow sticky traps to monitor emergence of adults (small, black sawflies) to help time sprays; sprays are only effective on adults or before the larvae tunnel into the leaves.

Leaves Skeletonized

Birch skeletonizers are yellowish green, $1/4$-in. caterpillars. Adults are moths with white-lined brown wings and $3/8$-in. wingspans. Larvae chew the undersides of leaves, which then turn brown. BTK (*Bacillus thuringiensis* var. *kurstaki*) or summer oil works against skeletonizers, especially if applied as soon as pests appear in midsummer.

Plants Defoliated; Tents in Branch Crotches

Tent caterpillars spin silken tents in crotches and emerge on dry days to feed on leaves. East-ern tent caterpillars are hairy, black, 2-in. caterpillars with narrow brown and yellow lines and blue spots along their sides. Western caterpillars are orange-brown with blue dots on their backs and sides. The caterpillars are 2 in. long. Adult moths are reddish or pale brown with $1 1/4$-in. wingspans. Caterpillars chew holes in leaves, often skeletonizing them. Tent caterpillars return to their tents during cool, wet weather or in the evening; to control them, prune and destroy the nests during these times. Apply BTK in early summer when eggs are first hatching.

Disease Control

Swollen, Cracked Lesions at Branch Crotches or on Trunks

Canker is a fungal disease that attacks birches at the branches near the forks or on the trunks. Infected wood swells and cracks open; a thickened callus may form around the infected area. Cankers on trunks cause flattened or bent areas. Cankers can girdle and kill branches or entire trees. Preventive measures are useful: Plant birches in well-drained soil rich in organic matter, avoid damaging the trunk with mowers and other equipment, and keep trees healthy and well watered. Remove and destroy branches killed by cankers. Heavily infected trees should be cut and burned.

Branches Die Back

Birches whose branches gradually die over a single season or several seasons may be infected with dieback, a fungus disease with symptoms similar to those of bronze birch borer. Preventive measures are best. Plant birches in well-drained soil rich in organic matter, keep plants well watered during drought, and prune out infected branches and burn them to stop the spread of the fungus.

Buxus spp.

Boxwood

Fertilizing

Apply balanced organic fertilizer in early spring as needed.

Insect Control

See "35 Common Garden Pests," on page 230, for additional information and control measures for the insect problems listed below.

Yellow Foliage

Plants weaken; bumps on stems and leaves. Scales suck sap from stems and leaves, causing plants to weaken. Leaves may turn yellow and drop. Adult scales look like many whitish to dark brown bumps on stems and leaves. Spray with dormant oil or lime sulfur during late winter when plants are dormant to kill overwintering scales. Remove badly infested growth. Spray immature scales, called crawlers, in spring with insecticidal soap.

Leaves yellowed. Psyllids are small jumping insects resembling tiny cicadas with whitish, waxy filaments. They suck sap, causing leaves to discolor and cup, and plants to weaken. Sooty mold may accumulate on the honeydew they secrete. If boxwood psyllids become a problem, spray with insecticidal soap.

Leaves stippled with tiny yellow dots; webby foliage. Spider mites suck sap from leaves, causing them to become stippled. Leaves may appear distorted. Webs may be present. Control overwintering eggs of spider mites with dormant oil spray applied in late winter just before buds break. In summer, spray plants with a strong jet of water or with insecticidal soap to control pests. For severe infestations, spray with abamectin, neem, pyrethrin, or rotenone.

Water-Soaked Blotches on Undersides of Leaves

Boxwood leafminers larvae tunnel through leaves, feeding on plant tissue. Leaves may turn brown and collapse. Control boxwood leafminers with neem extract or summer oil. To be effective, sprays must be timed for when adults emerge in spring. Use yellow sticky traps to monitor emergence of leafminer midges to help time sprays.

Disease Control

Dead Twigs; Leaf and Twig Dieback; Browned Foliage

Both sunscald and winter damage from cold temperatures cause diseaselike symptoms in boxwoods. New growth produced too late in fall and growth produced too early in spring are most susceptible to cold damage. Cold, dry winter winds can turn leaves brown or red. This is especially a problem on warm days in winter when the ground is frozen and roots can't take up enough water to replace that lost through the foliage. Cultural controls are effective: Discourage late-season growth by fertilizing in spring or very late fall after plants are dormant, mulch plants heavily in fall, and don't plant boxwoods in windy areas. In the North, provide protection in winter with burlap windbreaks or spray with an antidesiccant such as Wilt-Pruf.

Leaves Pale; Lesions on Leaves and Stems

Canker causes leaves to turn pale green, then tan, and curl upward; small, pink, waxy pustules may be present. Bark at the base of branches peels off easily and the wood underneath is gray or black. New growth is delayed and weak. Prune away dead branches; cut out small cankers. Burn infected trimmings and leaves, or put them out in sealed containers for disposal. Spray in spring, midseason, and autumn with lime sulfur or bordeaux mix. Thoroughly clean up all fallen leaves and those in branch crotches.

Leaves Bronzed; Growth Stunted; Lack of Vigor

Feeding by nematodes causes leaves to turn bronze; growth may be stunted and weak. Roots develop galls and die; root system may be densely branched and stunted. Treat soil with parasitic nematodes or with a chitin source; increase humus content.

Shrubs Wilted; Foliage Yellows

Boxwoods afflicted with root rot wilt suddenly; leaves will turn yellow, and the plants die. There is no cure once the disease attacks; remove and destroy rotted shrubs. Plant boxwoods in well-drained soil rich in organic matter. Solarize the soil and improve drainage by adding organic matter before replanting.

Camellia spp.

Camellia

Fertilizing

Apply acidifying fertilizer such as cottonseed meal about 6 weeks after blooming or in late summer. Don't overfeed.

Insect Control

See "35 Common Garden Pests," on page 230, for additional information and control measures for the insect problems listed below.

Foliage Curls, Puckers, and Turns Yellow

Aphids suck sap from leaves, stems, and blossoms, causing foliage to curl, pucker, and turn yellow. Leaves and buds may become stunted. Foliage may be covered by honeydew, which encourages sooty mold. Avoid excessive nitrogen fertilizer and overpruning. Both can create lots of succulent new growth that will attract aphids. Spray with a strong jet of water. En-courage populations of native beneficial insects. Summer oil sprays will also control aphids.

Plants Weaken; Bumps on Leaves and Twigs

Scales suck sap from stems and leaves, causing plants to weaken. Leaves may turn yellow and drop. Adult scales look like many whitish to dark brown bumps on stems. Spray lime sulfur or dormant oil to smother overwintering scales during dormant period. Prune out badly infested growth.

Stippled Leaves; Stunted Growth

Southern red mites, a species of spider mite, suck sap from plant tissues, causing speckled foliage, weakened plants, and stunted growth. Control overwintering eggs of spider mites with dormant oil spray applied in late winter. In summer, spray plants with a strong jet of water to control pests. For severe infestations, spray with abamectin, neem, pyrethrin, or rotenone.

Disease Control

Flowers Turn Brown and Fall Off

Flower blight causes flowers to develop brown spots; veins may be dark. Spots enlarge, turning the whole flower brown, which then drops. The rest of the plant is unaffected. Preventive measures are effective for controlling this fungal disease: Pick off all flower buds as they fade; mulch plants heavily with wood chips (3-in. layer) to prevent fungal spores from moving from soil to plants. Carefully remove infected plant parts, including all fallen flower buds. If blight has been a past problem, use a preventive spray of bordeaux mix in the spring. To avoid bringing the fungus into the garden, plant only bare-root camellias and pick off all flower buds showing color before planting.

Leaves Mottled with Yellow

Infection by camellia yellow spot virus causes leaves and flowers to become flecked, striped, or spotted with white or yellow. Afflicted plants are more susceptible to sun scorch than uninfected ones. The virus is transmitted when plants are grafted. There is no cure once plants are infected; dig and destroy them. Spraying plants with chelated iron can camouflage symptoms.

Leaves Wilt; Stem Browns

Canker is a fungal disease that causes leaves to wilt and brown and branch tips to die back. Stems dry and turn brown. The fungus enters through wounds, such as those caused by poor pruning, frost cracks, or a bad graft. Cut away any injured or weak branches. Spray with copper fungicide or bordeaux mix in late winter or early spring to prevent further infection.

Leaves Small and Yellow; Roots and Branches Die

Plants affected by root rot have leaves that are dwarfed and yellowed, and that eventually fall. Branches may die. Roots decay; lesions may form near soil line. Prevention is the best approach. Plant camellias in well-drained soil rich in organic matter.

Cornus spp.   Dogwood

Fertilizing

Apply balanced organic fertilizer in early spring or late fall as needed.

Insect Control

See "35 Common Garden Pests," on page 230, for additional information and control measures for the insect problems listed below.

Yellow Foliage

Foliage curls, puckers, and turns yellow. Aphids suck sap from leaves, stems, and blossoms, causing foliage to curl, pucker, and turn yellow. Leaves and buds may become stunted. Foliage may be covered by honeydew, which encourages sooty mold. Aphids may indicate too much nitrogen fertilizer or excessive pruning, which creates lots of succulent new growth. Encourage populations of native beneficial insects. Spray with a strong jet of water or with insecticidal soap. Apply dormant oil in late winter before budbreak to smother overwintering eggs.

Plants weaken; bumps on twigs. Scales suck sap from stems, twigs, and leaves, causing plants to weaken. Leaves may turn yellow and drop. Adult scales look like many whitish to dark brown bumps on stems. Dormant oil or lime sulfur spray works against scales when applied in late winter while plants are still dormant. Apply summer oil or insecticidal soap in spring as buds burst to control immature scales, called crawlers. Repeat in the summer.

Bark Falls off Trees; Twigs and Branches Die

Several species of borers attack dogwoods. Adult dogwood borers are 1-in., wasplike moths with clear, blue-black wings marked with yellow; they lay their eggs on tree bark. The light brown larvae enter the tree through wounds or scars in the bark or at limb crotches and tunnel through the sapwood. Full-grown larvae are white with pale brown heads. Afflicted trees lose their bark; twigs and branches die back from ends. Dogwood borers attack new transplants; wrap entire trunk of young dogwoods with burlap wrap or other barrier for first 2 or 3 years to prevent borers from gaining entry. Cut out borers with a sharp knife. Use preventive measures to discourage borers: Water trees well and provide good fertility, don't damage trunks with the lawn mower, and protect trees from deer and rabbit injury.

Distorted Twigs with Galls or Swollen Areas

Gall midges are gnatlike, $1/4$–$1/8$-in., red-brown midges with long legs and antennae. Their whitish or pale orange larvae enter twigs in midspring and cause pimple- or wartlike galls to form. Leaves may become distorted, wilted, or brown. Plants may become dwarfed. Remove and destroy galls before the eggs hatch.

Disease Control

In addition to the diseases listed below, decline has become a serious problem for flowering dogwoods (*Cornus florida*). Recently, the problem has appeared on kousa dogwoods (*C. kousa*), formerly thought to be immune. For more on this syndrome, see "Tree Stress: Symptoms and Solutions" on page 368.

Sunken Black Spots on Leaves

Anthracnose may appear as moist, sunken, black spots along veins on leaves; leaves may fall. The fungus may also affect terminal shoots where pink spores may be present; twigs may die back. Other fungi cause yellow, brown, or black spots on leaves, but are controlled in the same way as anthracnose. Keep dogwoods healthy with regular watering and feeding. Prune away infected branches and twigs and carefully clean up and destroy all debris in fall. Prune off watersprouts. Be sure plants aren't in complete shade, where leaves are more likely to remain constantly moist. Spraying lime sulfur or bordeaux mix during dormancy may give some control.

Leaves Small, Light Green; Swollen Growth on Lower Trunks or Roots

Crown canker, especially on newly transplanted trees, appears as small, light green leaves, which turn red earlier than normal in late summer. Twigs and branches die. A canker develops on the lower trunk or on main roots; this will eventually girdle the tree and kill it. This fungal disease strikes already weak or injured trees; avoid mechanical injury, such as by lawn mowers, and take steps to prevent borer infestation.

Leaves and Growing Tips Shriveled

Dieback is a fungal disease that causes leaves to discolor at the margins or tips and spots to develop. Leaf stalks and twigs also become infected. Prune out afflicted stems. Bordeaux mix is effective if applied at the first sign of the disease as new leaves emerge.

Cotoneaster spp.

Cotoneaster

Fertilizing

Cotoneaster is a light feeder. If necessary, apply balanced organic fertilizer in early spring or late fall.

Insect Control

See "35 Common Garden Pests," on page 230, for additional information and control measures for the insect problems listed below.

Yellowed Foliage; Weakened Plants; Bumps on Twigs

Scales suck sap from stems and leaves, causing plants to weaken. Leaves may turn yellow and drop. Adult scales look like many whitish to dark brown bumps on stems. Prune out severely infested limbs. Apply dormant oil sprays in late winter when plants are dormant; for serious infestations, apply for several consecutive winters. Insecticidal soap in mid-May and again in June helps control immature scales, called crawlers.

Pale, Mottled Leaves

Adult and nymph lace bugs suck sap from leaves, leaving brown excrement on leaf undersides. Upper surfaces of leaves become pale and mottled. Avoid excessive nitrogen fertilization because it can aggravate the problem. Use yellow sticky traps to monitor populations. Spray upper and lower surfaces of leaves with insecticidal soap as soon as nymphs are seen in spring.

Red or Brown Spots on Leaves

Pear leaf blister mite feeding causes $1/8$-in., red or brown, thickened or raised blisters on leaves. Mites overwinter on buds and infest new leaves as they appear in spring. Spray plants with lime sulfur in late winter when plants are dormant. For severe infestations, spray with abamectin, neem, pyrethrin, or rotenone.

Disease Control

Leaves, Flowers, and Branches Blackened

Fire blight is a bacterial disease that causes flowers and new leaves to suddenly wilt and turn blackish; these remain on branches. Bark of affected branches becomes dark brown or purple and sunken; cracks may be noticeable around diseased area. Brown ooze may be present. Good air circulation and careful pruning help prevent the disease. Don't overfertilize, since the disease quickly infects lush new growth. If disease does occur, remove infected limbs, cutting at least 6 in. beyond the discolored area, and spray copper or bordeaux mix the following spring during blossoming.

Crataegus spp.

Hawthorn

Fertilizing

Hawthorn is a light feeder. Feed with balanced organic fertilizer or well-rotted compost in spring or late fall as needed.

Insect Control

See "35 Common Garden Pests," on page 230, for additional information and control measures for the insect problems listed below.

Foliage Curls, Puckers, and Turns Yellow

Aphids suck sap from leaves, stems, and blossoms, causing foliage to curl, pucker, and turn yellow. Leaves and buds may become stunted. Aphids produce honeydew, which will drip from tree branches and encourage the growth of sooty mold. Aphids may indicate too much nitrogen fertilizer or excessive pruning, which creates lots of succulent new growth. Control aphid infestations with high-pressure water sprays or insecticidal soap as necessary; dormant oil before budbreak in spring smothers aphid eggs. Encourage populations of native beneficial insects.

Leaf Spots

Mottled leaves. Adult and nymph lace bugs suck sap from leaves, leaving brown excrement on leaf undersides. Upper surfaces of leaves become pale and mottled. Spray with insecticidal soap or pyrethrin as soon as lace bugs appear. Be sure to spray the undersides of leaves.

Leaves stippled with tiny yellow dots; webby foliage. Spider mites suck sap from leaves, causing them to become stippled. Leaves may appear distorted. Webs may be present. Control overwintering eggs of spider mites with dormant oil spray applied in late winter just before buds break. In summer, spray plants with a strong jet of water or with insecticidal soap to control pests. For severe infestations, spray with abamectin, neem, pyrethrin, or rotenone.

Plants Defoliated; Tents in Branch Crotches

Tent caterpillars spin silken tents in crotches and emerge on dry days to feed on leaves. Eastern tent caterpillars are hairy, black, 2-in. caterpillars with narrow brown and yellow lines and blue spots along their sides. Western ones are orange-brown with blue dots on their backs and sides. The caterpillars are 2 in. long. Adult moths are reddish or pale brown with 1¼-in. wingspans.

Caterpillars chew holes in leaves, often skeletonizing them. Tent caterpillars return to their tents during cool, wet weather or in the evening; to control them, prune and destroy the nests during these times. BTK (*Bacillus thuringiensis* var. *kurstaki*) applied in early summer when eggs are first hatching is an effective control.

Disease Control

Leaves, Flowers, and Branches Blackened

Fire blight is a bacterial disease that causes flowers and new leaves to suddenly wilt and turn blackish; these remain on branches. Bark of affected branches becomes dark brown or purple and sunken; cracks may be noticeable around diseased area. Brown ooze may be present. Careful cleanup, good air circulation, and reduced nitrogen fertilizing are helpful. Prune away all blighted twigs and branches, at least 6 in. beyond infection. Use a pruning knife to carve away cankered bark down to healthy wood. Be sure to disinfect tools in a household bleach solution (1 part bleach to 9 parts water) as you work. Spray with bordeaux mix the following spring to help prevent recurrence on new growth.

Spots on Leaves; Blighted Foliage

Several fungi cause spots on hawthorn leaves. Spots may run together and entire leaves may become blighted. Fruit sometimes becomes spotted. Fungi overwinter on fallen leaves; clean up and dispose of leaves in fall. If leaf spot has been severe the previous season, control with copper fungicide at bud break and again 10 days later.

Twigs, Leaves, and Fruit Deformed; Orange Spores

Several rust fungi attack leaves and fruit, causing defoliation and deformation of fruit and twigs. Leaves may have orange-red, gray, or brown pustules. Orange spores may be noticeable; fruit may have white, elongated formations on them. If possible, control rust by removing

junipers and other host plants from within several hundred yards of hawthorns. Apply copper or wettable sulfur every 10 days beginning at bud break and continuing for 4 or 5 weeks.

Euonymus spp.

Euonymus

Fertilizing

Apply balanced organic fertilizer every spring as needed to speed growth.

Insect Control

See "35 Common Garden Pests," on page 230, for additional information and control measures for the insect problem listed below.

Plants Weaken; Yellowed Foliage; Bumps on Stems and Leaves

Several scale species suck sap from stems and leaves, causing plants to weaken. Leaves may turn yellow and drop. Adult scales look like many whitish to dark brown bumps on stems and leaves. Treat scales by pruning away heavily infested parts and spraying dormant oil or lime sulfur in late winter or early spring. Follow up with an application of summer oil or insecticidal soap in early summer to control immature scales, called crawlers.

Disease Control

Tumorlike Swellings on Roots, Trunks, or Branches

Crown gall causes tumorlike swellings with irregular rough surfaces to form on roots and stems. Bacteria enter through wounds, so prune carefully; disinfect pruning shears in a household bleach solution (1 part bleach to 9 parts water) before working on undiseased plants. Avoid damaging shrubs with lawn mowers or string trimmers. Inspect plants at purchase and buy only healthy stock. For mild infestations, prune away diseased growth; destroy severely infected plants and wait several years before replanting susceptible plants in that location.

White Powdery Covering on Leaves

Powdery mildew is a fungal disease that causes a white powdery covering to form on leaves. Keep plants properly pruned to allow good air circulation around foliage. Use sulfur sprays to reduce infections.

Fagus spp.

Beech

Fertilizing

Apply balanced organic fertilizer every other fall or early spring as needed.

Insect Control

See "35 Common Garden Pests," on page 230, for additional information and control measures for the insect problems listed below.

Clusters of White Bumps on Trunks and Branches; Plants Weaken

Trees that have groupings of tiny white scale insects clustered on lower branches and the trunk are infested with beech scale. Scales suck sap from plants, causing them to weaken. Scales are a particular problem on beech; infestations lead to beech bark disease. Spray branches and the trunk with lime sulfur during late winter to kill overwintering eggs; avoid horticultural oil sprays, which may damage beech trees. Use insecticidal soap on immature scales, called crawlers, in late summer and again in early fall.

Small Holes or Cankers on Trunks and Branches

Borers will invade unhealthy, weak, or damaged trees. Small exit holes made by emerging adults or seeping cankers on branches and the trunk are symptomatic. They tunnel through the sapwood; twigs and branches of afflicted trees die back. Use preventive measures to discourage all types of borers: Water trees well during periods of drought, provide good fertility, use care when trimming or mowing around trees to avoid wounding the trunks or surface roots, and protect trees from damage by animal pests.

Disease Control

Swollen, Seeping Growth on Lower Trunks or Roots

Bleeding canker is a fungal disease that causes cankers in the bark that seep light or red-brown liquid. Twigs and branches may die; cankers on lower trunk or on main roots can eventually girdle the tree and kill it. Prune away and burn infected branches; cut and burn severely infected trees. This fungal disease strikes already weak or injured trees; avoid mechanical injury, such as by lawn mowers, to trunk and surface roots. Take steps to prevent borer infestation.

Trees Die Suddenly; White Scales on Trunks and Branches

Beech bark disease is a fungal disease that attacks trees through the puncture wounds caused by beech scale. Infected trees die quickly after the fungus invades the bark. There is no cure for the fungus once trees are infected; control the scales to prevent infection.

Fraxinus spp.

Ash

Fertilizing

Ash tolerates poor fertility. Feed every other spring or late fall as needed.

Insect Control

See "35 Common Garden Pests," on page 230, for additional information and control measures for the insect problems listed below.

Plants Weaken; Bumps on Twigs

Scales suck sap from stems, twigs, and leaves, causing plants to weaken. Leaves may turn yellow and drop. Adult scales look like many dark brown bumps on stems. Supply plants with plenty of water and good fertility to help them withstand infestation. For scales, spray dormant oil or lime sulfur in late winter just before trees

Fertilizing Trees and Shrubs

Many gardeners make the mistake of applying fertilizer and mulch in a small circle around the base of a tree or shrub. However, tree and shrub roots generally extend at least to the outer edge of the foliage cover (known as the dripline), and frequently far beyond it. For best results, you should fertilize the entire zone within the dripline. Fall fertilizing is best. You can choose from four methods: broadcasting, drilling fertilizer into the ground, flooding, and foliar feeding. All are effective, and you can try combining the methods. Broadcasting is the most common way to feed trees and shrubs because it is easy and effective.

Remember these pointers about tree and shrub fertilizing:

🐛 It's not necessary to feed established trees and shrubs every year, especially if you have a good soil management plan. Trees and shrubs have miles of root hairs that are constantly extracting food from the soil. Overfertilization can stimulate lush foliage that attracts pest insects and can cause the tree or shrub to grow too large for its site. Fertilizing every two or three years is sufficient, unless you are planting into poor soil or your plants are growing poorly.

🐛 You can broadcast compost around trees and shrubs any time of year at a rate of up to 10 cubic feet per 1,000 square feet. Leave an unmulched gap around tree or shrub trunks to prevent disease and insect problems and help protect against rodent damage.

🐛 When you broadcast a blended organic fertilizer, cover the entire area under the plant canopy. The application rate will vary depending on your soil's condition: A general rule of thumb is to apply 50 pounds per 1,000 square feet of 3-4-3 or similar analysis organic fertilizer.

🐛 Where thick lawns are competing with your trees and shrubs, surface feeding is less effective. Try injecting fertilizer below ground instead. To do so, use an auger or a sharp steel rod or pipe to poke holes in the ground 1 to 2 feet apart, following the dripline. The holes should be 1½ inches in diameter and 1 foot deep. Fill each hole with organic fertilizer and water it in with compost tea or dilute fish emulsion.

🐛 Flooding the area under the canopy with compost tea or a solution of fish and kelp is also effective for level planting sites. Mix the solution in a 5-gallon pail or 30-gallon trash can (depending on the size of the plant) and irrigate thoroughly.

🐛 Foliar feeding with kelp and fish extracts will give a quick response if a tree or shrub is stressed or growing poorly. Use a fine-mist sprayer and apply the fertilizer in early morning or evening. For taller trees, you'll need to use a power sprayer.

---

leaf out. Use insecticidal soaps or summer oil to control immature scales, called crawlers.

Knotlike Swellings on Branches and Trunks; Branches Break Off

Lilac borer adults are clear-winged moths that lay eggs on bark. The white, 1-in., brown-headed larvae tunnel into trunks and branches. Tunnel entrances may be surrounded with saw-dust and sap. Leaves may wilt; branches break off at the knot caused by the borers. Probe in borer holes with flexible wire to kill the larvae. Prune away infested limbs.

Webs on Branches; Leaves Skeletonized

Webworms feed at the tips of branches under the protection of webs. Leaves in webs are tied together with silk and skeletonized.

Control webworms by spraying foliage forcefully with BTK (*Bacillus thuringiensis* var. *kurstaki*) as soon as webs appear; repeat every week until feeding stops.

Disease Control

Leaves Grow in Clusters; Witches'-Brooms Form at Base of Trunks

Infection by the ash yellows mycoplasma, a viruslike organism, causes decline and sometimes death. Growth may be slow and twisted to one side. Brooms may develop, usually around the base of the trunk. Leaves are few, small, folded, and bunched together. Air pollution and drought weaken trees, leaving them more susceptible to ash yellows disease. Keep the trees well watered and fed to improve vigor.

Spots on Leaves

Trees infected with leaf spot may have small purple to brown spots with yellow borders on leaves. Spots may join together to form large, brown areas; leaves may fall prematurely. Keep trees well watered and increase soil organic matter.

Rake up and destroy leaves and fallen branches in fall. Periodic sprays with bordeaux mix give some control.

Yellow Powder on Twigs; Distorted Leaves and Twigs

Rust causes leaves to become distorted and brown and green twigs to swell. Yellow-orange spots may be present. Trees may look scorched. Spraying with sulfur or bordeaux mix provides some control. Keep tree well watered and increase soil orangic matter. Destroy leaves and fallen branches in fall.

Sunken Areas on Trunks; Twig Dieback

Several fungi cause cankers on branches and the trunk. Afflicted trees may have pale, stunted leaves that eventually turn brown and fall off. Twigs may die back; sunken areas may be present on the trunk. Prune and destroy infected branches. This fungal disease strikes already weak or injured trees. Keep trees well watered and fed; avoid mechanical injury, such as by a lawn mower; and take steps to prevent borer infestation.

Gleditsia spp.

Honey locust

Fertilizing

Fertilize with balanced organic fertilizer every other spring or fall as needed.

Insect Control

See "35 Common Garden Pests," on page 230, for additional information and control measures for the insect problems listed below.

Ragged Foliage; Silken Bags on Branches

Bagworms are brown moth larvae that feed from inside silken, 2- to 3-in. bags covered with bits of leaves and twigs. The bags resemble pine cones and enlarge as the larvae grow. Larvae move slowly about the plant stripping leaves, giving the tree a ragged appearance. Adult male moths have black wings; females are wingless. Handpick and destroy bagworms. Spraying with BTK (*Bacillus thuringiensis* var. *kurstaki*) in early spring when the larvae are young is the best control method.

Bleeding Holes in Limbs or Trunks

Honey locust borers tunnel into trunks and branches. Entrances may exude sap. Adults chew notches in foliage. Severe infestations may cause branch dieback. Use tree wrap to protect young trees from these pests. Primarily a problem on unhealthy, drought-stressed trees; keep plants well watered and fed to help prevent infestation. If infestation does occur, use a wire to kill the grubs as they burrow under the bark.

Distorted Leaves with Tiny, Wartlike Growths

Gall midges are gnatlike, $1/4$–$1/8$-in. red-brown flies with long legs and antennae. Their whitish or pale orange larvae enter twigs in midspring and cause pimple- or wartlike galls to form. Plants may become distorted, wilted, or brown. Plants may become dwarfed. Remove and destroy galls before the eggs hatch.

Leaves Stippled with Tiny Yellow Dots; Webby Foliage

Spider mites suck sap from leaves, causing them to become stippled. Leaves may appear distorted. Webs may be present. Deeply water trees infested with spider mites since moisture stress encourages the pests. Spray with strong jets of water or with insecticidal soap or summer oil. A late winter spray of dormant oil takes care of the eggs.

Webs on Branches; Leaves Skeletonized

Webworms feed at the tips of branches under the protection of webs. Leaves in webs are tied together with silk and skeletonized. Control webworms with a forceful spray of BTK as soon as webs appear; repeat every week until feeding stops. If possible, give trees an open exposure where the pests will have trouble finding sheltered sites to overwinter.

Disease Control

Sunken Areas with Sap; Discolored, Wilted Leaves

Several species of fungi cause cankers on honey locust. Small, slightly sunken, tan to black lesions merge and girdle the trunk or branch. Wood underneath has red-brown streaks. Sap may ooze from wound. Leaves may be discolored, wilt, and drop. Growth may be sparse and small. Branches or entire tree may die. Prune and burn infected branches. Fertilize and water properly to encourage new, healthy growth and healing of the wounds.

Black Spots on Lower Leaf Surfaces

Tar leaf spot appears as many black spots on the lower surfaces of leaves. Avoid serious problems with this fungal disease by carefully cleaning up leaves in the fall. Burn all litter or put it in sealed containers for disposal with the household trash.

Hydrangea spp.

Hydrangea

Fertilizing

Hydrangea is a heavy feeder. Apply balanced organic fertilizer in spring.

Insect Control

See "35 Common Garden Pests," on page 230, for additional information and control measures for the insect problems listed below.

Foliage Curls, Puckers, and Turns Yellow

Aphids suck sap from leaves, stems, and blossoms, causing foliage to curl, pucker, and turn yellow. Leaves and buds may become stunted. Avoid excessive pruning or overfertilizing with nitrogen; the resulting succulent new growth encourages aphids. Encourage populations of native beneficial insects. Control aphid infestations with high-pressure water sprays or insecticidal soap as necessary.

Leaves Stippled with Tiny Yellow Dots; Webby Foliage

Spider mites suck sap from leaves, causing them to become stippled. Leaves may appear distorted. Webs may be present. Control overwintering eggs of spider mites with dormant oil spray applied in late winter just before buds break. In summer, spray plants with a strong jet of water or with insecticidal soap to control pests.

For severe infestations, spray with abamectin, neem, pyrethrin, or rotenone.

Disease Control

Buds and Flowers Become Spotted and Rot

Blight causes flowers to develop spots, which run together to form blotches. Flowers rot rapidly. This fungal disease is especially a problem in damp weather. Pick and destroy rotting flowers. Increase air circulation around plants by pruning.

White Powder on Leaf Undersides

Powdery mildew appears as a white powder on the undersides of leaves. Upper surfaces may turn purplish brown. Buds and new growth may also be infected. Spray afflicted plants with sulfur spray or dust. Clean up plant refuse thoroughly, since it harbors the disease organisms.

Ilex spp.

Holly

Fertilizing

If necessary, apply cottonseed meal or other acidifying organic fertilizer in late winter or early spring. Avoid excessive feeding. Don't feed in fall.

Insect Control

See "35 Common Garden Pests," on page 230, for additional information and control measures for the insect problems listed below.

Blackened Rolled Leaves at Tips of Branches

Bud moth larvae are small, greenish white to gray-green, ³/₈-in. caterpillars. They feed at the tips of branches, sheltering themselves with rolled leaves tied in silk. Caterpillars eat shoot tips, causing rolled leaves to blacken. Prune away terminal leaves infested with bud moths, and clean up debris. Apply dormant oil in spring before growth resumes and eggs hatch.

Leaves Covered with Tan to Brown Blotches; Serpentine Tunnels in Leaves

Leafminer larvae tunnel through leaves, feeding on plant tissue. They leave serpentine mines or brown blotches in leaves, which may turn brown entirely and collapse. Pick and destroy infested leaves. Adults emerge in spring when plants have 3 or 4 new leaves. Look for small

(continued on page 390)

The Trouble-Free Trees and Shrubs

Botanical Name	Common Name	Comments
Acer buergerianum	Trident maple	
Acer campestre	Hedge maple	
Acer griseum	Paperbark maple	
Aesculus flava (=*A. octandra*)	Yellow buckeye	Not as troubled by foliar diseases as other *Aesculus*
Albizia julibrissin 'Charlotte'	'Charlotte' mimosa	Wilt-resistant clone but susceptible to webworm
'Tryon'	'Tryon' mimosa	Wilt-resistant clone but susceptible to webworm
Asimina triloba	Pawpaw	
Betula nigra 'Heritage'	'Heritage' birch	Resistant to bronze birch borer and leaf spot
Betula platyphylla var. *japonica* 'Whitespire'	'Whitespire' birch	
Carpinus betulus	European hornbeam	
Cercidiphyllum japonicum	Katsura tree	
Chionanthus virginicus	White fringetree	
Cladrastis lutea	Yellowwood	
Cornus kousa	Kousa dogwood	More disease-resistant than *C. florida*
Cupressocyparis leylandii	Leyland cypress	
Eucommia ulmoides	Hardy rubber tree	
Euonymus alatus	Winged euonymus	Resistant to scale
Evodia danielli	Korean evodia	
Ginkgo biloba	Maidenhair tree	
Gleditsia triacanthos var. *inermis* 'Moraine'	'Moraine' honey locust	Webworm tolerant
Gymnocladus dioicus	Kentucky coffee tree	
Hydrangea quercifolia	Oakleaf hydrangea	Fewer problems than other hydrangeas
Ilex cornuta	Chinese holly	No serious pests; may get scale

Botanical Name	Common Name	Comments
Ilex pedunculosa	Longstalk holly	
Magnolia spp.	Magnolia	
Malus	Crabapple	Check with local suppliers for the most trouble-free cultivars for your growing area
Nyssa sylvatica	Tupelo, sour gum	
Oxydendrum arboreum	Sourwood, sorrel tree	
Parrotia persica	Persian parrotia	
Phellodendron spp.	Cork trees	
Pinus koraiensis	Korean pine	
Platanus × *acerifolia* 'Bloodgood'	'Bloodgood' London plane	Resistant to anthracnose
Prunus sargentii	Sargent cherry	Fewer problems than other cherries
Pyracantha 'Fiery Cascade' 'Mohave' 'Rutgers'	'Fiery Cascade' firethorn 'Mohave' firethorn 'Rutgers' firethorn	Good disease resistance Resistant to scab and fire blight Good disease resistance
Quercus acutissima	Sawtooth oak	
Sciadopitys verticillata	Japanese umbrella pine	
Stewartia spp.	Stewartias	
Styrax japonicus	Japanese snowbell	
Syringa reticulata	Japanese tree lilac	Most trouble-free lilac
Ulmus 'American Liberty'	'American Liberty' elm	Dutch elm disease resistant
Ulmus parviflora	Lacebark elm	Resistant to Dutch elm disease and elm leaf beetle
Viburnum spp.	Viburnums	Relatively free of insect and disease problems
Zelkova serrata 'Village Green'	'Village Green' zelkova	Highly resistant to Dutch elm disease and to leaf-eating and bark beetles

flies around leaves and tiny pin pricks on foliage, then spray plants with summer oil or neem extract. Leafminers also infest deciduous hollies—winterberry (*Ilex verticillata*) and inkberry (*I. glabra*); treat these plants as well to prevent reinfestation.

Plants Weaken; Bumps on Leaves and Twigs

Scales suck sap from stems and leaves, causing plants to weaken. Leaves may turn yellow and drop. Adult scales look like many whitish to dark brown bumps on twigs and leaves. Summer oil sprays will help control scales. Overwintering eggs can be smothered with dormant oil in late winter before growth resumes.

Leaves Stippled with Tiny Yellow Dots; Webby Foliage

Spider mites suck sap from leaves, causing them to become stippled. Leaves may appear distorted. Webs may be present. Control overwintering eggs of spider mites with dormant oil spray applied in late winter just before buds break. In summer, spray plants with a strong jet

of water or with insecticidal soap to control pests. For severe infestations, spray with abamectin, neem, pyrethrin, or rotenone.

Disease Control
Spots on Leaves

Several fungi cause brown spots on holly leaves. Spots may join together to form large, brown areas. Pick off and destroy infected leaves. Keep trees well watered and increase soil organic matter with oak leaf mold or cottonseed meal. Rake up and destroy leaves and fallen branches in fall. Soil improvement and other cultural controls are best; spraying with bordeaux mix may damage foliage.

Seeping Lesions on Branches; Branch Dieback

Several fungi cause cankers on branches and twigs, which can girdle and kill branches. Keep trees healthy and well watered. Remove and destroy branches killed by cankers. Heavily infected trees should be cut and burned.

Juniperus spp.   Juniper

Fertilizing

Apply acidifying organic fertilizer, such as cottonseed meal, in early spring or late fall every other year.

Insect Control

See "35 Common Garden Pests," on page 230, for additional information and control measures for the insect problems listed below.

Needles Ragged; Silken Bags on Branches

Bagworms are brown moth larvae that feed from inside silken, 2–3-in. bags covered with bits of needles and twigs. The bags resemble pine cones and enlarge as the larvae grow. Larvae move slowly about the plant stripping needles, giving the tree a ragged appearance. Adult male moths have black wings; females are wingless.

Handpick and destroy bagworms. Spray with BTK (*Bacillus thuringiensis* var. *kurstaki*); early spring when the larvae are young is best.

Plants Weaken; Bumps on Stems

Scales suck sap from stems and needles, causing plants to weaken. Needles may turn yellow and drop. Adult scales look like many whitish to dark brown or black bumps on stems. Use dormant oil or lime sulfur spray in late winter before growth starts to control scales; insecticidal soap or summer oil works in spring after plants resume growth. Repeat in early summer when the young are crawling.

Yellowed Needles; Webs Present

Spider mites suck sap from needles, causing them to become yellowed and stippled. Webs may be present. Control overwintering eggs of spider mites with dormant oil spray applied in late winter just before buds break. In summer, spray plants with a strong jet of water or with insecticidal soap to control pests. For severe infestations, spray with abamectin, neem, pyrethrin, or rotenone.

Webs on Branches; Needles Brown

Webworms feed at the tips of branches under the protection of webs. Needles in webs are brown or stripped. Remove webworms by pruning or spray forcefully with BTK, summer oil, or pyrethrin as soon as the pests appear.

Disease Control
Galls on Branches

Red cedars (*Juniperus virginiana*) are alternate hosts for cedar apple rust fungus, which does extensive damage to crabapples and apples (see page 346 for information about this disease on apples). Infected plants produce large, 1-in.-wide galls on branches; galls later develop bright yellow-orange, spore-bearing filaments, especially during warm, rainy weather. Branch tips may die. Usually this disease is harmless to red cedars. Cut out the galls of cedar apple rust in late winter, before spore-bearing filaments form.

Magnolia spp.

Magnolia

Fertilizing

Apply balanced organic fertilizer or well-rotted manure every other spring.

Insect Control

See "35 Common Garden Pests," on page 230, for additional information and control measures for the insect problem listed below.

Plants Weaken; Bumps on Twigs

Scales suck sap from stems, twigs, and leaves, causing plants to weaken. Leaves may turn yellow and drop. Adult magnolia scales look like round, dark brown bumps on twigs. When natural enemies don't control scale, apply dormant oil spray in late winter just before new growth begins. Spray for several consecutive years if scales are a serious problem; lime sulfur is also effective. Use insecticidal soap spray to control immature scales, called crawlers, in late summer.

Disease Control
Sooty Mold on Leaves
Several fungi can cause black, sooty mold on magnolia foliage, especially in the Southeast. Spray plants with sulfur fungicide when symptoms appear.

Spots on Leaves
Several fungi cause brown spots on magnolia leaves. Spots may join together to form large, brown areas; leaves may fall prematurely. Pick off diseased leaves and discard them. Spray plants with bordeaux mix when symptoms appear. Keep trees well watered and increase soil organic matter. Rake up and destroy leaves and fallen branches in fall.

Malus spp.   Crabapple

See "Apple" on page 343.

Picea spp.   Spruce

Fertilizing
Apply acidifying organic fertilizer such as cottonseed meal in late fall or early spring as needed.

Insect Control
See "35 Common Garden Pests," on page 230, for additional information and control measures for the insect problems listed below.

Cone-Shaped Galls on Base of New Shoots
Spruce gall aphids suck sap from needles at the base of terminal shoots. Their feeding causes $1/2$–1-in. pine cone- or pineapple-shaped galls to form over feeding aphids. Later, the galls brown and crack open; mature aphids lay cottony-covered eggs near the base of buds. Spray dormant oil in early spring before new growth begins or summer oil later in the season to kill aphids. Don't use oil sprays on blue spruce, as it causes foliage to discolor. Insecticidal soap or rotenone also works, if sprayed just as new growth emerges, before galls have formed.

Trees Ragged
Trees ragged-looking or defoliated. Sawfly larvae feed heavily on needles and may

defoliate plants. Handpick sawflies, or spray with summer oil, neem, or rotenone as soon as they are spotted. Don't use oil sprays on blue spruce, as it causes foliage to discolor.

Ragged foliage; silken bags on branches. Bagworms are brown moth larvae that feed from inside silken, 2–3-in.-long bags covered with bits of needles and twigs. The bags resemble pine cones and enlarge as the larvae grow. Larvae move slowly about the plant stripping leaves, giving the tree a ragged appearance. Adult male moths have black wings; females are wingless. Handpick and destroy bagworms. Spraying with BTK (*Bacillus thuringiensis* var. *kurstaki*) in early spring when the larvae are young is the best control method.

Discolored Needles

Numerous small holes in branches; needles discolored. Spruce beetles are small, black beetles with reddish wing covers. They attack weak, older spruce trees. Beetles create small, round holes in twigs and branches that have gum and sawdust around them. Needles may fade; trees may weaken. Spruce beetles usually attack already weakened trees; provide adequate fertility and moisture, and keep plantings thinned. Remove weak or old trees. For light infestation, cut out infested twigs or branches.

Needles stippled with tiny yellow dots; webby foliage. Spider mites suck sap from needles, causing them to turn yellow. Webs may be present. Control overwintering eggs of spider mites with dormant oil spray applied in late winter just before buds break. In summer, spray plants with a strong jet of water or with insecticidal soap to control pests. For severe infestations, spray with abamectin, neem, pyrethrin, or rotenone.

New Growth Deformed

New growth deformed or eaten; wilting. Spruce budworms are dark, red-brown, $^1/_2$–$^3/_4$-in.

caterpillars with yellow spots and black heads. Moths are gray with brown patches and 1–1$^1/_5$-in. wingspans. Caterpillars feed on terminal shoots and new or old growth, usually webbing needles together with silk while feeding. Trees wilt; new growth may become deformed. Pheromone traps are available to monitor or control spruce budworm if handpicking is not sufficient. Spray caterpillars with BTK while they are still feeding on the needles.

Terminal leader damaged or killed. White pine weevils attack pines and spruces. Adults are $^1/_4$ in. long, brownish, and mottled with light and dark scales. Larvae are pale yellow, $^1/_3$ in. long. Larvae bore into terminal shoots; resin may be noticeable. The terminal leader is distorted and eventually turns brown and dies. Adults leave holes in bark when emerging in late summer. Cut away and destroy infested terminal shoots well below damaged wood as soon as symptoms appear. To replace the damaged leader, tie a lateral branch to a stake, fasten it upright, and cut off other laterals that compete with it.

Disease Control

Branches Die Back; Needles Fall; Resinous Cankers Develop in Bark

Cytospora canker causes branches to turn brown and die, usually beginning with the lower branches. Needles may fall. Resin may be present on bark of infected areas along with hidden cankers. Diseased areas may have tiny black cones or yellow ooze on them. Preventive measures are effective: Feed and water trees to keep them vigorously growing; avoid wounding trees with a lawn mower or through bad pruning practices. Remove afflicted branches and twigs. Cut away diseased tissue on trunk, and carve away 2 in. of healthy bark from the perimeter of the infected area. If the tree is severely infected, remove and destroy it.

Pinus spp.

Pine

Fertilizing

Feed with acidifying organic fertilizer, such as cottonseed meal, in late fall or early spring.

Insect Control

See "35 Common Garden Pests," on page 230, for additional information and control measures for the insect problems listed below.

Small Clumps of White Powder under Limbs and on Trunks

Pine bark adelgids, formerly called pine bark aphids, suck sap from the undersides of pine limbs and the trunk from the ground up. They cover themselves with white powdery material, which may be noticeable under limbs and on the trunk; the trunk may have a white-washed look. Spray dormant oil or lime sulfur in late winter before growth begins. Or use summer oil for control during the growing season; insecticidal soap or rotenone also works.

Needles Chewed

Needles chewed or trees defoliated. Gypsy moth caterpillars have gray, hairy bodies with rows of blue and red spots along the sides of the back; they grow to 2½ in. Adult male moths are brown; females are whitish with dark markings. They have a 1½-in. wingspan. Caterpillars feed in masses on foliage, often defoliating plants. Scrape brown or yellow egg masses off trunks into a bucket of soapy water. Wrap tree trunks with burlap skirts in June to trap the insects. Spray young caterpillars with BTK (*Bacillus thuringiensis* var. *kurstaki*), repeating at weekly intervals.

Trees ragged-looking or defoliated. Sawfly larvae feed heavily on needles and may defoliate plants. Handpick sawflies, or spray with summer oil, neem, or rotenone as soon as they are spotted.

Webs on branches; twigs stripped of needles. Pine webworms feed at the tips of branches under the protection of webs. Dead needles and frass are present in webs. Remove webworms by pruning or spray with BTK in spring when larvae are young and before they produce webs. Later in the season, apply BTK, summer oil, or pyrethrin weekly with a forceful, high-pressure spray until feeding stops.

Holes in Bark or Shoots Bored

Holes in trees; reddish sawdust and sap near holes. Bark beetle larvae tunnel through bark, primarily attacking weak or dying trees. Adults also chew holes in bark, leaving reddish sawdust at entrances; sap may exude from wounds. Foliage may turn yellow or red. Keep trees well watered during droughts, and fertilize if the tree has been injured or subjected to similar stress.

Shoot tips die back. Pine tip and pine shoot borers are the larvae of several species of small moths. The larvae are dark-colored caterpillars that bore into the bases of needles or buds and tunnel through the shoots, causing shoot tips all over the trees to die back. Cut off and destroy infested twigs as soon as you spot them. Spraying BTK may give some control if applied before caterpillars bore into shoots.

Terminal leader damaged or killed. White pine weevils attack pines and spruces. Adults are ¼ in. long, brownish, and mottled with light and dark scales. Larvae are pale yellow and ⅓ in. long. Larvae bore into terminal shoots; resin may be noticeable. Terminal leader is distorted and eventually turns brown and dies. Adults leave holes in bark when emerging in late summer. Cut away and destroy infested terminal shoots well below damaged wood as soon as symptoms appear. To replace the damaged leader, tie a lateral branch to a stake, fasten it upright, and cut off other laterals that compete with it.

Needles Yellowed or Covered with White Bumps; Plants Weaken

Scales suck sap from needles and stems, causing plants to weaken. Needles may turn yellow and drop. Adult scales look like many whitish to dark brown bumps on stems. Use dormant oil or lime sulfur spray in late winter before growth starts, to control scale; spray insecticidal soap or summer oil in spring to control the young, called crawlers. Repeat the spray in early summer.

Disease Control

Sunken Lesions Exude Resin; Cankers on Branches and Trunks

Several fungi cause cankers on pines. The cankers are sunken openings in the bark that usually ooze sap. Bark turns reddish brown, and needles turn brown or yellow. Shoots wilt and tips droop. Infection by canker can also cause deformed, stunted growth, dieback, and death. Unhealthy, weakened, or damaged trees are most susceptible. Preventive measures are useful: Plant pines in well-drained soil rich in organic matter; avoid damaging the trunk with lawn mowers and other equipment; treat injuries promptly if they occur; and keep trees healthy by proper feeding and watering. Remove and destroy branches killed by cankers. On valuable specimens, cut out infected tissue on the trunk and carve away 2 in. of healthy bark from the perimeter of the infected area. Heavily infected trees should be cut and burned.

Needles Become Discolored and Drop Off

Needle blights are fungal diseases that may cause needles to turn reddish or develop brown streaks or spots and become distorted; needles may fall. Terminal buds may die. Spray twice with bordeaux mix in spring, 3 weeks apart.

Red Needles; Twigs Fall Off

Pine twig blight starts at terminal buds and works downward. Needles turn red and die. Black or brown and green spots appear on twigs; twigs may fall off. Remove and destroy infected cones, branches, and twigs; treat wounds with wound dressing to prevent reinfection. Maintain vigorous growth by fertilizing and watering well. If twig blight has been a problem previously, spray bordeaux mix when new candle growth starts, again when candles are half-grown, and a third time 2 weeks after that.

Yellow-Orange Blisters on Bark

A serious disease of white pine, white pine blister rust causes swollen cankers, which may exude resin, to form at the base of branches or on the trunk. Pale yellow-orange blisters develop in cankers and release yellow powdery spores. Cankers may enlarge to girdle the branch or the trunk, eventually killing the branch or the tree. Needles on infected areas turn yellow-brown and droop; growth is slow. Cut off infected branches. Strip away diseased bark on the trunk and carve away 2 in. of healthy bark from the perimeter of the infected area. Coat wounds with wound dressing to prevent reinfection. Currants and gooseberries are the alternate hosts for this fungal disease; don't plant them within 200 ft. of pines.

Platanus spp.

Sycamore

Fertilizing

Feed balanced organic fertilizer every other spring or fall as needed.

Insect Control

See "35 Common Garden Pests," on page 230, for additional information and control measures for the insect problems listed below.

Yellow Foliage

Foliage curls, puckers, and turns yellow. Bark aphids suck sap from sycamore twigs, weakening plants, and producing honeydew, which will drip from tree branches and encourage the growth of sooty mold. Control aphid infestations with high-pressure water sprays or insecticidal soap as necessary; dormant oil before bud break in spring smothers aphid eggs. Encourage populations of native beneficial insects.

Plants weaken; bumps on twigs. Scales suck sap from stems, twigs, and leaves, causing plants to weaken. Leaves may turn yellow and drop. Adult scales look like many whitish to dark brown bumps on twigs. When natural enemies don't control scale, treat with dormant oil spray in late winter or spring for several consecutive years. Use insecticidal soap to control immature scales, called crawlers, in early spring.

Yellow or reddish spots on leaves. Adult sycamore plant bugs are $1/8$-in. brown bugs with dark brown spots on wings; immature bugs are yellow-green. They suck sap from the upper side of leaves. Infested leaves develop yellow or reddish spots, which eventually fall out, leaving holes in leaves. Spray infested plants with insecticidal soap or summer oil; 2 applications at 2-week intervals are best.

Holes in Limbs or Trunks; Bark Darkens; Limbs Die or Break Off

A variety of borers tunnel into sycamore trunks and limbs. Tunnel entrances may be surrounded by gummy sap. Bark darkens and dies. Infested limbs may die; serious infestations may kill the tree. Borers are most likely to attack trees already weakened by fungal diseases or stress. If possible, prune out damaged wood in winter and burn or destroy it to stop the infestation cycle. Also gather and burn or discard fallen twigs, which may be infested. Increase fertility and watering to build the tree's overall health and vigor. Where pruning isn't an option, kill the borers in their tunnels with a flexible wire, or inject parasitic nematodes into the entry holes, then plug the holes with putty.

Disease Control

Leaves Brown; Branches Die Back

Anthracnose, also called leaf and twig blight, is a serious disease that causes clusters of emerging leaves to brown and die. Older leaves develop dead areas near veins and may fall. Tan-colored formations may appear on the undersides of leaves or on bark. Severe defoliation may occur. Buds and terminal shoots die. Cankers may form on twigs and kill them. New growth may be stunted. To control, spray with lime sulfur or copper fungicide just before buds break. Repeat 2 weeks later, and again 2 weeks after that. Fertilize heavily in late fall and again the following spring to help the tree recover. Clean up fallen leaves and twigs thoroughly in fall.

Sparse, Yellow Foliage; Elongated Cankers

Canker stain is a serious disease that causes leaves to turn yellow; foliage is small and sparse. Trunks and large branches develop elongated sunken areas with cracked or rough, callused bark; these may enlarge to girdle the branch or tree. A cross-section of the infected area would reveal reddish brown or bluish black, wedge-shaped discolorations. Preventive measures are useful: Avoid damaging the trunk with lawn mowers and other equipment; treat injuries promptly if they occur; and keep trees healthy and well watered. Remove and burn seriously infected trees. Sterilize pruning tools that may be contaminated in a household bleach solution (1 part bleach to 9 parts water) before next use.

Populus spp. Poplar

Fertilizing

Most species tolerate poor soils. To encourage growth of young transplants, feed with balanced organic fertilizer in early spring.

Insect Control

See "35 Common Garden Pests," on page 230, for additional information and control measures for the insect problems listed below.

Yellow Foliage

Foliage curls, puckers, and turns yellow. Aphids suck sap from leaves and stems, causing foliage to curl, pucker, and turn yellow. Leaves and buds may become stunted. Aphids produce honeydew, which will drip from tree branches and encourage the growth of sooty mold. Control aphid infestations with high-pressure water sprays or insecticidal soap as necessary; dormant oil before bud break in spring smothers aphid eggs. Encourage populations of native beneficial insects.

Plants weaken; bumps on twigs. Scales suck sap from stems and leaves, causing plants to weaken. Leaves may turn yellow and drop. Adult scales look like many whitish to dark brown bumps on stems. Use dormant oil or lime sulfur spray in late winter before growth starts, to control scale; insecticidal soap or summer oil works in spring after plants resume growth, repeat in early summer when the young are crawling.

Webs on Branches; Leaves Skeletonized

Webworms feed at the tips of branches under the protection of webs. Leaves in webs are tied together with silk and skeletonized. Control webworms with a forceful spray of BTK (*Bacillus thuringiensis* var. *kurstaki*) as soon as webs appear; repeat every week until feeding stops.

Leaves Stuck or Rolled Together with Silk

Leafrollers protect themselves when feeding by rolling terminal leaves into tubes and binding them with strands or webs of silk. Spray with dormant oil just before bud break to kill egg masses. Handpick caterpillars. Spray with BTK, pyrethrin, or rotenone when larvae start feeding, before they are protected inside rolled leaves.

Holes in Trunks; Bark Darkens

Larvae of both flatheaded and roundheaded borers tunnel into wood of trunks. Tunnel entrances may be surrounded by gummy sap. Bark darkens and dies. In severe instances, the tree may be killed. Keep trees vigorously growing by providing good fertility, water, and light to prevent these pests. Avoid mechanical injury to the trunk, such as by lawn mowers. Cut off and destroy infested branches as soon as you see holes and chewed wood.

Disease Control
Seeping Lesions on Branches and/or Trunks

Several fungi cause cankers on poplars. Cankers, from which sap oozes, appear at the base of the trunk or on twigs and branches. These can girdle and kill branches or the entire tree. Cytospora canker causes brown, sunken areas to form. These may have tiny brown, gray, or black bumps that may later produce red to yellow filaments. Other symptoms include wilting, dieback, and a thinning crown. Infected inner bark is red-brown. Preventive measures are useful: Avoid damaging the trunk with lawn mowers and other equipment; treat injuries promptly if they occur; and keep trees healthy and well watered. Remove and destroy branches killed by cankers. If possible, cut out infected tissue on the trunk, and carve away 2 in. of healthy bark from the perimeter of the infected area. Heavily infected trees should be cut and burned. When planting new trees, choose cultivars less susceptible than Lombardy and other silver-leaved species.

Prunus spp.

Flowering cherry

See "Cherry" on page 351.

Pyracantha spp.

Firethorn

Fertilizing

Apply balanced organic fertilizer every other spring or fall, as needed.

Insect Control

See "35 Common Garden Pests," on page 230, for additional information and control measures for the insect problems listed below.

Yellow Foliage

Foliage curls, puckers, and turns yellow. Aphids suck sap from leaves, stems, and blossoms, causing foliage to curl, pucker, and turn yellow. Leaves and buds may become stunted. Aphids produce honeydew, which will drip from branches and encourage the growth of sooty mold. Avoid excessive pruning or overfertilizing with nitrogen; the resulting succulent new growth encourages aphids. Use a strong jet of water to control aphids. If the problem persists, spray with insecticidal soap. Encourage populations of native beneficial insects.

Plants weaken; bumps on twigs. Scales suck sap from stems and leaves, causing plants to weaken. Leaves may turn yellow and drop. When natural enemies don't control scale, treat with dormant oil spray in late winter or spring for several consecutive years. Use insecticidal soap to control immature scales, called crawlers, in early spring.

Mottled Leaves

Adult and nymph lace bugs suck sap from leaves, leaving brown excrement on leaf undersides. Upper surfaces of leaves become pale and mottled. Apply insecticidal soap to the tops and the undersides of leaves infested with lace bugs.

Disease Control
Flowers and Shoots Wilt Suddenly in Spring

Fire blight causes new shoots to wilt suddenly in late spring, turn black or brown, and eventually die. Prune infected branches, removing at least 6 in. of uninfected wood beyond the discolored area. Prevent further problems by improving air circulation, cleaning up debris, and reducing nitrogen fertilization. For further prevention, apply bordeaux mix in early spring the following year.

Scabby Lesions on Leaves and Fruit

Plants infected with scab have dark, scabby areas on leaves and berries. Leaves turn yellow, then brown, and eventually fall. Clean up infected berries in fall. Spray plants twice, 2 weeks apart, with bordeaux mix in spring to help prevent the disease.

Quercus spp.

Oak

Fertilizing

Apply low-nitrogen, high-phosphorus organic fertilizer every other year in late fall to keep established trees healthy.

Insect Control

See "35 Common Garden Pests," on page 230, for additional information and control measures for the insect problems listed below.

Leaves Chewed

Gypsy moth caterpillars have gray, hairy bodies with rows of blue and red spots along the side of the back; they grow to 2½ in. Adult male moths are brown; females are whitish with dark markings. They have 1½-in. wingspans. Caterpillars feed in masses on leaves, often defoliating plants. Spraying BTK (*Bacillus thuringiensis* var. *kurstaki*) is effective against young gypsy moth caterpillars. Scrape brown or yellow egg masses off trunks into a bucket of soapy water. In spring, catch young larvae in burlap bands tied around the trunk; crush or handpick them.

Western tussock moth caterpillars also chew oak leaves. Male moths have brown wings with gray markings; females are gray and wingless. They lay eggs on old cocoons or bark. Larvae are gray, ³/₄–1-in. caterpillars with red and yellow spots, 2 black tufts of hair at the head, and 1 black hair tuft at the end. They feed on leaves, leaving behind a dry leaf "skeleton." Scrape off cocoons before eggs hatch in spring. Spray trees in early spring while larvae are young with BTK or insecticidal soap.

Asiatic oak weevils feed on leaves; the larvae feed on roots. Adults are metallic. The weevils are dark red or black, 1/4-in. beetles with long antennae. Control Asiatic oak weevil with rotenone spray.

Plants Weaken; Bumps on Twigs and Leaves

Scales suck sap from stems and leaves, causing plants to weaken. Leaves may turn yellow and drop. Adult scales look like many whitish to dark brown bumps on stems. Use dormant oil spray during dormancy to smother scale eggs; later in the season, use summer oil or insecticidal soap to control crawling stages.

Warty or Large, Rounded Growths on Twigs

Both mites and insects cause galls to form on oaks. Some do not harm plants; others will kill twigs and branches. Prune out and destroy galls when they appear. A dormant oil or lime sulfur spray in late winter will kill many gall-forming pests that overwinter on oaks.

Disease Control

Sunken Spots on Leaves

Infection by anthracnose fungi causes leaves to develop moist, sunken spots with fruiting bodies in the center. Dead areas form along veins; leaves may become distorted and fall. Pink spores may appear on terminal shoots; twigs may die back. Prevent the disease by thoroughly cleaning up leaves and dead wood. Thin the crown to improve air circulation. Spray with bordeaux mix when symptoms appear; if anthracnose has been a problem in previous years,

spray with bordeaux mix or other copper fungicide at bud break.

Swollen or Seeping Lesions on Branches and/or Trunks

Several fungi cause cankers on oaks. Cankers, from which sap oozes, appear at the base of the trunk or on twigs and branches. These can girdle and kill branches or the entire tree. Other symptoms include wilting, dieback, and a thinning crown. Infected inner bark is red-brown. Preventive measures are useful: Plant oaks in well-drained soil rich in organic matter; avoid damaging the trunk with lawn mowers and other equipment; treat injuries promptly if they occur; and keep trees healthy and well watered. Remove and destroy branches killed by cankers. If possible, cut out infected tissue on the trunk, and carve away 2 in. of healthy bark from the perimeter of the infected area. Heavily infected trees should be cut and burned.

Yellow or Orange Spots on Leaves

A serious disease that also infects some pines, fusiform rust spends 2 of its stages on oak leaves, causing powdery yellow or orange spots to form on the undersides of leaves, which may fall. Prune away and destroy infected leaves; clean up debris such as fallen leaves and destroy them. Spray infected trees with bordeaux mix.

Leaves Blistered and Curled

Leaf blister appears as yellow-white blisters up to 1/2 in. in diameter on upper leaf surfaces, with corresponding yellowish brown depressions on leaf undersides. This fungal disease is common after cool, wet springs. If leaf blister has been a problem the previous season, apply lime sulfur or bordeaux mix just before buds swell.

Leaves Turn Brown and Collapse

Oak wilt causes leaves to curl, brown, and droop. Sapwood may turn black or brown. Disease may progress downward until all branches are infected. Trees may die rapidly, usually within a year. Cut and burn trees severely infected with this disease because there is no cure. Dig a narrow, 36–40-in.-deep trench between any remaining infected and healthy trees to cut any root grafts through which the fungus can travel, and then immediately backfill the trench. To slow the spread of the disease, prune oaks only when they are dormant.

Rhododendron spp.

Azalea and Rhododendron

Fertilizing

Apply cottonseed meal or other acidifying organic fertilizer in spring and midsummer as needed.

Insect Control

See "35 Common Garden Pests," on page 230, for additional information and control measures for the insect problems listed below.

Leaves Yellow

Leaves turn pale; holes in trunk. Rhododendron borer adults are small, wasplike, clear-winged moths that lay eggs on trunk scars or in branch crotches. Larvae chew into and tunnel through wood. Leaves of infested shrubs turn pale green, then yellow. Trunks will have holes surrounded by sawdust. Prune and burn branches infested with borers. Water deeply and fertilize well to help seal wounds and keep plants growing vigorously.

Plants weaken; bumps on leaves and twigs. Scales suck sap from stems and leaves, causing plants to weaken. Leaves may turn yellow and drop. Adults look like whitish to dark brown bumps on stems, twigs, and leaves. Many native beneficial insects feed on scales. Insecticidal soap controls immature stages of scale, called crawlers. Cut away badly infested branches. Test insecticidal soap on a small part of one plant before spraying, as some azalea cultivars do not tolerate soap sprays. Apply summer oil in spring just as buds begin to break, to eliminate eggs.

Weakened plants; leaves yellowed. Whitefly nymphs and adults suck sap from leaves, buds, and stems, causing leaves to turn yellow and the plant to weaken. Set up yellow sticky traps to monitor whitefly populations and take steps to control pests before they become a problem. Insecticidal soap, summer oil, or rotenone-pyrethrin spray controls whiteflies. Test insecticidal soap on a small part of one plant before spraying, as some azalea cultivars do not tolerate soap sprays.

Mottled Leaves

Pale, mottled leaves. Adult and nymph lace bugs suck sap from leaves, leaving brown, sticky excrement on leaf undersides. Upper surfaces of leaves become pale and mottled. Apply insecticidal soap to undersides of leaves as soon as eggs hatch in spring. Test insecticidal soap on a small part of one plant before spraying, as some azalea cultivars do not tolerate soap sprays. Repeat, as necessary, if pests spread to new growth. Spraying summer oil will also help control lace bugs. For severe infestations, spray with pyrethrin or rotenone.

Leaves stippled with tiny yellow dots; webby foliage. Spider mites suck sap from leaves, causing them to become stippled. Leaves may appear distorted. Webs may be present. Spray plants weekly with a strong jet of water to control these pests. For severe infestations, spray with abamectin, neem, pyrethrin, or rotenone.

Plants Defoliated or Wilted; Tunnels in Roots and Stems

Adult weevils chew holes or notches in leaves; some species roll or curl them. Larvae burrow through roots, fruit, or stems. Plants may become defoliated or may wilt or be easily uprooted. Handpick or shake off black vine weevils at night when they are active, and apply parasitic nematodes to control larvae in soil. Coat shrub stems with a sticky substance such as Tanglefoot to trap weevils as they try to climb up plants. Several rhododendron hybrids resist root weevils.

Disease Control

Leaves and Growing Tips Shriveled

Dieback may first appear as a discoloration in the tips and margins of leaves. Spots form and spread over entire leaves. Terminal buds and leaves may turn brown, roll up, and droop. Stems may shrivel and cankers form, which gir-dle the plant. Keep leaves dry when watering. Prune and destroy dead branches. Reduce moisture stress in summer and freezing stress in winter. Spraying with bordeaux mix may prevent spread of the disease; apply after plant blooms and again 10 days later.

Spots or Blotches on Flowers, Buds, and Twigs

Azalea flower spot or petal blight first appears as small pale or brown spots on inner surfaces of petals. These spots rapidly enlarge and cause the flower to collapse. Petals are slimy, and infected flowers remain on plant. Destroy all infected flowers; rake up and destroy litter beneath the plant and replace with clean mulch.

Leaves Become Spotted, Turn Brown, and Fall Prematurely

Several fungi cause spots on rhododendron and azalea leaves. Spots may be yellow, brown, or black and can run together, and the entire leaf may become blighted. Afflicted leaves may fall. Fungi overwinter on fallen leaves; clean up and dispose of leaves in fall. If leaf spot has been severe the previous season, spray with copper fungicide at bud break and again 10 days later.

Rosa spp.   Rose

Fertilizing

Rose is a heavy feeder. Apply organic high-phosphorus blended fertilizer in early spring and again at blossom time.

Insect Control

See "35 Common Garden Pests," on page 230, for additional information and control measures for the insect problems listed below.

Foliage Curls, Puckers, and Turns Yellow

Aphids suck sap from leaves, stems, buds, and blossoms, causing foliage to curl, pucker, and turn yellow. Leaves and buds may become stunted. Aphids produce honeydew, which will drip from tree branches and encourage the growth of sooty mold. Handpick caterpillars. Avoid excessive pruning or overfertilizing with nitrogen; the resulting succulent new growth encourages aphids. Control aphid infestations with high-pressure water sprays or insecticidal soap as necessary; dormant oil before bud break in spring smothers aphid eggs. Encourage populations of native beneficial insects.

Leaves Chewed

Adult Japanese beetles skeletonize foliage and eat flowers; larvae feed on roots. Handpick Japanese beetles. For long-term control, apply milky disease spores and/or parasitic nematodes to surrounding lawn areas to combat the grubs.

Rose chafers are tan, $1/4$-in. beetles with long legs. They skeltonize foliage and eat flowers. Handpick rose chafers or spray with rotenone. Milky disease spores applications for Japanese beetles will also control grubs of these pests.

Leaves Stippled with Tiny Yellow Dots; Webby Foliage

Spider mites suck sap from leaves, causing them to become stippled. Leaves may appear distorted and may be spotted with red, yellow, or brown; leaves may fall. Webs may be present. Knock off spider mites by forcefully spraying leaves with water. Resort to insecticidal soap if water doesn't seem to do the trick. Control overwintering eggs of spider mites with dormant oil spray applied in late winter just before growth resumes.

Brown Edges on Blossoms

Thrips cause flowers to develop brown edges; infested buds fail to open. Buds and new growth may be deformed. Thrips burrow between petals, where they are difficult to reach with sprays. Encourage lacewings and other predators to help keep thrips population under control. Use yellow sticky traps to monitor populations; as soon as pests appear on traps, spray with insecticidal soap, rotenone, sabadilla, or ryania every week as needed.

Disease Control
Black Spots on Leaves

Black spot is a fungal disease that causes black spots with yellow margins to develop on leaves. Leaves later turn yellow-pink and fall off. Preventive measures are effective: Plant disease-resistant cultivars; keep leaves dry when watering; prune plants to improve air circulation; clean up and destroy infected leaves as they appear; and do a thorough end-of-season cleanup. If black spot has been a previous problem, use preventive sprays: After pruning but while plants are still dormant in spring, spray thoroughly with fungicidal soap or wettable sulfur, then spray plants with dormant oil. Once growth begins, spray weekly with fungicidal soap or wettable sulfur.

Plant Grows Poorly; Tumorlike Growth on Roots

Crown gall causes rough swellings to grow on roots or lower stems. Plants grow poorly. Prevent the disease by not wounding stems and roots; inspect plants carefully at purchase. Cut away galls, making sure to leave only healthy growth. Dig and destroy severely diseased plants.

Discolored or Dead Areas on Canes

Many fungal cankers may trouble roses. Canes may develop swollen or discolored dead areas that may split open. Leaves and flowers may develop spots or turn brown. Check plants for signs of disease at purchase; prune away and destroy infected canes.

White Powder Covering on Leaves

Powdery mildew appears as a white or ash gray powdery covering on leaves and canes. As the fungus spreads, leaves become distorted and may drop off. Flowers may also be infected. Pick off and destroy infected leaves. If mildew has been a previous problem, apply preventive sprays: After pruning but while plants are still dormant in spring, spray thoroughly with fungicidal soap or wettable sulfur, then spray plants with dormant oil. Once growth begins, spray weekly with fungicidal soap or wettable sulfur.

Leaves Pale Above with Orange-Red Blisters Beneath

Rust is a fungal disease that causes pale areas to appear on upper leaf surfaces, with corresponding orange-red blisters on leaf undersides; later, blisters may appear on top. Canes may also be infected. As soon as symptoms appear, spray thoroughly with wettable sulfur or fungicidal spray.

Salix spp.   Willow

Fertilizing

Fertilize with balanced organic fertilizer as necessary every other year.

Insect Control

See "35 Common Garden Pests," on page 230, for additional information and control measures for the insect problems listed below.

Yellow Foliage

Foliage curls, puckers, and turns yellow. Aphids suck sap from leaves, stems, and blossoms, causing foliage to curl, pucker, and turn yellow. Leaves and buds may become stunted. Aphids produce honeydew, which will drip from tree branches and encourage the growth of sooty mold. Avoid excessive pruning or overfertilizing with nitrogen; the resulting succulent new growth encourages aphids. Control aphid infestations with high-pressure water sprays or with insecti- cidal soap as necessary. Encourage populations of native beneficial insects.

Plants weaken; bumps on twigs. Scales suck sap from stems and leaves, causing plants to weaken. Leaves may turn yellow and drop. Adult scales look like many whitish to dark brown bumps on stems. Treat scale with dormant oil or lime sulfur in late winter. Insecticidal soap is effective against immature scales, called crawlers; spray in midspring and again in late spring.

Branches Swollen and Distorted; Holes, Sawdust, and Sap Stains at Base of Trunks

Poplar and willow borers tunnel into branches and trunks, causing rough, swollen growth. Entrances may be surrounded with sawdust and may exude sap. Leaves may wilt. Wood lesions may be evident. Where pruning isn't an option, kill the borers in their tunnels with a flexible wire, or inject parasitic nematodes into the entry holes, then plug the holes with putty.

Disease Control
Spots on Leaves; Cankers on Twigs; Leaves Wither and Die

Several fungi cause diseases that attack willow leaves, ultimately weakening trees. Upper leaf surfaces develop dark brown spots; leaves droop and curl. Later, whitish to gray, elliptical, sunken areas with black borders appear on twigs and leaf stalks. Tiny black or brown fruiting bodies grow in the stem lesions; masses of pink spores may be released in wet weather. The tree may die after several attacks. During dormant season, prune out infected branches. Rake up and destroy leaves and prunings. Spray with bordeaux mix after new leaves appear and repeat twice at 10-day intervals.

Seeping Lesions on Branches and/or Trunks

Several fungi cause cankers on willows. Cankers, from which sap oozes, appear at the base of the trunk or on twigs and branches. These can girdle and kill branches or the entire tree. Cytospora canker causes brown, sunken areas to form. These may have tiny brown, gray, or black bumps that may later produce red to yellow filaments. Other symptoms include wilting, dieback, and a thinning crown. Infected inner bark is red-brown. Preventive measures are useful: Avoid damaging the trunk with lawn mowers and other equipment; treat injuries promptly if they occur; and keep trees healthy and well watered. Remove and destroy branches killed by cankers. If possible, cut out infected tissue on the trunk, and carve away 2 in. of healthy bark from the perimeter of the infected area. Heavily infected trees should be cut and burned.

Syringa spp.

Lilac

Fertilizing

Lilac is a light feeder. No fertilizing is needed under most circumstances.

Insect Control

See "35 Common Garden Pests," on page 230, for additional information and control measures for the insect problems listed below.

Holes Surrounded by Sawdust on Trunks

Lilac borer adults are clear-winged moths that lay eggs on bark. The white, 1-in., brown-headed larvae tunnel into trunks. Tunnel entrances may be surrounded with sawdust and sap. Leaves may wilt. Plant may topple easily or be susceptible to disease. Remove branches infested with lilac borers and keep plants otherwise well pruned. Or, kill the borers in their tunnels with a flexible wire. Then plug the holes with putty.

Plants Weaken

Scales suck sap from stems and leaves, causing plants to weaken. Leaves may turn yellow and drop. Adult scales look like many whitish to dark brown bumps on stems, twigs, and leaves. Many native beneficial insects feed on scales. Treat scales with dormant oil or lime sulfur in late winter. Insecticidal soap is effective against immature scales, called crawlers; spray in mid-spring and again in late spring.

Disease Control
Brown Spots on Leaves

Several fungi cause brown or black leaf spots on lilacs. Clean up debris and improve air circulation. Use bordeaux mix in spring if the disease has been serious in the past; spray when leaves are beginning to uncurl and again after they are fully open.

Stems Die Back, Leaves Brown and Rolled

Phytopthora blight infection causes terminal buds and leaves to turn brown, roll upward, and droop. Stems may be killed to the ground. Use bordeaux mix in spring if the disease has been serious in the past; spray when leaves are beginning to uncurl and again after they are fully open.

Leaves Spotted or Shriveled; Shoots Blackened

Bacterial blight appears as brown or black spots on leaves, which eventually turn black and dry. Shoots develop black stripes or blackened ends. Flowers turn brown and collapse. This bacterial disease is likely if nitrogen is excessive. Prune out infected branches. Keep plant properly pruned to encourage good air circulation. Spray with bordeaux mix as soon as the disease occurs.

White Powder on Leaves

Powdery mildew appears as a white powdery covering on leaves. Leaves may fall. This fungal disease is unsightly, but doesn't severely harm the plant, especially when it occurs late in the season; if control is necessary, spray with sulfur or garlic extract as soon as disease occurs.

Thuja spp.

Arborvitae

Fertilizing

Feed established trees with an acidifying organic fertilizer every other spring or in late fall.

Insect Control

See "35 Common Garden Pests," on page 230, for additional information and control measures for the insect problems listed below.

Plants Weakened

Foliage curls, puckers, and turns yellow. Arborvitae aphids suck sap from foliage, stems, and roots, causing plants to yellow and weaken. Where arborvitae aphids are a problem, spray with insecticidal soap or summer oil spray.

Plants weaken; growth stunted. Scales suck sap from stems and foliage, causing plants to weaken. Foliage may discolor and drop. Adult scales look like many whitish to dark brown bumps on stems. Treat scales with dormant oil or lime sulfur in late winter. Insecticidal soap is effective against immature scales, called crawlers; spray in midspring and again in late spring.

Ragged Foliage; Silken Bags on Branches

Bagworms are brown moth larvae that feed from inside silken, 2–3-in.-long bags covered with bits of leaves and twigs. The bags resemble pine cones and enlarge as the larvae grow. Larvae move slowly about the plant stripping leaves, giving the tree a ragged appearance. Adult male moths have black wings; females are wingless. Handpick and destroy bagworms. Spraying with BTK (*Bacillus thuringiensis* var. *kurstaki*) in early spring when the larvae are young is the best control method.

Holes in Branches or Trunks; Sawdust and Sap near Holes

Cedar bark beetles and their grubs bore beneath bark in characteristic featherlike patterns. Reddish sawdust and sap may appear near holes. Bark is loosened; branches die. Foliage is stunted and discolored. Prune off twig ends killed by cedar bark beetle and increase water and fertilizing to strengthen the tree and assure that larger limbs and the trunk aren't attacked.

Leaves Blistered, Curled, and Brown at Tips

Leafminer larvae tunnel through needles, feeding on plant tissue. Needles may become blistered or curled, turn brown, and collapse. Prune away infested foliage in which larvae

overwinter. Hang yellow sticky traps to monitor populations. Adults are gray, $1/3$-in. moths; when first adults appear on traps, apply pyrethrin or neem extract to kill adults and young larvae before they enter foliage.

Needles Turn Gray or Brown; Webby Foliage

Spider mites suck sap from foliage, causing it to turn gray or brown. Foliage may appear distorted. Webs may be present. Control overwintering eggs of spider mites with dormant oil spray applied in late winter just before buds break. In summer, spray plants with a strong jet of water or with insecticidal soap to control pests. For severe infestations, spray with abamectin, neem, pyrethrin, or rotenone.

Disease Control

Tips of Twigs Turn Brown and Die Back

Blight may cause needles on tips of branches to turn brown; fungus may appear as black specks on needles. Prune away and destroy infected branches; be sure to cut 6 in. beyond infected, discolored wood. Spray with bordeaux mix monthly during summer.

Tilia spp.

Linden

Fertilizing

Fertilize with a balanced organic fertilizer every other spring or fall as needed.

Insect Control

See "35 Common Garden Pests," on page 230, for additional information and control measures for the insect problems listed below.

Yellowed, Stunted Plants

Aphids suck sap from leaves, stems, and blossoms, causing foliage to curl, pucker, and turn yellow. Leaves and buds may become stunted. Aphids produce honeydew, which will drip from tree branches and encourage the growth of sooty mold. Avoid excessive pruning or overfertilizing with nitrogen; the resulting succulent new growth encourages aphids. Control aphid infestations with high-pressure water sprays or insecticidal soap as necessary; dormant oil before bud break in spring smothers aphid eggs. Encourage populations of native beneficial insects.

Holes in Trunk; Bark Darkens

A variety of borers tunnel into linden trunks and limbs. Tunnel entrances may be surrounded by gummy sap. Bark darkens and dies. Infested limbs may die; serious infestations may kill the tree. Borers are most likely to attack trees already weakened by fungal diseases or stress. If possible, prune out damaged wood in winter and burn or destroy it to stop the infestation cycle. Also, gather and burn or discard fallen twigs, which may be infested. Increase fertility and watering to build the tree's overall health and vigor. Where pruning isn't an option, kill the borers in their tunnels with a flexible wire, or inject parasitic nematodes into the entry holes, then plug the holes with putty.

Leaves Skeletonized; Trees Weakened

A variety of caterpillars chew linden foliage. Repeated infestations cause trees to weaken, and die if severely infested. Use BTK (*Bacillus thuringiensis* var. *kurstaki*) to control most kinds of chewing caterpillars.

Leaves Stippled with Tiny Yellow Dots; Webby Foliage

Spider mites suck sap from leaves, causing them to become stippled. Leaves may appear distorted and will turn brown and dry up. Webs may be present. Control overwintering eggs of spider mites with dormant oil spray applied in late winter just before buds break. In summer, spray plants with a strong jet of water or with insecticidal soap to control pests. For severe infestations, spray with abamectin, neem, pyrethrin, or rotenone.

Disease Control
Brown Spots on Leaves

Anthracnose symptoms include small, brown spots with dark edges on leaves near the veins. Pink blisters may appear on leaves. Leaves may fall, and branches may wilt and die. Prevent the disease by thoroughly cleaning up and burning or disposing leaves in fall. If the disease persists year after year, spray with bordeaux mix in spring, just as leaves emerge, and again 10 days later.

Tiny Reddish Orange Spheres on Branches; Sunken Lesions

Several types of canker affect lindens. Symptoms may include the appearance of tiny red-orange to tan formations on twigs and branches, lesions near wounds or dead branches, sunken cankers with concentric rings of callus, or branch dieback. Prune and burn infected branches.

Brown Spots on Leaves

Leaf blight appears as many brown spots with dark borders developing on leaves. Leaves may turn brown and fall. Infection is more serious on younger trees. Gather and burn or dispose of leaves in fall. If the problem persists, spray with bordeaux mix in spring, just as leaves emerge, and again 10 days later.

White Powder on Leaves

Powdery mildew appears as a white powdery covering on leaves. Leaves may fall. This fungal disease is unsightly, but doesn't severely harm the plant, especially when it occurs late in the season; if control is necessary, spray with sulfur or garlic extract as soon as disease occurs.

Tsuga spp.

Hemlock

Fertilizing

Apply cottonseed meal or other acidifying fertilizer in early spring or fall to speed growth.

Insect Control

See "35 Common Garden Pests," on page 230, for additional information and control measures for the insect problems listed below.

Tree Defoliated

Adult hemlock loopers are small tan moths with dark, wavy stripes. The 1-in. larvae are brown to yellow-green with black spots. They walk in a characteristic looping motion. Larvae eat parts of needles, causing them to turn brown and fall; defoliation, especially of outer twigs, is common. Control hemlock looper with sprays of BTK (*Bacillus thuringiensis* var. *kurstaki*) as soon as pests appear. On small trees, handpicking may provide adequate control.

Yellowed Foliage

Plants weaken; bumps on needles and twigs. Scales suck sap from stems and foliage, causing plants to weaken. Needles may turn yellow and drop. The feeding females look like many whitish to dark brown bumps on stems. Hemlocks are also attacked by woolly adelgids, sucking insects formerly called aphids that cover themselves with tufts of cottonlike coating. Apply dormant oil spray before new growth begins in spring to control both pests; use insecticidal soap or summer oil for immature scales, called crawlers, during summer.

Yellow needles; webby foliage. Spider mites suck sap from needles, causing them to turn yellow. Leaves may appear distorted. Webs may be present. Control overwintering eggs of spider mites with dormant oil spray applied in late winter just before buds break. In summer, spray plants with a strong jet of water or with insecticidal soap to control pests. For severe infestations, spray with abamectin, neem, pyrethrin, or rotenone.

Disease Control

Diseases are rarely a problem on hemlock.

Needles Yellow

Rust may appear as reddish filaments on the undersides of needles, new shoots, and cones. New tip growth may be twisted. Needles and twigs may yellow, twigs may droop, and needles may fall. Prune out any infected twigs.

Ulmus spp.

Elm

Fertilizing

Feed every other year with a balanced organic fertilizer to maintain good vigor and disease resistance.

Insect Control

See "35 Common Garden Pests," on page 230, for additional information and control measures for the insect problems listed below.

Foliage Curls, Puckers, and Turns Yellow

Aphids suck sap from leaves, stems, and blossoms, causing foliage to curl, pucker, and turn yellow. Leaves and buds may become stunted. Control aphid infestations with high-pressure water sprays or insecticidal soap as necessary; dormant oil before bud break in spring smothers aphid eggs. Encourage populations of native beneficial insects.

Holes in Bark; Buds and Twigs Damaged

European elm bark beetles and their grubs bore through branches or trunks of recently cut, dying, or dead trees. Newly emerged adults may feed in twig crotches of healthy trees, and thus may infect them with Dutch elm disease. European elm bark beetle usually attacks weak trees; destroy their breeding ground by removing dead and dying trees nearby.

Leaves Chewed or Skeletonized

Foliage skeletonized; trees defoliated. Several caterpillars chew elm foliage. Cankerworms are striped brown or green, 1-in. inchworms. They move by looping their bodies and hang by silk threads. Adult moths are gray; females are wingless. Caterpillars feed heavily on leaves, causing trees to weaken and die if severely infested. BTK (*Bacillus thuringiensis* var. *kurstaki*) sprays work against cankerworms and other caterpillars. Scrape off any egg masses that are apparent during the winter.

Rectangular areas chewed in leaves; leaves become skeletonized, then dry up. Elm leaf beetles are yellow to yellow-green, 1/4-in. beetles with yellow legs and a black stripe on the edge of each wing. The 1/2-in. larvae are pale yellow with 2 dark stripes and black spots. Adults chew rectangular holes in leaves. Later in the season, larvae feed on lower leaf surfaces and skeletonize them; leaves may die and drop. Plants may become defoliated and weakened. To control elm leaf beetles, spray with BTSD (*Bacillus thuringiensis* var. *san diego*), or as a last resort, with ryania. For best results, apply just at the end of peak egg hatching when the insects are most susceptible.

Plants Weaken; Bumps on Leaves and Twigs

Scales suck sap from stems and leaves, causing plants to weaken. Leaves may turn yellow and drop. Adult scales look like many whitish to dark brown bumps on twigs and leaves. Spray dormant oil or lime sulfur spray in late winter to control scales; spray insecticidal soap or summer oil in spring after plants resume growth, repeat in early summer when the young scales are crawling.

Leaves Covered with Tan to Brown Blotches; Serpentine Tunnels in Leaves

Elm leafminer larvae tunnel through leaves, feeding on plant tissue. Leaves may turn brown and collapse. Leafminers may cause leaves to fall prematurely. Although new leaves usually re-grow, the damage stresses the tree. Use summer oil, neem extract, or rotenone, if necessary, to control severe infestations. Use yellow sticky traps to monitor emergence of adults (small, black sawflies) to help time sprays; sprays are only effective on adults or before the larvae tunnel into the leaves. Spray in early May when the first brood begins feeding on new leaves; spray in early to mid-July to control the second brood.

Disease Control
Leaves Wilted, Curled, and Yellowed; Branches Die

Dutch elm disease is spread by bark beetles or by root grafts from one infected tree to another. Leaves wilt, yellow, curl, and may fall;

eventually the entire tree dies. Elliptical depressions are present at crotches of young twigs; dark spots or streaks are present on wood. Keep elms healthy and vigorous by regular watering and feeding. Remove diseased branches as soon as possible after diagnosis. Prune radically to remove 10 ft. of undiseased wood beyond the discolored area. Remove all diseased or dying elms promptly and burn them to prevent the spread of the disease. Or dig a narrow, 36–40-in.-deep trench around the infected tree, just under the dripline, to sever all root grafts. Backfill immediately. Some species are resistant to the disease.

Viburnum spp.

Viburnum

Fertilizing

Feed young plants with acidifying balanced organic fertilizer.

Insect Control

See "35 Common Garden Pests," on page 230, for additional information and control measures for the insect problem listed below.

Foliage Curls, Puckers, and Turns Yellow

Aphids suck sap from leaves, stems, and blossoms, causing foliage to curl, pucker, and turn yellow. Leaves and buds may become stunted. Puckered leaf edges protect the pests while they feed. Aphids produce honeydew, which will drip from branches and encourage the growth of sooty mold. Control aphid infestations with high-pressure water sprays or with insecticidal soap as necessary; be sure to coat the undersides of leaves so the spray reaches the pests. Encourage populations of native beneficial insects.

Disease Control

Spots on Leaves

Bacterial leaf spot causes round, water-soaked spots on foliage. Spots may join together to form large, brown areas; leaves may fall prematurely. Pick off and destroy infected leaves; clean up debris in fall. In severe cases, spray weekly with bordeaux mix.

White Powder on Leaves

Powdery mildew appears as a thin, white, powdery covering on upper surfaces of leaves. Spray with sulfur or garlic spray as necessary. This fungal disease is unsightly, but doesn't severely harm the plant, especially when it occurs late in the season; if control is necessary, spray with bordeaux mix or garlic extract as soon as the disease occurs. Do not use sulfur sprays on viburnums; they will cause black spots followed by defoliation.

CHAPTER TWELVE

Lawns

By Anna Carr

Contrary to popular belief, it is possible to have a lush, weed-free lawn without using synthetic chemicals. And once you've converted to organic lawn care, you'll find that a chemical-free lawn requires less time and effort to maintain. Organic lawns are slower growing so they need fewer mowings. They also have deeper roots so they need less water and are better able to withstand all sorts of stresses. Because they're healthier to begin with, organic lawns develop fewer pest and disease problems. If problems do arise, they are handled in safe ways that pose the least threat to you and the environment.

Whether your lawn has been "chemicalized" or just neglected over the past few years, you can correct the damage in a couple of seasons. All it takes is a commitment to stop relying on quick-fix chemicals and to start building your soil organically and using natural pest and disease controls. This may sound like a lot of work, but it ultimately takes less time and money than the chemical lawn eats up. It's simply a matter of treating grass like the living thing that it is. Nurture it, as you do the garden, and it will return the favor with a safe and beautiful turf.

THE WELL-CULTURED LAWN

It's all too easy to take your lawn for granted. But whatever its size, that green expanse contains hundreds of little plants that need proper care and attention to thrive. Proper plant selection along with good cultural practices—watering, aerating, and mowing—are essential for a chemical-free lawn. With a little bit of planning and care, you'll be able to grow a beautiful lawn that will have good tolerance of insect and disease problems.

Choosing the Right Grass

Selecting the right grass or mixture of grasses for your area is an important first step if you're planting a new lawn or reworking an older one that's been plagued with problems. Grass experts recognize two major groups of lawn grasses—cool season and warm season. There are also cultivars of grasses that resist insects and diseases. For more information, see "Resistant Lawn Grass Cultivars" on page 422.

Cool-season grasses, which are best for the northern half of the country, typically grow the most in spring and fall, but may remain green all winter. In midsummer, they generally become brown and dormant. Cool-season grasses include Kentucky bluegrass, perennial ryegrass, and fine fescues. Fine fescues include red or creeping fescues, Chewings fescues, and hard fescues.

Warm-season grasses, best for the desert southwest and Sun Belt, are more heat tolerant than cool-season grasses. They're dormant in winter, may turn brown when dormant, and don't begin growing until early summer. All are more drought tolerant than cool-season grasses. These include centipedegrass, zoysiagrass, St. Augustinegrass, and bermudagrass.

Gardeners living in the transition zone between North and South—as well as in the west and Great Plains—should use a mix of cool- and warm-season grasses. In the East, mixes often consist of improved tall fescues along with small amounts of other grasses such as bluegrass and annual ryegrass. In the western part of the transitional zone, two native warm-season grasses—buffalograss and blue gramma-grass—are good choices, especially for unwatered lawns. Crested wheatgrass is another excellent grass for lawns that will not be irrigated.

Care Basics

You may be surprised to learn that some tried-and-true lawn practices are actually harmful to your lawn. Daily watering, close mowing, and removing grass clippings from the lawn all serve to weaken your lawn, not strengthen it. A healthy, chemical-free lawn actually requires less work than a highly manicured, chemically maintained lawn.

Watering. Don't sprinkle your lawn every evening. Pleasant as it is for the gardener, it's deadly for the grass. The blades will dry slowly, or perhaps remain wet throughout the night, creating favorable conditions for disease organisms. Even more damaging, a light, daily watering encourages shallow roots that are unable to withstand the stresses of heat and drought and that ultimately weaken the turf.

Instead, water deeply and infrequently. Soak the soil to the depth of the roots—at least 3 inches. Don't water again until the top inch of soil is thoroughly dry. This encourages deep-rooted plants that are more drought tolerant. Where disease is a problem, water in the morning so that the blades dry out quickly.

Aerating. Lawns that are heavily used or are on heavy soils may need periodic aeration to loosen the soil and encourage the roots to grow deeper. Landscapers use power-driven aerating machines to spike the soil on playing fields. You can rent a motorized or manually powered aerator for your own yard. Or, if you have only a small lawn, you can try a more primitive method. Insert a spading fork in the turf at a 45-degree angle, and push it until the tines penetrate about 4 inches. Push down slightly on the handle to loosen the soil, and pull out the fork. Repeat this technique every foot or so all over your lawn. To cover larger areas with less work, you can drive 4-inch spikes into a board. Lay this on the lawn, and invite the kids to parade over it.

Mowing. Mowing the lawn can be hard on the gardener and is definitely stressful for the grass. It makes the blades dry out and temporarily sets back root growth. You can minimize stress for you and your lawn by keeping mower blades sharp and adjusting the mower height according to the species and possibly even the season.

The shaved look is great for the golf course,

but unless you are growing a specialty turf such as bentgrass, lawns cut higher are healthier. In the North, a taller lawn has deeper roots and will stay healthier and greener during hot, dry summer months. In fall, you may mow more closely, as the lawn is being prepared for winter.

Warm-season grasses perform best when cut shorter in summer. They are growing fastest in the hot months and may tend to accumulate thatch if kept too high then. But don't cut them shorter than ¾ inch, or you may chew up their stolons. In fall, raise the mowing height slightly. See "Suggested Mowing Heights," below, for specific recommendations on mowing height for different types of grasses.

FERTILIZING

The beauty of a chemically fertilized lawn is only blade deep. Synthetic chemical fertilizers —especially highly soluble forms of nitrogen —quickly green up the lawn, but they do so at the expense of good root development. The result is shallow roots, excessive thatch (a layer of dead grass and bits of grass roots that builds up on the surface of the soil), and eventually more problems with many pests and diseases. If you're lucky enough to have loamy soil that is naturally rich in organic matter, these problems may not develop for many years. But unless you renew the organic matter content of the soil

Suggested Mowing Heights

How frequently and to what height you mow is important to your lawn's health. Grass that is cut too short will be weak and more prone to insect, disease, and weed problems.

Just how often to mow depends on how fast your lawn grows. A good rule of thumb is to mow frequently enough that you never cut more than one-third of the grass height at each mowing.

Grass	Summer Height (in.)	Spring/Fall Height (in.)
COOL-SEASON		
Bentgrass	1	¾
Canada bluegrass	4	3
Creeping red fescue	2½	2
Kentucky bluegrass	3	2
Perennial rye	3	2
Tall fescue	3½	2½
WARM-SEASON		
Bermudagrass	1½	¾
Buffalograss	2½	2
Centipedegrass	2	1½
St. Augustinegrass	2½	1½
Zoysiagrass	1½	1

Controlling Thatch

Thatch is nothing more than plant debris that hasn't yet decomposed. A little thatch is a good thing. It protects roots and helps the lawn retain moisture. But a thicker layer creates all sorts of problems.

If you have a well-maintained organic lawn, you should never encounter thatch problems. But, if your lawn has been neglected or treated with chemical fertilizers, you may need to dethatch. If your lawn feels spongy when you walk on it, it may have excessive thatch build-up. Look closely at the base of the grass blades: If you see ½ in. or more of densely packed organic matter surrounding them, your lawn has too much thatch. Air, water, and fertilizers don't readily penetrate such a barrier. Grass-eating insects, most notably chinch bugs, can hide and flourish in the thatch. It favors the development of brown patch, dollar spot, and other lawn diseases. Weeds can infiltrate a lawn weakened by thatch.

To keep thatch to a minimum (a layer less than ½ in.), try top-dressing in spring or fall with a microbial humus builder such as Ringer's Lawn Restore or Lawns Alive! Sprinkling a compost activator such as BioActivator will supply beneficial microbes that break down the thatch.

If your lawn is suffering from severe thatch build-up, you may need to periodically remove some of the thatch. In a small yard, you can thin a heavy layer by raking with a special thatching rake. These sturdy iron rakes are available from nursery suppliers and mail-order tool companies. For very large lawns, you will need to rent a dethatcher.

Either dethatching method will leave the lawn looking terrible temporarily. There will be gaps, bare spots and areas where the roots of healthy turf are torn or shredded. Dethatching is very stressful to the lawn, so it's best to do it in the cool, moist seasons when recovery will be quickest. Dethatch cool-season grasses in early fall and warm-season grasses in early spring. Immediately afterwards, top-dress the lawn with rich humus and make the necessary fertility adjustments to your soil. Then overseed with fast-growing, good-quality seed. Keep the lawn deeply watered as it re-establishes itself.

To prevent future problems with thatch, mow a bit less frequently while still keeping the grass height appropriate for the species in your lawn. Where compatible with the grasses' requirements, adjust the pH so that it is between 6.5 and 7.5. At this level, thatch materials decompose most rapidly. Don't worry about lawn clippings—they rarely contribute to thatch. In fact, they are good for the lawn. If you're planting a new lawn or overseeding, choose cultivars that tend to produce less thatch.

---

beneath the grass, you'll eventually end up with a weak, chemical-dependent lawn.

Slow-release, organic fertilizers benefit the soil as well as the lawn. They improve soil structure and have long-lasting beneficial effects on soil microbes. Used in combination with the right cultural practices, such as aeration and proper mowing, they go a long way toward making your lawn less labor intensive.

Doing without Fertilizer

It is even possible to maintain an acceptable lawn for some time without any fertilizers—organic or otherwise. This is particularly true of mixed lawns that contain a good amount of clover. Clover is a legume, which means its roots grow in close association with soil bacteria, which can convert nitrogen from the air into nitrogen compounds that can be used by plants. It's difficult to overseed clover in an established lawn, but if you are starting a new lawn, try including clover in your seeding mix.

Leaving grass clippings to decompose on the lawn also provides some nitrogen and other nutrients. A mulching mower that chops the clippings and evenly spreads them speeds their decomposition. These practices, plus a topdressing of humus every few years may be all that your lawn requires. Set your own expectations and monitor your lawn for signs of nutrient stress before you decide on a fertilizing program. Don't just fertilize because the neighbors are doing it.

It's a good idea to have your lawn soil analyzed before you begin a new fertilization program. See "Having Your Soil Tested," on page 48, for more information about soil tests and directions for preparing a soil sample for testing. When you gather samples from the lawn, preserve the sod by carefully cutting it, rolling it back, gathering the sample, refilling the hole, unrolling the soil, tamping it in place, and watering the area.

Adjusting pH

Most lawn grasses do best in slightly acid or neutral soils. Centipedegrass and buffalograss are exceptions. Centipedegrass needs acid soil, and buffalograss does best in alkaline soil. For other species, adjust the pH to between 6.0 and 7.0. If you live east of the Mississippi River, you'll probably have to apply ground calcitic or dolomitic limestone to raise the pH. Soils west of the Mississippi tend to be alkaline. Usually these can be corrected by choosing acidic organic matter as your soil builder. Topdressing your lawn with cottonseed meal, leaf mold, or sphaghnum peat moss will slowly moderate an alkaline soil, and any humus-based product will have the same effect. Applying sulfur is only necessary in areas with very alkaline soils, as in some parts of the southwest United States.

Increasing Organic Matter

Lawns that have been neglected or treated only with synthetic chemical fertilizers will benefit from a topdressing of rich humus before fertilizer is applied. You can apply humus with a lawn spreader or broadcast it by hand. Spread a $1/4$- to $1/2$-inch-thick layer of fertile loam, compost, dehydrated cow manure, or mushroom soil over your lawn. (See "Computing Compost Coverage" in the box, on page 68, for an easy way to figure out how much compost or other material you'll need to spread to get a layer of the proper thickness.)

Most of the commercial blended organic fertilizers perform just fine on the lawn. Aim for an NPK (nitrogen-phosphorus-potassium) ratio of about 3-1-2 or 4-1-2 depending on your soil's fertility. (See "Mix and Match," on page 89, for recipes for homemade blended organic fertilizer.) Nitrogen is the most important nutrient for lawn grasses because it feeds the fast-growing blades and keeps the lawn green. Potassium is a close second, especially just before the grass goes dormant and needs to build up its roots.

Some companies manufacture organic lawn fertilizers that contain beneficial soil microorganisms and help eliminate thatch. Broadcast these products, Sustane or Lawns Alive!, for example, to rejuvenate a tired turf or help any lawn recover from aerating or dethatching. For lawns that are already in pretty good shape, a dose of one of these bio-activated humus builders once every year or two may be all that is needed to keep grass healthy. For a really green, lush turf, spray your lawn with liquid kelp or fish emulsion in spring or fall. These fertilizers green up the grass in a hurry and even give some disease protection.

Chelated trace mineral sprays can help supply nutrients that may be lacking in poor soil. Chelated iron dramatically greens up the lawn and also helps it resist drought, disease, and pest stresses. However, use these materials as a supplement to your soil-building program. Don't expect them to take the place of rich humus and balanced organic fertilizers.

Figuring Out Fertilizer Needs

Just how much fertilizer your lawn needs depends on the quality of your soil and on the type of grass you are growing. The typical lawn needs 2 to 4 pounds of nitrogen per 1,000 square feet of turf annually. Lawns in very sad shape may require much more the first season. Well-established lawns, growing in rich, humusy soil may need just 1 pound per 1,000 square feet per year.

Fertilize when the lawn begins its most active growth, but don't feed it during stressful times. In the North, fertilize in spring and early fall. Healthy lawns need only one yearly feeding; this is best done in fall. Avoid the temptation to feed the lawn in summer, especially if you are using fairly quick release fertilizers. The grass may look like it needs a boost then, but more nitrogen is the last thing it needs. Fertilizers applied in midsummer will only stress a cool-season grass, which grows best in spring and fall, is slow-growing or dormant in summer, and stays green in winter. Summer fertilizing forces these grasses to put forth new growth when they are trying to conserve energy and survive dry, hot weather. Wait until daily temperatures fall below 50°F and the grass's growth has slowed considerably, but hasn't stopped.

In the South, spring and summer feedings are great, but fall feeding can be disastrous. Warm-season grasses, which grow best during summer and turn brown when the weather turns cool, need their first feeding in early spring. Fertilize again in midsummer. Avoid any fertilizing after August. Too much nitrogen may weaken warm-season grasses at this time, making them more vulnerable to winter kill.

When to fertilize lawns in a mid-length growing season area (see the map on page 30 to see what growing season area you live in) depends on the types of grasses grown. (If you don't know what type of grass you have in your lawn, refer to "The Chemical-Free Gardener's Library," on page 431, for titles of books that include photographs or illustrations of lawn grasses.) If the lawn is made up of cool-season grasses such as bluegrass, perennial ryegrass, and fescues, feed it during fall and spring. If growing warm-season grasses such as bermudagrass, St. Augustinegrass, and zoysiagrass, feed in spring and summer.

Some turf specialists recommend changing the fertilizer formula for different times of year, especially in the North. Give grasses most of their nitrogen needs during active growth, and use a more potassium-rich fertilizer just before dormancy in the fall. This will help to build up the roots, strengthening the plant before harsh weather sets in.

FIGHTING INSECT AND DISEASE PROBLEMS

Most insect and disease problems of lawns affect more than one species of lawn grass and occur across broad areas of the country. The listings that follow key you in to problems with brief descriptions of symptoms. The insect or disease causing the problem is described along with suggested prevention and control measures. These measures are almost entirely cultural or biological. While there are organically acceptable insecticides that will kill some lawn pests, save them for very severe situations. These compounds are toxic to people and animals, and it's not a good idea to be spraying them on areas where you, your children, or your pets could be walking, playing, or sitting.

"Resistant Lawn Grass Cultivars," on page 422, provides the names of many cultivars that have been bred for resistance to some common lawn pests and diseases. Many are available only to landscapers, nursery owners, and specialists who buy in bulk, but others are included in

But What about the Dandelions?

If you're making the switch to organic lawn care, one of your biggest questions may be how to control weeds without chemicals. It's not surprising that chemically maintained lawns need regular doses of herbicides. When lawns are shallow-rooted with little resistance to drought or pest problems, weeds can move right in.

In the organic lawn, weed control is not a matter of quick-fix, short-lived solutions. It is an integral part of the entire soil-building, lawn management process. At the heart of the approach is the recognition that extensive weed growth is almost always the sign of some deeper problem. A vigorous stand of grass can choke out most weed species. It stands to reason that where weeds have taken hold, the turf just isn't as healthy as it should be. Reduce the stress, and you'll often take care of the weed problem.

The most common condition that encourages weeds is compacted soil, but this isn't the only cause. Too much or too little fertilization, a build-up of thatch, bad mowing practices, poor drainage, or just the wrong choice of grass species may also stress the lawn enough to allow weeds to take over. Identify the important causes on your lawn by first noting where most weeds are growing. Is it a heavily trafficked area? Is the grass species planted there one that is unable to handle such use? Does the sprinkler routinely miss this spot? Is it thinly seeded? If the conditions causing stress aren't readily apparent, look more closely at the weeds growing there. Knowing what sort of environment they prefer may point to the problem. See "Weeds as Soil Indicators," on page 60, for a list of common weeds and the growing conditions that favor them.

Once you've identified the conditions that let weeds get started in the lawn, you can set about changing them so that grasses, not weeds, are encouraged to grow. Adjusting the mowing height, watering, fertilizing, dethatching, aerating, topdressing, and overseeding can go a long way toward eliminating weeds.

In more severe cases, where you haven't caught the problem early on, you'll have to destroy the weeds before these cultural methods can really help the grass re-establish itself. Organic gardeners who don't want to use chemical herbicides can choose from several effective products and methods. Chapter 5 contains detailed information on these methods and products.

Where the weed situation is very serious and the turf is sickly and sparse, the best approach is often a complete lawn restoration.

---

seed mixtures sold for home lawns. Ask your local supplier about resistant cultivars, or request that he stock one listed in the table.

Insect Control

Insect pest problems will diminish as your lawn becomes less chemical dependent and more naturally maintained. Also, good management practices such as dethatching, using organic fertilizers, and supplying adequate water all encourage beneficial organisms and help keep insect populations at a manageable level.

But even when resistant grasses are used and the lawn is well maintained, some insect pests will occasionally pose a threat.

Bare or Ragged Patches

Armyworms chew grass blades down to the crowns, leaving bare areas or ragged patches of

This involves tilling up the entire yard, working in plenty of organic matter (that is free of weed seeds) and rock fertilizers, and reseeding.

Don't try this in midsummer. Wait until fall in the North and early spring in the South. In fact, it is even wise to avoid any extensive weeding during a very hot, dry summer, since you'll be creating a bare spot that needs replanting. Keep the annual weeds mowed so that they don't go to seed, maintain good moisture levels, and continue to top-dress with humus-building substances throughout the hot summer months. Then, do the major weeding and reseeding in the cooler, wetter months of fall.

Once the weeds are gone, loosen the soil with a spading fork or pick and hoe. Work in the richest topsoil and humus-building material you can find, along with any amendments your soil analysis suggests. Choose a high-quality grass seed appropriate for the conditions in your yard. Weed seed content is listed on the seed bag label. Inexpensive mixes may contain a high percentage of weed seed. Use a mixture of different species since that tends to create a turf most resistant to weeds, insects, and diseases. Some companies offer special fast-growing seed mixtures designed for filling in patches. These contain mulch and a water-retaining substance that helps the grass estab-lish itself within two weeks. You might also want to use this reseeding time to introduce some of the endophyte-containing cultivars into your lawn. The important thing is to choose your seed carefully—the wrong species or a poor-quality seed will mean more weed problems down the road.

While you're at it, top-dress surrounding areas with an organic soil-building product such as Lawn Restore, and overseed sparsely covered areas with the new seed. Water all the seeded areas deeply. A piece of floating row cover stretched over the most heavily seeded areas will encourage rapid seed germination.

In the South, make overseeding a regular part of fall lawn care. Cut bermudagrass and centipedegrass very close in late fall, then overseed with annual rye. This not only keeps out weeds, but greens up the lawn for winter.

Virtually all of the techniques for good lawn management help keep out weeds, just as they discourage insect pests and disease. Focus on aeration, topdressing, overseeding, and proper mowing to maintain healthy, vigorous turf that chokes out weeds. Maintain sufficient nutrients throughout the growing season, and periodi-cally check the pH. Never use fresh manure or cool-temperature compost on the lawn, because these may contain weed seeds.

grass. They are a common pest on bermudagrass during cool, wet periods. Spray affected areas with parasitic nematodes while pests are still in the larval stage. For best results, apply the nematodes in late afternoon or evening to avoid the drying effects of direct sunlight. Spraying larvae with BTK (*Bacillus thuringiensis* var. *kurstaki*) is also effective. Remove dead areas of turf. Reseed or overseed with resistant grasses such as the high-endophyte-level cultivars.

Yellowed Grass; Thinned, Brown Turf

Bermudagrass mites are microscopic white mites that suck sap from grass blades, causing them to turn yellow or straw-colored. Heavy infestations can kill plants, leaving grass looking brown and sparse. The mites thrive on poorly fed lawns and during dry conditions. The best controls are to improve fertility and keep the lawn well watered during dry spells.

Yellow or Brown Patches

Billbugs are cream to brown or almost black, $1/4$–$1/2$-in. weevils. Their larvae, which are white grubs with yellow-brown heads, feed on grass stems, causing shoots to turn brown and die. In warm weather, the grubs tunnel into the soil and feed on roots and rhizomes. Control billbug grub problems by aerating the lawn, watering deeply in spring to encourage deep root growth, and removing thatch. Reseed or overseed with resistant cultivars.

Yellow Circular Patches

Chinch bugs have $1/5$-in. black bodies with a black triangular pad between white, folded wings. They are a serious pest of lawns throughout the country, especially in dry conditions. The adults suck plant sap; infested grass turns yellow and patches may die off. The nymphs, tiny bright red insects with a white band across their backs, also suck sap, and are responsible for the most damage. The pests usually congregate in open, sunny parts of the lawn. They also smell bad, especially when crushed, and you may be able to detect the odor simply by walking across a severely infested lawn. You can also check for chinch bugs by using water to force them out. Remove both ends from a large coffee can. Push one end 2 in. into the sod, using a knife to cut a path for it or a board to hammer it in place. Fill the can with water and within 10 minutes, chinch bugs will float to the surface.

In moist soil, a naturally occurring fungus keeps chinch bugs under control. Chinch bugs coated with a fuzzy material have been infected by the fungus. Big-eyed bugs also attack chinch bugs. If you have chinch bug problems, try to control them by keeping the soil very moist. Wet it to a depth of 6 in., and maintain that moist condition for 3 or 4 weeks. If chinch bugs are still present after the water treatment, try trapping them by drenching the infested area with soapy water and catching the bugs on an old

| Endophyte Grasses Fight Pests |

A new group of pest-resistant grass cultivars, the endophyte-containing grasses, has recently come onto the market. These grasses are hosts to fungi that produce a substance that deters feeding by some insect pests and is actually toxic to other pests. The toxin also will cause serious illness in sheep and cattle and cause pregnant mares to fail to develop milk. Don't seed endophyte-containing grasses in areas where these animals might feed.

Endophyte-containing cultivars have some resistance to most pests that feed on the crown and lower stem of the grasses. Chinch bugs, sod webworms, billbugs, and armyworms fall into this category, but grubs don't. Many of the endophyte-containing cultivars are only available wholesale, but more are coming on the market every year and are slowly making their way to homeowners. So far, grasses with the highest levels of endophyte are all perennial ryes, but breeders hope to develop endophyte-containing Kentucky bluegrasses and fescues within the next few years. A good nursery should be able to help you find a blend that includes endophyte-containing cultivars. Since these grasses have less than a 2-year shelf life, buy only the freshest seed.

flannel sheet. (For more details on this method, see "Chinch Bug Traps" on page 210.) Seed or reseed with resistant cultivars.

Chewed Grass

Grasshoppers chew on grass, but are not often a serious threat to an entire lawn. The protozoan *Nosema locustae* kills grasshoppers, but the effects aren't usually realized until the second summer after application. Broadcast the bait as soon as grasshoppers emerge in the spring.

Irregular Streaks or Brown Grass through the Lawn

Mole crickets are 1½-in., light brown insects with short forelegs, and shovel-like feet. They are serious pests of lawns in the South. The crickets tunnel under the lawn and feed on grass roots. Infested grass wilts and turns brown, so irregular dark streaks appear on lawns. Parasitic nematodes are an effective control. Water the soil well before and after application. Apply during late afternoon or evening to avoid the drying effects of the sun.

Small, Dead Spots

Sod webworms sever grass blades just above the thatch line and pull the blades into a silken tunnel in the ground to eat. As they feed and tunnel, irregular, dead patches appear in the lawn. They are most commonly a problem on bluegrass, hybrid bermudagrasses, and bentgrasses in the South. Hot, dry conditions and a buildup of thatch encourage the pests. Control webworms by saturating infested areas with a soap drench (2 Tbsp. liquid detergent to 1 gal. water) to float the larvae to the surface. Rake the pests into a pile and dump them into a bucket of soapy water. Use insecticidal soap to ensure the pests are killed. Applying BTK or drenching the soil with parasitic nematodes when pests are in their larval stage (usually about 2 weeks after moths appear) are also effective controls. Spray with liquid pyrethrin solution (2 oz. 2-percent pyrethrin to 1 qt. water) if all other attempts at control fail. Limit spraying to areas severely infested with webworms. Endophyte-containing cultivars of fine-bladed fescues and perennial ryes are resistant to sod webworm.

Irregular, Brown, Dead Patches

White grubs are the curved, fat, whitish larvae of Japanese beetles and other beetle species. They chew on grass roots, leaving sections of lawn that appear burned and can be easily lifted from the ground. Ten or more grubs per square foot is a serious infestation. Japanese beetle grubs are most common on cool-season grasses. Other species such as scarab beetle grubs, European chafer, and oriental beetle feed on bentgrasses, Kentucky and annual bluegrasses, and fescues. A simple way to fight grubs is to walk the turf in spiked sandals made for the purpose (available through mail-order catalogs). For a large lawn, apply milky disease spores. This will eliminate Japanese beetle grubs over a few seasons. Apply the material in late spring or fall when soil temperature is at least 70°F, but while grubs are still present.

Predatory nematodes also control both Japanese beetle grubs and other white grubs, but they may not have the long-lasting effect that milky disease spores have. Watering the soil well before and after the application improves results.

Disease Control

If your lawn has disease problems, it's a sure sign that you need to change the ways you are caring for and feeding it. Improper mowing, too much or too little water or fertilizers, and poor aeration are common causes of disease. Use good management tactics and disease shouldn't become a serious problem. Be sure you're growing the best species of turf for your location. If your existing lawn isn't an appropriate species mix, you have two options. You can till it under and start from scratch, or gradually replant with new, improved grasses in bare areas, and overseed the existing grass. Plant a mixture of grasses, including cultivars that have some disease resistance, and the chance of problems is further diminished. Most turf specialists agree that one of the turf-type tall fescues is the best bet not only for disease and pest resistance, but also for general adaptability and low maintenance in most areas of the country.

(continued on page 424)

Resistant Lawn Grass Cultivars

Plant breeders are coming out with new cultivars of grasses every year. Most of these show excellent disease resistance and an overall hardiness that also makes them less susceptible to insect damage. They tend to be low-maintenance grasses with less exacting water and fertilizer needs and produce a lush turf with little care. For the best choice for your lawn, talk to your local Cooperative Extension agent or a nursery owner or lawn-care expert familiar with the latest developments in lawn grasses.

Cultivar	Diseases Resisted	Comments
BERMUDAGRASS		
'Midiron'		Cold tolerant
'Tifway'		Resists bermudagrass mite
FESCUE		
'Apache Tall'	Brown patch	Performs well at low nitrogen levels; good weather resistance
'Arid Tall'	Brown patch	Good color and density
'Aurora Hard'	Dollar spot, leaf rust, leaf spot, pink snow mold, powdery mildew, red thread	
'Aztec Tall'	Brown patch, leaf spot	Good color and density
'Biljarthard'	Dollar spot, pink snow mold, red thread	
'Bonanza'	Brown patch, crown rust, net blotch	Good weather resistance; performs well at low nitrogen levels
'Cimmaron'	Brown patch, crown rust, net blotch	Good weather resistance
'Crossfire Tall'	Brown patch	Good color and density
'Jaguar II Tall'	Brown patch	
'Kentucky-31'		Resistant to sod webworm
'Longfellow Chewings'	Dollar spot, leaf spot	
'Olympic Tall'		Drought tolerant; consistently good performance
'Rebel II'	Brown patch, crown rust, net blotch	Good weather resistance; performs well at low nitrogen levels
'Shenandoah Tall'	Brown patch, leaf spot	Good color and density
'SR 3000 Hard' (crusader mix)	Anthracnose, dollar spot, leaf spot, net blotch, pink snow mold, powdery mildew, red thread	High endophyte level; somewhat resistant to most lawn insect pests
'Victory Chewings'	Dollar spot, powdery mildew, red thread	Good density
'Wrangler'	Net blotch	
KENTUCKY BLUEGRASS		
'A-34'		Good in shade; very aggressive

Cultivar	Diseases Resisted	Comments
'Adelphi'	Dollar spot, pink snow mold, red thread	
'America'	Dollar spot, leaf spot	
'Banff'	Leaf spot	Cold tolerant
'Baron'	Dollar spot, gray snow mold	
'Bristol'	Dollar spot, leaf spot, pink snow mold, powdery mildew, red thread	Shade tolerant
'Coventry'	Leaf spot	
'Dawn'	Dollar spot, leaf rust, leaf spot	
'Eclipse'	Dollar spot, leaf spot, red thread	Shade tolerant
'Fylking'	Leaf spot	
'Glade'	Leaf spot, powdery mildew, stripe smut	Shade tolerant
'Midnight'	Leaf spot	Good summer performance
'Monopoly'		Withstands poor fertility; stands up to hard wear
'Touchdown'	Dollar spot, leaf spot, powdery mildew, red thread, stripe smut	Very aggressive
'Victa'	Dollar spot	Tolerates lower pH than other cultivars
PERENNIAL RYEGRASS		
'Citation II'	Brown patch, leaf spot, stem and crown rust	High endophyte level; somewhat resistant to most lawn insect pests
'Commander'	Brown patch, leaf spot, red thread, stem and crown rust	High endophyte level; somewhat resistant to most lawn insect pests
'Manhattan II'	Brown patch, stem and crown rust, winter brown blight	
'Palmer'	Brown patch, red thread	
'Pennant'		High endophyte level; somewhat resistant to most lawn insect pests
'Regal'	Red thread	Drought tolerant; high endophyte level; somewhat resistant to most lawn insect pests
'Repell'	Red thread	High endophyte level; somewhat resistant to most lawn insect pests
'Saturn'	Brown patch, dollar spot	High endophyte level; somewhat resistant to most lawn insect pests
'SR 4000' (crusader mix)	Brown patch, leaf spot, net blotch, stem and crown rust	High endophyte level; somewhat resistant to most lawn insect pests
ST. AUGUSTINEGRASS		
'Floratam'	St. Augustinegrass decline	Resists chinch bug
'Raleigh'	St. Augustinegrass decline	Cold tolerant

If disease does occur, make a careful diagnosis before treating. A kit put out by Agri-Diagnostics Association (see "Sources," on page 426, for the address) contains simple chemical tests for detecting 3 common lawn diseases—brown patch, dollar spot, and pythium blight. More tests may be available soon. Once you've identified the disease, follow these guidelines to cure it in the least toxic way.

Brown, Circular Patches

Brown patch appears as brown or dead, circular areas of grass up to 2 ft. in diameter. Grass in the infected patches will be thin. The fungus tends to attack bentgrass, bermudagrass, ryegrasses, St. Augustinegrass, tall fescues, and zoysiagrass, especially during hot, humid weather. Close cutting, poor drainage, overwatering, excessive nitrogen, and low pH all contribute to brown patch. Control the disease by reducing nitrogen fertilization, mowing less frequently, aerating, and dethatching. Top-dress with humus-building material. Water less frequently and only during the day so grass dries off quickly. Spot treatment with a product containing microorganisms and organic matter such as Ringer's Dispatch helps stop the disease early on. Rake out dead grass and replant bare spots with brown patch resistant grasses.

Small, White, Circular Patches That Turn Brown

Infection by dollar spot fungus causes tan or straw-colored spots the size of silver dollars to appear on the lawn. The fungus occurs widely on golf greens, but may also be a severe problem on poorly drained lawns that are low in nitrogen. Aerate the soil and improve drainage by top-dressing with organic matter. In the meantime, keep soil well watered. Apply a high nitrogen fertilizer; applying liquid seaweed is also helpful. Mow less frequently if possible. Organic lawn products that contain beneficial soil organisms and enzymes, such as Ringer's Lawn Restore, Lawns Alive!, and Vitabuild, may help provide control. Overseed in fall with resistant cultivars.

Green Spots Outlined with Brown

If your lawn has bright green circular areas that seem to be growing more rapidly than the rest of your lawn, the grass is probably infected by fairy ring fungus. A ring of grass around the green spots turns brown; the green areas eventually will brown out also. A circle of mushrooms usually develops around the edge of the infected area. Rake and discard the mushrooms as they appear. Spike the area with a spading fork every day. Water well. Encourage beneficial soil microbes by applying organic fertilizers and topdressing with a humus builder such as Vitabuild, Lawn Restore, or finished compost. You can try to dig out the diseased soil in the fairy ring, but this is not easy. If you leave any infested soil behind, the rings will probably recur. Dig down 2 ft. in the area of the ring and extend the hole outward at least 1 ft. from the ring. Remove the soil carefully, being sure not to spill any infected soil on the healthy lawn. Fill in the hole with the best humusy topsoil you have, adding a microbe-rich humus product or finished compost, and reseed.

Reddish Brown, Tan, or Yellow Patches

Fusarium blight is fairly common on Kentucky bluegrass during periods of hot, humid weather. Infected lawns develop 2–6-in.-diameter spots of reddish brown grass that later turn tan and finally yellow. Roots will be rotten and may be covered with pink mold. Heavy thatch favors growth of the fungus, so dethatching and aerating are control measures you should consider. Apply 1–2 in. of water each week. Raise the mowing height in summer. Avoid fertilizer applications in late spring or early summer. Rake out dead grass and replant dead patches with Fusarium resistant cultivars.

Dark Spots on Grass Blades

Several fungi cause leaf spot and leaf blight diseases in lawns. Common symptoms include reddish brown to black spots on the leaf blades, shriveled blades, and rotted crowns and roots. These fungi are favored by hot, humid weather. Fight leaf spots and blights by building soil fertility, particularly with fast-acting nitrogen sources. Set mowing height as high as recommended for the species being grown. If possible, don't mow during outbreaks of disease, because it may further spread the fungi. Keep soil evenly moist. Restore diseased areas by raking around the area and by top-dressing with a humus builder such as Lawn Restore, Lawns Alive!, or Vitabuild. Reseed or overseed with resistant cultivars.

Water-Soaked, Blackened Grass

Pythium fungi cause a disease known as cottony blight or greasy spot. The initial symptom is patches of grass that have turned black and look water soaked. In humid conditions, a cottony mold may appear on the grass. The disease usually occurs in wet, poorly drained areas that have been excessively fertilized. Once established, it can spread very rapidly. It is most common in warm, wet weather on bentgrass, bermudagrass, bluegrass, fescue, and perennial ryegrass. Alkaline soils and calcium deficiency encourage the disease. If pythium blight appears on your lawn, aerate and dethatch as needed. Run a soil analysis, and correct calicium deficiency if necessary. Reduce nitrogen fertilization, particularly in fall. Keep soil evenly moist. Maintain slightly acid soil. Treat affected patches with a product containing microorganisms and organic matter such as Ringer's Dispatch. In severe cases, where the lawn has been completely infected, it may be necessary to replant. Improve soil drainage before replanting by enriching the soil with organic matter.

Circular, Scorched Patches or Pink, Gelatinous Masses

Lawns infected by red thread fungi have circular patches of dried grass that have red or rusty threads on the blades. Lawns suffering from pink patch will develop pink, gelatinous masses on leaf blades. These 2 fungal diseases are common on bentgrass, bluegrass, fescues, and ryegrass, especially in cool, humid regions. Low fertility aggravates the problem. Apply an organic fertilizer with nitrogen in readily available form such as a seaweed foliar spray. Mow regularly to remove the infected leaf tips.

Yellow to Rusty Red Powdery Blisters on Grass

Infection by rust fungi causes yellow to rusty red powdery spore blisters to appear on leaf blades. Seriously infected lawns turn yellow and wither. Rust typically occurs in late summer on dry lawns lacking nitrogen. It is particularly common on bluegrass in the North and zoysiagrass and ryegrass in the South. To help prevent rust, water well in the early morning. Fertilize northern lawns in early spring and southern ones in fall with a liquid kelp or other nitrogen-rich fertilizer. If rust invades your lawn, mow regularly to a height appropriate for the species of grass you're growing. Rake out dead grass and overseed with resistant cultivars.

Sources

Seeds and Plants for Disease- and Insect-Resistant Cultivars

The following companies sell seeds and plants of many disease- and insect-resistant fruit and vegetable cultivars. The numbering here corresponds to the numbers in the listings of resistant cultivars in the tables in chapters 8 and 10. Many of these companies also offer flower seeds as well as trees, shrubs, and perennials.

1. Adams County Nursery, Inc.
P.O. Box 108
Aspers, PA 17304

2. Ames' Orchard and Nursery
6 East Elm Street
Fayetteville, AR 72703

3. Bear Creek Nursery
P.O. Box 411
Northport, WA 99157

4. W. Atlee Burpee & Co.
300 Park Avenue
Warminster, PA 18974

5. C & O Nursery
P.O. Box 116
Wenatchee, WA 98807

6. Country Heritage Nursery
P.O. Box 536
Hartford, MI 49057

7. Cumberland Valley Nurseries, Inc.
P.O. Box 471
McMinnville, TN 37110

8. Farmer Seed and Nursery Co.
818 N.W. 4th Street
Faribault, MN 55021

9. Henry Field Seed & Nursery Co.
P.O. Box 700
Shenandoah, IA 51602

10. Foster Nursery Co., Inc.
P.O. Box 150
Fredonia, NY 14063

11. Gurney Seed & Nursery Co.
2nd and Capital Streets
Yankton, SD 57078

12. Harris Seeds
P.O. Box 22960
Rochester, NY 14692

13. Hastings
P.O. Box 115535
Atlanta, GA 30310

14. HollyDale Nursery
P.O. Box 26
Pelham, TN 37366

15. Johnny's Selected Seeds
Foss Hill Road
Albion, ME 04910

16. J. W. Jung Seed Co.
335 South High Street
Randolph, WI 53957

17. Kelly Nurseries
Highway 54
Louisiana, MO 63353

18. Orol Ledden & Sons, Inc.
P.O. Box 7
Sewell, NJ 08080

19. Liberty Seed Co.
P.O. Box 806
New Philadelphia, OH 44663

20. Earl May Seed & Nursery L. P.
208 North Elm Street
Shenandoah, IA 51603

21. J. E. Miller Nurseries, Inc.
5060 West Lake Road
Canandaigua, NY 14424

22. New York State Fruit Testing Cooperative
Association, Inc.
West North Street
Geneva, NY 14456

23. Nichols Garden Nursery
1190 North Pacific Highway
Albany, OR 97321

24. North Star Gardens
19060 Manning Trail North
Marine on St. Croix, MN 55047

25. Northwoods Nursery
28696 South Cramer Road
Molalla, OR 97038

26. Park Seed Co.
P.O. Box 31
Greenwood, SC 29647

27. Pinetree Garden Seeds
Route 100
New Gloucester, ME 04260

28. Raintree Nursery
391 Butts Road
Morton, WA 98356

29. Rayner Bros., Inc.
P.O. Box 1617
Salisbury, MD 21802

30. Southern Exposure Seed Exchange
P.O. Box 158
North Garden, VA 22959

31. Southmeadow Fruit Gardens
Lakeside, MI 49116

32. Stark Bro's Nurseries & Orchards Co.
Louisiana, MO 63353

33. Stokes Seeds, Inc.
Box 548
Buffalo, NY 14240

34. Territorial Seed Co.
P.O. Box 27
Lorane, OR 97451

35. Thompson & Morgan, Inc.
P.O. Box 1308
Jackson, NJ 08527

General Gardening Equipment and Supplies

Many organic gardening products are not readily available at local garden centers. Fortunately, there are many fine mail-order suppliers. The following companies offer a wide range of merchandise including botanical poisons, biological controls, composting equipment, copper and sulfur fungicides, floating row covers, insect traps, organic soil amendments and fertilizers, soil test kits, sprayers, tillers, tools and accessories, and watering equipment.

Agri-Diagnostics Association
2611 Branch Pike
Cinnaminson, NJ 08077

Bio-Dynamic Preparations
P.O. Box 133
Woolwine, VA 24185

The Clapper Co.
1121 Washington Street
West Newton, MA 02165

Gardener's Supply Co.
128 Intervale Road
Burlington, VT 05401

Green Earth Organics
9422 144th Street E
Puyallup, WA 98373

Harmony Farm Supply
P.O. Box 460
Graton, CA 95444

The Kinsman Co., Inc.
River Road
Point Pleasant, PA 18950

A. M. Leonard, Inc.
P.O. Box 816
Piqua, OH 45356

Mantis Manufacturing Corp.
1458 County Line Road
Huntingdon Valley, PA 19006

The Natural Gardening Co.
217 San Anselmo Avenue
San Anselmo, CA 94960

Natural Gardening Research Center
Highway 48
P.O. Box 149
Sunman, IN 47041

Necessary Trading Co.
703 Salem Avenue
New Castle, VA 24127

North Country Organics
P.O. Box 107
Newbury, VT 05051

Ohio Earth Food
13737 Duquette Avenue NE
Hartville, OH 44632

Peaceful Valley Farm Supply Co.
P.O. Box 2209
Grass Valley, CA 95945

Smith & Hawken
25 Corte Madera
Mill Valley, CA 94941

The Urban Farmer Store
2833 Vicente Street
San Francisco, CA 94116

Fertilizers and Soil Amendments

Some organic soil amendments and fertilizers are not generally available at garden centers or from general gardening supply mail-order companies. This list includes several manufacturers or suppliers of these hard-to-find products.

Agronics (formerly FarmGuard Products)
701 Madison Street NE
Alburquerque, NM 87110
(Humates)

Erth-Rite
R.D. 1
Gap, PA 17527
(Aragonite and other amendments)

The Fertrell Co.
P.O. Box 265
Bainbridge, PA 17502
(Granite meal)

The Guano Company International, Inc.
3562 East 80th Street
Cleveland, OH 44105
(Guano)

J & J Agriproducts & Services
220 South Second Street
Dillsburg, PA 17019
(Enzyme products)

Marcona Ocean Industries, Ltd.
P.O. Box 1189
Apopka, FL 32704
(Aragonite)

Nitron Industries
4605 Johnson Road
Fayetteville, AR 72702
(Feather meal, enzyme products)

Insect Predators and Parasites and Other Biological Controls

These companies offer microbial disease products, pheromone traps, and insect predators and parasites. Insectaries specialize in rearing pest predators and parasites. Some rear several species at their facilities, while others raise only one or two, and buy the other species they offer from other insectaries. When you place an order, ask whether the insectary raises the predator or parasite you're interested in on site. If not, try to find a direct source from which to order. The less shipping involved, the better for the health and viability of the organisms. If you live in the United States and plan to order organisms from a Canadian firm, you must apply for a permit from the U.S. Department of Agriculture. Write to U. S. Department of Agriculture, Plant Protection and Quarantine/APHIS, Federal Center Building, Hyattsville, MD 20782; ask for application form #526. There is no fee for the permit, but it will take from 10 days to 2 months to receive the permit after you submit an application. The permit allows you to import the organisms you specify in your application for a period up to one year from the date of issuance of the permit.

Applied Bio-Nomics Ltd.
P.O. Box 2637
Sidney, B.C.
Canada V8L 4C1
(Insect predators and parasites)

Beneficial Insectary
14751 Oak Run Road
Oak Run, CA 96069
(Insect predators and parasites)

BoBiotrol
54 South Bear Creek Drive
Merced, CA 95340
(Insect predators and parasites)

Foothill Ag. Research
510½ West Chase Drive
Corona, CA 91720
(Insect predators and parasites)

Growing Naturally
P.O. Box 54
149 Pine Lane
Pineville, PA 18946
(Insect predators and parasites, biological controls, and parasitic nematodes)

Hydro-Gardens, Inc.
P.O. Box 9707
Colorado Springs, CO 80932
(Insect predators and parasites and parasitic nematodes)

Nature's Control
P.O. Box 35
Medford, OR 97501
(Insect predators and parasites)

Rincon-Vitova Insectaries, Inc.
P.O. Box 95
Oak View, CA 93022
(Insect predators and parasites)

Ringer Corp.
9959 Valley View Road
Eden Prarie, MN 55344
(Biological controls and botanical poisons)

The Chemical-Free Gardener's Library

Books

Bush-Brown, James, and Louise Bush-Brown. *America's Garden Book*. rev. ed. New York: Charles Scribner's Sons, 1980.

Campbell, Stu. *Let It Rot: The Gardener's Guide to Composting*. Charlotte, Vt.: Garden Way Publishing, 1975.

Carr, Anna. *Good Neighbors: Companion Planting for Gardeners*. Emmaus, Pa.: Rodale Press, 1985.

Coleman, Eliot. *The New Organic Grower: A Master's Manual of Tools and Techniques for the Home and Market Gardener*. Chelsea, Vt.: Chelsea Green Publishing Co., 1989.

Cox, Jeff, and the Editors of Rodale's *Organic Gardening* Magazine. *How to Grow Vegetables Organically*. Emmaus, Pa.: Rodale Press, 1988.

Damrosch, Barbara. *The Garden Primer*. New York: Workman Publishing, 1988.

Ellis, Barbara W., ed. *Rodale's Illustrated Encyclopedia of Gardening and Landscaping Techniques*. Emmaus, Pa.: Rodale Press, 1990.

Flint, Mary Louise. *Pests of the Garden and Small Farm: A Grower's Guide to Using Less Pesticide*. Oakland, Calif., ANR Publications of the University of California, 1990. (Available from Publications, Division of Agriculture and Natural Resources, University of California, 6701 San Pablo Ave., Oakland, CA 94608.)

Gershuny, Grace, and Joseph Smillie. *The Soul of Soil: A Guide to Ecological Soil Management*. 2nd ed. St. Johnsbury, Vt.: Gaia Services, 1986. (Available from Gaia Services, R.F.D. 3, Box 84, St. Johnsbury, VT 05819.)

Hall-Beyer, Bart, and Jean Richard. *Ecological Fruit Production in the North.* Trois-Rivières, Quebec: Jean Richard, 1983. (Available from Bart Hall-Beyer, 163 McNamee, Scotstown, Quebec, Canada J0B 3B0.)

Halpin, Anne Moyer, and the Editors of Rodale Press. *Foolproof Planting: How to Successfully Start and Propagate More Than 250 Vegetables, Flowers, Trees, and Shrubs.* Emmaus, Pa.: Rodale Press, 1990.

Hamilton, Geoff. *The Organic Garden Book.* New York: Crown Publishers, 1987.

Minnich, Jerry, Marjorie Hunt, and the Editors of Rodale's *Organic Gardening* Magazine. *The Rodale Guide to Composting.* Emmaus, Pa.: Rodale Press, 1979.

Mother Earth News staff. *The Healthy Garden Handbook: An Illustrated Guide to Combating Insects, Garden Pests, and Plant Diseases.* New York: Simon & Schuster, 1989.

Page, Stephen, and Joseph Smillie. *The Orchard Almanac.* 2nd ed. Rockport, Maine: Spraysaver Publications, 1988. (Available from Spraysaver Publications, P.O. Box 392, Rockport ME 04856.)

Rodale's *Organic Gardening* Magazine Editors. *The Encyclopedia of Organic Gardening.* Emmaus, Pa.: Rodale Press, 1978.

Schultz, Warren. *The Chemical-Free Lawn: The Newest Varieties and Techniques to Grow Lush, Hardy Grass.* Emmaus, Pa.: Rodale Press, 1989.

Smith, Miranda. *Greenhouse Gardening.* Emmaus, Pa.: Rodale Press, 1985.

Stebbins, Robert L., and Michael MacCaskey. *Pruning: How-To Guide for Gardeners.* Los Angeles: HPBooks, 1983.

Yepsen, Roger B., Jr., ed. *The Encyclopedia of Natural Insect and Disease Control.* Emmaus, Pa.: Rodale Press, 1984.

Identification Guides

Borror, Donald J., and Richard E. White. *A Field Guide to the Insects of America North of Mexico.* The Peterson Field Guide Series. Boston: Houghton Mifflin Co., 1970.

Carr, Anna. *Rodale's Color Handbook of Garden Insects.* Emmaus, Pa.: Rodale Press, 1979.

Muenscher, Walter Conrad. *Weeds.* 2nd ed. New York: Macmillan Publishing Co., 1955. (Reprint, with forward and appendixes by Peter A. Hyypio. Ithaca, N.Y.: Comstock Publishing Associates, 1980.)

Smith, Miranda, and Anna Carr. *Rodale's Garden Insect, Disease, and Weed Identification Guide.* Emmaus, Pa.: Rodale Press, 1988.

Westcott, Cynthia. *The Gardener's Bug Book.* Garden City, N.Y.: Doubleday & Co., 1973.

———. *Westcott's Plant Disease Handbook.* 5th ed., rev. by R. Kenneth Horst. New York: Van Nostrand Reinhold Co., 1990.

Periodicals

Common Sense Pest Control Quarterly, Bio-Integral Resource Center (BIRC), P.O. Box 7414, Berkeley, CA 94707

HortIdeas, Greg and Patricia Y. Williams, Rt. 1, Box 302, Black Lick Rd., Gravel Switch, KY 40328

National Gardening, National Gardening Association, 180 Flynn Ave., Burlington, VT 05401

Organic Gardening, Rodale Press, Inc., 33 E. Minor St., Emmaus, PA 18098

Garden Workbook Forms

On the following pages, you'll find blank forms to help you keep track of your gardening plans and activities from year to year. Make photocopies of these handy forms as needed, and keep them together in a garden workbook to chart your progress.

❧ *Rotation records.* Use this form to keep track of your crop plantings in the vegetable garden. Label each garden bed, or label a diagram of your garden to make it simple to record the location of each crop. Note the location of each crop in your garden in the first column. Then, each year, enter the information about the crops you plant in successive columns. Over time, you will create an easy-to-read history of the rotation pattern in each part of your garden. See page 27 for a sample form that has been filled out.

❧ *Soil records.* Keep the soil test results and recommendations you have received from soil testing laboratories in your garden workbook for handy reference. Use the soil records form to keep track of the soil amendments and fertil-izers you add and any green manure crops you plant, and make notes on your observations of changes in your soil and crop responses. Keeping track of what you add to your soil over the course of time will help you judge what soil management practices are most effective for your yard and garden.

❧ *Weather and garden diary.* Keep a record of garden and weather conditions on this form. These records will help you evaluate the pest control methods and products you use and figure out what role environmental conditions might be playing in the problems that occur in your yard and garden.

❧ *Cultivar comparison.* Note cultivar names, planting and harvest dates, and your comments on the performance and problems of each culti-var you try growing in your garden on this sheet. This storehouse of data will help you discover which cultivars perform best in your particular weather and soil conditions.

Rotation Record

Location	Year 1	Year 2	Year 3	Year 4

Soil Records for Year _____

Section of Yard/Garden	Soil Type, pH, Last Test Date	Amendments/Cover Crops	Comments

Weather and Garden Diary

Date	Weather Conditions	Pest Problems/Treatments	Comments

Cultivar Comparison

Cultivar	Date Planted	First Harvest Date	Comments

Index

Note: Page references in boldface indicate illustrations.
Italic references indicate tables.

green peach, summer oils and, 213

herbal sprays and, 217

insect fungal diseases and, 189, 192

insect growth regulators and, 227

insecticidal soaps and, 215

lacewings and, 182

minute pirate bugs and, 183

neem and, 225

nicotine and, 225

pine bark, 394

pyrethrins and, 221

quassia and, 226

reflective mulch and, 167

root, nicotine and, 225

rotenone and, 223

ryania and, 223

sabadilla and, 224

spruce gall, 392

starch spray and, 228

summer oils and, 212

tomato leaf sprays and, 216

tulip bulb, 338

water sprays and, 195

water stress and, **164**

water traps and, 203

yellow sticky traps and, 200

Aphid midges, 174, 180

Aphidolete aphidimyza. See Aphid midges

Aphytis melinus, 181

Apium graveolens var. *dulce. See* Celery

Apple, 343–46

pests and diseases of, 343–46

pomace, 87, *92*

Apple maggot(s), 15, 207, **231,** 344, 362

control methods, *231*

garden sanitation and, 165

traps, 202–3

Apple scab, 131, 345–46, 361

Aquatic insects, and insect fungal diseases, 192

Aquilegia spp., 307–8

pests and diseases of, 307–8

Aragonite, *92,* 99–100

Arborvitae. *See Thuja* spp.

Arborvitae aphids, 406. *See also* Aphid(s)

Archips argyrospila. See Leafrollers

Arctiidae family. *See* Webworms

Armoracia rusticana. See Horseradish

Armyworms, **231,** 276, 418–19, 420. *See also* Beet armyworms; Fall armyworms

Bacillus thuringiensis and, 186

baculoviruses and, 192

control methods, *231*

Artichoke plume moth, 207

Ash. *See Fraxinus* spp.

Ash yellows mycoplasma, 385

Asiatic oak weevils, 400

Asparagus, 135, 254–55

pests and diseases of, 254

Asparagus beetles, 254

floating row covers and, 196

nicotine and, 225

spotted, 254

Asparagus officinalis. See Asparagus

Aster, annual. *See Callistephus chinensis*

Aster leafhoppers, 311. *See also* Leafhoppers

Aster yellows, 133. *See also specific plants affected*

Australian lady beetles, 181–82. *See also* Lady beetles

Austrian pea, 114

Azalea. *See Rhododendron* spp.

Azalea flower spot, 402

Azalea petal blight, 402

B

Baby's-breath. *See Gypsophila* spp.

Bacillus lentimorbus. See Milky disease spores

Bacillus popilliae. See Milky disease spores

Bacillus thuringiensis (BT), 184–87, 192

pests controlled by, 186

var. *israelensis* (BTI), 185–87

var. *kurstaki* (BTK), 185–87

var. *san diego* (BTSD), 185–87

Bacterial cultures, adding to soil, 76

Bacterial diseases, 131–33. *See also specific diseases;* Disease controls, 133

Bactericides, spray application and weather, 349

Baculoviruses, 188–89, 192

Bagworms. *See also specific plants affected*

Bacillus thuringiensis and, 186

Baited traps, 207–9

Baking soda, 157

Bark beetles, 394. *See also* Beetles

Barriers for pest control, 24–25, 196–200

Bat guano, *92, 102*

Bean(s), 148

lima, 255–56

pests and diseases of, 255–56

pod borers, 255–56

snap, 257–58

pests and diseases of, 257–58

Bean mosaic, 133. *See also specific plants affected;* Mosaic viruses

Beating tray, 193–94, **194**

Beauveria bassiana, 189, 192

Beds

preparing new, 67–72

weed control in, 124

Beech. *See Fagus* spp.

Beech bark disease, 383

Bees

citrus oils and, 226

rotenone and, 223

Beet, 259–60

internal black spot of, 262

pests and diseases of, 259–60

Beet armyworms

abamectin and, 228

Bacillus thuringiensis and, 186

thuringiensin and, 229

Beetles, 175–76. *See also specific beetles*

damage symptoms, **162**

shaking, 193

tree bands and, 197, 198

Begonia × *tuberhybrida,* 308–9

pests and diseases of, 308–9

Bemisia tabaci. See Whiteflies

Cabbage root maggots, 143, **233,** 261, 290, 299
    control methods, *233*
    crop residues and, 156
    dehydrating dust and, 199
    diatomaceous earth and, 213
    floating row covers and, 196
    insect parasitic nematodes and, 191
    time of planting and, 167
    water traps and, 203
    yellow sticky traps and, 200
Cabbageworms. *See* Imported cabbageworms
Calcitic limestone, 77, **93,** 100
Calcium, 79, 82–83
    deficiency, *64, 65,* 80, *138, 139,* 262, 263
        in celery, 267
        in tomato, 297
Calendar of garden management, 29–42
Calendula officinalis, 309–10
    pests and diseases of, 309–10
Calirua cerasi. See Sawflies
Callistephus chinensis, 310–12
    pests and diseases of, 311–12
Camellia spp., 377–78
    pests and diseases of, 377–78
Cane galls, 347
Canker, 376, 378. *See also specific cankers; specific plants affected*
Canker stain, 397
Cankerworms. *See also specific plants affected*
    Bacillus thuringiensis and, 186
Canna × *generalis,* 312
    pests and diseases of, 312
Capsaicin dusts, 218
Capsicum annuum, Grossum group. *See* Pepper
Carpenterworms, insect parasitic nematodes and, 191
Carrot, 167, 265–66
    pests and diseases of, 265–66
Carrot rust flies, **233,** 265, 267
    control methods, *233*
    dehydrating dust and, 199
    floating row covers and, 196

time of planting and, 167
    yellow sticky traps and, 200
Caterpillars, 312, 408, 410. *See also specific caterpillars*
    Bacillus thuringiensis and, 192
    damage symptoms, **162**
    floating row covers and, 196
    insect disease viruses and, 188
    insect fungal diseases and, 189
    lacewings and, 182
    minute pirate bugs and, 183
    neem and, 225
    protozoan insect diseases and, 190, 192
    quassia and, 226
    ryania and, 223
Cattle flies, insect growth regulators and, 227
Cauliflower. *See* Cabbage
Cedar apple rust, 346, 361, 391. *See also* Rust
Cedar bark beetles, 407. *See also* Beetles
Celery, 267–68
    cracked stem of, 262, 267
    pests and diseases of, 267–68
Celery leaftiers, pyrethrins and, 221
Centipedegrass, 413, 416
Certified disease-free plants, 137
Chafers, 191, 354, 421
    insect parasitic nematodes and, 191
Chamomile, 59
Cheese whey, as soil amendment, 87
Chelated trace minerals, 90–91
    sprays, 83, 416–17
Chemical controls
    for disease, 129, 154–58
    for insects, 160, 211–29
    synthetic, 9
    for weeds, 105, 125–26
Cherry, 351–53
    pests and diseases of, 351–53
Cherry fruit flies, 207, 351
    traps for, 203
Chicory, 59
Chilean nitrate of soda, 101

Chilocorus nigritus. See Lady beetles
Chinch bugs, 420
    neem and, 225
    sabadilla and, 224
    traps for, 210
Chinese cabbage. *See* Cabbage
Chinese praying mantids, 177
Chitin, 136
Chlorine excess, symptoms of, *64, 65*
Chlorosis, 287
Chrysanthemum gall midges, 313
Chrysanthemum lace bugs, 314
Chrysanthemum leafminers, 313
    abamectin and, 228
Chrysanthemum spp., 313–14
    pests and diseases of, 313–14
Chrysobothris femorata. See Boring beetles
Chrysopa carnea. See Lacewings
Chrysoperla rufilabrus. See Lacewings
Cicadellidae family. *See* Leafhoppers
Citrullus lanatus. See Watermelon
Citrus oils, 226–27
Citrus thrips, sabadilla and, 224
Citrus trees
    sabadilla dust and, 224
    scale predators and parasites and, 180–81
    sticky tree bands and, 209–10
    summer oil and, 213
    tree bands and, 197
Clay soils, 76, 78
Clematis spp., 314–15
    pests and diseases of, 315
Click beetles, 209. *See also* Wireworm(s)
Clover, 72, 415–16. *See also specific clovers*
Club root, 131. *See also specific plants affected*
Coccoidea superfamily. *See* Scales
Codling moths, 207, **234.** *See also specific plants affected*
    Bacillus thuringiensis and, 186
    baculoviruses and, 192
    control methods, *234*
    cover crops and, 173
    dormant oils and, 212

Elm leaf beetles, 410
Bacillus thuringiensis and, 186
Elm leafminers, 410. *See also*
Leafminers
Encarsia formosa. See Whitefly parasitic wasps
Endophyte grasses, 420
Entomophthora spp., 190, 192
Environmental conditions
for disease control, 141–46
dormancy of seeds and, 106
insect resistance and, 166–67
stress and, 135, 373
Enzyme products as organic
fertilizers, 97
Epicauta vittata. See Blister beetles
Epilachna varivestis. See Mexican
bean beetles
Epitrix spp. *See* Flea beetles
Epsom salts, 83, *94,* 100
Equisetum arvense, 155
Euonymus spp., 382
pests and diseases of, 382
European chafers, 421
European corn borers, 207, **236,**
269, 286
Bacillus thuringiensis and, 186
control methods, 194–95, *236*
crop residues and, 165
ryania and, 223
sabadilla and, 224
Trichogramma wasps and, 183
European elm bark beetles, 410
European pine shoot moth, 207
European red mites, **247.** *See also*
specific plants affected; Mites
control methods, *247*
spider mite predatory mites
and, 180
Euxoa spp. *See* Cutworm(s)
Evergreen needles as mulch, 81

F

Fagus spp., 382–83
pests and diseases of, 383
Fairy ring fungus, 424
Fall armyworms, 207, 269, 295. *See*
also Armyworms
abamectin and, 228

citrus oils and, 226–27
insect parasitic nematodes and,
191
Fall webworms, 345. *See also*
Webworms
Bacillus thuringiensis and, 186
Feather meal, *94,* 101
Fertilizers, 12, 24, 84–91. *See also*
specific plants
for flower gardens, 317
formula for making, 89
for lawns, 75, 414–17
organic, *92–96*
organic matter as, 70
reading package labels on, 85
synthetic, 48
for trees and shrubs, 384
Fescue meal, *94*
Field crop pests, and *Trichogramma*
wasps, 182–83
Fine fescues, 413
Fire ants, and abamectin, 228
Fire blight, 346, 362, 380, 381, 399.
See also Blight
bacteria life cycle, **132**
Fireflies, 176
Firethorn. *See Pyracantha* spp.
Fish emulsion, 12, 81, *94,* 101–2
Fish extract, 81
Fish meal, 81, *94,* 102
Flatheaded borers, 371–74, 398
Flea beetles, **236.** *See also specific flea*
beetles; specific plants affected
control methods, *236*
damage symptoms, **162**
floating row covers and, 196
neem and, 225
rotenone and, 222
trap crops and, 210
Fleas
diatomaceous earth and, 213
insect growth regulators and,
227
Flies. *See also specific flies*
beneficial, 174
insect disease viruses and, 188
insect fungal diseases and,
189
pyrethrins and, 221
quassia and, 226

Floating row covers, 24, **112,** 143,
196–97
disease prevention and, 154
Flower(s), 302–41. *See also specific*
flowers
buying healthy, 306
garden
fertilizing, 317
sanitation, 144
soil care, 317
transplants, 280
Flower blight, 378
Flowering cherry. *See* Cherry
Flowers of sulfur, *94,* 100
Flower thrips, 323, 330. *See also*
Thrips
Foliar feeding, 24, 88, 148–49
Foliar nematodes, 314
Food by-products as organic
fertilizers, 97
Fragaria × *ananassa. See* Strawberry
Fraxinus spp., 383–85
pests and diseases of, 383–85
Fruit flies, 207. *See also specific fruit flies*
abamectin and, 228
Fruits, 342–65
Fruittree leafrollers, 207. *See also*
Leafrollers
dormant oils and, 212
Fruit trees, 83. *See also specific fruit*
trees
planting, 344
pruning for disease control,
152, 358
Fungal disease(s), 129–31. *See also*
specific diseases; specific plants affected;
Disease
baking soda and, 157
bordeaux mix and, 158
control, 130
copper sulfate and, 158
horsetail spray and, 156
insect, 189–90, 192
prevention, 130, 141–42
stinging nettle spray and, 155
sulfur and, 157
weather and, 143
Fungi, 129–31
life cycle, **130**
moisture and, 148–49

Juniper. *See Juniperus* spp.
Juniperus spp., 390–91
    pests and diseases of, 390–91

K

Kale. *See* Cabbage
Kelp, 82, 83, 90
    -derived spray, 82
    extracts, 88, 89, 104
    meal, *95*, 104
Kentucky bluegrass, 413
K-Mag, 83

L

Lace bugs, **238.** *See also specific*
    plants affected
    control methods, *238*
Lacewings, 176, **176,** 182
Lactuca sativa. See Lettuce
Lady beetles, **175,** 177, 180–81. *See*
    also Australian lady beetles
Lagenidium giganteum, 189, 192
Land plaster. *See* Gypsum
Landscape fabrics, 113
Langbeinite, 83, 104
Larkspur leafminers, 319. *See also*
    Leafminers
Late blight, 43, 131, 289, 297. *See*
    also Blight
Lawn(s), 412–25
    aerating, 413
    care basics, 413–17
    characteristics of organic, 412
    chinch bug traps, 210
    competition with trees and
        shrubs, 384
    disease control and, 421–25
    grasses
        cool-season, 413, *414*
        disease-resistant, *422–23*
        warm-season, 413, *414*
    milky disease spores and,
        187–88
    mowing, 373, 413–14, *414*
    overseeding, 419
    preparing new, 67–72
    protozoan diseases and, 190
    restoration of, 418–19

thatch control on, 415
topdressing, 75
watering, 413
Leaf, 73, 86, 99
    analysis for nutrient content,
        63–66
    indicators of nutrient im-
        balance, 63
    mold, 81, 99
Leaf blight, 408, 425. *See also* Blight
Leaf blister, 400
Leaf curl virus, 351
Leafhoppers, **238.** *See also specific*
    plants affected
    control methods, *238*
    cover crops and, 173
    damage symptoms, **162**
    floating row covers and, 196
    garlic oil sprays and, 216
    minute pirate bugs and, 183
    nicotine and, 225
    pyrethrins and, 221
    rotenone and, 223
Leafminers, 173, **239.** *See also specific*
    plants affected
    abamectin and, 228
    control methods, *239*
    damage symptoms, **162**
    neem and, 225
    nicotine and, 225
Leafroll, 133
Leafrollers, **239.** *See also specific*
    leafrollers
    abamectin and, 228
    Bacillus thuringiensis and, 186
    control methods, *239*
    damage symptoms, **162**
Leaf spot. *See also specific plants*
    affected
    angular, 271
    bordeaux mix and, 158
    lime sulfur and, 158
    septoria, 297
    sulfur and, 157
    tar, 386
Leaf weevils, damage symptoms,
    162
Leather meal, 98, 102
Leeks, 291
Legumes, 72, 73, 81

Leptinotarsa decemlineata. See Colo-
    rado potato beetles
Leptomastidea abnormis, 182
Leptomastix dactylopii, 182
Lespedeza hay, *95*
Lettuce, 148, 274–77
    pests and diseases of, 275–76
Lice, and diatomaceous earth, 213
Lightning damage to trees, 373
Light traps, 204
Lilac. *See Syringa* spp.
Lilac borer, 384, 405
Lilium spp., 327–29
    pests and diseases of, 327–29
Lily. *See Lilium* spp.
Lima bean. *See* Bean(s), lima
Limax maximus. See Slug(s)
Limestone, 77–79, 100
Lime sulfur sprays, 158
    with dormant oil, 212, 222
Limonius agonus. See Wireworm(s)
Linden. *See Tilia* spp.
Lindorus lopthantae. See Lady beetles
Liquid fertilizers, 88–89
Liriomyza spp. *See* Leafminers
Listroderes difficilis. See Weevils
Litmus paper soil test, 59
Loganberry. *See* Bramble fruit
Long-season garden calendar, 31–42
Lumbricus rubellus, 77
Lycopersicon esculentum. See Tomato
Lygus lineolaris. See Tarnished plant
    bugs

M

Maggot flies, and baited traps, 207
Magnesium, 83
    deficiency, *64, 65,* 79, 80
    excess, 61, 80
Magnolia spp., 391–92
    pests and diseases of, 391–92
Maize dwarf mosaic, 269. *See also*
    Mosaic viruses
Major plant nutrients. *See* Mineral(s)
Malus pumila. See Apple
Manganese, excess, symptoms of,
    64, 65
Manure, 82, 86, *93, 95, 96,* 97, 164
    tea, 90, 102

Maple. *See Acer* spp.

Maple phenacoccus scales, 370. *See also* Scales

Map of season lengths, **30**

Marigold. *See Tagetes* spp.

Masked chafers, and insect parasitic nematodes, 191

May beetles, and milky disease spores, 187

Mealybug(s), 173. *See also specific plants affected*
    alcohol sprays and, 216
    dormant oils and, 212
    excess nitrogen and, 164
    insecticidal soaps and, 215
    neem and, 225
    predator and parasites, 181–82
    summer oils and, 212

Mediterranean fruit flies, 207. *See also* Fruit flies

Meloidogyne spp. *See* Root-knot nematodes

Melon, 277–79
    pests and diseases of, 277–79

Melon fly, 207

Melonworm, and *Bacillus thuringiensis,* 186

Metaphycus helvolus. See Parasitic wasps

Metarrhizium, 190, 192

Metaseiulus occidentalis. See Spider mite predatory mites

Methoprene, 227

Mexican bean beetles, 227, **240.** *See also specific plants affected*
    bug-juice sprays and, 218
    control methods, *240*
    floating row covers and, 196
    handpicking and, 193
    neem and, 225
    pyrethrins and, 221
    ryania and, 223
    spined soldier bug and, 183
    trap crops and, 210

Microbial inoculants, 98

Microbial insecticides, 183–92

Microbiotic activity in soil, 73

Micro-herd. *See* Microorganisms in soil

Micronutrient(s), 62, 83, 104
    deficiencies, and chelated trace mineral sprays, 90–91
    phosphorus excess and, 81, 82

Microorganisms in soil, 73, 76, 78–79
    as plant pathogens, 183–92

Midges, and insect growth regulators, 227

Midlength season garden calendar, 31–42

Mildew. *See also* Downy mildew; Powdery mildew
    bordeaux mix and, 158
    garlic oil and, 157
    lime sulfur and, 158

Milkweed bugs, and ryania, 223

Milky disease spores, 187–88
    applicator for, 187–88

Milky spore disease. *See* Milky disease spores

Mimosa. *See Albizia julibrissin*

Mimosa webworms. *See also* Webworms
    Bacillus thuringiensis and, 186

Mimosa wilt, 371

Mineral(s), 49, 59–66, 77–83
    disorders, 59–66
    imbalances, correcting, 81–83
    supplements, 24

Minute pirate bugs, 183

Mites, 176. *See also specific mites*
    dormant oils and, 212
    insecticidal soaps and, 215

Moisture sensor, 56

Mold. *See* Gray mold; Sooty mold

Mole crickets, 421
    insect parasitic nematodes and, 191

Molybdenum deficiency, symptoms of, *64, 65*

Monitoring insect populations with traps, 200–210

Monitoring soil moisture, 56

Mormon crickets, and protozoan insect diseases, 190, 192

Mosaic viruses. *See also specific plants affected*
    coleus, 313
    cucumber, 133, 272, 334

    life cycle of, **134**
    maize dwarf, 269
    tobacco, 133, 298, 334
    turnip, 300
    yellow, 287

Mosquitoes
    Bacillus thuringiensis and, 186, 192
    insect fungal diseases and, 189, 192
    insect growth regulators and, 227
    pyrethrins and, 221

Mowing, 413–14, 418

Mulch, 84, 113
    crown rot and, 328
    disease control and prevention and, 141–42, 144
    flower gardens and, 317
    fruit trees and, 344
    living, 114–15
    organic, 99
    perennial weeds and, 113–14
    permanent plantings and, 73–75
    reflective, 167
    synthetic, 111–13, **112,** 143
    to improve soil structure, 67
    to suppress insect damage, 167
    as weed control and prevention, 17, 110–15

Mulching mower, 416

Multipurpose controls, 222

Mummy berry fungus, 348

Mushroom compost, 87, 98

N

Narcissus bulb flies, 329

Narcissus spp., 329–30
    pests and diseases of, 329–30

Nasturtium. *See Tropaeolum majus*

Natural insecticides. *See* Botanical insecticides

Navel orangeworms, and insect parasitic nematodes, 191

Neck rot, 283. *See also* Rot diseases

Nectarine. *See* Peach

Needle blights, 395. *See also* Blight

Neem, 224–25
  nematodes and, 136
Nematode(s). *See also specific plants affected;* Bulb nematodes; Foliar nematodes; Root-knot nematodes
  damage symptoms, 135
  insect-parasitic, 14, 190–92
  neem and, 136
  soil solarization and, 152
Neoaplectana carpocapsae, 190–92
Nicotine, 225–26
Nitrogen, 81, 100–102
  deficiency, *64, 65,* 139–40
  excess, 61, 81, 139, 262
    vulnerability to pests and, 163–64
Nomuraea rileyi, 192
Noninsect pests, *247–48,* **247–48**
Northern blight, 269. *See also* Blight
Nosema locustae, 190–92
Nuclear polyhedrosis viruses (NPVs), 188, 192
Nutrient(s)
  availability, 62
  crop rotation and, 148
  deficiencies, 135, 262–63, 372
  imbalances, 139–40
    home tests for, 63
    symptoms of, 63, *64–65*
  requirements, crops, 149
  tea, how to make, 90
Nut shells, as soil amendment, 87

O

Oak. *See also Quercus* spp.
  leaves, *95*
Oak wilt, 400–401
Oats, 72, 115
Obliquebanded leafrollers, 207. *See also* Leafrollers
Oil sprays. *See* Petroleum oil sprays
Okra, 279–82
  pests and diseases of, 281–82
Oleander hawk moth, and *Bacillus thuringiensis,* 186
Omnivorous leaftier, 207
Onion, 282–84

pests and diseases of, 282–83
  wireworms and, 283
Onion flies, and yellow sticky traps, 200
Onion maggot(s), 282
  "hot" dusts and, 218
  insect parasitic nematodes and, 191
  resistant cultivars and, 166
  traps, 209
Onion thrips, 282. *See also* Thrips
  sabadilla and, 224
Orangedog, and *Bacillus thuringiensis,* 186
Orange tortrix, 207
Orchard. *See also specific fruit trees*
  mulch, 344
  pest control
    apple maggot traps, 203
    cherry fruit fly traps, 203
    herbal sprays, 217
    horticultural oils, 212–13
    lacewings, 182
    minute pirate bugs, *179, 183*
    oil and lime sulfur sprays, 222
    petroleum oil sprays, 211–13
    pheromone mating disrupters, 228
    pheromone traps, 206–7
    ryania, 223
    spider mite predatory mites, 180
    sticky tree bands, 209–10
    Trichogramma wasps, 182–83
  sanitation, 143–44, 165
Orchard grass hay, 95
Organic fertilizers, *92–96*
Organic gardening, 9–18, 19
Organic matter
  in soil, 49, 78–79
  as soil amendment, 47, 66–76, 80–81, 91–99, 416–17
Organic mulches, 73, 99, 112
Organic pesticides, 22, 211, 219–26
Oriental beetle, 421

Oriental fruit flies, 207. *See also* Fruit flies
  neem and, 225
Oriental fruit moths, 207, **240.** *See also specific plants affected*
  baculoviruses and, 192
  control methods, *240*
  dormant oils and, 212
  pheromone mating disrupters and, 228
  ryania and, 223
Oriental poppy. *See Papaver orientale*
Orius tristicolor. See Minute pirate bugs
Ostrinia nubilalis. See European corn borers
Overseeding lawns, 419
Overwintering diseases, 143
Oyster shells, *95,* 100
Oystershell scales, 345, 347, 358. *See also* Scales

P

Paecilomyces farinosus, 189, 192
Paeonia spp., 330–31
  pests and diseases of, 330–31
Panonychus ulmi. See European red mites
Pansy. *See Viola* spp.
Papaver orientale, 331–32
  pests and diseases of, 331–32
Parasitic insects. *See* Beneficial insects
Parasitic nematodes, 14, 190–92
Parasitic wasps, 169, 172, 176, 181, 182–83
Pasteurization of soil and compost, 280
Paths and borders, beneficial insects and, 172
Pea, 148, 284–86
  pests and diseases of, 284–86
Pea weevils, 285
Peach, 357–59
  pests and diseases of, 357–59
Peach leaf curl, 131
  copper sulfate and, 158
  fungi blister, 359
Peachtree borers, 352, 357
  Bacillus thuringiensis and, 186

of insecticides, 211
of neem, 224, 225
of nicotine, 225, 226
of pesticides, 220–21
of pyrethrin, 220
of quassia, 226
of rotenone, 222
of ryania, 223
of sabadilla, 223–24
of starch sprays, 228
of thuringiensin, 229
Trace elements, 62, 79
Transplants, 112, 151, 280
Trap crops, 210
Traps (insect), 200–210
Tree(s), 366–411. *See also* Fruit trees
    bands, 24–25, 197–98
        sticky, 209–10
    care of, 112, 152, 384
    diagnosing problems of, 372–73
    resistant, *388–89*
    stress and, 368–69
Trellising, for disease control, 142
Trialeurodes vaporariorum. See
    Whiteflies
Trichogramma wasps, 176, 182–83
    tomato leaf sprays and, 216
Trichoplusia ni. See Cabbage loopers
Tropaeolum majus, 337
    pests and diseases of, 337
True bugs, 175
Tsuga spp., 409
    indicating acid soil, 59
    pests and diseases of, 409
Tuberous begonia. *See Begonia* ×
    tuberhybrida
Tuber rot, 309
Tufted apple bud moth, 207
Tulip. *See Tulipa* spp.
Tulipa spp., 338
    pests and diseases of, 338
Tulip bulb aphids, 338
Turf-type tall fescues, 421
Turnip, 299–300
    pests and diseases of, 299–300
Turnip black heart, 262, 299
Turnip mosaic, 300. *See also* Mosaic
    viruses
Tussock moths, and handpicking,
    193

Two-spotted spider mites, **248.** *See
    also* Spider mites
    control methods, *248*
    neem and, 225
    thuringiensin and, 229

U

Ulmus spp., 409–11
    pests and diseases of, 410–11
Undercover test, for soil condition,
    57–58
Underseeding, 114
Urtica dioica, 154

V

Vaccinium spp. *See* Blueberry
Vacuuming insect pests, 195
Vairimorpha necatrix, 190, 192
Variegated caterpillar, and *Bacillus
    thuringiensis,* 186
Vegetable(s). *See also specific vegetables*
    disease-resistant, 291
    garden, 253–301
        green manure crops in,
        73
        sanitation, 143–44
        soil care, 275
    nutrition, 262–63
    pest-resistant, 291
    transplants, 280
Vegetable weevils, 265
Velvetbean caterpillar, and baculo-
    viruses, 192
Verbena × *hybrida,* 339
    pests and diseases of, 339
Verticillium lecanii, 192
Verticillium wilt, 131. *See also specific
    plants affected*
Viburnum spp., 411
    pests and diseases of, 411
Vinegar, for weed control, 126
Viola spp., 340–41
    pests and diseases of, 340–41
Violet sawflies, 340. *See also* Sawflies
Viral decline, 329–30
Viral diseases, 133. *See also specific
    plants affected;* Mosaic viruses
    insect, 188–89

Visual traps (insects), 200–204
Vitis spp. *See* Grape

W

Walnut husk fly, 207
Wasps, 169, 172, 176, 182–83
Water
    for beneficial insects, 172
    deficiency, in trees, 372
    drainage tests, 56
    in soil, 49, 54
    sprays for insect control, 195
    stress, and vulnerability to
        pests, 164
    traps, 203–4
Watering, 26, 56, 142, 164, 413
Watermelon, 300–301
    pests and diseases of, 300–301
Weather
    diary, 17, 27, 433, **436**
    insects and, 160
    pesticide sprays and, 349
Webworms, **244.** *See also specific
    plants affected; specific webworms*
    control methods, *244*
    sabadilla and, 224
Weed(s)
    annual, 106, **108**
        control methods, *118–19*
    beneficial function of, 110
    biennial, 107, **108**
        control methods, *119–20*
    control, 23–24, 105–27, *118–21,*
        418–19
        tools, 25, 124–25, **124**
    grass, 107
    hay mulch and, 87
    identification of, 105, 106–9
    perennial, 106–7, **108**
        control methods, 113–14,
        120–21
        tilling, 116
    prevention, 16–17, 109–10
    problems caused by, 105
    soil compaction and, 110, 418
    as soil indicators, 59, *60–61*
    soil solarization and, 152
    test, for soil condition, 56
    winter annual, 107

Weevils, **245,** 402
    control methods, *245*
Western pine shoot borer, 207
Western spruce budworm, 207
    Bacillus thuringiensis and, 186
Western tussock moth, 399–400
Wheat, 96
Wheat stem sawflies. *See also* Sawflies
    and crop residues, 165
White clover, 59, *96,* 114. *See also*
    Clover
Whiteflies, 173, **245.** *See also specific*
    plants affected; specific whiteflies
    alcohol sprays and, 216
    control methods, *245*
    garlic oil sprays and, 217
    insect fungal diseases and,
      189, 192
    insect growth regulators and,
      227
    insecticidal soaps and, 215
    neem and, 225
    parasitic wasps and, 177–78
    pyrethrins and, 221

rotenone and, 223
starch spray and, 229
summer oils and, 212–13
vacuuming and, 195
yellow sticky traps and, 200
Whitefly parasitic wasps, 177–78
White grubs, 288, 421
White pine, 59
White pine blister rust, 395. *See also*
    Rust
White pine weevils, 393, 394–95
White rust, 292. *See also* Rust
Willow. *See Salix* spp.
Willow borers, 404–5
Winterberry. *See Ilex* spp.
Winter cress, 107
Winter damage, 372–73, 376
Winter mulch, 84
Winter rye, 114, 115
Wireworm(s), **246.** *See also specific*
    plants affected
    control methods, *246*
    insect fungal diseases and,
      190, 192

insect parasitic nematodes and,
    191
traps, 207, 209
Wood ashes, 79–80, 82, *96,* 104
Wood chip mulch, 73, 87, 99
Woodchucks, 356
Worm castings, *96,* 99
Worms. *See* Earthworm(s)

Y

Yellow mosaic, 287. *See also* Mosaic
    viruses
Yellow rot, 325
Yellow sticky traps, 14, 180, 200–202
Yellow woollybear caterpillars, 316,
    339

Z

Zea mays var. *rugosa. See* Corn
Zinc, *64, 65*
Zinnia spp., 341
    pests and diseases of, 341
Zoysiagrass, 413